James Dodson is the author of the bestselling *Final Rounds*, which was named the Golf Book of the Year in 1996. His other books include *The Road to Somewhere: Travels with a Young Boy Through an Old World*, *Faithful Travelers* and *The Dewsweepers*, together with *A Golfer's Life*, a collaboration with Arnold Palmer which was a *New York Times* bestseller. A multiple winner of the prestigious Golf Writers of America Award for his column in *Golf Magazine*, and numerous other literary prizes, Dodson lives with his wife and children on the coast of Maine.

Ben Hogan

· THE AUTHORISED BIOGRAPHY ·

JAMES DODSON

First published in Great Britain
2004 by Aurum Press Ltd
7 Greenland Street, London NW1 0ND
www.aurumpress.co.uk

This paperback edition first published 2005

Published by arrangement with Doubleday, a division of The Doubleday
Broadway Publishing Group, a division of Random House, Inc.

A catalogue record for this book is available from the British Library.

ISBN 978 1 84513 109 8

3 5 7 9 10 8 6 4
2007 2009 2011 2010 2008

This book is printed on paper certified by the Forest Stewardship Council as
coming from a forest that is well managed according to strict environmental,
social and economic standards.

Design by Amanda Dewey
Printed in the UK by CPI Bookmarque, Croydon, CR0 4TD

To Fans of the Hawk

Every man's task is his life preserver.

—RALPH WALDO EMERSON

Happiness is a thing of gravity. It seeks for hearts of bronze,
and carves itself there slowly; pleasure startles it away
by tossing flowers to it. Joy's smile is much more
close to tears than it is to laughter.

—VICTOR HUGO

CONTENTS

ACKNOWLEDGMENTS

This story simply could not have been told as comprehensively as it is without the valuable assistance of many people.

To begin with, the author wishes to thank Valerie Hogan for being such a diligent archivist of her husband's remarkable playing career. Without her extraordinarily revealing scrapbooks and tireless efforts to preserve his legacy, the intimate portrait contained herein would not have been possible.

I wish to thank Valerie Harriman, her niece and a true daughter of the West, for showing me a Ben Hogan rarely seen, as well as her children, Lisa Scott and Sean Anderson, for their critical assistance in this project. Representing the Hogan estate, Fort Worth attorney Dee Kelly could not have been more supportive and helpful. I am grateful to former Sleeping Bear editor Brian Lewis, who conceived this project and helped convince the Hogan estate that the timing was right for a more comprehensive view of Ben Hogan's life.

Several of Hogan's closest friends were kind enough to go over the manuscript in part or full with a fine-tooth comb, offering vital insights and corrections, and I am deeply indebted to them. They include Gary Laughlin, Rayburn Tucker, Gene Smyers, Marty Leonard, Dan Jenkins, Mike Wright, and Sharon Rea. Dr. William Mallon, former Tour player and U.S. Olympic historian, was invaluable to this project from beginning to end. Former *Golf Journal* editor and U.S. Open historian Robert Sommers was extraordinarily thorough in his examination of this biography. His dedication and assistance are deeply appreciated by the author.

In addition, there are a number of other people who knew Ben Hogan on a personal or professional basis and contributed wonderful insights and information to this project. Among those who gave generously I especially thank Jackie and Robert Towery, Dr. David Corley Jr., Charissa Christopher, David Corley Sr., W. A. "Tex" Moncrief Jr., Dr. James Murphy, Ben Fortson, Elizabeth Hudson, Willie Mae Green, Pat Martin, Doxie Williams, Dawn Coleman, Nick Seitz, Barney Adams, Ronnie McGraw, Roger West, Rees Jones, John Griffith, Jules Alexander, Terry Freschette, Jerry Austry, Tom Stewart, David Chapman, Mike Murphy, Jody Vasquez, Wendell Waddle, Bobby Goodyear, and Patricia Robinson.

From Merion Golf Club I wish to thank John Capers, Dick Barush, Irwin Brooks, Scott Nye, and Peter Zimmerman; from Northwood Club, H. Bruss Billingsley; from Riviera Golf Club, Todd Yoshitake; from the Tarrant County Historical Society, Suzy Pritchett; from the Dublin Library, Janella Hendon; also Gene Meone of the Hershey Resort and Greenbrier pro Robert Harris and historian Robert Conte. Senior Minister R. Scott Colglazier of University Christian Church was most helpful.

There are many to thank from the world of golf, beginning with the other members of golf's greatest triumvirate, the late Sam Snead and the ageless Byron Nelson. I wish to thank Sam and Byron both for the generosity of their time and candor of their opinions over many years of conversations. The late Paul Runyan was also an invaluable personal resource, a little man with loads of charm and fabulously clear memories of golf's golden years. The world won't see their kind again anytime soon. Ditto Tommy Bolt, who was kind enough to sit for an afternoon and spin his marvelous tales.

Author Curt Sampson, an old friend and colleague, was generous with both his notes and his insights from his own expedition down the Hogan trail, and I am forever grateful to Herbert Warren Wind for the lunches and conversations we've had over the years regarding the golf world he helped illuminate better than anyone. Ditto CBS broadcast legend John Derr, a man I'm privileged to call a good friend. I am also grateful for the insights of the late Ike Grainger.

A special thanks to Arnold Palmer, Ken Venturi, Harvie Ward, Jack Fleck, Mike Souchak, Jack Burke Jr., and Skee Reigel—gentlemen who were extremely kind with their time and insights. Also thanks to Peggy Nelson, Dave Anderson, Ben Crenshaw, Fred Simmons, Tom Kite, Eldridge Miles, Shelley Mayfield, Ernie Vossler, Eddie Vossler, Bill Campbell, Frank Stranahan, Billy Casper, Laird Small, Eddie Merrins, Bob Rosburg, Jerry Pittman, Jim Finegan, Marino Parascenzo, Doc Giffin, Rand Jerris, Nelson Silverio (PGA Tour), Irwin Smallwood, Karen Bednarski, Bob Russell, Chris Doyle, Martin Davis, Ron Mack, Sandy Tatum, Frank Chirkinian, Julius Mason (PGA of America), Johnny Palmer, Tommy Albin, Patrick McDaid, Marty Parkes, Kris Tschetter, Bob Farino, George Peper, Bob Ford, Jim Langley, Lee Pace, Ben Wright, Craig Harmon, Alastair Johnson, Dow Finsterwald, Tom Weiskopf, Donald Steel, Tim Rosaforte, Tim Nehr, Barry Van Gerbig, Mike Towle, Brian Morrison, Jon Sager, David Desmith, Bryan Andrew, George Sine, and Larry Reid.

Finally, I am deeply indebted to Doubleday editor Jason Kaufman for his patience and impressive skill at bringing this tale to life, and to my longtime friend and agent, Virginia Barber of the William Morris Literary Agency, for her tireless work on behalf of this book. I also wish to thank my golf-mad wife, Wendy, who cheerfully put up with her husband living Ben Hogan's life these past three years.

Voices of a
Summer Day

SOMEWHERE IN THE middle of the afternoon, Mike Wright glanced up from his pro shop counter and discovered Ben Hogan standing in front of him. Hogan was wearing one of his famous gray sweaters with the thinning elbows, clutching his flat linen golf cap and an old persimmon driver.

"Mr. Hogan," he said with surprise. "It's great to see you again."

"Thank you, Mike," the old man replied quietly. "Good to see you too."

It had been months since anyone had seen Hogan around Shady Oaks Country Club, perhaps even the better part of a year. Rumor had it that the club's most distinguished member had rapidly deteriorated since an emergency appendectomy and subsequent surgery for colon cancer. More discouraging to Wright, there were whispers that Hogan's mind had grown so frail, his memory so poor, that his wife, Valerie, no longer trusted him to leave the house even in the company of his full-time caretaker.

During this period of withdrawal, the great man's golf clubs had sat idly in their accustomed place at the back of the club storage room, looked after

Overleaf: Ben Hogan, Winged Foot Golf Club, summer 1959 *(Jules Alexander)*

by Wright, awaiting their owner's return. Inside Hogan's double lockers stood ranks of powders and unguents, the boxed painkillers and salve heat rubs and elastic bandages that spoke of Hogan's long journey through life and golf, his rise from West Texas obscurity to worldwide fame. Extra flat linen caps—the Hogan signature—and his famous English-made golf shoes were there too, spit-polished to perfection, deeply creased by years of trudging fairways.

"Would you like me to set up your golf clubs on a cart and get some practice balls for you?" Wright proposed, remembering how it wasn't so long ago that you could set your watch by the Hawk's daily arrival from the Ben Hogan Company for lunch with his Shady Oaks friends. Over the years, only the faces gathered around him at the large circular table by the picture window changed slightly; the ritual itself never varied. Back then, when his friends returned to work, Hogan always set out for the "little course," the club's par-3 course, or to a spot he favored between the 13th and 14th holes where he could spend hours hitting balls and testing golf equipment by himself. As a rule, Shady Oaks members knew better than to interrupt Hogan during these private interludes, for practicing—shaping shots, tinkering with grips and swings, watching balls do precisely what he wanted them to do in the wind— was Hogan's first and final love.

Hogan waved a hand.

"That won't be necessary, Mike."

As Wright watched, Hogan limped slowly out the pro shop door, scooped three golf balls from a range bucket, then proceeded in the direction of the 10th tee.

"I couldn't imagine what he was up to," Wright recalled a decade later to a visiting reporter. "I mean, it had been so long since anyone had seen him at *all*, even longer since anyone had seen him actually hit a golf ball. But you could see he had something really weighing on his mind. I couldn't take my eyes off him."

As Wright watched, Hogan went to the back of the 10th tee and teed up one of the balls. He took a couple of preliminary warm-up swings with his driver, as if limbering up before a round.

Then, with little ado, he smacked a ball down the fairway.

The swing wasn't as fluid as it used to be, but it was unmistakable Ben Hogan: the flat takeaway plane angle, the powerful hinging of the wrists at the top and delay through the descent upon the ball, the late release of his powerful workingman's hands just prior to impact, followed by the fine elevated finish so familiar to millions in the elegant black-and-white photographs of the man at the summit of his power.

"Given that this was a man over eighty who'd been seriously ill and hadn't hit a golf ball in goodness knows how many months, effectively *years* with any kind of regularity," mused the pro to the reporter, "I was, to say the least, *deeply* impressed. It was still a beautiful swing. It almost gave me chills to watch. It was the Hogan everyone remembers."

Out of sheer curiosity, Wright picked up the binoculars he kept behind the pro shop counter and found Hogan's golf ball resting a couple of yards into the first cut of rough on the right side of the fairway, about 250 yards out.

The club's 10th hole doglegs slightly left into a dominant south wind, and the green sits somewhat up the slope and back to the left. Hogan had put the ball in nearly the ideal spot from which to attack the flag. "Under the circumstances, it was great. But I could tell from his body English that Mr. Hogan wasn't particularly happy with it."

As Wright continued watching, the old man teed up a second ball and sent it away into the pale afternoon. Wright lifted his binoculars a second time and discovered this ball lying several yards ahead of the first one, positioned even better in the short grass. The young pro shook his head in amazement.

A moment later, Ben Hogan teed up a third ball and sent it into the summer sky.

"If you can believe it, the third ball landed a couple more yards into the fairway, just past the second ball. They were all out there together, each one slightly better than the one before it. It gave me goose bumps to see this—and even to talk about it now. You could have placed a small blanket over all three shots."

With that, Hogan picked up his tee and walked slowly down the 10th fairway. "This was something he always insisted on doing—walking after his practice shots to pick them up, purely for the exercise. In telling my wife about this later, I remember saying that it was almost like he—I don't know—just wanted to somehow *remind* himself what it was like to hit a golf ball again."

Recalling the moment, Wright's voice trails off and he stares down Shady Oaks' empty 10th fairway as if he can almost still see the finest shotmaker in the history of the game limping after his remarkable tee shots like just another elderly member out for a little fresh air and exercise on a hotly flaring Texas afternoon.

"Why *three* golf balls?" Wright wonders quietly. "I've asked myself that often, since then. Why not five or six or even just one? Mr. Hogan never did anything by accident, and there definitely seemed to be a point to three. I mean, wouldn't you have loved to climb inside his head and hear what he was thinking? Can you imagine the voices in there?"

Their brief encounter ended when Hogan returned to the pro shop a little while later, heading back to the bag room to put away his driver.

"It's nice to see you again, Mr. Hogan," Mike repeated.

"You too, Mike," Hogan replied, and waved good-bye.

As far as anyone knows, Ben Hogan never hit another golf shot.

FOR WELL OVER half a century, the golf world at large—generations of magazine writers and broadcasters, at least two ambitious Hogan biographers, millions of fans, and devoted students of the Hawk, as Hogan's friends and fellow Tour professionals Jimmy Demaret and Claude Harmon first called him, owing to the raptorlike way he descended on tournament fields and picked apart golf's toughest courses—have wished they could do nothing less than what Mike Wright wistfully imagined doing that slow summer day at Shady Oaks in the early 1990s: find a way to climb inside Ben Hogan's remarkable head and hear the voices speaking there.

Perhaps, if they could, so much would finally be revealed and understood about golf's most elusive star, the enigmatic little man who for all intents and purposes invented—and at the very least inspired and refined—modern professional golf as we know it today.

For the most part, like field archaeologists digging for traces of a lost advanced civilization, fans and students of golf's most venerated figure have been forced to gather clues to the man within wherever they can find them—amid the record books and flickering video newsreels of his major championship campaigns or in collections of yellowing newspaper clippings that convey the *how* but scarcely the *why* of his extraordinary life; in the parsed and careful utterances of his rare public interviews or from the qualified reminiscences of his Tour contemporaries who came to admire and respect and even fear Ben Hogan but rarely, it seems, fully understand or know him intimately.

Accordingly, they have studied and dissected his incomparable golf swing as with no player before or since, memorized the dates and scores and details of his extraordinary major triumphs, committed every characteristically blunt remark to memory, and pored over Hogan memorabilia and artifacts like a saint's holy relics. Ultimately, they have meditated upon the regal gray figure depicted in a thousand black-and-white snapshots of golf's most accomplished shotmaker in his prime (it's a revealing curiosity that Hogan was possibly the last great American athlete to look far more *natural* in black and white than full color) in what often amounts to a quixotic hope to draw closer to the intensely private little man who reshaped professional golf but kept the world that came to worship him at arm's length.

True to form, Hogan himself always argued that his playing record explained all that anybody needed—or had a right—to know about him.

So begin there.

Between 1940 and 1959, excluding nearly two years he was out of action serving in the U.S. Air Corps during World War II, Ben Hogan won sixty-eight golf tournaments and dominated professional golf as no one before ever had, a total that included four United States Opens, a pair of PGA Championships, two Masters Championships, and the only British Open Championship he ever played in. Only four times has a PGA Tour player achieved double-digit victories in one calendar year. Hogan did it twice—thirteen wins in 1946 and ten wins two years later.

Five times he was the coveted Vardon Trophy winner and the Tour's leading money winner, four times PGA Player of the Year. He played on three victorious Ryder Cup teams and captained two more. Out of 292 career tournaments he entered, he finished in the top ten an unprecedented 241 times. In nearly one-third of those tournaments he finished no worse than third, a winning percentage no modern player is likely to eclipse anytime soon.

Equally impressive over that same span of time, in the sixteen U.S. Opens in which he competed, Hogan never finished less than fifth place. At one point he won four of the six National Opens he entered and captured eight of eleven majors he played, and if an unknown Hogan disciple named Jack Fleck hadn't come out of the San Francisco sea mist to beat him in a play-off at Olympic Golf Club in 1955—an otherwordly upset that ranks with young Francis Ouimet's victory over Harry Vardon and Ted Ray at Brookline—Hogan would have collected an unprecedented fifth National Open championship. Even so, by his own firm reckoning and that of many who agree with him, Hogan's galloping win at the 1942 Hale America Open—the wartime event staged by the USGA in place of the suspended National Open—counted as a major win, the first of his Open titles.

In all, he won nine professional majors, placing him third on the all-time list, a career summary that would likely have been even more luminous if World War II, life-threatening injuries, or simple bad timing hadn't cost him the opportunities to compete in more than a dozen other major tournaments in his prime, a lost opportunity that included six U.S. Opens and at least four Masters. As many have noted, Hogan and his peers had the unfortunate timing to play in an era when the scheduling of the PGA Championship and British Open either directly overlapped or began days apart, a circumstance that made playing in both events impossible. Despite winning two PGA Championships, the grueling matchplay format was never Hogan's particular favorite. This and other factors, including his general dislike of the sponsoring organization, caused Hogan to skip at least eight PGA Championships during his peak playing years.

Without doubt, the Hawk's greatest moment of personal triumph came in 1950 at the U.S. Open at Merion Golf Club, in Ardmore, Pennsylvania. Just sixteen months after his collision with a Greyhound bus that destroyed the circulation in both legs and nearly killed him, Hogan defied dire medical predictions that he might never even walk again and limped through the languid Pennsylvania heat to capture his third National Open title—an epic moment capped for eternity by photographer Hy Peskin's famous snapshot of Hogan striking his immaculate one-iron to the 72nd hole.

For most mortals, Merion would have been enough. He'd come back from the dead to prove he was the greatest player since Bobby Jones, and Hollywood promptly announced plans to make a major motion picture of his inspirational return to glory.

On another level, perhaps only in America could a man who not so long ago was regarded as a cold, implacable scoring machine with little or no visible charisma become a sporting icon whose weekly exploits suddenly nudged rumors of wars and affairs of state below the fold of the nation's leading daily newspapers. Cheating death and climbing back on top made "Bantam" Ben Hogan the patron saint of ambitious underdogs everywhere, a headline writer's dream come true, a national icon who embodied so many traits of the ideal American—the dirty-face runt who never gave up on his dream, the reluctant champ who overcame every sort of adversity to become the people's hero. For millions of readers in a nation supposedly comprising hardworking loners and rugged individualists, Hogan's long rise from obscure West Texas childhood, conquest of an elite rich man's game, and comeback from the dead touched a mythical grace note of achievement—was, in short, nothing less than a primer in the virtues of hard work and absolute self-reliance, a shining American life.

But to the little man himself, limping on legs that would ultimately betray him, winning big golf tournaments remained all that really mattered, and the same accident that numbered his days, curiously enough, also rendered him a more dangerous raptor than ever.

The very next summer, at fierce Oakland Hills outside Detroit, Hogan successfully defended his title and demolished a golf course many felt was the strongest track the bluecoats of the USGA ever mounted in defense of a National Open Championship, commenting dryly afterward, "I'm glad I brought this course, this monster, to its knees," a characteristically chilly postmortem that once upon a time might have been considered par for the course from the tough little Texan but was now affectionately regarded as part of the gathering "mystique" of modern golf's greatest player.

Maybe even more impressively, forty-eight months later, following a year in which his game seriously faltered and many longtime Hogan watchers speculated he would soon retire from view, Hogan not only stunned the golf world by capturing titles in five of the six tournaments he entered in 1953, including the Masters, the U.S. Open, and the British Open at Carnoustie, but shattered scoring records at three of the most difficult courses in the world.

This triumphant year—by his own admission the most satisfying of his life—gave the Hawk victories in all of golf's so-called major events (what some would soon begin to call the "Career Grand Slam"), and provided a fitting swan song to the end of his extraordinary run of majors. At least three more times he would contend for that elusive official fifth National Open he desperately wanted, and for several years running he sent electrical charges through the worshipful galleries at Augusta National whenever he got anywhere near a Masters lead.

After Fleck pulled off his extraordinary upset at Olympic in 1955, a visibly spent Ben Hogan announced his official retirement from the game and essentially withdrew from public view to focus on building the equipment company that would bear his distinctive signature till the end of his days and commit his reflections on the golf swing to paper in the form of the best-selling game instruction book of all time, *Five Lessons: The Modern Fundamentals of Golf.*

MASTERS FOUNDER and amateur deity Bob Jones once commented that a player can truly only be judged by the quality of the men he competed against. Underscoring these accomplishments, it's worth remembering that the Age of Hogan—as *Sports Illustrated* writer and Hogan's collaborator Herbert Warren Wind first labeled this remarkable period of sporting dominance—unfolded against the spectacular exploits of Hogan's friend and caddie-yard rival Byron

Nelson and Virginia's sweet-swinging hillbilly phenomenon, Samuel Jackson Snead. Between the three of them—America's first great professional triumvirate—Hogan, Nelson, and Snead officially collected 208 tournament victories and 17 majors and, more lastingly, transformed American golf from a largely sleepy rich man's country club game into a national obsession and major spectator sport—quadrupling postwar purses and galleries in less than two decades on the job.

Of the three, though, it was dark and broody and ostensibly misanthropic William Ben Hogan—clearly the least naturally gifted, certainly the hardest-working, by far the most difficult to fathom—who ultimately exerted the most lasting impact on the game.

Before the Great American Triumvirate began winning golf tournaments at a breathtaking clip in the early '40s, professional golf was a moderately popular fringe sport played by nomadic club pros over the lengthy winter hiatus between their club's closing day and springtime opening event—its rough practitioners considered more like itinerant carnival performers than serious sportsmen. Amateur golf, symbolized by the graceful exploits of Atlanta's urbane and educated native son Bobby Jones, was by far considered the highest expression of the game.

By the time Hogan withdrew from the game, however (following his triumphant ticker-tape parade down Broadway during the summer of 1953, the first bestowed on any golfer since Jones), a new generation of Tour stars was beginning to emerge who based their style points and work habits unapologetically on Hogan's—the incomparable way he prepared and practiced for battle, the unprecedented way he concentrated during competition, even the way he dressed and conducted himself around the golf course. Hogan protégés popped up like secular apostles in the form of Jack Fleck, Gardner Dickinson, Tommy Bolt, and young Kenny Venturi.

As a result of his glittering accomplishments and the inspiring elements of his story, the pro game boomed, the amateur game dimmed, and many aspiring professionals never had to work a club job a day in their lives.

"There's no doubt in my mind that Ben Hogan played a key role in transforming professional golf into something different than it had been, a much bigger game with all kinds of new commercial possibilities," says Arnold Palmer, the most notable of the young Turks who came along just as the Age of Hogan was closing and took the game to even more unimagined heights.

"Love or hate him, most of us were frankly in awe of the man for what he'd done—even before we realized the huge debt of gratitude we owed him."

. . .

WHEN A PUBLISHER representing the heirs of Ben Hogan's estate approached me in late 2001 with the invitation to write an "authorized" biography of golf's greatest shotmaker, I was deeply intrigued but not a little wary of such a major undertaking.

To begin with, with the possible exceptions of Arnold Palmer and Jack Nicklaus, more has been written about the career of Ben Hogan than any other player of modern times, including a pair of thin early biographies that cast him in an almost laughable pulp-fiction light, two instruction books marginally "authored" by Hogan himself, a 1978 biography by Fort Worth newspaper man Gene Gregston, and Curt Sampson's best-selling 1996 biography *Hogan*, to date the most comprehensive examination of what surely is the most complex, remarkable, and self-determined life anyone ever fashioned for himself in any sport.

What more, I wondered from the outset, both as a pretty fair student of the man and his era as well as his potential biographer-in-waiting, could an "authorized" account of golf's most ultra-private legend possibly offer that hadn't already been amply conveyed and thoughtfully reflected upon by Sampson and company, including a pair of recent fine glossy tabletop tomes by Martin Davis featuring a host of Jules Alexander's unpublished photographs plus Valerie Hogan's warm reminiscences of her late husband through the redoubtable pen of *Times* columnist Dave Anderson?

The answer, as it turned out, proved a great deal more than I or anyone else could have expected. But it took nearly two years of diligent footwork to reach the fertile hidden terrain that lies between myth and man and an almost medieval roundelay of conversations with Hogan's remaining family and friends—each one growing more revealing and intimate than the previous one—for a far more complex, vulnerable, and revealing man to appear.

The problem with writing in depth about Hogan the golf star is the very mystique that envelops him like a mist from Mount Parnassus—a seemingly impenetrable curtain of silence that protected the man's oft-proclaimed right to privacy. Hogan the perfectionist simply couldn't abide any perceived mistake in the reporting of his carefully chosen remarks or his playing exploits, and his closest friends and family strictly honored his wish to be left alone by the world at large, even following his death. After her husband's death in the summer of 1997, for example, Valerie Hogan positively bristled at anything that conveyed Hogan in less than a heroic light.

From the biographer's point of view, the maddening dichotomy between the man and the mythology that Hogan and those around him carefully crafted to deflect deeper inquiry has always been the greatest impediment to finally understanding and appreciating how and why he managed to transform himself from a shy backwoods loner with a violent hook swing into the most dominant golfer of his time and one of the sporting world's most revered and influential figures, a little man who still fascinates and inspires millions by his indomitable spirit and refusal to give up. Ironically, perhaps the only other champion who rose from such humble beginnings and triumphed over such forbidding odds and terrible adversity to cast such a dominating spell over the national imagination was another undersized competitor named Seabiscuit, the tenacious little thoroughbred who began racing and capturing hearts the year after an unknown Bennie Hogan lit out for a second (unsuccessful) attempt to make it on the fledgling professional golf tour. In some ways the parallels between Hogan and Seabiscuit are downright eerie. After years of repeated failure, bad luck, and near-misses, Seabiscuit's trainer, Tom Smith— a reticent westerner who refused to ever explain himself to the press—sensed he might just have the greatest little racehorse on earth on his hands and trained the thoroughbred in secret workouts to become one of the most intimidating finishers in track history. Smith, it was said, derived pleasure from fooling turf scribes and track handicappers, allowing them to dismiss his horse as a "cripple" (owing to his unorthodox choppy gait and undistinguished past) and predict that the big-hearted little horse, despite his incredible work ethic, would probably never make it in big-time racing. "Seabiscuit and Greta Garbo can be coupled in the betting form from now on," wrote a columnist for the *Los Angeles Times*. "Both want to be let alone." Just over a decade later, another reporter from this same newspaper used almost identical words to describe Hogan's reticence to explain himself and his unfriendly passion for practicing in private, openly questioning whether "Bantam" Ben—who had failed in clutch situations before—had what it took to chase the "best field ever assembled" for the National Open that summer at long and tough Riviera Country Club. Driven by a flaming will, Hogan went out and attacked the course from the start, birdieing three of the first four holes of the competition, galloping home to win his first United States Open Championship, and setting two scoring records that would last a generation.

Finally drawn as I was into the project by the hint of never-before-seen personal correspondence and unrestricted access to his personal affairs (only some of which in fact turned out to be helpful; Hogan, for example, kept minutely

detailed expense and travel diaries and derived great pleasure from dispatching formal letters and puckish notes to his friends but rarely if ever committed his deeper feelings to paper) and family members who were said to be
willing and even eager to finally break their silence on the Garbo of Golf, the
last thing I had any interest in becoming—the explicit danger of all "authorized" biographies—was a mouthpiece for a floodlit monument.

Somewhere between the black numbers of Ben Hogan's extraordinary playing record and the blinding white floodlights of his sustained mystique I
hoped to discover a figure who was far more a man than a myth and to place
in proper context the hundreds if not thousands of famous Hogan anecdotes
and stories that almost everyone in golf knows some colorful shirttail version of.

Thanks to the good faith and unflinching honesty of Hogan's surviving
family members, Valerie Hogan's magnificently detailed personal scrapbooks,
and several of Hogan's closest surviving friends who believed a more full and
open accounting of Hogan's remarkable journey was overdue and could only
serve to deepen the world's respect for a little man they believe is genuinely
heroic but largely misunderstood, I eventually did find that meeting ground
between light and dark, between man and myth. In the process, it was a particular pleasure to encounter a Ben Hogan who was far more full-blooded
than cold-blooded, a complex yet remarkably modest man whose *lifelong*
struggle to overcome personal adversity, both hidden and seen, will likely surprise as many fans as it inspires. It certainly did me.

THE VISIBLE MILEPOSTS of that life, as his second biographer Sampson
aptly put it, resonate for most Hogan worshipers like the Stations of the
Cross—a childhood steeped in rural happiness followed by unspeakable family tragedy, his repeated failure to succeed as an aspiring pro, his breakthrough
and eventual triumph on tour, the accident that nearly killed him at the peak
of his craft, his "miraculous" comeback and the public's adoration, the creation
of his golf equipment company, and the enduring public fascination with his
so-called Secret.

Given all of this and the powerful reluctance of the man himself to offer
anything more than a maddeningly vague framework for his genius, is it any
wonder that tales of Hogan's life have grown into the Homeric tales of modern sport?

No teacher, the story goes, ever gave him a lesson, and everything he managed to learn about the golf swing—which apparently was twice as much as anybody ever had before him—he *dug out of the dirt* by practicing until his hands bled. When the skin of his palms blistered and cracked open, he soaked his hands in pickle brine to toughen them for the long haul. After almost nine years of unrelenting effort and disappointment, he cured his tendency to hook the ball under pressure and finally won his first golf tournament, transforming himself into a precision golfing machine and the most feared competitor of his day, almost as if he had discovered a formula for golfing perfection, a "secret" of some sort for playing the game better than anyone had before him.

He was almost thirty years old when this first win finally arrived in the drowsy pines at Pinehurst—late for a champion, slightly older than Bobby Jones when he won his mighty Grand Slam and decided to retire before winning golf tournaments became more important than playing in them.

Ben Hogan was no Bobby Jones, the eloquent, schooled scion of the American country club, the highest expression of ideal amateurism. When winning finally came to him, Hogan, self-made refugee from a brutal childhood, counted every win as one more step away from his emotionally destitute past. He played golf for hire, as the popular saying went of touring club pros beating the highways from one swayback tournament town to the next, and at age thirty, the moment of his breakthrough, unlike Jones, he was just getting started—a fact proven by the relentless way he continued to practice, hour after hour, day after day, year upon year. "The more I practice," he tersely explained when reporters first commented on this visible obsession, "the luckier I get." He later added with the economy of *Poor Richard's Almanac*, "Every day you miss practicing, it will take you one day longer to be good."

"Before Ben Hogan started doing it," says Tommy "Thunder" Bolt, the flamboyant Arkansan shotmaker and club-thrower extraordinaire Hogan came to regard as one of his closest friends on tour, "nobody in their right mind regularly went to Misery Hill. That was our nickname for the practice tee, see, because that was where guys went to try and figure out what the hell was wrong with their swings. Hogan, on the other hand, went there to figure out what was *right* about his golf swing. Take it from me, brother. That was revolutionary! And by practicing as much as Ben did, which I swear was twice as much as anybody I ever saw, he basically reduced the margin for human error to damn near nothing. There was no shot he hadn't already hit a thousand times already out on Misery Hill. Nothing was ever a surprise to Ben Hogan in a golf tournament. That's the first thing that set him apart."

As Bolt and others point out, if Hogan didn't invent the pre-shot routine that's standard procedure with tournament players and most good amateurs, he certainly popularized the practice. Famously, he also disdained yardage books and unsolicited advice from caddies and claimed to have no clue about the distances of his individual clubs. He chose instead to memorize every relevant feature of a golf course before playing it in competition and to compute the distances in his mind, visualizing every possible shot and matching it to the proper club, making precise mental footnotes on every dangerous spot or advantageous angle to a putting surface. According to Gardner Dickinson, who held a degree in psychology and served for a while as his first assistant at a Palm Springs golf club on the eve of his greatest year in golf, Hogan, who dropped out of high school to chase after a life of tournament golf, possessed an IQ at least fifteen points higher than genius level.

During competition, Hogan's mental absorption was so complete that he seldom spoke to playing partners or even appeared to notice his own friends and family tagging along in the gallery. For years another unlikely Hogan sidekick, Houston's colorful and voluble Jimmy Demaret, dined off the same joke about his frequent four-ball partner's dour public face and reticence to speak. "Old Ben was talking up a storm on the golf course today."

"Really? So what did he say?"

"You're away."

Hogan's concentration was so intense, the story goes, that he once failed to notice playing partner Claude Harmon score an ace at Augusta National's infamous 12th hole. As they walked off the green together, Hogan turned to Harmon and remarked, "That's the first time I ever birdied that hole, Claude." Harmon, shaking his head in disbelief, could only smile.

"Ben has the kind of will that makes the rest of us look like carefree schoolboys," Demaret observed in his chatty memoir *My Partner, Ben Hogan*, describing their years bumping along the potholed roads of the early PGA Tour together. "He doesn't ignore people. He just doesn't see them. Hogan simply divorces himself from the rest of the world when playing in a tournament. He is completely and absolutely detached from everything but that golf game of his."

Off the course, Hogan's reputation was scarcely better—and sometimes even more forbidding to encounter. He typically avoided small talk like the plague and disliked having to sit for interviews that lasted for more than a few minutes or probed beyond the visible facts. He preferred simple yes or no answers and, if displeased, offered replies that verged on icy curtness. What many saw as bluntness he viewed as simple honesty.

If Hogan liked you and saw some benefit in being warm and personable, to be sure, he could be as warm and courtly as a luxury hotel doorman; if he didn't see the point, however, he was as cold as the hotel dining room flatware—Hogan Lite and Hogan Heavy, as golf writer and Hogan authority Mike Towle once named the phenomenon. The man, his surviving intimates concur, had no visible tolerance for intrusive fans or lazy reporters who never left the comfort of the clubhouse and—worst of all—scribes who posed ridiculous questions or simply made up things they wished he'd said in the aftermath of competition, a fairly commonplace practice in the casual postwar years of sports journalism, when telling a good tale was at least as important as quoting the man with reasonable accuracy.

The Wee Ice Mon, as the admiring Scots of Carnoustie dubbed him after his extraordinary conquest of Britain's toughest links land, could halt a runaway tongue or freeze a questioner's stomach with a mere glance of his penetrating blue-gray eyes. When Hogan chose to elaborate, he did so with the exactitude of a nipped approach shot to the 72nd hole of a major. "Life's too short to go around explaining myself," he once told an interviewer with an unmistakable note of irritation. "A lot of people don't understand modesty. Not everybody wants publicity, you know."

"He would answer questions carefully, politely, and quietly," *The Guardian* correspondent Pat Ward-Thomas wrote of him a decade after his last great triumph, at Carnoustie, "but always with a full stop at the end, as if wary of the ebb and flow of ordinary conversations."

On the most visible level, Hogan's distinctly moderate tastes seemed to corroborate his claim of personal modesty—or, perhaps more calculatingly, as more cynical sorts suggested, were designed not to detract from the Archimedean beauty of his shotmaking. His chosen attire was simple, expensively made, immaculately maintained, and almost always muted in shade. "The first thing that struck me about Hogan when I saw him in person for the first time," says Tom Weiskopf, "was his perfect clothes. I'd never seen shirts that fit so beautifully on a human being before. His shoes were immaculate, his belt always looked brand-new. Crazy as it sounds, I studied every detail of the man. The creases in his pants looked as if they'd *just been pressed*. I couldn't take my eyes off him. Nobody ever looked the way Hogan did."

Flannel gray and muted blues were Ben's preferred battle hues—the colors of a Confederate officer's dress uniform or a bank president's suit—and no commercial logo ever graced a garment the Hawk wore in the public eye or in competition. Moreover, he routinely snipped labels from the shirts and traditional cardigan sweaters he favored, a peculiar habit, he once attempted to explain somewhat unsatisfactorily when word of the odd habit got out, that was aimed "at not giving offense to anybody"—presumably someone who couldn't afford the custom Oxxford-made clothing he wore almost from the moment he started winning golf tournaments.

A stickler for proper dress and proper public behavior, Hogan's trousers were made with old-fashioned button flies that prevented accidental openings, and his shoes were custom-made by a prominent London boot maker and came equipped with a mysterious extra thirteenth spike. For grinding opponents into the turf, it was sometimes rumored.

He consumed alcohol—early on, at least—sparingly, and never to public excess, detested long hair of any kind, always stood when a woman entered the room, and bristled at the use of profanity in the presence of women and children. "Old Ben could cuss like a sailor among the boys," says one of his closest lunch chums. "But send a woman or a child into the room and he was as smooth as a Spanish diplomat."

Finally, there were the man's golf clubs. Also the stuff of legend. Probably *unplayable* by anyone but Ben Hogan himself.

His persimmon-headed driver was forty-five inches long with the stiffest custom-flex available, its face turned slightly open at address, its oversized cord-textured grips cranked slightly counterclockwise to promote the delayed release he favored. His irons were believed to be the heaviest *ever* used in competition, forged and bent anywhere from three to six degrees flat depending on the club, scarred beyond belief from their owner's constant abuse of them, lead taped, guaranteed *never* to hook.

A close and longtime friend of Hogan's owns one of his cherished drivers and enjoys puckishly placing the hallowed instrument in his guest's hands at Cypress Point Golf Club's 12th hole—Hogan's favorite driving spot on the famous Monterey seaside course. "Try and hook a ball with this," Texas oilman Gary Laughlin says with a wry little smile. He stands back and his guest settles the club, strengthens his grip, and makes a pure hook swing. The ball scoots out low and long, fading to the right rough at the end of its flight. "Don't feel so bad," Laughlin says with a chuckle, taking back the treasured artifact, noting that he's invited maybe twenty-five great players to try to hit the club over the years. "Nobody can hit a hook with it. Davis Love put it in almost the exact spot you did."

. . .

"I ALWAYS BELIEVED there were really *two* Ben Hogans," Sam Snead reflected when I telephoned him in Florida shortly before his own death, to seek his thoughts on an authorized biography of his greatest rival in golf, the little man whose casket Valerie Hogan invited him to help carry one blazing hot morning in the summer of 1997. As a golf journalist, I'd been fortunate to get to know Sam pretty well over the years and hoped he would not only give me his usual blunt assessment of the proposed project but perhaps shed a little more earthy insight on the subject of his greatest competitor.

One of the surprising tidbits I'd picked up from conversations with Hogan's closest friends and several Tour veterans was that Hogan and Snead were intense and friendly competitors but never really more than that. Perhaps this shouldn't have been any great surprise. Both came out of the Darwinist realm of the club caddie yard and wore class chips on their shoulders their whole lives, but as chatting with Sam reminded me, all similarities basically ended there. One was a natural introvert, the other a born showman. One dressed rather flamboyantly, the other to avoid giving offense. One talked up a blue streak, the other used words like darts thrown at a board. Snead explained everything, Hogan revealed nothing.

Like Sarazen and Jones, though, Hogan privately found Snead's colorful japery deeply irritating at times, his disarmingly crude locker-room wit a walking offense to the dignity of the game. For his part, Snead could never get over the fact that, by his count, he won nearly three dozen more tournaments and beat Hogan more times than he lost in their head-to-head confrontations, but the "press boys" (as he called them) generally seemed to respect Ben a great deal more for winning four National Opens, the major title Snead always seemed to find a creative way to blow. "I'd give up half my wins for just *one* of them National Opens," he told me in a serious moment during an earlier autumn afternoon out on his beloved Old White Course at the Greenbrier Resort in West Virginia. "And when Ben won once in 1950 and got Player of the Year over me, well, hell, I damn near wanted to throw up and hang it up." Sam, the Tour's leading money and Vardon Trophy winner that particular season of 1950, won eight official tournaments, including Hogan's own backyard Colonial National Invitational. Ben's sole win that season came at the U.S. Open at Merion. But what a win it was.

And yet history had intimately joined the pair like few rivals in any other game, and their towering respect for each other's playing skills and individual marks on the game were unmistakable. Without the slightest hesitation, Snead once told me Hogan was the finest player golf ever produced, and Ben once famously remarked of Snead that if he'd only had Sam's swing and his own brain, why, the rest of the field would always be playing for second place.

"There was *Hogan* the golf champ and *Ben* the man. That's the way I always looked at it," observed the Slammer with gracious enthusiasm the afternoon I phoned him to talk about the proposed Hogan project. "The two weren't much alike, in the opinion of some people who knew both of them . . . different as night and day. But I knew 'em both. The public side of Ben Hogan was tough and hard to get close to—like I once said to some reporters, Hogan was about the *only* thing I ever feared on a golf course. Golf tournaments were all business to him. Nothin' more, nothin' less. He couldn't relax for a minute and enjoy them, even when everything was going his way. He played golf like he had a grudge against the game.

"The *Ben* most people never saw, on the other hand, was a very decent man, a lot of fun to be around when he wasn't kicking your pants, with a hell of a good sense of humor. I believe the publicity that the rest of us kind of liked and needed—well, ole Ben *hated* that. For some reason he couldn't put his guard down and let folks see the fella he was away from the golf course. I honestly don't know why."

Snead paused and thought for a moment, then added almost wistfully: "That's a damn shame, really. It would probably have been good for his fans, and Ben himself, to let the world get closer."

Not long after Snead passed away, on a rainy winter afternoon out in Roanoke, Texas, while I was sitting in a wooden rocker beside a blazing fire with Byron Nelson, I posed this same question to the other surviving member of America's great professional triumvirate. Nelson smiled his lazy ranchman's smile.

"Ben and I were always friendly and fairly close when we started out together on tour, but I wouldn't have described us as close lifelong friends," Nelson said by way of diplomatic prefacing. "And yet, due to our growing up together in Fort Worth, caddying at Glen Garden, and later competing against each other and so on, I think I have a pretty solid understanding of what made him tick. It was always my view that Ben was a good man who for some reason never wanted the world to see who he really was—perhaps never wanted people to know that about him.

"He was a lot friendlier and more complex than folks realized, not the Hogan you read about in books so much. But there was something inside him—a fear of being thought of as weak or vulnerable maybe—that made him appear so tough and unforgiving. I always thought it had something to do with that childhood of his, losing his father the way he did. . . ."

Lord Byron adjusted his lap blanket and stared for a moment at the scrolling flames of the fire his wife, Peggy, had kicked up a bit. Then the last member of the great triumvirate glanced over at me and smiled gently again, looking like a Roman emperor in winter.

"Ben was a great mystery to a lot of people, maybe even to himself. For some reason, I don't know why, he wanted it that way. He wouldn't let people in. That much, the tough side of Hogan, is pretty well known. It would be very good, I think, for people who admired him to finally have a better picture of him."

THROUGH THE VOICES of those who knew him best, the Ben Hogan you'll encounter in these pages may both startle and pleasantly surprise you. He is tough, brutally guarded, and absolutely unrelenting in the exercise of his will to succeed at the hardest game anybody ever played.

But he's also funny, unbendingly honest, deeply sentimental, remarkably engaging and generous, a tough guy with a tender spot for children and dogs and strangers in need, an old-fashioned American who was fanatically loyal to the people he employed and chose to reveal himself to—including, and maybe especially, his wife, Valerie.

For all his fame and the enduring mystique of his sporting achievements, this Ben Hogan was a genuinely modest man who constantly expressed surprise that the world at large even remembered his name in the decades after he left the game, a man who never permitted himself the luxury—or trap—of believing he was anything truly special, possibly because, deep down, he never felt worthy of such popular adoration. "I don't want to go up there and be eulogized," Hogan remarked with honest bewilderment to friends after declining Jack Nicklaus's invitation to be honored at one of the first Memorial Tournaments at Muirfield Village in Ohio. "Why, I'm not even dead yet."

The simple key to understanding William Ben Hogan, I discovered in the course of my lengthy and intimate explorations of his life, and the pivot point that explains everything about the man, from his incomparable practice routines to his Mandarin powers of concentration, his relentless search for technical perfection to his fanatical need for absolute privacy, his careful selection of mentors and friends and even a worshipful spouse, his meticulous manner of dress and unbending standards of public behavior, his obsessive need for rituals, scrupulous business acumen, and powerful but largely hidden tenderness and spirituality—all evolved from the same terrible family tragedy that shaped every aspect of his life after age nine.

In a nutshell, Hogan's real *secret* had little to do with any technical refinements he'd worked out during his arduous climb to golf's summit, and entirely to do with a boy's endless search for the vanished happiness of his rural childhood. Until the moment a confused and dispirited Chester Hogan placed a .38 to his heart and pulled the trigger one darkening winter afternoon in 1922, possibly with his youngest and most impressionable child looking on, Ben's life as a blacksmith's boy was largely something of a rural American idyll. After that instant of unimaginable horror, his life became a Dickensian ordeal of survival, a personal quest to somehow get back the perceived paradise he had suddenly and savagely lost. The engine of this holy quest, riven with secrecy and shame, was a pathological yearning that quickly honed his survival instincts but left him feeling somehow complicit in his father's death and dogged to the end of his days by a fear of never quite measuring up.

Over the course of a lifetime, the Ben Hogan you'll meet here, for example, only spoke a few times about his beloved father's death and in doing so always carefully avoided mentioning the way Chester died or the possible causes, choosing instead to fondly dwell upon how he loved sharing the saddle of a horse with his late father. The family secret held such painful dominion over him, in fact, that Valerie Hogan never learned anything about the circumstances of Chester's death until she and Ben had been married more than a decade—and only then because she overheard his mother and sister discussing the suicide at a family holiday gathering during the late 1940s.

It was only during a moment of bittersweet unburdening near the end of his life to his constant companion and daily caretaker, a delightful woman named Elizabeth Hudson, that the Garbo of Golf, the little man in search of his vanished boyhood, finally spoke openly of his father's death and how it changed his life. In doing so, he perhaps finally exorcised the demons of self-doubt that had doggedly pursued him for more than seventy-five years.

Poignantly, fittingly, Hogan's greatest triumph over the fear of failure he allowed to powerfully motivate but never fully consume him came in a room about the size of a PGA tournament scorer's tent, in the company of a woman who cared far more about the progress of his soul than the purity of his sporting legacy.

This Ben Hogan, you will learn, as I did, loved to play practical jokes on his friends and dispatch short, wryly typed notes on company stationery to acquaintances playfully signed "Henny Bogan"—his sentimental alter ego for the boy whose childhood didn't abruptly end when the bullet passed through his father's heart, the man Ben Hogan most dearly wished he could have been.

Not surprisingly to any modern psychologist worth his shingle, the man he selected to make his surrogate father and primary mentor was one of Fort Worth's most beloved figures, a kindly department store magnate and Colonial Country Club builder, Marvin Leonard. And this secret yearning also explains why his best friends on Tour were the most colorful, accomplished, and friendly characters in the game—the tumultuous Bolt and jesterly Jimmy Demaret, the gritty and loyal Jackie Burke Jr. Before they came along, he styled himself after the elegant-swinging Macdonald Smith and tough but regal Gene Sarazen, with invaluable assistance from suave Henry Picard. As his reign ended, Hogan developed close friendships with promising younger players in whom he saw vivid glimpses of himself, guys like Mike Souchak and Ken Venturi and Gardner Dickinson.

This Hogan loved going out to romantic movies, listening to his close friend Bing Crosby's records for hours, and hoofing to big band standards with his wife or the wives of his closest friends at the country club dance. Once, at a crowded debutante ball in Dallas, he suddenly hoisted himself up on a buffet table and performed an impromptu version of the Twist, to the delight of a teenage crowd and their chaperoning parents.

When he was pleased or delighted by something, this Ben Hogan often clapped his hands together with a gleeful, childlike innocence and, symbolic of his lost childhood, conferred particular fondness on young children and animals, especially little girls and stray dogs. He lavished attention on his two nieces—the closest thing he had to daughters—and once instructed his lawyer to make provision in his will for taking care of a pair of stray dogs that hung around Shady Oaks.

He got down on his knees and wept when those dogs died.

This Ben Hogan liked scrambled eggs for lunch and homemade peach ice cream after dinner. Ditto a well-made vodka martini. He took great pleasure in grilling his own steak (medium rare), driving his beloved black Cadillac everywhere he went, and watching the evening news while he chain-smoked Chesterfields or Camel cigarettes.

He started out a Roosevelt Democrat. He ended up an Eisenhower Republican.

His favorite color was not gray. It may really have been red.

He was far more religious than anybody but a handful of people realized. On his way to practice at Colonial or Shady Oaks, he often slipped unobtrusively into a rear pew of University Christian Church just after the service commenced, then slipped out again before the service ended. Tellingly, he left a million dollars—about one-thirtieth of his estate—to the church in his will.

The Army Air Corps taught him to fly an airplane, but Henny Bogan battled a lifelong dread of heights, flying in commercial aircraft, cameras clicking in his face, and large crowds of strangers of any sort—further telltale signs of a life psychologically rooted in the forfeited happiness of his childhood.

For these reasons alone, he preferred to stay home and seldom went on vacation. He once dropped out of a prominent Fort Worth social club, not because he was antisocial, but because the club moved to the top floor of one of the city's tallest buildings.

Financially, he selectively invested in oil wells, never in volatile stock equities, and invested conservatively for the long haul in only gold-backed municipal bonds. Like many children of hard times and the Great Depression, even after he became wealthy beyond his wildest hopes, Hogan was quietly besieged by an unreasonable fear of losing everything and having to start over, dogged by the constant specter of failure. And yet, equally revealing of a man who'd learned the hard way that character really does help determine one's fate, he refused to permit his name to be sold for endorsing products he didn't actually use or believe in. Once turning down a lucrative offer to put his name on a national chain of golf instruction schools, his reasoning was simple: "There's no way I could physically give every lesson and I wouldn't want to do it—it wouldn't be worth it to the customer—if I couldn't give the lessons."

Even at the height of his fame, unlike almost every other marquee player who followed him, Hogan refused to have a business manager or sports agent running his affairs or representing his interests. His personal secretary made all of his travel arrangements, and Hogan himself negotiated his own best terms with the doggedness of a Baghdad rug dealer. "He was a tough but honest negotiator," remembers a Texas oil broker who did a lot of business with him in the late 1980s. "He studied drilling histories and geology reports and had everything down to the smallest detail. You really had to be on your toes with Ben."

Contrary to the popular image of Hogan as the Garbo of Golf, this Ben

Hogan greatly enjoyed signing autographs for fans who were respectful enough to place their requests in writing, and he set apart a portion of each day in his office to fulfill dozens of such requests. He made his signature one of the most recognizable and distinctive in sports, more aware than anyone of what its street value had cost him.

Henny Bogan's loyalty to Ben Hogan Company employees was legendary, and his passion for designing and testing clubs was nearly all-consuming. "He could see things in a golf club nobody else could see," says Ronnie McGraw, a Hogan Company club designer who learned his craft directly at the master's elbow. "No one ever understood how a golf club works any better." For a man of supposedly few words, he relished giving inspirational talks at amateur golf banquets and the address to the troops at his annual Company sales conference dinners, impromptu speeches that were remembered by many as leaving few if any dry eyes in the house.

The first house Ben and Valerie purchased on Valley Ridge Road in Fort Worth's Westover Hills, only months before his near-lethal car accident, was a classic suburban colonial straight from Ozzie and Harriet, a model of good American middle-class tastes, and the second home he built a decade later on Canterbury Drive—designed by a man he met while serving in the Air Corps—was a pretty brick affair, roomy but by no means extravagant by the standards of today's PGA Tour homes.

As his regular Shady Oaks lunch cronies learned, this Ben Hogan was a soft touch for people down on their luck, particularly those he read about in the *Fort Worth Star-Telegram* who faced some unexpected hardship or personal adversity. On a dozen different occasions, Hogan passed the hat among his pals at the famous round table overlooking the club's 18th hole, raising thousands of dollars for people he never met. Without anyone knowing about it, he also picked up the medical bills for several Shady Oaks employees and once bought a tailored suit of clothes for his favorite waiter. The man later insisted on being buried in his "Hogan" suit.

Like many journeyman golf pros of his generation, he detested giving formal golf lessons—a holdover from his days as a young club pro hungering to practice on his own—but savored the opportunity to analyze a promising player's golf swing in detail or fix a child's or member's clumsy swing if he happened to spot them, all the better if the player in question happened to be young, female, and attractive. During the last two decades of his life, he rarely played a full round of golf. But his love of practicing shots remained undiminished by advancing age and the cruelty of whatever claimed his short-term memory.

FOLLOWING HIS surprise appearance at Houston in 1970, Hogan granted *Golf Digest* editor Nick Seitz a rare interview at his home on Canterbury Drive—the house Hogan built, so the story went, with only one bedroom so the misanthropic owner wouldn't have to put up with overnight guests.

The truth was more complicated than anyone but family members, a small handful of Hogan friends, and the ever-changing domestic staff could fathom, a circumstance that, combined with his own childhood fear of exposure and failure, explained so much about Hogan's obsessive need for privacy.

The problem concerned Valerie Hogan, the worshipful little woman who abandoned her own ambition to be a Fort Worth society columnist and shunned the spotlight to devote every moment of her life to helping Ben Hogan achieve his dreams. Like Pat Nixon, wife of another celebrated loner who reached the top of his profession by outworking every competitor on the turf, Valerie Fox Hogan was the picture of the perfect postwar wife: disarmingly shy, gorgeously dressed, a gracious wife and hostess who stood loyally by her famous husband's side but rarely expressed more than a few upbeat and supportive words in public.

As age and infirmity descended upon her, though, the diminutive woman Hogan once described as "my best friend in life, perhaps my only true friend in life," became increasingly convinced the world was out to claim the man she helped transform into a sporting deity, and her natural wariness of people in general grew into rank paranoia that manifested in an obsessive need to control every aspect of her husband's legacy and remaining life—where he went and what he did, who he saw, even what he ate.

At least three times during their long and successful married life, Hogan quietly moved out of the couple's home to a Fort Worth motor inn for various intervals of time, to cool off and think. At least once, Hogan seriously contemplated the possibility of divorce, only to change his mind and come home again to the only person who had believed in him from the beginning. "Of all of the human virtues Ben admired," muses one longtime Hogan friend who was privy to these private struggles, "loyalty was the one thing he respected most. If you showed him true loyalty, he never let you down. For better or worse, as Ben knew, nobody was more loyal to him than Valerie."

Nevertheless, as Hogan's health declined and his mental frailness increased, owing to the onset of an officially undiagnosed ailment that could have been either dementia or Alzheimer's, Valerie Hogan's intense loyalty grew into an obsession that prompted her to dismiss a stream of housekeepers and medical staff who might have made the Hawk's declining years much more comfortable and far less lonely at the end.

In a sad if well-intentioned desire to try to protect the man she worshiped from damaging his own meticulously crafted legacy, she adopted the role of a fierce gatekeeper and finally isolated her husband from the people and things he loved and needed most—his two grown nieces and their families, his beloved practice sessions and fellowship with his Shady Oaks lunch pals, finally even his beloved Cadillac and cigarettes.

"Whatever else is true about Uncle Ben and Aunt Valerie," says Charissa Christopher, Hogan's great-niece, who remained unusually close with both Hogans right up till their respective deaths in 1997 and 1999, "I think they were, originally at least, ideally suited for each other. He gave her the strength she needed to face people, and she gave him the unqualified belief in him that helped Uncle Ben become the Ben Hogan people now read about.

"For better or worse, life had taught them both to be caretakers, to fight for everything and keep their emotional distance but protect everything around them no matter what, including and maybe especially the people they loved. The irony is, people thought he was cold and aloof, but he really wasn't. He was shy and very sweet. As he got older, this sweeter side of him came out. Unfortunately, Aunt Valerie went exactly the opposite way. I don't know why Aunt Valerie did what she did, but I don't think it was meant to harm or smother him. I believe her intentions were honorable but she didn't know any other way."

WHICH, ODDLY ENOUGH, brings us back to the lengthening shadows of that summer afternoon at Shady Oaks, Ben Hogan's final golf shots, and Mike Wright's haunting question: Why *three* golf balls?

Perhaps they were symbolic of the three major attempts it took for Ben Hogan to catch on and make a good life for himself in professional golf, or maybe they were symbols of another summer's glories forty years before—the three unforgettable championships of his greatest year and last hurrah, a sentimental old champion's poignant salute to his incomparable performances at

Augusta, Oakmont, and Carnoustie—three balls, three shots, each one more perfect than the one preceding it. A final bit of perfect symmetry by the Archimedes of golf.

Hogan worshiper Tom Weiskopf once observed that his hero liked to play three balls in practice—one for each side of the fairway and a third straight down the middle—so that no approach to the green would be unknown to him in competition. Does this explain those three valedictory swings?

Or perhaps Mike Wright simply had it right from the beginning. For one final moment in time, as he slipped from sunlight to shade, *Ben* just wanted to remember what it felt like to be *Hogan* again, the greatest shotmaker who ever lived.

"We lost the Unicorn," the late Dave Marr summed it up nicely to *Golf World*'s Bill Fields when word got out that Hogan had passed away in July 1997.

"Did he *really* exist? . . . People wanted to see him, but Ben never understood that. He was a fabled animal, a fabled man. He was the one by whom all great ball-strikers will be judged."

ONE

God's Country

DATING FROM THE LATE 1880s, a U.S. federal surveying map of West Texas lands summarizes the isolated village of Dublin rather simply and starkly as "a moderately prosperous railhead located on the edge of formerly occupied Indian territories."

In fact, since its establishment by Irish immigrant farmers a decade before the outbreak of the Civil War, eighty miles southwest of Fort Worth and nearly at the geographical center of the state of Texas, Dublin had been an oasis of protection and shade in an unforgiving sea of scrub oaks and native grasslands. It occupied a limestone rise of forested hills that were notable for their clear running creeks and abundance of wild turkey, prairie chicken, and free-ranging buffalo.

The Comanche, Kiowa, Lipan, and Apache tribes who hunted these bleak surrounding lands, undisturbed for centuries before white settlers pushed into the region, were more than a little reluctant to give them up to the newcomers, and thus Dublin's early town records are filled with vivid accounts of

Overleaf: Chester and Ben Hogan, 1913 *(Courtesy Hogan Estate)*

deadly skirmishes between uninvited homesteaders and native inhabitants, family massacres, and revenge killings.

As late as the start of the twentieth century, surviving elements of these "pacified" native peoples periodically committed violent raids on Dublin township for horses and cows, and a year seldom passed without the murder of a farmer or disappearance of a town resident caught unaware in some isolated outlying area. "My grandmother used to say this was God's country," remembers a modern resident of Dublin whose family roots burrow back to the town's formation. "He put this nice little Christian town smack in the middle of a country that was meaner than hell. Reckon only *He* could truly love it."

One popular account of how Dublin got its name holds that it came from the shouted alert to "double in the wagons! Indians a'comin'!" though the abundance of Irish surnames in local graveyards suggests the founding fathers were probably more intent upon honoring their distant homeland when Dublin actually appeared on government land maps around 1860. A less likely if more colorful theory holds that the name derived from the raucous Double Inn Hotel that opened up about the time the railroad arrived to serve the needs of a more prosperous crossroads economy, a notorious roadhouse that specialized in strong drink and cheap beds.

Five years after the Yuma Stagecoach Line made Dublin a regular stop in 1874, the Texas Central Railroad surveyed a line straight through the heart of town and opened a small depot there in 1881, prompting an influx of cattlemen and cotton farmers aiming to seek their fortunes on the edge of a wild new country. One of those who came to town was a young, rawboned Mississippian looking for a new start. William Alexander Hogan had spent a year serving as a blacksmith in a Confederate cavalry unit before taking a bride four years his senior and settling down to try to raise cotton on rented land back in Mississippi. After five years of hard tenant labor that left the Hogans with little or nothing to show for their efforts, William and Cinthia Hogan pulled up stakes and joined the migration to the promised land of west Texas, arriving in Dublin sometime after 1870 with their four young children: William, Josephine, Martha, and Mary. According to Sunday school records, they joined the First Baptist Church almost immediately upon arriving in town, and William abandoned farming in favor of the trade he'd learned in the Confederate Army.

Whether by chance or design, the opening of a new blacksmith shop on Elm Street, just a block or so from the center of town, was fortuitously timed because the same railroad that brought settlers into the formerly untamed region also brought cattle ranchers and cotton farmers in growing numbers, people who relied heavily on the horse for their livelihoods and transportation needs.

On February 2, 1885, a fifth and final child was born to the Hogans, a solemn dark-eyed boy they called Chester, possibly after the outgoing president of the United States. At an early age, according to early family lore— what little of it managed to pass down the line—Chester Hogan was drawn to the dust and bustle of his father's workplace, often spending his days at the blacksmith shop tending horses and watching customers come and go. He was said to be an unusually sweet-dispositioned child given to periods of prolonged silence.

In 1889 a spur of the larger Fort Worth–Rio Grande Railroad reached Dublin and an opera house opened its ornate doors, featuring dance hall girls and the kind of rowdy frontier melodramas that soon attracted patrons from as far away as Fort Worth and Dallas. One of those who found himself attracted to the town's mix of the Old West and the new ways was Sam Houston Prim, a former bookstore owner who contracted to produce and bottle a carbonated concoction that was all the rage down in Waco, a sweet soda beverage called Dr. Pepper. Sensing an opportunity to get the jump on merchants restricted to peddling the newfangled soda drink from their traditional lunch counters around the Lone Star State, Prim opened his small bottling plant with the greater ambition to make Dr. Pepper available at every general store and grocery purveyor in west Texas. To do so, he hired his brother and a nephew to mix chilled carbonated water and flavored syrup in Hutchinson bottles, which could then be sealed with wire corks and shipped imperishably anywhere there were good roads or rail lines. The idea caught on like a fever, and Prim was soon expanding his operation and looking for extra hands to bottle and ship his soda. In due course, Prim hired the quiet but hardworking youngest son of William Hogan to wash returned bottles, refill and cork them, and crate them up for shipment.

Chester Hogan was believed to be twenty years old and already married the spring he briefly left his father's blacksmith shop to bottle Dr. Pepper, and in a famous photograph that the *Dublin Progress* newspaper published in 1955— half a century later—the youngest Hogan appears erect and taciturn, with an almost Lincoln-like solemnity and bearing about the eyes, remarkably like the two sons he would father within a decade. Not long after the photograph appeared in print, the newspaper's editor received a pair of politely worded letters from golfer Ben Hogan, the first requesting a "glossy print of this original picture at your earliest possible convenience," the second a short while later expressing the letter writer's deep appreciation for a prompt reply and dispatch of the photograph in question. Neither letter made even passing reference to the fact that the man in the photograph was Ben Hogan's father.

Chester Hogan, in any case, was married to the former Clara Williams, third child of a Dublin cotton buyer who grew up in a rented house on nearby Grafton Street, a short time after he went to work for Sam Prim. Her father, Ben Williams, a prominent member of the Baptist church, was remembered as being a fastidious dresser and a quick-witted man who could instantly work out the most complicated math problems in his head even while simultaneously transacting purchases of bundled bails of raw cotton that were brought from the fields by the wagonload to the Dublin train depot. It was Williams's job to grade and purchase bails of raw cotton fiber, then mark and ship them on for processing to northern clothing and thread manufacturing companies. For his trouble, he collected 10 percent of every consummated purchase.

Cotton was king across much of the American South in those days, and Ben Williams had social ambitions that probably didn't include his pretty, spirited daughter marrying the silent heir of the village smithy shop.

As a Fort Worth reporter snooping around in Ben Hogan's mysterious early life in the late 1950s first discovered—but chose not to reveal—there was apparently no marriage certificate between Chester Hogan and Clara Williams filed anywhere in the courthouse records of Erath or neighboring Comanche County, leading some to surmise that the young couple may simply have eloped or quietly gone off and married in a hurry, owing to an impending arrival. In any case, from family sources it's known that Clara was eighteen in 1908 when she gave birth for the first time to a boy she rather fancifully named Royal Dean. Two years later a daughter was born at home, probably at the young couple's modest wooden frame house on Camden Street. Projecting her ambitions for a more refined life on her first and only female child, Clara named the girl Chester Princess.

Finally, on August 13, 1912, a few days after the Bull Moose Party nominated Theodore Roosevelt for president and advocated a platform promoting women's suffrage and sweeping election reform, Clara Hogan delivered a second son at the new women's infirmary in nearby Stephensville, the county seat. For reasons unclear—possibly having to do with her natural distrust of strangers or the dying western tradition that held all newborns should be properly named at home (it was bad luck to do otherwise)—Mama Hogan chose not to give the baby a formal name until she brought her infant male home to Dublin.

Both Royal Dean and Princess were remembered by Dublin elders as lively babies who seemed to possess their mama's extroverted nature, but the third Hogan issue had both his father's calm and watchful personality and his mother's imposing blue-gray eyes. Clara eventually decided to call him William Ben Hogan, after both his grandfathers, the diligent blacksmith and the enterprising cotton broker, a pretty good choice considering the way young Bennie turned out in life.

EXCEPT FOR HIS modestly phrased letters of inquiry and gratitude to the *Dublin Enterprise*, sent and received during the summer of 1955—the year he just missed winning a record fifth National Open and announced his intention to "retire" from full-time professional golf to pursue "other interests"—Ben Hogan rarely acknowledged his blood connection to the rough little pioneer railhead of his birth on the edge of former Indian country. In light of what followed nine years after his birth, it's not too surprising that he flatly refused to ever publicly mention the circumstances that drove the family from the town, and never even spoke of it to the woman he chose to court and marry until his own mother let the secret out many years later.

"One of the first things I learned about our family was that nobody talked about the past or wrote things down unless it was completely necessary, and certainly not *that*," reflects Jacqueline Hogan Towery, Royal Hogan's only daughter and one of two nieces Ben Hogan came to regard as if they were his own daughters. "For the Hogans, Dublin was essentially the end of the line. And the way they looked at it, if you wrote something down it might later be used against you. So there was no chance of family history ever being written. Growing up, I never heard my grandmother say anything about my grandfather, her late husband. Chester was the man *never* mentioned in our house. All we knew was that he'd somehow gotten sick and eventually died. And then she'd brought her family to Fort Worth to get on with things, to start a new life."

Before that abrupt and violent partitioning from their birthplace took place, by all accounts the three Hogan children experienced fairly ordinary and even happy childhoods in the quiet oak-shaded streets of Dublin. Once Chester returned to take over his father's blacksmith shop on Elm Street, shoeing horses provided sufficient income to permit Chester and Clara to own a second small rental house, and for many years the family wasn't anywhere nearly as destitute as later accounts of Hogan's early childhood days present them as being.

On the contrary, life for the Hogan charges appears to have been something of a rural American idyll, with picnics by Clear Creek and evening suppers at the Baptist church. An early newspaper advertisement for the family business, for example, includes a photograph of the Hogan children bundled together on a pony wagon draped with a Fourth of July parade sign that cheerfully reads: "PAPPA'S A BLACKSMITH. LET HOGAN SHOE YOUR HORSE!"

The oldest boy, Royal Hogan, was remembered as a natural athlete who organized neighborhood teams and pitched a mean sandlot baseball game; Princess, who had her mother's gregarious personality, stern good looks, and no shortage of the Williams charm and ambition, sang at church and even earned a few bit parts in musical productions at the old Dublin Opera Hall. Neighbors from those years who knew the family often remembered that quiet little Bennie Hogan seemed to be his father's boy to the core, a thoughtful lad who was shy but unfailingly polite around adults, a bit of a happy loner who loved to poke around his father's busy blacksmith shop, where he calmed the horses as they waited to be shoed and fed scraps of his lunch to the village dogs that always congregated there on hot summer days. Tellingly, decades later, Ben Hogan's favorite keepsake from this faraway childhood—his most prized family possession—was a small black-and-white photograph that shows him sitting peacefully on his father's lap, astride a chestnut mare. Bennie was maybe a year old at the time, being cradled between his father's belt and the saddle horn, already clutching the reins like a true son of the West. Father and son are both looking away from the camera's lens, as if scanning some unknown horizon, but the spiritual connection between them is unmistakable. Their expressions and profiles are serenely calm, and nearly identical.

As his father had been, young Bennie was a bit undersized for his age, the classic neighborhood runt, and some recalled that he seemed destined to grow up in Royal's shadow, reduced to playing the "pigtail" during sandlot games where Royal was always pitching, the extra boy who chased down errant throws the catcher missed, just waiting for his chance to get invited into the game. For other entertainments, the Hogan children swam in Clear Creek and went to the open-air movie theater just off Dublin's dusty main square on Friday nights, plunking down a nickel for a seat on a hard bench to watch Douglas Fairbanks in *The Knickerbocker Buckeroo* or Charlie Chaplin's *Shoulder Arms*. Even then, Bennie Hogan shared his big sister Princess's fascination with the magic of Hollywood movies, in thrall of a world of glamour and fortune that felt about as far away as one could possibly get from the dust and heat of God's country and their father's already dwindling blacksmith trade.

. . .

THE YEAR 1920 was a watershed year for America in general and for Texas in particular. The "Great War to end all wars" had claimed the lives of five thousand Texans but ended with the signing of the Armistice in 1918. By 1920 the war's end had produced a manufacturing boom and a revolution in goods and services back home that promised to transform the American landscape as never before, beginning and ending with Main Street itself.

As wartime price restraints were lifted, milk and steel prices suddenly rose for the first time in six years, Congress ratified the Nineteenth Amendment to the Constitution officially granting women everywhere the right to vote—immediately raising both hemlines and fierce editorial debates about a woman's proper place in emerging American society—and a sweeping civic folly popularly called Prohibition went into effect, ostensibly aimed at puritanically ridding the nation's streets of cowboy saloons and crime elements once and for all, an ambitious bit of social engineering embraced nearly two-to-one by hard-drinking, God-fearing, predominantly Baptist Texans.

Meanwhile, a rage to own electrified washing machines and illuminate ball fields and amusement parks in small towns where the sidewalks had always been neatly rolled up at sunset were merely two indications of what George Babbitts everywhere unapologetically hailed as "America's New Prosperity," a flood of new money that had Main Street hopping and Wall Street humming. Even if brokers in New York were officially prohibited from celebrating a rampaging bull market and the vast whirlwind fortunes being made overnight with their favorite tipple, the historic run-up in stock and bond values was so swift and pervasive that some otherwise prudent editorialists essayed, a bit erroneously as it happened, that due to the momentum of Jazz Age prosperity, the good times simply couldn't abate anytime soon.

One notable impact of this sudden surge in personal wealth and the leisure time it created was the public's sudden renewed interest in professional sports, initially baseball but also the once-sedate realm of tournament golf. While fans of Boston's hapless Red Sox spent the first summer of the century's third decade wondering if the team's owners had scored a financial coup or made an appalling mistake by unloading the hefty playing contract of one George Herman "Babe" Ruth on the rival New York Yankees for a princely $125,000, members of Toledo's redoubtable Inverness Club, sensing the winds of change upon them, voted boldly to break with tradition by inviting contestants for the

U.S. Open Championship into the clubhouse and granting them full use of all of the club's facilities for the very first time.

As if to punctuate this end of an era, six-time British Open champ Harry Vardon, fifty years old but graceful as ever with his Norfolk jacket and stylish form of play, put on a gallant effort to capture the coveted American title he'd won exactly two decades before, only to discover himself agonizing over three-foot putts down the stretch and battling a right forearm that twitched so violently, owing to jittery nerves, that he was forced to lurch at several key putts. Still, gamely, Vardon finished with a respectable four-round total of 296, one thin stroke back of his longtime touring rival Ted Ray, who at age forty-three became the oldest man in U.S. Open history to win America's national golf championship. With that, golf's Grand Old Man tipped his canvas travel hat and promptly boarded an ocean liner home to England and was never seen in the game's Brave New World again.

In Vardon's wake, curiously, not only had record crowds turned out to watch a pair of thick-waisted, middle-aged English gents perform their hickory-shafted artistry one final time, but Toledo police reported a new social phenomenon in conjunction with, of all things, a *golf* tournament. The tournament, it seems, had caused one of the sporting world's first major *traffic jams*.

Down in the lonely, sun-mused hinterlands of West Texas, on the other hand, it's highly doubtful that Bennie Hogan, who turned eight the same day Ray beat Vardon at Inverness, knew much about sea changes at the National Open or the gathering populist interest in golf tournaments, or even anything of the buzz surrounding the amateur exploits of a formerly hotheaded, club-throwing Atlanta boy named Bobby Jones who'd finally conquered his volcanic temper, passed the Georgia bar exam, and begun to make people forget the names Vardon and Ray.

The closest golf course to Dublin was eighty miles away in Fort Worth, and most hardworking Texans, it was safe to say, if they thought of golf at all, regarded the sport as the province of wealthy swells who had the time and money and natural lack of gumption to chase a silly little ball over a field where you might otherwise raise a decent crop of cotton.

Even so, the passing of the guard was seen and felt in many other ways on even the remotest of the Republic's main streets. Home electrification and flush toilets reached a record number of American homes in 1920, and the number of public street lamps quadrupled—cutting petty crime, it was estimated, by one-third. For the first time ever, the U.S. Census Bureau reported that more Americans now resided in cities rather than the countryside, and while newspaper editorialists from Bakersfield to Bangor fretted about the negative impact of such a large-scale migration upon America's agricultural output, preachers across the nation inveighed from the pulpits against the dangers to be encountered by impressionable farm youth rushing to the city.

"Transportation and access were necessary in a state where the population was scattered across immense distances," notes T. R. Fehrenbach in *Lone Star: A History of Texas and the Texans.* "At the start of the century some farmers had to haul cotton more than 100 miles to gins and markets. . . . The automobile, in a very real sense, replaced the horse in both social function and symbology." In other words, the vast Lone Star nation went from being a horse culture to an automobile culture, Fehrenbach asserts, "in one fell swoop."

With dizzying alacrity, America's new and sudden prosperity was felt most profoundly by owners of livery stables, livestock feed suppliers, and blacksmith operations everywhere. Within five years, it's been estimated, almost half of the nation's traditional horse-based businesses failed and closed their doors. The owners either found something new to grab hold of to ride the wave to survival and tomorrow or simply let go, dried up like jimsonweed in a drought, and vanished.

DURING THE LONG hot days of 1921, the same summer Henry Ford produced a record number of his "affordable" $600 Model Ts and Cal Coolidge's new secretary of commerce, Herbert Hoover, proudly boasted there were now over nine million automobiles on America's ever-expanding network of paved roads and highways—prompting a frenzy of municipal paving, a rush to join the future—Clara Hogan quietly packed up her young family's belongings, placed the Hogan house on Camden Street up for sale, and moved her husband and three children to a small rented house at 305 Hemphill Street on the southeast side of downtown Fort Worth, not far from the handsome new ornate Texas & Pacific train station.

For the record, if any of her friends or neighbors dared openly to question why on earth such a pragmatic woman would do such a headstrong and possibly reckless thing, Clara simply explained that the blacksmith operation Chester inherited from his father wasn't working out anymore and left it at that. Life was too short, she believed, to go around explaining yourself to people. But anyone with eyes could see the truth for themselves. The coming of Mr. Ford's affordable automobile had occasioned the recent construction of a new state highway that connected Dublin directly to the bright lights of Fort Worth, and that's where, Clara decided, her family's best hope of survival lay.

Mostly, though, Clara offered only her firm, level smile and said nothing at all about the family's sudden turn of fortune. At just five-foot-two, as everyone in town understood, Mama Hogan was neither a woman to be trifled with nor a lady who wasted much time or oxygen on failure. In her pioneer vision of the world, golden opportunity was overlooked by most folks because it usually came dressed in overalls and resembled hard work. Times were tough down on the farm, but the opportunities were out there if you were willing to go out and find them.

The private, deeper explanation for the family's sudden bold relocation was considerably more complicated—and desperate—than anyone who knew the Hogans perhaps could have guessed, though the signs of trouble were unmistakable if you knew what you were looking at. A failing blacksmith shop was either the consequence or triggering mechanism of a far more elusive and pernicious malady of the spirit that brought out the finest pioneer survival instincts in Clara Hogan but unleashed demons of pure self-loathing in her decent, hardworking husband, Chester.

Over roughly a year and a half before the family pulled up stakes, as the horse trade dwindled and debts mounted, Chester Hogan became so despondent that he could barely lift a hammer and some days didn't even bother leaving the family house to open up for work. There is more than anecdotal evidence to suggest that Chester had always been (along with the children) the faithful churchgoer in the family, but suddenly even that staple of life dropped off precipitously, and he may have turned to the whiskey bottle for a little aid and comfort from the anguish of both his failure and the gathering antipathy of his wife.

In short, what Mama Hogan steadfastly declined to reveal to a soul was that Chester was mentally "depressed" and slowly coming apart from the inside out, tumbling into a void of emotional blackness and acute personal desolation that endangered all of their lives. In 1920 even the most forward-thinking country physician was ill equipped to deal with the ravages of mental illness of any kind, especially one that preyed rather amorphously on the life and prospects of an entire family. Standard medical texts of the day still typically referred to mental depression in the scented antique language of the pre-Victorian era. Some called it "melancholia," others a "nervous disorder" or "malady of the spirit." Whatever the label, there were few if any known cures for the elusive ailment of mind and spirit and only a few places where a sufferer could seek anything resembling help. Most of these institutions were "back east" in the traditional urban centers of commerce and education, where bold new psychotherapies were emerging to try to attack the growing problem of mental dislocation that appeared to accompany surging prosperity in Western industrial society.

As it happened, though, bustling Fort Worth had a hospital and a handful of trained physicians who specialized in the care of "humours of the mind" and "troubles of the spirit," as the medical guide of Dublin's own town doctor referred to the mysterious condition. This was the only such facility in all of west Texas.

Not only did Mama Hogan have the natural gumption to take the problem in hand and do something about it before it was too late, but she also had a means of supporting her young family while she took Chester there and sorted him out. Even before arriving on Hemphill Street, she landed a job doing alterations at Cheney's Department Store in downtown Fort Worth, a store that catered primarily to the clothing tastes of the city's well-to-do matrons.

"Without a doubt," says her granddaughter Jackie Hogan Towery, "Mama Hogan was the finest seamstress I ever saw. When I was twelve, she taught me to sew, and I learned in no uncertain terms that you didn't dare cross her. When the seam wasn't perfectly done, she ripped out the entire hem and made me do it completely over.

"She wasn't a woman who did *anything* with halfway measures," Towery elaborates. "If it was done at all, it was done right. Both my father and Uncle Ben learned that lesson directly from her. She could be sweet and friendly as the day was long if it suited her purposes, but she was also the toughest little person I ever met. A woman determined to survive."

IRONICALLY, diagnosis and treatment of the mentally ill were also at a major turning point in America the summer Clara Hogan relocated her brood to Hemphill Street on the teeming, low-income south side of the most notorious cow town in Texas, the self-described "Place Where the West Begins," the "Queen City of the American Prairies."

By 1922, there were several hospitals and private infirmaries in the rapidly growing metropolis of 150,000 people but only one institution that specialized in the treatment of nervous disorders and mental maladies, the Arlington Heights Sanatorium, an old-fashioned, mansard-roofed therapeutic asylum built on the western fringes of the city out near Camp Bowie, the former training facility of the U.S. Army's Thirty-sixth Division during World War I.

As irony would have it, the region's only mental hospital occupied land that had once been the site of Fort Worth's first planned suburban housing project, an ambitious schematic that included, among other things, the construction of the city's first private golf club, a grandiose blueprint that never left the drawing board, owing to the rapidly changing fortunes that were common to the movers and shakers and fortune seekers of notorious Cowtown.

Though no official records remain to confirm it—the asylum was eventually closed and torn down and its patient logs were either lost or destroyed—it's likely that Clara Hogan brought her husband to Arlington Heights for treatment of his mental depression, probably on an outpatient basis, simply because there were no other such facilities anywhere near the Queen City of the Prairies and no physicians beyond that institution's trained in the few treatment remedies available.

As Edward Sorter points out in his definitive *History of Psychiatry*, depression as a major psychiatric illness has been known for centuries—mentioned as far back as the writings of Herodotus—but the standard treatment of individuals suffering from the commonly accepted symptoms of the disease—bleakness of mood, acute self-loathing, inability to experience pleasure, periods of grandiosity accompanied by suicidal thoughts—had scarcely evolved in well over a century from the fundamental ideas pioneered by London physician William Battie, the man who advocated removal of a disturbed patient from the hustle and grind and pressure of his daily life in hopes that regimented isolation and a "calming" routine might eventually restore a balanced state of mind and the patient's mental equilibrium.

"The rise of the asylum," Shorter notes, "is the story of good intentions gone bad." By World War I, he points out, asylums and mental hospitals in America had "become vast warehouses for the chronically insane and demented." And in quest of what was commonly called the "rest cure," better equipped facilities (which Arlington Heights appears to have been) offered amenities like gardens, billiard rooms, staff counselors, and a host of physical therapies ranging from mineral baths to mild electrotherapy. Alkaloid sedatives, sodium bromide, the liberal administration of laxatives—"Diarrhea is often a natural cure for insanity," wrote another famous British doctor whose celebrated quackery became a major impetus for an appalled Sigmund Freud's groundbreaking efforts to get at the problem's taproots—and a heavy reliance on

chloral hydrate, so-called knockout drops, were among the common approaches applied to a host of related symptoms that had no official clinical
identity.

In any case, owing to vanished records and Clara Hogan's icy self-imposed
silence on the subject and the distance of eighty years, it's impossible to know
exactly how Chester Hogan's depression fully manifested or what regimen of
treatment, if any, he received under a doctor's care at Arlington Heights.

But as second Hogan biographer Curt Sampson and others have noted,
with the benefit of hindsight and the spyglass of modern psychoanalysis, there
are revealing clues about what was bugging Chester Hogan. According to
those who witnessed his odd behavior and steady decline back in Dublin, his
"black moods" appeared to come and go with periodic intensity, suggesting
that Chester's ailment was not the unipolar form of depression, which would
have forced him to be institutionalized and perhaps even shackled to the floor
(a widespread practice) for indefinite periods of time, but rather the phantom
of bipolar depression, which comes as unbidden and mysteriously as an
evening fog, causing euphoria one day and utter hopelessness the next.

What is known about Chester's progress toward sorting himself out is that
five months after the family relocated to Fort Worth to seek treatment and
start a new life, apparently following several months of seeing a specialist and
being unable to locate work as an automobile mechanic, Chester Hogan
abruptly returned alone to Dublin and reopened his blacksmith shop on Elm
Street, determined to have another go at the only trade he really understood,
the only work that had ever truly given him peace and happiness.

People who knew the family back in Dublin later reported that by Christmas Chester seemed very pleased to be back in the little town of his birth,
working hard to reopen his shop, and talking eagerly of bringing Clara and
the children back to where they belonged, possibly as soon as the new year's
arrival.

A month later, with a mood still elevated by the prospect of getting his old
life and family back, Chester took the afternoon train up to Fort Worth aiming to convince Clara that he was "cured" and it was time to move back home
with the children.

No one knows exactly what transpired next. As a chilly winter dusk settled
over Cowtown on the evening of February 13, 1922, a Monday, the eve of Saint
Valentine's Day, a bitter argument erupted in one of the front parlor rooms of
the tidy frame house at 305 Hemphill Street. What passed accusingly between
husband and wife can only be surmised. Chester undoubtedly pleaded his case

for the comforts and memories of Dublin, while Mama Hogan refused to give an inch from her position that nothing like this could even be considered until the school term ended in the spring. By one family account, the children sat in other rooms listening mutely to the growing tumult. At some point during their argument, with the demons of his greatest fears unleashed with a vengeance once more, Chester picked up his carpet bag and stalked out of the room.

In his bag was a loaded .38 revolver, and following him into the room where he fled was possibly his greatest comfort in life, the quiet little boy he'd once cradled in the saddle of a chestnut mare during a much happier time of life, his pride and joy, little Bennie. Moments later, a single pistol shot rang out.

Hours later, a small headline from the Valentine's Day edition of the *Fort Worth Record* read: "Child of Six Sees His Father Shot."

The accompanying story described how no one but Chester Hogan's "six-year-old son" (Bennie was actually nine) had been present in the front parlor room when his wife and two other children heard a gunshot, rushed in, and discovered Hogan lying on the floor, mortally wounded. According to the newspaper, the bullet entered Hogan's body just above the heart and exited below his left shoulder blade, clearly self-inflicted.

"It was stated by physicians at the hospital," wrote the reporter on the scene, who probably got his facts straight from the ambulance attendant or the first policeman who was summoned to the residence—"that while his condition is critical he has good chances for recovery."

In fact, by the time the newspaper hit the teeming streets of Cowtown, Chester Hogan, who had turned thirty-seven just eleven days before the shooting, was dead. News of the tragedy appeared three days later in the *Dublin Progress* and gave a slightly more detailed, if somewhat curiously altered, account of the terror that took place at 305 Hemphill Street, explaining that Chester and Clara had fiercely tangled over his desire to move back to Dublin. At some point, according to this account—which many believe Clara Hogan actually had a hand in writing or at least editing—Chester was alone in a separate room of the house and suddenly pulled a pistol from his grip and placed the muzzle to his chest just as his "twelve-year-old son Royal" entered the room and demanded, "Daddy, what are you going to do?" The gravely wounded man was taken to Protestant Hospital, where, according to the *Progress* account, Chester Hogan died twelve hours later after declaring, "I wish I hadn't done it."

Finally, there was this brief coda to the almost operatic tragedy: "Mr. Hogan

had been in bad health more than a year and had been from time to time under medical treatment in a Fort Worth Sanatorium. It is believed this ailment
from which he could secure no relief, was one of the contributing, if not the
prime cause of his rash act."

Assuming Mama Hogan supplied her own take on events to the *Progress* reporter, one must pause to wonder, how could she have possibly mistaken her
eldest son's age (Royal was actually thirteen) and placed *him* in the room with
his suicidal father when the actual police report from the scene of the tragedy
had a much younger boy witnessing the shooting?

The accounts, in short, simply didn't jibe. Was it Clara's poor if well-
intentioned attempt to shield the quieter and more impressionable Bennie
from the avalanche of sorrow that was certain to follow from his beloved
father's suicide, or simply a case of a reporter rushing to get the story down before he could double check his facts?

"I always had the impression that it really was Uncle Ben who was in the
room and saw what happened," supplies Jackie Towery. "It wouldn't surprise
me at all if Mama Hogan wanted people to think it was Royal, though. He was
older and a lot more like her. I mean *tough*. Even then, he could handle anything life threw at him. I remember, many years later, she told him she
thought he was the hardest man she ever knew—that he'd have made a perfect prison warden. I don't think she was joking either."

Whoever saw Chester Hogan put a bullet through his own heart, as both
Heroditus and Chester's Arlington Heights physician would no doubt concur,
suicide was nothing less than a pox upon a household in Jazz Age America, an
ailment from which there was no relief. Time, as one survivor of the ordeal
liked to say, could ease the pain but never remove the stain.

Whatever else can be said about that rash and unspeakable act in Cowtown's chill winter dusk, the joy and safety and innocence Bennie Hogan had
always felt in his life up till then was shot clean through the heart too.

As the sound of the shot faded through the house, his childhood ended on
the spot, and his greatest fear became his greatest strength, the angel's wings
that eventually lifted him up and protectively carried him to distant worlds he
never could have imagined.

TWO

Welcome to Cowtown

T HE FUNERAL was more than little Bennie could take.

 "Ben's father was his idol," Valerie Hogan told Dave Anderson of the *New York Times* shortly before her death in early 1999, "and his father's death just hurt Ben so much . . . they were not able to get Ben to go into the church . . . he couldn't bear to see the casket." She and Ben had been married "many years," she also confided to Anderson, before she learned about Chester's suicide, a reflection of the event's powerful significance in her husband's life. As Valerie speculated to her younger sister, Sarah, and others, she probably would never have heard a whisper about the family's darkest secret if she hadn't overheard Princess Hogan discussing Chester's death with Mama Hogan at a family gathering in the late 1940s. "In all the years we were married," Valerie amplified to Anderson, "he only talked about his father's death a few times, about how he remembered his father and remembered being on a horse with his father."

Overleaf: Hogan home, East Allen Street, Fort Worth, circa 1924 *(Courtesy Hogan Estate)*

In any case, less than two weeks after Chester's body was brought home on the Frisco train and buried in a family plot at Dublin Memorial Park, Clara Hogan packed up and moved her family out of the Hemphill Street house to a temporary accommodation, an apartment on Taylor Street, on the edge of downtown Fort Worth. Taylor Street was a few blocks closer to Cheney's, but it was also within easy walking distance of Striplings and Meachums, the other major department stores, where she could pick up extra seamstress work to augment the family's modest income flow.

Though she was a Baptist and not a particularly religious woman, the trauma of Chester's death also prompted her to install Princess and Ben in the Sunday school at one of Cowtown's more affluent Methodist parishes, where she soon heard through the grapevine about a small frame house up for rent out in the quieter reaches of the Morningside neighborhood, a couple of miles southeast of the Texas & Pacific depot.

This location would require Clara to take the streetcar to work, but the pretty little house at 1613 East Allen Street had a decent yard and a shade tree or two plus a neighborhood full of kids around it. That would be a better environment for Bennie and Princess, she decided, and she didn't hesitate to sign a lease and uproot her brood again. Not long after the trio moved in, Clara enrolled her youngest two in the Baptist church Sunday school only a few blocks away from East Allen. No sense wasting good money by taking the streetcar to church, she told a neighbor, when they could walk to services. The downtown church had served its purposes quite nicely. Besides, Hogans had always been Baptists.

Despite these marginal improvements, the family's financial plight grew more severe by the day until Clara finally agreed to allow Royal, who was then almost fourteen, to drop out of school and take a full-time job delivering office supplies for Bert Pollard & Company on his bicycle. He also sold copies of the *Fort Worth Star-Telegram* on a street corner near the busy Westbrook Hotel, occasionally pumped gasoline at a service station on Lancaster Avenue, and soon began attending night school three days a week to learn bookkeeping and accounting. Like his maternal grandfather the cotton broker, Royal Hogan possessed a spectacular head for numbers, and like his mother, an indefatigable work ethic. "He became my Rock of Gibraltar," Clara Hogan fondly reminisced three decades later to a reporter from the newspaper whose long-ago receipts helped pay the family's early rents. "Without him I hate to think what might have happened to us."

When Bennie, a fourth-grader at Carroll Peak School on Elmwood Street, volunteered to help out too, Clara reluctantly agreed to permit him to contribute by hawking newspapers after school on the busy passenger platform at the T&P depot, a reasonably safe public spot, she calculated, where she or one of her older children could collect the small boy on their way home each evening. Princess, meanwhile, helped out by babysitting neighborhood children and, a bit later, working part-time at a local drugstore.

Bennie took on his task of selling newspapers with industrious solemnity, hustling straight from school yard to train platform to peddle the late edition of the *Star-Telegram* among the trains arriving and departing through the afternoon into the night, waving the newsprint over his head and broadcasting the day's headlines—"Lillian Russell Dead at Sixty-one!" "King Tut's Tomb Found in Egypt!"

On one of these first few afternoons of his adulthood, barely four feet tall and scarcely sixty pounds, the story goes, the diminutive nine-year-old had to use his fists to defend his chosen spot on the train platform against the predations of an older newsboy. "That station was where I learned to take pretty good care of myself," he boasted gently—almost fondly—to an interviewer in the early 1950s. "It toughened me up real fast. You either fought for your turf and won or you went someplace else. I wasn't about to give up."

Like Oliver Twist, the plucky and determined survivor of Charles Dickens's classic tale of an orphan's life on the mean streets of Industrial Age London, Bennie Hogan believed—at least in his own worried mind—that his survival in teeming Cowtown depended on selling those newspapers and taking home the receipts. More than one observer of the dark turn of events that quickly transformed Bennie Hogan from a gentle country field mouse into an enterprising city street rat has in fact glimpsed a powerful parallel to Charles Dickens's own struggle with the lost innocence of his childhood and the breakdown of a beloved father.

When Dickens's father was cast into debtors' prison in the mid-1820s, twelve-year-old Charles was forced by his mother, Elizabeth, to quit school and work for six shillings a week at a boot blacking factory in London's Strand, a personal humiliation he never forgot—or forgave her for. "I suffered in secret," he later wrote, "suffered exquisitely. . . . No words could express the secret agony of my soul. My whole nature was so penetrated with grief and humiliation. . . . Those trials made me as I am today."

After working as a court stenographer and parliamentary reporter, Dickens employed the keen powers of human observation he developed through his early labors to produce *Sketches of Boz*, a series of humorous London carica-

tures that propelled him to instant fame. Though he eventually found a dot-
ing wife and produced ten loving children, apparently experiencing great devotion and happiness during the early years of his marriage, Dickens
remained haunted by what he called the "battle of life" and driven by ghosts
of his forfeited childhood, a Calvinist workaholic whose mental toughness,
ravenous appetite for success, and obsessive search for love and public acclaim
made him the greatest author of his age—and an emotional wretch who ultimately deceived his wife and family and perished in a fever of frustrated self-
loathing.

In fiction if not in life, Dickens learned early that he could control events
and at least determine a happier outcome for his characters. Not surprisingly,
his finest works, *Oliver Twist*, *Great Expectations*, and *David Copperfield*, are
dark anthems of boyhood paradise lost and human dignity eventually recovered. In real life, however, relentless hard work became Charles Dickens's
solely perceived means of personal salvation, the only thing he believed would
ultimately save him from a childhood shame he was never in fact quite able to
outrun.

One hundred years later, working the swarming crowds on the platform of
Fort Worth's ornate Texas & Pacific train depot, little Bennie Hogan had an
emerging mind-set—and world—that was not a whole lot different from
young Charles Dickens's in London's bustling universe around the blacking
factory in the Strand. From his mother and older brother he quickly learned
the art of street survival, adopting their work habits and unsentimental attitudes. Among other things, according to his sister, Princess, and other family
sources, Bennie never again permitted himself the luxury of crying in public,
prematurely developing a heightened sense of adult responsibility and self-
protectiveness—the thick skin of an Oliver Twist—that hid his natural boyish
exuberance and native glee and tenderness, which instantly manifested, for
example, around animals or even while watching certain romantic Hollywood
movies with a noble message or ending. These traits in his son also became ca-
sualties of Chester Hogan's rash act of self-destruction, banished to the attic of
little Bennie's emotions for safekeeping under lock and key until he was a late-
middle-aged man, put out of sight the way Miss Havisham put away her beautiful untouched wedding cake and waited for a handsome groom who never
arrived.

"Sometimes it would take him all night to sell his newspapers," recounts his
early biographer Gene Gregston, a newspaperman who knew his subject reasonably well. "More than once Royal or a friend found Ben, his old aviator cap

pulled down over his ears, curled up asleep on a waiting-room bench, his head resting on his stack of newspapers."

As with Charles Dickens before him, the downside of learning to survive on his own was that he forever carried a resentment toward his mother for being the agent of these hard and necessary lessons. Also, while her indefatigable will to survive brought them all to Cowtown to seek new opportunities, it didn't escape his notice that her good intentions directly resulted in the loss of his father, the gentle soul Bennie most loved and trusted in life. "There is no doubt in my mind," says Clara Hogan's granddaughter Jackie Towery, "that Ben respected his mother and loved her the way any dutiful son would. But it was my impression that it wasn't anything close to the way he loved my grandfather. That was something special and very private. Beyond his loyalty to her, there was a distance between Mama Hogan and Uncle Ben you could always see—and feel."

AT LEAST SEVENTY trains a day arrived or departed from the Texas & Pacific depot, telling the tale of a city on the move. With its booming population and sprawling streets of brick and mud, the Queen City of the Prairies still unapologetically claimed to be America's leading cowboy town. Just north of the Trinity River, to be sure, the infamous stockyards still processed two-thirds of the livestock that left the state of Texas for northern slaughterhouses, and remnants of the Old West were evident in the violent antics of the cattlemen who routinely packed the sawdust-covered saloon floors of Hell's Half Acre, the notoriously squalid district just off the Old Chisholm Trail, where drinking and prostitution flourished at Twelfth and Commerce Streets.

If the arrival of a new century had brought with it certain civilizing influences and a more refined civic vision from a sudden influx of ambitious outsiders who perceived nothing but golden opportunity in the place where Broadway met the range and the West was said to begin, the chance discovery of oil at Ranger, Texas, ninety miles due west of downtown Fort Worth—just as the Great War ended and the troops came home to nearby Fort Bowie—produced the biggest oil boom in the nation's history and unleashed even greater forces of change in brawling Cowtown.

Within weeks of the Ranger discovery, every major oil company and hundreds of independent drillers and operators—so-called wildcatters hoping to drop a drill bit and strike it rich—dashed to open branch offices in downtown

Fort Worth, followed by merchants of every stripe aiming to cash in on servicing the boom.

To feed and clothe this black gold rush, national grocery store chains like the mighty Atlantic & Pacific Company and Memphis-based Piggily Wiggily quickly identified the booming Fort Worth marketplace as the place they needed to be and introduced self-service and lower prices to the city's growing ranks of shoppers. In reaction to their arrival, most of Cowtown's long-established merchants went even more upscale in goods and services, hoping to secure loyalty among the city's more affluent buyers.

One of those who resisted this temptation was young Marvin Leonard, a shy but thoroughly likable sort who, shortly before Christmas 1918, having already twice failed to make it in the general merchandise business in northeast Texas, opened up a small, unpretentious general store on North Houston Street in the shadow of the ornately carved Tarrant County courthouse. Unlike the better-known newcomers, Marvin Leonard's merchandise was largely salvaged at bargain prices from surplus stock in the city's vast railroad warehouses—"razors and cheese," as he later playfully described it, "cabbage and canned peas." About the time little Bennie Hogan began peddling Amon Carter's *Star-Telegram* newspaper at the Texas & Pacific depot, Leonard was joined in this enterprise by his younger brother Obie, and the brothers Leonard perceived their own golden opportunity to uniquely position the store that bore their family name in a manner that would touch every life in town, regardless of income.

Instead of going upscale and offering goods and services on credit, as most of their famous competitors were doing, Marvin and Obie continued salvaging everything they could lay hands on at a cut-rate price and offering it to their growing ranks of customers at a significant discount, opting to build a devoted following among the city's rapidly growing minority and immigrant communities, factory workers, and farm families.

Whether it was slightly dented cans of condensed milk or a shipment of surplus oranges, rubber work boots, or bails of barbed range wire, Leonard Brothers expanded into whatever commodity for home or farm they could acquire by the cheapest means, then peddled it exuberantly to their devoted customers with dash and imagination, stacking merchandise high and crowding unexpected bargains onto cluttered store counters to add an element of the hunt to the ordinary shopping experience, a festive Old World bazaar of cut-rate goods that often tumbled straight out the front door into the busy street.

"By selling both necessities and semiluxuries at bargain prices," said Leonard's biographers, Victoria and Walter Buenger, "Marvin allowed the less affluent to share the 1920s consumer culture." Later in life, Ben Hogan fondly recalled to a reporter that stepping into the Leonard Brothers store of the late 1920s was like "going to another world, some place you liked to be, almost like home." Exactly the kind of place, in other words, that would have appealed to a boy who had lost both home and father.

Where other retail brokers simply promoted low-price goods and volume, the Leonards offered something intangible and irresistible: *value* and an unerring knack for connecting with customers that directly reflected the genial personality and core values of "Mr. Marvin" himself. Over the subsequent decade, buying up unclaimed freight, salvaged stock, distressed goods, and the inventories of competitors who went belly up in the intensely competitive environment, the Leonards slowly but surely became a Fort Worth institution and a million-dollar emporium that eventually gobbled up an entire block of Houston Street, a big-city department store that acted more like one big friendly country general store peddling everything from Bluebird washing machines to the finest imported silks, from office furniture to 175 varieties of cheese, from ball bearings to long johns.

Fort Worth's original wealth had come principally from cattle and railroads, money that tended to be conservative and largely homegrown in nature, solid fortunes amassed over time by men who were largely risk-averse and careful in their financial calculations, builders of grange halls and stockyard associations, joiners of Christian churches and civic organizations.

These solid citizen types, these old-line Fort Worthians, built their sensible houses in the new affluent neighborhoods that sprang up in the pretty forested hills southwest of downtown and in time were the guiding force behind the formation of the Queen City's fancy opera house, its various civic improvement organizations, and the creation of parks and ultimately the city's first "country" clubs. To their ilk, Marvin and Obie Leonard quickly came to symbolize everything that was good and decent about life in Cowtown—hard work, honest value, no flash, a fortune being made the old-fashioned way.

The newly arrived oil barons, by contrast, who were taking hold with a vengeance the same summer impressionable Bennie Hogan was peddling newsprint on the T&P platform, were far more interested in making a quick killing than finding a good bargain on roof nails or cut-rate overalls.

A large percentage of the city's newcomers were high rollers who had no fear whatsoever of putting everything they had down a dusty hole on the

prairie in hopes of striking it rich. As a result, by 1922, despite the more genteel ambitions of the Queen City's traditional wealth, crude oil was suddenly
king and Fort Worth, according to city historian Oliver Knight, "was drunk
at the shrine of the Oil Goddess."

At one point during the oil frenzy, for example, petroleum speculators
seized control of the ornate lobby of the sleepy Westbrook Hotel where Royal
Hogan sold newspapers before heading off to his evening accounting classes.
They chased hotel guests from the establishment and pitched every piece of
lobby furniture save a large statue of a naked Greek goddess into the street to
make room for a noisy makeshift trading floor.

During that first long hot summer following Chester Hogan's suicide when
young Bennie was struggling to make his own way and some sense of the
seething human cauldron he'd been pitched into, the headlines he broadcast to
passing strangers were dominated by sensational oil fraud trials as one bogus
operator after another—including a man who claimed to have found the
North Pole and was willing to sell parts of it to the highest bidder—ran headlong into the traditional values of *old* Texas and was tried, convicted, and sent
off to the newly expanded Tarrant County jail.

The other dominant local news item that summer concerned the colorful
ongoing affrays between the Reverend J. Frank Norris and Cowtown's seed-
ier elements as well as the Queen City of the Prairie's ruling civic authorities.
Despite the lofty intentions of Prohibition, Jazz Age speakeasys and saloons
openly flourished in Fort Worth, and most of the city's big hotels regularly
hosted card games attended by some of the slickest card players in America.
Street crime and prostitution flourished in Hell's Half Acre, among other
places, and police could be persuaded to look the other way for the modest liberation of a five-dollar bill, while bootleggers were said to be doing a brisk
business selling homemade whiskey in fruit jars to none other than Reverend
Norris himself—so he could impress and inspire his growing revival flocks by
theatrically smashing them to bits.

Norris's preferred targets ranged from Catholics to country club patrons,
from city fathers to foreign immigrants. From his pulpit at Fort Worth's influential First Baptist Church, the gangly, consumptive itinerant preacher violently attacked everything from picture shows to lingerie ads in the
Star-Telegram, openly flirted with the Ku Klux Klan, started the nation's first
radio ministry, shot a man dead who stormed into his office to protest one of
his sermons, and built a bedrock following of true believers that was said to
number over twelve thousand strong—"the world's largest Protestant congre-

gation," as the Reverend Norris himself liked to boast. "A veritable ocean liner of the saved, crossing to Jordan River to salvation."

THE SAVING INFLUENCE on Bennie Hogan came from Cowtown's most enterprising merchant, Marvin Leonard, and oddly enough, it was golf—a rich man's game neither man nor boy had played much before they met—that brought them together in an unlikely friendship that changed both their lives.

After two years of peddling newspapers at the train depot, Bennie heard from Royal—whom he called "Bubber"—that boys his age were out at the Glen Garden Country Club pocketing 65¢ for simply carrying a bag around eighteen holes of golf. Royal might have gone out to Glen Garden to investigate the rumor for himself, but he was now sixteen and working full-time in the office of a downtown business supply firm, wearing long pants and rapidly moving up as a shop clerk.

Bennie had heard of golf, even seen pictures and read stories about Walter Hagen and the accomplished young amateur Bobby Jones in the sports pages of the *Star-Telegram,* but he'd never actually seen the game played. Furthermore, Glen Garden was nearly a six-mile walk from his house on East Allen. Still, 65¢ was two bits more than he made on a good afternoon flogging Amon Carter's newspaper. So one summer day Bennie hiked out to Glen Garden to see what all the hubbub was about.

Glen Garden was neither Fort Worth's oldest nor finest golf course. That distinction belonged to the Rivercrest Country Club, which formed in the western suburbs in 1910 when one hundred prominent local members organized to purchase 625 acres of land and form a club. Glen Garden, which organized three years later, was three miles past the city limits on the largely middle-class southeastern side of town, on 111 acres of idle prairie land once owned by the OK Cattle Company, close to the Interurban shuttle train that operated between Fort Worth and Dallas and just off the old state road to Cleburne. Glen Garden's first clubhouse—a rustic Craftsman-style ranch structure with a large porch supported by open beams, rafters, and fieldstone—opened in 1914 with 350 members, including many of Fort Worth's newest and most addicted golfers.

The original layout was an unremarkable nine holes of hard-baked prairie grass with slightly pushed-up sand greens, but big changes were already under way when Bennie Hogan wandered up to investigate the employment possibilities shortly before his twelfth birthday. The club was in the process of switching over its putting surfaces from sand to grass, and lucky for him, membership had experienced a recent uptick, owing to the growing national fascination with Bobby Jones, the splendid Georgia amateur who had become an instant media darling by winning his first National Open Championship at Inwood Country Club on Long Island in 1923, and who just missed successfully defending his title at Detroit's Oakland Hills just days ahead of Bennie Hogan's first walk out to Glen Garden.

The problem on the ground for Hogan was quickly apparent. "When I arrived," he explained many years later, "I found there was no shortage of caddies, and those already there tried to discourage every new boy who showed up. They ran me through their 'kangaroo court,' rolled me down a hill, and ran me through a paddle line. After that, as was customary, I was required to fight a boy who was a little bigger than me. Thanks to my experiences at the depot, I was handy with my fists and gave my opponent a pretty good working over. So I was accepted."

Well, not quite as simple as that.

The best accounting of what Bennie Hogan was up against comes from another caddie hopeful who showed up just weeks ahead of Bennie, but who scarcely noticed the broody undersized kid for the first few months they were working together that summer.

John Byron Nelson was a tall, gangly farm boy in denim overalls and a big, floppy straw hat who'd just survived typhoid fever and been baptized when he presented himself to club caddiemaster Harold Akey. Akey explained to him that the club had more caddies than players and advised Nelson to come back on weekends and holidays. It took six trips before Nelson finally got a bag to carry. Akey clearly liked the kid, who was polite and well-spoken, smiled a lot, and didn't swear. Those were sterling and somewhat rare qualities in a caddie at Glen Garden, which had official prohibitions against bag carriers cursing and gambling, most of which the caddies blithely ignored unless Akey or club manager James Kidd, a stern Scotsman who went by the moniker "Captain Kidd," were anywhere in view.

With his natural ease around people and sunny farm-boy disposition, Nelson easily stood out from the club's run-of-the-mill caddies. Unlike the belligerent newcomer Hogan, Byron even managed to evade the full fury of the "kangaroo court."

"It was like a fraternity initiation," Nelson recalled in his engagingly homespun memoir *How I Played the Game*. "They'd form two lines, and we'd have to run between them while each one gave us a good hard lick with their belts as we ran by. Sometimes they'd get a barrel and put a new kid in it and roll it down a hill the clubhouse sat atop of. That was even worse than running the gauntlet, but for some reason they never did that to me. They did try to run the new boys off, but I didn't run off very well. After I became a regular caddie, I never did pick on the younger boys, because I hadn't liked it when they did it to me and didn't think it was right."

Bennie Hogan, on the other hand, was a natural target for their initiatory hazing rites. He was nearly too small to even carry a golf bag, and to make matters worse, he seemed to arrive with a big chip on his slim shoulders, defying anyone to try to knock it off—just the kind of punk it was fun to torment and send running home to mama.

They began by yanking off his aviator's cap and throwing it down the hill. Then they taunted Bennie and pushed him around and finally picked him up and shoved him into the stayed barrel and rolled it down the rain-rutted slope by the practice range, a jarring descent that never failed to reduce a victim to rubble and tears. What they learned, though, was that Bennie Hogan didn't cry for anybody. Finally, they made him fight an older boy to prove he belonged. With his oversized fists, he quickly reduced the older boy to a coiled and blubbering heap in the dust, and that was that. He'd won his place in the caddie yard.

Byron Nelson didn't witness Bennie Hogan's initiation ordeal because he was already out on the golf course earning money. Not surprisingly, Byron was already a popular looper with several prominent members, including a local judge who offered him employment doing odd jobs away from the course. These members, many of whom were excellent golfers, also gave bonny young Byron valuable pointers on the game and even loaned him equipment and sometimes—whenever they were out of sight of the tyrannical Kidd, who kept a small apartment on the top floor of the clubhouse—even encouraged him to play along with them on the course.

Like most private clubs of the day, Glen Garden observed strict rules about caddies playing with members. Caddies were officially permitted to play the course only on Saturday mornings before members arrived, Saturday being a workday (or at least half of one) for most people in Cal Coolidge's America. In his memoirs, Nelson recalls that he played his first full round of golf there during the annual Christmas caddie tournament the first year he arrived, using a borrowed set of clubs. He shot 118—"but that didn't count the times I whiffed the ball completely." With saved-up money from caddying, though, he soon purchased his first golf club, a used hickory-shafted five-iron, and also picked up a secondhand edition of Harry Vardon's golf instruction book and set about teaching himself the fundamentals of a serious golf swing.

That next spring, Ted Longworth, Glen Garden's head professional, offered the club's standout caddie a regular position in the pro shop cleaning and repairing golf clubs. Nelson jumped at the opportunity to leave the caddie yard behind and learn a trade he calculated would eventually pay him far more than carrying some businessman's golf bag. He quickly became so skilled at working on members' golf clubs that Longworth invited him to help assemble the set of clubs he planned to take with him to the National Open up at Oakmont Country Club in Pennsylvania later that summer. When the pro invited Byron to tag along to Dallas for the 1927 PGA Championship at Cedar Crest Country Club, Byron began to feel like a genuine protégé, a kid with a future in golf.

Over in Dallas, Byron fell in behind Al Espinosa and the great Walter Hagen during the semifinal round of the tournament, studying every move they made. At one point when the Haig (the eventual winner) faced an approach shot directly into the broiling Texas sun, the affable Nelson spoke up and offered the living legend his own sweat-stained baseball cap. Hagen, grinning, placed the cap jauntily on his smoothly pomaded head and struck a sweet little approach shot that wound up eight feet from the flag, handing fifteen-year-old Byron Nelson his golf cap back with a wink, the thrill of his young life.

Nelson recalls being only dimly aware of the dark-haired kid he would face in the annual caddie tournament later that year, the inward, undersized boy who stuck to himself but always seemed to be hanging around Glen Garden's practice range whenever Nelson had a moment to work on his own evolving swing. The Glen Garden range was a hard, grassless plot where Kidd conducted "caddie school" (explaining the protocols of caddying, the rules of the club, and so on) and permitted the boys, between loops, to hit balls back and forth to soup cans stuck in the ground.

Nothing about Hogan's golf swing initially made an impression on Byron, or on anybody else around Glen Garden, but the saga of Hogan's battle to get down the basics of a grip and swing remains one of the more beguiling mysteries to emerge from this time. Hogan claimed he was a natural lefty—probably true—but in those days left-handed clubs were rare to nonexistent. The story goes that Ted Longworth was the first to place a right-handed club in Ben's oversized hands and correct his awkward "hog-killer" grip. Hogan himself cites brother Royal Hogan (who took up golf about this same time) as the one who actually switched Ben from left- to right-handed playing, assuring him no athlete was ever successful playing left-handed. "I was a southpaw who never stopped playing baseball right-handed until my brother, Royal, made me switch," he told reporters following his breakthrough win at Pinehurst in 1940. "My brother would slap me every time he saw me use that right." Still others maintain it was Longworth's newly arrived assistant Jack Grout (who much further down the fairway would shape the swing of a promising Ohio youngster named Jack Nicklaus) who realized the game would be a lot easier for him if Bennie Hogan played it from the right side.

Whoever finally got Hogan squared away, the early switch in part explains the incredible power he was always able to generate from his left side, including his tendency to hook the ball. Years later, Hogan ruefully joked that he wished he'd been born "with two left hands," reflecting the commonplace view that a dominant left hand was an asset to the right-handed golf swing. Many years later, however, Johnny Bulla—the first player on Tour to fly his own airplane to tournament sites and Sam Snead's best friend and former traveling pal—claimed Ben was never a pure southpaw, as everyone thought. Citing some obscure physical doctrine he called "the Mendelian Law," Bulla argued that only 4 percent of the human species takes after their grandparents and natural left-handedness often skips a generation. He posited, from studying Hogan closely at his peak and talking with him on the subject over their years traveling together, that he merely *inherited* a strong left side from one of his grandparents but was actually a natural right-hander, which accounted for his great strength from the left side but his ability to hammer the ball with his right hand. (If it all sounds a tad esoteric, take comfort from the fact that Sam Snead, among others, admitted he never understood what the hell Bulla was going on about. "I sometimes wish Ben had played left-handed," Sam once drawled with a sly grin. "That way, maybe he would have been less of a headache for me in National Opens.")

Young Byron Nelson, at any rate, first became fully aware of Bennie Hogan's presence not during regular golfing hours but rather at the club's annual caddie boxing contest at Christmas. There he watched Hogan go toe to toe with a much bigger kid called Joe Boy for nearly fifteen full minutes, neither boy giving an inch, until the match was ruled a draw and the members congratulated both combatants.

What struck Byron as most impressive about the smaller boy was the large size and strength of his arms and hands and the unremitting nature of his attack. Hogan's hands were enormous, almost out of proportion to his compact and skinny body. Not a boy's hands at all. And his eyes "looked as hungry as anything I'd ever seen."

When Hogan and the other caddies weren't flinging dice out of Captain Kidd's view, they played a driving game for pennies on the club practice field. Each boy drove a golf ball as far as he could, and whoever hit the shortest distance had to go and pick up all the other balls, typically being hectored by the others. Early on, Bennie lost nearly every time, and many years later Nelson attributed Hogan's rapid improvement and reputation as a power hitter to the sting of that ridicule by the other boys on the Glen Garden practice field. When Bennie couldn't stand being the butt any longer, he started putting in more time beating balls and fiddling with his grip and swing to maximize the velocity of his club head at impact. "He found if he turned his left hand over on the club and gave himself what we call a strong grip, he could hook the ball and make it roll quite a way on that hard, dry ground," Nelson says. "So he didn't have to go chase balls much after that."

"That's probably what kept me going," Hogan reminisced to *Sports Illustrated* in the mid-1950s, looking back on a childhood he was reluctant to explore in any depth. "I began copying the good players and I started hitting a much longer ball. . . . You learn how to take care of yourself and how to think when you're out on your own. I was too old for thirteen."

LEARNING GOLF, at heart, is pure mimicry. The summer Byron Nelson went indoors to make clubs for Ted Longworth, Bennie Hogan caddied regularly for a member named Ed Stewart, perhaps Fort Worth's top amateur player at the time, whose brisk and handsy, low-angled swing he admired and began to seriously emulate during his own practice sessions on the Glen Garden range.

On other long summer mornings, Bennie looped for a pleasant, talkative kid named Dan Greenwood, a friendly teenager whose papa dropped him off at Glen Garden for the entire day. It was an unwritten rule that no caddie liked to carry the bag of another kid, especially "rich" kids, who seldom tipped and were generally pains in the ass to be around.

But an unexpected friendship developed between Greenwood and Hogan, boys of about the same age. Dan disarmed a wary Bennie, the story goes, by handing him a golf club and ball and inviting him to "play along" once the pair were safely out of the view of Captain Kidd. Many years later, a commonly held opinion among the club's former caddies was that these unauthorized rounds may have constituted Hogan's first real shots on a regulation golf course.

Decades later, during Hogan's big welcome-home celebration after capturing the British Open at Carnoustie in 1953, the last of his major championships, an aging Captain Kidd claimed to a Dallas reporter that he actually *encouraged* Glen Garden caddies—Bennie Hogan included—to play whenever there weren't any members' bags to look after. But few of the surviving caddies seemed to recall it this way.

Whatever the truth of the matter, by this time in his rapid development Hogan possessed only a couple of secondhand hickory-shafted irons of his own, scrounged from dime-store barrels for a dollar apiece; playing with a real set of clubs would probably have been a temptation he simply couldn't resist. When Byron Nelson got caught wielding a client's clubs on the course, he was reprimanded and even briefly suspended from the premises. This fate, however, never fell on Bennie Hogan's head, who was either too lucky or too careful to get caught playing with Danny Greenwood's golf clubs.

The Glen Garden practice range became Ben's home away from home, his favorite place to spend time while waiting for a paying bag to come along, the only place he was free to hit as many golf balls as he could physically tolerate. As Jack Grout heard from some of the other boys in the caddie yard, nobody had ever seen a kid who loved the range as much as Bennie Hogan did. His desire for hitting balls was insatiable, almost spooky. The kid could stay out there forever, beating balls from the dusty hardpan and hiking out to pick them up, walking back, and beating them from the dust again.

DURING THE EARLY PART of that summer of 1927, a fairly nonathletic neophyte showed up at Glen Garden hoping the game of golf and a little fresh country air and exercise might be just the cure for what ailed him.

His stomach ached and his legs felt weak, but Marvin Leonard's business was going great guns down on North Houston Street. He and Obie were preparing to take over two new retail spaces that would give Leonard Brothers ownership of an entire city block between Houston and Weatherford, and already in the planning stages was an ambitious new Christmas toy display that would become, in short order, a cherished Fort Worth tradition. But the long hours of work and constant salvaging were exacting a toll on Marvin's chronically frail stomach and constitution, so he went to see his doctor. "After he had quizzed and examined me," Leonard explained some years later, "he told me I could keep on working in the store fourteen or sixteen hours a day and die within a few years, or I could go outside and take some exercise and live a much longer time. He recommended that I take up golf . . . a game I had never played nor to which I had paid any particular attention."

Leonard purchased a cheap set of golf clubs and took a few starter lessons from Ted Longworth. His swing was loopy and erratic. But he kept doggedly at the game and soon adopted the habit (not uncommon among beginners who don't wish to draw attention to themselves) of showing up at Glen Garden before dawn for a quick nine holes prior to work.

Because of his size and personality, Bennie Hogan rose hours before the sun did and set off on foot through the darkness for Glen Garden to get the jump on the older, larger caddies. More than once, he even slept in a sand bunker to be the first in line to claim a bag. Not surprisingly, the first caddie Leonard found waiting to carry his bag was Bennie Hogan.

"I'm not much of a player yet, son," Leonard informed the fourteen-year-old. "But I'd be glad to have you go along."

"That's okay, sir," Bennie supposedly replied solemnly. "Maybe I can show you something."

So off they went together, the runt caddy and the genteel groceryman, a match that eventually did them both a world of good.

"Every morning I got up in time to be at the course about sunup and play nine holes," Marvin recalled two decades later. "Then I'd go home and eat a big breakfast and sail off to work feeling like a new man. Golf not only saved my life, but it restored my health and gave me a new interest."

A couple of important things were happening in Bennie Hogan's life at precisely this moment too.

The first was that his growing ardor for golf was knocking holes in his newspaper earnings. Down at the circulation office of the *Star-Telegram*, office manager Clyde Milliken noticed an annoying pattern developing. Whenever it rained, Bennie Hogan was at his post on the T&P platform selling papers to beat the band; when the sun shined, though, he was nowhere to be found—until Milliken discovered he was out at Glen Garden Country Club hitting balls or hustling up caddie jobs. When Milliken presented the boy with a choice between toting golf bags for hire and selling newspapers, Hogan chose golf.

For her part, Clara Hogan wasn't the least bit pleased to learn that Bennie had quit the paper to pursue caddying. "Why don't you quit fooling around with golf and get an honest job?" she scolded him, according to Royal. "Your brother is working hard while you're off playing a silly game."

As Marvin Leonard discovered during their early morning perambulations together, though, there was nothing silly about golf to Bennie Hogan; the boy regarded the game as seriously as Leonard took selling groceries. What the pleasant if reserved Leonard may have glimpsed in Hogan was an undersized version of himself—an enterprising kid who was willing to hike half a dozen miles on foot through the darkened streets just to beat the other caddies to an honest buck.

Leonard could certainly relate to that, and admire it. As a kid growing up in a farm town near the Arkansas border, he'd been a sickly and somewhat lonely boy, the son of a hardworking man who abandoned his failing grocery business in the economic downturn of 1893 to go back to farming vegetables and cotton. On his way to becoming a marketing force who redefined Fort Worth's commercial shopping habits (and to some extent America's), Marvin Leonard dropped out of school and bought and sold anything he could get his hands on just to make ends meet. He showed up early, stayed late, and was naturally wary of credit and positively terrified of debt. He worshiped his mother and suffered from a declining, Bible-reading father whose Old Testament wrath was meted out with unsparing harshness. As a young man, Marvin bore his father's righteous outbursts without rancor, internalizing his anger, counting the days until he could finally strike out on his own.

Though Marvin couldn't have detected it then, the parallels to his young Glen Garden caddie's life would prove remarkable over the fullness of time. Both men would emerge from difficult childhoods to find salvation in the rigors of hard work and later marry emotionally needy women who hid their mental distress from the world at large, a lifelong burden each man carried with great dignity and composure.

Both became benign autocrats and natural caretakers of every detail in the lives of the people around them. Leonard would go on to have four daughters and no sons; Hogan would have neither but expressed a lifelong affection for children, a tenderness that manifested in the lavish treatment of his two nieces. Once their separate successes finally arrived, both mentor and charge chose to live a discreet and relatively modest material life, acting generously—if quietly—as a benefactor to the community, donating liberally to charities, hospitals, and churches, the fundamental institutions of a solid American life, always without any need or desire for personal publicity.

Was it a mere coincidence that Marvin Leonard's father, John, passed away from heart disease the same summer he moseyed out to Glen Garden to check out golf and discovered a kindred spirit and unlikely protégé in the person of young Bennie Hogan?

Probably not. Marvin Leonard, then in his late twenties but feeling much older, dreamed about finding a wife he could dote on and settling down to have a family. Bennie Hogan, ten years his junior, was a boy in search of a father just like Marvin Leonard aspired to be. The kid's eyes were sharp and his instincts for improving himself were even sharper, qualities that mirrored Marvin's own survival values. In many ways, theirs was a match made in heaven—if not the Glen Garden caddie yard.

What Bennie saw in Marvin Leonard, of course, though he may not have recognized it at the time, was the mentor he desperately needed to fill the cindered black hole Chester's suicide left in him.

Beyond these not insignificant attractions, contrary to Mama Hogan's chaste assessment of golf as an idle rich man's game, everything about the game thoroughly appealed to Hogan's personality and nature, beginning with the solitary quality of the game itself; the fact that winning or losing a match didn't depend on the unpredictable actions of a teammate, just on the simple execution of one's own acquired playing skills; and the game's governing rules, which, in a world that struck Bennie as cruelly unfair, promoted fairness (and penalized cheats) and operated with a definite protocol of rights and wrongs.

On a different level, Hogan instinctively understood that golf attracted a lot of influential people and successful businessmen like Marvin Leonard and that one's chances of self-improvement in the company of men like Leonard could be measured in ways that far exceeded the simple numbers scratched on a scorecard.

GLEN GARDEN's Christmas caddie tournament of 1927 became the stuff of legend. By tradition, caddies signed up to use members' clubs, and members not only volunteered to carry the bags of their favorite loopers but also threw a lavish turkey dinner and distributed small gifts afterward.

Bennie Hogan surprised everyone, and possibly even himself, by firing 39 over nine holes, two over par, though Nelson, who matched him by sinking an impressive thirty-foot birdie putt on the final hole to force a tie, later insisted in his memoirs that they actually tied with scores of 40.

In any event, someone in a position of authority quickly proposed a nine-hole play-off, and as the two competitors walked to the 10th tee, the story goes,

Hogan shook his head in dismay and remarked to Byron, "Well, good luck. I didn't think you could make that putt."

He probably hadn't intended any slight and was merely expressing his view of the situation exactly as he saw it, an emerging Hogan trademark. And to be fair, given the circumstances, the smaller Bennie wouldn't have been human if he hadn't felt a little cheated by Byron's last-moment heroics. To compound matters, both boys were under the impression that they were playing a sudden-death play-off, and when Ben scored a 4 and Byron a 6 on the 1st hole, Hogan mistakenly assumed he'd won for a *second* time. Several Nelson partisans, however, pleaded for a full nine-hole play-off, and it was decided the boys should play on in the spirit of the occasion. Something perhaps faltered in the fatherless Hogan after that, to whom fortune showed no grace and every step in winter felt like two. Nelson ultimately sank another long putt on the final hole of their Christmas match to register a score of 41, beating his smaller competitor by a slender stroke. Before the turkey dinner was served, the players were each presented with new golf clubs—Byron the winner received a mashie iron or five-iron; Ben, the runner-up, was given a two-iron. "Well, I already had a five-iron," Nelson recounts cheerfully in his memoirs, "and he already had a two, so we traded clubs."

After this, it was remembered, everybody went inside the clubhouse for punch and food to celebrate Christmas—all except Hogan, who never fully explained why he declined to participate in the festivities or where exactly he went off to with his new five-iron, but possibly to the cold comfort of the darkening practice range. "I felt I already had my party when I tied Nelson," he amplified a bit defensively many years later, sounding a little like Ebenezer Scrooge looking back on a moment of painful youthful pride, and left matters at that. Under the circumstances, it would have been hard not to resent Nelson's popularity and easy success, a frustrating pattern that was to characterize their evolving friendship and rivalry for the next twenty years.

The following spring, however, Ted Longworth brought fifteen-year-old Bennie Hogan into the Glen Garden shop and showed him how to repair and build clubs too. "On weekends I polished clubs until three in the morning. Boy, I would look at those clubs and they were the most beautiful things, Nickels and Stewarts, all made in Scotland," Hogan remembered decades later. "I found that working on those clubs, usually alone and sometimes late into the evenings, gave me tremendous personal satisfaction and a much better understanding of the game."

Every year, Glen Garden members voted to honor their most deserving caddies with a junior membership and full playing privileges, and that same spring Hogan went into the club shop, Captain Kidd was asked to submit a worthy candidate's name. Without hesitation he nominated Byron Nelson, noting with a Scot's moral pragmatism: "He's the only caddie who doesn't drink, smoke, or curse. I think he should have it."

Once again, Bennie Hogan was left out in the cold, a stinging second to Nelson's charm and sunny popularity. Byron won a small tournament out at nearby Katy Lake Golf Course and, when he wasn't mowing greens to earn extra money from Longworth, soon dropped out of school to take a full-time job as a file clerk for a prominent Glen Garden businessman. As a new junior member of the club with folding money in his pocket, Byron suddenly had his afternoons and weekends free to play all the golf he wanted, and a place where he was entitled to play.

His game naturally progressed with vigor, and a little later that same year Nelson won several members-only tournaments around Fort Worth while Hogan continued caddying and polishing clubs until the wee hours in back of Ted Longworth's shop. Given his lowly status as shop assistant, Bennie wasn't eligible to play in Glen Garden events, nor was he on the receiving end of invitations to play at other clubs. He polished his clubs and bided his time, wondering what Byron had that he didn't, determined to follow suit.

At Christmas, despite her low opinion of where golf might lead her youngest son, Clara Hogan scraped together forty bucks and bought Bennie his first full set of golf clubs from a downtown hardware store. She was working exclusively at Cheney's now, making better money at the high-end ladies' shop on Main Street. Royal was bringing home almost $20 a week. After years of painful struggle, the family's situation had more or less stabilized.

To replace his lost income from the *Star-Telegram*, Ben took an evening job as a doorman at the Hippodrome Theater in downtown Fort Worth. Now sixteen, he'd reached his full height of five-foot-eight and 135 pounds. He had sharp angular features, a full head of dark hair, a mouth full of straight white teeth, a broad smile, and the kind of lean good looks that made some of Clara's customers think her son looked like a young George Raft. In his regal gold-piped doorman's uniform, the young man often stood at the rear of the darkened auditorium and watched movies the way he had as a dreamy kid on a hard wooden bench beside his sister, Princess, long ago and far away, in a place called Dublin. When people commented that he was handsome enough to be in the movies, young Bennie sometimes permitted himself to fantasize about what being a movie star would be like.

Something else was already crowding that childhood fantasy, though—a fate he perhaps already held in his oversized hands.

Many years later, Clara explained to a Fort Worth newspaperman that upon receiving her Christmas gift of a new set of golf clubs, Bennie solemnly declared, "Mama, I'm going to be the greatest golfer that ever lived." She also remembered how whenever she sent him to the store for a loaf of bread or pound of butter, he hit shots from yard to yard the entire way there and back, like a boy thoroughly possessed by the game.

Ben Hogan later denied ever saying this.

"I never did decide that golf was going to be my life," he told *Sports Illustrated* in a famous interview near the end of the fifties. "I loved the game when I first started caddying, but in high school I tried to play football. I was too small, and baseball just didn't catch my fancy. Why golf did, I don't know. But I just loved it."

THE SUMMER AFTER his sophomore year at Paschal High, where he recorded spotty attendance and only mediocre grades, failed to make any athletic teams (nobody had a golf team in those days), joined no clubs or organized school activities of any kind, and scarcely made an impression on any of his classmates, Bennie Hogan followed his friend and rival Byron Nelson's lead and quit school, promising his mama he would make up for the lack of a diploma by working doubly hard and constantly improving his mind by reading books and newspapers. He pragmatically understood, as she did, that for a poor kid from Morningside, college simply wasn't an option—that if he was going to make anything of himself in life, it would be through his own sweat and hustle. If one part of Bennie resented his mother for effectively sending him out into the cold cruel world to earn his keep, another part of him was grateful to her for the self-reliance that hard experience had taught him. "I feel sorry for kids these days," Hogan remarked in an interview in the early 1970s. "They don't know what it's like to learn that you can survive almost anything."

On the positive side of the ledger, Bennie played in his first real golf tournament away from Glen Garden, at the public links championship in Waco, bumming a ride to the tournament from another promising amateur named Matty Reed. For his efforts, the Glen Garden shopboy placed second and collected thirteen new balls for thirteen birdies. He promptly sold the golf balls for two bits apiece to other competitors before heading home and pocketed the proceeds. Golf balls were relatively easy to come by.

The summer following that, as his practice rituals grew longer and more self-absorbed, just prior to his seventeenth birthday, Bennie hitched another ride one hundred miles east to Shreveport, Louisiana, and actually made it to the finals of the Southwestern Amateur, losing down the stretch to a fine young player from Dallas, nineteen-year-old Gus Moreland. During their match, the long-hitting Hogan, a Shreveport daily reported, was repeatedly in trouble off the tee with prodigious drives, constantly having to scramble from the woods and deep rough to keep up before losing the match, 4 and 3.

Too broke to pay his caddie for his services, and rather honorably in retrospect—a glimpse perhaps into the evolving rigid moral code that made the hungry young man view most things starkly in black-and-white terms and make snap judgments of either right or wrong, proper or improper—Bennie hocked his runner-up prize on the spot, a wristwatch, paid his caddie what he owed him, and thumbed his way home to East Allen Street.

"After that," Hogan later explained, "I decided amateur golf was fine, but if I wanted to continue playing golf, I'd have to make some money."

On the face of it, this wasn't an entirely crazy proposition, because Bennie Hogan had regularly begun to beat the better players at several courses around Fort Worth, picking up the odd five or ten bucks off money matches at Katy Lake Golf Course and another layout called Z-Boaz out in the suburbs. As his play at Shreveport indicated, given the right circumstances, Bennie could hold his own against the region's top prospects, whether gangly Gus Moreland or soft-spoken Ralph Guldahl or the hard-edged Mangrum brothers, Ray and Lloyd, from over in Dallas. Some Glen Garden members in fact believed Hogan's potential matched or even exceeded that of Byron Nelson, though he clearly lacked the kind of support systems Byron and the others enjoyed—enthusiastic supporters who wrangled them invitations to compete at the area's top clubs and (in an age before such strict prohibitions) helped finance such expeditions, or supportive family members who had the time and means to fund improved equipment and transport them from one amateur event to another. For this reason alone, Nelson, Guldahl, and the Mangrums rose much quicker through the ranks of Texas amateur golf and saw their names posted on professional scoreboards well before Bennie Hogan did.

Ted Longworth admired Hogan's intense work ethic and was the first to admit the wiry teenager had loads of raw potential too, though his putting stroke was, at best, highly inconsistent—a direct reflection of how little time, relatively speaking, Bennie had been able to practice on real grass putting surfaces.

A year after the members voted to make Byron a junior Glen Garden member, on the other hand, golden boy Nelson qualified for his first Texas Open pro-am and got his first real taste of major tournament competition, displaying a ball-striking ability and confident putting stroke that made a host of Lone Star believers and belied Byron's usual tournament stomach jitters. Less than two years later, after winning a number of small amateur tournaments and members-only events to which Longworth had wrangled his most promising protégé invitations, Byron qualified for his first U.S. Amateur Championship up in Chicago and made his first trip out of Texas, a wide-eyed and deeply grateful young man who couldn't say thank-you enough to anyone who had helped him along.

Not long after that, in November 1932, after winning Fort Worth's Rivercrest Invitational, and with $75 in his pocket and little more than the faith of a mustard seed and the worried prayers of his parents to go on, John Byron Nelson decided to make a go of it playing tournament golf for money. Ted Longworth had recently accepted the head pro's position at Texarkana Country Club, which was putting on the $500 golf tournament where Byron was headed. But Longworth hadn't exactly forgotten his other protégé. By the time he left Cowtown, Longworth had been part-owner, for well over a year, of a raw new nine-hole layout near downtown Fort Worth called Oakhurst, which gave a hardworking former shopboy named Bennie Hogan the opportunity to move up a peg and actually run a pro shop, selling balls and equipment, giving lessons to anyone who was willing to pay for them.

The Oakhurst job paid less than thirty bucks a week and didn't have a lot of other perks, but it at least gave Hogan a foot in the door of his chosen profession, permitted him to call himself a "professional" for the first time ever, and provided him unlimited opportunity to beat balls till his hands bled when there weren't paying customers around.

As advancement opportunities went, the Oakhurst job couldn't have come at a more unpromising moment in American life. The prosperity that once seemed so real and boundless had basically disappeared overnight following the stock market crash of 1929. Three years into the deepest financial crisis in the nation's history, according to the *New York Times*—the same week, as it happened, that grateful, wide-eyed Byron Nelson boarded his bus with high hopes for Ted Longworth's Texarkana tournament—an estimated twelve million people were out of work across depression-strapped America, daily breadlines in some cases stretched dozens of blocks in most major cities, and millions of solid family men who not so long before had fancied themselves the gatekeepers of the American dream had simply taken to the rails and vanished, many leaving their wives and children behind to fend for themselves.

For what it's worth, golf courses and country clubs were among the hardest hit by the ripple effect of the tumultuous stock market crash. More golf clubs and courses actually closed their doors and ceased operations than opened them during this bleak interval, and at one famous club north of Manhattan, in the wake of Black Tuesday, more than one-third of the wealthy membership was never seen again.

In his inaugural address beneath dark swirling clouds that mirrored the mood of the nation at large, just days before Byron Nelson got off the bus in Texarkana, the man on whom most Americans pinned their hopes to somehow save them, former New York governor Franklin D. Roosevelt, assured his worried countrymen that the only thing they needed to fear was fear itself.

Back in Cowtown, meanwhile, good-looking nineteen-year-old club pro Bennie Hogan took an additional nighttime job to help make ends meet. With his quick head for numbers and a nearly photographic memory, Hogan was a natural for dealing cards at the Blackstone Hotel, a job he was initially too embarrassed to tell his own mother about. Displaying the same qualities that made Byron such an appealing caddie for hire—he didn't drink or cuss and had the kind of hard poker face nobody was inclined to try to hustle—Bennie proved such an adroit card manager that he was soon offered broader employment opportunities as a stickman at a craps table at a famous roadhouse between Fort Worth and Dallas.

He took the job—for a while at least—and although the position soon paid well enough for him to be able to afford his own set of wheels and occasionally take the pretty brown-eyed girl he'd started seeing on a regular basis to the movies and out to eat, being a croupier in a jackleg casino wasn't something he planned to do for long. For years, in fact, both before and after his fame and wealth arrived, Hogan flatly refused to even acknowledge his erstwhile career as a card dealer and stickman. He spoke of it only now and again to his closest friends or a few trusted fellow journeyman pros (most of whom had far worse skeletons than professional card-dealing hanging in their closets), mentioning it in the slightly regretful tone of a necessary youthful indiscretion.

In an odd sort of way, President Roosevelt might have even had an industrious, hardworking bootstrap guy just like Bennie Hogan in mind when he made his famous reassuring remarks about fear being the only thing Americans really had to fear, in the face of sweeping economic convulsions that showed no sign of letting up anytime soon.

Thanks to the cards life had long ago dealt him, there was hardly anything Bennie Hogan genuinely feared. Even fear itself.

And as the impressive new president battling his own physical frailties took pains to constantly remind so many good folks temporarily down on their luck, this was still an America where faith, hard work, and perseverance always made the difference.

With a pretty girl suddenly on his arm who believed he could do most anything he put his clever mind to, why, there was just no telling how far a young man like Bennie Hogan could really go.

THREE

Nothing Divided
by Nothing

According to Valerie Hogan, she met Bennie Hogan the summer he turned fourteen, the summer before he began carrying Marvin Leonard's golf bag and copying Ed Stewart's polished golf swing at Glen Garden Country Club. She was already fifteen, a rising freshman at Fort Worth's Central High School. "I knew Ben played golf," she said. "He talked about it all the time, but at the time I really knew nothing about golf. All I knew was that golf was his life. He just loved it."

The most popular version how the two shy youngsters first met maintains they were introduced in Sunday school at the Morningside Baptist Church when Ben was twelve or thirteen and became nearly inseparable after that. This may or may not be true. People remember things differently, and many years later Hogan explained to a local reporter that the two really got to know each other at Jennings Junior High School the year before Valerie moved on to the ninth grade at Paschal High, which more or less jives with her account of their first meeting.

Overleaf: Ben Hogan, aged sixteen *(Courtesy Hogan Estate)*

In all likelihood, the first time they set eyes on each other was probably in the quiet street that divided their houses. According to the Fort Worth city directory of the late 1920s, Claude Fox and his wife Jesse had been living at 1341 East Allen Street with their two young daughters, Valerie and Sarah, for several years already when Mama Hogan moved her devastated family into the small frame house diagonally down the block at 1316.

Claude Fox was the projectionist at the New Liberty Street Theater, a big friendly Irishman who bore an uncanny resemblance to his hero Harry Truman and liked to show off his strikingly pretty daughters. On Claude's modest income of $35 a week, the family was by no means well off, but Jesse Fox, a fiery rancher's daughter who hailed from the wilder reaches of West Texas, had a reputation for dressing them in the latest fashions of the day.

"Even as teenagers, those Fox girls were very well known around Fort Worth," recalls a woman who knew the family only by reputation in those days. "Always dressed to the hilt, white gloves and hats, bitsy waists just like their mother. I remember how striking the pair of 'em were—perfect little china dolls with coal-black hair. The older one—I believe it was Valerie—was much quieter, never said boo. The younger one, though, was Miss Personality, a real extrovert just like her mother. Everybody in our part of town knew the Fox girls."

Though nobody could have guessed as much to look at them, just like the hardworking Hogans down the block, the Foxes had a lively frontier past of their own to contend with, including a family scandal that ultimately sent Jesse and Claude scurrying for a new start in the relative anonymity of Cowtown.

Back in Mineral Wells, a prosperous farming town 50 miles west of Fort Worth, Jesse's father, a passionate Norwegian rancher named J. D. Pederson, caused quite a local stir when he suddenly up and divorced Jesse's mother, Nana, then whipped out his Colt sidearm and shot her lawyer dead as the two men sat in his office negotiating the terms of the pending legal separation. "I thought he was going for his shooter," J. D. Pederson explained simply to the arresting authorities shortly before he was arraigned and sent off to Austin to stand trial for murder.

The rancher had to sell just about everything he owned to pay for his defense, but after a sympathetic jury acquitted Pederson of all charges and released him—the general feeling was that *he* was the injured party, being shaken down by a shyster lawyer representing a woman who probably had no business even being in West Texas—Pederson returned triumphantly to Min-

eral Wells on the train to start rebuilding his life, arriving home to a warm surprise celebration that featured the town brass band and the gift of a new buggy
from his admiring neighbors. By this point in the drama, Jesse's terrified and
bitter mother had already fled home to the bosom of her family somewhere up
in the godless reaches of New York State, leaving her only issue behind.

"My grandmother dearly loved her father and was his only child," explains
Valerie Harriman, Jesse's granddaughter (Valerie Hogan's niece). "He raised
her to do everything better than a man—to ride, rope, and shoot. She was the
belle of the local rodeo and a true daughter of the West."

Like her papa, Jesse Pederson was incredibly headstrong, and not too long
after her father returned home acquitted of all charges against him and her
mother left town, the belle of the rodeo met and fell in love with a friendly ap-
prentice movie projectionist named Claude Fox. They were both eighteen
years old—this was just about a year before they gave birth to their first child,
Valerie, in 1911. Claude had a job offer from a new theater up in Fort Worth.
And in no time flat, the couple decided to elope on a northbound train.

"The story my grandmother told me," says Valerie Harriman, "was that
just as the train was pulling out her father appeared and took a seat on the
hard bench directly across from the surprised couple. He wasn't a bit pleased
with the light of his life running off to the big city with some slick young man,
a movie projectionist no less! And I gather he sat and glared at them all the
way up to Fort Worth. I suppose he thought that might help change their
minds. It didn't work."

Many years later, Ben Hogan, Valerie Harriman's uncle by marriage,
greatly loved hearing the Fox family's rowdy tale of frontier love and justice.
"I think it reminded him in some positive way of the mythical Old West he'd
come from, a small town where passions were real and justice rather simple."
Harriman also remembers that Valerie Fox Hogan, her mother's more socially
sensitive older sister, disliked ever hearing any mention of her mother's frontier past and the checkered family history before coming to Cowtown.

"As a lot of people in Fort Worth saw for themselves, my mother [Sarah
Fox] and Aunt Valerie couldn't have been more different if they'd hailed from
different planets. Only the way my grandmother dressed them made them
somewhat alike. My mother was outgoing and optimistic. She resembled her
own mother in a lot of wonderful ways—they both had a magnetic warmth
that drew people to them and made them so much fun to be around, true cowgirl spirits. They were passionate and fun-loving, and I think that's why Uncle Ben worshiped them both.

"Though she was the oldest sibling, Aunt Valerie, on the other hand, was wary and painfully reserved. It took me many years and a lot of conversations with my own mother to realize that her apparent shyness—and the very proper, ladylike appearance she always carefully maintained—hid a deep embarrassment of our family's past, the stuff that happened down in Mineral Wells and another hush-hush story about one of our New York relatives, a son I believe, going off his rocker and blowing a great deal of the family's money and having to be institutionalized."

These difficulties, Harriman maintains, prevented any hope of Jesse Pederson and her eldest daughter ever being close. "Aunt Val was much too embarrassed by the force of my grandmother's personality, her natural cowgirl honesty and colorful ways. Beneath it all, I also think she was absolutely terrified that the family's streak of hidden madness would somehow catch up to her. My mother had this same fear, by the way, but she never let it come to rule her life the way Aunt Valerie did. As a result of these things, both ladies developed a keen sense of proper appearances. But as they got older, my mother grew more extroverted and friendly—less worried about what people thought of her, less on guard. Aunt Valerie, unfortunately, went the other direction."

The transition from rancher's daughter and rodeo belle to Fort Worth housewife, at any rate, wasn't an easy one for Jesse Pederson Fox, and early on at least, before Claude had established himself and Jesse could afford better, both her young daughters rebelled at wearing the secondhand dresses that mysteriously showed up on East Allen Street in packages postmarked from New York, charity from their mysterious unmet grandmother Nana.

"They were clothes that had obviously belonged to unknown cousins," says Valerie Harriman with her own coy cowgirl smile. "Neither my mother nor my aunt ever forgot this because the minute they could afford better things they both made a beeline to Neiman Marcus and supported that place devotedly for the rest of their lives."

JESSE FOX TOOK a shine to fourteen-year-old Bennie Hogan almost the instant she laid eyes on him, her granddaughter thinks, because of the careful attention he paid to such things as his appearance and his manners and the nice way he treated her pretty, if somewhat emotionally fragile, older daughter.

"I think she saw immediately how good Ben was for Valerie," says Harriman. "He was strong, good-looking, and obviously a take-charge kind of guy—not unlike her own father. Apparently behind closed doors Aunt

Valerie could be hell on wheels if she didn't get her way, a constant trial to both her parents. The problem was, she seemed to have no capacity at all for dealing with change of any sort, including the idea of a rival for her parents' affections."

Among the more unsettling particulars Valerie Harriman picked up from "adult" conversations with her grandmother that took place during her own teenage years, a young and jealous Valerie—then about four years old—once dumped an entire box of talcum powder on the sleeping infant Sarah's head when nobody was looking. Another time, Jesse Fox discovered a feather pillow resting over the baby's face and quickly deduced that Valerie had crept into the room and placed it there. "After that, my grandmother told me, she never felt comfortable leaving Aunt Valerie in a room alone with her newborn sister. The irony is, my mother not only turned out to be Aunt Valerie's best friend in life after Uncle Ben, but as *he* frequently recognized over the years— especially as both women aged—Sarah was the one person who could control Aunt Valerie, calm her down, and handle her difficult personality. That's why they lived so near each other for most of their lives. What the outside world saw of Valerie Fox Hogan was a terribly shy, beautifully turned out, and loyal wife, the quintessential private woman behind the public man who never had a hair out of place or an ill word to say. What they *didn't* see, both my mother and grandmother used to say to me, was Aunt Val's lifelong struggle to control everything around her, including Uncle Ben. As time went on, that became our family's *other* little secret."

So what, it begs to ask, did young Bennie Hogan see in sweet, shy Valerie Fox that drew him so powerfully to her? By all accounts, not long after they met and began spending time together, the two formed an emotional attachment that was as fiercely protective and devoted as anyone had ever seen.

"I think it was really pretty simple," speculates Valerie Harriman, who is named for her maternal aunt. "He gave her strength and character, she gave him loyalty and unwavering devotion. Those were highly valued qualities in a western marriage. She was very pretty, and he was a courtly young man, wise beyond his years, who was clearly going somewhere in life. Human chemistry is a mysterious thing. They suited each other perfectly and fell in love almost instantly, my grandmother told me, filling a powerful void in each other that no one else could fill."

The teenage couple's first official date was a stroll to the movies with a stop at a neighborhood lemonade stand during the walk home. "When we got home," Valerie Hogan explained many years later, "he said, 'May I kiss you?'"

" 'I don't think so,' I said. 'But thank you for a wonderful evening. I enjoyed it.'

"I didn't know that my sister Sarah, who was four years younger than me,
was listening through the open window. As soon as I got in the house, Sarah
started imitating us: 'May I kiss you goodnight? I don't think so.' I adored
Sarah, but she did that so often in the next few days that my mother had to tell
her to stop. My mother and father liked Ben right away.

" 'That little Ben Hogan,' my mother often said, 'is the nicest fellow that
comes to our house.' "

As the Roaring Twenties ended and punishing days of economic
hardship descended, Claude Fox accepted a better-paying projectionist job
over in Cleburne, a prairie town about an hour's drive south of Fort Worth,
and soon moved his wife and youngest daughter there to start the position.
Within a year, Valerie Fox had finished high school and enrolled at Texas
Christian University to study journalism, thinking she might someday become
a society page writer for the local newspaper, a job that would suit her ambitions and refined sensibilities very nicely.

She continued to see Bennie Hogan—whom she had called "Ben" almost
from the day they met—on weekends and whenever her studies permitted or
he wasn't busy tending the shop at Oakhurst or playing wager matches out at
Katy Lake or Z-Boaz or working nights at his mysterious "downtown" job at
the Blackstone Hotel, the two were inseparable. After church on Sundays, Ben
sometimes drove Valerie out to her parents' house in Cleburne in his new secondhand jalopy, where he almost always stayed for supper and struck up a
deepening friendship with Jesse and Claude Fox. She later remembered that
he was the "most reliable young man I ever met."

During a cold and dreary week in February 1930, Hogan and Ralph Guldahl hitched a ride in Ted Longworth's Ford to San Antonio's Brackenridge
Park, where each teenager slapped down $5 on the tournament registration
table and officially declared himself a professional tournament golfer, the only
formality in those days required to make the leap from amateur to professional. When the registration official asked Bennie's name, he answered "Ben
Hogan," using the more grown-up and serious-sounding name Valerie
preferred. He was here to officially start his professional tournament playing
career and make some serious money. In terms of this ambition, *Ben* sounded
more convincing than *Bennie*.

Walter Hagen and Gene Sarazen, the two top professionals of the day, were missing from the field of contenders at the 1930 Texas Open, but according to the *San Antonio Light*, several seasoned tournament journeymen like "Wild Bill" Mehlhorn, the red-hot Horton Smith (he would capture seven out of eighteen tournaments that year), and wiry New Yorker Bobby Cruickshank were on hand to headline a field composed of touring veterans and promising newcomers, including Dallas's gentle, stoop-shouldered reigning city champ Ralph Guldahl and Fort Worth's promising long-hitting Ben Hogan.

Newspaper photographs accompanying their professional debuts reveal both teenagers wearing handsomely pressed plus fours and rather unhappy expressions, Guldahl because he apparently suffered severe pangs of doubt about giving up his amateur status, and Hogan because he had absolutely nothing to lose but a lot of nothing. Royal Hogan had a favorite expression his younger brother adopted about this time and used for the rest of his life to express his contempt for failure of any kind and people he thought were phonies or deals that were worthless. "Nothing divided by nothing is nothing," Royal would say bitterly if something didn't turn out the way he hoped or expected. But brother Ben, in his immaculate duds, had definitely come all the way down to San Antonio for *something*—to officially commence a professional playing career and seize a chance to measure his game's progress against the best sticks in golf, to make a little money and earn the respect of the folks back home, among whom only Valerie Fox seemed to fully comprehend and support his compulsion.

As Open tournament venues went, Brackenridge Park probably wasn't the worst track the pros of the early Great Depression played on during the loosely allied winter circuit of tournaments, beginning out in Los Angeles in early January and meandering back east to the balmy latitudes of Florida around middle March. But despite the fact that the municipal course had been designed by the renowned designer A. W. Tillinghast, poor weather and hard economic times had combined to make Brackenridge's wheat-colored grass so thin on the damp and chilly afternoon Ben Hogan made his professional debut in competition that the fairways had to be marked off with work ropes in order to identify them.

Hogan, playing with silent and thin-lipped Ray Mangrum of Dallas, split the fairway and finished his first nine holes as a pro with a decent score of 38, followed by a 40 on the back side for an opening total of 78. This score ate him up inside, particularly in light of the fact that the unfriendly Mangrum shot 71 while languid and diffident Ralph Guldahl managed 74.

The next day, after sharing a $2 boardinghouse room with Guldahl, Hogan bettered his mark by three strokes, good enough to make the halfway cut in his first professional outing. Without explaining why, though, he suddenly withdrew from the field and headed home without a word to anyone.

"I found out the first day I shouldn't even be out there," he said simply many years later about this surprising development, the start of a pattern of abrupt withdrawals that plagued his early playing career and helped form his reputation as a brooding loner. When asked for more clarification on the problem, Hogan admitted he was nearly overcome in his professional debut by "jumpy nerves" that caused him to savagely hook the ball out of play, devastating his confidence and dashing any hope he had of contending. "Nothing divided by nothing is nothing," he summed up the dispiriting Brackenridge experience. "Right then and there I decided, if I couldn't learn to handle the pressure and play any better than that, why, I had no right to be out there at all."

It was a hard, self-imposed verdict, to be sure, but on the face of it not all that unique among players. Ironically, another beginner, a chatty club-spinning youth from Houston who within a matter of years was destined to become Hogan's closest ally on the early tournament circuit, shot exactly the same opening score as Ben did but waited an additional round before he withdrew too.

Before Jimmy Demaret started winning tournaments and could afford to stick around simply to shoot the breeze with tournament officials and party after-hours with reporters, he had a near-addiction to suddenly pulling out of any golf tournament where he wasn't playing particularly well. "If I had no chance of winning or even being in the money," he reasoned, "there was no sense in paying for a hotel room and a half-starved caddie. Better to see what's waiting for me at the next stop." Few of the scribes, it seems, held this against friendly Jimmy Demaret, because he was everybody's drinking pal and an upbeat character who made friends wherever he went.

Hogan was another story. His abrupt withdrawal from the Texas Open of 1930 signaled something darker than simple pragmatic economics at work. His withdrawal was based on a foreboding sense of personal inadequacy, a crushing feeling of failed hopes and expectations—it was an act of almost desperate self-loathing. At the outset of the tournament, he was the very picture of groomed confidence in the city's leading newspaper, while halfway through the tournament weekend he was just another Dust Bowl loser with his thumb jerked out on a desolate highway headed home.

A week after his sputtering debut at Brackenridge, determined to try again, Hogan took a train to Demaret's hometown and played poorly in the Houston pro-am and even worse in the tournament's opening rounds, 77-76. He withdrew for the second time in less than two weeks and caught a ride back to Fort Worth, quietly vowing to his girlfriend, Val, never to show his face at a professional tournament again until he could subdue the jittery nerves that unraveled him in competition.

Two weeks, two tournaments, and nothing to show for his efforts but dust and heartache—nothing divided by nothing.

THE PROFESSIONAL golf tour of the early thirties that Hogan was so desperately hungry to catch hold of the way Pecos Bill lassoed the twister was a peculiar blend of elements—part itinerant caravan of serious club pros beating across the western landscape to try to augment their modest salaries during the winter hiatus before they had to return home and open up their clubs, and part traveling circus of vagabond golf hustlers and trick-shot artists who probably would have been riding the rails or doing time on a chain gang if "golf for hire" hadn't provided a convenient way of keeping one step ahead of the law.

As the toughest years of the Great Depression struck, golf's image problems were compounded when amateur sensation Bobby Jones, after capturing both the Open and Amateur championships of Britain and America in 1930—a feat sports editor Grantland Rice hailed as the "Grand Slam of golf"—shocked the world by announcing he was officially "retiring" from tournament competition to practice law and get on with his life. Following a boisterous ticker-tape parade down Broadway in New York City, the polished Georgian held to his word by graciously heading to the sidelines at the peak of his craft to practice law, make instruction films, and help transform the grounds of a former commercial nursery down in Augusta, Georgia, into a living shrine to the game's master practitioners. Ironically, the films he made compromised his amateur status.

In the public's mind, Jones's classy departure left a sentimental void nobody could honestly hope to fill in tournament golf, but it certainly wasn't for lack of trying on the part of wily old pros and hungry-eyed newcomers to the circuit. Despite the fact that most tournaments slimmed down their payouts to try to stay alive during the leanest years of the Depression, the number of tournament events actually expanded as worried town fathers and civic promoters suddenly viewed pro golf as a means of boosting flagging public morale and providing a little relief to so many unemployed men. One tournament venue out west, for example, offered free lunch and dinner with every paid admission, and another rather innovatively set up tents staffed with local volunteer doctors who provided free medical exams to customers and their families. In other places, farm livestock, tractors, and donated automobiles (from unsold inventories) were frequently raffled off to benefit local feeding programs at two bits a ticket.

On the positive side of the pro game in 1930, though he hadn't won a tournament of major status in many years, golf's incomparable first full-time touring professional and largest box-office draw, flamboyant Walter Charles Hagen, aka the Haig, winner of two U.S. Open and four British Open titles, five-time USPGA champion, still showed up from time to time to delight paying customers with his brilliant shotmaking (his forte was the recovery shot) and the kind of debonair showmanship that won young Byron Nelson's heart the instant he offered the living legend his ball cap for shade in the broiling Texas sun. "Never hurry, never worry" was the Haig's philosophical approach to both life and golf, and the fact that he still bothered to come out to play made every Hagen sighting a special occasion.

At his peak during the 1920s, Sir Walter raked in more than $300,000 a year from tournament winnings and lucrative exhibition matches, a fortune in the world of professional sports and as much as any athlete in the world made at that time. "I never wanted to be a millionaire," he confided on the cover of his best-selling autobiography. "I just wanted to live like one."

Whatever else was true, professional golf owed Sir Walter a debt far greater than probably the average tournament competitor and patron could even begin to appreciate. In the course of lavishly entertaining galleries on both sides of the Atlantic (golf historian Al Barkow credits him with personally "Americanizing" the game abroad), the game's first professional superstar established the benchmark for how touring professionals would be regarded and treated in decades to come by tournament sponsors and hosting clubs. Through his flamboyant tastes and media-savvy stunts, golf's Gatsby undertook successful campaigns to break down barriers of snobbery and prejudice and elevate the visiting pro's status, particularly among the game's ruling elite. When, for example, he was appalled to discover that competitors at Deal, southwest of London, in 1920 were not permitted to change inside the clubhouse and were relegated instead to a dim, tiny service room adjacent to the head professional's shop, Sir Walter placed his footman conspicuously on guard beside his chauffeur-driven Daimler and changed inside his car, creating a furor in London's daily broadsheets and scandal-hungry tabloids. At the British Open at Troon two years later, then-defending champion Walter Hagen declined an invitation into the clubhouse for the presentation, archly noting that he'd been handsomely entertained all week by his many supporters in a local pub. If the stags of the Royal & Ancient Golf Club of St. Andrews wanted to present the tournament's runner-up with something, said "man of the people" Sir Walter, they could go *there*. His point wasn't missed by anyone, and not too long after these unforgettable performances, even the most snooty British clubs abandoned their practice of denying professionals access to their clubhouses.

But as a worrying new decade dawned and steel shafts suddenly began to replace traditional hickory ones in the hardware of the game's leading practitioners, the problem for both tournament organizers and die-hard fans of the Haig alike was that their man hadn't won a major championship since the 1927 USPGA, a small eternity in golf.

Not to put too fine a point on the problem, but on a good day the aging Hagen could make more dough playing golf with a couple of tubby Chicago tycoons than by winning *both* the National Open and the USPGA. Moreover, these motivations notwithstanding, after two decades of delighting golf fans on two continents with his stylish shotmaking and roguish lifestyle, Sir Walter's game skills were unmistakably in decline à la Harry Vardon's at the beginning of the previous decade. By 1930, in short, the sharp winds of change were blowing fiercely again—through the Dust Bowl of the nation's troubled heartland, to be sure, and even through the game of golf.

Fortunately for American golf in general and a bitterly discouraged but highly impressionable Ben Hogan in particular, Gene Sarazen was approaching the peak of his form, with a rags-to-riches story of yeoman determination that was almost as compelling as Hagen's rise from obscurity to worldwide fame.

When reigning champ Sir Walter controversially decided to skip defending his title at the 1922 PGA Championship at Oakmont in favor of a lucrative exhibition match in Buffalo, Sarazen, a former Bridgeport caddie and carpenter's son who captured both the PGA title and his first National Open that summer, adroitly exploited Hagen's snub by pluckily offering to meet his "boyhood hero" at Oakmont and Westchester in a staged, head-to-head, thirty-six-hole "grudge match" the New York papers quickly leapt upon and drummed as the "World Championship of Golf." As pure golf theater went, the regal Haig versus the cocky Italian upstart had it all—glamour, drama, and a decent pile of cash, plus Sir Walter's usual entourage of pretty women.

The Haig went five up on the gutty new National champion early in their match, it was remembered, but twenty-year-old Sarazen showed the kind of grit that would soon make him the first player ever to win each of the four major championships of modern golf at least once, achieving the so-called career Grand Slam. Deep into the match, and five down to his hero, Sarazen rallied to win their head-to-head match, 3 and 2. A year later, at Pelham Country Club in New York, just to prove the win was no fluke, he repeated as PGA champion in 1923—nipping none other than Walter Hagen.

Now, as the Haig withdrew and the uncertain thirties advanced, Sarazen was essentially the lone monarch of the professional game, considered the man to beat during any given week by the oddsmakers, despite a host of talented, colorful challengers who rattled down the highway from one swayback tournament town to the next in hopes of knocking the arrogant self-styled "Squire" (so named after he purchased a large grape farm in upstate New York) off his perch.

To begin with, there was Ky Laffoon, the first player to go a full season with a stroke average under 70 and record the lowest seventy-two-hole total for a tournament (266 at the Park Hill Open in Denver in 1934), a man who showed extraordinary promise but was cursed with a volcanic temper that had cost him a host of top-flight tournaments. For decades after he abandoned the Tour game for a safe-paying club job, the story circulated that Laffoon, who was nicknamed "Chief" owing to his high cheekbones and partial Cherokee Indian heritage, once got so mad at his faltering putter that he tied it to a well rope and dragged the offending article down Route 66 behind his yellow tobacco juice–stained Cadillac, throwing up a fantail of sparks that woke a startled young player sleeping in the backseat. That player was named Ben Hogan.

As he later insisted to early Tour chronicler Al Barkow, Laffoon was simply using the highway's surface to creatively grind down the flange of his pitching wedge, not abuse his putter. Whatever the truth of the matter, Hogan not only eventually purchased his own Cadillac for cross-country travel—he believed, as Laffoon and other top players did, that the Cadillac's suspension system made it the smoothest long ride available—but also adopted the practice of honing the edges of his own wedges to almost scalpel-like severity.

The same year Hogan ventured out to try to catch hold of the Tour, Wild

Bill Mehlhorn, another top player of the twenties who always seemed to wind up in second place through nobody's fault but his own, was also saying good-bye to pro golf. Like Walter Hagen, Mehlhorn was a fabulous ball-striker who came to golf from baseball, and he had no shortage of intricate theories about the golf swing and what made it either flop or work. Among other things, Mehlhorn believed a free and natural swing was the only way to effectively hit a ball to the target. But even more important, after playing with Harry Vardon in 1921, Mehlhorn worked for thirteen months to replace his natural hook with a consistent left-to-right motion—à la Vardon—he came to believe was essential for reliable shotmaking, a controlled fade.

One of the no-name hopefuls of the new decade who watched Mehlhorn and attempted to copy his powerful sideways swing before he vanished from the Tour for good was young Ben Hogan, a voracious learner who not only took note of Wild Bill's careful playing action but paid particular attention to the highly analytical manner in which Mehlhorn considered the golf swing, broke it down, and attempted to figure it out in minute detail. Hogan later said that Mehlhorn was the first "theorist" who got him thinking in depth about the physics of the golf swing.

THE ROUGH-AND-TUMBLE Tour life that both Ben Hogan and Byron Nelson aspired to was hardly an easy-paying proposition. Depression-era tournament purses were generally paltry (only the top eight or ten finishers collected any payout—another reason Demaret and others made their calculations early and didn't hesitate to vamoose if their game failed to click), and tournament playing conditions were typically, in the words of one surviving veteran, "okay to simply goddamned awful."

A decent rooming house bed went for three bucks a night, a good meal for half that. There were no commercial sponsors and few if any perks for players. More than one promising stick came out to the circuit brimming with hope and confidence only to linger for a few weeks on the fringes of poverty, then thumb a ride straight home, as Hogan did. "It took a certain breed of cat willing to leave everything and ramble after golf," Sam Snead once said. "If you were lucky, you made a few bucks and kept going. If you were *really* lucky, you failed and went home and got a decent-paying club job for your family."

The more fortunate pros held down respectable club positions that provided a modest income base from May to October, then larkishly set off in the fall hoping to generate some quick tournament revenue against traveling expenses and make a name for themselves in the big-city newspapers, though only a handful of talented aspirants, like "Lighthorse" Harry Cooper, Henry Picard, and tiny Paul Runyan, managed to accomplish this feat on anywhere near the level Sarazen and Hagen had done on the hustings prior to them— or Nelson, Snead, and Hogan did after them.

"The touring days were tough but kind of fascinating," said Paul Runyan, who won fourteen events in 1933 and '34 and went on to become a Hall of Famer and a pioneering teacher over the next five decades. "There was so damn little money around, we didn't really take ourselves too seriously. We fought like cats and dogs for titles, you better believe it, but the money didn't seem to make that much difference then. You had a little bit one week, none the next. Somehow, though, you kept going. Guys slept in chicken coops or the backseat of some buddy's car. I knew fellas who always headed straight to bars the second they hit a tournament town—looking for a woman who would take 'em home for the week, provide a bed, some home-cooked food, maybe even a little sympathetic entertainment."

In a productive year on the winter circuit, Runyan calculated, only nine or ten of the Tour's top players in those days cleared enough to meet expenses and take a few dollars home to their club jobs and families. (In 1934, for instance, Runyan was the Tour's leading money winner with $6,767.) The rest of the field scrounged for peanuts week to week, bumming rides on somebody else's wheels, sharing everything from gas money to flophouse beds. On nights when they didn't have to drive till dawn to reach a tournament site, these winter vagabonds often got stinking drunk; on days when they didn't have a tournament to play, they scrounged up local "pigeons" and hometown high rollers to wager against. During tournament play, even many top-tier players routinely split purses—they agreed before the start of a tournament to "pool" winnings from which proceeds were evenly distributed afterward, a common practice the Tour eventually outlawed.

"It wasn't an easy life," reflected Paul Runyan, "but it was sometimes kind of fun. Most of us were pretty young and flexible. Given the hard times, what else would we have been doing? Besides, I think in back of all of our minds, each one of us perhaps thought we could be the next Walter Hagen. Even Sarazen wanted that."

Even as he receded into the parched and withered landscape, Sir Walter remained the patron saint of this iconoclastic breed of wandering sportsmen. It was a well-known secret that the Haig kept a tooled-leather notebook filled with names and comfortable beds from coast to coast.

"Of course," Runyan added, "no one could have guessed how this would all eventually play out and change in ways none of us could have imagined— thanks largely to three guys named Nelson, Snead, and Hogan."

THOUGH HE PUBLICLY refused to ever say much about the long two years following his bitter forays to San Antonio and Houston—his failed first attempt to make a living playing golf—Hogan later told friends that these difficult days were probably the reason he eventually went as far as he did in life, and golf.

Living at his mother's house on East Allen, hiding out in his old back bedroom, he continued working on weekends out at Ted Longworth's Oakhurst course between Belknap and the Trinity River and picking up money wherever he could find it as long as it didn't cut into his practice and playing time.

"Not much of a job," Hogan recalled of his first club pro job to an interviewer in the late 1940s. "Practically all of my revenue came from selling golf balls by the dozen to one rich foursome, and by winning bets from them. The bets those fellows made on me taught me how to play under pressure, though. One man would back me against another of the foursome, and if I won, see, my backer would give me some of his winnings. I had to handicap myself in every way you could imagine. I've won money playing every stroke of an eighteen-hole round standing on one foot, and by playing a round with only two clubs while my opponent used a bagful." He paused and shook his head at the memory. "It was pretty bad."

For a while, to augment his measly weekend income from Oakhurst, he mopped floors through the week at a popular downtown restaurant and hauled bags at the Blackstone Hotel, where he also dealt poker hands at night. For a short time he tried parking cars and working as a hired field mechanic in the bleak oil fields outside of town. When Royal found him a job doing nine-to-five maintenance work at a local bank, he did the job until it began to cut into his afternoon matches at Oakhurst, Z-Boaz and Katy Lake, matches he counted on to keep his game sharp and bring in a few extra bucks.

With his share of a $1,600 bet collected off a couple of wealthy Fort Worth swells out at Oakhurst, though, Hogan was finally able to purchase a three-year-old Hudson roadster that enabled him to see Valerie Fox more often and drive her to Sunday lunch at her parents' home out in Cleburne.

Combined with his natural talent for handling cards and numbers, this new mobility led to his brief career as a stickman out at the Top of the Hill Terrace, an infamous gambling joint off the main highway between Fort Worth and Dallas. Despite the best efforts of Reverend Norris *and* civic booster Amon Carter, Fort Worth was still a wide-open place where gambling, crime, and vice flourished. The toothless Volstead Act was still three years away from being officially repealed by Congress, and bootleg hooch was flowing like water from a spigot—into the cocktails at Rivercrest bridge games and in the flesh parlors of Hell's Half Acre—filling the pages of Amon Carter's *Star-Telegram* with lurid accounts of sensational shooting sprees, bank heists, and flimflam games gone horribly wrong. During Prohibition, one northern wag wrote, Fort Worth became the town "where the West started all over again."

During one of his money matches at Oakhurst, Hogan himself nearly became a casualty of the vice range wars when he and his playing partners happened upon a daring daylight robbery in progress—two desperadoes holding "hoglegs" (long-barreled .45s) on a foursome of startled businessmen who'd just teed off. As Hogan and company watched from a slope adjacent to the first fairway, the bandits looted the golfers of their wallets and gold watches, then fled to a waiting getaway car. According to his playing partners, Hogan suddenly turned to go fetch the .30-caliber rifle he'd begun keeping on the floorboard of his roadster for security purposes, but they succeeded in preventing him from giving chase. "Ol' Ben was hot to go after them desperadoes like a one-man posse," one of the playing partners remembered many years later. "Good thing we stopped him or he might not be here today."

"Hogan," says his biographer Gene Gregston, who understood Ben's natural reticence to elaborate on what he considered his most compromising years of survival, "was not proud of this period of his life. For a man whose sole desire was professional golf success, they were years of dissatisfaction and disillusionment. He believed he should have been on the professional golf circuit winning tournaments."

TOWARD THE END of the summer of 1931, not long after he took Byron Nelson to National Open qualifying in Chicago and Ben Hogan turned nineteen, Ted Longworth offered Hogan another crack at professional golf, inviting Ben and Ralph Guldahl to accompany him to St. Louis for the Open tournament being staged there.

Both young men enthusiastically went along. Guldahl finished in the money; Hogan once again came up with lint-filled pockets. Longworth, who'd left Glen Garden ten months before to accept the head professional's post at Texarkana, subsequently invited his two protégés to head out west with him for the start of the approaching winter circuit. The three of them, he proposed, could at least share expenses and maybe even split a few purses if Lady Luck smiled on any of them.

Hogan had nothing to share, but also nothing to lose, save a few crummy day jobs. So he went to brother Royal and borrowed a little grubstake of money, $25, for his first trip west. Though the investment came up empty, Hogan never forgot his brother's critical early support.

By this point in time, as seamstress Clara Hogan was quick to point out to her well-heeled patrons at Cheney's, eldest son Royal was doing quite handsomely for himself, not only managing the office supply firm where he'd worked since age fourteen but also pulling down enough regular income to play golf for *fun* on weekends out at Glen Garden and occasionally at the even snootier Rivercrest Country Club.

Ironically, Royal Hogan's golf game had progressed so rapidly that many who'd watched both Hogan brothers play maintained that Royal was actually the more promising player of the two—by a wide margin. Many years later, after he'd collected numerous club championships at Colonial Country Club and even reached the early stages of the National Open, Royal Hogan was prone to rattle the ice melting in his whiskey glass, gaze out at Colonial's magnificent sun-splashed 18th green, and comment ruefully to anyone who would listen that the "only thing that got between me and a pro golf career was having to make a responsible living."

The other backer Ben Hogan quietly approached for a modest starter loan was his old friend and de facto mentor Marvin Leonard. Despite the effects of the Depression on most merchants in Texas, the brothers Leonard, to no one's real surprise, were doing exceedingly well down on Houston Street. Their colorful country store now sprawled over four city blocks of downtown Fort Worth, delighting loyal patrons with a blizzard of daily promotional stunts and seasonal cut-rate bargains.

Despite a workload that was more demanding than ever, Marvin Leonard had taken his physician's advice to heart and was spending less and less time on the store's crowded floor and more and more time on the golf courses at Rivercrest and Glen Garden.

What began for him as a cheap means of getting some useful exercise and much-needed fresh air had quickly grown into an expensive, all-consuming sporting passion that would rapidly transform Leonard, during the course of the next ten years, from a successful businessman into an influential community leader and ultimately a sponsoring pioneer of the tournament golf world.

By 1932 Leonard was on the board of directors at Glen Garden, aggressively promoting a bold experiment to see whether bentgrass greens could possibly survive Fort Worth's long and sensationally hot summer weather. Better courses in the North and West, he'd learned from following his late-in-life golf addiction all over the map in recent years, typically featured lush bentgrass greens, and he saw no reason why Fort Worth's golfers should be deprived of the smoothest putting surfaces available.

Under direct pressure from Leonard, who offered to underwrite the entire expense of a test, Glen Garden's 18th green was replanted with bentgrass and extensively watered, producing one of the finest putting surfaces in all Texas.

Simultaneously, the story goes, Leonard made the same bold offer across town at Rivercrest Country Club, where he was also a prominent member in good standing, calmly proposing to the club's board of governors that if they would only permit him to convert two or three of the club's greens to bentgrass, he would, once again, pay the entire cost of the experiment. Most of the golfing elites there, however, hadn't traveled much and remained unconvinced that bentgrass had a respectable future in the Lone Star State, while others didn't want the annoyance of having their golf course ripped apart just to satisfy the nutty curiosity of a relatively recent convert.

"Marvin, if you like bent greens so damned much," the president of Rivercrest reportedly grumbled to Leonard, "why the hell don't you go *build* your own goddamn golf course!"

"Good idea," Leonard reportedly replied, unfazed, and embarked on an extensive tour of famous western golf courses to gather ideas for a true bentgrass championship layout somewhere in Cowtown.

Leonard, as it turned out, dreamed as big in golf as he did in groceries—he was soon in possession of 157 acres of land along the Clear Fork of the Trinity River near the Texas Christian University campus and Forest Park subdivision. In late 1934 he hired Texan John Bredamus and Perry Maxwell of Oklahoma to assist in the design and construction of his unnamed championship golf course, asking each man to submit five alternative plans for the course. Bredamus was known for his fine layouts around Galveston and Houston; Maxwell was the architect of the new Southern Hills layout that was garnering eye-popping praise up in Tulsa. Borrowing ideas from both men and adding a few nuggets of his own, Leonard asked each designer for five *more* workups and finally got down to work constructing his layout in early 1935.

To create the bentgrass putting surfaces he so ardently desired, Leonard's construction crews planted a combination of seaside bentgrass (not unlike the kind found at Pebble Beach and the better golf courses developing in the California desert around Palm Springs) and lavish amounts of sand and cow manure. To combat heat, he kept the spiky new greens heavily watered, sometimes showing up in the evenings after work to stand and water them himself.

By the end of that summer—this was the same year the PGA Tour began to keep official prize money records, as it happened, and total purses scaled above $134,000—Leonard had erected a stately, colonial-style clubhouse to preside over his new golf course and offered the first memberships with no initiation fee save a $50 security deposit against future charges to the club. Unlike most private clubs in Texas, and in keeping with Leonard's personal beliefs, Colonial didn't exclude Jews and Catholics from applying for membership. But blacks and Hispanics weren't allowed because segregation ruled the South—and most of the rest of America too for that matter.

When the doors finally opened for business on January 29, 1936, near the bottom of the Depression, more than one hundred Fort Worthians came forth to plunk down their fifty bucks and join the new Colonial Country Club. Many of them braved below-freezing temperatures and a rare blanket of snow to attend Leonard's opening soiree, though no one brought along their golf clubs, and a few even cheekily brought along sleds. One of the club's first memberships, not surprisingly, went to a pair of discreet newlyweds for whom fortune was suddenly picking up. Their names were Ben and Valerie Hogan.

By the time he opened Colonial for business, Leonard had an even more audacious plan in mind. Within two years, the indefatigable groceryman would begin a dogged five-year campaign with the U.S. Golf Association to bring the National Open, golf's most prestigious event, to Fort Worth.

To help make that happen, he enlisted the help of Amon Carter, the Queen City's most successful pitchman, who happened to be working on a grandiose showcase of his own for Fort Worth at precisely that same moment. A year after Colonial officially opened, Carter paid pint-sized Broadway impresario

Billy Rose a thousand dollars a day for one hundred days to produce and direct "the show of shows for the city's celebration of the Texas Centennial," a sprawling *carnivale* of lush "Broadway-style" entertainments, spread over a former forty-acre cow pasture west of downtown Fort Worth, that featured, among other dazzling delights, a "true Western dance hall" and a topless burlesque revue called the "Nude Ranch," topped off by an elaborate musical rodeo somewhat surreally encircled by a six-thousand-gallon artificial moat that featured singing gondoliers floating past between acts. An illuminated spray of fountains served as the curtain for the "largest outdoor theater on earth," and one thousand patrons a night were cordially invited to stick around following the performance and dance beneath the Texas stars on the "biggest revolving stage floor in the world."

Despite its outrageous costs and ludicrous scale, in a state where "big" held more than symbolic meaning, Amon Carter's over-the-top Casa Mañana, or "House of Tomorrow," was one *big* horse opera really aimed at outdoing the centennial observance of Texas statehood in neighboring Dallas, conveniently substantiating Fort Worth's longtime claim to be the place where "Broadway meets the West." To the delight of its irrepressible ten-gallon-hat-wearing creator—also the son of a failed blacksmith who came to Cowtown penniless and parlayed his persuasive salesmanship into a newspaper dynasty—Casa Mañana received generally positive theatrical notices from Los Angeles to faraway Paris (as in France). As outlandish and comical as the entertainments were, on some basic level they seemed to express a growing populist hope that Texas, maybe even America itself, was finally beginning to claw its way out of the Depression.

Meanwhile, Carter's business connections to the nation's leading columnists and sports stars proved an invaluable service to Marvin Leonard's lobbying juggernaut as well. He had the sizable task of convincing USGA president Harold Pierce that upstart Colonial could hold its own with the likes of mighty Oakmont, Baltusrol, Merion, and Winged Foot—places knicker-deep in golf tradition—and that Texas in June wouldn't wipe out innocent National Open patrons with heat stroke. When Leonard personally guaranteed an unprecedented purse of $25,000 for the right to host the National Open, the deal was cinched and the Colonial Country Club was selected, not without controversy, as the site of the U.S. Open Championship for 1941.

By then, seven years of thinking big and working hard had paid off handsomely for both Marvin Leonard and Amon G. Carter.

Maybe not so surprisingly, after eight long years of hard work and repeated failure, dreaming big and working hard had finally paid off for young Ben Hogan too.

"I sometimes wondered why Ben never approached my father for a job during those lean hard years around 1931 and '32," muses Marty, a Leonard daughter, one of four, who later became one of the city's more accomplished amateur players in her own right. "But I think there was such powerful respect between the two men, almost a father and son kind of relationship, and playing professional golf was everything to Ben. My father knew that. Amateur golf wasn't going to do it for Hogan, so I suppose that's why Dad never offered him a full-time job. He knew Ben had his eyes set on the Tour, so he made him a small loan to try and help him out. It's a measure of the mutual respect Ben had for my father that he insisted the loan be recorded, and a measure of my father's admiration for him that he forgave the debt the moment Ben tried to repay it.

"That was just one more thing they managed to keep between them."

Marvin Leonard made his initial investment in Hogan's second shot at the professional winter golf tour near the end of 1931, allowing Hogan to launch himself out of Cowtown with a grubstake of fifty bucks from Leonard and an additional twenty-five from his brother, Royal. "I left here with $75 in my pocket," he told Ken Venturi in a famous televised interview in 1981. "Would you try that today?" In Phoenix, Hogan won another fifty—his first actual winnings as a professional. By the third week of December, though, he was down to just 15¢ in his pocket, forced to eat oranges he picked off trees along the fairways of the California courses where he played. He reluctantly wrote his Texas patron asking for another loan. Less than two weeks later, Leonard sent a check for an additional $75 to Los Angeles, where Hogan made zilch. By the time Hogan limped back to the annual Texas Open shindig down in San Antonio in late January 1932, he was flat broke again, shot 75-80, and withdrew from the tournament.

Hardly anyone noticed his withdrawal, however, because the buzz of the tournament was created by the sensational early play of amateur Byron Nelson and Gus Moreland, old Hogan rivals suddenly coming into their own. Nelson eventually faded, but Moreland grabbed national headlines by tying former U.S. Open champ Gene Sarazen for second place in the tournament some called the "mother event" of the winter tournament season.

Dwindling funds aside, one wonders how he had the gumption to keep on trying, week after dreary week. Yet Ben somehow made it out of Texas and on to New Orleans for the next tournament stop. It didn't go well. He came up lint-pockets yet again—nothing divided by nothing.

"After New Orleans, I wasn't in the money and I was broke," Hogan told Venturi in his famous TV interview with a grimness that was still evident fifty years after the fact.

"I had to come home."

FOUR

The Turning Point

A NY NORMAL MAN might well have given up right there.
Fortunately, that same spring, through his future father-in-law Claude Fox, Ben heard about an opening for a professional at the tiny Nolan River Country Club out in Cleburne and immediately drove down and applied for the job.

The position was pretty much a one-man operation, but the take-home pay was decent at about $35 a week. At least the whole shop would be his, and there turned out to be a few unexpected side benefits as well. To begin with, the club was relatively new, its membership small and composed largely of local farmers and their spouses, most of whom had little or no interest in obtaining formal golf lessons and could divide a dollar a dozen ways, and thus wouldn't dream of purchasing fancy new equipment when their old hickory-shafted shooting irons would do nicely.

As the age of steel shafts had suddenly dawned, however, several frugal-minded members brought old clubs to Hogan asking that they be reshafted

Overleaf: Ben and Valerie Hogan, Hershey Hotel, 1938 *(Courtesy Hogan Estate)*

and regripped. Hogan spent much of his time taking apart golf clubs and putting them together again, fiddling with equipment, trying this and that, using his strong hands and nimble scientific mind to decipher the art of clubmaking—deepening both his knowledge and love of club construction, a skill that proved invaluable over the fullness of time.

The job also provided plenty of time for Hogan to beat balls on the practice range and contemplate his failures and inability thus far to subdue his tournament jitters and wrestle his wayward hook into line, a process he found somewhat akin to taking apart golf clubs, seeing how they work, and putting them back together again.

Hogan paid a nominal rent on a small spartanly furnished room at the back of the club and was spared complete social isolation by the fact that Valerie came home to her parents' house most weekends from Texas Christian. He never declined Jesse Fox's generous invitation for a home-cooked meal.

"Whenever he came to our house at night," Valerie told Dave Anderson six decades later, concerning the nearly two years Hogan spent out in Cleburne, "he would say, 'Mrs. Fox, do you have anything left from your dinner?' and Mother would say, 'Yes, son, sit down.' She already had the table set. After dinner one night, he told me, 'I'm going in and ask your mother if we can get married. I don't have much, but I'm so lonely, I just can't stand it any longer. I want you with me.' My mother told me later that when Ben asked her about marrying me, she started to say, 'Ben, this is so sudden,' but then realized he wouldn't like the teasing. Instead, she said, 'Well, son, you know how I feel about you, but you'll have to ask Valerie's father,' and Ben said, 'Yes, ma'am, I intend to do that.' My father always liked him."

That autumn of 1932 in Mr. Roosevelt's America, Ted Longworth invited Hogan up to a $500 tournament that members were putting on at the Texarkana Country Club. He also wrote and invited Byron Nelson, and it was during the lengthy bus ride to Texarkana that Nelson made up his mind to ditch his clerk's job at a Fort Worth business publication and chase his own big dream of golf for hire. "I got to thinking about that prize money," he later wrote. "I knew you couldn't make much of a living playing professional golf, but there was some pretty good money going at these tournaments, and I felt I was good enough to have a chance at some of it."

His hunch proved correct. Nelson finished third in Texarkana and pocketed $75 in prize money. Ben Hogan, who'd been officially playing for prize money for almost two years already, finished third in the qualifier but failed to make any money in the tournament because only the top six spots paid off.

Within weeks, on a grubstake of $500 provided by several of his prominent Fort Worth friends, young Nelson headed for California to try his luck on the winter tour—particularly aiming for the Opens at Los Angeles and Long Beach and the lucrative pro-ams to be held at Hillcrest and Pasadena. Overwhelmed by the palmy splendor of California and the headiness of the competition—seeing Gene Sarazen almost put him into a swoon, he admitted to someone later—Byron placed no higher than twelfth place in any tournament he entered that winter, battled homesickness and a dodgy stomach, and soon ran out of money and was fortunate to catch a ride home with a Fort Worth businessman who happened to be returning from a West Coast sales trip.

"By the end of January 1933 I was back home, practicing and playing at Glen Garden, helping around the house and garden, milking the cow and so forth," Nelson recounts, noting how he subsequently wrote to Ted Longworth detailing his experiences in California and soliciting his old golf mentor's advice on what to do next.

In golf and life, timing is everything. A short while later, Longworth wrote back with the news that he was about to accept a better head professional's post at the Waverly Country Club out in Portland, Oregon, and he wondered if his top Glen Garden protégé might wish to apply for the vacant job in Texarkana—a job that would provide a steady income through most of the golf season and free Byron to try the winter golf tour once again.

Byron didn't hesitate. In April he boarded the bus to Texarkana for the second time in a year with little more than his golf clubs, high hopes, and a suitcase stuffed with Sunday clothes in tow. His mother told him to take good care of himself and be sure to present himself to the local Church of Christ at the earliest possible opportunity. She had worries about the life of an itinerant golf professional, the drinking and rough carousing she'd heard so many stories about. Good son that he was, though, Byron assured his mama that he would locate a church and join it at the earliest possible convenience.

For the first few weeks in Texarkana, battling loneliness and homesickness, the personable, sunny Nelson walked everywhere he had to go in town until he met a salesman who agreed to sell him a used royal blue Ford roadster with cream wheels and top, for no money down and whatever he could afford to pay at no interest—the kind of neighborly terms that desperate car dealers were throwing at almost anyone who could walk and legibly sign his name during perhaps the bleakest summer of the Great Depression.

"I suddenly felt like everything was going to be all right," Nelson remembered fondly seventy years further on, as if it had been only minutes ago. "Especially after I took my mother's advice and went to church."

One Sunday morning he met an attractive, wrenlike girl named Louise Shofner, the daughter of a local grocer, who invited him to a picnic that the church's youth group had planned for that very afternoon. The first time Byron asked Lousie out, after first carefully complimenting her on the quality of her angel food cake, she flatly turned him down. She already had a boyfriend, she politely explained. The next Sunday Byron and Louise sat together in church, though, and suddenly the boyfriend vanished.

Almost exactly one year later, on a track nearly identical to the one Ben and Valerie were on down in Texas, Louise and Byron got married (to save money) in her parents' living room in Texarkana. Shortly after Christmas 1934, with a loan of $660 from Louise's father, the newlyweds shoved off for Byron's second shot at the western golf circuit.

This time he played with more confidence and managed at least to meet living and traveling expenses and earn enough bread, owing to a pair of late-season top-five finishes in Galveston and San Antonio, to march straight through the door of Papa Shofner's grocery store and pay back his father-in-law's loan.

During their long rides through the cold clear western nights from one Tour stop to the next that following winter, at times using heated bricks wrapped in blankets or newspapers to keep themselves warm in the unheated little Ford roadster, Byron first sketched out for his bride his secret dream of making enough money in golf to someday purchase a cattle ranch, settle down, and maybe have a family.

The highlight of this season of 1935 came when Nelson upset reigning American and British Amateur champ Lawson Little in the San Francisco National Match Play Open and earned an unexpected invitation to a new gathering of golf champions and promising amateurs that Bobby Jones and Clifford Roberts put together on the golf course they built in the sleepy pines of Augusta, Georgia.

Nelson finished ninth in the second Masters of 1935—the one in which Sarazen holed his miraculous four-wood for a double eagle to win the tournament, the "shot heard round the world" that helped place the Masters tournament on the map—and collected $137 for his efforts. Better yet, through his new friendship with Augusta National head professional Ed Dudley, a future president of the PGA, Byron met a man who offered him an even more promising club job opportunity up at the prestigious Ridgewood Country Club in New Jersey. "I think back on that year, and I realize how extraordinarily happy I was," he observed many years later, glancing out the window of his pretty Roanoke ranch house and recalling with a modest smile how he boasted rather uncharacteristically to Augusta head pro Ed Dudley, as he departed the beautifully groomed grounds, that he hoped to win Bobby Jones's cozy little Invitational sometime in the "next three years."

As it happened, Nelson beat his own bold prediction by a year, firing 283 to capture his first Masters title in 1937. After that, financially and in almost every other way, Byron and his bride never looked back. Their new car had a proper heater, and the ranch he secretly dreamed of someday owning was a major step closer to being his.

A COUPLE of weeks after good things happened to Byron Nelson down at Augusta, something good *finally* happened to Ben Hogan too.

At the stroke of 12:30 in the afternoon on April 14, 1935, in the front parlor of Jesse and Claude Fox's modest home on Prairie Avenue in Cleburne, Ben Hogan and pretty Valerie Fox got married by the local Baptist minister. According to the *Cleburne Times-Review*, the young bride wore an attractive white tailored crepe frock with white accessories and carried a spray of pink rosebuds and other spring flowers. Only a few relatives were in attendance, including the bride's parents and Royal Hogan and his wife Margaret. Sarah Fox served as her sister's bridesmaid. Royal Hogan acted as Ben's best man. "The bridegroom is a well-known golf professional in Fort Worth," the newspaper noted, failing to mention Ben's recent stint in Cleburne, also mangling Valerie's name into "Valeria."

Revealingly, there was no mention of Clara Hogan being present at her youngest son's nuptials, leading some to surmise by her absence that Mama Hogan and Valerie Fox didn't exactly see eye to eye on certain things, including the marriage.

In fact, though she wasn't overly fond of Valerie Fox, whom she considered prissy and a snob, Mama Hogan was temporarily staying out west in Los Angeles with her daughter, Princess, and her new husband, Dr. Charles Ditto, a son of Arlington, Texas, who had a fine job at one of L.A.'s leading hospitals. Perhaps she simply couldn't get back to Texas in time for the wedding, or perhaps under the circumstances she felt she ought to make her feelings known by simply staying put in California.

In either case, an even stronger glimpse of the natural tension that existed between Clara and her new daughter-in-law comes from Jackie Towery, Royal's first child, who was born in the late 1930s and observed the family interplay at a critical moment in Ben Hogan's professional evolution.

"Mama Hogan could be either the most charming person you ever met or a living terror, depending on what she really thought of you," says Towery. "She never shied from giving an opinion on any topic, and I think Valerie Fox was one of them. The Hogan nature was so strong, and I'm sure Mama Hogan, initially at least, thought Valerie might be a burden to Uncle Ben—that he would have to spend all his time and money, in other words, trying to please her and living up to her standards. It was only over time that we learned that beneath that sweet shy exterior she was tougher and more demanding than he was."

Over these years, Ben and Valerie Hogan were frequent dinner guests at the home of Royal and Margaret Hogan on Pulaski Street. "They came quite regularly at this time because my mother was such a fabulous cook," says Towery, "and because, despite what you've read in places, my father and Uncle Ben were very close almost all their lives. Royal was terribly proud of Ben, even if he couldn't express it. And Ben felt like he owed Royal a great deal for his help and support. To be honest, Mama Hogan wasn't much warmer to my mother, but it certainly didn't help Aunt Valerie's cause that she was basically hopeless in the kitchen."

According to the Fort Worth city directory of 1935–36, Valerie and Ben Hogan's first marital address was 1316 East Allen, Mama Hogan's house, but if the newlyweds resided there while she was safely out west, it was only until they could rustle up enough cash to afford a place of their own.

Sometime in late 1936 or early '37, Ben and Valerie moved into the same Forest Park Apartments where Marvin Leonard and his wife, Mary, were living. The twelve-story building was considered one of the city's better residential addresses. To meet expenses, Valerie and Ben invited single gal Sarah Fox to move into a two-bedroom apartment with them. With Ben's weekend Oakhurst income and a part-time office job Royal helped him find at a downtown petroleum company, combined with the sizable winnings he took off wealthy members at Colonial or over at Rivercrest from time to time, and assisted by Sarah Fox's modest earnings from a local dress shop, two Hogans and one Fox were surviving rather handsomely the same summer Amon Carter opened up his extravaganza Casa Mañana to the world. Though nobody but Valerie and Sarah was privy to his plans, Ben was saving up dough for a third assault on the western golf tour and still dreaming of a Casa Mañana of his own.

The picture that emerges from this interval is one of pleasant if slightly unconventional domestic life. "As I understood from both my mother and grandmother," Valerie Harriman picks up the tale, "the three of them were basically inseparable. They went everywhere together—to the movies, out to dinner, probably even to Casa Mañana, as Uncle Ben in particular was always taken with theater and movies. This was a period of time when they met important people and formed friendships that lasted the rest of their lives."

Many years later, a persistent myth surrounding their decision to marry centered on a purported agreement the couple made beforehand to remain childless so that no offspring would interfere with Hogan's golf career. Though the hard pragmatism of such a deal fits the neat scenario of absolute sacrifice some Hogan students prefer, there is no evidence to suggest such a radical agreement took place. If it did, no family member was ever privy to it, though the tenuous nature of their financial situation as newlyweds may have prompted such early discussions. Furthermore, within a decade or so Valerie granted newspaper interviews in which she talked quite comfortably of both her and Ben's desire to settle down, own a home, travel less, and possibly start a family of their own. Was it mere wishful thinking or some romantic projection on her part? Possibly so. Looking back on their childless marriage some years further along, both Ben and Valerie were quick to acknowledge that having children would have been a difficult proposition. Yet curiously, as his playing days wound down, Shady Oaks friends of Ben's remember a quiet desire he expressed to produce an heir, and they even recall a bizarre incident in the late 1950s when he showed up at the club to hand out Cuban cigars, apparently under the impression Valerie—who would have been at least in her middle forties and far beyond conventional childbearing years—was pregnant. Others remember he was adamantly opposed to the notion of adopting. In any case, they insist, either by design or nature's verdict, their failure to have children was one reason Ben lavished such tender attentions on his two nieces, Jackie and Valerie.

"I'll let you in on a little family secret, though," Valerie Harriman says, recalling those early apartment-sharing days in Fort Worth. "My mother did most of the cooking and housekeeping at the apartment they shared, either because Valerie couldn't or wouldn't do it and I seriously doubt they could afford a maid. This led to some amusing moments. Uncle Ben, for example, had a passion for scrambled eggs, and my mother would get up early and make them just the way he liked them. But it was always Aunt Valerie who served him breakfast—as if she'd been the one who made them. He was so focused on golf and other things, I don't know if he ever learned the truth about those scrambled eggs and what the beautiful and clever Fox sisters were really up to."

BY MOST INDICATIONS, it was also during this pleasant time of new married responsibilities and multiple income sources that Hogan's daily practice routines developed into an almost religious regimen. Typically he commenced these lengthy workouts ranging at least an hour and sometimes two in length with his pitching clubs (almost from the beginning Ben's favorite club was his pitching wedge, a tool he wielded with such surgical precision that he and others eventually took to calling it his "equalizer"), then methodically and unhurriedly worked his way down through the bag from high to middle and low irons, expanding the swing pattern as he went, developing a standard drill for each club that led him to the fairway woods, and finally the driver itself, the club he believed to be the most important tool in the bag—and the one that seemed to cause him the most heartache in competition.

"The driver is what puts you in play," he told an interviewer in the early 1960s. "You control that, you control your play."

From the beginning of his Tour quest, despite the prodigious length his oversized golf swing was capable of producing, Ben's major problem in tournament play—and the real source of his unsettled nerves and loss of competitive confidence—had been a consistent inability to control his driver when it counted most.

Nelson and Ralph Guldahl both saw this tendency and understood that the challenge of sorting out his driver would be either Hogan's demise or salvation, his tireless quest's triumph or Waterloo, when the three of them briefly barnstormed over the Southwest in early 1934. "We traveled together for a short while to save expenses," Byron recalled. "All of us were basically broke and trying to make some sort of impression. We had some pretty good conversations, and I came to know Ben and like him better than I ever had. Neither of us had any money to spend, you see, so we practiced a lot. Truth is, we kind of fed off each other that way. We were both pretty hungry."

"Despite his many defeats," Jimmy Demaret, who joined the pro ranks that same autumn, amplified in his 1953 memoir *My Partner, Ben Hogan,* "Hogan was continually improving his game. He had no money to spend while he was on tour, so he put all his free time into practice. He and Nelson would spend hour after hour on the practice tee, something unheard of in those days. The old timers in golf rarely practiced. They'd take a few swings to limber up and then go out and play a tournament. Hogan and Nelson began almost a new concept with those lengthy practice sessions."

Thanks to his maturing practice routine, during the summer before his marriage to Valerie, shortly after moving back to Fort Worth from Cleburne, Hogan actually made it through sectional qualifying to reach the first stages of the U.S. Open Championship at the Merion Golf Club, outside Philadelphia. That was the good news. The bad news, per usual, was that tattered nerves and a plunging loss of confidence got the better of him and he hooked half a dozen tee shots into the punishing Open rough and carded dismal back-to-back 79s, missed the cut, and promptly went home on the train, more furious with himself than ever.

Like a dog that retreats to lick his wounds and heal up, as Ben and Valerie adjusted to their new life together and saved money for a third and more comprehensive assault on the pro circuit that had thus far eluded him, Hogan divided his busy working hours between Oakhurst and the petroleum company, consulted with Marvin Leonard on the dream course he was building on the Clear Fork, and for nearly a full year played in only regional golf tournaments of little or no consequence, none of which he won. In the early summer of 1935, despite regular practice tutorials that gave him a sense of comfort and far more command of his shots than ever before, he even failed to qualify for the Open up at Oakmont too. For some reason, he confided to Valerie on the heels of these brief and unpromising sorties, he was unable to marshal his concentration sufficiently in the heat of competition to make the kind of clutch shots he knew he was capable of making under pressure.

"Then maybe, Ben, you should just practice until you don't really have to think about how to hit the shots during a tournament," she rather pragmatically suggested.

It was a small and somewhat obvious observation on her part. But in due course, it became a nugget of wisdom that changed both their lives.

Contributing to her husband's growing frustration and isolation in late 1935 was a gnawing sense of urgency compounded by the sudden breakthrough successes of Ben's boyhood contemporaries. Nelson, Guldahl, and even Houston gadfly Jimmy Demaret were suddenly all over the sports section of Amon Carter's *Star-Telegram*.

Jimmy Demaret won the first of his six Texas PGA titles in 1935 and played well enough in half a dozen other winter circuit venues to shelve a promising big-band crooning career in favor of full-time employment in tournament golf. Byron Nelson, for his part, won the New Jersey State Open that same year.

Ralph Guldahl, meanwhile, who not so long before had expressed serious misgivings about even turning pro, was making tremendous strides too. He seriously contended in several leading Tour events and finally broke through by winning both the prestigious Western and Metropolitan Opens in 1936. He followed this up with a flurry of sensational finishes that included winning two more Western Opens (at that time, along with Pinehurst's North and South, the Western was widely regarded as one of golf's "major" events) in consecutive fashion. At supposedly invincible Oakland Hills outside Detroit in 1937, Ralph shattered scoring records by firing 281 to beat another promising newcomer named Sam Snead by two strokes and take possession of the most coveted prize of all—his first National Open title. Even more impressively, just one year later, Hogan's former equally impoverished traveling companion did something only the great ones seemed capable of doing: he successfully defended his National Open title at Cherry Hills, in Denver, romping past talented Dick Metz and the rest of the field by a margin of six strokes.

If Hogan (who, as it happens, wasn't doing too badly himself by this point) begrudged Ralph his novalike success—and there is no direct evidence he did—there was soon a valuable lesson to be gained from Ralph's difficult experiences with sudden fame and wealth. A river of commercial opportunities flooded Guldahl's way, all of which proved mentally distracting to the naturally shy and amiable Texan, among them the lucrative proposition to translate his winning golf touch into an instruction manual. Guldahl, the son of hardworking Norwegians, applied himself diligently to the task of breaking down and explaining the components of his winning golf form. But somehow in the process of trying to explain the physics of his winning unorthodox swing—someone described it as a "gangly sledgehammer lunge"—Ralph altered the form that carried him to the summit, lost direction and confidence, and effectively destroyed his game.

After capturing his lone Masters title in 1939, never complaining but struggling poignantly to rediscover his winning form and losing his competitive fire with each passing year, brilliant Ralph Guldahl became a casualty of his own big success and soon abandoned the professional game entirely.

. . .

BEN HOGAN WATCHED his friend's meteoric rise and fall very carefully, one can surmise from comments he made later on, and eventually took from Ralph's cautionary tale the wisdom of remaining focused and perhaps even working harder to protect whatever got you to the trophy ceremony. "The minute you believe whatever they write about you and let that change things," he remarked a decade later, more or less at the center of the same kind of media storm that had enveloped and ultimately undone likable Ralph Guldahl, "is the minute you go no further."

In the early summer of 1936, Hogan bagged a pair of promising 71s to take low qualifying honors at the regional National Open qualifying round in Dallas and qualified for his first trip to the U.S. Open Championship in two years, being staged that year up at Baltusrol's Upper Course in Springfield, New Jersey, twenty miles outside New York. He asked Valerie to accompany him. She hated to travel, routinely getting carsick on trips over ten or twenty minutes, but agreed to go along.

"I had gone with Ben's mother to see him play an exhibition in Fort Worth," Valerie remembered. "That was all the golf I knew. But now that he was going to play in the U.S. Open, I was excited about traveling with him." With new optimism and a more reliable set of wheels, the determined couple set off for New Jersey in their newly purchased, secondhand, maroon-colored Buick sedan. Two days later, they checked into a modest hotel just two miles from Baltusrol's front gate.

The first thing Ben did, according to his wife, was pick up the telephone and call Byron Nelson. Nelson, who also qualified for the Baltusrol Open, had just become the first assistant professional at Ridgewood (New Jersey) Country Club. "Byron and his wife, Louise, came over to see us that night and Louise and I just right away liked each other," Valerie remembered. During their lengthy dinner conversations, Ben casually mentioned to Byron and Louise that Valerie had always wanted to see New York City, but he couldn't afford to take time away from his pretournament practice sessions to take her there.

"I'll take her," Louise cheerfully volunteered.

The next day, the story goes, the two women took a ferry across the Hudson River and window-shopped for hours on end, arm in arm, buying nothing but becoming fast friends. "Louise and Valerie liked each other right off, and their friendship was much closer than anything Ben and I had ever known," Byron said many years later. "I think that particular U.S. Open created a pretty good friendship between the girls and even Ben and me for a time."

The friendly interlude certainly wasn't memorable for the golf either man played over Baltusrol's difficult Tillinghast-designed Upper Course. Hogan shot 75–79 and missed the thirty-six-hole cut; Nelson 79-74, and likewise. So on the Saturday night after Tony Manero closed with a 67 to shatter the old Open seventy-two-hole record by four strokes (his 282 total would hold up until Guldahl beat it by a stroke one year later) and capture his one and only national championship, the Hogans and Nelsons all took the ferry back into Manhattan for a night on the town before heading home. Tony Manero's wife, Agnes, a stylish and popular woman, was one of the Tour wives who warmly befriended Valerie that week, easing her fears that she wouldn't be accepted. "Imagine," she wrote her mother, Jesse Fox, on motel stationery before she and Ben headed for the long road back to Texas. "I'm a friend of the U.S. Open champion's wife."

BY THE TIME the bluebonnets had come and gone again down in Texas, Ben and Valerie Hogan had saved up $1,450 and were ready to take on the western tournament circuit.

"It's now or never," Ben reportedly told Valerie in July 1937, at which point they loaded up the Buick and drove for two solid days to reach Niagara Falls, Ontario, for the General Brock Open. The journey came to a halt in front of a beautiful ivy-covered hotel.

"This place looks too expensive for us, Ben," Valerie pointed out to her husband. By mutual agreement, she had been designated traveling secretary and official exchequer of their road odyssey. Hogan, meanwhile, had begun the routine of keeping a small black personal diary of his daily expenses, jotting down winnings and expenses in immaculate twin columns.

As Valerie waited in the car, Ben went inside the hotel to check and reemerged smiling broadly. A doorman approached to take their bags.

"They've got a special rate for golfers. Our room is only two dollars."

Hogan tied for eleventh place at the General Brock—the same old same old—and won just $60 for his efforts.

On a more positive note, though, he placed second to Jimmy "Siege Gun" Thomson in the tournament's driving contest, pounding out several 300-yard drives that put an extra $50 in his pockets and made him a gallery favorite for one of the first times in his career. "Possibly because of his size," Valerie speculated later, "Ben had the crowd behind him." Unlike other Tour wives who tagged doggedly along fairways after their husbands and turned out for any special event where there was the possibility of free food and extra money, Valerie Hogan witnessed neither Ben's tournament play nor his second-place finish in the long driving contest. She stayed put in their pretty hotel room, knitting socks for her husband and reading local newspapers, clipping any item that mentioned her husband by name, avoiding the tournament hubbub and forced fellowship of the waiting game, establishing a pattern she would follow his entire career.

Some years later, Hogan explained to reporters that his wife was simply too "nervous and shy" to follow him in tournament play. But others deduced a natural reluctance on Valerie's part to mingle with certain Tour wives who were as earthy and loud at parties as they were loyal on the golf course. "Valerie Hogan?" one of these better-known party girls was heard to quip at a hotel cocktail party. "Why I wouldn't know the girl if her husband won the U.S. Open!"

Whether it was nerves or snobbery or some combination of both, Valerie missed her husband's prodigious driving exhibition but afterward took special care in pasting the local newspaper account of his heroics into an oversized black scrapbook she'd brought along for their journey, hoping to fill its pages by trip's end. Hogan's drives were only four yards shorter than the mighty Thomson's, and more tellingly, unlike every other contender, none of his launches had gone out of bounds. "Now he is on the tournament trail and unless we are mistaken," noted one of several newspaper accounts Valerie clipped that week by the famous falls, "that beautiful swing of Hogan's should really soon take him places."

Jimmy Demaret also saw evidence of Ben's newfound confidence and optimism. " 'I've got the secret of this game now,' " he quoted Hogan as saying as they warmed up together on the range at Niagara Falls. "But if Ben found the secret at that time," Demaret later wrote, "he lost it again immediately. It was the same story, and a heartbreaking one, for the Hogans. Ben tied for eleventh in the General Brock, he came in ninth in the Shawnee Open, he placed ninth in the Glen Falls Open. And so it went."

Well, not exactly. Ben's tidy pocket ledger told a slightly more encouraging story.

Two weeks before Glen Falls, Hogan climbed up to seventh place at the St. Paul Open, followed by an encouraging third at the Lake Placid Open—almost $600 in earnings for less than two weeks' work. Not great, but a whole lot better than starving. After sliding back in Glens Falls, the couple's Buick rumbled down through the Poconos to Hershey, Pennsylvania, for the impressive $5,000 Hershey Open.

While Valerie waited in a quiet corner of the pretty clubhouse, Ben scraped out a pair of uninspired rounds of 71-75 while tall, regal, fluid-swinging Henry Picard, Hershey Country Club's own sharply dressed head professional, set a new halfway scoring record of 11 under par.

Picard, a taciturn New Englander who previously worked out of the elite Charleston Country Club, was one of the Tour's steadiest players, a gracious man who made playing golf look effortless through a personality that never appeared the slightest bit ruffled. He captured a dozen tournament titles in the thirties, including the 1938 Masters. But more important, his guidance quietly exerted major influence on a pair of struggling Tour beginners who would eventually change the face of the game.

The first was a silky-swinging hillbilly from West Virginia's Greenbrier Resort named Samuel Jackson Snead, aka "Sammy," who made his professional debut at the Hershey tournament in 1936, finished fifth, and won $285. Snead's power attracted crowds from the first day he stepped out on Tour, while his incredible finesse with a chipping iron and putter and engaging homespun personality made him an instant gallery favorite. Snead's only problem, like Hogan's, was the dreaded hook, an affliction that had him so down in the dumps after only a few months out on the circuit that he considered giving up the $45 a month windfall the Greenbrier was paying him to represent the resort on Tour and going home to teach hotel guests.

Prior to the start of the 1937 Los Angeles Open, however, Picard had loaned Snead a heavy George Izett driver that weighed fourteen and a half ounces and had a swing weight of E-5, eight degrees of loft and an ultra-stiff steel shaft.

With this monster of a club, Snead's driving woes vanished and his confidence soared. "The harder I swung," Snead said later, "the straighter the dang ball flew." Sure enough, one week later, Henry Picard was leading the Oakland tournament when Snead blasted past him with a final-round 67 and won his first professional tournament and $1,200 in prize money. Three weeks after that, down in Rancho Santa Fe, Sammy did it again—68 to win the first Bing Crosby pro-amateur tournament, a one-day affair that paid $500. Snead later told George Mendoza, who helped him write his autobiography, that he collected a *thousand* dollars at the first Crosby clambake, but no matter. Sammy decided there was no way he could part with Henry Picard's Izett driver and gratefully paid the elegant Hershey pro who kindly placed it in his hands (and possibly saved his career) $5.50 for the magical driving instrument.

In June 1938, at Oakland Hills, Snead drove the ball flawlessly with his Izett driver only to lose the National Open by a whisker to defending champion Ralph Guldahl, the beginning of golf's most famous streak of failures. (In the long and illustrious career that followed, Sam would never manage to win the United States Open, though nobody had more chances to do so.) Despite the loss, pro golf suddenly had its most appealing star since the salad days of Sir Walter Hagen.

Much of Snead's popularity lay in his sly plowboy charm and a butter-greased swing that made golf look as easy to play as, say, struggling Ben Hogan's made it look difficult. PGA publicist Fred Corcoran, for one, imme-diately recognized the marketability of these star qualities and soon had "the Dan'l Boone of Golf" plastered across every newspaper in America. The day after his breakthrough win at Oakland, for instance, Corcoran presented Snead with a New York newspaper featuring a photograph of the Tour's newest winner signing his victorious card at a scorer's table. "Hey, Mister Cor-coran," Snead declared—or so Freddie Corcoran widely broadcast the birth of a rube—"how'd they get my picture in New York? I ain't ever even been there!" It was all a joke. But the public ate it up.

Within a year or so, Ben Hogan would also be a grateful recipient of Henry Picard's guidance and largesse, but not before he and his gal Val ran out of money and tournament stops in the fall of 1937. Registering no higher than a tie for twelfth place at the Miami Biltmore Open two weeks prior to Christ-mas, they aimed their road-worn Buick for home to take stock of their dismal financial situation and talk about whether it made sense to head west for the start of the winter circuit in California immediately after the holidays.

A touring professional needed to earn a minimum of $3,000 a year just to break even, but Hogan's six-month grand total amounted to just $1,164 in winnings. According to the careful calculations of his pocket diary, he spent slightly more than $1,600 in traveling and living expenses, so he was almost $500 into their joint next egg by the time he and Valerie got home to their apartment in Cowtown.

As Henry Picard later told Jimmy Demaret, a few days after Christmas he and former Glen Garden assistant Jack Grout were passing through Fort Worth on their way west to join the winter tour out in Los Angeles when he happened to see Valerie and Ben Hogan seated together at a table in the same Blackstone Hotel where Hogan had not long ago dealt cards in order to eat.

Grout and Picard both strolled over to offer a friendly hello, and a clearly agitated Hogan revealed to them that he didn't have enough money to go back on Tour *and* take his wife with him.

"I want him to go alone," Valerie reportedly told them. "I'll stay and find a job."

"In that case," Hogan supposedly dug in his heels, "I won't go. We both go or nobody goes. I want you with me."

Picard liked what he saw of Hogan, a hardworking guy he believed just needed a break or two to get his career in gear the way Nelson and Guldahl and Snead had.

As Picard later told golf historian Al Barkow, it was his impression that Hogan's mind was all but made up to quit tournament golf—and undoubtedly he would have if Valerie hadn't been adamant that he should go on alone out west without her.

"All right. Let's end the argument here and now," Henry told the arguing couple. "Ben, take Valerie with you and go out west and play. If you need anything, come and see me. If you run out of money, I'll take care of you. You've got my word on that."

Ben Hogan stared at Picard. He wasn't the kind of guy who accepted charity from anyone, but Henry Picard was arguably the best player in professional golf at that moment and everything Ben Hogan hungered to be—urbane, polished, a proven champion who never seemed the slightest bit rattled by whatever took place on the golf course.

In some fashion, though Ben probably failed to realize it then, Picard filled the same void Marvin Leonard had begun to fill a decade before. Neither older man gave Hogan much more than his quiet assurance that he believed wholeheartedly in his abilities—something that meant far more to the complicated psychology of Ben Hogan, as it turned out, than mere money.

"Knowing that help was there helped me forget about my troubles," Hogan asserted a decade later in his own first instruction book, *Power Golf*. "The support and confidence Henry expressed in me meant all the difference in the world," Hogan told another interviewer when the best-selling book came out.

And so, instead of tossing in the towel, Ben and Valerie decided to head for California and see how far their remaining life savings could take them as they took one last shot at the big time. If they went broke, as Ben half-expected them to, he decided they would sell the Buick for train fare back to Fort Worth, and he would get a full-time job in the oil business and forget about playing professional golf.

They agreed to go as far as the Oakland Open.

The final Hogan quest began at Los Angeles, where Ben failed to place in the money. With living costs running about $150 a week, their dwindling nest egg took a major hit. At the second Crosby clambake in Rancho Santa Fe, Hogan finished eighth, good enough for $75, barely enough to cover lodging and food and gas. A week later, he pocketed just $67 for tenth place in Pasadena. Two more circuit stops followed that, with no payout in either place.

"I don't want to worry you," Hogan told Valerie as they headed north to the Oakland Open, the designated end of their odyssey. "But we've got less than $100 left." For the first time ever she wavered, according to her husband, wondering aloud if they should just call it quits and use the last bit of operating cash to get home on. That way they could at least keep the car.

"No, honey," Hogan replied, finally. "We made a deal to go as far as Oakland. If we don't make any money there, I'll sell the car, and we'll go home, and I'll never mention golf to you again."

They checked into the most inexpensive respectable hotel they could find in downtown Oakland and went out to find a decent diner. Years later, reflecting on these early struggles, a wealthy and famous Ben Hogan smiled and confessed that as a result of having to "eat cheap," he possessed a special fondness for the daily specials found at roadside diners—scrambled eggs, bacon, toast, and coffee, "good honest food for a fair price."

On the morning play was scheduled to begin in Oakland, Ben walked across the street to the lot where the couple's Buick was parked and was startled to discover the car's rear end sitting on cinder blocks. Overnight, thieves had made off with two tires. One account says Hogan threw up his hands and marched straight back to the hotel and told Valerie, "That's it. We're finished," and that she replied, "Nonsense. We'll just find someone to give you a ride to the golf course and we'll worry about the car later."

This story is probably true, although Hogan, in several interviews years later, couldn't recall the precise details of what happened that morning. The bitter irony of this final indignity must have been nearly blinding to him, and he always credited Valerie's clear thinking with saving the day—and probably his career as well.

As it turned out, reigning Masters champion Byron Nelson (who played in twenty-five tournaments and won two of them that year) was staying not far away and drove Hogan to the Sequoia Country Club that morning. Despite these pressures and the bleakness of his situation—or maybe *because* of them—Hogan was able to marshal his concentration and played decently for three rounds and fired 67 in the final round, which was good enough for sixth place and a payout of $285.

"We thought we were rich," Valerie Hogan remembered.

"It was the biggest check I'd ever seen in my life," Hogan observed, his voice catching, in his famous television interview with Ken Venturi in the early 1980s. "And I'm quite sure it's the biggest check I'll ever see."

This modest windfall enabled Ben and Valerie to put replacement tires on the Buick and go another week—on to Sacramento, where his concentration again was pretty solid, he finished third, and he made $350.

A month later, seemingly out of the blue, undoubtedly through the influence of his quiet benefactor Henry Picard, Hogan was approached at a tournament and offered an assistant professional's job at the Century Country Club in Purchase, New York, a prominent club founded by 100 wealthy Jewish members.

He leapt at the opportunity, which paid $500 a month plus anything he could earn giving lessons at $2 an hour. Two months later, en route to report for work in Purchase, Hogan played in his first Masters golf tournament, where Henry Picard won and Ralph Guldahl placed second. Hogan tied for twenty-fifth place.

By Christmas of 1938, the Hogan Buick had more than 3,600 additional miles on its odometer and nearly bald tires, but Valerie Hogan's large ornate scrapbook was thickening with clips of respectable showings at St. Petersburg and Miami and a few other places along the golf trail.

Back in September, something extraordinary had taken place. Henry Picard had unexpectedly invited Hogan to play with aging, silver-haired Tommy Armour in the Hershey Round Robin Four-Ball, a seven-day shindig in which eight teams made up of the Tour's top sixteen players competed to split $2,000 first-place prize money. Just prior to the event, the forty-three-year-old Armour, a red-faced, heavy-drinking Scotsman who allegedly once hurled his irons in disgust from the Firth of Tay railroad bridge, a former British Open, U.S. Open, and PGA champion, broke a bone in his hand and notified officials that he intended to withdraw.

A twenty-five-year-old virtual unknown from New Jersey, pleasant Vic Ghezzi, was penciled in as Armour's replacement—a stroke of great fortune for Ben Hogan, as it turned out.

Before the proceedings, Picard buttonholed his boss, Milton Hershey, and suggested to the famous chocolate baron that he keep an eye on the up-and-coming Ben Hogan, whose rapidly evolving golf swing, Picard quietly evangelized, was overdue to start producing tournament wins. "He's a self-made guy who lives clean and works harder than anybody out here," Henry told his employer.

Hershey, a self-made Quaker orphan who failed two or three times himself before finding the formula for getting rich in America, made a careful note to watch Hogan and see how he stood up to the best players in the game. Realistically, nobody gave the team of Hogan and Ghezzi much hope of winning the star-studded four-ball. The oddsmakers had them listed, in fact, dead last at 200 to 1.

Ben and Vic shocked the field—and possibly themselves—by firing a blistering 61 best-ball in the opening round and didn't let up their assault on the field until they were 53 strokes under par for 126 holes of play. Only Sammy Snead and short-game wizard Paul Runyan came close to matching them.

Followed by a gallery that the local *Hershey Bugle* estimated at four thousand strong, long-striding Ghezzi was beaming unstoppably as he strode toward Mr. Hershey's final green, raking back his sun-streaked hair and waving gratefully. Hogan, on the other hand, appeared oblivious to the applause and revealed nothing but a grim determination beneath his gray banded fedora hat. As if trudging into a private wind, unsmiling and all business despite a cushy four-stroke lead, perhaps he fully expected that having come so far and worked so damned hard, something or *someone*—shades of Byron and the infamous Glen Garden Christmas tournament of 1927—would appear at the last instant to deprive him of his first win of any kind.

There was another possibility too. Maybe Ben Hogan was finally just successfully blocking out the world at large and fully concentrating the way Valerie Hogan suggested he needed to in order to play his best.

"If we had lost," Ghezzi later confided to Jimmy Demaret, "I am quite certain that he would have jumped out a window."

But they didn't lose.

For their impressive collaborative efforts, each member of the winning team collected $1,000 plus an extra $100 each for the aggregate low-ball total.

For the week, Ben Hogan scored thirty-one birdies—six more than anyone else in the field. Milton Hershey was the first man to congratulate the broadly smiling little Texan. "I heard from Henry that you were the man to watch this week," he told Hogan.

"Thank you, Mr. Hershey," Hogan replied. "I'm glad I didn't let Henry down. Or you either."

"Maybe we should stay in touch," Hershey told him.

"Yes, sir. I'd like that."

For the year 1938, the very moment many observers believed America began to finally shake off the gloom of economic depression and get back on its feet, Ben Hogan finished thirteenth on the official money list of professional golf with $4,794.

He later described this as the turning point of his career.

The PGA tournament circuit was indeed now Ben Hogan's own Casa Mañana, his personal House of Tomorrow, and even Mama Hogan was somewhat impressed.

"Valerie is the only one who can honestly say, 'I told you so,'" she replied when a local reporter asked her about the role her reticent daughter-in-law had played in Hogan's breakthrough.

"The rest of us hoped Ben would make it," she expanded, graciously eating a little crow. "But Valerie was always sure he would."

FIVE

Vindication

ON THE COOL rain-splashed morning of Sunday, April 30, 1939, the same day the Soviet Union formally invited Great Britain and France to join an alliance against the gathering menace of Nazi Germany, a quarter of a million wide-eyed patrons traipsed into the sprawling 1,200-acre grounds of the most ambitious World's Fair ever mounted, an exhibition of technological extravagances that promoters optimistically called the "World of Tomorrow." As one Texas editorialist wryly noted, someone had taken Amon Carter's gaudy little Cowtown pageant and created *many* houses out of tomorrow.

Everywhere fairgoers looked they were dazzled by pavilions filled with dazzling geegaws and startling consumer wonders—model households that operated on timer switches and something called "electronic computers"; clothing made from a new wonder fabric called "Nylon"; various conveniences predicted to "liberate housewives from the slavery of the kitchen once and for all!"; telephones that could span the breadth of the nation in a matter of seconds (90 percent of Americans had yet to make a long-distance phone call); and a thrilling new technology called "Victrola television," which broadcast live moving pictures from a converted Manhattan sound studio directly to a cabinet-enclosed electronic screen, a contraption futurists boldly predicted would be in half of America's homes within the decade.

So what if storm clouds of war were gathering rapidly over Europe and nearly nine million Americans were still looking for work owing to a decade of severe economic convulsion? The runaway popularity of John Steinbeck's *Grapes of Wrath* and David O. Selznick's *Gone with the Wind*—unabashed anthems both to America's instinct for surviving the wretched excesses of its own recent past—suggested that most fairgoers at least were ready to believe tomorrow really was going to be a better deal for them, a vindication gained solely on the pure American virtues of hard work, self-sacrifice, and human innovation. As one famous New York commentator summed up rather breathlessly the emerging national mood on the eve of President Franklin Roosevelt's official opening of the fair, "With a vision to chase their dreams and an unbending will to succeed, the human being may stand on the very threshold of achieving a kind of unimagined perfection."

Thirty miles away, in his new job as assistant pro at the sedate and leafy Century Country Club in suburban Purchase, Ben Hogan was having thoughts along those same lines about the evolution and prospects of his emerging golf game and life. Hope gained through hard work, vindication achieved from never giving up.

Though he failed to break through and actually win a golf tournament in 1939, the technical improvements in Hogan's game were sufficient to suggest that the hungered-for moment was merely days rather than weeks away. Hogan's modest $500 seasonal salary and a scattering of second- and third-place finishes out on the Tour, including a second place to Byron Nelson at Phoenix early in the year's campaign, had marginally eased his financial worries. But the lessons he was required to teach under the terms of his contract with the Century Country Club paid a pittance and remained more of an intrusion on his valuable self-tutorials, each hour of which he fervently believed drew him closer to success. More than once he privately commented to Valerie that every time he had to try to teach some bored bridge-playing bond matron or half-interested banker's brat to swing a golf club, a little bit of him withered up and died inside.

As Valerie admitted to Louise Nelson, her husband was only truly happy out on the tournament circuit chasing that elusive first win, a personal torch song to the highway life that was repeated week after week through the long tournament seasons of 1938 and 1939 as the Hogans' aging maroon Buick bumped along roads behind Byron and perky Louise Nelson in their shiny new Studebaker President.

The closeness of the traveling foursome didn't escape the notice of the dozen or so other vagabonding Tour wives, who complained to each other that neither couple seemed particularly interested in joining the wider social aspects of life on tour, or as Tommy Armour's spirited wife was supposed to have tartly remarked over cocktails, "Those boys and their wives wouldn't know a good time if it walked up and kicked them in the shins."

True enough. By personal temperament and the dictates of his boyhood faith, genial and ever-smiling Byron didn't drink or smoke and simply wasn't the carousing type who placed a lampshade on his head and grabbed somebody's wife for a spin around the parquet to Tommy Dorsey.

Poker-faced Ben, who consumed alcohol only sparingly and smoked addictively but was otherwise engaged on a self-improvement campaign that made Mahatma Gandhi's self-denial look indulgent, could be friendly enough when it suited his purposes or there wasn't a golf club in his hand, but as their husbands routinely pointed out, there was no such thing as a casual friendship with Ben Hogan—only polite acquaintances and people getting in his way. "Playing golf with Ben is kind of like going to the dentist," Sam Snead drew a laugh by quipping to someone. "You don't say a helluva lot. You just sit there and wait for the pain to be over. It seems to hurt him as much as it hurts you." Years later, though, when asked by a reporter to name the player he most enjoyed playing with in his long career, Sam would offer a more sober assessment. "That's easy. Ben Hogan. First, because he always brought out the best in me. Second, because even though he said next to nothing, he was never anything less than a perfect gentleman."

Not surprisingly, almost from the moment they met out west—possibly at Bing Crosby's clambake—the engaging rube from Virginia was a major irritant to Hogan, though Snead's sudden, breakthrough, dazzling early success, velvety natural golf swing, and vast popular appeal with galleries waiting for another Walter Hagen to emerge probably contributed more than anything else to Hogan's initial dislike for the Dan'l Boone of Golf. He also found Sam's locker-room bonhomie crude and unbecoming for a major league sportsman in the public eye.

For a while, on the other hand, Byron Nelson occupied a unique niche in Hogan's narrowly circumscribed world on tour. Nelson's farm-boy charm stemmed from his genuine Christian modesty and a determination to give the least offense to anyone if possible—something Ben greatly admired in him and even copied—qualities that made every win Byron notched feel like a gift from the Almighty.

Hogan's unexplained aloofness, on the other hand, increasingly masked an almost pathological need to focus entirely on the task at hand, like a seamstress doing the finest piecework by hand. He had the curse of the underdog who had to toil twice as hard to get where he wanted to go, a need Valerie appears to have spotted early. She helped him overcome it with her casual but astute insight about the value of practicing his swing until it became second nature and made him immune to tournament jitters—the emerging Hogan formula for success, if there was such a thing.

Despite the fact that he was playing the finest golf of his life, nothing divided by nothing still constantly echoed in the corridors of his mind. On one occasion about this time, after coming close but faltering yet again and bitterly wondering aloud to his bride, "Why the hell can't I make more birdies, Val?" she provided yet another insight that on the face of it seems almost laughably obvious—yet made complete sense to workaholic Hogan. Decades later, he described her casual response as one of the prime reasons he became such a competitor in due course, a story he told over and over with relish and an unmistakable note of wonder to friends and interviewers—as if the answer to his trouble had been there all along, the forest hidden by the trees.

"Why, Ben," she supposedly replied calmly, "why don't you just hit it closer to the hole?"

As he related the moment years later, he thought about her comment for a moment, then smiled at her across the bench seat of their elderly Buick and said, "You know, Val, you're right. I think I'll do that from now on."

Was it really that simple? Probably not. But on the other hand, like the broad guiding principles of a modern self-recovery program, this profoundly simple notion gave Ben an invaluable concrete objective on every shot, a means of staying entirely in the moment instead of getting ahead of himself and fretting about the outcome—an undeniable means of producing more birdies and therefore finally winning. Like an alcoholic whose mantra becomes "one day at a time," Hogan's path to recovery and breakthrough became "one shot at a time," a credo that not only transformed him in due time but laid the foundation for the modern performance psychology of the game.

Beneath Hogan's increasingly chilly tournament exterior—which was really a kind of protective yogic trance he was learning to project himself into in order to replicate the peace and solitude of the practice range, where every shot seemed possible and rattled nerves were rarely if ever part of the equation—Hogan remained a man of desperately bundled emotions. On the surface, for example, he wrestled with a genuine wariness of strangers in particular and crowds in general, a direct result of his abruptly forfeited childhood. And somewhere just below that were the deeper festering wounds of a fatherless son who never felt truly accepted and admired by anyone except perhaps his equally needy wife.

On the most visible level, Ben's and Byron's respective family histories and starkly different personalities (and even their marital choices—painfully wary Val versus sunny, take-charge Louise) made them highly unlikely companions in their shared quest for golf stardom—more Mutt and Jeff than Hope and Crosby. On a personal level, however, Byron's natural ease offset Ben's innate tension, while Ben's growing obsession with practice rubbed off and clearly improved the quality of Byron's game.

True to their natures, though, with each win Nelson grew more gracious and charming, almost awestruck at what faith and hard work could produce, while with every near-miss Hogan seemed to become even more of a loner—withdrawn, detached, and introspective.

For a while, undergirded by little more than their shared nostalgia for the old Glen Garden rivalry and mutually shared tastes for the same kinds of hotels, clothing, and social entertainments, this peculiar dynamic of friendship worked pretty nicely for both men and their spouses and made them oddly ideal traveling mates and temporarily comfortable allies, a perpetual party of four against the world at large.

"There's no question they stood off from us," Paul Runyan of the neighboring Metropolis Club remembered. "Particularly Ben. He let it be known early that he was all golf and no fooling around. Some of the fellas began to even fear getting near Hogan—that icy look he would give you that said, 'That's far enough, friend.' He could be very friendly if he liked you. He and I got along pretty well, probably because we were both small guys trying to compete against the big guns. Besides, he had Valerie. She seemed to be his only real close friend out there."

As their travels together entered a second winter season, the wives drew especially close; Louise Nelson's plucky charm counterbalanced Valerie's natural reticence and reminded Valerie of her closeness to sister Sarah back home in Texas (to whom she regularly jotted postcards and whom she phoned before and after almost every tournament). During tournament play, wives who didn't have the nerves or physical stamina to tread the golf course after their husbands normally congregated in a lounge at the clubhouse, shared lunch, and played a little bridge or mah-jongg. They passed the tense hours of waiting beneath a clock by learning to knit or crochet, quietly swapping gossip or news from home, reading the occasional book or newspaper (clipping any item that mentioned Ben, in Valerie's case), and writing letters, all the while dressed in their Sunday best in case one of their golfing Lochinvars did something truly noteworthy.

Byron did something noteworthy often in 1939, especially during that long last summer of the Great Depression. After tying for second at the Crosby, he won in a gallop (by 12 strokes over a faltering Hogan) at Phoenix, took the lustrous North and South Championship at Pinehurst, nipped past Snead and Guldahl to win his first National Open at Philadelphia's Spring Mill course (best remembered as the tournament Sam Snead blew by scoring an 8 on the par-5 72nd hole), and finished up the year with a pair of scintillating victories at the Massachusetts and venerable Western Opens. At the PGA Championship at Pomonok, he narrowly lost to Henry Picard on the 37th hole.

Nelson's smashing breakthrough—he finished no worse than a tie for tenth place all season long—only underscored, and deepened, Hogan's gloom over achieving a win he could call his own. "I'll never be anything that matters if I don't figure out how to finish off a tournament," Ben complained to Valerie during their drive from Philadelphia to Byron and Louise Nelson's place in Reading, Pennsylvania, where Byron was the new head pro, for a brief respite from tournament action, having made his first thirty-six-hole cut ever at the U.S. Open but finishing in a miserable tie for *sixty-second* place on Open Saturday at Spring Mill.

"Yes, but you've finished second three times in the past six months," said Valerie, attempting to put a good face on the situation. "And every time it has been to someone different. No one is winning everything, Ben."

True, he reluctantly conceded. But even if no one player was dominating things, almost every other Tour son of Texas but he had broken through to win and seemed, on the whole, to mount his best effort at the Tour's major events. First it was Guldahl at the National Open in 1937 and '38, now it was Byron at Spring Mill. Demaret was always in there, and so were Dick Metz and even hard-ass Lloyd Mangrum. At Spring Mill, both Hogan's strengths and weaknesses had been emphasized. His early iron play at times had been nothing less than superb, but his driving was all over the place. The culprit was the hook that wouldn't go away no matter how hard he concentrated and blocked out the world.

No player in the professional ranks, it's safe to say, had come as far and improved himself as much by watching better players perform and refining their techniques than Ben Hogan. "Ben wasn't unique in having to watch others to learn that swing of his," observed Sam Snead, who enjoyed the luxury of having one of the most natural and supple swings God ever gave to a Homo sapien. "But he sure as hell was probably the best at copying and refining what he saw. Nobody helped anybody much in those days, brother. If you did get some advice from somebody, you didn't advertise it much. It was basically each man for himself out there."

"On the contrary," counters feisty Jackie Burke Jr., "in those days hotels didn't have air-conditioning and TV sets, so almost every evening the players gathered in the hotel lobby to gamble, play cards, drink booze, and shoot the breeze. For guys with wives, that's about all there really was to do. I remember being about ten years old, traveling with my father, in some hotel lobby out on the circuit, and there was Hogan, Ky Laffoon, Henry Picard, Jack Grout—all swapping ideas to beat the band, trying this or that, trying to get some edge up. These guys were all club pros, remember, who made their money giving lessons, so sharing ideas wasn't the least bit unusual for them. The Tour was a laboratory for 'em, and Ben was probably the best of the bunch at picking things up and trying them out. He saw everything with those eyes of his—the reason they called him the Hawk. He saw the slightest change in some guy's address, or the faintest pressure he applied to the club with his fingers, things most of the others just couldn't see if they looked all day. Ben did, though. He took it and tried it and used whatever worked."

Early in his career, Hogan studied almost every movement Walter Hagen made on a golf course, quickly coming to the conclusion that the Haig possessed the finest natural rhythm and playing tempo any champion ever displayed—which he attempted to copy. In a remarkable handwritten, fourteen-page letter to a friend in the late 1960s, using a "stick figure" he drew to illustrate his point, Hogan explained the grip and fundamentals of "a sound driver swing" he claimed to have developed directly from conversations with the aging Hagen, detailing principles of a proper grip, finger pressure, alignment of shoulders and feet, flex of knees, position of the body and head through the swing, position of the left hand during the backswing, transfer of weight, and a high finish that encouraged the hips and shoulders to fully turn into the shot. Hogan advised: "Keep on file and refer to when in doubt. If used correctly you can belt the ball a country mile (Drive for show and putt for dough)," then concluded his remarkable tutorial by offering a detailed if somewhat unorthodox way of verifying the correctness of one's backswing: "At the top of the backswing the groin muscle on the inside of your rt leg near your right nut will tighten. This subtle feeling of tightness there tells you that you have made the correct move back from the ball. Ben Hogan."

Early on, he also absorbed insights from the fluid swing of Carnoustie-born Macdonald Smith (a thirty-time winner on the U.S. tour who never managed to win any of the big ones) and inspiration from the game of inaugural Masters winner Horton Smith. Once Hogan was established on tour, he closely observed the way Johnny Revolta and Paul "Little Poison" Runyan compensated for their lack of distance off the tee by chipping and putting better than almost anyone. English-born Harry Cooper—who once pointed out to the ascendant Hogan that he weirdly released the club at the top of his backswing and re-gripped it with a stronger grip that promoted a right-to-left trajectory—hit such low-rising, straight line drives and possessed such a fine repeatable golf swing that the press dubbed him "Robot Man" and joked about Cooper having to be plugged into a wall socket and recharged every evening.

All of this, it appears, made strong impressions on Hogan. Through a wreath of cigarette smoke, he observed and memorized every feature of Cooper's machinelike swing and processed his advice too, like one of those wondrous new computers running the lights in the houses of tomorrow.

Quiet Densmore Shute, the '33 British Open and PGA winner of 1937 and 1938, an angular suburban Boston pro who stroked low irons as effortlessly and effectively as anyone who played the game, was another early swing influence. The Hawk's gaze feasted on Shute's slow takeaway and his high, flawless finish. As his form improved, though, Hogan particularly took a shine to the way Gene Sarazen, another little man on top of his game, strutted into a locker room and got down to business on the golf course, grinding opponents and courses to a pulp. Almost from their first encounter, Sarazen's confident, Napoleonic swagger, expensive clothes, candid opinions, and respect for tradition deeply impressed Ben and showed him a picture of who he could someday be with enough hard work and polish.

By the summer of 1939, Hogan's short game skills, particularly his wedge play and putting stroke, were already making admirers out of some leading competitors. Crouched slightly over his bent knees with his feet close together in a slightly open attitude, Ben presented a classic tripod position over the ball, with his weight almost entirely distributed to his left side, employing a reversed overlapping grip that permitted him to place all five fingers of his right hand on the putter's grip. His backstroke was typically on the short side, but he followed through boldly with his right hand, believing that weight on the right and a strong right hand balanced out the putting stroke. As a result, Hogan's balance over the putt was superb, and when he was off target, he tended to push putts slightly to the right. When he was on, he was deadly accurate, rarely touching the sides of the cup, particularly from inside twelve feet.

Sarazen, whose own work habits became legendary as he chased his hero devil-may-care Walter Hagen around the tournament circuit of the twenties, proclaimed Hogan's putting technique the best he had ever seen on tour but admitted the Texan's addiction to practice left him bone-weary.

"It exhausts me, and most other professionals, just to watch Ben practice, and there are occasions on which I think that even the superdisciplined Hogan leaves his finest strokes on the practice grounds." According to Sarazen, players loathed billeting in hotel rooms near the Hogans because the persistent *thump-thump-thump* of Ben's endless late-night carpet putting sessions robbed them of sleep. The Squire liked to recount how he encountered the broody Hogan stalking a dim hotel corridor late one night in his pajamas and bathrobe, pacing angrily over the carpet. "What's wrong, Ben?" Sarazen claims he asked the unhappy Texan. "I just three-putted twice in my room," Hogan spit out dejectedly. "I think he *sleeps* with that putter of his," Sarazen capped off the tale, with a twinkle and robust laugh.

In the midfifties, Jimmy Demaret told of vacating the grounds at Oak Hill after dusk had settled in, flipping on his car's headlights, and suddenly seeing his pal Hogan illuminated out on the practice tee, striking ball after ball into the night. Demaret supposedly climbed out of his jalopy and hiked over to discover Hogan had been on the tee hitting practice balls since finishing his round several hours earlier.

"Ben, you made *ten* birdies today and shot 64. What the hell are you trying to prove?"

Hogan, a cigarette dangling from his lip, glanced at his talented, fun-loving friend from Houston, one of the few guys he felt genuinely drawn to and wished he could be more like—pro golf's living incarnation, in a way, of Henny Bogan.

For Demaret and a majority of the tournament's competitors, evening was the time to unwind and let their hair down, grab dinner, get drunk, play poker, chase broads, do anything but mentally dwell on the riddle of figuring out mighty Oak Hill. But not Ben Hogan. The more he practiced, as he tersely put it, the luckier he got, though *luck* was simply the name he gave to his scientific method of reducing the margins for mistakes. Like Salk with the polio scourge, he simply couldn't let it go. Tournaments were won or lost, he had come to believe, building on his wife's original insight, almost entirely in the preparation stages, the reason he developed a ritual during nontournament days of hitting at least six hundred balls twice a day, three balls every minute for three and a half hours in the morning, followed by three and a half hours of practice in the afternoon. Playing in the actual tournament became, he insisted, "almost secondary," an anticlimax for him—"simply going through the motions," as he put it. Improving equipment and better course conditioning were fine and dandy, but the only thing a serious golfer needed, as he stated again and again over the next half-century, was "more daylight."

For its part, the golf press marveled at Ben's holy obsession with practice, wondering what it was the fedora-wearing Texan found so comforting in hour upon hour of lonely ball-striking.

"I always wished the days were longer so I could practice and work," Hogan told the *Dallas Morning News* not long before his death in 1997, going straight to the heart of what set him apart from everyone else, still savoring his famous monkish interludes on Misery Hill decades after they ended. "I always enjoyed practicing more than playing because I could prove and disprove things."

"Jimmy," Hogan supposedly replied amid the evening shadows at Oak Hill when his friend wondered what more he could have desired from a round that included ten birdies and no bogeys, "if a man can make ten birdies in a round, there's no reason in this world why he can't birdie *every* hole."

Demaret laughed and shook his head at this impossible grail, later recalling that Hogan didn't even crack a smile when he made the comment. "I get the feeling he really believes it," Demaret told the others in the locker room out of Ben's earshot. "And he fully expects to be that man."

IN THIS QUEST for personal swing perfection, an item from Valerie Hogan's traveling scrapbook from the closing years of the decade leaps out most revealingly. It happened in St. Petersburg in late 1938. "Hogan Hits Flags" read the headline of the local paper. "Ben Hogan, Fort Worth, Texas, twice hit flags on 11 and 16. His second hit struck and if it had been in the hole straight the ball might have dropped in for an eagle. On the sixteenth, he pitched his third right to the pennant and it struck the rod and rolled twenty feet back." The reporter concluded, "He really goes for the pins, this Hogan."

Therein lay another valuable lesson on the road to vindication—the need for caution. By Hogan's own calculations, striking flagsticks with his increasingly accurate approach shots—hitting balls *too* close, as irony would have it—cost him at least half a dozen opportunities to make birdie and win his first tournament as early as 1938, the year his contemporaries Guldahl and Nelson seemed to either challenge or win everything in sight and he, a harder worker than both of them put together, wound up in fifth place for the Vardon Trophy. Stung by the consequences of perhaps *too* much accuracy, he began aiming for the flattest portions of every green *nearest* the hole, preferring to leave himself a short uphill putt for birdie.

Among other things, some insist that this small adjustment in thinking and strategy explains why Hogan scored so few aces in PGA competition. One of the persistent myths of golf holds that the game's greatest shotmaker failed to ever score an ace in competition. But he did, at least twice, one at the 10th hole of the Texas Open in 1934, another at the 4th hole at the Esmeralda Open in Spokane, Washington, in 1947.

Whatever the truth of his conclusions regarding shooting for flagsticks, as his confidence and shotmaking skills markedly improved and his desire to finally break through scaled to a fever pitch, around 1939 Hogan suddenly began making more birdies than almost anybody else in golf.

So it was no surprise when, ruthlessly pragmatic as he was, Ben turned to his original tour benefactor, the suave and unflappable Henry Picard, for insight on the only remaining problematic part of his game, a driver that had a maddening tendency to hook under pressure.

Before the start of the PGA Championship that summer at Pomonok Country Club, in Flushing, New York, Hogan confided to Picard that his untimely hooks were making him crazy. By one account, Picard cogitated for only a moment before replying, "Ben, in your case, it's pretty simple. You'll never win until you learn to slice the ball."

Taking Hogan to the range, Picard used a five-iron to show him exactly what he meant, shifting Hogan's powerful blacksmith hands to a more neutral, even slightly "weak," position on the leather club handle. In a photograph of this interlude, taken by a wire service photographer, the elegant, necktie-wearing Picard tilts forward to adjust Hogan's powerful left hand toward the forward portion of the shaft. A closer examination reveals that Hogan, with his shirt collar open and his shirtsleeves rolled up for work, his head bowed in a posture of almost prayerful concentration, stands with his feet slightly open at address—the classic setup for a workable fade, which he would soon adapt as his own, refining and perfecting it like a surgeon wielding a scalpel.

Fifteen years later, when *Life* magazine published, to great accompanying fanfare, an article over Hogan's byline proclaiming "This Is My Secret," Ben explained to the world that the better a player got in terms of ball-striking, the more he had a tendency to hook the ball from right to left. "Most of the players on tour today are fighting a hook," he essayed. "They fight it on almost every shot they make. When they miss a shot you will find them missing the green on the left." In his famous exegesis, he went on to reveal that he was battling a "low, ducking, agonizing hook, the kind you can hang your coat on," as late as 1946 and tried a host of conventional approaches for curing it— opening his stance, weakening his grip, using more left arm and a cutting descent at the ball. "They all worked, but in the process they cut down my distance by five to ten yards. Five yards is a long way. You can't give anybody five yards. You can't correct a fault with a fault."

Using close-up photographs of Hogan's hands at the top of his backswing, the editors "revealed" that in his driver swing—presumably his flawed *pre*-1946 technique that nevertheless won twenty-two PGA events and an "unofficial" National Open championship—the master's left wrist remained straight, while employing an "antiquated" technique called "pronation," brought to American shores by immigrating Scottish pros but later basically abandoned by mainstream teachers. It permitted the same wrist to bend backward and inward, forming a slight V, which prompted the hands to roll gradually to the right, opening the face of the club at the top of the swing. This fractional cupping of the left wrist—invisible to all but the most astutely tutored eyes—combined with a slight shift of his left-hand grip an eighth to a quarter of an inch to the left, allowing his thumb to rest on top of the shaft, supposedly explained his spooky accuracy. It was this final "secret" that purportedly let him finally develop a "hook-free" swing and a distinctive boring low trajectory of flight that sent his ball on a rope toward the target, where it momentarily appeared to hover at its apogee before settling with a tiny fade onto the green. This was the technique, he claimed to millions of eager readers, that he used "ninety percent of the time" in competition.

Maybe so. But for ordinary mortals, it was far too much to comprehend, much less effectively copy. Some of Hogan's better-known Tour competitors in fact openly belittled *Life*'s revelations and Ben's so-called secret, implying he'd taken the magazine for a joy ride, while pocketing its dough, by making the act of swinging a driver sound more complicated than fashioning an atomic bomb from scratch in your basement.

The truth is, whatever nuggets Henry Picard conveyed to Ben that afternoon on the practice tee at Pomonok provided the first step toward discovering a final solution to his problem with the hook and certainly appeared to suddenly make a big difference in the way Ben subsequently performed under pressure, producing spells where he was chillingly accurate off the tee, driving the ball with a newfound confidence.

On his own, Hogan had come to the fervent belief that a long straight drive was essential to the proposition of winning. A crushed tee ball intimidated an opponent and invariably shortened the approach to the green, improving percentage with every yard gained. Initially at any rate, Picard's teaching seemed to produce sparkling results. When play at the 1939 PGA Championship opened, Hogan went out and fired impressive matching rounds of 69 to share the thirty-six-hole qualifying honors with Ky Laffoon, Chuck Kocsis, and Dutch Harrison. He missed exactly three fairways in thirty-six holes of play. During the first round of match-play competition, for example, he positively demolished a talented Springfield, Ohio, club pro named Steve Zappe 7 and 6 and went on to face Paul Runyan, the tournament's reigning champ, aka "the Cyanide Kid," in the tournament's quarter-final round.

Hogan's driving was peerless in their match, once more a tribute to Picard's astute coaching and the student's keen ability to quickly process information, and on half a dozen greens Hogan was ten to fifteen feet inside Runyan, putting for birdie. As he'd done to other big hitters like Snead and Johnny Bulla and Lawson Little, though, Runyan used his famous metal-spooned putter to rattle half a dozen monster putts into the back of the cup, proving Willie Park's maxim that a man who can putt is a fair match for anyone.

"That sort of thing," Hogan confided to a local reporter, slumped on a locker-room bench after Runyan had narrowly disposed of him, "repeated on hole after hole, chokes the heart out of you. At least five times the gate was wide open for me, but Paul wouldn't let me through."

Hogan lost 2 and 1 to Runyan, but during their drive back to Purchase, a surprisingly upbeat Hogan confided to his wife that the draining experience had been a positive learning experience in more ways than one. "Runyan knows how to finish a match better than anybody I've ever seen," he explained to her. "It's his focus. Paul's concentration is so absolute he doesn't seem to see anything but the next shot. He wasn't the slightest bit intimidated by my drives. He controlled his mind *and* mine."

Hogan gripped the steering wheel, staring out at the lonesome highway as if one more critical truth—another scientific breakthrough leading directly to the World of Tomorrow—had been revealed to him and fallen in place at last.

"If I'm going to win," he said, "I've got to be able to do that too."

PERFECTION, OF COURSE, is a cruel god. It requires the kind of absolute devotion and daily sacrifice that is the sworn enemy of personal emotion and intimacy with others, even—and maybe especially—one's loyal ladywife.

Before the PGA Championship, commenting in a national magazine on the growing number of wives who insisted on tagging along with their husbands out on the wearying tournament circuit, Gene Sarazen stirred up a hornet's nest by declaring that golf wives were effectively a "burden and distraction and really ought to stay home." He bluntly proposed that their primary duty was to procreate the race and keep the home fires burning.

Among those who took exception to the little squire's domestic advice were none other than Mrs. Byron Nelson and Mrs. Ben Hogan, who, photographed wearing smart matching outfits and identical two-toned designer shoes at the Dapper Dan Championship, politely declined to take direct issue with Sarazen's ridiculous assertions, preferring their attractive high visibility to speak for itself.

And yet, like many of the fifteen or so other dutiful "fairway wives" who regularly drummed the circuit with their spouses, both Louise Nelson and Valerie Hogan were rapidly growing weary of life in a four-door sedan, drafty roadside hotels, lumpy beds, and the same dull restaurant menu day after day.

"No, it's not too grand an experience living in suitcases and traveling 18,000 miles every winter," Valerie admitted to New York journalist Arch Murray from a wicker chair on the veranda of the elegant Carolina Hotel in Pinehurst for the North and South tournament during the spring of 1939, almost a year to the day before her husband broke through and won. "It was a thrill at first but that's long since worn off." She explained to Murray that the primary job of a fairway wife was to "hide her boredom and mental fatigue from her husband at all costs, to keep smiling and encouraging him no matter what anyone says.

"A golfing wife has to be a combination of many things—nurse, masseur, comforter and whipcracker—but most of all she has to be a psychologist," she observed. "Your reactions to your husband's moods are vital."

Among other things, displaying a heretofore unglimpsed volubility and dexterity with words, Valerie Hogan pertly explained that she could tell exactly how her husband Ben had played simply by watching him approach the home hole of any round. Her barometric readings came from studying his shoulder posture and the speed of his walk. If his pace was brisk and his head was up, his "jaw thrusting forward," there was no doubt Ben was in top form. If his head was down and his gait slower, "he's probably shot 75."

Late that next October, following Hogan's lessons at Spring Mill and Pomonok, as his second season working for the Century Country Club was drawing to a close and a new winter circuit loomed, journalist Murray followed up with another visit to tournament golf's most prominent groomsman and found Valerie Hogan "quietly dreading the closing up of their snug little apartment" on the grounds of the Century Club and heading back to the grind of hotels and highways.

Her husband, by contrast, was practicing more diligently than ever and "bristling like a bulldog to get back at it, to attend a couple of college football games and then head to Florida for the start of the winter season and the big swing out West."

"I think this year is going to be the vital one for me," Ben confidently told Murray. "I have been knocking at the door too long now. I'm going to develop a finishing touch. I've had too many fellows in the trap, only to let them get away. That has to stop."

DURING THE THREE weeks the couple was back home staying with Margaret and Royal in Fort Worth for the holidays, Valerie spent her afternoons shopping for clothes with her sister, Sarah, while Ben played practice rounds at Colonial with Royal and Marvin Leonard.

Among other things, Ben was intrigued to learn that Leonard's charm offensive to bring the National Open south of the Potomac River for the first time ever was paying dividends. As Leonard tweaked and fussed with Colonial, he and Amon Carter used their contacts to promote Colonial's cause with golf's ruling elites. At one point Leonard dialed up USGA president Harold Pierce at home in Boston and spent more than a half-hour making his case long-distance on the telephone. Among other blandishments, Leonard promised Pierce record crowds, fabulous playing conditions, incomparable southern hospitality, and a guaranteed windfall to the coffers of golf's governing American body of at least $15,000 in cold hard cash—possibly profits in the unheard of range of $25,000. Pierce and the USGA finally submitted, and for many years, the story went, Leonard's long-distance sales pitch was the most expensive phone call to ever leave the state of Texas.

By 1940 Marvin Leonard was a tough man to say no to. And so was his former Glen Garden caddie, Ben Hogan.

One Colonial member recalled seeing the lone figure of Hogan practicing wedge shots for the length of an entire morning during that particular Christmas interval, taking a lunch break with Leonard, then getting straight back to business with his favorite club in the bag, trying shots from every kind of lie imaginable.

When the member asked him about it later, Ben patiently explained that a good short-iron player, particularly with a timely pitch of the wedge, could equalize any advantage and make up for a mistake. But his calculations didn't cease there.

One year later, this same Colonial member watched Hogan devote an entire morning to drilling four-woods on the range, take a thirty-minute breather for a Coke and Hershey bar, then pass the length and breadth of a cool winter afternoon working the same four-wood left and right, using a caddie armed with a catcher's mitt out at the 200-yard mark for a movable target.

Most of the time, the member recalled, after Hogan motioned where he intended to hit his next shot, the ball catcher shifted little more than a step in one direction or the other. When the member asked Ben, why such dedication to a four-wood, Hogan looked at him neutrally and explained, "I just lost a tournament last summer up in Chicago due to a poor four-wood shot. I don't want that happening again."

"Hell, Ben. You hit that four-wood better than most Tour players hit their wedges."

"Apparently it wasn't good enough."

When the tour of 1940 resumed play in Los Angeles for the winter schedule three days into the new decade, winless Ben Hogan was hitting his tee shots longer and straighter than ever, as he proved by placing second once again to golf's Jimmy "Siege Gun" Thomson during a pretournament "bombing party" staged by Freddie Corcoran at the Los Angeles Coliseum.

Thomson's longest effort cleared the concrete wall at the west end of the arena and flew into the empty spectator seats, 265 yards from the temporary tee built on the Coliseum peristyle.

"Little Benny Hogan, the 138-pound marksman from White Plains," as the *Los Angeles Times* somewhat erroneously identified him that year, 70 pounds lighter than Thomson, was the only other player to clear the wall and reach the seats, prompting Hogan to speculate that someday a player who stood six-foot-three and weighed 220 pounds would routinely drive the ball at least 350 yards. Even some old tournament hands laughed at this outrageous suggestion, assuming "Bantam Ben" was making an uncharacteristic funny. He couldn't have been more serious.

Hogan's best effort measured 255 yards, a blast for which he picked up 150 extra bucks and the dubious title of "pound for pound the longest driver in golf." Byron Nelson won the accuracy segment of the contest by driving three balls between the uprights of the football goalposts 225 yards from the tee. With the extra cash in hand, the Hogans and Nelsons splurged on a fancy Hollywood restaurant, and Valerie and Ben afterward went to see a screening of *Gone with the Wind*.

"I think Ben felt he was due at any moment," Nelson recalls of that moment. "You couldn't argue with the way he was striking the ball. You could see the confidence building in him right along. Most of us thought, as the newspaper fellas did, that his breakthrough would come any day about then."

Nine days later up at Oakland, with Nelson not in the field, Hogan finished second to Jimmy Demaret, who less than a week later also captured the San Francisco National Match Play Open. When the winter argosy paused down the coast at Crosby's clambake in Del Mar, it was long-hitting Ed "Porky" Oliver's turn to beat out a fast-closing, long-driving Ben Hogan. Close again, a tie for third, but no cigar.

Less than eight days later in Phoenix, Oliver blistered the Country Club of Phoenix for a final-round 64, maddeningly making Hogan a bridesmaid once again. Other players noticed that the closer he came to winning week after week, the less Hogan said about *anything* either on or off the golf course.

"Jimmy Demaret Has Averaged $100 per Day So Far in 1940," bugled the sports pages of the *San Antonio Express* when the Tour caravans rolled into Brackenridge Park for the 1940 edition of the Texas Open. Demaret was the Tour's leading money winner and odds-on favorite to win the tournament in his own backyard, but it turned out to be the *other* native sons, Nelson and Hogan, who rapidly seized the spotlight.

Amid heavy downpours and high winds, Hogan posted a brilliant pair of closing 66s to tie the tournament record of 271. As he sat in the locker room waiting for the final group to finish, rubbing lineament on a hand that had cramped up from signing so many autographs, Lawson Little, Horton Smith, and others came forward to offer him their congratulations. The moment was a long time coming, Smith told someone, and nobody would have blamed Ben for feeling vindicated. His hard luck had finally been overcome by his hard work.

But Hogan would have none of it. Unwilling and unable to accept the verdict until the final group was off the course, shades of his sober victory walk up the final fairway at the Hershey Four-Ball, Hogan shook each man's hand but sharply dismissed any idea that he had won. He sat alone, rubbing his hand, smoking a cigarette, looking into the middle distance like a man awaiting a jury's verdict.

Sure enough, minutes later, word came that reigning National Open champ Nelson, the new head pro at Toledo's prestigious Inverness Club, playing in the day's final group, needed only one birdie in the wintry dusk on the final hole to catch Hogan in the clubhouse and force a play-off.

"Then I hope he either gets a 66 and wins, or takes 68 and second so there will be no play-off," Hogan remarked to a reporter from the *Express*. He undoubtedly had a sense of déjà vu but thought for a moment more, softened a bit, and added: "But if he wins, there's no one I'd rather lose to than Byron, for he's one of the best friends I'll ever have."

As it turned out, Byron made his birdie putt to tie and force a play-off. A little while later, after both men had showered and changed, they rode together to a San Antonio radio station for a live evening interview. Two of the Lone Star State's most accomplished sons were going after the biggest prize in Texas golf. Nelson was asked for his feelings about being in a play-off, of all things, with childhood friend Ben Hogan.

True to form, Byron responded, "Anytime you can tie Ben or beat him, it's a feather in your cap, because he's such a fine player."

The interviewer smiled and turned to Hogan. "How about you, Ben? What's it feel like to be going head to head with Byron?"

True to nature, Ben thought for a moment and reflected, "Byron's got a good game. But it'd be a lot better if he'd practice. He's too lazy to practice."

A moment of dead air followed, a startled silence after which the interviewer pushed on, talking about the week's nasty weather conditions and the unlikelihood of a better forecast for the play-off.

Many years later, Hogan attempted to explain that he was merely attempting to lighten an otherwise difficult moment by poking a small needle at them both—Nelson for his relaxed approach to tournament preparation, Hogan for his relentless practice rituals that exhausted anyone who watched him.

It may well have been a genuine attempt at humor on Hogan's part, though public humor wasn't often attributed to Ben by anyone who knew him and had felt his glacial guardedness. Whatever his true intent, the remark came off not a little sanctimonious and evidently both surprised and stung Byron Nelson. Some say their relationship was never quite the same after the radio interview, though others suggest that the intensely competitive atmosphere both men faced on a week-to-week basis now was largely responsible for eroding whatever comfort and pleasure they'd once found in each other's company on the road. "I think Ben always had some resentment about their early years together, due to Byron's early success," said Sam Snead. "And tournament golf will only magnify that sort of thing. Some fella you think is your best pal one day, well, hell, you'd cut his throat the next to have half a chance of winning some tournament. It's just the nature of the game."

Maybe so. But Valerie Hogan was also to play a key role in the perhaps inevitable estrangement of Ben and Byron. Outside of her younger sister, Sarah, she considered Louise Nelson the closest thing she had on earth to a friend and confidante, a person who fully appreciated the sacrifices she was making in behalf of her husband's ambitions. Though nothing remotely alike in personality, the two women shared opinions regarding a woman's place in marriage, had the same tastes in fine clothing and decorating, and expressed a desire to someday have a home and perhaps even a family. Though neither would conceive and bear children, the far more adaptable Louise Nelson, thanks to Byron's relatively rapid success in golf, would soon have her dream home and a widening circle of friends outside the golf world, enabling her to leave the rigors of road travel behind forever.

Not so Valerie Hogan. She had at least another fifteen years of hard labor ahead of her serving as Ben's sole traveling partner, advice counselor, scrapbook maker, and head cheerleader, a role she was born to play but clearly paid a price for in terms of her own inward tendencies. When Louise left the Tour wife circuit for good in 1945, nobody replaced her in Valerie's loyal affections. The two women remained good friends, despite a palpable chill in relations between their world-famous husbands, until Louise's death and Byron's eventual remarriage to a much younger woman, at which point, friends say, Valerie Hogan wanted little or nothing to do with Byron Nelson, primarily due to remarks Byron made about Ben in the newspaper.

But all that was yet to come.

At the Texas Open of 1940, at least as the local press flogged the banner headline story, two sons of Texas were going to renew their bitter childhood rivalry and settle "bragging rights" once and for all.

Curiously, in golf it's the rare play-off that isn't a disappointing spectator affair. Hogan arrived two hours early at Brackenridge and warmed up in a cocoon of unapproachable silence. Nelson arrived an hour behind him, admitting he hadn't slept well at all. Neither man, to judge solely by their visible moods and body English, was happy about the prospect of reprising the Glen Garden play-off of Christmas 1927.

The play-off, Hogan's first ever as a professional, went off sharply at 1:00 P.M. on Monday, February 12, with an estimated crowd of two thousand spectators swaddled in overcoats and fedoras watching beneath damp and gloomy skies. Spectators had to shell out an extra $1.10 for admission.

Owing to nerves and playing conditions, which heavy downpours and rising winds had made significantly worse overnight—throughout the tournament players had been forced to hit their tee shots from rubber mats like the ones found at commercial driving ranges—neither man produced memorable golf. On turf that felt like glue underfoot and permitted no roll on the ball, par was about the best to be hoped for.

Ben was briefly up by a stroke halfway through the first nine holes but gave back the 7th and 9th holes to fall a stroke down. By 15, he'd regained the momentum and his one-stroke advantage—only to drive his tee ball into a muddy, poorly filled-in fairway divot. His approach shot came out heavy and landed short of the green in a tributary creek of the San Antonio River, earning an additional penalty stroke.

He made bogey to Nelson's par. Byron then birdied the 16th to go one up in their match. Both men finished with workmanlike pars, Hogan for an even-par 71, Nelson a one-under 70. Byron had won, though he looked more relieved than happy.

"It seems as if I played better against Ben on the average than I did against anybody else," Byron wrote in his autobiography, remembering the difficulty of the moment. "I tried harder against him because I knew I had to."

The two men shook hands, and Hogan graciously peeled off his broad-brimmed hat for a photographer, showing his gritted movie star teeth.

The Glen Garden rivals stood briefly side by side while flashbulbs popped and someone asked the new Texas Open winner what he planned to do next. Byron smiled modestly and explained that even though he was dead tired from the play-off, he was committed to drive that night up to Dallas, where the Ryder Cup team was supposed to play a selected group of top Texas amateurs on Tuesday.

"How about you, Ben?" someone thought to ask the silent runner-up.

"Houston," he replied tersely, then turned and headed for the locker room to collect his stuff.

"You can't blame Ben," Byron commented to the local reporters. "He's been close more than anyone lately."

A sports writer followed and was surprised to discover Hogan loading some of Nelson's equipment into his own car trunk. Byron had asked if Ben would consider taking his excess clubs, balls, and other effects on to Houston for the Western Open, and Ben hadn't hesitated to oblige.

"That's awful decent of you, Ben. Not every guy would do that for the guy who just beat him out of an important golf tournament."

"Really?" Hogan replied, glancing incredulously at the reporter. "Well, we're friends." He thought for a moment, then added, "It's just a golf tournament. There will be others."

True enough. For the moment at least, they were friends. Loyalty meant the world to Ben Hogan; it was a quality he admired more than any other in a man. Byron was nothing if not loyal, and vice versa. Still, inside he was dying over *another* second-place finish to Byron, an otherwise decent man he appeared destined to be forever measured against. But he wasn't about to reveal this private angst to anyone save perhaps Valerie. The truth was, there would be other golf tournaments and soon—if hard work and the law of averages meant anything—he would come out on top.

At that same moment up in Cowtown, Royal Hogan was phoning up the sports desk at the *Star-Telegram*, wondering if their man on the scene or the Associated Press might have results of the play-off down in San Antonio.

"It's Byron by one," the night sports editor broke it to him. During the previous weeks of the Tour's western swing, Royal had taken to regularly phoning the news desk for results, making something of a pest of himself. Each time, it seemed, Ben had wound up second or third.

"Son of a bitch," Royal swore when he heard Ben had lost to Byron. "I think I'm jinxing Ben."

BY THE TIME the Tour invaded North Carolina in mid-March, the dogwoods were budding and Hogan had officially recorded six second-place finishes to six different champions in the previous fourteen months, including seven top-ten finishes in just eleven starts for 1940. On the positive side of his immaculately kept pocket ledger, he already ranked second in the prize money with $3,038. On the negative side, *he still hadn't won a golf tournament.*

"Ben Hogan was starving for a tournament triumph as the 1940 tour began," wrote Gene Gregston, noting that Hogan rationalized to Valerie that the "only way" he would ever win was to get so far ahead of the field in any given tournament that nobody would be able to catch him at the finish.

A popular myth that still pops up from time to time is that Hogan arrived in Pinehurst so frustrated by his inability to finish off a tournament and win that he was seriously thinking of giving up tournament life.

On the contrary, following the Thomasville Open in Georgia, possibly at the suggestion of his brother, Royal, Ben opted to do something that would soon become a standard procedure in his major tournament preparation. He canceled a pair of lucrative exhibition matches in Georgia and South Carolina that would have paid him $250 apiece—serious money for a day's work— drove straight to Pinehurst, and checked into James Walker Tufts's elegant Carolina Hotel, where the rest of the Tour was not scheduled to arrive for more than a week.

The North and South Open at Pinehurst was one of tournament golf's most anticipated events, a beautifully run tournament most marquee players regarded as only a whisker below the National Open and the PGA Championship in terms of prestige and stature. The players loved the North and South because Pinehurst was America's most elite golf spa, a sleepy southern crossroads where old money met gracious charm beneath the whispering longleaf pines. Tufts housed and fed the players and their wives at no cost to the participants, and the tournament was played on one of the finest layouts in America, Donald Ross's splendid No. 2 course, which the creator himself was forever tweaking to perfection. Ross, a Pinehurst winter resident, would be on hand to present the tournament trophy to the winner.

Players' wives adored the North and South because the tournament's hosts treated them like visiting royalty, providing manicures and massages, lush buffet luncheons, special teas, garden tours, horseback rides, and black-tie socials and dinners in the elegantly draped dining room of the Carolina. There were always fresh spring flowers waiting in the guest rooms, along with imported bottles of French mineral water, and guests were invited to take in polo matches off the hotel's vast side porch or attend evening band concerts in the village square.

By the time Byron and Louise checked into the Carolina on March 16,

Valerie had been enjoying the hotel's charms for over a week and Ben had memorized nearly every feature of Donald Ross's No. 2 masterpiece.

Byron had something to show Ben—a pair of new custom-made drivers he'd just picked up from his equipment sponsor, the MacGregor Sporting Goods Company of Ohio. Ben was under contract to MacGregor too, having signed a modest $250 contract with the company's tournament rep Toney Penna in late 1937, but MacGregor treated Byron differently than Ben.

Byron was an easygoing National Open winner who expressed only gratitude for the equipment the company had custom-made for him at the factory. Ben was Mr. Second Place—formerly just another Tour nobody, albeit a damned hardworking one, who seemed almost impossible to please when he made his first trip to MacGregor to be fitted for a set of clubs. The company was already enjoying dividends from its association with Byron—a set of Byron Nelson clubs was in the planning stages—but Ben was your basic long shot, money flung at a classic dark horse, an intense, little, hard-to-please guy who might suddenly break through and win one or fizzle out and never be heard from again.

Byron offered Ben the driver he liked least, a heavy fourteen-ounce model with a beautiful black lacquered head. "The minute I swung that club," Hogan said later, "I knew it was something special." Ben took it straight to the Pinehurst range and practiced with it until dark.

The next morning, dressed in gray slacks, a dark green sweater, a white shirt, and a navy blue necktie, wearing the white linen cap he'd taken to sporting out west during the warmer stretches of the Tour, Hogan split the fairway of No. 2's first hole with a long straight drive, struck a seven-iron approach to twelve feet, and rattled his birdie putt into the back of the cup. He birdied the second hole too—three of the first opening four in fact.

Ben Hogan was on a tear, or maybe a holy mission.

The Tour's top money winner, Jimmy Demaret, was back home attending to business in Houston, but the North and South field was probably better than it would be at Augusta in three weeks' time, including Sam Snead, Gene Sarazen, Lawson Little, Jug McSpaden, Craig Wood, Johnny Revolta, Paul Runyan, Horton Smith, and big-shouldered local favorite Clayton Heafner, the Charlotte native and Linville (North Carolina) Country Club pro many in the galley specifically shelled out $1.25 admission to watch win.

By the 4th hole, Hogan was three under, driving the ball flawlessly with his borrowed MacGregor driver and putting like a man on fire. Over one putt of less than an inch, for instance, he went through the painstaking routine of lining up a twenty-footer before tapping it in. Nothing was left to chance. Striking shots and walking briskly, leaving a trail of burnt Chesterfields behind him, head up and chin thrust forward in an attitude Valerie could have recognized from 300 yards, he tore a smoldering hole through the crisp spring morning, didn't miss a fairway all day, compiled six under 66, and tied the competitive course record set just one year before by robot man Harry Cooper.

"There's something about this new driver that fits me like a glove," he glowed afterward, heading off to the practice range. "I tell you, I've never driven the ball better." That evening at dinner with Louise and Byron, Byron told Ben the driver was his to keep. When Ben insisted on paying him for it, Byron smiled and shook his head. "I hope it works out for you, Ben," was all he said, ever his Christian mama's good-hearted boy.

The next day, Hogan fired 67 to widen his lead by four strokes over Snead and Revolta. People were buzzing in the lobby of the Carolina, but Squire Gene Sarazen was convinced he'd seen it all before. "He [Hogan] has never won before, he won't win this time," the little maestro predicted. "Hogan's been out front before. Someone will catch him."

But they didn't. Not this time. By lunchtime after the morning round of the final day, a Thursday, Ben held a commanding six-stroke lead over his closest challengers, Snead and Sarazen. A birdie on 16 put him 11 under par heading into the final round of play, and two pars to finish nipped two strokes off Vic Ghezzi's glittering 1938 tournament record.

"Don't pinch me," Valerie Hogan remarked to a reporter as she went out to greet her husband on the final fairway. "I'm afraid I'll wake up."

The little man from Fort Worth had finally won. The long wait was over. Vindication was his, a victory so sweet it almost ached.

As Ben disappeared into the locker room to comb his hair and straighten up his necktie for the presentation of the tournament trophy, Valerie turned to another reporter and explained with a rare burst of public emotion, "Ben's been so close so many times only to see one shot crumble all his hopes. He's never given up trying, though, even in his darkest hours. That's why I'm so proud of him now."

A telling comment. A few minutes later, sipping a glass of cold milk shortly before he was presented with the trophy and shook hands with Donald Ross, a visibly relieved Hogan made an eerily similar assessment of the situation, proving how close husband and wife truly were in their thinking.

"I was beginning to think I was an also-ran," he admitted. "I needed that win. They've kidded me about practicing so much. I'd go out there before a round and practice, and when I was through I'd practice some more. Well, they can kid me all they want because it finally paid off. I know it's what finally got me in the groove to win."

As darkness slipped over the Carolina sand hills, a young sportswriter named John Derr pushed his jalopy over the pine-girdled back roads to Greensboro, the Tour's next scheduled stop, where he raced to his desk at the *Greensboro Daily News* and rapped out his account of the little Texan's extraordinary breakthrough at Pinehurst, then sent it flying down the tubes to the composing room. An hour or so later, when the morning's first edition came up around midnight, Derr was horrified to see the first run of his story bearing the headline "Hagen's 277 Leaves Snead Three Strokes Back."

"I phoned downstairs and told them they'd gotten it wrong," Derr remembers. "It was Ben *Hogan*, not Walter Hagen!"

"Hogan?" the typesetter bellowed back at him. "Who the hell is *Hogan?*"

WITHIN DAYS, the sports world at large learned an awful lot more about *Hogan*.

At Starmount Forest Country Club in Greensboro, two days after Pinehurst closed, Hogan and Clayton Heafner opened with 69s to tie for the lead in the Greater Greensboro Open, and then something most peculiar happened.

It snowed three inches in the early afternoon, halting play for the day with fourteen threesomes still out on the golf course. "Okay, fellas," Sarazen quipped, "let's ski it off."

Another day of waiting was required before play could resume; Hogan passed the time playing gin rummy with Valerie and putting in his hotel room at the fading but elegant O'Henry Hotel—so named for the hometown boy and famous author of "The Gift of the Magi" whose tales always had a surprise ending—eight miles from the golf course. Rounds three and four, it was decided by the sponsoring Jaycees, would be played on a Thursday, causing the official start of the Land of the Sky Open in Asheville to be pushed back and delayed until Friday.

There was no surprise ending in Greensboro. Hogan fired a 68 in the second round of the GGO, scoring three birdies and no bogeys, to vault over Sarazen and Guldahl and lead by three at the halfway point.

The tournament moved out to the elegant, Ross-designed Sedgefield Country Club for its concluding rounds, a beautiful course that wound through the stately pines, and Ben showed the bosses at MacGregor Sporting Goods and anybody else who was interested that he was no fluke, posting blistering rounds of 66 and 67 to shatter the old tournament record and collect his second win in less than a week.

"It's easy to see why we can't catch that fellow," Johnny Revolta remarked to John Derr. "The way that sumbitch is playing, you can't beat perfection."

Back home in Fort Worth, Royal Hogan was on the phone almost hourly to the *Star-Telegram*, prompting an editor to joke that maybe the paper ought to demand a steep discount on its office supplies—or simply hire Royal to cover Ben's career.

Seventy-two hours after he won Greensboro, Ben carved out a pair of brilliant closing 69s to overtake Ralph Guldahl and pocket another $1,200 first-place check at the Land of the Sky Open too.

In just ten days, Ben Hogan had won the first three professional golf tournaments of his life, something no player had ever done so quickly before, possibly the most sensational stretch of tournament golf anyone had ever played, a fact borne out by the statistics of his remarkable breakthrough.

Over 216 holes of competition, in three straight tournaments, he was an eye-popping 34 under par, breaking 70 on all but two of the twelve rounds. During the course of this violent assault on Old Man Par, he three-putted just two greens, both in Asheville, and, maybe most amazing and revealing of all, missed only two greens in regulation over the entire stretch of play.

In Richmond, where the Hogans drove so Ben could play an exhibition match at the Country Club of Virginia the day before he and Valerie turned around and headed south for Augusta National, Hogan gave his first, if somewhat scant, public analysis of his suddenly red-hot golf swing to the national media, explaining that his unusual power came from having "extremely supple wrists," which permitted him "to delay the break and put extra snap on the ball at contact." His impressive accuracy, he explained simply, came from "many hours of practice with irons."

On the drive up to Richmond, Ben decided to double his exhibition rate from $250 to $500, and while there, among other things, the hottest figure in sports showed off his winning form for his first print ad ever, a true sign of hitting the big time in Mr. Roosevelt's America—a magazine spot for Bromo-Seltzer!

The ad, trumpeting the unprecedented exploits of golf's "Mighty Mite," appeared ten days later in the pages of the venerable *Saturday Evening Post*.

" 'You can't play a good game of golf when you're upset by a headache. I always take Bromo-Seltzer,' says Ben Hogan."

By the time Ben and Val rolled into Augusta on April 3, another New York ad agency was hot on his heels wanting him to promote Rheingold extra dry ale for a princely fee of three grand. Hogan liked beer and was even willing to drink Rheingold for that kind of dough—decent payback for years of toiling for peanuts while being ignored, even mocked, for his lonely work habits by some members of the national press corps.

Amid the sudden hoopla, what Hogan discovered he didn't care for was not being able to properly prepare for a major golf tournament the way he had learned paid handsome returns at Pinehurst—carefully, unhurried, and *alone*. He'd scarcely gotten unpacked at the Bon Aire Hotel and dashed to the practice tee, where a photographer and reporter from the *New York Journal-American* were waiting to photograph his golf swing and scribble down a few comments on his amazing juggernaut, before he was forced to head straight to the first tee to begin the tournament.

This was just Hogan's third appearance at the Masters, and shaking hands with Bobby Jones was still a distinct thrill for him. Ditto chatting with Grantland Rice, the dean of America's golf writers. Finding a way to win the Masters, he admitted confidentially to Rice, was almost as high on his list of priorities as winning the National Open.

Hogan's relentless practice had finally brought about near-perfection and three record-shattering wins in a row. His name was in newspapers around the world. Commercial offers were flying his way like parade confetti. Kids were thrusting autograph books at him, reporters calling, "Hey, Ben, gotta minute?" Why, even Toney Penna was slapping him warmly on the back and asking if his clubs were okay or needed any tweaking. He knew how Ben loved to tweak his clubs.

But every angel is dangerous. The dark side of such divine success was clear. The same hard work that had made all of this "sudden" success possible—settling his nerves, removing destructive doubt—unexpectedly overwhelmed his ability to shut out the world around him and focus entirely on his game. The physical fatigue and emotional expectations that come with being the center of the sports world also took a predictable toll. His performance slumped.

At the Masters of 1940, Hogan closed with a disappointing 74 to finish in distant tenth place. The good news was that his friend Jimmy Demaret won.

• • •

AFTER AUGUSTA, Ben and Valerie set off immediately for their "cozy cottage" at the Century Country Club and a week out of the spotlight before the start of the Goodall Round Robin, a tournament many considered the toughest event in golf, given the 126-hole marathon format and the unusually high caliber of the field on hand. Only the Tour's top fifteen players were invited to compete, an all-star field that drew huge galleries and press interest from nearby New York City.

Each man was required to play a full eighteen-hole match against every other competitor in the field, pitting leading money winner Demaret and Hogan directly against each other for the first time that season. The likes of Snead, Sarazen, Runyan, Nelson, and Picard highlighted the rest of the impressive field.

With four days of rest behind him and no cameras clicking in his face, Hogan went out on the opening Thursday and blitzed Clayton Heafner and Craig Wood and went on to capture ten of his fourteen matches, amassing 23 points to Sammy Snead's 19—to collect his fourth win of the year.

The quality of this win, picking up right where he left off at Asheville, made Ben the odds-on favorite to take the National Open at Cleveland's Canterbury Club during the first week of June.

Less than a week later, he finished second at the Metropolitan Open in Bloomfield, New Jersey, and drove straight to sectional qualifying at Mount Vernon Country Club in New York. During the qualifying round, however, he was forced to call a one-stroke penalty on himself for a ball that moved upon address (shades of Bobby Jones in his prime—nobody else saw it move), causing him to miss qualifying for the National Open by a single stroke.

Hogan cited his "fatigue" and a sudden poor stretch of putting for his failure to earn a trip to Cleveland, but he managed to gain entry to the Open field as a first alternate when another qualifier, Joe Strafacci, suddenly dropped out. The relief among Tour reporters was palpable, and they quickly established Hogan and reigning champion Nelson as the men to beat.

It didn't happen. On Open Saturday, Ben cobbled together a pair of indifferent rounds of 72-73 to wind up in fifth place, his best Open showing ever but a dismal eighteen strokes behind winner Lawson Little.

Then it was on to Chicago for the Windy City's Open—and that poorly struck four-wood that left him in a disappointing tie for second place.

During the first week of August, for the PFA Championship at Hershey

Country Club, old nemesis Ralph Guldahl eliminated him 3 and 2 (3 up with two holes to play) in the tournament's quarter-final round of play. Byron Nelson won the tournament 1 up over Sam Snead.

Ben Hogan was visibly tired. But he was also visibly happy for the first time in anyone's memory. With $10,655 in official earnings in the bank and an exhibition rate that was more than double what it had been just nine months before, Ben Hogan was the Tour's new leading money winner, a dark-horse winner who was determined to push himself even harder in the days ahead.

"I've set my sights on winning major golf tournaments, and I still have yet to do that," he explained to a syndicated columnist who flew down from New York to catch up with golf's newest star at home in Texas, fresh from a season-ending third place at the Miami Open, before he ventured west for the start of the winter circuit.

Their conversation took place in the members' grill at Colonial Country Club, after Hogan had lunched with his friend Marvin Leonard and heard the latest plans for the National Open scheduled to come to Cowtown the next summer.

"This year was very gratifying," Hogan admitted to his interviewer. "But until I manage to win a major tournament, I really won't be happy."

And with that, Bantam Ben thanked the reporter for coming so far just to have a friendly chat, offered a polite but firm handshake good-bye, then headed straight back to the place that made him happiest in life—the practice tee.

SIX

One Man's War

Accompanied by a week of lavish beef barbecues and cocktail fetes that drifted past midnight, Marvin Leonard's big coming-out party—aka the forty-fourth United States Open Championship, the National Open of 1941—got under way beneath slightly threatening skies on the warmly flaring morning of June 5, with a field that included the Open's three previous champions and the hottest player in golf, hometown hero Ben Hogan.

In fourteen starts from January to June, Hogan had already logged six second-place finishes and was never worse than sixth place. On his way down the golf trail to Colonial, he'd teamed with former role model and skeptic Gene Sarazen to run away with the Miami Four-Ball, narrowly missed successfully defending his titles at both Greensboro and Asheville, and even improved his showing at the Masters by six places, finishing fourth.

Hogan had momentum, but he didn't have what he now wanted most—a major tournament title. Good players won golf tournaments, but great players won major golf tournaments, especially the most coveted prize in golf, the

Overleaf: Ben Hogan, Army Air Corps, 1943 *(Courtesy Hogan Estate)*

United States Open Championship. Byron Nelson already possessed one (the Spring Mill Open that Sam Snead booted away in '39; Nelson also owned the '37 Masters and '40 PGA). If Snead had yet to capture his first major championship, Sam still had twenty victories and a pair of narrow runner-up finishes to Nelson in both his major championships to prove he was on the threshold of greatness.

Before the start of the Open, the serious wagering money was on Nelson, Snead, and Hogan, in that order, though some gave Hogan the sentimental edge owing to the storybook setting. Just weeks before, Hogan had breezed through Cowtown on his way to Augusta, bearing a freshly signed contract to represent Hershey Country Club, and paused long enough to hammer out a spectacular 65 over Marvin Leonard's demanding, tree-girdled 7,000-yard layout—a new Colonial course record.

The new Hershey contract, estimated to be worth at least eight grand a year, called for Hogan to simply "represent" the famous candy company on tour and make himself available to socialize with members whenever he was back in the tidy Pennsylvania town. He wasn't required to give lessons, run the pro shop, clean clubs, or do anything but fraternize with members and maybe play a little recreational golf if the spirit moved him.

Once again, the unseen broker, the guardian angel behind this sweet deal, was Henry Picard, the "Chocolate Soldier" himself, who had left Hershey that spring to accept a $10,000 post at Canterbury Country Club in Cleveland, a prestigious private club on the National Open rota, after personally recommending his up-and-coming friend Ben Hogan to Milton Hershey.

The terms of employment were ideal for Hogan, for at this point all he wanted was to be left alone to practice shots till daylight expired and a major golf tournament finally submitted to his will. He'd be friendly enough to Hershey members as long as they didn't disturb his tireless preparations. Playing with hackers was out of the question, though. Ben Hogan had neither the time nor the interest in playing "recreational" golf with anybody.

Too much was at stake. Tournament golf was personal warfare, and capturing the National Open was the only way Ben Hogan could begin to win the war quietly raging within him.

Not surprisingly, before dawn on the morning following his long train ride home to Fort Worth from the Goodall Round Robin, forty-eight hours before the Open's first grouping teed off and a couple of hours before he was scheduled to play a practice round with brother Royal (Colonial's new club champion and the city of Fort Worth's reigning amateur champion), Ben was found by a local reporter poking about before official business hours in the repair room at the Colonial pro shop. The Hawk was pounding a two-by-four against the head of his MacGregor five-iron, trying to flatten the club's lie angle by several degrees.

Noting the young reporter's perplexed expression, Hogan, a cigarette dangling from his lip, explained to him that the clubs his equipment company sent him were always several degrees too upright. This caused the ball to come off the club face with a right-to-left spin that promoted a hook, something he feared more than a coiled rattlesnake at his feet. For this reason he also filed most of the bounce off his wedges. Bounce promoted a hook, Hogan believed. That was also why the leading edges of his clubs were sharp as a carpenter's plane. He wanted a blade that cut like a Buck knife.

Pausing in his exertions, Hogan lit a fresh cigarette, inhaled half its length in two drags, and asked a black shop attendant standing nearby to go find some brass and someone with a blowtorch so he could "put some power" on the back of his wedge and nine-iron. Ben liked his clubs as heavy as possible— otherwise, he couldn't "feel" them.

With that, Hogan picked up his crude lie angle tool and got back to work, surprising the young reporter by inviting him to stick around and ask anything on his mind. This unexpected invitation came as a pleasant surprise to the reporter, as he wrote later, because he'd been led to believe that the hottest player in the game was one tough SOB, a nightmare to interview.

"Well," the younger man ventured, "so how's your game shaping up for the Open?"

Without looking up, Hogan smiled. "Not as good as I'd like it to be," he replied mildly. "Been playing a lot but not practicing enough." Giving the club another whack, he added almost offhandedly, "I'm battling the hook again like life and death."

The reporter smiled, waiting. He'd heard from old Hogan hands that it was wise to either wait for Ben to speak or at least ask him something reasonably intelligent. If you asked him something reasonably stupid, Hogan would freeze you out, and that would be the end of your interview.

Hogan finally glanced at him.

"I'm going out to the 9th green and give this a try," he said, stubbing out his cigarette. "Want to tag along?"

The young reporter's smile broadened.

"Sure, Mr. Hogan," he replied, thinking that Hogan was nothing like the bastard he'd heard about.

• • •

BEN'S IMAGE PROBLEMS began during his fevered breakthrough the previous season, on the heels of a couple of well-publicized incidents down south and in the Midwest, where Hogan skipped town after winning a tournament, either intentionally or inadvertently snubbing the local press in the process. "Frankly I was so excited to get to the next tournament and see what I could do," he attempted to explain, rather late and a trifle ineffectually. "I just forgot to stick around for the interviews." With a defensive edge that failed to play well in Peoria, he added, "Didn't mean to offend anybody."

Weeks before returning home for Marvin's National Open, as he playfully called it, following the Miami Four-Ball he won with Sarazen, it happened again. Hogan pocketed his share of the winnings and scooted away to catch an early train before local writers had had the opportunity to interview the tournament winner. Yet again he left a trail of miffed sponsors and bruised feelings in his wake, a developing problem.

"Hogan may be finally winning golf tournaments," grumped one influential midwestern columnist to his Sunday morning readers, "but he isn't winning any friends where it counts. He may have the game to win a number of golf tournaments, but not yet the grace to be a champion."

This criticism apparently stung Hogan, but it didn't really surprise him. When he attempted to explain, albeit tardily, that the slights were purely unintentional, the gaffes mere oversights due to his enthusiasm to compete, few of his critics were mollified or particularly sympathetic. His uncooperative behavior was something they'd observed slowly building for years, like a grudge between two natural adversaries, and even before he began winning tournaments at a frightening gallop some of them took an intense dislike to the little Texan who set himself apart from the other tournament players. They vowed to punish him for his eternal mortician's face and maddening one-word replies.

From the view of certain golf writers, Hogan appeared to derive perverse pleasure from making a beat reporter's life hell. That was gratitude for you, they decided, having given him (in recent years) the kind of coverage money couldn't buy, basically turning lemons into lemonade where the sour personality of Ben Hogan was concerned. They'd given him monikers that half the kids in America knew by heart—"the Century Club Sharpshooter," "the Wasp-Waisted Warrior," and "Battling Bantam Ben," just to name a few. And the coverage didn't end at the golf course. In purple prose that rendered him a cross between Jack Armstrong and Seabiscuit the race horse, they wrote flattering portraits that overlooked his wintry nature and put appealing flesh, so to speak, on his chilly bones, giving the otherwise colorless little guy some much-needed personality and humanity, especially now that he was winning. When Hogan and Ted Williams bumped into each other at Toots Shor's place in Manhattan earlier that spring, for example, to nobody's surprise, a news photographer was right there to capture the moment as the two renowned sluggers paused and shook hands.

Williams was off to the hottest year of his career (he would finish 1941 with a .406 batting average), and after their brief encounter, someone promptly asked Williams what shaking hands with Hogan was like.

"Like bands of steel," replied Ted, who was nearly as laconic as Hogan.

For his part, the evidence suggests that Hogan, early on at least, really was surprised by the vigor of the developing press antipathy toward him. What pressmen regarded as a cold brush-off and clear intent to make their quote-harvesting jobs harder, Hogan viewed simply as one man's honest efforts to do his best and get the job done the only way he knew how—to stay focused only on the task at hand, to put every other distraction on or near the golf course completely out of his mind. His replies to questions, for example, were generally quick but well thought out, and honest to the point of bluntness—the way, say, a surgeon with poor people skills might brutally describe how he extracted a suspicious lump. Having spent most of his life facing one difficult reality after another, Hogan simply saw no point whatsoever in sugarcoating the truth as he saw it.

Though armed with an earthy wit few were ever permitted to see in the public realm, Hogan at this stage of his evolution was incapable of softening his responses with jocular intimacies and locker-room bonhomie. In the right company, to be sure, he could appreciate a blue joke and savor a cold beer in the seclusion of the clubhouse, but fellowship went only so deep and lasted only so long. "When Ben's around," one of his equally famous contemporaries observed, not unkindly, "you can almost hear his watch ticking." If and when a beat reporter joined the party, Hogan's interests often noticeably waned. He appeared suspicious of every reporter's true intent, on guard against their efforts to mythicize the smallest accomplishment, constitutionally incapable of swapping personal favor for colorful copy because explaining himself was the toughest thing on earth for a natural loner like Ben Hogan to do.

Life had not equipped Ben to be a confessor, a backslapper, an easy joiner, or even really one of the boys in the locker room. That was because, on a much deeper psychological level, as the glare of the national spotlight finally turned intensely and directly upon him, even the most casual inquiry from a reporter held the dangerous potential of exposing Bennie Hogan's darkest secret to the world at large, the boyhood shame that drove the grown man forever after some elusive grail, some unobtainable victory. The war was now seething both within and out.

Moreover, one reason Ben was so irresistibly drawn to spirited and entertaining players like Jimmy Demaret and Byron Nelson early on, and Jackie Burke Jr., Mike Souchak, and Tommy "Thunder" Bolt a bit later on, was that he genuinely admired the easy way they maneuvered through a difficult world fraught with fresh dangers around every dogleg. Though he admired aspects of their individual personalities, much as he admired Marvin Leonard for his avuncular grace, Hogan simply wasn't hardwired like any of his closest companions, equipped to take whatever was thrown at him and keep on smiling, ignoring the bullshit and chasing Old Man Par, giving good quotes and having a little adult fun in the process—or in Tommy Bolt's case, pitchforking an occasional golf club down the fairway just to blow off steam and delight the press. In a sense, Ben Hogan simply couldn't afford the luxury of real intimacy with anybody other than Valerie. Otherwise, someone might discover that he didn't feel worthy of consorting with some of the finest ball-strikers and nicest guys on tour. Henny Bogan wanted to be just like them. But Ben Hogan believed he had to work twice as hard as they did just to keep up with them.

On the broader public level, Hogan's views of the press and its role weren't terribly unique. A fairly common view among many of these same top-tier players, as expressed by Gene Sarazen on more than one occasion, was that sports reporters were generally a decent if slightly predatory species that fed off someone else's hard work and glory, deadline panhandlers whose bosses were far more interested in getting quick colorful copy than the facts perfectly aligned, a winking proposition most players were happy to oblige as long as everything was going their way.

But for a man who played every shot and expressed his thoughts with the sober exactness of an approach iron to the 72nd green of a tournament he was leading, the somewhat checkered tradition of American newspapering—creating heroes out of the flimsiest material, embellishing facts to make a story more readable—was bound to cause problems.

He was, in sum, a literal-minded creature caught between *their* desire to know the bigger story and *his* need to protect the truth at all costs. As a result of this evolving struggle of wills, Hogan learned he had no tolerance for trivial questions from any reporter who hadn't expended the basic energy to follow him around the golf course and witness events for himself.

If a question annoyed or particularly bothered him, for example, he simply ignored the questioner or, worse, fixed him with a brief stare of contempt that wirebrushed the foolish inquisitor into silence. If it bothered some reporters that Ben was reluctant to yield more than a few miserly words about his performances, it bothered Hogan even more when some of these same deadline scribes took what he considered extravagant liberties with his careful comments—either directly misquoting, altering, or casually applying his words to captions or headlines he judged to be out of proper context and inaccurate. His greatest indignation, however, was reserved for the widespread newspaper practice of attributing quotes and using his likeness to convey "swing tips" to the reading masses.

Hogan, in short, had a different standard on the press than other high-profile players. Byron, for example, appeared to sympathize with the deadline reporter's plight, often making himself available to the press and rarely if ever criticizing the resulting news copy. Snead and Demaret seemed to thrive on being the center of attention. They jumped at the opportunity to play the court fool and didn't appear to give a damn how the media represented them ("Say anything you want, boys," Snead once drawled, "just spell my name right so my mama don't get madder 'n' hell at me"). Hogan, by contrast, simply couldn't abide anything less than a watchmaker's strict accounting of his words and deeds and found, as a consequence, probing interviews of almost any duration nearly unbearable to take for one simple reason: the more he expressed, the more likely the interviewer was to take his words and use them against him.

Underscoring this growing estrangement was the damage to Ben's reputation when, on his way back to Colonial for Marvin Leonard's National Open jamboree, and clearly out of frustration over the aforementioned affrays, he put out the word to the press corps that henceforth he would "prefer" to do interviews only in the confines of the locker room immediately following each day's play and immediately upon the tournament's conclusion—an effort at pragmatic appeasement that promptly blew up in his face.

In being the first player ever to attempt to formalize what had always been a relaxed and gentlemanly interviewing process, Hogan viewed his proposal as a pragmatic means of assuring every reporter equal access to his thoughts, but it was more broadly interpreted as one more example of his growing need to control every aspect of his exposure to the press, including the duration and nature of his comments. As far as anyone knew, this was the first time any golf champion had put such strict limitations on his interactions with the press, and it frankly didn't earn Ben Hogan a lot of friends among those with deadlines to make.

Thus, when the young Fort Worth reporter snooping about Colonial before-hours for a human interest piece on the Open stumbled upon Hogan pounding his five-iron into submission early that June morning, it's no wonder that he braced for the worst but found himself utterly disarmed by Ben's friendly before-hours chat, and was positively thrilled to tag along with him to the golf course.

There, Ben dumped a sack of shag balls into the glistening frog hair at the edge of the 9th green and began chipping with his newly "flattened" five-iron, then switched to a six. He popped several of the chips straight into the cup.

Next, as the scribe silently took it all in, Hogan climbed down into the deepest green-side bunker and blasted shots out until he realized the fiercely spinning balls were making too many gouge marks in Marvin Leonard's perfect putting surface.

"Let's go to the range," he said.

George Barclay was already waiting for him at the end of Colonial's practice tee. Barclay, one of the club's most popular caddies, had once looped with Ben and Byron during their Glen Garden days. "Tell me, George, is the swing anything like it was back in our caddie days?" Hogan posed this question to Barclay with a chuckle, after a few warm-up shots, purely for the benefit of the observing reporter.

Barclay smiled lazily. "No, I'd say it's improved quite a bit, Ben," he replied, glancing at the kid, who was busy scribbling everything down.

A maintenance truck suddenly pulled up, and a man came over bearing a portable welder's rig.

"Now *that's* what I call deluxe service," Hogan grinned as he watched the man solder a lump of brass onto the back of his nine-iron. He reached into his pocket and asked the workman what he owed him for the work.

"Nothing, sir, it's on the house."

"No," Hogan protested, pulling several bills out and handing them to the workman. "This welding job may mean a thousand dollars to me."

A small cluster of early risers had begun to gather at the fence behind the tee, a gang of local boys who caddied at Glen Garden and Z-Boaz and had come out to watch their hometown hero practice. After Hogan hit several balls and paused to wipe mud off a club face, one of the younger boys brazenly asked for his autograph. The reporter recalled that Hogan stared over at them for a moment with a cigarette dangling from his lip. His contempt for anyone who interrupted his heuristic practice sessions was part of the growing Hogan legend too.

But unexpectedly, once again, Ben smiled, dropped his cigarette and stepped on it, then strolled over and "signed several autographs as if he had all the time in the world instead of a United States Open to prepare for," to quote the impressed young reporter on the scene.

"You're gonna win, aren't you?" one of the boys asked the Hawk.

"I sure aim to," Hogan replied, smiling a little. "It's about time I did, don't you think?"

Several heads bobbed vigorously.

"You don't wear a glove," a smaller boy remarked with a note of wonder, staring at his hero's heavily calloused hands. Hogan smiled again, opening his palms. The Hawk had tough hands but a soft spot for kids.

"I can't use a glove," he explained to them. "These old bare hands will have to take it."

THE U.S. OPEN of 1941 didn't have the storybook ending that thousands of Hogan's hometown fans desperately hoped for that week—or Byron's and Demaret's sizable coteries either, come to that.

As national golf theater goes, however, the forty-fourth National Open was a fitting Cinderella story for another fine Tour journeyman who'd paid heavy dues and was equally desperate for his first major win.

When he showed up in Fort Worth aiming to capture golf's biggest prize (wearing a special lady's corset owing to a recent back injury), long-hitting Winged Foot pro Craig Wood was finally enjoying the kind of season Ben Hogan believed he was on the threshold of experiencing himself. Starting in 1933, when he lost a dispiriting thirty-six-hole play-off to Boston's Densmore Shute, Wood narrowly lost the PGA Championship to Paul Runyan in '34 and was by all accounts cruising to the Masters title in 1935 when Sarazen made his extraordinary double-eagle shot and eventually won in a playoff. An even more bitter failure followed in 1939, when Byron drained a snaking twenty-footer for birdie on the 72nd hole of the U.S. Open at Philly's Spring Mill to force a play-off, which Wood lost convincingly the following afternoon.

In April 1941, about a month before Marvin Leonard's National Open party, Wood finally won the Masters.

Then, as the Open marched into its second morning of play under gathering rain clouds and Marvin Leonard's watchful eye, Fate smiled on likable Craig Wood again. His rapidly stiffening back caused him to seriously consider withdrawing during a lengthy thunderstorm delay that swelled the nearby Trinity River over its banks and made spectator paths and the low area around the 9th green, where Hogan had practiced his five-iron chipping from the frog hair, into a mucky quagmire. Leonard's grounds crews hurriedly fanned out to spread a combination of cottonseed hulls and dried cow manure to firm up footing. Tommy "Silver Scot" Armour, knocking back restorative nips from the medicinal flask he always carried to ward off the chills during rain delays, prevailed on Wood, who opened with a disappointing 73, to soldier on.

A wise choice, as it turned out. With a restricted swing that markedly improved his accuracy over a golf course where strategic placement was critical, Wood finished round two with a handsome 71 and added a pair of even finer 70s during Saturday's rain-delayed double round to post 284 and beat his former British Open nemesis Denny Shute by a margin of three strokes.

Pretournament favorite Byron Nelson was never really a factor. The only player who managed a better finish on Colonial's soggy Open Saturday, as the Texas sun finally bobbed out from behind ragged wool clouds and heated up the turf so pungently a wag from New York playfully dubbed Leonard's dream course the "Colonial Stockyards," was one Ben Hogan, whose closing 68-70 left him in a tie for third. Hogan's tournament summary actually beat those of the Open's *three* previous champions, and his final day's play seemed to indicate conclusively that he now understood how to finish off a major championship with a killer's cold efficiency. Colonial was his best finish ever in an Open, coming on one of the toughest courses the pros had ever seen up till then.

As if he needed it, there was a clear message in Craig Wood's dogged perseverance. Golf tournaments, certainly majors, particularly U.S. Opens, were endurance contests won far more often than not by the plodding tortoise than the bolting hare. Every time Hogan inched closer to attaining his goal of winning a major golf tournament, every time he crept a little higher in the final standings of a major championship leaderboard, his confidence grew exponentially and that precious ground carried him one step closer to victory.

"The greatest thing Ben finally had to overcome," says Jackie Burke Jr., Masters and PGA champ of 1956, who became one of Hogan's closest tournament friends and preferred practice partners, "was the powerful insecurity he'd battled most of his life. There was no question he had all the shots by

1940—nobody was better prepared in that regard than Ben, frankly. But winning major championships requires a special kind of confidence few players ever acquire, and those who acquire it never seem to be able to keep it long. That's what finally made Hogan so unique. Once it finally came together, once he got those big hands of his around it, once he found *that* kind of confidence, hell, he almost couldn't be beaten. And he kept it longer than just about anybody."

Nelson, among others, addressed this elusive topic many years later when he said to golf historian Al Barkow, "Is there a psychology for winning? I don't understand the psychological function of the human mind sufficiently to answer that very well, except to say that winners are different. They're a different breed of cat. I think the reason is, they have an inner drive and are willing to give of themselves whatever it takes to win. It's a discipline that a lot of people are not willing to impose on themselves. It takes a lot of energy, a different way of thinking."

A small postscript to the National Open of 1941 poignantly illustrates the relevance of both Burke's and Nelson's observations—and the sad consequences of what happens when an Open winner's confidence vanishes like moonlight on an ocean tide.

Shortly after accepting his National Open trophy, Craig Wood was driving back to his hotel in downtown Fort Worth to collect his things with Tour publicist Fred Corcoran and a Boston reporter when they happened to pass a public driving range. Corcoran turned to Wood and asked, smiling, if America's new national golf champion wanted to stop and hit a bucket of balls just to keep his back loose and his swing grooved. Corcoran later said he was really only joking.

"You're right," Wood agreed with a rueful laugh. "It comes and goes. It's the kind of thing you can't turn loose once you've got it going or it might never come back."

To the surprise and astonishment of half a dozen weekend hackers and the driving range's manager, the new national golf champion promptly got out, doled out his money, and hit a full bucket of balls.

Perhaps Wood appreciated how lucky he'd been at Colonial, trussed up in a corset and hitting every fairway. Or perhaps he simply sensed, as he later told companions, how quickly the magic of success appeared and vanished in American sports. Today's news was tomorrow's fish wrapper, especially in the lonely world of tournament golf. Maybe, in fact, he had a premonition that his wonderful game was about to leave him and never come back to greatness.

Six months to the day later, in any case, the Japanese bombed Pearl Harbor, and America was suddenly thrust into World War II. Golf tournaments were suddenly about as relevant as pole-sitting marathons, and the blazered aristocrats who ran the USGA promptly suspended the National Open "until further notice," ironically anointing Craig Wood "champion for the duration" until play resumed in 1946.

Wood's reign lasted half a decade, but he never managed to capture the bottled lightning of another major golf title, his championship ball-striking and confidence all but vanishing during the lengthy hiatus.

To a great extent, like the passing of a soldierly generation, a number of other top stars of Depression-era America saw their games fade and fortunes dim during the lengthy break in the action. Lawson Little, Denny Shute, Henry Picard, and Ralph Guldahl were proven champions with consummate skills who somehow lost their winning touch during the long days of war and never quite recovered the magic of moonlight on the water.

HOGAN, BY CONTRAST, was just getting a good Vardon grip on the confidence Byron had discovered when he captured the 1937 Masters and claimed he felt like he was "suddenly walking with springs on my feet," the kind of confidence he would certainly need to catch Byron and Jimmy and join the ranks of major tournament winners, the real measure of a golfer's worth.

Within three weeks of the 1941 U.S. Open, his best showing ever at a major tournament, Ben struck twice more with lightning efficiency—first in Nelson's own backyard at the Inverness Four-Ball in Toledo (blitzing the field with flamboyant, club-twirling Jimmy Demaret as his new partner), followed by the Chicago Open, flashing a four-wood that performed better than most players' wedges.

Disappointingly, he failed to last beyond the quarter finals of the PGA but completed the remaining schedule of 1941 with a win at Rochester and five more runner-up finishes, collected his second consecutive Vardon Trophy, and captured the Tour money title with $18,734 in official earnings.

WITH AMERICA officially at war, most of golf's stars wondered if there would even be a professional tournament circuit for the year 1942. Most if not all of the marquee players expected to be drafted at any moment, and because of the travel restrictions imposed by civilian mobilization, the season was shortened to just twenty official events and a handful of exhibition fund-raisers.

In place of the National Open, the USGA announced it was joining forces with the PGA and the Chicago District Golf Association to put on something called the Hale America National Open, with all proceeds going to benefit the USO and the Navy Relief Society.

Along with 31 million men who registered for the draft after Pearl Harbor, Byron Nelson and Ben Hogan dutifully filled out their draft registration forms later that year in Fort Worth, but Nelson was immediately disqualified from active service owing to a blood disorder that was judged to be borderline hemophilia.

Hogan not only was eligible for the draft but fully expected to be inducted before year's end, which only deepened his resolve to capture either the Masters of PGA Championship before Hitler and Tojo stopped all tournament play dead in its tracks.

"You know, I don't mind going into the army," Hogan mused to New York columnist Bob Brumby at dinner one night in Miami, a few weeks after Pearl Harbor. Brumby had been one of those who initially stirred Hogan's ire by publicly describing him as an "uncooperative star," but he was also one of the few reporters whose opinions and accuracy Hogan genuinely respected. "It's something that has to be done and something anyone should be proud to do. But I'd gladly give everything I've got, gladly start all over again, if this hadn't happened."

Hogan was on the threshold of turning thirty, the prime of a golfer's life. After two failed attempts to make the Tour and years of relentless hard work, he'd finally started winning. How cruel was the timing? It was do or die, now or never, and in addressing Hogan's well-deserved reputation for dodging reporters during his breakthrough run, Brumby sympathetically, and accurately, changed his tune on the little Texan: "If they could have looked into the heart of the man who was to become one of the most dramatic figures in sports," he wrote after that night, "they might have seen fright. The fear of failure, of slipping back into the hunger and frustration he had known so long, constantly plagued Hogan.

"Here was a man who had fought hard to pull himself up from mediocrity," Brumby went on, "now on the verge of attaining security for himself and the wife he loved so much, facing a future from which there might be no return. That night, I think, I began to understand the real Ben Hogan. A man outwardly cold and calculating, but inwardly warm and determined to protect the girl he loved very much."

Hogan's private war for major acceptance in 1942 began at Los Angeles, where he sculpted a brilliant low-iron shot to the 72nd green at the Hillcrest course and two-putted for a birdie to tie Jimmy Thomson, then went on to beat him in a play-off—the first of Hogan's playing career. A good omen indeed.

The battlefield shifted up the coast to Oakland, where Nelson won with a five-stroke rout of the field. The next week, across the bay in San Francisco at the California Country Club, where Franci Ouiment's pie-faced caddie Eddie Lowery was now a prominent member and a growing friend to both Byron and Ben, it was Hogan's turn to win again, despite the dreaded return of a hook that compelled him, according to Nelson, to aim well right of fairways just to locate the short grass.

The pair seesawed their way from Bing's pro-am through Texas to Florida, where they commenced the southern leg of the circuit by teeing it up in the second unofficial Seminole Invitational and Ben was reintroduced to Oklahoma oilman George Coleman, a fine amateur player he'd first met (and immediately liked) at the Agua Caliente Open back in 1932, the second official tour event of Ben Hogan's twice-faltering early playing career.

Hogan fell hard for Seminole, a lush Donald Ross course he felt demanded every shot in the book, and placed third in the club's unofficial event. More important, he hobnobbed with several prominent members and men of substance and rekindled his friendship with Coleman, a worldly man of means who was destined to become one of Ben's closest friends and advisers.

Two weeks later, Hogan captured his second North and South Championship in three years (Nelson was third), then steered his new Cadillac on to Greensboro, where he nearly won the GGO again (Hogan was second, Nelson was fourth). Days later, he claimed Asheville's Open title for the third time in a row (Byron was third). Finally he turned toward Augusta National with only one thing on his mind. It certainly wasn't Georgia.

DURING HIS OWN train ride down to the pines of Augusta, Byron and Inverness playing pal Harold "Jug" McSpaden calculated that if they could each bank one hundred grand during their careers they could live comfortably off the interest for life and never have to travel the tournament circuit again. As

Nelson remembered it, the conversation was more playful than serious, but it does reveal a growing discomfort Byron felt with tournament life and the direction his life was generally taking.

So much travel was slowly grinding Nelson to the bone, and privately he could see the day fast approaching when all he would want to do would be to buy a little spread of Texas turf like the one his folks had dreamed of owning, tend a few beef cattle, and show up only to play in those major golf tournaments that caught his fancy. Though he never showed it on his almost perpetually smiling face, Byron Nelson's urgency to win—and win *big*—was nearly equal with Ben Hogan's.

This set the stage for maybe the most sensational tournament clash in years: Hogan versus Nelson at the Masters, on the golf course Bobby Jones built as his personal shrine to the game, pro golf's two heavyweights center stage in the most theatrical setting in the game.

Conveniently paired with his buddy Jug McSpaden in the first round, Nelson sped out to a sensational 68 and seemed to take command of the affair with an even better 67 in round two. Hogan struggled with his putter in both rounds, finishing 73-70.

Sharp and swirling winds played havoc with round three, creating hard greens and difficult approaches. Only a trio of players managed to beat Nelson's even-par 72, a rumpled Arkansas pro named Ernie Joe "Dutch" Harrison and Scotland's venerable Bobby Cruickshank, both of whom fired 71, and Ben Hogan, who matched Nelson's opening round with a brilliant 67 of his own.

In the locker room after his marvelous round, now in second place and just three shots behind his erstwhile road partner, Hogan described his performance as "the best managing I ever did. I mean manipulating the ball, allowing for wind and roll." The reporters at Augusta dutifully wrote that down. The golf world had a new word for the surgical way Ben Hogan attacked a golf course under the most extreme of conditions. It was called "managing" a round, and he'd done it that day better than anyone else, including the leaders.

Despite a broadly sensed shift in momentum, Byron gamely held on to his lead through the third round but made a cluster of costly bogeys during the final circuit that let Ben take the tournament lead into the clubhouse on Sunday afternoon. As Hogan disappeared into the locker room to have a cold beer and wait, his partisans turned and hurried back out to follow Byron home.

As Byron stepped onto the tee at the long and difficult uphill 18th hole, he needed no worse than par to tie Hogan, who'd finished with 280, or a birdie to win outright.

His foot slipped on the downswing of his drive, though, and his ball flew into the pines on the right. "The ball was just sitting on the ground nicely," he recalled, "and there was an opening in front of me, about twenty feet wide, between two trees." Using his five-iron, Byron fashioned a brilliant low running hook shot around a pine tree that flew up the fairway and onto the green, drawing a thunderous ovation from the gallery. He nearly drained the fifteen-footer but settled for a tap-in par and a tie at 280 with Ben.

Their play-off, yet another reprise of the 1927 Glen Garden Christmas caddie tournament and the miserable Texas Open rolled into one on golf's most majestic stage, was scheduled for 2:30 P.M. Eastern War Time the next afternoon.

That morning at the Bon Air Hotel, where most of the players and their wives billeted, Ben discovered that Byron spent much of the previous night throwing up and had already lost his breakfast that morning as well.

Ben offered to postpone their match; Byron declined the offer because his stomach frequently acted up on the eve of important matches, and curiously enough, it sometimes meant he was going to play his best. To ease his nerves and keep his strength up, though, Byron managed to eat a chicken sandwich and drink a cup of hot tea before their face-off began.

"This was probably one of the most unusual play-offs in golf," he explained many years later, "in that at least twenty-five of the pros who had played in the tournament stayed to watch us in the play-off. I don't recall that ever happening any other time. Ben and I were both very flattered by that."

Privately, Ben dreaded having to play Byron for a title he wanted almost as much as a National Open—it felt like San Antonio all over again. The inescapable truth was that Ben had never beaten Byron in a head-to-head match, and he frankly would rather have faced anyone in golf but his oldest rival. As the two men shook hands to start play, Byron later said he felt Ben's determination like an electric current.

The parry and thrust of their play-off reflected its powerful importance to Hogan. He played rock-solidly for the first four holes, Byron more like a man reeling from a nasty case of stomach flu. Pushing his opening tee ball into the pine grove on the right, Byron found his golf ball lodged against a pine cone and finished the first hole with a double bogey to Ben's par. They matched pars on holes 2 and 3, and then Byron misjudged the distance to the par-3 4th, bunkered his tee shot, and made 4 to Hogan's 3.

"It looked like Ben was going to run away and hide with it by the turn," remembers a longtime Augusta member. "He was absolutely in control of things—cruising."

At the par-3 6th, though, Byron, who always had a nimble talent for coming back from the edge of disaster, laid his tee shot ten feet from the cup and smoothly drained the putt; Ben missed left and made 4. Following matching pars at 7, Nelson eagled 8 after a stunning approach shot, and Hogan could manage only birdie. They were all square, playing in a cathedral silence punctuated only by the whisper of spectator feet shuffling over groomed beds of Bob Jones's succulent pine needles.

During the next five holes, Byron picked up three shots on Ben, including a tee shot that nearly went in the cup on the beautiful par-3 12th. Hogan's ball wound up on the bank at Golden Bell, as the hole is called, but he nearly chipped in for 2. The gallery was buzzing from the heroic back-and-forth.

The two old friends and adversaries arrived at the 18th tee with Byron leading by 2. Byron intentionally played short of the green on his approach shot, astutely avoiding the protective front bunker at all costs. Afterward, he told the press that this was his "secret" for successfully maneuvering around Augusta National—always shoot for greens, avoid bunkers, and never go directly for a dangerous flag.

The flag was positioned low on 18, but Hogan had no choice but to go for it; he overclubbed (as he sometimes did intentionally, aiming to execute a more controlled shot) and flew his approach shot to the upper tier of the putting surface, leaving himself a long, dangerous, downhill putt for birdie. Byron chipped short and missed his par, tapping in for 5. Ben two-putted for 4 and lost—once again—by the breadth of one stroke.

Among the spectators above them, having just vacated their quiet perches in the clubhouse and filtered out to greet their husbands, dressed as usual in nearly identical spring frocks, Valerie Hogan and Louise Nelson embraced and kissed each other's cheeks.

Amid the sustained applause of their admirers, Byron and Ben stood on the 18th green and shook hands. Byron removed his hat. He looked more relieved than pleased, someone remembered. Hogan finally removed his cap too, palming his sleek black hair as the two men left the green to total up and sign their official scorecards.

Ben was smiling, flashing his movie star enamels once again, the soul of a gracious loser. But inside, as the clock ticked away and shadows of war gathered, he was positively seething, kicking himself for the overdone approach shot at 18—exactly the kind of dumb mistake he simply couldn't permit himself if he ever expected to win a major golf tournament.

NINE WEEKS LATER, he got a bit of a reprieve from this agony. Following a month of well-paying exhibition matches and nearly three weeks of intensive practice at his new home course in Hershey, Pennsylvania, Hogan appeared at the Hale America Open, an event backed by a national health organization and staged at Ridgemoor Country Club in suburban Chicago, shot a blistering 62 in the second round, and cakewalked past a highly respectable field that included the Tour's top players and even a rare appearance by Bobby Jones. When a reporter asked him if he felt this win constituted a major championship, the winner faltered only a moment, a nerve touched. "Yes," he answered quickly, but then hesitated. "I think given the quality of this field it's a major championship." He gave a wintry smile and added, "At least I feel that way. Don't know about you boys." Most of them, it turned out, didn't share this view. And neither did the sponsoring USGA.

Beyond his sterling play, one of the more interesting items to come out of the Hale America was the news that Hogan's red-hot Spalding putter fetched $1,500 in a post-tournament auction for charity relief. Figuring he would receive his own draft notice any day, Hogan decided to let the putter do some patriotic service of its own, raising money for the troops. The gesture was genuine, though maybe not as altruistic as it seemed on first glance. For weeks Ben had been practicing with a more center-shafted brass-headed model made from a melted-down door knob. He liked it—loved its feel and brassy heft—and decided if golf got back into civilian clothes anytime soon, he would use this putter instead.

As the media buzz over his sensational Hale America win rapidly faded under the weight of news accounts of the U.S. Marines' assault on Guadalcanal, hints of untold Nazi massacres in the occupied low countries, and growing consumer shortages of gas, butter, and metal appliances on the home front, Rosie the Riveter quickly replaced Ben Hogan as a symbol of hard work and self-sacrifice. Major League Baseball steeply cut its admission prices to keep up spirits and attendance, the jitterbug craze started among teenagers who needed to work off pent-up energy, and 20 million victory gardens popped up across America's fruited plain, including hundreds on temporarily appropriated golf courses.

Only Ben Hogan and his most ardent fans were still thinking about the

meaning of Hale America when he finished his own golf career "for the duration" with a final win at Rochester a few weeks later, a title that gave Hogan
his third Vardon Trophy in a row and the abbreviated season's money title
($13,143) over Byron Nelson and hard-charging Sam Snead, respectively, a
tidy glimpse of the postwar world to come.

Curiously, in the weeks before the Tour formally shut down for the duration, a gentlemanly debate continued in back sports editorials regarding the
Hale America, fueled by those who loved the little Texan and those who
didn't.

Perhaps significantly—or not—the handsome bronze-struck Hale America
medal presented to Ben in Chicago was nearly identical in every way to those
awarded to National Open champions, and considering the strength of the
field the event had attracted, as the winner himself was quick to point out, despite a somewhat lackluster golf course, many were saying this should count
as Hogan's first major win.

Hogan agreed with them, passionately so, though not many reporters
changed their position on the subject. This was a sweet revenge for many of
them—payback for Ben's efforts to control them.

"It's just Hogan's luck," observed one of the few national columnists who
was mildly sympathetic to his cause. "He joins the dance just as the band is
boxing up and going home."

WILLIAM B. HOGAN reported for active duty on March 25, 1943. According to his wife, Valerie, who drove him down to the Tarrant County courthouse, where the inductees were required to report in order to be bused to
boot camp, Ben requested service in the Army Air Corps but nearly wound up
in the Navy. " 'I don't want to wear that blue suit,' I remember him saying,"
Valerie said. "But the day he went in to sign up, the officer there was about to
stamp his papers for the Navy when Ben said, 'Just a moment, sir. I requested
the Air Corps, not the Navy.' He got the Air Corps."

The night before he reported for duty, according to his wife, he did a highly
romantic thing. He presented Valerie with a star sapphire ring, which she put
on her finger and never took off again.

"I don't know if I'll ever be able to give you another gift," he told her. "So I
want to give you this before I go." The next morning, she drove him to the
courthouse to start his military career.

He asked her to leave before his bus arrived.

"I don't want to leave," she dug in her heels and told him. "I want to stay until the bus pulls away."

"I want you to leave," he repeated.

"I realized," Valerie said later, "he didn't want to tell me good-bye with the bus there."

Lacking a high school graduation certificate, Hogan was assigned the standard rank of private, and as it turned out, he didn't have far to ride—just out to the newly renamed Army Air Forces basic training facility at Tarrant Field on the outskirts of Fort Worth.

Why the Army Air Forces? For years, that question puzzled a handful of Hogan friends who knew that he suffered from a dread of heights and that flying caused him jitters. The conclusion they finally reached was that the Air Forces was the most glamorous of the military branches, the most likely to keep him nearest to home in Texas as well, and the least likely to send him into combat, if things came to that. Learning to fly—and confronting a secret fear head-on, as he'd always done in life—was precisely the kind of intellectual challenge that would absorb his detail-oriented mind until he could get back into civvies and chase his missing major.

"Ben spent his whole life confronting his fears and beating them to a pulp," says one of his Shady Oaks golf partners later in life. "Learning to fly an airplane was all about taking control of that fear and beating it down. Doesn't surprise me one bit that he chose the Air Forces."

Hogan hinted at this motivation himself. "I've never really flown very much," he admitted to a Dallas reporter attending his induction. "And I'm eager to see what flying is all about. A number of golfers have taken to flying between tournaments. Perhaps, if I become a pilot, I might also."

Under the terms of his enlistment, he was required to reside at the field's barracks for six weeks of intensive basic training, and his family wasn't a bit surprised to learn that upon discovering that his barracks latrine was short of cleaning supplies, Private Hogan secured a pass and went off-base and purchased the supplies out of his own pocket.

He went off-base for other things too, including a Red Cross benefit at Colonial featuring Bob Hope, PGA president Ed Dudley, and his own commanding officer, Colonel Henderson. If his comrades in arms minded his special treatment, few if any ever publicly grumbled about it. "Ben's a pretty regular guy," a fellow private was quoted by the Associated Press as saying. "Except he keeps his uniform much neater than any of us."

"I'm eager and willing to do whatever the Army needs me to do," Hogan told the *Star-Telegram* shortly before shipping out to officers' candidate school in Miami, adding, "and I'm pretty sure that doesn't mean playing much tournament golf. From now on, I think most of my golf is going to be played only on Sundays."

In November 1943, Valerie pinned the gold bars of a second lieutenant's rank on her husband's shoulder. The graduation ceremonies were held at nine on a warm Saturday morning at a Miami community golf course that had been commandeered by the Army and converted into a parade ground, where, as newly designated squadron officer, Lieutenant Hogan had become obsessed with winning the weekly marching pennant. "Our squadron hasn't won the pennant yet," he complained to his newly arrived wife, noting how he was drilling his men so aggressively that he expected to make up for that shortfall any day. "He really worked his men," Valerie remembered. "One of them was Mark Payne, the architect who years later would design our Fort Worth home. Mark later told me, 'Ben was the toughest officer we had. He nearly killed us.' And finally, Ben's squadron won the marching pennant. He was so happy, and so typical. Golf or marching, he had to win something."

Fort Worth friends who knew Hogan during this period say he wasn't fully consumed by a desire to get back to tournament golf—as is frequently asserted in accounts of his military service. "I sometimes think he enjoyed being *out* of golf," remembers a man who knew the Hogans socially at Rivercrest and Colonial. "It took some of the pressure off, and I got the impression that he liked wearing the uniform. Ben was very patriotic, old-fashioned in that way. Whenever he got a leave, he and Valerie would show up for dinner at the club and even a few dances. He always wore his uniform. Ben liked to dance. Not many people knew that. Much later he even took dance lessons so he'd be better than any other fella out there."

With his new officer's commission, however, Ben got placed in the newly formed Civilian Pilot Training Program—a unit specifically designed to rapidly pump out interim flight instructors who could train younger combat pilots—and sent to Kilgore, Texas, for a month of basic flying instruction, then on to air bases in Louisiana and Texarkana for further instruction; then finally on to the Spartan School of Aerodynamics in Tulsa for more advanced training as a flight instructor.

On a far lesser scale, like Byron and Jug McSpaden, he was able to keep his golf skills reasonably sharp and earn a few war bonds by doing the occasional Red Cross exhibition. At one of them near Tulsa, a beautiful young woman named Patricia Robinson marched up to Hogan and congratulated him on his success and wondered if he had any advice for someone her size trying to play golf. She stood just a whisker over five feet tall and was delicate boned, not to mention extremely pretty. Hogan liked pretty women. Furthermore, she was "mad for golf," and her husband was a Navy officer taking flight training nearby. Some years later, Robinson would help organize and run the Ryder Cup festivities at Wentworth in England—the one, as it happened, that fell at the end of Hogan's most sensational year in 1953. Unfortunately, a weary Ben Hogan chose not to participate, a personal blow to pretty Pat Robinson.

"Madam, look at me," he commanded her. "And tell me what you see."

"A very fine golfer," she replied.

"That's true. But I'm not much bigger than *you*. Permit me to show you something. . . ." And with that, he teed up a ball and drilled it over the back of the practice range.

"Never let *anyone* tell you you're too small, madam," he inveighed gently. "The one thing you must not do is give up. Never *ever* give up!"

"He was terribly persuasive," she remembered many years later. "And most attractive as a person."

While he was in Tulsa, Lieutenant Hogan did indeed learn to fly an airplane, receiving certification as a copilot in light propeller aircraft, but he never had to teach anybody else to fly as he thought, and perhaps expected, he would do.

"Having known Ben for most of his life," wrote the president of the Fort Worth National Bank in a letter of recommendation to Hogan's superiors, "as far as this military conflict is concerned, I can't think of any young man more qualified to lead other men. Ben has the natural quality of command." Oil wildcatter W. A. Moncrief and others, including Marvin Leonard, wrote similar letters supporting Ben's character and fitness to lead.

"Hogan Gives up Golf," reported the *Tulsa World* a short time later, noting that Ben Hogan had nevertheless managed to play "more than two dozen charity matches during his year of flight training but was now fully concentrating on aviation," expecting the quality of his golf game to "rapidly deteriorate until I'm able to get back at golf full-time." The patriotic champ's only complaint, the paper noted, was that he and Valerie were having a tough time finding a good apartment near his Tulsa base, where he expected shortly to be training young flyboys for active combat duty.

Probably because of his age and fame, that duty never transpired, and the couple didn't have long to search for digs. Hogan's assignment was supposed to last nine months, but it lasted instead only a dozen or so weeks. The reason was a blessing in disguise to Hogan's mothballed tournament game. By early 1944, experienced combat veterans were being furloughed in droves and returned stateside to take over combat flight training, allowing 'older, hastily trained fill-ins like Hogan to be sent home with basically nothing to do but polish their shoes and wait for the second front.

Back in Fort Worth, with Ben free to dress in civilian clothes and live wherever they chose, Valerie and Ben moved back into a pretty garden apartment near Camp Bowie Boulevard, and Ben resumed a routine of regular practice and playing at Colonial that some weeks rivaled his prewar form. He was even able to venture off to several special "victory" tour events staged in Chicago and Dallas, where he appeared with Bob Hope and Bing Crosby and played scores of private matches with his brother, Royal, and other worthies at Rivercrest and Colonial, all the while girding himself for the moment victory in Europe and Japan was declared and another kind of warfare resumed.

Weeks before he mustered out to civilian life, Ben and Valerie spent ten days down in San Antonio with Sarah Fox and her husband, Ralph Walters, a business machine executive. Hogan practiced every morning and played golf every afternoon with a local club pro and used his evenings to get better acquainted with his young niece, Valerie.

"We played hide and seek, and I remember hiding from him beneath my bed and suddenly seeing the most beautifully polished pair of shoes I'd ever seen standing beside my hiding place," recalls Valerie Harriman. "Suddenly the entire bed lifted up, and there stood this man smiling down at me. 'There you are, I found you!' he would say with a huge surprised smile. We played this game over and over. He was so warm and friendly. Children have a natural instinct about these things. It was clear that this man, who my mother said was my uncle Ben, really loved children."

Shortly before signed papers came through honorably discharging Hogan back to civilian life and the recently resumed PGA Tour in August 1945, Lieutenant Ben Hogan was promoted to the rank of captain and presented with a personal letter of gratitude from President Harry S. Truman, his father-in-law's personal hero.

"I'm damn glad it's over," he confided to Valerie as they drove over one evening to join Marvin and Mary Leonard for dinner at Colonial.

But in fact, one man's war for respect was really just resuming.

· · ·

HOGAN WASN'T ALONE in his desire to get back to tournament life and resume his quest for a major championship. Sam Snead spent most of the war giving golf lessons to Navy brass in Norfolk, collecting used golf balls he scavenged and kept in a shoe box due to rubber rationing, and counting the days until he could bolt back to defend the PGA Championship he'd finally won at New Jersey's Seaview shortly before play was suspended for the duration. Before this breakthrough, Snead had been in the same boat as Ben—the top player in golf who *hadn't* won a major—and considered his thrilling win over a promising newcomer named Jim Turnesa, a small, dark-skinned, Hogan-like Army corporal stationed at nearby Dix Hill—yet another of the fabulously skilled Turnesa brothers—the most satisfying moment of his career thus far. "If nothing else, that PGA finally got them newspaper boys off my back a little bit," he remembered many years later. "Up till then they liked to say I was a hex-haunted hillbilly who couldn't finish off the big ones. Well, that win at Seaview gave me some boost in confidence, I can tell you, and I spent most of my time in the Navy thinkin' about nothin' else but gettin' out and winning me a National Open and a Masters or two to go with it. Ben was probably even more anxious about that subject than I was because he didn't have a national title either and was getting the same business from the press as I was before the PGA come along."

The war's end brought a bevy of hungry veterans and a few promising newcomers to give chase to glory. Not only were Demaret, Lew Worsham, and Herman Keiser also just out of Navy blue—Demaret joked that he "spent the whole war inside Sherman's in San Diego—not the tank, friends, the *bar*"—but the Coast Guard was releasing "Siege Gun" Thomson, and Lloyd Mangrum was back bearing a leg wound and a Purple Heart from the Battle of the Bulge, as was Jay Herbert from the landing at Iwo Jima. Clayton Heafner, Dutch Harrison, Vic Ghezzi, Jim Ferrier, and Horton Smith (who spent time playing golf with Hogan in Miami) were suddenly back in spikes and civilian duds too, raring to chase themselves down a championship of any kind.

The immediate challenge for most, aside from tournament games that had grown a bit rusty, was that tournament golf had basically belonged to Byron Nelson and his lantern-jawed Kansas sidekick Jug McSpaden, the so-called Gold Dust Twins, who, thanks to medical deferments, spent the war years crisscrossing the country to raise money for the USO and the Red Cross and pocketing the lion's share of whatever prize money was available (almost all of it in war bonds), keeping alive the radically reduced tournament circuit and patriotically performing something like 110 separate exhibitions. In a somewhat bitter *Saturday Evening Post* essay that appeared in 1947, McSpaden complained that the $18,000 worth of war bonds he collected in 1944 amounted to only $134.55 when he cashed them in a few years later.

Beginning at flamboyant George May's Tam O'Shanter tournament in July 1944, just weeks after the Normandy invasion to liberate occupied France, Nelson went on a breathtaking run of tournament wins and near-wins like nobody in golf had ever seen.

After collecting an unheard-of check for $10,000 from May, a short, potbellied former Bible salesman and self-made millionaire who threw money around like confetti but introduced several genuine innovations to tournament life (including the first television coverage of golf), Nelson went on a tear, winning half of the next twelve tournaments he entered. Counting the Miami International Four-Ball Championship he won with McSpaden in the spring of 1945, he then won a record-breaking eleven tournaments in a row, finishing the year with eighteen titles in all to his credit. He also won a 19th event on the Jersey shore that the PGA Tour refused to count.

During 1944, impressively, Nelson was over par only three times in the twenty-one tournaments he played and earned more than $37,000—twice as much as anyone had ever earned in a single season of golf—and won the coveted Associated Press Athlete of the Year Award. Among other things, the windfall enabled Nelson, then thirty-two, to resign his club pro position at Inverness—"I had already realized I didn't want to play tournament golf forever or be a club professional all my life," he revealed in his autobiography—and travel the circuit in more comfort, even as he calculated how to leave the game. Privately, Nelson viewed 1945 as his swansong year in pro golf, and in reviewing the small record book he kept for the first time, detailing the highlights of every round he played, Byron discovered that "poor chipping" here and a "careless shot" there had cost him a number of other titles and even more money. Thus, for 1945, he resolved not only to improve in these finesse categories but to try to establish a scoring average that would send a clear message to the hotshots returning from military service.

After winning his fifth tournament in a row down in Atlanta (where he broke the existing seventy-two-hole scoring record with 263), Byron was approached by a representative from Wheaties cereal, who invited him to appear on the box cover of "the Breakfast of Champions." Nelson made his own deal with the cereal firm, accepting $200 for his likeness and a six-month supply of free Wheaties, most of which he was forced to give away before it spoiled.

After his Atlanta win, Nelson later revealed, the pressure he felt from the press and fans alike to keep on winning became so oppressive that there were days he confided to Louise that he hoped he would blow up and shoot himself out of contention, thereby ending the fevered public expectation that only mushroomed every time he teed up a ball.

By the ever-important PGA Championship that summer, Byron's back was aching from so much play. He required lengthy osteopathic massages every night following his rounds ... then went on to extend his streak to nine in a row by knocking out former Yankees player Sam Byrd in the finals, with 30,000 spectators hugging the fairways, a wild throng of Nelson fans restrained by gallery ropes for the first time ever.

Two weeks later, dodgy back and all, he was at it again at George May's orgy of golf capitalism, now portentously recast as the All American Open, firing 269 to lap the nearest competitor by eleven strokes.

The press had a new moniker for the wondrous Byron Nelson, blissfully unaware that he was about to leave the pro game in his dust and go find his cattle farm. They called him "Mr. Golf."

AS IT HAPPENED, Ben Hogan was the man Nelson beat by eleven strokes at May's lavish Roman spectacle of golf.

Almost unnoticed in the excitement surrounding Byron's streak, Ben finished only his second tournament back from wartime duty with a highly respectable 280 and narrowly admitted to a reporter in the locker room afterward, while taking off his new custom-made British golf shoes with an added spike for more traction, that he'd had "just about enough of all this Mr. Golf business."

Byron was counting the days till he and Louise could purchase their dream ranch in the pretty country north of downtown Fort Worth, while Ben was counting the days until he and Byron could go head to head again.

"There now was not much love lost between Nelson and Hogan," noted Hogan biographer Gene Gregston, who knew both men fairly well at their peaks. "Their rivalry was too intense for the close friendship to survive. Nelson backers said Ben in action and word showed he resented the success Nelson had attained in the war years. Hogan backers explained that he was too combative to be a buddy to the man who stood between him and his goal."

At Knoxville a month later, a week after Fred Haas halted Byron's streak at eleven straight, the two former travelmates were at it again. Mr. Golf won, and Mr. Hogan finished third.

Former Seaman First Class Samuel Jackson Snead wasn't exactly sitting idly on the end of his golf bag humming "The Merry Widow Waltz" either. Since leaving the Navy in late 1944, Snead had rapidly made up ground by capturing an impressive five of the first six tournaments he entered, including the Tour's opening event for 1945, the Los Angeles Open, where he beat Mr. Golf by a stroke. By the time Hogan was fully back in action that July, Snead had notched three more wins, to Nelson's neat baker's dozen. Pro golf, as someone said, was "a three-man affair."

A week later in Nashville, Hogan led off with 64 and carved his way to 265 and a four-stroke victory over runner-up Nelson.

The next week down in Dallas, it was Snead's turn to win by four. Days later, the Slammer beat runner-up Bantam Ben by a whopping nine at Tulsa. Then, as the Tour swung west, it was Nelson's turn again at the Esmeralda Open.

Much to the delight of the golf-starved, war-weary tournament patron, from August 1945 to September 1946, Hogan and Nelson and the insurgent Sam Snead waged a furious guerrilla war for the number-one spot in golf.

Hogan won eighteen times, Nelson ten, Snead eight.

The most extraordinary moment for Ben and his revitalized partisans came at the Portland Open, where he put together four extraordinary rounds (65-69-63-64) to shoot an unearthly 261 and clip four strokes off Nelson's record and establish the lowest seventy-two-hole score in Tour history.

"Nice going, Ben!" Jimmy Demaret claimed he congratulated the Invitational's winner after his stunning, record-breaking performance, Ben having beaten Byron by a whopping fourteen strokes.

Hogan, he says, simply stared at him and offered only a wan smile.

"I guess that takes care of this Mr. Golf business," said Ben.

But it didn't. Two weeks later, Nelson roared back with a 259 (62-68-63-66) to take the Seattle Open by thirteen strokes. "I was so embarrassed at having Hogan beat me by fourteen that I might not have played as well at Seattle if I'd only been two or three shots back at Portland," Byron explained some time later.

Reporters demanded to know how long Byron thought his new scoring record could stand—especially with Hogan and Snead running wild and the game's best players returning plus a crop of hungry newcomers coming to the circuit.

Byron, ever true to form, smiled and politely repeated almost verbatim what he had said a fortnight before in Portland, vis-à-vis Hogan. "You don't know in this game. The record could be broken next week. Or maybe not forever." (As it happened, Nelson's masterful 259 endured for nearly a decade, until Mike Souchak shot 257 at Brackenridge Park in the Texas Open.)

Two weeks after Seattle, Ben won the Richmond Invitational, then went to Pinehurst hoping to add another North and South to his expanding trophy collection. He wound up a disappointing third, then finished third at Durham and Mobile as well. Byron was missing from all of these fields, having already slipped home to Fort Worth to quietly scout about for ranch land.

Someone joked that Captain Hogan couldn't muster the enthusiasm to win if his archrival Lord Byron wasn't on the battlefield. But Ben won again at Orlando, the distant forerunner of Arnie Palmer's Bay Hill Classic, before going home to finish the season in a head-to-head match with Byron.

The event was the first Glen Garden Invitational, and it was held just two weeks shy of the Christmas break. Hogan wanted nothing more than to beat Byron where their career in golf began.

But maybe the ghosts of Christmas Past were simply too much for Ben. He played poorly over the modest little course where once upon a time both he and Byron began as caddies, putting together one of his highest four-round totals of the year, 287—good enough for only a sixth-place tie.

As bittersweet irony would have it, Byron Nelson prevailed and won by a convincing fourteen-stroke margin over the field. It was a firm reminder to the world in general, and Ben in particular, that—for the moment at least—Byron was *still* Mr. Golf.

SEVEN

Three Putts

APPROACHING THE halfway mark of what many had already begun to call the American Century, the postwar United States stood alone in terms of power and prestige at "the summit of the world," to quote a grateful and admiring Winston Churchill. America's farms and factories were operating at maximum capacity, and the nation's treasury was overflowing for the first time in decades.

As Averell Harriman, Harry Truman's newly appointed ambassador to the worryingly expansionist Soviet Union, summed up the emerging peacetime mood of late 1945, the vast majority of Americans simply wanted to go out to the movies, drink a Coke, and "have a good time being themselves again."

Among the other "ordinary" pleasures once again available to the masses, the Professional Golf Association resumed play in 1946 with its most ambitious offering of tournaments ever, including more than twenty-five open field events, half a dozen invitational tournaments, and a record amount of prize money topping $400,000.

Overleaf: Ben and Byron, Augusta National, 1946 *(Corbis)*

From the outset, a direct reflection of the nation's elevated hopes due to the outbreak of peace, everything about the resumption of golf's most cozy rite of spring, the 1946 Masters, appeared over the top and slightly surreal, beginning with a purse inflated to $10,000 and feverish anticipation of watching golf's leading rivals, Nelson, Snead, and Hogan, go at each other under the tranquil Georgia pines. Indicative of how deep passions were running, a pair of prominent Augusta members laid fifty grand apiece on Hogan to win in a gallop, taking four-to-one odds on their man, while much of the other big money flying around at the Bon-Air Hotel's infamous Calcutta auction—a Rio-style *carnivale* of white-man gambling openly tolerated by local lawmen and even routinely covered by the *Augusta Chronicle* and other prominent newspapers until the increasingly image-conscious USGA and USPGA banded forces to end the practice—fell on the shoulders of Nelson, Snead, and showman Jimmy Demaret.

Some of the high rollers felt that Hogan's low-ball game, not to mention his history of faltering badly in the late stages of Masters past, mitigated his chances of achieving his long-awaited breakthrough in an event that had always conveyed something of the cloistered air of a club final but suddenly gained "major" status upon the return to peacetime prosperity. Other oddsmakers decided that Nelson and Snead, given their better Augusta vitas, were simply unstoppable forces. All but invisible in the jamboree of wagering and prefiguring was a fidgety, sallow-faced Missouri pro nicknamed "the Missouri Mortician," who once upon a time served as a setup man for the infamous roving golf gambler "Titanic" Thompson (he'd scout up wealthy pigeons at private clubs before Thompson appeared in town and proceeded to empty their money clips) and spent the early days of his military career as a petty officer marooned on a Navy cruiser out in the Pacific Fleet.

Like several of his better-known contemporaries, including Snead and Hogan, round-faced Herman Keiser spent the final few months of his military service idly waiting to muster out and working on his wobbly backswing at the same Norfolk Navy Yard where Snead spent his latter wartime years giving swing tips to admirals and regaling visiting brass with jaw-dropping dirty jokes.

Listed by the Bon Air bookies at twenty-to-one, Keiser, who received one of the last invitations issued by Jones and Roberts that year, gamely plunked twenty bucks on himself and promptly went out and fired opening rounds of 69-68 to vault over the field and lead Ben Hogan by seven shots at the tournament's halfway mark.

As Keiser explained decades later to Masters chronicler Curt Sampson, following his brilliant second round the Missouri Mortician was collared by a powerful local bookie who informed him that a pair of the club's biggest fish had laid fifty grand apiece on Hogan—the implicit advice being that if Keiser desired to ever be invited back to lovely Augusta National, he well might consider the career advantages of *not* beating the Hawk.

Confirming Keiser's suspicions that a conspiracy to boost Hogan to his first major was afoot, tournament officials declined Keiser's not unreasonable request for a new caddie. Herman himself was one of the game's most notorious slowpokes (rivaling Ralph Guldahl and Cary Middlecoff in this department), but his assigned bag carrier hobbled around the course like a Bombay cripple, unable to even keep pace with his employer at several key moments. A further indignity was dumped on the leader when tournament officials made an unannounced change in Keiser's scheduled final-round starting time—moving him forward by half an hour—nearly causing the anxious, high-strung Missourian to miss his final-round starting time.

To compound matters, during the round itself the tournament's longest shot, playing with more deliberation than usual, glanced over to find national sportswriter and unapologetic Hogan cheerleader Grantland Rice closely shadowing him. When he spoke cordially to Rice, the dean of America's sportswriters supposedly advised him sharply to "get a move on before they penalize you." Keiser later said he felt it was yet another gambit to unravel his game and give Hogan a chance to catch him.

If true, the irony on the ground was that Ben Hogan was perhaps the most deliberate and periodically the slowest player in any major field, fully capable of keeping official timekeepers in suspended animation thanks to a playing aura that was as forbidding as an Arctic sunrise.

Was there indeed a gentlemanly cabal hatched in the corridors of the old Bon-Air or the private corners of the Augusta National locker room to keep Herman Keiser out and help Ben finally over the hump to major stardom? To this day, no one but the Missouri Mortician seems entirely certain of it.

In any event, rattled by these distractions and the crushing pressure of leading his first Masters, including the silent insult of being the tournament's final-round leader by five strokes but being assigned a starting time that was at least half an hour *earlier* than the day's final pairing (which just happened to include Hogan), Keiser sprayed drives left and right with his punchy swing and managed to par on only two of the first nine holes, scrambling for three birdies and four bogeys en route to an outward 37. After a bogey at the opening hole, Hogan cruised to 35 on the first nine.

"So far as I know, and certainly so far as I have observed," wrote *Atlanta Journal* reporter and Bob Jones biographer O. B. Keeler, following along in the huge spectator galleries estimated at over 7,500, "there never was such a finish in major league golf."

Herman's nerves settled a bit on Augusta's dangerous back nine. He played steady par golf until the 72nd hole, the difficult uphill 18th. At that point, brilliantly striking the flagstick on his approach shot from the short left-hand rough, he simply needed to coax his ball twenty feet down the lightning-fast green to make birdie and seal his victory. Instead, Keiser rolled his ball five feet past the cup and missed the comeback putt for par. It was his first three-putt of the tournament.

Dejected and still stewing over his perceived shabby treatment by tournament officials, Keiser disappeared into the locker room and was unable to even make himself watch as Hogan calmly stood on the middle tier of the same green half an hour later, just thirty inches above the cup, assessing the two and a half feet of grass needed to claim his first major golf title.

Three birdies on the back nine had brought him level with Keiser, and a spectacular five-iron approach to the final green placed him in the driver's seat. From ten feet or less, nobody was a surer bet than Ben Hogan and his beloved door-knob putter.

"The greens were so slick, you could almost hear them crackle," Hogan recalled the moment afterward, noting that he nudged the ball lightly enough to get it moving so slowly he could actually read the MacGregor label as the ball lazily turned over on its agonizing journey down the slope. To a sudden cascade of long gasps, the ball grazed the cup and rolled another four feet below the cup.

Hogan stood immobile in the Sunday afternoon shadows, the dark blue-gray eyes lacerating the ball with an unblinking raptor's stare. The vast crowd, having witnessed the utterly unthinkable, whispered and murmured and attempted to settle itself down.

A few moments later, after taking even more than his customary sweet time lining up the short putt to tie and force a play-off, Hogan missed the short uphill putt as well. As he stood looking at his ball, even more gasps and murmurs of disbelief rose. Having just three-putted away the Masters championship, Hogan rapped his final putt firmly into the cup and walked quickly up the hill toward the clubhouse, his slightly oversized head tilted down and his face set in stone, walled off from the world by his worst failure ever, the crowd respectfully parting as he proceeded.

O. B. Keeler, who called it the "most fantastic finish" he'd witnessed in forty years of covering golf, later recalled that no one in the horrified gallery dared move for almost a full minute, as Hogan picked up his ball and departed the green with his head tucked down, oblivious to the soft patter of applause that broke out.

Inside the clubhouse, it was genial Henry Picard, of all people, who delivered the news of yet another major Hogan failure to the wan and lingering Keiser.

"Congratulations, Herman," Picard said, slapping the Missouri Mortician on the back. "The little man really took the choke. Those were the three worst putts I've ever seen him hit."

So, YET AGAIN, a major disappointment—more nothing divided by nothing. Not surprisingly, given the revival of the game from its wartime slumbers, the old question surfaced with stinging freshness: when would Ben Hogan, the so-called human shot machine, now widely considered the finest ball-striker since Walter Hagen, win a Masters, PGA Championship, or U.S. Open, golf's most coveted tournaments?

Hogan's win totals were matched only by Nelson and to a lesser extent by Snead over the previous three seasons of regular tournament competition, yet none of those wins were considered major status, unless one cared to count the Hale America as a major championship (which only Ben and a few other partisans did).

On the way home to prepare for Marvin Leonard's new invitational golf tournament at Colonial, now traveling almost exclusively by sleeper train in hopes of easing the wear and tear both he and Valerie increasingly felt, Hogan made up his mind to spend the next month at home, keeping a low profile and preparing for his next opportunity to get the major monkey off his back, June's National Open at Cleveland's Canterbury Golf Club.

Time away from the public's scrutiny was critical for the Hawk. He had much to think about and, though a faltering putter had been the culprit at Augusta, an old problem to try to finally rid himself of once and for all.

Though few but the closest Hogan watchers noticed it, the little man's dreaded hook had begun to reassert itself at critical moments in his game, often when the tournament hung in the balance, and despite a shorter, more controlled backswing and the important grip alterations Henry Picard had helped him make to achieve a controlled fade, by Ben's calculations he'd thrown away half a dozen tournaments in the previous sixteen months, including at least a couple of major championship opportunities, owing to his old nemesis, Captain Hook.

"I left the tour [in 1946] and went home to Fort Worth about as desperate as a man could be," he recounted in *Life* magazine in 1955. "I sat and thought for three or four days. I did not pick up a golf club, although I wanted to in the worst way. One night while laying awake in bed I began thinking about a technique for hitting a golf ball that was so old it was almost new."

The technique was called *pronation*, an old Scottish technique that rolled the hands on takeaway, permitting the face of the club to open slightly at the top. Was *this* the much ballyhooed Hogan "secret" for incomparable ball-striking? Many thought so, and Hogan rather coyly claimed it was, though in the same article he warned that the maneuver—widely discredited by most modern teachers of the day—could actually promote a hook. Hogan admitted that his refinement required "two further adjustments" that rendered the technique, at least on paper, "hook-proof." These two adjustments, he vaguely elaborated, "were so delicate that no one would ever think of looking for them—and I certainly was not going to tell anybody where to look."

The first was Picard's Pomonok lesson: a slight weakening of his left-hand grip by placing his thumb almost entirely on top of the shaft. The second— "which is the real meat of the 'secret' "—was nothing more than a virtually imperceptible twist or cocking of the left wrist backward and inward, which formed a slight V, a "cupped" attitude, at the top of the backswing.

"No matter how much wrist I put into the down swing," he wrote, "no matter how hard I swung or how hard I tried to roll into and through the ball, the face of the club could not close fast enough to become absolutely square at the moment of impact."

The result of this Archimedean inquiry, as he described it, was a spectacularly high and straight-flying shot that seemed to hover briefly over the target area before "coming down light as a feather" with a slight fade—"that lovely long-fading ball which is a highly effective weapon on any golf course," as he extolled the technique's virtues. Best of all, the harder he struck the ball, or so he claimed, the better the "secret" worked.

For a man who believed his only chance at salvation lay in slavish rituals of hard work, this self-revelation was no small evolutionary advance toward his desired state of perfection. In the '30s, sitting with Valerie in her father's empty darkened movie theater, an unknown Ben Hogan had studied Movietone footage of Jones, Hagen, and Sarazen in their prime to learn proper hip-turn technique and balance. During his embryonic days on tour, he'd studied Mac-Donald Smith's beautiful swing and spoke with "Wild Bill" Mehlhorn about his cerebral analytical approach to the game. Later, he blended elements picked up from Ky Laffoon and Lefty Stackhouse and Jack Burke Sr.; Paul Runyan's short-game wizardry, Picard's unruffled ease, Denny Shute's mastery with a two-iron, and Johnny Revolta's pre-shot waggle also all played an invaluable role in Ben's self-tutorials in the field, his driven experimentation to create a swing that wouldn't wilt under pressure.

"With Hogan," says Tommy Bolt, "you got the feeling everything was his real so-called secret. By that I mean, piece by piece, nothing too small was considered and either used or discarded. And once he took it and learned and refined it, brother, it was *his*."

Though Ben failed to reveal as much in his famous *Life* article, anyone who had watched the evolution of his swing from his breakthrough in 1940 to his postwar stature near the summit of the game in 1946 knew he'd also considerably shortened the monstrous backswing that once pounded balls out of the Los Angeles Coliseum. The newer, tighter leverage action gave him the control he craved by reducing the variables of spin on the ball. His extraordinarily supple wrists remained the key, however, to his unearthly length with a driver—a delayed release that sent the ball scorching off the tee, producing a sound generations of players claimed was unique to Hogan. "If you ever heard Hogan hit a ball," says Ben Crenshaw flatly, "it was like no other sound in golf."

In *Life*, Hogan asserted he took his "secret" discovery of late 1946 straight back to the Tour to test it under tournament conditions, which worked so magnificently he promptly won George May's Tam O'Shanter.

Or so he recalled.

Apparently his discovery did work splendidly—whatever he managed to teach himself that he didn't already know about his superbly calibrated swing—but it wasn't May's gaudy golf spectacle he won with his latest technical refinement. Hogan in fact placed fourth at that tournament. (Since the piece was written nearly a decade after the fact, it's possible Ben was thinking of another May spectacular, the World Championship of Golf, which he won in late September the following year.)

More than likely, in any case, as friends' memories and his own meticulously kept travel diary seem to indicate, this important interlude of scholarly self-enlightenment took place during the month he spent around home between his Masters failure and his appearance at the first Colonial National Invitational Tournament in Fort Worth, Marvin Leonard's latest effort to capitalize on the goodwill and superb reviews that flowed from the National Open of 1941. The new Colonial NIT was simply Leonard's latest effort to place Cowtown permanently on the golf map—the way, say, a little invitational called the Masters had done for the tiny river hamlet of Augusta, Georgia.

Borrowing touches innovated by the elders of Augusta National and Chicago impresario George May, Colonial officials not only put up the third-largest purse being offered on the circuit that season ($15,000 in official prize money, with a first-place check of $3,000—second only to the PGA Championship) but strictly limited the field to thirty-six top players—twenty-four professionals, twelve amateurs—making Colonial one of the most prized invitations in golf.

To add further luster to the proceedings, Leonard enhanced spectator viewing areas with better seating and first-rate concession stands, roped off galleries to provide a more ordered flow, strategically placed leaderboards out on the golf course, and added mobile player standards so his paying customers would never have to guess who they were watching.

If a new spirit of optimism was blowing through America in general and pro golf in particular, it didn't hurt Leonard's evangelizing efforts one bit that the opening edition of the Colonial NIT showcased the game's hottest players, two of whom hailed from Cowtown, and one of whom, following a script straight from Hollywood, actually won.

During a stretch of beautiful May weather, Hogan used his newly reworked golf swing to blitz the field, capping off the performance with a scintillating final-round 65 that set a new course record and beat the other hometown favorite, Byron Nelson, by six strokes. Nelson disappointed his local partisans by winding up in a tie for ninth place.

During his brief acceptance comments by the 18th green, a visibly elated Hogan reflected that because of his longtime close association with Marvin Leonard, he'd rather have won the first Colonial than even the National Open that season—a slight bit of embroidery perhaps, due in part to the deep gratitude and admiration he felt toward his old benefactor, which was far keener than anyone listening save perhaps Valerie or Mary Leonard could have fathomed.

For all its polish and luster, the Colonial NIT wasn't considered a major championship. But as the year advanced, no single tournament other than the U.S. Open would mean more to the emerging mythology of Hogan's playing career—or his well-hidden emotions.

THE START OF 1946 brought another kind of unexpected epiphany that would have considerable impact on the length and nature of Hogan's playing career from that point on.

When Sam Snead's pal Johnny Bulla offered to fly a group of the top pros and their wives out west to an upcoming tournament, charging them less than the airlines would, Hogan, still certified to copilot light military aircraft, had wound up sitting in the copilot's seat of Bulla's newly purchased DC-3.

"When we got to Arizona," Hogan confided with a chuckle to sportscaster Jack Whitaker at a tribute dinner decades later honoring former Colonial champions, "I had to make an emergency landing, and I damn near crashed the airplane. It would have wiped out half the golf tour. That was the end of Golf Tour Airlines."

Even before his return to civilian life in 1945, as it happens, Hogan indicated to several friends in Fort Worth that he was looking into the possibility of flying his own airplane on tour; air travel would render the grind of the circuit less taxing on his mind and body than switching from cars to trains for longer hauls. Thanks to the technical expertise he'd picked up in the Air Corps and due to his far more demanding playing schedule, Ben found himself up in the air more and more often, able to suppress his natural flight jitters with the same iron will he used to block out distractions in golf tournaments.

The frightening incident involving Bulla's plane, however, evidently marked the abrupt end of the Hawk's brief flirtation with the idea of owning and flying his own plane. Pilots who make mistakes don't stay pilots for long, as they say in aviation circles, and the thrill of an emergency landing appears to have muted any enthusiasm Ben had for owning and operating his own wings. Besides, Valerie's intense dislike of flight dwarfed her husband's, and at heart both were seasoned veterans of America's highways, those long-ago caravans bumping down the back roads of the Republic after Old Man Par.

Though Val was no particular fan of long-distance car travel either, Ben loved the feeling of freedom and independence that being behind the wheel of a fine motor car afforded him. Traveling by car meant he had hours and sometimes whole days alone to think and plan out his life, to listen to his buddy Bing Crosby croon on the radio, with no reporters bugging him or sticking annoying microphones in his face, no fans crowding him for autographs, and plenty of good roadside diners to scout for cheap scrambled eggs at any hour. At heart, Hogan was a deep sentimentalist who couldn't help associating a good roadside diner with the kind of homey comfort he needed most back when he was Mr. Nobody in big-time golf.

Not surprisingly, one of the first major purchases he made upon his return to civilian life was a beautiful ebony Cadillac, equipped with the latest creature comforts—roomier and plusher seats, a fine radio, and a suspension system said to be unrivaled in the automotive industry.

"I remember Ben talking about his first Cadillac one day at lunch," recalls an older member of Colonial. "He loved that thing—the idea of just getting in it and going anywhere he wanted to. But the longer distances, I guess, were getting to him and Valerie. He was always pointing out that he wasn't so young anymore. So he started riding Pullman cars to the more distant places—particularly the majors events. That way he could rest up and get there fresh, I guess. Anytime he went west, though, it was usually in that Cadillac of his." The member paused and shook his head wonderingly at some flare of memory.

"Ben loved going west for some reason. And I used to wonder if that love of driving west didn't nearly kill him."

By the time former Air Forces captain Ben Hogan and his wife climbed down from their sleeper car in Cleveland in mid-June 1946, a well-rested Ben had the Western Open and Winged Foot's grueling Goodall Round Robin safely folded beneath his handmade English belt and a refortified golf swing he believed was now essentially wiltproof under the heat of major tournament pressure.

It certainly needed to be. The temperatures soared that week in suburban Cleveland, nudging close to the century mark as a record number of spectators swarmed over the tight and hilly golf course, eagerly anticipating the latest grand installment of Ben versus Byron versus Sam.

In the opening round, striking his irons as beautifully as he ever had, Byron vaulted to the lead and scarcely missed a fairway, seldom facing more than ten-foot putts for birdie. The sweetness of his ball-striking matched the poignancy of his cause. Unknown to anyone but his wife, Louise, and a couple of members of his Sunday school men's discussion group, Byron had formally made up his mind to withdraw from professional golf. His instruction book, *Winning Golf*, was already scaling several national best-seller lists, and he was earning a quarter for every copy sold. "That doesn't sound like much," he noted years later, "but that royalty enabled me to buy my first fifty head of Hereford cattle when I did finally get to start ranching."

For Byron, it was more than a nervous stomach and the grind of the road that was finally penetrating his bones. Thanks to his record-setting accomplishments in 1945, Lord Byron was now at the top of his game, and the cattle ranch he'd always dreamed of owning was a reality at hand. Days before the Open commenced in Cleveland, he put down fifty-five grand on 630 acres out in rural Roanoke in the pretty rolling cow country north of Fort Worth. From Byron's perspective, all that remained was to relinquish the stage to Ben and Sam and Jimmy with his customary Sunday grace—and ideally, to make sure another national championship had Mr. Golf's name etched into the silver.

Hogan, who had other ideas, opened play in Cleveland with 72 and improved on day two with a 68. More than 12,000 spectators showed up for the Open's dramatic double round Saturday, clogging footpaths and forcing both contestants and their caddies to elbow their way through unruly crowds and to hit shots through funnels of forward-tilting fans. An unhappy incident on the 13th hole in round three, a dangerous par-5, may have cost Byron Nelson his glorious farewell Open.

As marshals struggled to clear space around his second shot on the hole, Byron's caddie ducked under a rope and inadvertently booted his man's half-hidden ball about a foot, leaving USGA official Ike Grainger no option but to impose what turned out to be a very costly penalty stroke. In the final round that afternoon, Nelson's beautiful three-wood shot to the 71st hole, a long par-3, had the misfortune of landing in a woman's hat on the edge of the green, and the resulting delay over the ruling and placement of his ball caused Nelson's concentration to waver and finally evaporate. He chipped, lipped out, and missed the three-foot return putt for a par that would have won the tournament.

Upset by this mistake, visibly irritated with himself for losing concentration, Nelson blocked his drive to the right side of the 18th fairway and was forced to hack out of the thick rough with an eight-iron and then missed a twelve-footer for par, an unlucky bogey-bogey finish that left him in a tie for the lead with Lloyd Mangrum and Vic Ghezzi.

A little while later, Ben Hogan and Herman Barron were both standing on the same green in the lengthening shadows of an Ohio Saturday afternoon, both with medium-size birdie putts to win the United States Open Championship outright.

Barron missed his birdie attempt, and Hogan, his famous hawk eyes shaded beneath his exquisite linen cap, appeared to study every blade of grass lying between his ball and the hole, a distance of just under eighteen feet—an almost eerie reprise of the situation he had faced two months before at Augusta National. Make it and the "major" weight would forever be off his back. Miss and he would be forced to join Ghezzi, Nelson, and gritty Lloyd Mangrum in a play-off for the national championship.

Three thousand wedged-in spectators fell silent as Hogan assumed his familiar slightly crabbed posture over the ball, glanced twice at the hole, and then gave his ball a gentle, wristy nudge down the hard-baked slope toward the cup. Someone let out a shout as the ball approached the cup, dipped fractionally into the hole, then lipped out, skidding to a halt four feet below the hole.

Hogan appeared absolutely unfazed, implacable.

The huge gallery groaned and murmured.

He marked his ball and stepped away and watched Herman Barron three-putt himself out of the National Open play-off. Then, playing a little quicker than normal, to the utter disbelief and astonishment of his assembled witnesses, Ben Hogan did exactly the same thing—missed his four-footer to join the Open play-off party.

DOWN IN FORT WORTH that same night, a pulpy Hollywood western called *Badman's Territory,* starring Randolph Scott and Ann Richards, was playing to a packed house at the Worth Theater for the third night in a row. "A Saga of land beyond the Law! See them all in action in one picture!" promised the movie's trailer. "The James Gang, the Daltons, Belle Starr!" But in rough-and-tumble Cowtown that evening, most in the audience had turned out to see an added black-and-white short feature called *Ben Hogan, King of Golf.*

A week later, Clara Hogan herself went to see the film, clipped the ad from the *Fort Worth Star-Telegram*, and mailed it to the Hogan cottage in Hershey, Pennsylvania, where Ben was already home diligently beating balls and inhaling packs of cigarettes at his favorite secluded spot out on Milton Hershey's golf course, a quiet wedge of Kentucky bluegrass and rye framed by spreading hardwoods between the 7th and 11th tees, the mighty smokestacks of the Hershey's candy factory bellowing chocolate-scented smoke in the near-distance.

Mama Hogan jotted in the margin of the newspaper ad: "I just went to see my child to-night on the screen. June 21, 1946." That was her no-nonsense way of acknowledging how proud she was that her boy had finally made it to the Big Screen.

By then, of course, Hogan was trying his best to forget what happened on the final holes at Augusta National and Canterbury. Those jarring three-putts were just another bitter pill he had to swallow as he forfeited the field of play on both afternoons, head cast down in Valerie's perfectly described attitude of defeat, followed by the disbelieving stares of his vastly disappointed fans, heading for the first train he could catch out of town.

For the record, the Open drama Ben left in his wake at Canterbury was a little anticlimactic, as most Open play-offs are, but at least it offered the poignancy of a passing legend.

In the aftermath of another three-putt disaster for Ben, decorated Battle of the Bulge survivor Lloyd Mangrum of Grapevine, Texas (the most underrated player of his day, according to Lord Byron), pieced together a scrambling 71 to beat Ghezzi and deprive a faltering Byron Nelson of his farewell national title.

Byron would never enter another U.S. Open field.

For Mangrum, on the other hand, the victory was both timely and sweet. He'd been toiling in both Byron's and Ben's shadows for years, a small lifetime of never quite making the grade or garnering the praise and attention he believed he was due.

A visible match for Hogan in terms of playing toughness, he of the center-parted hair, thin riverboat gambler mustache, and cigarette dangling from his thin, cool lips, Lloyd was the younger and far more accomplished of the Texas Mangrum boys and Ben's junior by only a couple of years, a sardonic joker who likewise disdained locker-room bonhomie and lengthy interviews of any kind.

Over time, Lloyd would be principally known, a bit unfairly, for depriving Nelson of his final Open opportunity and for shooting 64 at the 1940 Masters on the strength of a brilliant iron game that never seemed to waver under pressure. For what it's worth, he reportedly transported a loaded pistol in his golf bag and could drink the average Tour player under the table without slurring his words.

After winning the National Open of 1946, Mangrum's confidence soared, and he went on a tear of tournament victories that led him to the top of the money list and a pair of Vardon Trophies of his own during the following decade. Among other things, Wilson Sporting Goods signed him to a lucrative $5,000 contract to play its clubs, and enterprising George May paid him ten grand to represent Tam O'Shanter on tour. By the time Lloyd officially retired just over a decade later, golf's wisecracking tough guy had collected thirty-four Tour wins and teamed with Sam Snead to produce one of the most formidable Ryder Cup partnerships ever.

Though Byron had carefully dropped a few hints to reporters here or there during the summer of 1946 that he might soon begin to "gradually withdraw" from the active Tour and eventually play only a few select tournaments like the National Open, Masters, and Texas PGA Tour events, few of the regular golf writers who followed the circuit appeared to believe it would happen so soon, so swiftly, and on the heels of maybe the greatest year anybody had ever had in golf.

In mid-August, though, after Porky Oliver drained a wildly bending forty-foot putt to eliminate the defending champion from the quarterfinals of the PGA Championship at Portland Country Club, Byron and Louise drove home to Denton and started packing up their bungalow for the big move to the new ranch in Roanoke.

For more than a decade the Nelsons had endured cramped rental apartments and club cottages with spartan furnishings. Now they went on a furniture shopping spree like a pair of giddy newlyweds. "I don't recall a happier moment in my life," Byron said many years later.

His startling retirement announcement came just prior to another George May production at Tam O'Shanter outside Chicago a few weeks after the Portland tournament, a two-round "World Championship" match that featured four of the year's top money winners—Nelson, Snead, Mangrum, and Herman Barron. Ben Hogan, the logical fourth, declined an invitation to play owing to a "prior commitment" (translation: he intensely disliked George May and thought his Barnum-like innovations were an insult to the dignity of the game), and even Lord Byron later seemed to second-guess his decision to participate.

After stunning the reporters by explaining beforehand that it was time to finally hang up his MacGregors and go raise cattle, Nelson finished two shots behind Snead but collected nary a cent of May's $10,000 purse.

"Apparently it was a winner-take-all event," Byron wrote. "But the amazing thing is that I don't recall one single thing about playing in it whatsoever.

I guess the fact that I didn't win a dime kind of made me want to forget the whole thing."

Instead, he and his old Gold Dust Twin, Jug McSpaden, went elk hunting in Idaho with a friend who helped build Hoover Dam. Byron shot his first elk and had its head mounted and shipped to his father-in-law, who hung the head on a wooden post in his country grocery store for many years. Fittingly, Byron's final appearance that year was at the Fort Worth Open, an event he'd won the preceding year at Glen Garden, the place where his life in golf began.

He'd come full circle but finished a disappointing seventh.

"What a relief it was to have it all over with," he admitted in his memoirs. "I packed up my clubs, sent them to MacGregor, and told them to keep them till I asked for them, which wasn't going to be for a long time."

IN THE DAYS leading up to the PGA Championship at Portland Country Club, where Porky Oliver eventually sent Byron home to the farm, a family dispute that had simmered for years behind closed doors in professional golf suddenly threatened to erupt in a very nasty and public way.

The issue concerned the growing desire of seasoned full-time tournament players to manage and control their own affairs under the authority of an autonomously functioning Tournament Bureau. Through a series of smoke-filled locker-room gripe sessions at tournament venues along the Western and Grapefruit swings, the "tourist" insurgents hashed out their demands for more independence and less interference from the governing PGA and let their feelings be known that they were collectively prepared to split and form their own tournament organization if demands for self-determination weren't fully and reasonably met.

The man selected to convey this unyielding view to the PGA's powerful Executive Committee, when it convened that approaching November, was none other than Ben Hogan.

In 1946 the PGA had 2,168 regular dues-paying members, the vast majority of whom were club pros who never got anywhere near the first tee of an open or invitational professional golf tournament. They were the Johnny Appleseeds of the Scottish game—teaching the game to newcomers, looking after the needs and wants of the members who paid their salaries, conducting club championships, and peddling golf equipment. There were, at war's end, 4,817 golf courses in America but only an estimated two and a quarter million people actually playing the game of golf on a regular basis. If the game was go-

ing to grow as many hoped and projected it would with the return of the soldiers and the nation's expanding prosperity, the home pros believed, not without reason, that they would be the primary reason it did so.

As an operating body, the home pros believed that the circuit tourists—an
elite group who really numbered only a handful by comparison—were the
fortunate beneficiaries of the grassroots work they did back home.

Their argument was compelling. Whatever else was true, the PGA had
managed to keep the spirit of competition and tournament golf alive during
the bleakest days of the war break by putting on one war bond exhibition after another and holding tournaments with fields so thin they occasionally had
more money places than actual competitors to fill them.

Furthermore, prior to the war there had been only a handful of players who
managed to make a decent living playing golf full-time—and most, if not all,
had worked as club pros or enjoyed the financial benefits of some nominal
"club association" like Hogan's sweetheart deal with Milton Hershey. Part of
what made tournament life so difficult for Nelson, in fact, was the perennial
conflict he felt between his natural love of teaching the game to others and
working as a true club professional—a job he took quite seriously and performed ably, by all accounts—and his desire to win big-money tournaments
and buy the ranch of his boyhood dreams.

With the apparently broadening public interest in the game, marquee players like Hogan, Snead, and Demaret represented a new breed of pro who
maintained a lucrative club affiliation but basically didn't need a regular paycheck from the membership to keep going week after week. Though their
ranks were still relatively modest—Hogan estimated that a player had to earn
a minimum of $10,000 a year just to "meet basic expenses"—the tourist insur-
gents of 1946 believed the key to the pro game's future appeal, by contrast, lay
almost entirely in *their* hands.

They noted that as far back as 1934 Gene Sarazen, pro golf's leading stylist
and self-appointed social arbiter, incurred the wrath of the governing PGA by
openly grousing about unknown club pros who routinely showed up to "pay
and play" in PGA-sponsored tournaments. They were, the Squire argued, no-
name players who "generally lacked high standards of professionalism" and
ultimately hurt tournament golf because they sometimes prematurely filled up
fields, pocketed money, and went home as anonymously as they came. The
only fair measure of a player's fitness to compete in big-money tournaments,
Sarazen insisted, was how a man performed week to week on tour. Only that
kind of success built name recognition and fan loyalty, he maintained, archly

advocating the permanent separation of the home pros and the circuiting tourists before fans grew uninterested or the issue came to blows.

Time's passage made Sarazen's fighting words only more prophetic. For example, at the same PGA Championship where Henry Picard gave Hogan his lesson on fading shots, at Flushing's Pomonok Country Club, exactly that sort of dustup occurred when soft-spoken Denny Shute's entry application arrived a day after the official registration cutoff. Flexing its governing muscle, the PGA denied Shute entry into the Championship, setting off a firestorm of protest that several players took from the locker room straight to local bars. By the time accounts of Shute's "snub" reached the national papers, several prominent players (not including then-winless Ben Hogan, who wasn't about to let a dispute interfere with an opportunity to finally win) were threatening to go on strike unless Shute, the 1936 USPGA champ, was immediately reinstated to the field. "It was a showdown case of tournament players against PGA officials who were convinced they represented golfers at large," wrote Herb Graffis, the organization's official historian.

In the end, the PGA buckled and Shute played, but the unresolved issues and bruised feelings left in the incident's wake wouldn't soon be forgotten.

Ben Hogan, not surprisingly, took a negotiating line almost identical to that of his de facto style-meister Gene Sarazen. "Among the top playing pros," Graffis notes, "Sarazen and Hogan are, on the record, the coldest, toughest, most defiant proponents of the policy that tournament golf is a problem whose answers are worked out by clubs, balls, and the scorecard, instead of being a playground of the welfare state."

With forty-one tournaments and record prize money of $454,000 up for grabs in 1946, and its biggest star Byron Nelson dropping hints about possibly retiring from the active tour, PGA officials scurried to avoid a similarly unseemly fracas from erupting at Portland Country Club, site of their big tournament finale.

Even before play got under way, Hogan and others were assured by new PGA president Ed Dudley—the smooth-swinging Augusta pro who'd been so useful to Byron Nelson, ushering him into several lucrative club jobs—that the PGA was finally addressing their gathering concerns. A bold counterproposal, finally offering the touring professionals the virtual autonomy they craved, was working its way "out from committee" and would be on the table when players met with the Executive Committee come November.

For the moment at least, this promise cleared away any distractions from the quest for the Wanamaker Trophy and Byron's rumored fare-thee-well.

Most newspapermen anticipated—and hoped—that they would be treated to yet another Ben and Byron affair with a little homespun Sammy Snead thrown in for local color.

Just a year before, in a fever to reclaim his prewar form, Hogan fired a frighteningly low 261 over the same narrow and relatively short course to win the Portland Open Invitational, a breathtaking sequence that included rounds of 65-69-63-64. As some have pointed out, no other tournament golf course, with the possible exceptions of L.A.'s Riviera and hometown Colonial, would mean more to Hogan's playing career than Portland Country Club.

By the end of August, Ben was rested and ready, in part because the day after his last tournament appearance at the Winnipeg Open in early August, he and Valerie slipped away and spent a few days at a rented cottage beside Canada's Lake Minaki, angling for trout with a teenage guide. A local photographer captured them in a boat puttering about on the resort lake, Ben in his signature flat linen cap and usual immaculate golf mufti reeling in a large wiggling trout, Valerie in elegant sunglasses and a frock coat, dressed as if prepared for tea with royalty, looking as uncomfortable as a fish out of water. "It was the closest thing we'd had to a real vacation in over ten years," she later told friends.

Only defending champ Byron Nelson was exempt from the PGA's grueling thirty-six-hole Monday and Tuesday qualifier, a procedure in place since the inception of the tournament in 1916, and on the first day of match play reigning British Open champion Snead and his U.S. Open counterpart Lloyd Mangrum were both unceremoniously booted out. Nelson breezed through his first two days of matches, reaching the third round with impressive winning margins of 8 and 7, and 3 and 2, while Hogan struggled against a hard-slugging but virtually unknown club pro named Charles Weismer, taking his opening match by a relatively slim margin of 2 and 1.

After demolishing Art Bell 5 and 4 in the morning of his third round, Ben subsequently walloped William Heinlein and Frank Moore by similar wide margins to reach the thirty-six-hole semifinal match against his old friend Jimmy Demaret, at which point, playing his eleventh match of the week, Hogan produced another unearthly sequence of 33-32-31, ending the match, 10 and 9.

One Associated Press reporter compared the lopsided victory to the night Joe Louis knocked out John Henry Lewis, the heavyweight champion's one-eyed and elderly best friend, and others not so politely berated Bantam Ben for humiliating maybe his closest pal on tour. "Hogan," wrote Lawton Carver of the Independent News Service, "is the most ruthless, most cold-blooded and the least compassionate of golf foemen. He doesn't merely want to beat you. He wants to trample you underfoot."

The Bob Hope of tournament golf took it all in stride, though.

"Hey, Jimmy," one of the scribes said. "What was the turning point in the match with Ben?"

Dapper Demaret smiled lazily and drawled, "Ten o'clock this morning, boys. When the match started."

Another reporter wondered if his "best friend in golf" had said anything to him during their punishing encounter.

"Yes," Demaret deadpanned. "You're away."

The next morning it was Porky Oliver's turn to face golf's most intimidating figure. Affectionately called "Pork Chops" by his fellows pros, owing to his propensity for chowing down on plates of steak and spaghetti and a playing weight that wildly fluctuated between 200 and 270 pounds, Ed Oliver had been the first of the big-name pros to be drafted by the military and once offended—or delighted—a couple of hundred patrons of an important tournament by suddenly reclining on his side on the far edge of a putting green with his back mysteriously turned to the gallery. Questioned later about the bizzare maneuver, Oliver grinned sheepishly and admitted it was the only way he could think of to discreetly answer the call of nature and not have to expose himself to such a classy crowd.

In contrast to the gray and buttoned-up Hogan, Pork Chops was a friendly ape of a man who dressed himself almost as clownishly as Demaret did in his canary yellow polos and billowing maroon pantaloons. But as Ben knew from painful experience, there was nothing the least bit funny about Oliver's tournament game. He was prone to patches of brilliant play and putting streaks that could knock the breath out of you. Five years before at the Western Open of 1941, for instance, Ben finished the tournament with a three-stroke lead over the field, not unreasonably assuming he'd won, only to see Oliver come blazing home with a back-nine 28 to beat him by a stroke with 275.

Coming to the PGA finale, Porky also had momentum. With one lengthy stroke of his magical putter in the quarterfinals, after all, he'd dispatched Nelson, the tournament's reigning champ, the oddsmakers' favorite, and the gallery's runaway sentimental choice. Hogan understood that if his game and mental concentration weren't their sharpest ever, he could easily be Pork Chops's next victim.

Amusingly to some, the thirty-six-hole final pitted golf's lightest and heaviest circuit stars directly against each other, 220 pounds versus 137 pounds, respectively, clownish red against corporate gray, japing jester against somber would-be king of golf. In the morning circuit, Pork Chops's amazing touch with the flatstick put him 3 up by the lunch break. Hogan and his wife retreated to a quiet corner of the club dining room, where he ate some chicken broth and dry toast and drank a glass of chilled ginger ale (Ben believed cold ginger ale helped clear his sinuses, which often kicked up in late summer) and then spent nearly forty-five minutes before the afternoon match got under way silently rapping putts on the practice green.

After a season filled with such major disappointments, some observers felt another Hogan collapse might well be imminent—the set of Hogan's jaw, one witness recalled, was more severe than he'd ever seen it, his silence almost like that of a man grittily headed to the executioner's block. More likely, what they were witnessing was a cocooning of his formidable powers of concentration that rivaled his mindset at Pinehurst six years previously, a steeling of his will to finish off the tournament the way he knew a major championship had to be won.

In the afternoon, amid fluttering late summer breezes, Hogan's putter sprang to life, and he blistered Portland's opening nine by shooting 30 and leapfrogging 2 up over Oliver with nine holes to play. In the end, it was the lumbering Pork Chops who ran out of both stamina and magic. Ben nailed three birdies over the next five holes, four of which he won. The match ended on hole 32, with yet another Hogan birdie. After starting the round three down, Hogan won 6 and 4. Through fourteen holes, he stood a dizzying eight under par, one of the strongest finishes ever recorded in a PGA final.

Ben Hogan had finally won a major championship.

At the presentation of the Wanamaker Cup, Hogan stood erect and regal in his tailored gray blazer, his silk necktie perfectly knotted, not a single wisp of his gleaming, black, water-combed hair out of place. Next to him, sheepishly dangling a cigarette in his half-cupped hands, wearing an open-necked shirt over a wrinkled two-tone travel jacket that looked as if it might have been recently slept in, Porky Oliver grinned amiably and looked damned grateful to have the ordeal over with.

"It's impossible to explain how much this means to me," Hogan said to the fans and assembled reporters at the ceremony, momentarily falling into one of his customary difficult silences. He cleared his throat and added, "So I'll just say thank you to the PGA and my wife, Valerie."

His eyes widened a fraction and slid around the room until they located her standing next to Bob Hudson, the Oregon fruit baron who would pick up the entire tab on the travel expenses of the British Ryder Cup team and host them at this same Portland Country Club that fall when the famous biennial matches resumed. As usual, Valerie was dressed like a million bucks, beautifully turned out in a smart summer outfit with a corsage of roses on her lapel, flowers Ben had delivered to her at their hotel before coming to the club that morning. Far too shy to utter a response, Valerie merely smiled, blushed slightly, and nodded.

With that, the pressmen peppered Ben with questions about his drubbing of Porky, the relief of getting the major jinx off his back at last, his plans for the future, his goals for 1947.

"Easy, boys," Hogan said with a small laugh at one point, smiling, for once relishing the attention given to a major championship winner. They watched as he casually lit a cigarette and dutifully scribbled as he explained that he was tired but relieved to finally have a "national title." He said a few gracious words about Porky Oliver and remarked on what a difficult test the PGA was for anybody to win.

Then, after taking a few more questions and answering them with thoughtful replies, rather abruptly, he politely excused himself and went to collect his golf shoes from his locker. Some of the reporters thought it was another classic Hogan put-off. "Vintage Ben," grumbled a midwestern veteran of Hogan's terse interview routines who understood the significance of the moment and hoped to get something beyond the winner's standard clichés. "Another rebuff by golf's frigid midget."

In fact, though he failed to explain it as the reason for his hasty departure, an important phone call had been placed through to Fort Worth from the club secretary's office. Someone recalled Ben massaging his eyes as he took the call, either from fatigue or an emotion he didn't feel comfortable ever letting loose at a golf tournament.

It was Mama Hogan calling from Fort Worth, just to say how proud she was of him.

BEN HOGAN finally had his *official* major title to go with his unofficial national championship, and by the time he strode briskly into the corporate meeting room at Chicago's somber Bismarck Hotel to face the PGA Executive Committee over the demands of the circuit players for complete tour autonomy, on November 15, exactly three months after putting his hands around the Wanamaker Trophy, he'd also won four of the remaining seven tournaments on his schedule for that year, including another North and South Championship. In total, he'd concluded 1946 with thirteen wins and the most prize money any pro golfer had ever won, a record $43,212.

For the record, he had been second six times, third three times, and no worse than seventh in five other events. In other words, in more than half the tournaments he'd entered, Hogan either won or just missed winning.

In light of these accomplishments, many already considered Ben's blitz of the revived professional Tour, with its full fields and competition of unprecedented quality, at least the equal of Nelson's astonishing feat just one year before. As Hogan consort and golf writer Dan Jenkins has accurately noted, his remarkable tally for the year included the Western Open and North and South Championship, venerable tournaments many considered major championships in those days. "But for those two three-putt greens," Jenkins speculates, "Hogan might well have won five majors in that single year of '46. Yeah, five. So what would it have been called, the Grandest Slam?"

Whatever else was true about his stunning performance in the first full year back from war, Ben Hogan had clearly reclaimed golf's summit ground from his departing Glen Garden rival and maybe really was finally the "King of Golf."

With pro golf gaining fans and civic sponsors every day, the most enticing question for many to contemplate—what the boys back in Portland really wanted to know from the reluctant new PGA champion—was, who could possibly stop Hogan from winning everything of importance for the foreseeable future?

Nelson was gone, and Snead was coming on strong (he won six times in '46, including the British Open at St. Andrews) despite a remarkable penchant for blowing big tournaments, particularly National Opens, in creative ways. Even if he dressed himself like a human stoplight and clowned around when he ought to be practicing, Jimmy Demaret's game and tempo were for the ages—his was one of the sharpest games in golf. Jimmy already had one Masters and would soon have a couple of more green jackets in his closet.

And as events at Canterbury illustrated, Lloyd Mangrum was obviously now a major force to be reckoned with too, as were Porky Oliver, Dutch Harrison, Vic Ghezzi, and the fine Winged Foot club pro Claude Harmon. Herman Barron and George Fazio (whose swing was so infectiously rhythmic that Hogan sometimes sought him out for practice rounds) were guys who could juice up a scoreboard at any given moment. And even wily old vets like Paul

Runyan, Johnny Bulla, and Jug McSpaden were still around, always a threat to go low. But realistically, beyond Snead, Demaret, and Mangrum, there didn't seem to be anyone on or near the top tier—or on the horizon—who could match Hogan's intensity and performance standards, week to week.

As he faced the PGA execs at the Bismarck, Hogan himself saw the intrinsic danger of this situation, a problem he believed only bolstered his cause for tournament autonomy, the primary reason he'd come to cold Chicago on an airplane in November.

"There's a big need for young blood—it's wide open for those who can make the grade—but that need isn't being filled," Hogan warned in an article written for Detroit's *Free Press* several days after making his points to the PGA powers. As he bluntly warned, if something wasn't done to address simmering wounds and resentments, new stars and promising prospects would either stay put in the amateur ranks or retreat into safer club jobs. To give tournament golf the boost it needed and ensure the pro game's continued growth and popular appeal, Hogan insisted, the Tour's players needed—demanded—their very own organization.

"If you don't do this," he predicted flatly, sounding remarkably like his hero Gene Sarazen, "you're likely to soon have one hell of a civil war on your hands."

The clubmen of the PGA listened respectfully, clenching their teeth behind poker expressions. In the end, as Ed Dudley predicted they would, the committee fell in line and reluctantly proposed to establish the Tournament Bureau—a self-governing operation overseen by the PGA but essentially operated by the circuit travelers themselves.

Boston public relations man Fred Corcoran was appointed the de facto Tour manager of the new "players' organization," and though no one was entirely certain how the brave new experiment in tournament self-governance was meant to work—especially since no legally binding document to that effect was struck—for the moment at least the uprising among the palace guard was quelled.

With numerous issues remaining unresolved, the divisions between home pros and tour players widened over the next few years. Just weeks into the '47 season, for example, a frustrated Johnny Bulla sucker-punched Fred Corcoran, and Dick Metz, another veteran, slugged Corcoran on his Irish kisser, prompting the tournament manager to threaten lawsuits against both men. Hogan himself was not immune from these erupting affrays; he was accused, for example, of being the source behind an elaborate "poison pen" letter-writing campaign to oust Ed Dudley from the organization, a charge Hogan vehemently denied.

In any case, as peace broke out and prosperity spread through the heartland, the groundwork was being laid for a much larger and more comprehensive palace revolt that would occur a couple of decades further along the fairway, led by two gilded malcontents called Palmer and Nicklaus—a threatened rebellion that led directly, in turn, to the formal creation of a separate corporate governing entity called the PGA Tour.

Thus, in many ways, it could be argued, though he made himself few friends inside the cloistered ranks of the professional game's old guard and governing elite—largely underscoring his reputation for being one tough little SOB when it came to defending his turf both on and off the golf course— the year of Hogan's long-awaited major breakthrough also serves as a working birthdate for the modern professional golf tour.

EIGHT

Hogan's Alley

Wɪᴛʜ ᴀ Wᴀɴᴀᴍᴀᴋᴇʀ Tʀᴏᴘʜʏ in his hands and Byron Nelson officially down on the farm, many predicted that the expanded tournament season for 1947 would be a cakewalk for Ben Hogan, that he would leave
Snead, Demaret, and Mangrum to sweep up the crumbs.

Playing straight into Ben's steel-banded hands, as it were, the Tour's first
stop in early January was the Los Angeles Open, the season's opening event,
once again staged at the visually commanding Riviera Country Club at the
mouth of Santa Monica Canyon in luscious Pacific Palisades, the site where
Nelson beat him by a whisker in 1946 and, as it happened, one of Ben's favorite
teeing grounds on earth.

Hogan loved everything about playing in California in general, and in Tinseltown in particular, once commenting to *Time*'s bureau chief there that anyone who chose not to live in California was simply a "victim of circumstance."
Hogan's sister, Princess, and her husband, Doc Ditto, were unapologetic boosters of life in the City of Angels; southern California's warm dry weather suited

Overleaf: Ben Hogan, Los Angeles Open, 1950 *(Corbis)*

Ben's body chemistry; and rubbing elbows with movie stars and their ilk never failed to thrill the small-town Dublin boy. Still very much alive inside him was Henny Bogan, the solemn little guy who used to go off to the movies with his big sister and brother Bubber on hot Texas evenings, plunking down a nickel to sit on a hard bench and stare wide-eyed at thundering Lionel Barrymore or funny Charlie Chaplin.

During his tournament visit to L.A. in 1941, in fact, more to satisfy his childhood curiosity about screencraft than to explore any career alternatives, Hogan submitted to a major studio screen test. His broad tooth-filled smile and angular features photographed very well indeed—someone thought he looked a lot like tough-guy cowboy Alan Ladd—but the romance proved largely visual. Hogan's reserved demeanor and carefully modulated voice (bearing only the faintest traces of a Texas twang) were fine for making short instructional films à la Bobby Jones or brief scripted guest appearances on popular television shows (as he did on Ed Sullivan's show and others), but as one low-level studio exec was supposed to have chortled to his studio boss, "Watching Hogan try to act is about as exciting as watching Tarzan try to play golf."

Even so, as his sports star gained brightness, with each call he paid on Tinseltown Hogan was deeply pleased to find himself the object of almost fawning admiration by the biggest names in show biz. Bing Crosby and Bob Hope were close friends from many years of fellowship at the intimate Crosby clambake and numerous wartime exhibitions, and more than once Ben and Jimmy Demaret had slipped away to Bing's California ranch for a little hunting and fishing with Der Bingle. But now a host of other famed Hollywood tough guys, like Randolph Scott, Howard Hughes, and Bill Holden, were almost tongue-tied in Hogan's presence, invariably making themselves "available" for a game at Bel-Air Country Club whenever news dropped that the Iceman was back in town.

In Hollywood terms, golf's toughest little competitor had an unmistakable aura of self-possession, a captivating presence that prompted Bel-Air member Katharine Hepburn (who lived off the 14th fairway and insisted on playing from the men's tees) to invite Ben and Valerie to dinner at the Brown Derby. On one occasion, during a caddie fund-raiser that Hope, Crosby, and Hogan hosted at the "Country Club of the Stars" during one of his regular visits in the late '40s, middle-handicapper Jimmy Stewart followed Hogan around the course like an adoring schoolboy, marveling at his action. "I've never seen anyone do what he can do," Stewart politely gushed afterward. "Ben tops everybody."

"Hogan liked movie people," Paul Runyan observed. "He understood them and they understood him. I think he felt he could let his hair down among Crosby and Hope and the rest of them."

As for Hogan's growing tensions with the press and his determination to keep people out of his private affairs, more than one observer saw an uncanny resemblance between golf's most elusive star and Hollywood's original Frigid Midget, Humphrey Bogart, who once testily fired back at his critics for repeatedly dodging their in-depth interviews, "The only thing I owe the public is a good performance."

Even before Ben put his stamp on the place, Riviera's divinely shaped 245 acres were something special to him. Prior to flooding that devastated the course and forced several holes to be altered in 1939, Hogan considered the George Thomas–designed layout to be one of the top four or five in all of America—and it was still one of his favorites "after the flood."

Thomas, the nation's preeminent course architect, came out of retirement, the legend goes, from his hybrid roses and luxury yacht in the late '20s to create a 7,020-yard masterpiece that severely tested both the strength and shot-making moxie of all comers, a heavily bunkered, wildly varied, *barranca*-laced elysium so damned unforgiving it either made golf champions—or broke them in half.

At the inaugural event in 1929, Walter Hagen, golf's most celebrated showman, got unceremoniously roughed up by Riviera's devilish poa annua greens and sandy grottoes. He finished the tournament with a humiliating score and advised sponsors he probably wouldn't be back anytime soon. A year later, he returned to give his West Coast fans a charge but lasted only eight holes into the second round before withdrawing and hiking back to the majestic hilltop clubhouse for the aid and comfort of a double whiskey.

For the 1947 edition of the Los Angeles Open championship, listed just ahead of Snead and Demaret as the prohibitive favorites, Hogan began the tournament with a workmanlike 70, good enough for second place behind Toney Penna and a former U.S. Amateur Champion, Marvin (Bud) Ward. The concluding three rounds, however, belonged entirely to Ben Hogan.

The Hawk's blistering 66 in round two tied the course record, a marvelous exhibition of controlled shotmaking that included seven birdies and two bogies. As Riviera historian Geoff Shackleton notes, Hogan opened the long tournament season with commanding authority despite a host of relatively modest physical challenges—unexpected twitches, new aches and pains that came with growing older, plus a mystifying tendency to suddenly run out of steam. Notes Shackleton: "This was the same man who stopped twice on the No. 13 tee in the practice round because of a horrible twitch in his shoulder."

Although no one but Valerie really knew it, Hogan's slight, thirty-four-year-old body was beginning to let him know it had been through two decades of punishing physical abuse, in particular a regimen of practice that placed enormous stress on his joints and muscles on a daily basis. Though he looked like a poster boy for the virtues of clean living and staying in shape, Hogan was dealing regularly with painful spasms in his shoulders and fatigue that sometimes crept into his upper legs near the latter stages of a tournament, tell-tale signs that age was catching up and his tournament pace would have to slow down if he meant to go on for long.

After his superb steady play in rounds two and three, the outcome of the '47 Los Angles Open was really never in doubt. Toney Penna, the only player within striking distance, made a brief run at Hogan in the closing stages of the final round, but Ben finished with a 72 to beat Penna by three strokes, a total of 280. It was the Hawk's second L.A. title and his first win at gorgeous Riviera.

"Hogan is picking up where *both* he and Byron Nelson left off," wrote one of the city's top sports columnists. "The only real question is, can anyone catch him now?"

But they did. As popular expectations of Ben soared, stoked by such fish-wrapper encomiums, the remainder of 1947 became, in due course, one long personal disappointment—and silent physical ordeal—for Hogan. Twenty days after L.A., he won at Phoenix, where he snapped the shaft of the beloved MacGregor driver that Byron Nelson had given him at Pinehurst nearly a decade before. He quickly found a replacement and managed to win the tournament with it, but he explained some years later that it took nearly a decade of searching to find a driver "that felt as good as that one did."

A month after Phoenix, he teamed with Demaret to win the Miami Four-Ball, but one week later, up U.S. Highway 1 in Jacksonville—the prelude to that year's Masters—Hogan suffered one of the most embarrassing moments of his career. On a par-3 hole of just 140 yards, he dumped his tee shot into a small pond protecting the green. Four times he attempted to slash the ball out of the water before having to lift and drop. Then he flubbed his pitch shot and watched with visible contempt as his ball trickled back into the drink. He lifted and dropped again, got the ball on the green, and two-putted for *eleven*. (For the record, he followed up this embarrassing disaster with a pair of spectacular birdies.)

Other satisfying wins came back home at Colonial (his second) in mid-May, at Chicago in late June, at the Inverness Round Robin in mid-July, and finally at the unofficial World Championship of Golf (also in Chicago) that September.

But whether it was the new driver, the growing number of aches and pains, or something far more private in nature bugging him, Hogan's major championship campaigns were a collective bust. The Masters he so hoped to finally win was essentially a three-way horse race between Nelson (who always took his clubs out of mothballs for the Masters), Demaret, and a hardworking amateur named Frank Stranahan, a tempestuous Champion Spark Plugs heir who lifted free weights, lived off his daddy's money, and practiced nearly as tirelessly as Hogan.

There, getting off to a poor start—75—Hogan never found his stride and was thus never a serious threat to be measured for his first green jacket. Demaret, on the other hand, the crown prince of golf and that season's early money winner who'd already won three times in eleven starts, opened with 69 and together with dental school graduate Cary Middlecoff shared the lead at four under after thirty-six holes. In the third round, Jimmy pounded half his drives into the pines but preserved his lead by fabulously one-putting ten greens, good enough to give him a three-shot bulge over Byron and five over young Stranahan, the volatile golf scion Demaret loved to needle about his weights, skin-tight muscleman polo shirts, and clusters of admiring schoolgirls trailing him wherever he went. That fall, *Collier's* magazine dubbed Stranahan "Golf's Bad Boy" and described, among other things, how he swaggered around the golf course like a teenage hot-rod idol, generally behaving like the poor little rich boy he was. As a result of his unflattering exposure, Frankie's angry papa canceled $300,000 worth of advertising with the magazine.

On Masters Sunday, dressed head to toe in bright canary yellow, smiling pleasantly at galleries as if he didn't have a care in the world, and periodically humming big band standards as he traipsed along Augusta's treacherous back nine, Demaret cobbled together 71 to beat a faltering Nelson ("The fact is," Byron wrote in his memoirs, "I didn't care anymore . . . and the Masters in '47 showed me once again that I was definitely through with the tour") and fend off hard-charging Stranahan by two, earning a coveted second green jacket for his rainbow wardrobe.

Hogan finished in a tie for fourth place, irrelevantly at 284.

Six weeks later, Hogan's uninspired performance at the U.S. Open at St.

Louis Country Club—not a particularly stern test of the shotmaker's art—was even more baffling and revealing to some fans of the Hawk.

While Open venues like Colonial and Canterbury stretched to nearly 7,000 yards and challenged players on nearly every shot, St. Louis was your standard sweetheart country club track scarcely covering 6,500 yards with only a handful of hazards to speak of and wide-open driving lanes, a circumstance that permitted thirteen players to break par 71 in the opening round alone.

Among them were Sam Snead and Bobby Locke, the apple-jowled South African who dressed in old-fashioned knickers and four-in-hand neckties and wielded a wooden-shafted blade putter with such lethal unorthodoxy—first opening the blade on the backswing, then nearly hooking it closed with a wristy flip of the wrists as the blade came through the ball—that Hogan, ever the student of technique and something of a wristy thumper himself, was prompted to shake his head and marvel: "Locke holes everything he ever looks at."

Ben was also among those who broke par on day one—he shot 70, with thirty-five putts—but lost valuable ground with a shoddy 75 on day two. This poor effort didn't go unnoticed by the working press and seemed to support a startling revelation conveyed by powerful wire columnist Oscar Fraley on the eve of the golf tournament.

"Hogan to Call It Quits," read the banner over Oscar Fraley's blockbuster.

Ben Hogan, the miniature Irishman who ranks with the all time golfing giants, has just about reached the point today where he is ready to retire from tournament play. Hogan, like many of his illustrious predecessors, is deathly tired of the competitive fairways and greens. Others who reached that breaking point where they actually hated the game were Byron Nelson and Henry Picard—and they didn't hang around long afterwards.

The bantam Benny is hanging on because he wants one more crack at the U.S. Open and wants to try to defend his PGA title. After those two are over he is expected to say adieu, even though he won't admit it now.

Maybe most worrying of all to some longtime Hawk watchers, Hogan himself was conspicuously silent on any post-Open plans, taking pains to neither deny nor confirm Fraley's stunning assertion. After play got under way, not even his closest pals on tour had the nerve to directly ask Ben about Fraley's column.

Ironically, during this same National Open, for one of the first times ever, Ben was handsomely paid to produce his own account of the tournament in the form of a "personal diary" for the *St. Louis Star-Tribune* (which a staff reporter at the paper actually assembled from interviews following each round). Maddeningly, he gave no hint of either his majors doldrums or his future plans vis-à-vis tournament golf. With the care of a Hollywood publicist, reviewing every word before it was typeset and printed, he talked only about the relatively easy conditions players faced in St. Louis, the advance of beastly hot weather and its likely effects, and his belief that Ralph Guldahl's record of 281 would surely fall before a champion was crowned late Saturday afternoon. Among reporters he got along with, owing primarily to the depth in which he studied both Open sites and his fellow competitors' games, Hogan had a solid track record of predicting winning totals. Tellingly, he rarely put a name with the total, though he sometimes mentioned players whose games he felt suited a particular course. Fearing a jinx, he studiously avoided ever mentioning himself in this regard.

In the morning round of that Open Saturday, Ben seemed to briefly recover his form of a year before by carving out a one under 70. But after lunch, showing unmistakable signs of fatigue due to the damp waves of midwestern heat—at one point pausing, removing his cap, and massaging his back—he tumbled back to 74 and finished the event disappointingly tied for sixth place.

If Hogan's game that afternoon appeared to wilt under the layers of stifling heat or some other form of deflation, Slammin' Sam's appeared to be peaking at precisely the right moment to finally end his so-called Open jinx.

Burning a hole in the back of the Slammer's mind was the bitter memory of the way he had played his final round at Canterbury the previous summer. Starting his final loop just one stroke off the lead, Sam had missed nearly half the fairways that afternoon, putted atrociously, and staggered home with a ruinous 81, his worst Open score ever, yet another inexplicable collapse.

In St. Louis, however, Sam was encouraged by vast and devoted galleries who believed their man's velvety swing and homespun grace made him the natural foil to the faltering Hogan. And as the Open edged toward its finale, Sam didn't disappoint them; he was right in the thick of contention. With nine holes left to play on that hot Open Saturday afternoon, though, a twenty-nine-year-old Virginia club pro named Lew Worsham seemed to take command of the tournament with 33 on the outward leg of his final nine. Lew, the older brother of Arnold Palmer's future college roommate, slipped to 38 on the back side but finished at level par—a 280 total most observers felt would hold up even with the relatively easy playing conditions. At the very least, Hogan was once again cannily accurate in his forecast that Guldahl's record would fall.

Coming along half an hour behind Worsham, however, after draining a birdie on 15, Sam caught fire and pulled even with the clubhouse leader. Snead's rowdy followers tumbled along after their man with war whoops and cavalry shouts, trying to cheer him home to his long-overdue victory when he made par at the difficult 16th and groaning like a Trojan chorus when he made a foolish bogey on the short par-4 that followed.

After ripping off a 300-yard drive that found center-cut of the final fairway, Sam put his approach shot eighteen feet from the cup and boldly thumped his ball into the hole for a birdie that forced the National Open into overtime. Sam's fans were beside themselves with joy. For the second year in a row, the National Open championship would be decided in a Sunday play-off, and their man was on a roll!

The next afternoon, Snead was on top of his game for the first nine holes as well, sauntering out in a cool 34 that included brilliant birdies at 12 and 15 and eased the Slammer two strokes ahead of his virtually unknown opponent. With three holes left to negotiate, Sam looked fully in control of his destiny. "The only person who could really hope to beat Sam," one prominent wire scribe recounted devilishly afterward, "was Sam."

Then, at 16, Worsham made a meandering twenty-footer for birdie and Sam missed his attempt to halve. One stroke up now, two to play. Both men made poor drives at 17, but Lew reached the green in two and Sam missed wide; he chipped poorly, then failed to coax his six-footer into the cup for par and tried not to hear the demons whispering, "Here we go again," as he proceeded solemnly toward the final tee.

The stunning news of Hogan's predicted retirement had generated most of the early tournament buzz, but St. Louis's week in the national spotlight was memorable for plenty of other petty distractions and flaring controversies too, including loud complaints from numerous contestants that first-round challenger Bobby Locke should have been immediately disqualified when word got out that he improperly cleaned his ball on the green during sectional qualifying. (This was a violation under USGA rules, to be sure, but a procedure commonly permitted under PGA play; so many other pros were guilty of this breach, in fact, that the USGA was forced to temporarily relax the rule, prompting Locke to surmise, not inaccurately, that the slight had been personally directed at him, the American game's top "foreigner.") Moreover, several players neglected to remember the USGA's irksome fourteen-club rule and were summarily booted from the playing field.

As Snead might have put it, all of that was merely wind out of a duck's rump compared to what happened on the final hole of his Sunday play-off with Lew Worsham. For a change, the Open's conclusion was anything but anticlimactic.

The players reached the final green all square, and as Sam took his position and prepared to tap a short birdie putt down the slope into the cup for a par that would give him the lead in the one championship he wanted more than all others, Worsham, whose ball was also about two feet below the hole, suddenly cleared his throat and called out, "Wait a minute! Are you sure you're away?"

Sam stepped back, glowering.

Murmurs of surprise rippled among the 6,000 spectators packed around the green, and USGA rulesman Ike Grainger was summoned to formally measure distances with a steel tape and determine whose turn, in fact, it was to play.

Sam walked to the side of the green, shaking his head in disbelief, clearly seething at the interruption, trying desperately to maintain his focus. All he had to do, he told himself, was somehow get that damned two-foot putt down the slope into the cup and Worsham would be forced to make his on top of it.

After several agonizing moments, Grainger found that Sam's ball lay thirty and a half inches shy of the hole; Worsham's ball was twenty-nine and a half inches. Sam was away, after all—and not one bit happy about a stunt he and his followers forever viewed as pure gamesmanship.

Once again he took his stance over his ball and finally nudged his ball down the slope—a hair too gently, as it turned out. Failing to hold its line, Snead's ball turned away from the hole and stopped two inches below the cup. His emotionally drained followers released one final Greek chorus of sighs and groans for their man's awful luck.

Worsham, taking almost no time, stepped up and briskly rolled home his par putt to give him 69 to Sam's 70. The extraordinary Open jinx had struck again, and Sam, visibly devastated, could barely bring himself to shake Worsham's extended hand.

"There's never been any doubt in my mind that it was something Lew did to try and rattle me," Snead said one day while playing a round with a friend on his beloved Old White Course at the Greenbrier. "To be honest, there's not a day goes by I don't think about those lost Opens. Especially *that* one. St. Louis is the one maybe hurt the most. In my mind, I reckon I've made that damn putt ten thousand times."

As the peculiar injustices of golf go, the sport's all-time leading tournament winner would have at least four more excellent opportunities in his career to exorcise his Open ghosts and finally snag the one major championship he wanted most. "I figured it up once," Sam said, watching his golden retriever lope along one of Old White's creeks. "And I figured out that if I'd shot six-nine in the final round, I would have won *seven* National Opens." He shook his head, smiled ruefully, and added, "Hell, I'd give up half my wins for just *one* of them Opens—particularly that one at St. Louis."

Hogan, he said, went out of his way to commiserate with him.

DUE TO A scheduling quirk, the National Open and the PGA Championship were played that year within days rather than weeks of each other. Ben was knocked out in the first round of a PGA field by Toney Penna, the field boss of MacGregor's playing advisory staff, in a round that was so silently antagonistic that one newsman joked he thought it might actually come to blows. Privately, Penna didn't care for Hogan's cold and obsessive ways (translation: Ben constantly complained that the clubs MacGregor sent him never fit his specs and had to be "worked on" before they were "fit for playing with"), and Ben had never quite gotten over the slight of being considered second-class to Byron in MacGregor's pecking order of stars.

Coming close on the heels of his St. Louis flop and Oscar Fraley's bombshell, Hogan's abrupt dismissal from the PGA party, at any rate, prompted a new flurry of speculations and rumors that the Hawk was prepared to officially retire and follow Byron out to pasture grass.

True to form, Hogan offered no comment on the poor quality of his play or his future tournament plans.

Weeks later, ironically, on the eve of the Columbus Invitational, it was Valerie Hogan of all people who agreed to grant a rare sit-down interview at her hotel on the subject of life with Ben, travel in golf, and his widely rumored impending retirement from the tournament beat.

Among other juicy tidbits Valerie revealed to the society editor from the Columbus paper, she and Ben had talked a great deal about having children but "agreed that a golfer's life wasn't suitable for children." She revealed that Ben was keen to own a ranch and might even tend his own small herd of cattle someday.

"We haven't had a permanent home since we got married almost twelve years ago," she explained, noting that living in hotel rooms and the constant travel kept her from indulging her "love of cooking and homemaking." On the plus side, though, Valerie revealed, she and Ben had been planning their dream home for more than a year. "In two or three years," she explained a bit vaguely, "we'd like to build a small home in the country, just outside Fort Worth, with horses and things like that."

The resulting wire story only fueled broad speculation that Hogan, as Oscar Fraley predicted in St. Louis, would indeed soon hang up his sticks à la Byron and pursue other business interests—his new instruction book, *Power Golf,* was about to hit the shelves, and there was talk of a franchise of Hogan golf instruction centers in the works.

Briefly back in Hershey, packing up for the three-day train ride back to Portland, Oregon, to play in the Invitational at a course he greatly enjoyed— the site of the forthcoming Ryder Cup that autumn—Ben bristled when a member and casual acquaintance at the club where he regularly practiced (and where he declined to play with members) asked him if there was any truth to all the rumors that he was quitting the Tour. "People love to talk," he snapped. "But when I decide to retire, you'll know."

And yet, after teaming with Demaret to take another victory at the Inverness Four-Ball in mid-July, just days before Valerie sat down with the Columbus society writer and spilled the beans about cattle and dream houses, Hogan gave a tiny glimpse of where his thoughts were running by hinting he might not be returning to Inverness, an event that was historically one of his favorite and more successful (if physically demanding) tournaments on tour.

Furthermore, during the six weeks that immediately followed upon these scenes of hints and denial, the quality of his tournament play noticeably slipped another notch—he was ninth at Columbus, sixteenth at the Portland Invitational, fifteenth at the important Western Open. It wasn't until George May's gaudy World Championship in late September that he finally won again, pocketing $7,000 for just two rounds of work.

Afterward, Hogan granted only a brief ten-minute interview to the press before bolting for a train home to Fort Worth where he planned several weeks of rest and practice at Colonial to get ready for the Ryder Cup matches back at Portland Country Club. "So, Ben, is this going to be it?" one of the reporters in Chicago asked him. "The Ryder Cup, I mean?"

Ben gave his questioner a tight, mirthless smile, as unrevealing as any sphinx.

"Tell you what, boys. You'll know when I know," he replied, sounding only slightly irritated by the constancy of the question. "Or shortly thereafter."

• • •

THE RYDER CUP was desperately trying to recover its prestige and footing from the first-ever American victory on British soil back in 1937, a point at which the cup's fate had been left precariously dangling when competition was suspended indefinitely owing to an engulfing world war.

It's not stretching things to say that a whole new generation of American golf fans had never even heard of the biennial team classic begun at Worchester Country Club in 1927 by English seed merchant Sam Ryder to foster goodwill between the top professionals of America and Britain. (With the likes of Hagen, Sarazen, Wild Bill Mehlhorn, and Jim Turnesa, the Americans won the inaugural event handily, 9 and ½ to 2 and ½.)

Thanks to Oregon fruit tycoon Bob Hudson, however, new life was breathed into a venerable event on the verge of irrelevancy. Hudson not only offered his home club of Portland CC as a venue for the resumed competition but magnanimously offered to pick up all of the impoverished British squad's traveling expenses.

Also, in a move aimed at bolstering the public's interest in the affair, for the first time ever beginning in 1947 Ryder Cup teams were selected through a point system that gave winners of the National Open and the PGA one hundred points, respectively; the Masters champion, ninety-five; the Western Open, eighty; and all other PGA tournament events seventy points toward qualifying for the matches.

Things were proceeding smoothly until a controversy flared on the eve of the British team's arrival.

In a scathing letter to the Advisory Committee of the sponsoring PGA, journeyman Vic Ghezzi bitterly complained that the PGA had been intimidated by one man and ceded responsibility for determining Ryder Cup points entirely to him. That man was Ben Hogan.

Ghezzi contended that Hogan had discriminated against him by "eliminating certain invitational meets in which I had done well" and further charged that Hogan used his considerable influence with tournament powers to ease prohibitions against exactly the kind of groove-filing on wedges that Ghezzi himself was accused of earlier in the year—a procedure that put more backspin on balls and gave them added "bite" on slick greens.

Compounding matters was lingering ill will over British captain Henry Cotton's testy remark a month prior to the start of the affair that the American PGA was "violating the spirit of competition" by permitting the widespread discretionary use of "winter rules" in many of its top sanctioned tournaments, a policy that permitted contestants under certain extreme weather conditions to lift and clean and sometimes place their balls on fairways and greens. Like most Brits, Cotton was old school on this subject, a total proponent of "play as it lies."

When the Irish and English players disembarked from the *Queen Mary* and wended their way west on a train to Portland, however, Cotton attempted for the sake of harmony to downplay his earlier comments, asking only for "a good blow" and a "bit of British Open weather" to aid the visitors' cause.

As modern British golf historian Derek Lawrenson points out, they would need it. Tournament play in Britain had suffered mightily from being suspended for nearly a decade, a time during which many top-flight golf courses were left abandoned or turned into seaside fortifications. Many of Britain's most promising golf prospects went into military service and never swung a golf club for the duration, while others saw their games go to seed from lack of formal competition. In America, by contrast, even though the Tour operated on a vastly reduced level and many of its stars were absent, a number of the country's top golf courses had remained fully functional—used for Red Cross exhibitions and the like—and that, Cotton and others calculated, given the home field advantage, gave the Americans a distinct hand up.

Writing in the *Daily Telegraph*, British journalist Leonard Crawley, who accompanied the English and Irish squad on the train to Oregon as Ghezzi presented his gripes to the PGA board behind closed doors, soberly assessed the American force arrayed against the Brits and felt obliged to inform his readers back home, "This is as good a side as has ever played against Britain, and probably better." Crawley predicted the brave sons of Britain and Ireland would be fortunate to win "four matches out of twelve."

As things developed, they weren't even that lucky.

In an opening foursomes duel, which got under way after the PGA decided to take no action on Ghezzi's charges, Open winner Lew Worsham and Porky Oliver blitzed aging Henry Cotton and Arthur Lees, 10 and 9, while Snead and Mangrum ripped Fred Daly and Charles Ward, 6 and 5. Byron Nelson (playing by special invitation) and Herman Barron beat Dai Rees and Sam King 2 and 1, and captain Ben Hogan and his Inverness sidekick Jimmy Demaret finished two up over Jimmy Adams and Max Faulkner. Day one yielded four points for the Yanks. The rout was effectively on.

Day two was even blacker for the distinguished visitors. The Americans claimed seven singles matches out of eight for the most lopsided win (11 to 1) in Ryder Cup history. One British newspaper described the loss as a "disgraceful low point in British-American sporting relations," while more tempered editorialists in the United Kingdom appreciated the vast challenge their side had faced and used the drubbing to lobby for quick and much-needed improvements in conditions back home. Despite the shellacking, fruit tycoon Hudson spared no expense in entertaining and thanking the losing team, prompting Jimmy Demaret to joke about switching teams for the "free booze and food." Civility and goodwill ended up carrying the day at the Ryder Cup revival.

Obscured by the historic rout and all the accusations and controversies beforehand, a pair of revealing footnotes went all but unnoticed.

On the eve of the start of play, playing captain Hogan noticed that pasty-faced Herman Keiser, the "Missouri Mortician," looked even more down in the dumps than usual. When he asked Herm what was bothering him, the story goes, Keiser blushed and revealed that a girl he'd recently "dated" for a modest fee was suddenly making big trouble for him. Presumably having read about Keiser in the newspapers, she was threatening to go hire a lawyer and claim their brief interlude had really been one of forced intimacy. If she didn't get a thousand dollars fast, Keiser got to the point, she and her lawyer would go to the newspapers and cry rape.

Captain Hogan supposedly opened his wallet and counted out ten one-hundred-dollar bills to Keiser, then instructed him to go clean up his business before it became a distraction to the team, more bad publicity for an event that didn't need any more troubling headlines. When Keiser pointed out that he didn't have the dough to repay Hogan right away, Ben reportedly told him, "Pay me when you can, Herm"—a kindness that recalled Henry Picard's generosity to Hogan a decade before. It was a generosity Keiser talked about for the rest of his life. Ironically, as the drama played out, the sole bright spot for the British team came when Keiser lost in singles 4 and 3 to Sam King.

The other footnote of the revived Ryder Cup concerns Vic Ghezzi's controversial claim that Hogan filed his own wedges to gain extra spin on his balls. When asked directly about Ghezzi's assertion, Ben flatly denied ever filing the face of any of his irons in order to deepen or widen grooves.

In fact, though, he did file his clubs—just not his wedge or any of his irons, as Ghezzi claimed.

When a friend encountered Hogan in the Colonial clubmaking shop one morning around the subsequent Christmas break, two weeks before the Tour returned to Los Angeles for the start of the 1948 season, the Hawk was busy filing the face of his four-wood. "I once saw him doing the same thing," Mike Souchak says. "He was filing the faces of his three- and four-woods, to widen the grooves and give them a little more spin. That wasn't against the rules then, filing woods, and Ben could really make balls stop with his fairway clubs, better than anyone I ever saw. He'd do anything to get an edge inside the rules."

IN THE AFTERMATH of the contentious revival of old Sam Ryder's competition, back home in Texas for the quiet Christmas holidays, hoping to place the disappointing season and its failed major hopes and the pressure of distracting rumors safely behind him, Ben went to see a back specialist in Dallas and put himself through a comprehensive physical examination.

The tests concluded there was absolutely nothing wrong with his back that a little rest and relaxation wouldn't eventually clear up. The pains in his shoulders and neck were diagnosed as stress-related. The doctors prescribed a little aspirin and a lot of time off from the strains of tournament life. They advised him to go hunting or fishing for relaxation, to find some other hobby to briefly divert his attention.

Hogan was not a hobby kind of guy. For two decades every molecule of his being had gone into putting himself through the refiner's fire, transforming himself from a west Texas nobody into the most efficient killing machine ever seen in golf. Telling Ben Hogan to go find a hobby was like suggesting to Humphrey Bogart that he take up community theater for fun.

Even so, he did ramble up to Arkansas to chase a few whitetail deer through the brush with Jimmy Demaret during the holiday break from action. According to Demaret, they drank whiskey and sat by a fire under the stars, giving Demaret the perfect setting to ask Ben directly about the swirling rumors of his retirement and possible health issues.

"You know, Jimmy," Ben surprised his host by saying, "I feel better than I have in years. This break has been just the thing."

According to Demaret, the hunters spotted several trophy deer during their time together in the woods, but neither man brought one home to Texas, and in fact, Hogan never even fired his rifle.

TWO WEEKS LATER, in a stark reversal of his gloomy moods at the National Open and the PGA the previous summer, a positively beaming Ben Hogan showed up at Riviera Country Club in Pacific Palisades.

"I feel fine and the back trouble, whatever it was, is gone completely," he said as he chatted pleasantly with a cluster of deadline chasers from Tinseltown, relaxed and smiling after a morning practice round.

Maybe it was the doctor's verdict or the time away with Jimmy or simply being back in sunny dry California on a golf course he'd come to love that elevated both his energy and his spirits. *Whatever* had been eating at Hogan so powerfully in 1947, the tournament writers took note, appeared to be gone. Many quickly leapt to the conclusion that Ben's refortified attitude had something to do with the Masters and National Open titles still missing from his résumé. He was thirty-five years old, now considered one of the game's "old guard."

Not counting his Hale America National Open win in '42, in the seven National Open appearances he made prior to 1948, Hogan had never finished better than a tie for third place—a paltry showing for a man widely considered to be the best golfer in the world.

His Masters summary during this same period of time was more productive but equally frustrating: seven appearances, six top-ten finishes, two runner-up finishes, but no wins in a golf tournament he loved everything about.

While customers of his new best-selling *Power Golf* combed the pages for clues to the little man's incredible power and unearthly accuracy, anyone who'd watched golf's greatest practitioner perform his craft for any length of time began to understand that the key to fathoming Hogan's success—his real secret, as it were—lay not in the technical jargon of some fractional manipulation of the glide path of the golf club at impact, as his comments and writings on the subject would have you believe, but rather in the rarest combination of an extraordinarily disciplined brain and an undeniable willpower fueled by a fierce survivor instinct to prevail against any odds.

By nature and temperament, Ben Hogan was a friendly, tenderhearted, and highly sentimental man. But only a tiny handful of people knew this about him, a fact he entombed behind the hard shell of work and accomplishment. Friendliness and tenderness wouldn't win him a golf tournament (or much of anything else) in a dog-eat-dog world, a lesson he learned as far back as the Texas & Pacific depot platform. Tournament golf, as he once said, is a ruthless game of mistakes, and his own slavish work ethic was simply the lone bulwark he had against the specter of failure that constantly dogged him, a motivating detail he never felt the slightest bit inclined to reveal or explain to anyone.

The answer to his success—to finally winning the Masters and the National

Open and eventually being able to leave the game knowing he'd done everything he could possibly do to beat his demons—resided where it always had, in the dirt at his feet.

SWEET RIVIERA's dirt yielded up another spectacular win for Hogan that first week of the 1948 season. He toured the course in four beautiful rounds of 68-70-70-67 for a record-breaking 275, nine under par—a feat that would stand for the next quarter-century.

Hogan attributed his sterling play to fast greens and the subtle changes in his swing he'd begun making over the previous year, but he warned reporters not to jump to conclusions and be misled by his record-breaking Riviera performance, particularly as it related to the U.S. Open, which was scheduled to return to Riviera in mid-June.

The summer conditions and traditional punishing rough of the National Open, he predicted, would render Riviera a "very different place," at least six to eight strokes tougher for the eventual winner, he predicted. "Personally," he added, "I think a score of 282 to 284 will win the Open in June." Privately, though, as he confided to Valerie with a coy smile en route to sign copies of his book at Bullocks' Department Store in downtown Los Angeles, he couldn't wait to come back and chase the National Open over a difficult golf course he felt he understood better than anyone.

During his L.A. romp, one of his vanquished fellow pros was overheard in the locker room quipping that Riviera had become "Hogan's Alley," and an L.A. newspaperman took the moniker and ran with it, promptly designating Hogan the man to beat for the National Open of 1948.

By Masters time in April, however, Ben's game seemed to be mysteriously sputtering again. Over the span of six appearances along the tournament trail to Georgia, he'd done no better than winning the team portion of Bing's celebrity pro-am and only mildly challenging for the title at St. Petersburg.

As tradition dictated, Bobby Jones teed off first to open the first round of the twelfth edition of the Masters, the aging legend heading one of the most talented fields in years.

Jones was treated like a god by America's most astute galleries but played dismally (76-81-79-79) and promptly headed straight for the comfort of a padded chair and an iced-down old-fashioned in the locker room immediately following each round.

As players paused to chat and pay homage to golf's most venerated figure,

Bobby, who was forty-six, with a slight paunch and thinning hair, gently complained of soreness and stiffness in his right shoulder, a discomfort he referred to for years simply as "this little crick in the neck," a dark harbinger of things to come.

This would be Jones's final Masters as a competitor.

In another development before the tournament got under way, the most promising amateur since Jones, *Collier's* bad boy Frankie Stranahan, was summarily booted from the course, and his invitation yanked, for alleged repeated violations of the club's rule against hitting more than one ball during a practice round—a charge Stranahan vociferously denied—and for belligerent behavior when confronted by the course superintendent on the matter.

When no players rallied to his cause, Strannie threatened "serious repercussions." He purchased an admission ticket instead and waited around for several days, hoping to plead his case personally with Jones. But the bureaucrats of golf's various governing organizations, who might have interceded in Frank's behalf with either Clifford Roberts or the tournament's celebrated founder, stayed mum, and the wire services downplayed the unpleasant incident, as Roberts requested they do.

When Stranahan finally got his moment with Jones on the eve of play, requesting that he be immediately reinstated to the field, the elder statesman of golf explained that he routinely left all matters of tournament policy up to Cliff Roberts. The matter was closed. The gods had spoken. Frankie's suspension held.

Stranahan, who eventually apologized to Jones and Roberts in a letter handwritten on club stationery, would be invited to ten more Masters tournaments, but his relationship with the gods of Augusta remained stormy at best. Two months after the Masters in 1956, for example, Jones personally wrote Stranahan's father—the head of Champion Spark Plugs, who funded his son's amateur career—respectfully asking that the elder Stranahan straighten out his son once and for all on the matter of accepted Masters behavior. A flurry of tense letters passed between Stranahan minor and Jones before a typed pledge of good behavior—reportedly using words Bobby himself suggested—showed up in Augusta. By all accounts, Stranahan's Masters behavior was impeccable from that day forward.

Hogan, who found Frankie's "poor little rich boy" routine acutely distasteful and didn't lift a finger to help him out of his quandary, was never a factor at the 1948 Masters, which turned out to be one of the more memorable in tournament history. Winged Foot club pro and Hogan friend Claude Harmon breezed around the course four times with a record-tying 279 to beat one of the strongest fields ever assembled beneath the pines.

As Masters historian Charlie Price notes, the public at large assumed Harmon was just another flashy club pro who got a hot hand and rode it to the championship. But Harmon's winter club affiliation was Seminole Country Club, the fabulous Donald Ross–designed gem in North Palm Beach where Hogan had recently gone to tune up for Augusta and renew his friendship with Oklahoma oilman George Coleman. Coleman, who would join Seminole in 1954, later became president of the club; Hogan was made an "honorary member" in 1956. "Just before going to Augusta for the Masters," Price points out, "Harmon had been playing almost daily at Seminole with his old friend Hogan—'beating him as often as he beat me,' as Harmon would recall. 'When I began the last nine holes with a five shot lead at Augusta,' Harmon went on, 'I told myself that if I couldn't win this tournament I was in the wrong business.' "

One story holds that Hogan called on Harmon at his hotel the night before the final round, and the two friends enjoyed drinks and a friendly heart-to-heart chat about Claude's chances of finishing off the tournament in solid style, encouragement that apparently made a world of difference to the club pro. For the record, Ben Hogan finished in a tie for sixth, at 289, and warmly congratulated his Seminole playing pal on his big breakthrough.

After a two-week break, Ben played three events in a row leading up to the PGA Championship, finishing no worse than third. A rare flip-flop of scheduling had the PGA being played at Norwood Hills Country Club in St. Louis at the end of May, and Claude Harmon once again captured headlines by battling his way to the quarterfinals, surviving an epic duel with Sam Snead that went forty-two holes and nearly tied the PGA record for duration of a match.

The other three who reached the semifinals were Demaret, Hogan, and thirty-nine-year-old Mike Turnesa, the delightful White Plains club pro (and scion of a great golfing family that was perhaps even more accomplished than the Harmons) who once had Byron Nelson four down with five to play in a PGA match, played one under the remaining way, and still lost.

By the time Turnesa mounted a late rally to dismiss his hot-handed opponent Claude Harmon, one up on the 37th hole, Ben had already tossed out his Inverness buddy and '46 PGA opponent James Newton Demaret 2 and 1 (on his birthday no less) and hurried off to his hotel to rest, disappointing some pressmen and fans who fancied a duel in the sun between Seminole practice partners Claude and Ben. At the very least, though, events produced a fascinating title match between the tournament's odds-on favorite (Hogan) and a true Cinderella (Turnesa).

"I've got to wash out some socks tonight," Turnesa, who rarely played in major tournaments, quipped playfully to reporters as he prepared to meet his worst nightmare head to head. "Didn't plan to stay this long, fellas."

Most expected the final to be short work for Hogan, who soaked his bare feet in iced towels between rounds and grumbled throughout about the tournament's exhausting format. During their morning eighteen holes, followed by a gallery that grew to an estimated 5,000 by the time it ended, Turnesa was bothered by a frisky wind that repeatedly caused him to misjudge and underclub his approach shots.

Aided by his own long practice sessions in Seminole's difficult sea winds— no one in golf handled the wind better than Hogan, it was commonly believed—Ben had a brilliant 65 in the morning that put him four up over struggling Turnesa by the halfway mark, a lead he held through the afternoon's first nine holes, at which point he clipped off birdies on three successive holes to take possession of his second PGA Championship and end the ordeal by a yawning 7-and-6 margin. A jeep picked up the exhausted combatants on the 30th hole of their match and drove them back to the clubhouse.

The real surprise came as PGA officials presented Ben his second Wanamaker Trophy in three years.

"I know you all think I'm the great stone face," he told the crowd after first praising Norwood Hills Country Club and citing the courage and pluck of Mike Turnesa. "But this is a competitive game. I know the other fellow doesn't expect any quarter from me—and I don't give it."

Most curiously, he added: "You probably think I'm happy over winning this tournament, but I'm not. I hate to beat these men. They have to go back to their clubs and tell how they were beaten."

For one of the few times ever, Hogan let down his guard and peeled back the curtain on his complex psyche, aiming to show compassion for the challenge facing a young club pro like Mike Turnesa. In the aftermath of these remarks, he was dismayed to read that some reporters actually found his comments to be ungracious and condescending, an example of classic Hogan gamesmanship, possibly even a carefully worded effort to humiliate an up-and-coming competitor. It was exactly these kinds of distortions, or simple misinterpretations, that contributed to increasingly chilly relations between Hogan and some members of the press corps.

To compound matters in St. Louis, before heading off to catch a late train home to Fort Worth (for the start of the Colonial NIT), he dropped another little bombshell—noting that this would be his final appearance at a PGA Championship.

"The physical ordeal of the PGA just takes too much out of a man," he admitted. "I just don't want to put myself through that anymore." Having played in twenty-seven different PGA Championship matches over a seven-year span, some 718 holes of golf, including 12 qualifying rounds, capturing two championships, and producing better than an 81 percent winning total, Ben Hogan wasn't saying anything a dozen other top pros didn't routinely say. But coming from Ben Hogan, this sober assessment of the facts amounted to a slap in the face.

By the time his train had reached Fort Worth, Ben attempted to soften his departing remarks, which got splashed in heavy black ink—"Hogan Hates Winning!" "Bantam Ben to Quit PGA Forever!"—on broadsheets from Bangor to Bakersfield. "I still think the tournament is too long, but they can't do anything about it," he said, trying to hedge his bets. "But I may try again next year."

Hogan's words, as many had already noted, had an eerie way of becoming prophetic. But it wouldn't be the protracted ordeal of America's second-oldest major championship that prevented Ben from returning to defend his second major golf title.

It would be a ten-ton bus, coming out of nowhere.

As 160 COMPETITORS for the forty-eighth United States Open Championship assembled in Los Angeles, a suddenly familiar controversy flared—accusations that some players, including possibly the tournament favorite, facing Riviera's dauntingly small and fast greens, had shown up with more deeply grooved club faces than permitted under the rules.

In the wake of Vic Ghezzi's loud protestations the previous autumn, the irony that the sponsoring USGA, employing a newfangled device that accurately measured groove depth, advised forty competitors on the eve of play to file down their club faces didn't escape notice by anyone, including Ben Hogan, who arrived seven days early and checked into the Beverly Wilshire Hotel, fresh from a second-place win at Colonial, and went straight out to Riviera to see what all the ruckus was about.

Upon examination of their own shooting irons, even pre-tourny favorites Hogan and Demaret were asked by the USGA (which was eager to quell the controversy before it got out of hand) to make "modest alterations" to their clubs. No evidence remains that either man was sporting clubs with illegally widened grooves, but by displaying a firm public hand with *all* players before the start of play, the blazers in charge of finding a new National Open winner minimized any chances of a controversy popping up at the end.

In Ben's final Riviera practice round, he played with Demaret, Sarazen, and Bing Crosby, three of his better amigos in golf, and was trailed by a gallery that swelled to more than 3,000 at times. That evening at the Beverly Wilshire, he sat down for a full half-hour interview in his suite with two reporters from an L.A. newspaper he respected, who wondered, near the end of their conversation, if having reached the summit of the game Hogan had any ideas about how golf in general might be improved, particularly for the average Joe.

"The rules and equipment are fine," he replied after a second or two to think about it, perhaps reflecting on the "slight alterations" he'd been forced to make that week (though nobody to this day quite knows what they amounted to). "The only thing golfers really need is more daylight. There isn't enough time during the day to practice and play, to key one's game up to where it should be."

The reporters laughed; Hogan didn't.

"You're not joking," one of them said.

"No, I'm not," Hogan replied.

Valerie sat silently throughout this exchange.

Before the reporters left the couple, they asked if the paper's staff photographer might be allowed to snap a photograph of the Hogans together. Because of Valerie's shyness, only a few such pictures existed at that time. There was a wonderful shot of them as newlyweds starting out on tour, sitting together on a sun-splashed lawn somewhere up north, and another of them standing by their automobile outside the Hershey Resort Hotel the autumn Ben went to work for Milton Hershey. But aside from a few other snaps of them arriving at or departing a tournament site, there was no recent portrait of them enjoying the material rewards of Ben's success.

"I don't see why not," Ben agreed, adjusting the expensively made checked sports jacket he was wearing. He got up and walked over and stood by his wife, picking up his wedge and assuming the posture of an approach shot.

He gazed down affectionately at his wife, and she smiled adoringly back up at him.

The photograph appeared in the next morning's edition of the paper, the day the United States Open Championship for 1948 finally got under way.

• • •

Cool midsummer breezes wafted off the Pacific Ocean through Santa Monica Canyon on the first day of play, prompting Hogan to don a gray alpaca cardigan and a long-sleeved open-collar white shirt that perfectly matched his flat linen cap. Paired with amateur Bud Ward and old Texas rival Lloyd Mangrum, Hogan went off at 9:18 in the morning and began attacking Riviera's frighteningly small greens from the very start, birdieing three of the first four holes and completing the front nine with a scintillating 31 on his card.

He faltered slightly in the sticky three-inch kikuyu grass of the back nine but nevertheless finished his opening day's effort with seven birdies and three bogeys for a pace-setting 67.

With most eyes locked on the usual wagering favorites Hogan, Snead, and Demaret, not many gave defending champ Lew Worsham much of a chance to win in Hogan's Alley. Lew went off two hours behind Ben, with a gallery half the size of Hogan's, and played his own nearly flawless round, matching Hogan's 67 with some brilliant iron play and deft putting of his own. The press scarcely noticed him, though.

Neither Lew nor Ben played well the next day. Worsham fired a sloppy 74 and began a slow slide toward irrelevance, while Hogan, facing an afternoon tee time and even more of a Pacific breeze than on Friday morning, hooked his opening tee shot badly and escaped several wayward drives to get home with a one over 72 he summed up as "very lucky." His total dropped him just behind leader Sam Snead, who fired a second consecutive 69 for a new thirty-six-hole U.S. Open record. "Sam is running out of hair and time," wrote one wire reporter, cutting surgically to the heart of the Slammer's own motivation. "And there's maybe only one man in the field who's as hungry as he is to win this thing—Hogan."

Also near the top, though, were Locke, Demaret, and pleasant Jim Turnesa.

With the thirty-six-hole Saturday finale looming, most believed the National Open was a three-horse race between the best players in the game: Hogan, Snead, and Demaret. A fourth who might have also been in the hunt, Byron Nelson, tagged pleasantly along in the gallery, taking pictures with his new camera—his first trip to a U.S. Open strictly as a spectator.

The Dan'l Boone of Golf began his final-day assault by dropping a fourteen-foot putt on the first green for eagle and followed it up with a birdie on the long and difficult par-4 2nd hole—sending an early electric charge through the massive galleries assembled on Riviera's dramatic scruffy hillsides. Weeks later, Snead confided to reporters that he believed, foolishly as it turned out, that he had the Open "well in hand" at this point and would cruise to victory.

Sam hadn't counted on nerves betraying him, a series of small jerky motions he eventually called "the yips," which caused him to miss several critical short putts for par later that morning and into the breezier afternoon. Growing visibly agitated as the day wore along, Snead completed his morning circuit with a disappointing 73 and followed that with an insufficient 72 in the afternoon. Once again, cursed by the Open gods, Snead spiraled out of sight and finished in a tie for fifth place.

Hogan and Demaret, on the other hand, made it a two-man road show with matching 68s in the morning, Ben's two-shot lead at the lunch break giving him his best opportunity ever to win the championship. The highlight of Hogan's morning round came when he blasted a magnificent recovery shot from the depths of the peculiar bunker set in the heart of the 166-yard par-3 6th green and made the clutch putt to save par. By lunchtime, the only question being asked by the Tour writers was, could Ben close the deal?

Playing half an hour ahead of Ben in the afternoon, Jimmy Demaret briefly caught fire on holes 7 through 12, going four under for the stretch. For a little while, spectators loped back and forth between the Inverness teammates to see what would develop next. On 13, Jimmy put his second shot four feet from the hole but lipped out a putt that would have placed him in a tie with Hogan. As the sun began to dip into the eucalyptus trees along Riviera's narrow concluding fairways, something seemed to fade in Jimmy Demaret too. Despite several good opportunities to make birdie, he failed to mount a charge.

Despite a three-putt on the 69th hole, Ben went on to finish the Open the way he always knew he would have to do in order to win—coldly, methodically, as focused as a heart surgeon in the closing stages of a life-and-death operation. His clutch 69 and a 276 total lopped five strokes off the old mark set by Ralph Guldahl at Oakland Hills in 1937. Ironically, Demaret's 278 also shattered the old record, as did Jim Turnesa's 280. But the day, the National Open, finally belonged exclusively to Ben Hogan.

The victory meant far more than the $2,000 first-place prize money to the new, broadly smiling United States Open champion, the king of golf and Hogan's Alley. By even the most conservative estimates, the win was worth a minimum hundred grand in commercial endorsements and future paid appearances. His exhibition fee promptly headed for the stratosphere, representatives for Milton Berle, Jack Benny, and Perry Como sought him out for guest appearances, and his once-indifferent equipment sponsor, MacGregor Sporting Goods Company, promptly announced it would match every purse Hogan won.

At the height of a busy summer that saw mighty Citation gallop to the Triple Crown, Babe Ruth pass away from cancer, and Joe Louis knock out Jersey Joe Walcott, Bantam Ben Hogan seized the largest headlines of all, closing in on his own brand of immortality. Citation, Ruth, and Louis were all thoroughbreds, athletes who fascinated the public and enjoyed the limelight almost from the moment they stepped into the arena. Hogan was something very different—considerably older than Ruth and Louis at their peaks, with a heart more in common with Seabiscuit than Citation, a tough little cuss who'd made the world love him simply by never giving up and finally vanquishing all the giants around him. For what it was worth, the poor inward boy from Glen Garden was suddenly richer and better known than anybody in golf since Walter Hagen became the game's first millionaire, and his game, despite persistent rumors of retirement, suddenly seemed invincible.

Fifteen days after the National Open, the Ben and Jimmy show clobbered the competition to take their final Inverness Four-Ball Championship. "I'm very pleased to win this once again," Hogan stoked the fires of speculations by telling the crowd. "Especially since I won't be returning next year."

A week later, though, he beat Dutch Harrison in a play-off at the first Motor City Open in Detroit, sighed, and observed, "I want to die an old man, not a young one. But I'm not so old I won't be back next year."

Like headlines flipping in a Frank Capra film, on he raced to Reading, the Western Open, and Denver—three more weeks, three more wins. Records fell, headlines danced. It was six wins in a row, and his play-off win over Porky Oliver at the Western Open made Hogan the first player in history to hold the U.S. Open, the PGA, and the Western Open all in one season.

In her nationally syndicated column "Hi Ya," Babe Didrikson Zaharias (that summer's leading female pro golfer who earned a whopping $3,400, or roughly one-tenth of Hogan's record-breaking haul from the game) proposed: "If some bright person in Hollywood can find time to discover the forest through the trees, he will make a movie of the life of Ben Hogan."

"Who can possibly stop Ben Hogan?" wondered his one-man rooting section, Grantland Rice, watching Hogan's mastery of the pro game roll on, as summer waned, like the brand-new Cadillac Hogan had purchased back in Fort Worth just weeks after the end of the Open. This one came with a state-of-the-art two-piece curved windshield, a vast tinted rear window, tail fins inspired by Lockheed's famous P-38 fighter aircraft, and a purring Hydramatic automatic transmission that led the industry. The Hogans paid about $3,000 for their deluxe model, which included the finest radio available in any motorcar of the day.

As Ben and his gal Val barnstormed west, Granny Rice pointed out an interesting fact—nobody had won more golf tournaments in a shorter period of time than Hogan, forty-nine victories since 1940. The only cloud on the horizon appeared at Denver, where Ben, to nobody's surprise, won the tournament but slipped away once again before the mayor of the city could present him with a check and the winner's trophy, leaving 4,000 fans who'd paid $2.40 apiece to follow him around Wellshire Country Club cooling their heels in the Colorado heat while he raced to make a train for Salt Lake.

Those who detested Hogan—and there were many who considered his cold, efficient brand of golf an insult to the gracious standards set by Jones and Hagen—used this familiar faux pas to unload savagely on golf's most enigmatic star.

"Hogan's walkout," the *Rocky Mountain News* editorialized, "climaxed a long series of unpleasant incidents in which the Hershey prima donna let one and all know that he is good—and that he knows it." Among other things, the paper accused Hogan of dodging a free clinic, harassing photographers for taking his photograph without permission, blowing off several promised radio interviews, and telling a cute tyke with his autograph book to scram.

"The Greeks may not have a word to describe Hogan's kind," fumed syndicated columnist Jack Carberry, "but Americans do. But since the American word is not used in mixed company or the public prints, we'll content ourselves by referring to him as a stuffed shirt—one of MacGregor's stuffed shirts. You'll just have to supply the word we *mean* yourself."

Arriving in Salt Lake, Hogan strenuously denied most of the charges leveled against him by the *Rocky Mountain News*, explaining that he felt certain he'd actually *lost* the tournament in Denver when he left to catch the 5:30 Denver & Rio Grande express to Salt Lake. Back at his hotel, after being informed by Valerie that she'd heard on the radio that he'd in fact won, Hogan claimed he hurriedly phoned the president of the sponsoring Denver Civic Golf Association to convey his apologies for any misunderstanding and express his gratitude to the people of Denver—a message that apparently went astray. The official in question later confirmed the phone call from Hogan, but by then Ben's reputation—a bit unfairly this time—had once more taken it on the chin like a Joe Louis uppercut.

The nasty headlines out of Denver—"Hogan Blasted for Snub of Photogs and Fans," "Golf's Frigid Midget Strikes Again"—briefly bumped him off his winning stride in Utah, where he finished in a tie for ninth place, his worst showing since New Orleans back in February. Days later, though, he sprang back at the Reno Invitational, fired a blistering 269, and took away a pile of gold treasury coins valued at $3,500. Perhaps hoping to repair fences with the public, Hogan lingered after the tournament to greet fans and sign autographs. He also lavishly praised Reno's large galleries as "the finest I've ever seen in golf," a comment some seized upon as a slight to the savvy patrons at Augusta National and the National Open.

Hogan's final two events in his most fulfilling season to date were the Portland and Glendale Opens, held fourteen days apart in early October.

With two holes remaining to play in Portland (on a golf course that rivaled Riviera in Hogan's estimation), someone in the gallery informed Ben that he needed a pair of birdies on the final two holes to tie Freddie Haas Jr. for first place. He got them, indicating to some that golf's most intimidating shotmaker could simply summon whatever was needed in order to catch a frontrunner and win. But Haas won their play-off by a stroke.

Then, down in sunny Glendale, just outside Los Angeles, the place where he secretly wished he could spend the rest of his days, where he hadn't lost since 1946, Hogan displayed maybe his finest golf of the year.

Prior to heading out for his final competitive round of the season, he made a slight adjustment in his putting grip, "to avoid hooking putts," and canned twelve one-putt greens—"the finest putting round of my life," he boasted later—en route to a course record 64.

For this dazzling performance effort, he collected Glendale's first-place check of $2,450 and notched his tenth victory of the year. The win also gave him a third Vardon Trophy and the undisputed Tour money title for 1948 with a record $36,812 in tournament earnings.

In New York, meanwhile, Hogan's publisher, A. S. Barnes and Company, reported that sales of *Power Golf* had gone through the roof in the previous month as Hogan mania spread—more than 25,000 copies sold in less than three weeks.

Time magazine and *Esquire* both promptly issued press releases heavily promoting their forthcoming January (1949) profiles of golfer Ben Hogan, "the most exciting man in American sports," as *Time* called him.

"I'm tired, dead tired," Hogan told journalist Bob Lee as he prepared to head home to Fort Worth and put away his clubs for a bit, either unwilling or unable to utter the word "retirement" on the heels of such an extraordinary year.

He finally came out and said what many felt he'd been thinking all year long: "If something good comes along, I'd like to quit golf for keeps."

LOOKING A LITTLE like a formal wedding invitation, the "welcome home" party invitation was done on heavy stock cream paper and went to a who's who of Cowtown's social elite and anyone else who had ever been of help to the city's favorite son.

Colonial Country Club cordially invites you to attend a reception honoring Mr. and Mrs. Ben Hogan, Sunday, the twenty-eighth of November, nineteen hundred and forty-eight, from four until seven o'clock.

On a cool and overcast Sunday following Thanksgiving, 1,500 of Fort Worth's finest turned out to stand in the long reception line just to offer a few words of greeting and congratulations to Ben and Valerie. "Part family reunion, part coronation," was the way one Colonial member later put it. A beaming Mama Hogan was there along with Margaret and Royal Hogan and their daughter Jacqueline, Princess and her husband, Doc, Claude and Jesse Fox, and Sarah Fox Walters and her only child, ten-year-old Valerie.

Earlier that year, Sarah had fled a crumbling marriage to San Antonio businessman Ralph Walters, moved her precocious daughter to Fort Worth, and started spending most of their weekends at Jesse and Claude's house out in Cleburne. During this interval, they stayed with Valerie and Ben.

By returning to the family fold, Sarah and little Valerie could now travel on trains to tournaments with Ben and Valerie just the way Royal, Margaret, and Jacqueline had been doing for several years.

As everyone who knew the Hogans understood, Ben was extremely fond of both his nieces and took a great deal of pleasure in having them around him when he was home from the Tour, playing card games, playfully quizzing them about their schoolwork, lavishing his full and undivided attention upon them both.

"He had such an easy way with children, a genuine affinity for us," recalls Valerie, whose mother soon started dating and eventually married a popular

Dallas insurance man named Gordon Harriman. He was a Harriman from Boston, of *those* Harrimans, a first cousin in fact of Harry Truman's famous ambassador to the Soviet Union.

"I think we were a source of simple pleasure for him," speculates Jackie Hogan Towery, "because unlike just about everybody else around him, we didn't need or want anything from Ben Hogan except whatever attention he could give us. We adored him and he returned that affection, like we were his own daughters rather than nieces."

For the big welcome home party at Colonial, in a gesture many viewed as a direct thank-you to his longtime friend and mentor Marvin Leonard, Hogan had several of his championship medals and national trophies sent over to the club and agreed to let them be stored and displayed there indefinitely.

The Reverened Granville Walker was also in the celebrating crowd at Colonial that evening. Walker was the head minister at University Christian Church, near the TCU campus, a spellbinding preacher who played an increasingly important role in Ben Hogan's life and thinking. Whenever he was home on weekends, Hogan sometimes slipped into a rear pew of the beautiful southwestern-style church on his way to practice at the club, usually ducking out again after Walker gave one of his humdinger sermons and the collection plate was passed.

The Hawk's rarely-spoken-of spirituality was simply one more facet of a complex personality the public at large, and even many people who fancied themselves Hogan intimates, knew little or nothing about. A lifelong Baptist, he and Valerie had quit attending church until someone mentioned Granville Walker's oratorical gifts and the couple went to University Christian and had a look for themselves. Valerie reserved her church attendance for Christmas and other special occasions, but Ben attended fairly often during this period of his life, often showing up and departing before anyone realized he was there.

The new National Golf Champion and his wife stayed late into the night at their swank Colonial Country Club reception just after Thanksgiving, fielding praise and saying thank you to everyone who bothered to come out and anyone who'd ever meant anything to Hogan in his long climb to the game's summit.

Underscoring the mood of homecoming, that same night Ben and Valerie went home to their new house on Valley Ridge Road, a pretty two-story colonial in one of Fort Worth's finer western neighborhoods. The house had four nice-sized bedrooms, two up, two down, a nice large den, a screened back porch, and an expansive yard full of mature plantings.

If it wasn't exactly the sprawling ranch Ben Hogan had now and then talked about someday owning, it was at least a pretty suburban house straight out of Ozzie and Harriet, nothing too showy but roomy enough for house-guests and the occasional dinner party.

Valerie Hogan had spent weeks getting the place ready to move into, buying furniture and having the walls painted white and hiring black housekeep-ers she insisted upon dressing in traditional white maid's outfits. "My aunt," says Valerie Harriman, "had this idea that white was 'French,' and she loved anything that was 'French.' That was pure sophistication where Aunt Val was concerned."

In every way that appeared to matter, Ben Hogan had achieved the American dream. On paper at least, he was a millionaire; in golf, he was a national champion who'd won everything there was to win save one important golf tournament, the Masters. (Curiously, up until now, the venerable British Open, golf's oldest championship, provoked little or no interest in the Hawk. Like many others, he felt the tournament's low payout and travel challenges muted any appeal.)

He had a beautiful new home and a wife with impeccable French taste. He had powerful friends and a pioneer mama who was finally proud of him. In the midst of the homecoming festivities, when a few of his closest friends nudged him aside and discreetly wondered over their highballs if there was any truth to persistent rumors that his retirement might come any day, Hogan smiled and let a few Colonial cronies in on his actual thinking.

He evidently told Marvin Leonard and Fort Worth oilman W. A. Moncrief and even the Reverend Granville Walker that he didn't see any reason why a man who kept himself in top physical shape and his mind sharp couldn't go on indefinitely playing—and winning—golf tournaments, the ultimate mind-over-matter proposition.

."Don't believe everything you read in the papers," he said. "In fact, don't be-lieve any of it unless you see it with your own eyes, or I tell you about it." As a matter of fact, he added, he fully expected to go on playing and winning un-til he was fifty. Ironically, less than one year later and under vastly altered cir-cumstances, the Hawk expressed this same surprising notion to leading British golf journalists Pat Ward-Thomas and Henry Longhurst as they chatted pleasantly by the rail of a liner churning east to the Ryder Cup.

It's impossible, of course, to know what exactly was running through Ben Hogan's agile mind the night he stayed late into the evening at Colonial Country Club to say thank-you to all the folks who turned out to welcome him home after such an incredible year.

"Nobody goes through life without something happening to them. You just have to take those things as they come along, and go ahead with life," he would say a short time later. But his meaning would be something entirely different than winning golf tournaments at a clip nobody had seen since Byron Nelson left the game.

Not even a golf prophet as prescient as Ben Hogan could foresee the looming disaster that was only weeks away, a moment that would dramatically shatter and ultimately redefine the meaning of everything he'd worked so hard to achieve and believe, altering the history of the game he had finally conquered in the process.

NINE

Lucky Ben

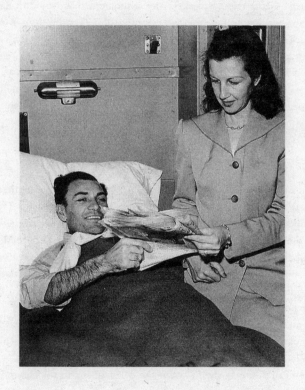

O N   T H E   S A M E   D A Y Hogan made his worst finish in more than a year, a disappointing tie for eleventh place at the Los Angeles Open, the Tour's opening event for 1949, the Hawk's beaming, angular movie-star face appeared on the cover of *Time* magazine, a somewhat surreal cartoon by artist Boris Chaliapin depicting his lean and slightly oversized head propped weirdly up on a golf tee, surrounded by a swing sequence of his vaunted driver. Silly as the illustrated Hogan looked—tiny drivers appeared to be sprouting out of his ears, giving him a faintly buglike countenance—the artist clearly intended to be saying something about Hogan's unprecedented mental mastery of the game, his left-brain dominance. The cover story was titled "Little Ice Water."

"If you can't outplay them," went the cover quote, in the chaste idiom of pure Hoganspeak, "outwork them."

Though colorful Tour newcomer Tommy Bolt was among the first to reveal that many pros loved watching Hogan practice because the diligence of

Overleaf: Ben and Valerie, two weeks following accident *(Courtesy Hogan Estate)*

his routines elevated the quality of their own focus and games, the *Time* article quoted a "top" unnamed touring professional as saying it was no fun whatsoever to play with Little Ice Water because he was so mechanically perfect and silent that "he seems inhuman," an intimidation factor that often caused tournament partners to flub shots and play poorly.

Down in Fort Worth, newsstands sold out of the newsweekly hours after it went on sale, prompting Mama Hogan to phone Hogan Office Supply and ask Royal to purchase half a dozen copies on his lunch hour and drop them off at her new apartment at the Westbrook Hotel. From Clara Hogan's point of view, having her hardworking little boy grow up and make it to the cover of the country's most prestigious news magazine was proof that both of them had survived the worst life could throw at them. For the time being, their shared knowledge of the true force behind Ben's rags-to-riches success was safely preserved by an impenetrable wall of silence, a conspiracy of wills so complete that not even Valerie knew the details of Chester Hogan's demise. Anecdotal evidence suggests that she learned the true nature of Chester's death that same winter of Ben's Colonial homecoming, possibly at a family holiday gathering at the Hogans' new home on Valley Ridge in a casual conversation with Ben's older sister, Princess, after she was interviewed by a local reporter who had gone snooping around down in Erath County to try to gain a fuller picture of America's newest sports idol. Valerie herself corroborated this fact when she admitted to Dave Anderson, not long before her death, that she was married to Hogan "for some time" before learning the facts surrounding his father's death.

In any case, a lighter moment occurred a few days after the *Time* cover story appeared. An Associated Press reporter at Bing's celebrity invitational playfully collared Ben in the buffet line and wondered if his poor finish in Hogan's Alley a few days before might have been the result of *too* much publicity—perhaps even a media "jinx." After all, more than one national sports idol or movie star had seen his or her fortunes radically dip after appearing on the cover of *Time* or its sister publication *Life*. The most notable example of late was Red Sox slugger Ted Williams, who, in the wake of batting over .400, received similar canonization, only to fall into a terrible batting slump that made him even more churlish and unapproachable than usual. At last glimpse, Williams, who bore more than a passing resemblance to Hogan, was *still* attempting to battle his way out of the batting doldrums.

"I don't think that'll be the case here," Hogan, dressed nattily in a wide-lapel houndstooth sports coat and a silk necktie, assured the reporter at Bing's outdoor gala. "For one thing, I'm feeling fairly rested—maybe better than I have in years. And I also enjoy playing out west," he added. "Last week was just one of those things."

Over the next three days, he underscored this notion by firing 208 to capture the individual portion of Crosby's clambake. He also took time out to ride horses with Bing at his ranch over in Nevada, deeply impressing his host with his knowledge of, and comfort around, horses.

Eight days later, down in Long Beach, Ben beat Jimmy Demaret in a playoff, then drove over the Chuckwalla Mountains to Phoenix, where Jimmy returned the favor, beating Ben in the Monday play-off. "The Two Man Tour" one of the local headlines dubbed the Ben and Jimmy Show. During drinks after their play-off, Jimmy asked Ben if he and Valerie were pushing on with the Tour to Tucson "for the rubber match."

"No," Ben replied. "Val and I want to get back to Fort Worth. No sense having a house if we don't live in it." Valerie, he explained, had just finished furnishing the house to her satisfaction and was eager to hold her first formal dinner party.

"What's the matter?" Demaret ribbed him, rattling the ice in his glass. "I beat you and you have to run home and practice for a month?"

Ben offered a thin smile. Once again, though he didn't say it, Hogan was tired. In the previous twenty-five days, he'd put almost 3,000 auto miles on his Caddy's odometer and played four Tour events, performed at least two free public clinics, played an exhibition match, and endured half a dozen sit-down interviews about his undeclared future plans. He'd also taken out time to make the first of several scheduled instructional films, won a pair of golf tournaments, and collected $4,000 in prize money—enough to lead the Tour's early-season money parade. As he confessed to *Time*, repeating comments he had first made in Detroit the previous summer, eerily presaging events, it wasn't playing the golf that was wearing him out. "It's the traveling. I want to die an old man, not a young one."

Without a doubt, unfinished business at Augusta was also weighing heavily on his mind. Hogan had seven top-ten finishes at Augusta, including a pair of razor-thin near-misses and the black memory of that choked four-foot putt in 1946 to obliterate. Given his present position atop the game in nearly every statistical category that mattered, it seemed utterly incomprehensible to many—especially Hogan himself—that he had yet to find a way to win Bobby Jones's splendid little invitational in the pines.

So the Hogans ambled east toward home in their purring new Cadillac, talking about furniture they'd ordered for the new house in Westover Hills and Sarah Fox Walters's deepening marital woes. Sarah and her husband Ralph, an alcoholic, had been arguing for months and divorce seemed inevitable, a personal abhorrence to Valerie Hogan. "It's a coward's way out, why would anyone who claims they are committed actually do such a thing?" she once remarked to a society page editor in a conversation about the undue stress that life from a suitcase seemed to put on Tour marriages. Yet even she was beginning to accept the fact that her sister Sarah's marriage to Ralph Walters was a hopeless cause. Ralph's rages terrified his wife and young daughter, and Sarah and little Valerie could stay with them until things could be resolved one way or another.

Ben was in favor of this plan because Valerie Hogan was always noticeably happier and more relaxed when her younger sister was around to help out with the details of domestic life. Ben loved having Sarah around because she was always the life of the party in a way Valerie never could be, a true compliment to their spirited cowgirl mama, Jesse Fox, the family's original belle of the rodeo. Sarah made Ben laugh and had even enthusiastically taken up playing golf, displaying quite a budding zest for the game. Early in their married life, Ben had tried to give Valerie lessons, but she never got beyond the initial frustrating lessons. "My arms weren't strong enough to swing the clubs the way Ben thought I ought to," she told someone. "And with Ben, you know, strength is everything."

ON TUESDAY, February 1, Ben and Valerie made the nine-hour drive from Phoenix to El Paso, veered south along the palely glittering Rio Grande River for a time, and kept rolling until they reached the modest El Capitan Motel in tiny Van Horn just after darkness fell.

They were almost exactly halfway between Phoenix and home now, and the El Capitan was both reasonably priced (rooms started at $4 a night) and popular among Tour caravans for its clean rooms and a diner that served wonderful homemade food and breakfast at any hour. Ben and Valerie had been stopping at the El Capitan for years, as had Byron and Louise Nelson, Jug McSpaden, and Porky Oliver, that colorful Tour trencherman who never forgot the location of a good cheap road meal.

At roughly 6:30 that morning, a cool misty Wednesday out in the desolate hinterlands of west Texas, Ben went to breakfast alone at the motel's coffee shop. Car travel often made Valerie queasy in the mornings, so she stayed in the room packing up their things and putting on her makeup while Ben went for his customary scrambled eggs and coffee and a quick scan of the El Paso newspaper before they hit the road.

Relatively speaking, it was a slow news day on February 2, 1949. The paper that morning carried wire reports of free-market Republicans sniping at President Harry Truman's scheme for a "planned economy" to try to blunt any future stock market debacles and accounts of the vast crowds of mourners gathering by the River Ganges to pray at the grave of Mahatma Gandhi on the one-year anniversary of the Hindu holy man's assassination. In other news, the nation of Hungary had just declared itself a "People's Republic," and Humphrey Bogart, the Ben Hogan of movie stars, was reported to be the highest-paid performer in Hollywood, raking in $467,000 before taxes.

On the calendar was also Groundhog Day, the day in popular American folklore when a furry rodent's seen or unseen shadow could auger either winter's dreary continuation or the arrival of an early spring. Ben was personally hoping for an early spring, crowned by a long-overdue victory at Augusta. It was also Chester Hogan's birthday. Had he survived, Ben's father would have been sixty-seven years old that winter day. Ben knew this date better than anyone, a private anniversary forever darkened by its own shadow.

After breakfast, Ben checked out and drove directly across Highway 80 to gas up the Cadillac. Then he returned to the motel and loaded up their suitcases and his golf clubs (which always went with him to the room), placing his sticks across the car's plush and spacious backseat. At 7:45, he and Val pulled out of the El Capitan Motel's parking lot, switched on the car's radio, and began the final leg of their drive toward home.

The weather along the Pecos River Valley was mostly clear and cool, though patches of dense ground fog soon began to wreathe the rolling scrub country east of Van Horn, heading toward the foothills of the Apache Mountains. Visibility quickly became a problem. After just ten minutes, Ben slowed down to thirty miles per hour on the narrow two-lane highway. Upon hearing a noise that sounded like a tire giving out, he pulled over to the shoulder to investigate. According to Valerie, he discovered the highway coated with a light glaze of ice—not uncommon in the cold winter mornings of west Texas. To be on the safe side, he switched on his headlights and reduced the Caddy's land speed, as he later described it, to "practically nothing."

• • •

IN THE DRIVER'S SEAT of Greyhound bus number 548, twenty-seven-year-old Alvin Logan, a substitute driver on the company's Dallas–El Paso run, was worried about running late and being docked in pay. Logan's normal route was Pecos to El Paso, a trip he made three times a week in just under two hours. Today, though, while pulling out from a service station in the tiny junction town of Kent thirty-seven miles east of Van Horn, he'd fallen in behind a lumbering six-wheel Alamo freight hauler that was taking its own sweet time negotiating the curves and dips in Highway 80. In the best of weather, this stretch of the road could be a trucker's nightmare, full of sudden rises and blind curves. But ground fog made traveling here doubly frustrating and dangerous.

As Logan later admitted to authorities, he knew that passing the truck was a risky proposition, but with each passing minute he and his thirty-four passengers were falling further behind schedule. Greyhound was a company that prided itself on on-time arrivals and drilled this performance goal into its drivers. The last thing Alvin Logan wanted was a reprimand or worse for another late arrival.

Approaching what appeared to be a long rise of Highway 80 with no one coming, Logan boldly swung his bus into the oncoming lane and gunned the vehicle's massive General Motors Super Coach engine, pushing the ten-ton vehicle up to fifty miles per hour as it sped up a slight incline. Over the rise, the road dipped fractionally toward a small culvert spanning a dry wash. Logan later said he thought he could see at least three to four hundred yards ahead through the fog and he saw absolutely no vehicles approaching. As Logan insisted to the authorities investigating the consequences of his poor judgment, he believed there was ample room to safely pass the lumbering truck.

A mere eighth of a mile away, proceeding cautiously up the rise into the same swirling patch of ground fog, Ben Hogan suddenly saw *two* sets of headlights bearing down on their Cadillac as it approached the culvert.

For an instant, the couple stared straight ahead in disbelief, unable to speak, until, according to Valerie, her husband said with almost eerie matter-of-factness, "Honey, I think he's going to hit us."

Valerie opened her mouth to scream, but no sound came out, and Ben later explained that seconds before impact he tried to calculate whether it would be possible to swerve off the highway and thus avoid a collision altogether. Unfortunately, the small bridge had thick steel guard rails that would have bounced them directly back into the path of the accelerating bus. Perhaps only a brain as agile as Hogan's could have sorted through their limited options and found the one maneuver that probably spared both their lives.

At the last possible instant before impact, Ben released the wheel and dove headlong to his right, hurling his body protectively over Valerie's terrified ninety-eight-pound frame.

The bus's front left bumper slammed ferociously into the front left portion of the Cadillac, shattering its distinctive grillwork, blowing out its revolutionary curved windshield, and jolting the 3,900-pound luxury sedan backward several yards, accompanied by a sickening thud of metal, crumpling the passenger compartment into a smashed concertina. Witnesses inside the bus reported that the Hogan vehicle ricocheted off the bus and skidded sideways to the right before slipping off the shoulder of the road and sliding back down the culvert grade into the wash, engulfed in steam and smoke.

Fighting to regain control of his vehicle, Alvin Logan managed to keep bus 548 on the highway until it plowed into a drainage ditch and rattled several hundred more feet before coming to a halt against a small embankment. Directly behind, the Alamo hauler jackknifed to avoid rear-ending the smoking bus, causing several following cars to collide as they rapidly braked to avoid a foggy pileup.

In a space of about three seconds, roughly one second more than it takes to swing a golf club, the collision sent the Cadillac's 500-pound V-8 engine smashing through the luxury car's thick protective firewall onto Ben's lower body, pushing the steering wheel straight through the seat where, an instant before, he had been seated. The rim of the wheel stabbed his left shoulder just below the collarbone, fracturing it severely. The left side of Hogan's face slammed the collapsing dashboard and his unconscious head tumbled into Valerie's lap. Her face struck something too—possibly the back of her husband's hard head—and she lost consciousness as well.

"The next thing I knew," she recalled, "I came to, but all I could see was the gray sky. I didn't know where I was. I heard Ben moaning and yelling, 'Get out! Get out!' He was afraid our car might catch on fire. . . . Somehow I got my door open and got out and looked around, but I still didn't know where I was."

The highway was strewn with wrecked vehicles and people already shuffling about in a daze. Miraculously, no one on the bus or in any of the other cars was seriously injured, though several reported small injuries, bruises and cuts. Alvin Logan was shaken up too. Among other things, his wristwatch got shattered in the impact with Hogan's Cadillac, freezing both hands of his timepiece. It was exactly 8:30 in the morning.

A number of minutes elapsed before anyone thought to check on the passengers in the Cadillac. Hearing Valerie Hogan's weak cries for help, two men slid down the gully and helped extract Ben's pinned legs from beneath the Cadillac's collapsed dashboard, then gingerly lifted him from the mangled passenger compartment. "I'm not hurt," he told them, grimacing. "Help my wife. I'll be okay." They placed his arms around their shoulders and carried him up the slope to another car, where a woman identifying herself as a registered nurse suggested they stretch him out on the backseat until an ambulance could be summoned.

"I don't know how the woman knew to call me Mrs. Hogan," Valerie remembered. "I hadn't told anybody our names. But everybody there seemed to know who we were because I remember them saying, 'Ben Hogan's been hurt.' Maybe the men had recognized Ben, maybe they had noticed Ben's golf clubs. But those wonderful people, they put Ben in the backseat of that woman's car and she took his pulse."

"Don't you worry," the woman assured Valerie. "He's going to be all right."

After a few minutes, Ben complained that his left leg was growing cold and numb. Someone fetched a lap blanket from the bus and placed it over him. The nurse recognized the signs of a man rapidly descending into circulatory shock—his blood pressure and pulse were both dropping like a stone.

Amid the confusion, no one thought to go find a phone and call for an ambulance for the better part of an hour. Finally, a Texas state police cruiser arrived and patrolman George Summerhill radioed for the ambulance. By this point, Hogan had lost and regained consciousness five or six times, each time growing a little bit grayer and colder.

As they waited for help to arrive, Valerie walked over and confronted Alvin Logan. "You coward," she spat at him. "Why don't you go over and see what you've done to my husband?"

Logan, who was later charged with failure to yield right-of-way and aggravated assault, both misdemeanors in the state of Texas, supposedly replied, "Your car was on the wrong side of the road, lady. You were skidding into *me*." Then he walked away from the grief-addled woman, shaking his head. Years later, following another bus accident in which Logan was at the wheel and two people were killed, the bus company finally fired him and officially apologized to the Hogans. ("I know I'm not being a lady," Valerie told the company's representatives. "But I despise you and your company. It's bad enough my husband was almost killed, but you kept that ornery man driving and now you've got two people's deaths on your conscience.")

As they waited endlessly in the gloom of the lifting fog for the ambulance to arrive, a man began to gather up Hogan's scattered golf clubs and put them back in his bag, so they would be there when, and if, he regained consciousness again.

MORE THAN NINETY minutes passed before an ambulance from El Paso arrived. With Hogan's vital signs perilously fluctuating, the attending physician, Dr. John Wright, an osteopathic physician who hailed from Van Horn, decided against giving the patient a painkiller but insisted on briefly pausing at the tiny clinic in Van Horn for an emergency X-ray to assess the level of internal bleeding before the ambulance sped on to the larger and better-equipped hospital Hotel Dieu (which means Inn of God) in El Paso, more than one hundred miles away. Wright used the interval to phone ahead to the hospital and give Dr. Lester Fenner there an update on Hogan's condition.

At one point during the interminable ride to El Paso, Valerie recalled, Ben opened his eyes and demanded to know where his golf clubs were. She assured him they were safe in the ambulance with them. Administered a moderate sedative to allow him to rest for the journey, he flexed his hands as if trying to grip an invisible club and slipped off to sleep again, murmuring about pulling a golf shot toward the gallery on the left.

During their brief stop in Van Horn, Valerie phoned Royal's office in Fort Worth, leaving a frantic message for her brother-in-law (who had stepped out to run an errand). Next she phoned her sister, Sarah, who'd just gotten little Valerie out the door to her new elementary school. Sarah promised to find Royal and catch the first flight available down to El Paso.

NEWS OF THE ACCIDENT broke across the national wire services about lunchtime back east. At Tucson Country Club, Jimmy Demaret was walking down the 6th hole of the tournament's pro-am with Toney Penna and New York Yankees owner Del Webb when the club manager came loping across the fairway, flushed and panting, to report that Ben Hogan had just been killed in a car crash somewhere in west Texas.

"I don't remember what I said exactly," Demaret remembered, "but I began walking to the clubhouse. I wanted to get at a phone. I remember Webb softly calling to the caddies and paying them off. I even recall his exact words. 'I think we'll forget about golf today.' "

At the clubhouse, Demaret phoned the Texas State Highway Department and asked if they had any report of Ben Hogan being killed in an auto accident. He was told someone would have to phone him back, so he left a number. "I hung up and stood there looking dumbly at the wall in front of me. Then the fellow called me back. 'Yes,' he said, 'Hogan was in the accident. But he's alive. He's at the Hotel Dieu in El Paso.' "

"It felt good," Demaret said later, "damned good, to know he was alive."

According to the first sketchy wire reports of the accident, however, believed to be the result of an excited motorist phoning a local newspaper to convey his account of the horror he'd just witnessed out on Highway 80, Ben Hogan had indeed perished in the auto crash north of the city. The erroneous story stayed out there only a short while before the *El Paso Herald* clarified matters, reporting that golf's premier player had been critically injured in a car crash just outside the hamlet of Van Horn. Among the factual errors reported an hour or so following the crash, the Associated Press reported that Hogan sustained three broken ribs, severe major chest injuries, and a broken back in the accident.

Anyone who saw the wreckage strewn on Highway 80 east of Van Horn might certainly have come to this conclusion on their own, or worse. A little while after the ambulance took the Hogans away, Herman Keiser and Dutch Harrison threaded their way through the scene of wreckage on their way to San Antonio. Harrison instantly recognized Hogan's new Cadillac, and they pulled over to find out what happened. Minutes later, Keiser, remembering Ben's various kindnesses to him over the years, including the classy way the Hawk handled Herm's unexpected win at the Masters, turned his own sedan around and accelerated toward El Paso.

About that same time, a young man hoping to break into the oil business named Gary Laughlin was driving an old pickup truck up Highway 80 to Fort Worth, passing slowly through the scene of smoldering metal. Laughlin, Amon Carter's nephew, was just out of the Marines, a former fighter pilot who was preparing to go into the well-drilling business with his older brother Phil. Five years down the road, Gary Laughlin and Ben Hogan would become fast friends and business partners. "That morning I happened upon the wreck, I'd never met Ben Hogan," Laughlin recalls. "Though obviously, like everybody else, I knew who he was, and I was shocked when I later learned that the wrecked automobile was his. I even took a photograph of the wreck that was later used in the lawsuit Ben filed against Greyhound. All I remember thinking was, *whoever* had been in that smashed Cadillac was probably dead by now."

Up in Fort Worth, Jackie Hogan got a note in one of her freshman classes at Paschal High (the former Central High that Valerie graduated from and where Ben rarely showed up for his classes before dropping out) informing her to immediately call her mother Margaret at home. "The minute I heard my mother's voice I knew something terrible was wrong. 'Come home immediately,' she said. 'Your Uncle Ben has been in a serious car accident.' That was all she said. But I remember that she paused and added sternly, 'And *you* drive carefully, young lady.' "

At that moment in time, Jacqueline Hogan was a girl in high cotton. She was about to turn fifteen and had her grandmother's prairie handsomeness, a flock of high school suitors, a feisty personality and a first-rate mind, a learner's permit, and a car of her very own—a pale green two-door Ford bought by her hard-assed daddy, Royal Hogan.

By the time she got safely home, though, her father was already on his way to the Fort Worth airport to catch the next flight out to El Paso, and Jackie was disappointed to learn that she and her mother would have to wait at home for a phone call from Royal with further news on Ben's condition. "We knew so little, just that there had been a terrible accident and Uncle Ben was in very bad shape. I don't recall there being any mention of Valerie's situation. It killed my mother and me to have to wait for Daddy's call. We thought that meant Uncle Ben had died."

Valerie Walters, a fourth-grader at Bradford Elementary School in the tony Dallas suburb of Highland Park, where she and her mother had just moved into an apartment, was surprised when her mother Sarah showed up at the door to her classroom. "Honey," Sarah told her daughter calmly, "I have to go down to El Paso. Grandmother Fox is going to come and stay with you until I get back."

Valerie wondered if her father might be going as well. Lately her parents had been bickering a lot, but there was talk of maybe moving to Atlanta for a "new start." Valerie loved her father, though she rarely saw much of him.

"No, honey," Sarah explained to her. "I'm going alone. Uncle Ben and Aunt Valerie have been in a terrible wreck. We don't know if he's going to make it."

. . .

ALMOST FOUR HOURS after the accident, Ben was carried on a stretcher into the Hotel Dieu Hospital in El Paso. The initial diagnosis was surprisingly encouraging. In addition to the fractured left collarbone, he'd suffered a double ring fracture of the pelvis and a broken left ankle, a broken rib, and several deep cuts and contusions around his left eye. By the time Royal and Sarah reached Ben's bedside several hours later that day, a large gauze bandage covered his swollen left eye (which had filled with blood), and he was sleeping peacefully under heavy sedation.

They found Valerie Hogan seated in a chair directly by his bed. Her injuries were slight—a bruised face, a twisted arm, a few small cuts here and there—but for the next few days, until she was completely convinced by doctors that Ben was safely out of the woods, Valerie refused to budge from the room for more than a few minutes at a time. When the ward's regular night nurse was forced to miss two nights of work because of a family emergency of her own, Valerie slept by her husband's bedside in an armchair.

On day two, when Herm and Dutch finally got to lay eyes on Ben, Keiser's first thought was: *He's not going to make it.* "He was all strapped down," he said later, noting that Ben suddenly opened an eye and motioned him closer. "Herman," Hogan croaked, "would you check on my clubs?" Keiser had to smile. Somehow, he decided on the spot, Hogan just might make it after all.

Later that day, Hogan's doctors asked the patient if he felt up to granting the press a brief interview. The hospital's waiting room was packed with reporters who'd flown or driven in from a dozen directions.

"I have nothing to say," Hogan replied, sounding more like his old self.

On Friday, after more X-rays were taken, Ben's battered lower body was placed in a pair of large plaster casts—one covering from chest to knees, another from calf to ankle. For the first time, in her husband's behalf, Valerie spoke to the waiting reporters, describing how the accident unfolded and Ben had hurled his body in front of hers to try to soften the blow of the collision.

Valerie's modest account of their ordeal went out in that evening's edition of the local paper and simultaneously filtered out over the national wire services, a breaking saga of survival that elbowed any number of important international news items from above the fold in many of the nation's leading dailies.

Her account, accompanied by stark wire photos of the demolished Caddy, had nothing short of a major impact on popular perceptions of her husband. Suddenly *Time*'s Little Ice Water, golf's most remote and chilly champion, had an entirely different kind of image: that of a man acting purely out of personal courage and compassion to save the little woman he loved. Across America, headline writers had a field day.

"Bantam Ben Hero, Says Wife," went one prominent headline back east. "He Tried to Save Me."

"Hogan's Greatest Win—Saving His Gal Val." This from Cleveland.

"The Little Champ with the Big Heart." Sacramento.

Another Texas paper summed up the view of the Hotel Dieu staff even more succinctly.

"Lucky Ben," it said.

The next day, Valerie accepted phone calls from concerned well-wishers. Demaret and Gene Sarazen were among the first to phone the hospital and get an update on Ben's condition. So did Byron and Louise Nelson, the Reverend Granville Walker, Henry Picard, Jimmy Thomson, Lawson Little, Claude Harmon, and Mr. and Mrs. Sam Snead. All conveyed their best wishes for a speedy recovery to the battered champ who was suddenly riding sky-high in the nation's prayers and affections.

Bing Crosby and Bob Hope both phoned to speak with Ben's gal Val, as did a number of the Hollywood elite, including Katharine Hepburn and Jimmy Stewart, even Hepburn's former beau Howard Hughes. Mountains of flowers arrived, which an irritated patient finally ordered taken from his room and given to the hospital staff. "This isn't a funeral," he grumbled beneath his bed-sheets, ". . . yet."

"The damage isn't as bad as we first thought," a normally grim-faced Royal, serving as official spokesman for the family, informed reporters with something resembling gritty optimism five mornings after the fearsome collision on Highway 80. "I think Ben is going to be all right." He confirmed that Ben's legs were "pretty beaten up" and would require "some hard work" to rehabilitate them, but he predicted Ben would not only soon walk and play golf again but might even be up to attending that approaching autumn's Ryder Cup festivities in England, "as a player." When they heard this pronouncement, several reporters glanced at each other with surprise.

Behind closed doors, Hogan's doctors were far less optimistic about his prospects of recovery, privately expressing doubts about whether the national golf champ would even be able to walk again without assistance, much less be able to endure the physical toil of a golf tournament.

In his private hospital room, redolent with spring bouquets sent over from every florist shop in the county, Lucky Ben was already sitting up eating chicken noodle soup, drinking ginger ale, and reading through some of the mountains of get-well letters and telegrams that began flooding the hospital's mailroom after word of the Hawk's accident got out. By day six, the volume was up to three hundred cards and letters per day, including a get-well telegram signed by most of the citizens of tiny Dublin, Texas, his hometown— a kindness for which the injured man personally later responded to every name by handwritten note.

When the volume of notes and letters became overwhelming, the hospital staff moved their famous patient to a larger room and found several cardboard boxes to pile unopened letters in as they arrived. That same afternoon, the cast of the Hollywood movie *El Paso* stopped by on their way to the premier of their film at a downtown movie house, the actor John Payne and the film's other stars clustering around the bedside of "America's newest hero" as the flashbulbs exploded.

"He's simply the *nicest* man you ever met," cooed one of the film's unknown starlets as they left. "You'd never know he was supposed to be so unfriendly."

PRIOR TO THE thunderous collision out on Highway 80, Ben Hogan was a bona fide sports star and a tough-skinned symbol of what an unflagging work ethic could do for a proverbial underdog. But he was hardly a hero in any classical sense because he showed no vulnerability and little or no emotion, the kind of humanness that makes a hero real.

Suddenly, however, across a nation that had thrown off the shroud of Depression breadlines and recently beaten back Nazi terror and was rushing pell-mell to embrace consumer prosperity and identify new cultural icons in the daily exploits of ball-field warriors like DiMaggio and Williams, Ben Hogan's sacrifice elevated him to new heights of popular fascination. DiMaggio's comeback from tendon surgery was heartwarming, and Williams's effort to regain his form was an inspiration to watch. But Ben's protective lurch, at least as the media portrayed it, was the kind of spontaneous, unthinking act any ordinary Joe could relate to and might have attempted under similar circumstances— to protect his favorite little gal from death.

The day following her interview with the press, reflecting on an unexpected deluge of get-well cards and letters from thousands of total strangers, Valerie told the *Fort Worth Star-Telegram*, "If there's one good thing out of this accident, it's been that Ben realizes how many good friends he has everywhere. People have been wonderful." She thought a moment and added: "I guess you don't know these things until something like this happens."

"Uncle Ben really was genuinely startled to discover what he meant to millions of people he'd never met," says Jackie Hogan Towery emphatically. "He simply had no idea how and why they cared about him. There's no doubt in my mind, as he later said himself, that this revelation provided the motivation to get back on his feet and play golf again. But it also put further responsibility on him—a greater sense of obligation he felt to all those people cheering him on."

Furthermore, acquaintances who knew a more private Hogan before and after the collision agree that the crash significantly altered his outlook in several ways—it made him a bit more sympathetic to interviewers, friendlier to the press in general, more tolerant of fans, and even less ill at ease in crowds of adoring strangers. "To a man who stared death in the face the way Ben did," says Ken Venturi, "battling to win a golf tournament and deal with all the distractions that go with it was nothing. That wreck made Ben pause and appreciate life a bit more, no doubt about it. But in the long run, it also only made him even more fearless in competition."

Critics and even some biographers of Hogan, on the other hand, dismiss the public's influence on Hogan's eventual comeback and rather narrowly contend that he dedicated himself to getting back on his feet and into the heat of major competition primarily because winning golf tournaments was all he truly cared about in life, and time was clearly running out on Little Ice Water's quest to be considered the finest player of his time.

But several factors suggest that Hogan's hospital-room revelations were indeed genuine and perhaps even life-altering.

To begin with, several members of the Hotel Dieu staff recalled that the patient, America's so-called Frigid Midget, propped up in his bed with one eye bandaged, grew visibly emotional while reading many of the more detailed cards and letters he received from thousands of admiring strangers, highly personal notes that poured out accounts of the author's own experiences with death or near-tragedy involving themselves or a loved one. Over the long months of his convalescence, Hogan, a stickler for proper etiquette, made replying to and thanking these individual letter writers a high priority, and when he was physically unable to respond to the flood of mail that continued to come his way, he hired a secretary to type out thank-you notes and personal letters, all of which he read and signed.

According to his family, Ben was most taken with those missives that revealed some adversity either a child or young athlete was struggling to overcome, and once he was back on his feet and traveling to tournaments again on a limited basis, Hogan even made an effort to visit several young people he'd heard about who'd found inspiration through his ordeal. When a reporter in Philadelphia, for example, discovered that Ben planned to visit a local hospital en route to Merion Golf Club in 1950, Hogan specifically requested that the reporter make no mention of his visit with the sick boy in question—partly because he feared the onslaught of requests that would come his way if the news got out, partly because he felt that the boy and his parents ought to be granted their privacy. The request was honored, but news of other bedside visits did filter out into the press, softening Ben's image even more, revealing a little champ who had a beating heart in his chest after all.

Hogan's closest friends from this time suggest, moreover, that the accident only served to stimulate his natural compassion for anyone who had a hard-luck story to tell, as if any ordinary person's tale of adversity reminded him of his own lonely struggle against the odds and the hand he'd been given up by Marvin Leonard and a few others. As the years unfolded, sometimes to the annoyance of his own wife, he sent money to people he read about in the newspaper whom life had dealt a raw deal, donated quietly but generously to children's charities and hospitals, even subsidized animal shelters. In virtually every case, either out of natural modesty or fear of being besieged by requests for similar assistance, he asked the recipient not to reveal the source of the help. Hogan's charity, in short, was as confidential as his churchgoing.

Following his accident, though the press had no inkling of it or simply chose to ignore this aspect of his private life, Hogan also grew more visible in the exercise of his faith—or at the very least, less concerned about shielding his spirituality from view. Following the long months of recovery at home, for instance, he began showing up even more regularly at Granville Walker's Sunday morning services at University Christian Church and in coming years even attended services at the Catholic church with his niece Jackie and her new husband.

The same critics who like to point out what a blunt, profane SOB Hogan could be with people he didn't care for or while fraternizing briefly with the boys in the locker room (always safely out of female earshot) typically neglect to mention the fact that upon his triumphant return to tournament golf slightly more than one year after the car wreck, Hogan thanked "the Lord" as well as his lifelong companion for helping him get back on his feet and win again—in precisely that order. For what it's worth, Ted Williams also claimed to have discovered the value of a spiritual life about this time, citing his experiences in the Korean conflict with bringing him to a heightened awareness of God's hand on his bat.

This fact leads one to surmise that even if the events that unfolded on Highway 80 weren't a complete road to Damascus experience for Little Ice Water, the accident and the deep personal reflection it sparked provided something critical to the length and purpose of Hogan's remaining days. Popularity was no substitute for personal excellence in Hogan's book, but armed with a newfound sense of his own value to people's lives, a sports hero admired at least as much for the content of his character as for the quality of his game can never really be the same man again.

Underneath it all, because of Chester's suicide, Hogan was plagued by the hollow feeling of always being the odd man out and unworthy of anyone's genuine admiration—a void perhaps only truly filled by the constancy of Valerie's unblinking worship and the intimate friendships he sought among men of "substance" who were considerably more comfortable than he was being themselves in the limelight. This explains why Marvin Leonard became his mentor and George Coleman his best friend, why the clownish Demaret and later the volcanic Tommy "Thunder" Bolt became his closest working associates, why Sarazen and Picard were his primary inspirations on tour. Ditto Hope and Crosby, America's original road-show duo, and colorful, bighearted car salesman Eddie Lowery, Francis Ouimet's suave, bucket-hatted looper. In his heart, Henny Bogan wanted to be exactly like them—guys who knew how to win with grace and style, men who enjoyed the spotlight but never lost the common touch.

Hogan's brush with death apparently helped him fully grasp, perhaps for the first time, why it was important to let his growing legions of fans and admirers see occasional glimpses of the real man within, not just the golf machine that won tournaments with intimidating mechanical precision.

Before the accident, Lucky Ben had come to the conclusion that he was not a popular champion. "Whether he exaggerated this in his mind," says his early biographer Gene Gregston, "Ben's judgment as usual was sound. He had given only a few people the opportunity to know him, fewer still the opportunity to like him." Slamming head-on into a bus captured Hogan's attention as little other than golf had done, and the aftermath gave him plenty of time to ponder what he might be missing. "Where the critics of the media had failed, the thousands of goodwill messages succeeded. Hogan, deeply moved by the expressions of kindness, began to feel that most people who admired his golfing ability also were prepared to like him as a person if given half a chance to do so. He decided he must learn to acknowledge the multitudes," Gregston adds. "It would be a marked departure from the past."

"If I ever get out of here," Ben reportedly told Valerie early on in his hospital stay, "I'm going to be more aware of people—and their kindness to me."

Americans love a winner, after all, especially one who turns out to have a working heart. That golf's most elusive star would gain a human face on the strength of near-tragedy simply gave the evolving Hogan saga another layer of mythical intrigue, a more appealing human dimension—something Hollywood itself might well have conjured up.

FEW WHO KNEW the man were really surprised that within eight days of his encounter with Alvin Logan's speeding Greyhound, Hogan's official condition steadily improved from "critical" to "fair" and finally to "good" and that the little champ himself was already talking about going home to Fort Worth and getting to work on his rehabilitation.

Four days after Valentine's Day, the private anniversary marking his father's suicide, and two days after doctors announced he would be allowed to go home to Fort Worth, Ben reported a sharp pain in his chest and was rushed to X-ray, where it was quickly determined that a pair of large congealed clots of blood were making their way up from his damaged left leg to his chest. The clots were floating time bombs in his circulatory system, large enough to block a key artery to the lungs and possibly kill him.

All talk of a quick recovery was moot. Ironically, the afternoon before Hogan's pulmonary embolism was discovered, Hogan's old four-ball partner, Jimmy Demaret, stopped by the Hotel Dieu and discovered Ben sitting up in bed waggling a putter, in such lively spirits it occurred to Demaret afterward to propose making Ben the nonplaying captain for the forthcoming Ryder Cup.

To add insult to injury, on the same day the clot was detected slowly working its way toward Hogan's lungs and heart, the couple's new home was burgled back in Fort Worth. According to police, who got their information from Mama Hogan, several valuable items, including Valerie's new silver tea service, were taken, along with jewelry and "other valuable household items." The burglars must have known whose house they were looting, police concluded, because several of Ben's clubs and tournament medals were stolen too.

Less than twenty-four hours later, Hogan's blood was thinned by physicians, but the lethal clots kept advancing, his condition taking a sharp turn for the worse. Ben's pulse became erratic and his blood pressure dropped precipitously. After a hurried telephone consultation with vascular experts at the Mayo Clinic in Minnesota, Hogan's doctors decided to put in an emergency call to renowned Tulane University surgeon Alton Ochsner, a pioneer in vascular surgical techniques who, among other things, founded the Ochsner Clinic and was the first to introduce medical blood transfusions to the United States.

, Ochsner agreed to fly to El Paso and perform an extremely risky emergency procedure in which the inferior vena cava, a primary conduit that returns blood from the pelvis region and both legs to the lungs and heart, would be tied off to prevent the advance of the dangerous blot clots. Though Ochsner was the leading expert in the radically invasive procedure, which called for the surgeon to slice through the patient's abdominal wall and peritoneum muscle to reach the dull purplish vein about the diameter of a half-dollar just right of the spinal cord and then use surgical thread to tie off the soft, pliable vein— "like turning off a faucet," as the acclaimed surgeon later explained it in layman's terms to the press—success was by no means guaranteed. Even if everything went according to plan and the smaller surrounding veins began to absorb the backed-up blood flow and expand to create new channels of circulation on their own, there could be dire consequences for the patient.

During their phone conversation, Ochsner outlined potential problems to both Valerie and Royal Hogan. Assuming that the patient in his rapidly weakening state managed to survive such a radically invasive procedure, the sharply decreased flow of blood circulation in his legs would undoubtedly make walking anytime soon extremely difficult, if not impossible. Also, with several tiny veins having to do the work of one large efficient artery in returning blood to the heart, the pain could be excruciating in the lower extremities. If the patient eventually did walk on his own again, he was likely to have major swelling in both legs and acute persistent pain for the rest of his life.

The other option was to do nothing, hope the clots disintegrated on their own, and probably watch Hogan die. To compound matters, while this discussion was going on, Ben's El Paso doctors detected a third blood clot making its way north to the lungs. The patient was fading fast. Time was running out.

By evening on the eighteenth, the decision was made to get Ochsner to El Paso as quickly as possible. A tropical weather system had drifted up from the lower Gulf, however, temporarily grounding all commercial flight all along the Gulf Coast. According to one account, in desperation, at 3:30 in the morning, Royal phoned his old Colonial exhibition partner Brigadier General David Hutchinson for help. In her own version of events, Valerie Hogan told friends that she contacted several Fort Worth friends who owned airplanes, but they were all out of town, at which point she—not Royal—contacted General Hutchinson. Whatever the truth of it, within hours, a B-29 crew was en route from Fort Worth to New Orleans, and seven or eight hours later a wailing El Paso police cruiser delivered a sleep-deprived Alton Ochsner to Hotel Dieu. "The first thing I need to do, Mrs. Hogan," Ochsner surprised Valerie by saying, "is get some rest. I've been up all night waiting for that plane to arrive."

As Ochsner grabbed a shower and a quick nap to refresh himself, Valerie slipped off to the hospital chapel in the Inn of God for some quiet reflection with her sister Sarah as a comforting companion. Though marginally raised in the church, she was not a particularly religious woman, but she later admitted to a Dallas reporter that she spent a "lot of time saying prayers" as the hospital's medical technicians prepared Ochsner's operating arena. Royal Hogan, meanwhile, went out to the hospital steps and smoked cigarettes while the staff prepped the patient for surgery by pumping three units of blood into his faltering system. Shortly after two that afternoon, delirious and murmuring about moving back the gallery for their own safety, Ben submitted to Ochsner's scalpel.

As he did so, the Associated Press released a sixteen-paragraph obituary of golfer Ben Hogan to member newspapers and radio stations with this advisory: "The following is a biographical sketch of Ben Hogan, professional golfer, now ill at El Paso. It is intended primarily for use in the event of his death, but excerpts may be used as background for current stories. Please preserve this copy. It will not be repeated."

"Ben Hogan Fights for Life and New Blood Clot Found in Lung Vicinity" read the somber headline out of El Paso as evening shadows spread over west Texas. Similar news bulletins interrupted national radio broadcasts, including *Amos and Andy* and *The Pepsodent Hour.* Some member newspapers went so far as to set the grim announcement of Hogan's death in bold headline type, preparing for the worst. As night crept over the East, millions of Hogan fans and others who'd never even held a golf club in their hands sat by radios awaiting further news on the brave little champ's fate.

Valerie Hogan's prayers were answered. After two hours of surgery, a weary but smiling Ochsner emerged to describe the operation as "a complete success" and predicted Hogan would recover in about a week's time and possibly be up and around, with limited mobility, "in several months."

As news of the successful emergency procedure was conveyed to the relieved and waiting press corps, Ben's physicians cautiously warned that a lengthy and difficult convalescence was ahead for the reigning national golf champion, and they judiciously avoided making predictions about his eventual fitness to play the game again.

Privately, however, they informed Valerie, Royal, and Sarah that Ben would be damned lucky ever to walk again without assistance, much less play in a golf tournament of any kind.

USING A NEW PUTTER and a considerably narrowed stance that placed his head further over the ball, Sam Snead won his first Masters golf tournament that spring down in Georgia, the start of his two best years ever in professional golf, a glorious run in which he captured twenty of the forty-two tournaments he played in between 1949 and '50, including a second PGA Championship, the Western and Los Angeles Open titles, and Hogan's own Colonial National Invitational. With his main competitor flat on his back and uncertain whether he would ever swing a golf club again, Slammin' Sam made the most of his golden opportunities, stepping up his practice sessions and even borrowing a page from his arch competitor's book.

"I was mostly known for the way I hit the driver," Snead said. "But the truth was, beginning in early '49, I begun concentratin' more on my iron play and puttin' than I ever had before. Most folks didn't realize that's what won all them tournaments for me, and why I had the lowest scorin' average in 1950. In some ways I owed that to Ben. He showed what a fella could do if he put his mind to it. If we hadn't been such competitors then, why, we might have become very good friends. But even when he was out of it I always knew he was out there watchin', countin' the days until he could get back."

Indeed he was. When nationally syndicated *Chicago Tribune* columnist Charlie Bartlett and *Golfing* editor Herb Graffis arrived to check up on the progress of the patient in room 301 at the Hotel Dieu a few days before Hogan was scheduled to be released and permitted to go home to Fort Worth, they found Lucky Ben squeezing rubber balls to strengthen his hands and a mobile chin-up bar dangling over his hospital bed.

The champ was seated in an armchair by the window of his sun-splashed, high-ceilinged room overlooking El Paso's busy Stanton Street, dressed in blue pajamas and a white polka dot dressing gown. The editors were shocked at Hogan's physical gauntness and the listlessness of his eyes.

"This wasn't the Hogan who came into the press room at Hollywood's Riviera Club and submitted to an hour quiz program by reporters on how he had won the National Open with a record score of 276," Bartlett later wrote. "This was a wan, weary little man who has now spent 41 days beating death, the roughest player of them all."

Though they tried not to reveal their own discomfort, Bartlett and Graffis couldn't help observing the grotesque swelling around Ben's ankles, the effect of his newly constricted blood circulation, and the difficulty that accompanied even the slightest movement of his legs. The champ's voice was flat, weak, and almost drowsy. It was only when the topic shifted to golf, Bartlett said later, that Hogan showed any spark of life. Prior to the interview, both Royal and Valerie Hogan specifically asked that the editors refrain from asking Ben about his golfing future, but Charlie Bartlett simply couldn't resist the temptation.

"Will you play golf again?" he said to Hogan gently near the end of their conversation, adding, "Not when, Ben, but *will* you play?"

Hogan stared at his questioner for a long moment with cratered eyes, as if absolutely nothing else had been on his mind since being hauled from under the collapsed dash of his Cadillac.

"I'm going to try, Charlie. It's going to be a long haul, and in my own mind I don't think I'll ever get back the playing edge I had last year. You work for perfection all your life, and then something like this happens. My nervous system has been all shot by this, and I don't see how I can readjust it to competitive golf. But you can bet I'll be back there swinging."

Coming from a man who appeared to be little more than a shell of himself, Hogan's bleak assessment left both editors with the parting impression he would never make it back to the game. While walking the visitors out of the hospital, though, Valerie, overlooking the fact that the subject had been broached with Ben, attempted to put a more optimistic spin on the situation. "Don't believe a word of it," she told Bartlett flatly. "It's going to take time, lots of it, but I am sure Ben will be himself again, bones, nerves, and all. He has shown me more willpower through this terrible spell than he ever did on a golf course."

An excellent sign of his recovery, she pointed out, was that he'd begun to grumble about the hospital food. Finicky as ever about what he ate, flapjacks from a nearby hotel kitchen were now sent over every morning in an effort both to build up his strength and to put back a few of the twenty pounds he'd lost since the accident. He was also bugging doctors to let him smoke again.

"I don't know if Ben will ever win a golf tournament again," she told the editors by way of good-bye. "But I can assure you he means to play golf again."

"I left the hospital," Graffis admitted afterward, "sick at heart, stomach, and head, but hoping for a miracle."

• • •

HOGAN DEPARTED the Inn of God on the morning of April 1, almost two months to the day after he entered the hospital, strapped to a mobile rolling gurney bed and accompanied by six large cardboard boxes filled with unanswered cards, letters, and telegrams. Royal Hogan flew back to El Paso from Fort Worth for the occasion, just to ride the train home with his brother.

Mama Hogan and a crowd that included Margaret and Jacqueline Hogan, Marvin and Mary Leonard, the Reverend Granville Walker, and half a dozen friends and reporters were waiting for them to arrive at the Texas & Pacific station in Cowtown. As Hogan's mobile bed was lowered to the train platform where he'd once flogged Amon Carter's newspapers, Ben greeted his entourage with a broad smile and optimistic wave of the hand.

"What I remember most about it," says Jackie Hogan Towery, "was how thin and drawn Uncle Ben looked. He looked worse than I expected him to. Happy to be home. But lucky to be alive."

Hogan *had* been fortunate—lucky to survive the crash that demolished his luxury automobile (which Ben credited with saving their lives and citizen Leonard promptly had hauled to Fort Worth and placed on display on a commercial lot near his store, using the crumpled automobile to warn passersby of the dangers of excessive speed) and maybe luckier still to have survived marauding blood clots that would have finished off most ordinary mortals in his situation.

Safely installed in the front downstairs bedroom of his pretty white colonial house on Valley Ridge Road, finally out of the view of cameras and curious prying eyes, Charlie Bartlett's haunting question came back to him with fresh and devastating clarity, and Lucky Ben faced perhaps the most daunting challenge of his adult life. Could he recover sufficient use of his damaged legs to even walk a golf course again, let alone compete in a major championship?

Months after the accident, his doctors were nearly unanimous in their professional judgments that he could not. But theirs was only a collective medical wisdom, failing to take into account the patient's various powerful, if less visible, motivations.

Ben Hogan had lived most of his life being written off as either too small or unfit to seriously contend for life's grand prizes, and the specter of another failure only strengthened his resolve to win. He was a man who was almost always at his best when the odds were most stacked against him. Aside from a second National Open Championship that would cement his supremacy and the unfinished business of claiming a Masters title, the moment the Hawk abandoned the practice routines that set him apart and gave up his quest to play golf better than anyone ever had before him, Ben Hogan's life would essentially be over.

His hospital-room epiphany, if that's what it was, seems to have played a significant role in reminding him of poignantly prescient comments he made at the tail end of his brilliant breakthrough season in 1946 when he finally addressed the swirling rumors that he was about to quit the tournament trail and follow Byron into semiretirement.

"No. I don't ever expect to quit tournament golf," he said emphatically then, hoping that would be the end of the discussion (which it wasn't). "I'm a pro golfer. That's my business. I guess I'll play golf as long as I can drag a leg out there."

MONTHS AFTER Sarah Fox Walters returned from Ben's bedside in El Paso, she and Ralph and little Valerie moved to Atlanta to try to make a "new start" at family life. Ralph had a new job, but his drinking continued, as did the further disintegration of the couple's marriage.

Early that summer little Valerie was sent off to a ranch-style summer camp in south Texas to learn to ride and rope like her grandmother Jesse. When she came home to start the fifth grade that August, Sarah surprised her daughter with the news that Ralph was staying put in Atlanta but she and Valerie were moving back to Fort Worth, for good. The couple had decided to divorce. Sarah and Valerie would live for the time being with Uncle Ben and Aunt Valerie on Valley Ridge Road.

"My mother always tried to find the positive aspect of anything that happened to us," Valerie Harriman remembers. "I remember how enthusiastic she was that we would be able to help look out after Uncle Ben and maybe even travel with him to tournaments if he was ever able to actually play again. I remember being sad about the divorce but very happy about moving back to Texas."

The house on Valley Ridge had two large upstairs bedrooms connected by a spacious bath and a downstairs bedroom with a bath that became Ben's recuperation suite. Valerie and Sarah moved into the other upstairs bedroom. For the most part, Sarah took charge of running the household while Valerie and a day nurse devoted their attentions to the patient.

Doctors told Hogan it would be at least five months before the swelling in his legs disappeared and he regained reasonable use of his legs. They advised walking every day to rebuild atrophied muscles, and Hogan, a model patient in every respect, quickly devised his own routine for pushing along his recovery plan. For the first few days, he woke around eight in the morning, soaked in a tub of warm water and Epsom salts to loosen his muscles, then walked "laps" around the house with the use of a cane until he tuckered out.

On April 5, he slipped an overcoat over his pajamas, placed a fedora on his head, and stepped outside for a short stroll around his new backyard—his first steps outdoors in over two months. The next afternoon, he repeated the procedure, hobbling a little farther around the yard to inspect the new bedding plants growing in the watery spring sunlight. At one point, carrying a pan of water, he stopped and sniffed several blooming flowers and watered them, then chatted with the new lawn man. Hogan had a lifelong interest in gardening but had never had the time to pursue it. Valerie later told a friend that the sight of Ben poking about in the yard like an old man with nothing else to do brought tears to her eyes.

Days later, on April 7, a Delta Airlines pilot showed up unexpectedly at the Hogan front door carrying a framed photograph of the entire Masters field and an engraved humidor full of fine cigars. The inscription read: "To our friend Ben Hogan. On the eve of the 1949 Masters, we send you heartfelt good wishes for a speedy and complete recovery."

On Easter Sunday, April 17, wearing street clothes for the first time since the accident, Hogan managed fifty laps around his living room and went for a half-block walk through Westover Hills with the help of his cane and his daytime nurse by his side. "At first he went out with the cane and eventually, to be less conspicuous," says Valerie Harriman, "he switched to using a golf umbrella. The walks became longer and longer down the block. I remember how panicky Aunt Valerie became every time he went a little bit further afield. She wasn't good at handling any kind of stress, especially where Uncle Ben was concerned."

On several afternoons while Valerie was out doing errands, he took himself off on unannounced voyages around the neighborhood, prompting his worried wife to come flying after him in their new Cadillac. In at least two instances, she found him waiting for her several blocks from home, grimacing from severe cramps in his overextended leg muscles, waiting for the pain to subside on the curb of somebody's house. "She would always scold him pretty good," remembers Harriman, "because he'd done something without her knowledge. It was the same thing with cigarettes. Aunt Valerie didn't want him to have them at all, due to his weakened state. But I think my mother may have let him have a few whenever her sister wasn't around. She was good for his recovery, he liked to say. Probably because she let him bend the rules a little."

On April 30, Hogan flew to the Ochsner Clinic in New Orleans for a comprehensive checkup and physical evaluation. Despite painful and constant swelling in his calves and lingering pain in his shoulder and right knee, the prognosis was fairly promising. Hogan returned home via train in excellent spirits and promptly doubled his chin-up, rubber-ball-squeezing, and weight-lifting regimen and added blocks to his voyages around the streets of Westover Hills, to his wife's chagrin.

A few weeks later, Hogan stunned USGA officials by mailing his entry form for the 1949 United States Open Championship to Golf House in New York City. His surprising entry was accompanied by a note requesting that the organization release nothing to the press about his ambition to play in the National Open. If the pace of his recovery enabled him to play, he reasoned, perhaps the fans would be both surprised and pleased; if not, nobody would be disappointed. The blue coats consented to his wish for confidentiality on the matter.

He didn't play, of course. By early June, Hogan's legs were capable of carrying him several blocks around Westover Hills, and he'd even made a few limited slow hikes over fairways at Colonial with Valerie following in the car, ostensibly to chip and putt and work on his short game. On the practice range itself, however, the Hawk had only limited range of motion on legs that were still wobbly and weak. He began experimenting with a swing that didn't require as much of a weight shift on his legs and at lunch with Marvin Leonard confessed to being so bitterly disappointed to miss the opportunity to defend his National Open crown up in Chicago that he couldn't even bring himself to listen to the radio broadcast of the event.

If he had, the Hawk would have heard the changing of the guard and another chapter in the saga of Sam Snead versus the U.S. Open.

Cary Middlecoff was a graduate of the University of Tennessee Dental College, a lean, gangly, affable, but highly skittish young man who'd won the 1945 North and South convincingly while still an amateur (beating Ben Hogan, no less, by six strokes) and had been a Tour pro for only two years. Among other playing curiosities, six-foot-two Cary was known for his fast, impatient walk and his agonizingly slow play, an indecisiveness about selecting clubs that put his nerves in knots and drove other players crazy, a pause at the top of his swing and a grunt at the bottom, but also an ability to hit long and wonderfully straight drives and crisp iron shots that were things of beauty. When his putting was on and his nerves weren't acting up, Middlecoff was capable of going on scoring binges that dropped jaws and left fields in his dust.

Opening with a fidgety 75 at Medinah, Cary settled down and put together masterful rounds of 67 and 69 over the next thirty-six holes to reach the Open's concluding Saturday round with the lead at 211, three ahead of volatile Carolinian Clayton Heafner and six ahead of the ever-present Snead. Unfortunately, Middlecoff's nerves returned in the afternoon round, and he staggered around the final eighteen in 75 strokes, a 286 total that left him two over par. Most observers felt that left the door wide open for either Heafner or the Sage of Hot Springs to finally get his National Open. By the 14th hole of his final circuit, Heafner had pulled even with Cary, but a bogey on the 16th and a missed birdie on the final hole left him at 287, one shy of the lead.

In his marvelous history of the U.S. Open, USGA author Bob Sommers relates yet another Sneadean tale of woe:

Sam still had nine holes to play when Middlecoff finished. Out in 36, he'd have to play the rugged second nine in 33 to catch up, and he hadn't shot under 71 so far. Suddenly the putts began to fall, and he birdied two of the next five holes, picking up the strokes he needed. If he could match par the rest of the way, he'd have the tie. Par on the 15th, and another on the 16th; two more to go. Before Medinah was revised in the early 1980s, the 17th was a dangerous par-3 of 230 yards with a massive carry across a wide body of water. A deep bunker guarded the front, and the rear of the green rose sharply. The tee shot was all carry, with no room for error. Snead hit a good-looking shot dead at the pin, but a slight wind blowing in his face held the ball back a trifle. It hit well to the front of the green, drew back down the incline, and rolled three feet off the putting surface.

A radio announcer on the scene whispered to his national audience that Sam Snead looked as if he'd stepped on a copperhead snake.

He seemed to be in no danger; he could either putt the ball or chip it. He chose to putt, planning to hit down on the ball and let it skim across the apron, which should brake it. It was a common shot, one used all the time, but Sam didn't notice that his ball was sitting in a small depression. When he stroked the ball, it popped up quickly, jumped across the fringe, and rolled eight feet past the hole. He missed his par putt, and now he needed a birdie on the 18th, a par 4 of a little over 400 yards with a gentle left to right swing. His approach skipped over the green, and his chip stopped three feet short. He shot 34 instead of 33, and finished with 70 and 287, one stroke too many.

Again.

Nervous Cary Middlecoff was the new National champion, and Sam Snead was never really quite the same in the tournament he wanted to win more than all others. True, four years later, at Pittsburgh's Oakmont, Sam would play heroically and wind up in second place for the final time in his storied career. But the little man who would limp around the golf course that unforgettable warm afternoon above the Allegheny would steal all of the spotlight and outplay the Slammer shot for shot, beating him by a wide margin of six strokes.

THAT SAME WEEK down in Texas, Culberson County Judge James A. Terrill presided over Alvin Logan's misdemeanor trial on charges of aggravated assault and failure to yield the right-of-way.

Logan's attorney argued to the jury of six white men that the Hogan Cadillac had been traveling in "excess of sixty miles per hour" as it approached the culvert, lost control, and swerved into the path of the oncoming Greyhound bus. The fog had played a major role in the mishap, he said, but Ben Hogan's anxiousness to get home had clearly caused the wreck.

The state countered with eyewitnesses who testified that Logan's bus had improperly attempted to pass the truck as it went up the incline, suggesting that Logan's recklessness—not Hogan's speed—was the real cause of the collision. The Hogan vehicle, the official investigation showed, had been doing "no more than twenty miles an hour" at the moment of impact.

After a fairly short deliberation, the jury ruled in favor of the state's case but gave Logan the lightest sentence permitted by law—a fine and court costs totaling just $127.

IN LATE AUGUST, with summer waning, Ben returned to New Orleans for another checkup with Ochsner, complaining of persistent sharp pain in his right knee. His walks were now up to a mile every afternoon, but the pain in his knee showed no signs of easing up. Ochsner found torn cartilage and recommended surgery to repair it. After sleeping on his decision for a night, Hogan decided to forgo surgery. He could live with pain—along with an elastic brace to support the knee and aspirin to dull the ache. What he couldn't live with was the modest risk that surgery on the knee might delay his comeback another day.

Back home, he extended the length and duration of his afternoon hikes, once or twice hobbling half the distance over to Colonial Country Club—a distance of more than three miles—before having to phone Valerie to ask her to come pick him up.

By September he'd put on ten pounds and was fit enough to travel to England on the *Queen Elizabeth* to serve as nonplaying captain for the American Ryder Cup squad steaming to Ganton Golf Club in Yorkshire. It was during this somewhat turbulent transatlantic crossing that he revealed his surprising thoughts about playing until fifty to Henry Longhurst of the *Times* and Leonard Crawley of the *Daily Telegraph*.

"He was still a cripple," Crawley wrote four years later, "and could only move around with difficulty, but my friend and colleague Henry Longhurst and I spent interesting hours talking to him. I have vivid memories of him telling us one night how he had planned before his accident, by a system of monastic self-discipline, to continue playing and winning championships until he was 50 years old; and before going to bed that same evening he said that he intended to play again and win another championship. Longhurst and I looked at one another, and when Hogan left us we said in the same breath: 'How pathetic.' "

It wasn't mere wishful thinking on Hogan's part. Any foolish assumption that Ben was no more than a sentimental selection for team captain quickly vanished beneath the hard regimen he instituted upon reaching British soil. Among other things, Hogan ordered his charges to rise and shine two hours earlier than normal, to practice for at least an hour before and after every match, and to go easy on the sauce and fraternizing at night.

"Hey, Hawk," Demaret asked, "we training for golf or for the Army?"

Then, as if to underscore the fact that he was back, just prior to the start of the competition at the fine old gorse-girdled course just outside the pretty market town of Scarborough, where Harry Vardon once served as head professional, Hogan upped tensions—and reopened old wounds—by charging, of all things, that certain British players were filing the grooves of their irons deeper than the rules allowed.

London's tabloids howled indignantly, labeling his protest nothing more than rank gamesmanship and payback for Henry Cotton's "reasonable" request to inspect golf balls and clubs used by the Americans at Portland two years before. Despite the angry editorialists arrayed against him and grumbles from prominent British players like Max Faulkner and '39 British Open champion Richard Burton (who reportedly used a drill to deepen the holes in his dot punch wedge), Hogan stuck to his guns, and the host team's armaments were submitted to inspection before the start of play. Accordingly, on the eve before the supposedly "friendly" team competition got under way, Ganton head pro Jock Ballantine stayed up half the night grinding down the faces of several sets of clubs.

The charge of illegal grooves was not the only flap to rise from Hogan's brutal captaincy. With wartime food rationing still in force across Britain, Captain Hogan insisted that the traveling Americans bring along their own field rations, a rich cache of foodstuffs that included fresh butter and eggs, half a dozen Virginia hams, thirty pounds of smoked bacon, and more than six hundred pounds of iced-down Texas sirloin, an all-American horn of plenty that flatly astonished most Britons who read about the provisions in the newspapers.

It also deeply embarrassed the British hosts. More than one official complained to the press that Hogan's aggressive captaincy was shifting Ryder Cup competition from its somewhat relaxed and clubby traditions toward something resembling warfare.

"If this is indeed a fight, as some would have you believe, what does Mr. Hogan intend to do with his splendid rations while his foot soldiers are elsewhere engaged?" wondered one London editorialist with his tongue only partly inserted in his cheek. "Post a military armed guard by the door?"

As the unexpected furor grew, however, Hogan suddenly defused the situation by calling a press conference and graciously offering to "share" the imported provisions with the home team. Feathers settled and play began.

Motivated by home pride and the bitter memory of an 11-to-1 shellacking at Portland, the hosts responded by brilliantly earning three of a possible four points during the first-day foursomes, including a stunning upset by a seething Dick Burton and Arthur Lees of the "unbeatable" Mangrum and Snead.

Johnny Palmer, who lost his opening foursomes match with partner Dutch Harrison 2 and 1 to Faulkner and Adams, remembers Hogan's blistering expression after he came off the field of battle. "When he gave you that look, you knew you were in trouble," Palmer remembered. "I don't remember a whole lot of laughs being had that week. I mostly remember Ben saying we simply had to get the job done."

Needing just three and a half points from the second day's eight singles matches to seize back old Sam Ryder's cup, many sensed a British and Irish romp in the making. But at the lunch break, according to Jimmy Demaret, Hogan laid down a little speech that lit a patriotic fire beneath the visitors.

After Dai Rees and Jimmy Adams disposed of Bob Hamilton and Johnny Palmer to move the home team to within a point and a half of returning the cup to Britain, Dutch Harrison demolished Max Faulkner (8 and 7) and Snead did a similar number on poor Charlie Ward. The final four matches were won convincingly by Clayton Heafner, Chick Harbert, Demaret, and Mangrum, a stunning reversal of fortune that gave America a 7 to 5 win and sent Sam Ryder's famous cup back to the colonies aboard the *Queen Mary*.

According to Demaret, one evening during the five-day return voyage and nonstop celebration party that ensued, with the largest passenger ship on earth rocking in heavy autumnal seas, he stepped out to take in some sea air and discovered a gray figure standing alone at the rail, contemplating the restless sea. It was Hogan, looking deeply worried and perhaps a little seasick, wrapped up in a gray wool sweater, cap, and trench coat.

"Come on, Hawk, I'll buy you a drink," golf's blithest spirit insisted, nudging his old four-ball mate toward the ship's main bar.

Inside, Hogan's spirits seemed to pick up slightly, Demaret recalled, until he happened to glance through an open door to the ship's rear deck, where several seamen in dress uniform and a Church of England minister were congregated at the rail.

"What's going on?" Ben wondered, and walked that way to investigate. Demaret followed him, cocktail in hand. They paused together by the door and watched a Union Jack–draped coffin being solemnly lowered over the side of the *Queen Mary*, the final act of a formal burial at sea.

For a moment neither man said a word. "I stiffened a bit and got set to turn right around and head back to the bar. But Ben grabbed me by the arm," Demaret remembered.

" 'Jimmy . . . please. Whatever happens to me, don't let them do that. You're my friend. Don't let them do that to me if I die on this thing.' "

Demaret thought Hogan was joking. But then he saw the genuine terror in his friend's eyes.

"Ben, don't you worry," Demaret attempted to console him in the only way he knew how, with a joke. "The water here is too *cold* for you. If anything happens, we'll wait until the ship gets into warmer water."

• • •

BACK HOME in Fort Worth, Hogan pushed his walking and strengthening routines to the limit, more than once setting off for Colonial Country Club on foot and then walking home, a distance of approximately seven miles.

Two weeks before Thanksgiving, he tentatively hit his first full shots on the club practice range, reportedly tumbling over on legs unaccustomed to the ferocity of the Hogan swing. During most of these outings, Valerie stood faithfully monitoring her husband's progress and looking deeply worried. She felt he was pushing too hard and risking further injury.

Since the accident, in addition to being Hogan's primary health care provider and chauffeur, she had assumed an important new function in Ben's life—the unbending gatekeeper of home life. Anyone who phoned the house to chat with Ben normally had to go directly through Valerie (who might or might not pass along the message, depending on her judgment of the call's importance), and more than one day nurse was dispatched for failing to perform up to Mrs. Hogan's standards of patient care. She also went through a series of cooks before finding one who pleased her. "Maids who messed up in the slightest way," remembers Valerie Harriman, "rarely got a second chance before she fired them."

In other ways, life looked up considerably for Ben and Valerie, as well as for Sarah and little Valerie. During the nine months Sarah and her daughter lived with the Hogans on Valley Ridge Road, "little" Valerie attended a school she loved and spent a great deal of time with her maternal grandmother while Sarah worked as a volunteer gray lady at Harris Methodist Hospital, joined the Westover Hills Garden Club, and even took golf pointers from Ben.

Soon after her divorce from Ralph Walters, Sarah started dating insurance man Gordon Harriman, one of her former husband's regular Brook Hollow golf pals. Harriman, Averell Harriman's cousin, was handsome and Andover-educated and quickly charmed everyone in the house on Valley Ridge Road.

"My mother told me to call him Uncle Gordon or Gunk, and I quickly came to adore the man. He was so kind and generous to us, I secretly wished he could be my father. I was thrilled when I learned that they planned to get married. Granville Walker married them right in the living room at Uncle Ben's house. Then my new father and mother built a house of their own just around the corner on Westover Road. It was the perfect situation for everyone."

. . .

ON DECEMBER 10, a Saturday, ten months and eight days following his collision with Alvin Logan's Greyhound bus, Ben Hogan played his first eighteen-hole round of golf assisted by a motorized scooter. Ridglea Country Club pro Ray Gafford, a Hogan friend since their caddying days, was invited to play along with Hogan and surprised his host by wondering, during a second loop of the course, if Ben had any intentions of trying to enter the Los Angeles Open, now only weeks away.

"I don't know. Why?" Hogan grunted.

"You'd sure shock a lot of people," Gafford replied, smiling.

Hogan stared hard at Gafford.

"You think so?"

"I do."

The story of their clandestine golf outing reached the pages of the *Fort Worth Star-Telegram*, crediting Ben with rounds of 71 and 72. When Hogan was asked about this impressive feat, he dismissed the report out of hand because, as he noted, "I didn't walk all of the way or finish some holes."

Golf tournaments require reliable legs, and despite his steady improvement, Hogan in fact feared he might never hold up under the rigors of tournament golf. After almost any walk of significant length, including his lengthy perambulations with an umbrella around the neighborhood streets of Westover Hills, both ankles and lower calves swelled painfully and his left knee sometimes buckled. Ochsner prescribed painkillers and a gentle diuretic to combat the swelling, but Hogan had a strong abhorrence for pills of any kind and would take only a single aspirin to knock the edge off his pain. At Ochsner's suggestion, he also took warm baths before and after his walks to try to soothe the muscles and reduce inflammation in the tissues.

Before playing golf, he also adopted the elaborate procedure of carefully bandaging his legs from upper thigh to ankle to try to keep swelling at bay; afterward he rubbed down his weary legs with strong liniments.

A week after news of his impressive rounds at Colonial broke, Hogan completed another eighteen holes of golf entirely on foot, and a day or so later, he quietly let it be known to officials at the Los Angeles Open that he was considering a late entry into their field—despite the fact that after his latest practice round his strength had been so compromised and his legs ached so fiercely that he went straight home and climbed into bed, telling Valerie the comeback cause was hopeless.

His decision to aim for an L.A. return didn't stay quiet long.

When Jack Murphy of the *Star-Telegram* phoned him to find out more about the rumored "California plans," Hogan cautiously informed the reporter that he wouldn't know if his game and legs were up to the undertaking until he reached Los Angeles and played a practice round or two at Riviera. Assuming they proved up to the task, he allowed, he might also try to play in Bing Crosby's pro-am and possibly even the newly renamed Phoenix Open—now called the Ben Hogan Tournament, directly in his honor.

The Bing Crosbys had invited Ben and Valerie to be their houseguests at Pebble Beach, Hogan explained to Murphy, and after the Monterey clambake, he and Val hoped to take a few days off and visit with their friends the Pollard Simons (of Dallas) at their winter home over in Palm Springs. If his legs failed to hold up out west, Hogan said, he would aim to make his comeback at the Colonial NIT.

"Don't waste your time writing about me, Jack," Hogan surprised the reporter by concluding. "People are tired of hearing about Ben Hogan. They're interested in the guys who are playing now.

"It won't be long," he added gloomily, "until they forget about me."

Colonial members who'd been discreetly monitoring Hogan's practice routines and feeding guys like Murphy impressions of the Hawk's medical progress couldn't have disagreed more with this wintry assessment. Though his drives were shorter and his damaged knee was clearly not allowing him to transfer his weight fully as before, the ball-striking they'd witnessed was as crisp and accurate as ever—maybe even more so.

Ten days before Christmas, sponsors of the L.A. Open officially invited Ben to serve as the tournament's honorary starter. Most people who'd heard about this knew it was simply a polite way of giving the fallen champ a graceful means of exit in case his legs weren't up to snuff.

"Honorary starter, hell!" Hogan complained to his wife. "If I go out there, I'm going to play."

"The only reason he wants to do this," his wife complained to her sister, "is the press and the public. For some reason he feels he *owes* it to them."

A few days after that, requiring the services of three porters to carry all of their baggage, Ben and Valerie boarded a morning train for California.

"It's a possibility I'll play," Ben told several Fort Worth reporters who turned out at the depot to see them off. "I'll have to wait and see how I'm feeling and how my game is working. One thing I can tell you for sure: I'm not going out there and shoot in the eighties."

• • •

THE ELEGANT little man who made a brief appearance at Riviera's player reception in Pacific Palisades two days after checking into the Beverly Wilshire Hotel was surprisingly thin and a little haggard, but otherwise his broad movie-star smile was exactly as everyone remembered.

Being back in California always lifted Hogan's spirits.

"Ben," a reporter asked him, "did you happen to see Louella Parsons's column this morning?"

"No, I didn't," he said.

"It said they plan to make a movie about your comeback."

"Is that a fact?"

That morning, the famous gossip columnist broke the news that several "major" studios had recently engaged in a fierce financial scrimmage for the rights to translate Hogan's amazing comeback story—the one everybody hoped and expected to begin momentarily in Los Angeles—to the silver screen.

In fact, negotiations had already been concluded in the matter, and Hogan had personally selected Twentieth Century Fox to make the film and his old Hollywood friend Sydney Lanfield to direct it. A dozen actors were already being considered for the roles of Ben and Valerie, and a trio of studio-employed screenwriters planned to follow the returning champ every step of the way around Hogan's Alley, hoping to gather good material for the as-yet-to-be-written movie script.

Under the terms of the new contract, which paid Ben and Valerie an estimated fifty grand, Hogan had complete script approval and would serve as paid technical adviser to the film, a deal worth at least another twenty grand.

"Well," he replied with grim relish, days ahead of the tournament's official start, "we'll see if there's any comeback worth making a movie about."

TEN

Merion

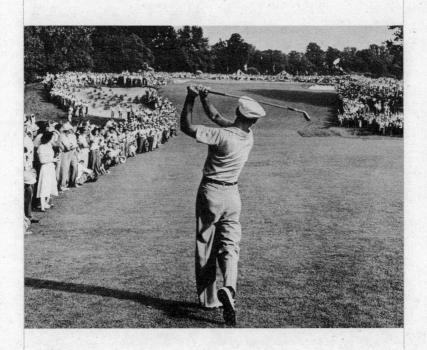

DURING THE OTHERWISE quiet week between Christmas and New Year's of 1949, pausing to rest his legs every few holes on a portable seat like those used by spectators at steeplechases, Hogan got around his first tournament practice round in nearly eleven months at Riviera Country Club accompanied by George Fazio and Sidney Lanfield.

As with most things, the choice of the Hawk's practice partners was far from accidental. Fazio's velvety swing and smooth playing tempo made him one of Ben's preferred warm-up partners and Lanfield, a high-handicapper with a brisk, abbreviated punch-swing, was the man Ben had hand-picked to direct his yet-untitled film biography.

Aside from Ben's rather startling thinness (his weight was still ten pounds below normal) and visible fatigue, longtime Hogan followers who turned out to watch their man's brave return to the links saw something else new. Gone were his cigarettes. In an effort to placate both Dr. Ochsner and Valerie, both

Overleaf: Ben Hogan, 72nd hole, Merion Golf Club, 50th United States Open Championship *(Time/Life)*

of whom believed Ben's comeback effort was seriously premature, Ben agreed to try to kick his three-pack-a-day cigarette habit, at least until he got what he called his "golf legs" back.

In another positive development, he also appeared to display a new ease with fans and press. After signing his card for an impressive 33-36 total of 69, a weary but relaxed and smiling Hawk posed for photographs with cute, tam-wearing Billy Seanor, age twelve, the new Los Angeles Open Mascot Trophy winner, signed autographs for nearly a half-hour, chatted with reporters about the season he'd just missed and the nature of his rehabilitation, and carefully avoided making any comment that could be construed as a commitment to play in the Tour's opening event for 1950.

"Say, Ben, 69 is quite a score," a reporter finally said to him, hoping he'd take the bait. "You really tore up the place out there."

Hogan glanced at his questioner and smiled thinly.

"I did a lot better than expected. But my legs bothered me."

"Still, you'll play . . ."

"Tough to say."

When news dropped that Hogan was back in town, the national wire services and most of the city's newspapers increased the number of reporters dispatched to Riviera, hoping to snag an exclusive interview with the returning star. As one UPI editor quipped, Hogan's sudden reappearance was the best news to hit the City of Angels—hell, *America*—in months, a welcome break from Alger Hiss's perjury trial and growing anxiety over Wisconsin senator Joe McCarthy's "search for Commies under every studio contract."

From both a filmmaker's and a newsman's point of view, whether he succeeded or fell flat on his face, Hogan's comeback attempt had all the elements of great drama—a fallen people's champ transformed by harsh adversity, a loyal wife, a storybook setting, and a challenge most observers realistically felt was well beyond the reach of even a gritty little fighter like Ben Hogan—and was just the narrative antidote for a nation fed up with news of red scares, hydrogen bombs, and crazed Maoists overrunning mainland China. Days away from a new decade that was supposed to signal the start of a wondrous age of technical innovation and human freedom, as Walter Winchell had recently observed, the world at large appeared to be rapidly going to hell in a handbasket. But at least Ben was *back*.

Thus, on New Year's Eve, when another young Mascot player named Bobby Hunter wandered innocently out of the Riviera locker room to meet his mother, not long after Hogan disappeared within to escape the crush of questions and have a much-needed cigarette, the waiting reporters pounced on the startled boy, pinning him to the wall with their rapid-fire questions—"Say, Bobby. What did Ben say in there? How's he feeling, eh? Did he let on if he intends to play or not? Did he mention the big movie deal?"

"Golly, Mother," Hunter addressed his mom as the pencils scratched furiously around him, "you shoulda seen Mr. Hogan's legs. They're *so* scarred. Why, I don't see how he can walk one hole of golf, much less a whole golf course."

It was the kind of moment a movie publicist lives—or dies—for. Lanfield's men didn't miss a detail.

The next morning, New Year's Day, Jimmy Demaret caught up with Ben at the club's practice range.

"Hey, Hawk, I hear you've been practicing and hitting 'em pretty well out there," he said with his usual bonhomie.

"Not really," Hogan replied with his usual reserve. "I'm just going to try my luck here, Jimmy."

The two men shook hands, and Demaret later told reporters the calluses on Hogan's mitts felt like "meat grinders," proof he'd been beating balls as if they "were going out of style."

"Are you free for a practice round this week?" Hogan asked him.

Jimmy grinned. "Like nothing better. Going to the Rose Bowl?"

"No."

Hogan dearly loved watching college football and sometimes even laid a ten-spot on the outcome. That afternoon undefeated Cal was set to go up against Ohio State over in Pasadena, a potential humdinger. But Hogan loved winning golf tournaments more than watching football, so he skipped the Rose Bowl and played an afternoon practice round with only his caddie Charlie Pollock for company. When a reporter afterward collared Pollock and asked how Hogan had played, Pollock only shrugged and smiled, pointing to the card. Hogan had shot 70.

Commencing his third practice round with Demaret, pro Bob Hamilton, and National Open champ Cary Middlecoff the next afternoon, Ben opened with three birdies in a row. But after another birdie at the 12th, he scored three consecutive bogeys and needed to rest on his stool.

"My legs hurt like hell, Cary," he admitted to Middlecoff.

"Let's call off the match, Ben," Middlecoff suggested; they had a $10 Nassau going, and Cary had just drawn even.

"No way."

Hogan got to his feet, Middlecoff dutifully reported afterward, fired an approach shot to twelve feet, then dropped the birdie putt to retake the lead.

"I'm satisfied with my game," Ben admitted to the press at the round's conclusion, a 75, wearily peeling off his linen cap, "but my legs hurt and after a round are swollen, so I must go home and lie down with them held higher than my heart to reduce the swelling. Not fun, fellas." Once again, maddeningly, he declined to reveal if he intended to actually play in the Tour's season opener.

The Hawk clipped off one more impressive practice round of 67, and it didn't escape the notice of veteran golf reporters that his four practice totals added neatly up to 281—three strokes better than the aggregate score of the tournament's reigning champion, Lloyd Mangrum. Ironically, Mangrum was an early scratch from the field owing to an aggravated shoulder injury.

For many observers, including the pretournament favorite Sammy Snead, who rolled into L. A. on New Year's Eve and stayed out late playing the glamorous hayseed, the cat-and-mouse game Ben was enjoying with the press simply indicated that he not only fully intended to play in the Tour's first event but was back to his old head tricks, attempting to keep everyone off stride and rattle his competitors with his usual cool evasions.

In fact, the growing suspense—and accompanying media frenzy—over Hogan's reluctance to officially commit to the event riled some tournament officials, who found themselves besieged by late requests for press credentials from as far away as Britain and Japan but unable to promise whether the little man at the center of the storm would indeed participate.

"You know, I've felt better every day," Ben remarked almost buoyantly after a fifth circuit of the golf course and a scorecard that read 68. "I didn't know if that would be the case or not by this point . . ."

And with that, Hogan mercifully ended the suspense about whether he would play in the twenty-fourth Los Angeles Open. According to *Examiner* columnist Mel Gallagher, Riviera's switchboard immediately lit up with hundreds of phone calls from people who'd heard the news that "Ben was in" and wanted to purchase additional tickets. The city announced it would put on a dozen more buses out to Pacific Palisades, and local camera shops reported a run on film and cameras. Like filmmakers and new editors, most golf fans believed history of some kind was about to be made.

When Snead heard the official news of Hogan's entry shortly after his own impressive warm-up round of 67, he simply offered a lazy I-told-you-so smile. "If he keeps them legs under him," drawled Sam as he ambled off for an early dinner with Mrs. Snead and the Randolph Scotts at the Brown Derby, "Ben'll be damned hard to beat out here, boys. As you know, Ben loves this place."

L.A. Times golf writer Chuck Curtis took Snead's handicapping to heart and promptly declared Ben, Jimmy, and Sam the men to beat—in that precise order of finish.

THE NECESSARY RITUAL of tournament preparation that Hogan had elevated to a personal art form began well before dawn in his suite at the Beverly Wilshire Hotel: a warm soak in the tub, soothing skin rubs with Ben Gay, a single aspirin taken with fresh-squeezed orange juice, a little coffee, his usual two scrambled eggs and well-done bacon, and finally the careful application of elastic bandages and special rubber support stockings similar to the kind used by old ladies with varicose veins to support their saggy thigh muscles.

He left for the golf course in Pacific Palisades before the morning traffic was out in Beverly Hills, advising his driver to "take it slow and carefully" as they wound along Sunset Boulevard toward the Pacific Ocean.

The excitement around Ben's comeback quest attracted a record first-day crowd of 9,000 spectators to Riviera that morning, a majority of whom appeared to wedge themselves creatively on the pavement bordering Riviera's dramatic elevated first tee in anticipation of Hogan's first competitive swing in nearly a year.

Ostensibly out of concern that he might falter and play badly—possibly even fall down and embarrass himself—Hogan, more image-conscious than ever, agreed to make a few posed swings before hitting his first drive but firmly requested of tournament officials that no photographs of him be taken at any point during his round.

To drive the point home, moments before he was introduced and teed up his ball, a boy appeared on the tee carrying a placard that read NO CAMERAS, PLEASE!!! PLAYER'S REQUEST, which visibly irked many of the sports editors, newspaper photographers, and national wire service people assembled beneath the warm winter sun.

As Ben slipped into his yogic pre-shot routine, a fan's movie camera, however, whirred somewhere softly above him, and the Hawk suddenly paused and took a step back, searching for the offender. Someone groaned. Others hissed their disapproval. The camera stopped. Moments later, Hogan blistered his first drive to the center of the fairway and the crowd let loose a sustained cheer.

Out on the fairway of the par-5 hole, though, Hogan paused again and exchanged sharp words with a small group of still photographers from an out-of-town newspaper who evidently either hadn't gotten the message or simply chose to ignore it.

"Can't you fellas read?" he demanded angrily, jerking his head at the trailing notice-on-a-stick. The exchange intensified—a "regular rhubarb developed," according to Mel Gallagher—until a group of Hogan fans, self-appointed enforcers, began to chant, "Take away the cameras!" and the photographers gave up and made a beeline for the tournament director's office.

By Hogan's seventh hole of play, a debate was raging full force across tournament director George Schneiter's desk between besieged officials and several news wire editors who believed the "ban" had been orchestrated by Hogan's chum Sidney Lanfield, the newly hired filmmaker who had preposterously offered his subject, among other things, use of a movie studio Jeep to ferry him around the golf course if his legs gave out, an offer Hogan wisely turned down. The scribes argued that Lanfield wanted no official documentation of Hogan's heroic comeback efforts in order to preserve the freshness of the tale for the big screen, a charge tournament officials were hard-pressed to deny. The editors didn't give an inch, arguing the unfairness of the prohibition. No other players had asked for or been granted such exclusion from full coverage. Why should prima donna Hogan? The tournament officials eventually caved.

As Ben approached the 8th tee, Schneiter used a walkie-talkie to remove the boy with the sign, effectively lifting the ban. Hogan, deep into his own head, gave no indication that he even noticed. Much as the reporters admired his gritty determination to play, the last thing they were willing to sacrifice was photographic evidence of possibly the year's hottest sports story. Later that day, a wire service photographer complained of being shadowed and constantly abused and harassed by a group of "angry Texans" after taking a photograph of Hogan hunched over a putt.

Following the completion of his round, though, Hogan met personally with Schneiter and the photographers in the pressroom to try to iron out their differences, before further misunderstandings arose. After a bit of friendly conversation about his surprisingly fine round—Ben pieced together a respectable opening 73—the Hawk conceded that it wouldn't be fair to prohibit pictures of him in action while other players were freely photographed, and he assured the irate lensmen that he wished to receive no special favors and held no ill will toward them for simply doing their jobs. In parting, he strenuously denied having said, during the brief "rhubarb" on the first fairway, that "there are no pictures or I won't play," and he attempted to smooth over any wrong impressions by clarifying. "What I meant to say was that I didn't want any pictures taken *before* I hit the ball."

The meeting, according to *Evening Herald* columnist George Davis, ended on friendly terms, but only when "the photographers assured Hogan this would not be done." One of the veteran Tour photographers dryly commented afterward, "Nothing's changed much, I'm afraid. He's thinner and a little friendlier but otherwise the same old Ben. He just smiles a little more and actually speaks to us now."

Ben's opening round of 73 was no thing of beauty, but for all its technical problems, the performance was not the least bit disappointing to the thousands who flocked to Pacific Palisades to see if their hero in gray still had any of his Riviera magic. The man they followed was admittedly not the same little bantam who electrified galleries with his precision shotmaking in '47 and '48. *This* Hogan was visibly jumpy, struggled to gain his putting touch on the tricky poa annua greens, and was clearly tuckered out by the back nine, even briefly lapsing into a nasty old habit—the dreaded hook off the tee.

Between holes, sometimes between shots, he rested himself for several minutes on his portable stool, looking glum and in desperate need of a Chesterfield or Camel. But still, considering all he'd been through in the previous year, for all the ups and downs of his ball on one of golf's most demanding courses, Ben finished his first tournament round back only five shots behind leader Ed Furgol, in a tie for sixteenth place. Not bad at all, under the circumstances.

"Ben is a walking miracle," Dr. Middlecoff observed with almost giddy admiration in the tournament locker room, just prior to ambling out to start his own first-round play that afternoon. "He couldn't possibly be on his game after that long layoff. If he wins this thing, believe me, it won't be with his game. It'll be with his heart. Bennie has more heart than anybody I've ever known."

Lanfield's scriptwriters jotted that pearl of dialogue down too.

In Saturday's second round, both Ben's game and his nerves finally settled down. When a mobile radio broadcaster's voice interrupted his putting routine on the 5th green, Hogan abruptly straightened and took a step back, glancing over at the sportscaster with a deadpan expression that actually cracked into something resembling a smile. Here, for an instant, was the *new*

Ben Hogan who'd stared down the Grim Reaper and learned the value of a smile in competition. A moment later, he resumed his stance and drained the putt for a birdie. The roar was thunderous.

His growing crowds ate it up, and the trailing press members quietly elbowed for a better view of the evolving drama. Ben completed the front nine of his second round in 34 strokes and made Cary Middlecoff look like a prophet by holing two long birdie putts as he trudged home for 35 and an impressive 69 total, good enough to vault him up to a tie for third place with Ellsworth Vines at the tournament's halfway post. Both men were at 142. Dapper Pasadena golf glove salesman and unapologetic Hogan disciple Jerry Barber (the only man in the field physically smaller than Ben) held the thirty-six-hole lead with 137. "I was thrilled to be leading," Barber remembered, "until I glanced back and saw who was closing like a thoroughbred on me."

A biblical downpour washed out Sunday's scheduled third round, flooding barrancas and forcing the tournament rules committee to scrap every round after only fifty-seven players managed to safely reach the clubhouse and seventeen others, including Hogan, were forced to pick up their balls. Out in the tumult, Jimmy Thomson, Snead, and Demaret actually snatched up their balls and vacated the course before play was officially suspended, risking disqualification, while Hogan, unable to proceed across a raging creek on the 11th fairway, hands on hips, glared like an Old Testament prophet for a moment at the seething waters before finally confronting a nearby tournament official. "My legs won't stand an attempt to broad-jump *that*," he insisted, adding irritably, "Get the tournament committee on the walkie-talkie and explain." Before a response could come, though, he too picked up his ball and set off at a slow hobble under his umbrella toward the clubhouse on the hill, shades of old Walter Hagen—a blessing, as it happened, because Ben had gone out in a sloppy 39 and felt creeping numbness in his hands.

The unexpected halt in play (which denied Barber a ten-stroke lead and probably cost him the $2,000 first-place check) allowed Ben to go back to the Beverly Wilshire and soak in a tub of Epsom salts, enjoy an early dinner with friends from back home in Texas, and get to bed before eight that evening.

Ben felt refreshed on Monday and proved it by bagging two birdies in the first seven holes of play, his jubilant galleries growing even more immense and noisy as word spread that something truly unprecedented was taking shape out at Hogan's Alley. Ben carved out another beautiful 69 and climbed to second place, within two strokes of Jerry Barber, who came in at 209. Five strokes back, all but invisible amid the Hogan hoopla, was the hottest player in the game at that moment, Sam Snead.

"I'm plenty tired," Hogan admitted at the three-quarter mark of his gallant comeback, fueling speculation that his legs might finally be spent. "I'm not even sure these old stems can go another eighteen." But the next day, tapping a reservoir of unexpected strength, he recorded a third straight round of 69 and signed his seventy-two-hole card for 280, then limped into the clubhouse tipping his cap politely, followed by the thunderous cheers of his followers. "The second coming of Lazarus," one of the radio commentators barked excitedly from the dramatic hilltop above the final green. "Why I wouldn't have believed it if I hadn't seen it with my own eyes!"

Sid Lanfield's secret battalion of scriptwriters could not have written a better Hollywood ending. At that moment, with Barber and Demaret and the other names having fallen back, the only player left on the golf course with a reasonable chance to catch the Hawk was none other than his archrival Snead, the man who would be king, who was three under after fourteen holes and needed two birdies in the four remaining holes simply to tie.

After failing to find them at 15 and 16, Sam turned to his playing partner, Hogan pal Jackie Burke Jr., and his own loyal gallery and ruefully remarked, "Guess I've got to knock a couple in to catch the Little Man."

Some of Sam's loyal followers tittered nervously at the comment, realizing what an uphill battle their man faced.

But nobody laughed, Snead recalled, when he got that first needed birdie at 17, his fourth birdie in six holes.

Riviera's 18th is a shameless spirit breaker, a 445-yard par-4 monster that plays uphill and slightly left to right, ending in a natural hillside amphitheater below the majestic clubhouse, one of the most picturesque finishes in all of golf. As Sam prepared to play the hole, 10,000 spectators covered the hillside around the green, and another 10,000 lined the fairway itself. "Most of 'em, you got the feeling, were waiting to pop the cork on Ben's big comeback win," Sam said later.

The Slammer drilled a magnificent shot 250 yards into the short grass slightly left of center, then artfully bounced his six-iron approach shot off the left slope to within fifteen feet of the cup, initiating a whooping cheer from his own rowdy partisans on the hill. As he was settling over the putt into his new narrowed stance, however, a limb cracked sharply and a spectator tumbled out of a nearby tree.

"Must be a Hogan fan," Sam drawled darkly. The gallery tittered. Sam stepped back and studied his critical birdie putt again, unwilling to make the mistake he'd made against Lew Worsham when he putted too quickly after an interruption, missing the short putt that cost him a National Open.

Even before the accident, Snead's rivalry with Hogan was such an ongoing saga that the producers of Ben's epic planned to make it part of their movie, hoping to convince Sam to play himself in the drama. It didn't come as a real surprise to anyone present that Sam was the only man left standing with any chance to catch Ben. Week to week, Sam Snead was playing the golf of his life and savoring every *gol-dang* moment of it. But this was Hollywood, where the sentimental favorite always won. The perfect ending to a magical week on the California Riviera would be for Sam to lip out his birdie putt and graciously congratulate Ben on his miraculous and successful comeback.

Upstairs at a window in the club's vast formal sitting room, where she had waited most of the afternoon on pins and needles, unable to concentrate on either her knitting or her popular romance novel, Valerie Hogan couldn't bring herself to watch the drama unfolding one hundred feet below. She turned away and sat down in an overstuffed armchair, listening for the crowd's reaction.

Downstairs by the tournament scorer's tent, an already showered and dressed Hogan had come out of the locker room to speak with tournament director George Schneiter and reportedly didn't flinch or even turn his head toward the final green when he heard a mighty shout go up from the multitudes on the hillside.

Someone jogged over, flushed and excited. The cheering came from Snead's rowdy partisans, the groans from Hogan's worshipers. There would have to be a Tuesday play-off.

Ben hastily retreated into the locker room to collect his topcoat and fedora. Several reporters gave pursuit, blowing past the L.A. policeman stationed by the door and going where few but the likes of regular golf writers and the cream of columnists dared tread without a direct player invitation.

"I wish Sam had won it out there," Ben admitted a few minutes later, pausing in front of locker 414, noting that the play-off would amount to his ninth round of golf in slightly more than a week—too much, the clear implication was, for one set of wounded legs to bear.

"I don't feel bad about Sam tying me," he amplified. "I just don't want to play another round. I'd rather Sam had won."

Someone asked if he planned to drive to the Crosby pro-am. As a rule, Hogan loathed pro-ams, but he loved playing in the relaxed Crosby affair, which always allowed him to fraternize and play with his good friends George Coleman and Eddie Lowery. After all the sustained drama and nonstop questions at L.A., the Crosby pro-am would be a walk in the park.

"I don't drive anywhere but home anymore, fellas. We're going up by train."

That night the Pacific rain swept back onshore with wild gusts and torrents, flooding Riviera's famous barrancas once again and washing out any hope of a play-off the following morning. A decision was made to postpone the clash between golf's titans for a week until the Wednesday following Crosby's clambake.

That would give Riviera time to dry out and, as Snead was quick to point out with a note of hillbilly sarcasm, Hogan the opportunity "to rest up them busted legs of his."

Hollywood having been denied the ending it craved, one of the wire services went a little bit over the top in labeling the rescheduled encounter the "Golf Match of the Century."

BY THE TIME Ben and Valerie reached the Salinas train depot, he felt a nasty head cold coming on. He considered dropping out of the pro-am upon his doctor's advice, but played anyway out of consideration for his host Bing Crosby and his budding friendship with many of California's movie colony types to whom golf was both a passion and a means of conducting business. As scriptwriters continued to invisibly dog him around the golf course, Ben finished up the three-day pro-am in a not-so-inspiring tie for nineteenth place, sniffling and pausing to blow his nose and genuinely looking miserable. He then boarded an evening train back to Los Angeles for his much-hyped play-off Match of the Century, his scheduled eighteen-hole encounter with the Slammer at Riviera.

On January 18, the same day the Texas Court of Criminal Appeals down in Austin reversed the guilty verdict against bus driver Alvin Logan based on a technicality involving jury selection, Hogan limped around Riviera to a disappointing five over 76; Snead played only slightly better in their predictably anticlimactic encounter, scoring 72 to collect the title and the $2,600 first-place check.

For their troubles, however, the participants got to split the gate receipts from the 2,091 fans who paid 60¢ apiece to traipse after a match that looked more like an annual club final than the professional golf match of the century.

Ben's comeback effort may have fallen short of Hollywood's expectations, but it wasn't short of cheerleaders who saw it as one of the great human interest stories of modern times.

"Nobody with the possible exceptions of the dying Babe Ruth and Lou Gehrig has so stirred the nation's heart as has Ben Hogan," trilled Pat Robinson of the International News Service afterward, sentiments that were commonplace in newspapers and radio broadcasts across the country. Ben's take on his long-awaited head-to-head with Snead was a little more tempered and, well, distinctly *old* Ben Hogan.

"It was just bad golf," he summed it up chastely. "I've obviously got a lot of work to do yet."

Even before the combatants could clear out of town, another news story broke: days before arriving in Los Angeles, Hogan and his lawyers had reached an out-of-court settlement with Greyhound Bus Company. Though the terms were officially "undisclosed," one source put the figure at $25,000 a year for life, a sum that meant if Ben Hogan never won another dime playing professional golf, he was still set for life.

During a brief rest with Dallas real estate tycoon Pollard Simons and his wife in sunny Palm Springs, Ben's head cold deepened. Valerie consulted with Princess's husband, Doc (Ben's sister and her husband had recently moved back to Texas, and he was now Ben's personal physician), and lobbied to take the train straight home to Fort Worth instead of pushing on to Phoenix just so Ben could fulfill his promise to appear at the newly renamed golf tournament, now called the Ben Hogan Open, in his honor.

By the time a somewhat wan-looking Hogan showed up to say thank you to the civic sponsors in Phoenix, he was lighting up cigarettes again with the gold engraved cigarette lighter Bing Crosby had given him for Christmas, thwarting the advice of both physician and wife, his tobacco addiction returning with a vengeance.

Proving he still had some work to do, and hoping the unexpected difficulty of his West Coast adventure hadn't compromised the physical stamina he knew would be critical two months later at the Masters in April, and the National Open come June, Ben finished play in Phoenix in a ho-hum tie for twentieth place, quickly catching the next train home to Fort Worth.

HE WAS HOME on Valley Ridge for several weeks, sleeping late and eating scrambled eggs, rebuilding his strength and putting on a bit of weight, taking brief strolls around the neighborhod, and pondering what he might do with all that settlement money besides dump it into oil, visiting his nieces and catching up on his fan mail, quietly resuming his lengthy practice rituals at Colonial Country Club, and, weather permitting, even playing a few afternoon rounds of golf with Royal and Marvin and others.

However welcome this respite, February in Texas made Ben's knees and calves throb with cold, his body simply refusing to warm up. He needed some good advice about the oil business and someplace warm to work on his game.

He got both warmth and advice two weeks before the start of the 1950 Masters when he and Valerie headed for Palm Beach, Florida, to visit his Wall Street broker Paul Shields and practice his game at Seminole Golf Club.

Built a year after the collapse of Wall Street by stock baron E. F. Hutton on prime coastal land he reportedly "stole" for ten bucks an acre, Seminole Golf Club featured a fine Donald Ross championship golf course, no formal tee times, a fabulous dining room, and a wealthy private membership that largely hailed from nearby Palm Beach's winter society but rarely showed their intensely suntanned faces around the place before the noon buffet, owing to seasonal hangovers. "Seminole has always been your basic afternoon club," insists one longtime member of high standing. "And the buffet is usually quite memorable."

Hogan loved everything about the place—the fine old course with its challenging Ross greens that placed heavy emphasis on the proper approach shot, the bending fairways that were normally so devoid of other humans on March mornings that he and a caddie could venture wherever "Mister Hogan" decided to go give chase to the prevailing right-to-left Atlantic breeze he preferred to practice against.

"I think privacy was one of the things Ben most liked about the place," says longtime Seminole pro Jerry Pittman, who succeeded Hogan's golf mentor Henry Picard as Seminole's winter head professional. (Like many private southern retreats of its ilk, the club closed every summer and reopened in the autumn.) "Everybody there gave him what he most craved. They left him entirely alone to practice all the golf he wanted."

When Ben and Valerie first came to Palm Beach in the late forties, they stayed either at the Breakers Hotel or rented a small apartment.

As the fifties unfolded, they often stayed with Ben's good friend George Coleman, who joined Seminole in 1954 and much later (1980–91) became Seminole's president.

As Ben's affection for Seminole's splendid isolation and dislike of Texas winter exponentially increased, not surprisingly, so did the duration of the Hogan late winter–early spring forays to south Florida, eventually stretching out to three or four weeks prior to the start of every Masters.

Two figures eventually came to mean a great deal to Hogan in Seminole's somewhat gilded outpost life.

The first was gracious, avuncular George Coleman, the former Sooner State Amateur golf champion and son of tiny Miami, Oklahoma (where his daddy owned the bank, the movie house, and almost every other business in town), who grew up to make a fortune of his own in the oil business, eventually becoming a major shareholder and director in the Penzoil Corporation.

A beloved figure for the compassionate way he treated both club employees and demanding members with equal parts polish and warmth, Coleman, though he was born the same year as Ben, was a younger version of Marvin Leonard and a logical choice as Ben's best friend.

The two shared identical opinions on matters such as marriage, politics, vodka martinis, and how the hell a great private club ought to be run. Their favorite golf game was to pick a score and place twenty bucks in the pot. Whoever came closest to achieving their predicted score without going under it, collected the loot. A player who played under his score had to cough up another twenty. "There was never much money in their games, unlike some others around here," says Jerry Pittman. "Ben and George never had anything to prove to anybody. It was more about the friendly competition than the money anyway. Their matches were close too."

The club's other memorable figure when Ben and Valerie began going there was debonair Chris Dunphy, a former Hollywood talent agent who traveled in elite society circles and lived exceedingly well off no visible means of support other than his golf winnings. "Dunphy got on the green committee and ran the place for years with a polite gloved fist," says another longtime Seminole member. "Everybody loved Chris, especially the Duke of Windsor. They were kindred spirits and real pals. Whenever the Duke came across the pond, they played golf, drank gin, dealt cards, and had one hell of a time together. They were two of a kind, except the Duke always played from the ladies tee, teed up his ball in the fairway, and used two caddies to get around the golf course—one to find his shot and tee it up, the other to pick his club. Hogan, as I recall, always thought that was hilarious—true English decadence."

Hogan liked Dunphy too but generally found him more entertaining than anything else, particularly appreciating the flattering attention he paid to

Valerie, who seemed to savor the sophistication of Palm Beach and its monied winter refugees.

Among other things, during Ben's lengthy visit to Seminole in March 1950, the persuasive Dunphy managed to convince Hogan to commit to playing in something called the "Spring Festival of Golf," a new event Dunphy had just been hired to promote at Sam Snead's Greenbrier Resort during the first week of May. That Hogan agreed to play probably had less to do with his interest in helping out Dunphy than taking advantage of an opportunity to get one back from Snead, who had spoiled his comeback plans at Riviera back in January.

Hogan never forgot a kindness—nor a grudge against someone he felt he should have whipped. Beneath the polite and even friendly respect Ben publicly displayed for Sam's growing prowess and presence atop the game, he seethed that the crude Blue Ridge hillbilly had taken his place at the summit of the standings, and in the hearts of many fans.

Thus, when Hogan suddenly showed up at Augusta's Bon-Air Hotel a week before the 1950 Masters commenced, he was not only tanned and well rested, displaying an almost startlingly upbeat frame of mind, but also willing to sit and chat pleasantly with news reporters he'd formerly avoided like the plague—taking a page, as it were, from Snead's own folksy playbook.

Reflecting on the challenge Augusta's rolling, pine-girdled hillocks presented to his weakened legs and rusty golf brain, Hogan sat for unprecedented spells after his early practice rounds drinking scotch and talking about his comeback's progress and his game's relatively poor "course management" thus far. Winning golf tournaments, he said, was "80 percent management and 20 percent physical." If his old game was based on a principle of numbing physical routine and absolute concentration, his "new" approach was to better *manage* how and where he played the course to minimize mistakes and maximize scoring opportunities.

Several who politely listened to this explanation, however, were hardpressed to see how this approach varied to any significant degree from the siege techniques Hogan had developed and refined over the years. "New words for the same old Ben," witty Tour rookie Tommy Bolt summed up Hogan's so-called "management" style. "He hits the ball wherever he wants. We should just aim for his divots."

Ben's opening three rounds did resemble nothing if not the Hogan of old—73-68-71. But his putter stroke balked and his stamina failed once again in the closing stages of this particular Masters; he finished round four with a bitterly disappointing 76 on his card, six strokes behind his pal Jimmy Demaret, who won his third green jacket with 283.

When a Dallas reporter asked a departing Hogan to assess his "course management" for the week, Hogan gave him a level glance and a vintage two-word answer.

"Damned lousy."

ONE EVENING a month later, Marvin and Mary Leonard came to dinner at the Hogan house.

It was the height of bluebonnet season down in Texas, and while their wives busied themselves in the kitchen, Ben and Marvin sat on the porch talking with vodka martinis in hand. Ben, a light social drinker, always insisted on making the cocktails himself. He playfully called them "see-throughs."

As he sat listening, Marvin aired some of his latest business ideas. With downtown Fort Worth booming and more national retail giants elbowing their way on to Leonard Brothers' turf every year, Marvin and Obie were thinking of starting up a customer shuttle service to their downtown retail landmark (the prelude to an elaborate customer rail system they would in fact create in the early 1960s, a shuttle train that generations of their suburban customers would come to affectionately call "the M&O Subway").

When the subject turned to golf, as it always did, Marvin admitted he was kicking around the idea of searching for some land for a private "members" course somewhere in California where he and Ben and others could retreat when the winter weather turned cold and unfriendly in Texas. He'd even looked into the prospect of purchasing Pebble Beach but found the $20 million price tag a little too rich for his blood. The father of four young daughters, Marvin's second oldest, Marty, was showing signs of being the family's budding links star.

The conversation shifted to oil, and Ben revealed to Marvin that he had more than a casually growing interest in the subject, the effect of having witnessed the Queen City's boom-or-bust oil frenzy back in his days on the Texas & Pacific passenger platform. A man who knew what the hell he was doing—and wasn't in a hurry to do it—could still make a fortune in oil, and Ben now had the kind of operating capital to finance a couple of gushers of his own, not to mention a crack industry mind like George Coleman to advise him.

But something else was on his mind.

"I'm sick and tired of haggling with MacGregor."

After a moment, Leonard asked him, "You want to start your own equipment company, Ben?"

"It's something I'm looking into."

Ben reminded Marvin that nearly every set of irons he received from the MacGregor factory had to be altered to his specifications, taken in the shop and bent or shaped to his satisfaction. For whatever reason, MacGregor seemed incapable of making his golf clubs exactly the way he wanted them. Furthermore, he argued, probably half the balls the company sent him were "out of round." To add further insult to injury, the new Ben Hogan signature iron the company was about to roll out was, in Ben's estimation, "worthless, a piece of junk. The kind of thing you can buy anywhere.

"Not only do I know how to make a good set of golf clubs," Hogan said, "I know how to make a great set."

"Maybe for you, Ben. But everybody else too?"

It was a reasonable question for a seasoned businessman to ask. The golf equipment world was dominated by MacGregor, Spalding, and Wilson, the three titans of sports equipment manufacturing. These firms had decades of experience marketing and selling golf equipment and powerful longtime relationships with most of the country's club professionals. Even if Hogan could find a way to set up a plant and start producing equipment under his own name, Leonard knew, how could even a Ben Hogan hope to compete with the likes of them?

For Hogan, the answer was as clear as the martini he'd just placed in Marvin's hand.

"I'll make better clubs than they do. For anybody who wants to play golf the way it ought to be played."

IN EARLY MAY, looking tanned and fitter than anybody could remember seeing him in quite some time, Ben stepped down from the train at the Greenbrier depot in White Sulphur Springs, West Virginia.

The Spring Festival of Golf was part of Chris Dunphy's scheme to bring the old society hotel gloriously back to life after it had been appropriated by the government to serve as a military hospital during the war. Resident sage Sam Snead was the official host of the golfing fete, and among the elite patrons who attended were Britain's Duke and Duchess of Windsor, who knew the Hogans well from their Seminole visits. The Duke was mad for golf, almost in awe of

Ben, and followed every step of the little golfer's attack on Greenbrier's Old White Course. By the time Ben was through carving up the somewhat short-ish but fine old course where Sam Snead had given his first golf lessons to pay-ing guests two decades previously, he'd posted eye-bulging rounds of 64-64-65-66.

His 259 total matched the seventy-two-hole record set by Nelson during his brilliant winning spree in 1945. Afterward, though, Ben downplayed the sig-nificance of his scoring jamboree, noting that Old White's modest length (ap-proximately 6,300 yards) wasn't nearly the survival test of Augusta or even his own approaching Colonial tournament. He would need something "much tougher" to prepare himself for the tests of golf to come later that season.

During a private dinner with his friend the Duke, Hogan admitted he was working hard to get himself into shape for the fiftieth United States Open Championship at Merion Golf Club outside Philadelphia. Every great player since the days of Harry Vardon had competed at Merion, and the USGA's gru-eling thirty-six-hole Saturday finisher dwarfed any obstacles he'd faced thus far in his comeback effort.

Snead, the tour's leading money winner but once again sentimentally the odd man out at his own party, sat listening to this conversation feeling almost as forgotten as he had in the early stages at Riviera, and not a little upstaged by all the flattering attention being paid his famous guest from Texas.

"I always thought it was kind of inconsiderate of Ben to come up here to West Virginia and score like that," Snead joked in the early 1990s, remember-ing the occasion in detail more than four decades after it happened. "If it hadn't been *my* tournament where he tied the record, I might not have gotten so damn annoyed with him. My own year wasn't going half-bad, you know."

Indeed it wasn't. After nipping Hogan in L.A., the Slammer had put his large supple hands around the trophies at the Texas Open, Miami, Greens-boro, Inverness, and Pinehurst's coveted North and South. Most Tour scribes had him already penciled in for a monster year and a cinch for the Tour's Player of the Year honors. Sam didn't disagree with them. And Jimmy De-maret wasn't lagging far behind. Ben, on the other hand, was miles back on the official money list and no real threat to Snead's dominance, week to week.

As if to remind the fans and the press of this fact, a fortnight after the Duke of Windsor presented Ben with his Greenbrier check and toasted him at the concluding gala dinner, Sam took the train to Fort Worth and shot a spectac-ular 277 to steal Marvin Leonard's trophy straight out from under Ben's nose. Colonial's flatness was a welcome break for Ben's aching legs, and as a former

National Open site, Colonial presented the player with a puzzle of leaning cottonwoods and multiple doglegs that forced him to work the ball left and right the way any contender would soon have to do at Merion. Hogan put together respectable rounds of 71-73-68-70 for 282, good enough for third place. It wasn't good enough for Hogan, though.

Merion loomed—the first place he ever teed up the ball in a United States Open Championship and failed miserably, way back in 1934, the same year he got to know George Coleman even better on the golf trail at the Galveston Open. He'd have to get a whole lot better, and certainly stronger, with a great deal more physical stamina, if he was to have any hope of winning the toughest tournament in all golf and the one thing he wanted even more than that missing Masters title.

BEN AND VALERIE checked into the stately Barclay Hotel, overlooking Philadelphia's sun-dappled Rittenhouse Square, a week before play commenced. The Barclay was Philly's "society" hotel—small, elegantly worn, sophisticatedly shabby, and probably twice the room rate of the other downtown hotels where the other name players and their wives dropped baggage. The hotel was a half-hour's drive out the Main Line by car to the golf course and home to Frank Sullivan, the crusty but brilliant bachelor lawyer who worked for Lippincott, publishers of Hogan's *Power Golf.* As Merion's genteelly Republican membership went, Sullivan was an unusual bird—a gruff, straight-talking city dweller who represented, among other notables, the state's brawling Democratic Party. He was, in short, Ben's kind of guy, a tough insider with no-nonsense, iconoclastic views. He also stirred one hell of a martini.

Hogan admired and gravely respected Merion, which at around 6,600 yards wasn't long by typical National Open standards but basically threw everything in the book at a player. Designed by an insurance man and club golfer named Hugh Wilson (who had a hand in shaping Pine Valley, a course Merion resembles), who spent seven months in England and Scotland studying great golf course design elements before agreeing to lay out then-Merion Cricket Club's "new" course in 1911, the par-70 Ardmore gem meandered over modest, thin, clay-covered hills and the rocky remains of an old granite quarry, an engaging mix of cleverly short par-4s that bent left and right, thoroughly testing par-3 holes of varying lengths, several tough par-5 holes including one stretching over 600 yards, and three concluding holes many regarded as the finest finishing trio in all of championship golf. To give the course the look and feel of its distinguished British antecedents, Wilson and the course's original superintendent, William Flynn, used bedsheets to strategically place bunkers in the most penal spots and loaded up the framing terrain with bursts of rough Scotch broom and spiky native grasses. As with all Open sites, Merion's tidy, marbleized putting surfaces and brutal rough made precision shotmaking critical. Intelligently plotting one's way around the golf course—what Hogan had taken to calling "course management"—was absolutely essential.

The story goes that during one of Ben's early practice rounds in the week before the 1950 Open festivities got under way, meticulously hitting three shots to different spots on every hole, playing mostly alone, he drove his ball to a plateau slightly over the right fairway bunker on the short and ingenious 8th hole, to a flat shelf just over the brow of the hill but well back of the spot where most players aimed to deposit their tee shots, sternly admonishing his young caddie to "carefully replace the divot, son, because I plan to be here every round."

Though no one has ever been able to confirm the story, the anecdote is a beloved part of Merion lore and certainly illustrates Hogan's methodical manner of strategically memorizing every feature of the golf course beforehand, selecting his preferred lies and directional angles to the flag and thoroughly digesting every possible variation so that no shot required of him during the tournament would come as a surprise.

Before the opening round of the National Open's golden anniversary edition got under way, in order to satisfy the sponsoring USGA's fourteen-club rule, Ben pulled the seven-iron from his bag proclaiming, "There are no seven-irons at Merion." In place of it, he inserted a one-iron, a bread knife for keeping the ball low and penetrating in the wind and a club few players had either the skill or nerve to carry.

Because he had gone from national champ to near-death and battled his way back to golf's most elite arena in just over sixteen months, perhaps more than any player before him—including Jones and Hagen in their prime—Hogan was now considered and treated like a demigod who gave the unassailable impression that he knew exactly what was humanly required to win. When reporters quizzed Ben on what score would take the Open, with or without a seven-iron in the bag, he declined to give a firm number but predicted the winning score would be "unusually high."

"From day one you got the feeling that everyone there was watching to see how Ben would hold up," remembers Skee Reigel, the '48 USGA national amateur champion who subsequently turned pro. "Sam was probably the favorite, and some thought Demaret and Mangrum would be right in it. But Ben was the one we were all really watching. He was like some figure from another planet."

When an obscure pro from Birmingham, Alabama, named Lee Mackey knocked off ten one-putt greens en route to a stunning 64 in the opening round of the tournament—a new eighteen-hole Open record—Ben was briefly paragraph-two news, especially after he limped home with a 72. Under normal circumstances, Hogan's two-over score would probably have placed him somewhere near the top of the leaderboard, but he was clearly having difficulties figuring out Merion's rock-hard greens and demanding slopes. At one point during the first round, facing a downhill putt, for example, he opted not to sole his putter so he wouldn't be penalized if the ball moved. It was a wise strategy, since his ball did exactly that, suddenly trickling down the hill and four feet closer to the cup. Hogan straightened and glanced sharply over at the watching USGA rules official, who informed him that no penalty would be leveled because he hadn't grounded his putter. Afterward, facing reporters in the warm and cramped players' locker room over the club pro shop, Ben told them that Merion's greens were as hard and fast as he'd ever seen at a National Open. Whoever won would have to find a way to handle them, he said flatly.

The next day, after being unable to sleep because of his excitement, leader Lee Mackey blew to an 81 and began a rapid disappearing act (he finished in a tie for twenty-sixth place), while Ben shot 69 and climbed into fifth place at 141 behind Dutch Harrison, Johnny Bulla, former PGA champ Jim Ferrier, and a darkly handsome accountant beginning his U.S. Open career, sweet-swinging Julius Boros. On the way out of Merion's main entrance, a wan Hogan suddenly instructed lawyer Sullivan to pull over. Overcome with nausea, he cranked open the car door and vomited in the grass. "When we heard about that," Skee Reigel remembers with a chuckle, "I told some of the caddies they ought to go mark the spot."

Back at the Barclay, Hogan unwrapped his throbbing legs and soaked them in a tub of Epsom salts for an hour. His 69 had not come without a price. The soaking reduced some of the swelling of his calves and ankles, but it didn't lessen the general fatigue he felt rippling dangerously through his body, which was why he and Valerie chose to eat early with Sullivan in the hotel's private dining room and turn in just after darkness fell on the lights of Rittenhouse Square. During their supper, Hogan admitted to Sullivan that he dreaded the next day's infamous double-round finisher. Privately, to Valerie, he expressed doubts about whether he would even be able to finish.

Hogan's preparatory routine—warm bath, stringent leg rubs, the elastic bandaging routine from crotch to ankle, downing a single aspirin with either fresh-squeezed orange juice or ginger ale—required at least two hours, followed by the thirty-minute drive to Ardmore Avenue. Accordingly, Ben rose at five-thirty and made it to the course by eight. Merion's one flaw was its lack of a serious practice area, so players warmed up at a flat spot above the left-hand fairway bunker on 18, where they were permitted to hit balls toward the 14th fairway. Hogan, some recalled, shortened his normal forty-minute warm-up routine in favor of more time on the practice green, trying to get a feel for Merion's murderous greens. Even as the first players teed off, the work crews of Merion superintendent Joe Valentine were busy dumping several wheelbarrows of fine beach sand onto the 12th green and working it into the turf with bamboo poles, watering and rolling the surface to make the lethally hard green even more hostile. On this same green later that day, Sam Snead rolled a short putt from three feet above the cup off the green and a dozen yards back into the fairway.

Saturday morning was lovely and warm in eastern Pennsylvania, with gentle warm breezes coming out of the southwest and puffy white clouds floating like dreamy battleships overhead. Thirteen thousand spectators wandered like ants at a picnic over Merion's tidy, magnificently groomed 108 acres, hoping to see history made on the National Open's 50th birthday.

The contenders all played cautiously that morning, including Hogan, who carded another 72 for a fifty-four-hole total of 213, three over par, placing him in a tie for second place with Johnny Palmer and his playing partner that Saturday, Cary Middlecoff, and two strokes behind the tournament's new leader, Lloyd Mangrum.

After a bowl of soup with Valerie on the club's covered terrace, Hogan started his afternoon round with a 4 on the 1st hole, a par. "I was terribly worried about him going back out," Valerie admitted to a Philadelphia society reporter who chatted briefly with her on the porch as she settled in to sip iced tea and wait nearly six full hours for her husband to finish whatever he was intent on finishing. "I don't think his legs are really up for this."

Her concern was well founded. As one by one the leaders gave ground to par, Hogan trudged slowly to an outward nine of 37, one over, and was visibly having difficulty as he paused for relief at several points and clasped his legs as he negotiated some of Merion's steeper hills. The front nine of his final round was far from spectacular, but under the circumstances it was considerably better than Mangrum's, Harrison's, or Middlecoff's. Fighting their own war of attrition, fidgeting Cary slipped to 39 while the others recorded disappointing 41s. By the turn, though he was now four over par for sixty-three holes, Hogan had backed into the lead of the golden anniversary National Open.

Almost entirely unnoticed in the excitement building in the huge throngs trailing Ben and Cary was the fine finish that scrap-metal dealer and part-time Cadillac dealer and PGA touring pro George Fazio made on the historic old course where, in the summer of 1930, Bobby Jones had capped off his own Grand Slam quest by whipping Eugene Homans 8 and 7 to win the U.S. Amateur Championship and subsequently announced his official retirement from the game. For his part, Fazio finished with 287, seven over par, and immediately went to get an iced cocktail in the players' locker room.

Jones's famous Merion match had reached its dramatic conclusion at the marvelous 11th hole, a 378-yard gem that conclusively established that a hole doesn't require length to be great. From the tee, the fairway rolls out rather innocuously for 200 yards before dropping to a lower shelf some 20 feet below and slightly to the left. The green from this point is no more than a stout pitching iron for most skilled players but reposes beguilingly above a narrow winding creek, flanked by a steep bunker on the left and trickling waters on the right and behind. "It is a teasing hole," writes USGA author Sommers, "that invites birdies but collects a stiff price from those who take the chance and fail."

It was precisely here in the Open of 1934, Sommers notes, that a cruising Gene Sarazen attempted to play cautiously with a two-iron off the tee, hooked his ball into the creek, took seven on the hole, and lost the National Open to Olin Dutra by a stroke.

Now, with a second National Open well within his grasp, Ben Hogan nearly failed to make it through the hole as well. His legs were so stiff and achy that Middlecoff had to lift his ball from the hole for him, as he'd already done at least twice in the previous holes. Hogan's face was a mask of stifled pain. He narrowly missed a birdie from twelve feet and hobbled through the little patch of hard woods to the 12th tee, now leading Fazio in the clubhouse by three, as the other contenders began to fall back.

"For by now," Philadelphia golf historian Jim Finegan wrote after watching the moment unfold before him, "every step had become agony. Hogan was managing to put one foot in front of the other, to advance down the fairway on a straight line—oh, he was striking the ball squarely and his swing still had the accustomed zip, the takeaway rather faster than most players could handle effectively, the exaggerated extension of the straight right arm far down the line on the follow-through swing something most players can only dream about—but here, obviously, was a man whose legs were near to buckling under him."

As Ben lashed his drive on 12, he felt both legs seize up in severe muscle spasms; he staggered and nearly toppled to the ground, only managing to spare himself that indignity by grabbing hold of someone's arm. "Let me hold on to you," he supposedly gasped, adding, "My God, I don't think I can finish."

"I thought he was going to collapse," Middlecoff said later.

Only those spectators who bothered to look back at the tee saw the little man stumble and nearly end his day and his Open comeback quest then and there. But muscle spasms were not the only reason he nearly fell: new turf had recently been installed by the club grounds crew, and the ferocity of his swing had caused the shaded turf beneath his spikes to slip. One of those who witnessed this incident was Bill Campbell, a fine amateur and the reigning West Virginia Amateur champion who'd fired rounds of 80-73 to miss the cut in his second U.S. Open effort. Campbell was standing only a few yards away and saw Hogan grab Middlecoff's arm, though other witnesses claimed it was a Hogan friend named Harry Radix (a wealthy Chicago golf enthusiast who paid for the diamond cuff links annually given out with the Vardon Trophy) whom Ben reached out to and seized. So much of what happened that day got wrapped in the gauzy fabric of legend. *Whoever* provided the supporting arm, as Campbell says, "Ben looked nearly finished. He couldn't even bend over to pick up his ball."

"The reason not many saw him stumble," injects Merion historian John Capers, "was because so many were already making a mad dash for the twelfth green." Campbell himself reached the green's edge just as Hogan was preparing to putt his ball twelve feet or so down the slope to the hole. His approach shot had been one of the few mistakes he'd made all day, leaving him dangerously above the hole on the stone-hard green. His ball rolled five feet past the cup, and he three-putted to reduce his own lead by a third.

Crossing sleepy Ardmore Avenue and ascending the steps to the slightly elevated 13th tee at the dazzlingly short par-3, Hogan's legs seized up again. He paused and rubbed his thighs. His caddie teed up his ball, and Hogan made a crisp swing that was remarkable, under the circumstances. His ball wound up ten feet from the cup. But after holing out for par and vacating the green, his legs seized up again, doubling him over.

"According to the story everyone tells around here," historian Capers picks up the tale, "Hogan turned to his caddie and said, 'That's it. I'm finished. You can take my clubs back to the clubhouse.'"

The caddie, whose name no one recalls, the Merion legend goes, supposedly turned to his client and said: "No, Mr. Hogan. You can't quit. I don't work for quitters. I'll see you on the 14th tee, sir."

Like so much else that people swore they witnessed that warm Saturday afternoon, the touching story may or may not be true. One account even has the incident taking place during Hogan's morning round. Regardless, after making his par at 14, Hogan limped on and played the daunting 15th nearly perfectly from tee to green, leaving himself a mere eight-footer for birdie. But then, unaccountably, he three-putted away the second stroke of his lead, missing a putt from less than eighteen inches.

The margin was now one, with perhaps the toughest three concluding holes in championship golf left to play. On the signature "quarry" hole at 16, his approach missed the green, but he chipped to within four feet and made the putt to save par. He bunkered his tee shot, however, on the long par-3 17th. He blasted to within six feet of the cup and took an unusual amount of time sizing up the putt to salvage another par, walking back and forth three times before he finally settled over his ball. He stroked the putt and saw it stop one full revolution shy of falling in the hole. Another bogey. His lead was officially gone.

At that instant, though he didn't yet know it, Ben's longtime Texas nemesis Lloyd Mangrum was already safely inside the Merion clubhouse with 287, tied with George Fazio and Hogan for the Open lead.

Now he faced the toughest tee shot on the golf course, a blind drive that required players to carry 220 yards up over the snarling rock lip of the old quarry to a heaving bosom of turf that would still leave the average Tour player a demanding long iron or fairway wood to the slightly elevated putting surface of the home hole. Hogan hit a beautiful drive that soared over the edge of the cliff to a flat spot on the brow of the hill. The gallery exploded in cheers and applause.

By the time he'd slowly made his way up the path to the upper tier of the fairway, his followers were preparing to close ranks behind him. Stopping by his ball, gray-faced and winded, pinching a smoldering cigarette, Hogan pondered what kind of shot he needed to hit to get safely home in two, and turned to see pro Jimmy Hines and Tour manager Fred Corcoran standing nearby in the gallery.

"What's low?" Hogan grunted at Hines, who told him 286.

"No," Corcoran corrected him, "287 is low. Fazio."

"Mangrum too," someone chipped in. Hogan gave a faint shake of his head. A par 4 would get him into the house in a tie with them at 287; a birdie would win it outright. But under the circumstances, the hole was probably among the toughest to birdie on the golf course.

As Hogan stared at Merion's final hole and considered his options, tournament marshals permitted spectators to fill in directly behind him. For the first and only time ever, the USGA had replaced the club's distinctive teardrop-shaped baskets with conventional flags, and the flag at 18 was fluttering in a light afternoon breeze up on the right rear portion of the green, guarded by a large bunker in front.

The math was pretty simple.

Par to tie, birdie to win.

Arguably nobody in golf ever hit the four-wood better than Hogan. But a four-wood shot that cleared the bunker and got back to the hole also risked the danger of running off the back side of the putting surface into the punishing rough. That would make a par, and a spot in a play-off, very hard to come by.

Though the idea of a Sunday play-off made him positively queasy to contemplate, Ben Hogan hadn't come as far as he had in golf—and in life—by taking ridiculous chances. Golf was a game of mistakes, and he was the man who normally came out on top by not doing something stupid when it counted most.

Hogan thumbed away his smoke and reached into his bag and pulled out his butter knife, the one-iron that had replaced his seven. In doing so, he chose wisdom over valor. If he aimed left of the bunker and hit it perfectly, the ball might reach the lower center of the green, leaving him a lengthy but reasonable shot at birdie, with little or no chance of running over into the deadly rough.

Kneeling just behind the Hawk, twenty-year-old Jim Finegan, a former caddie and a junior on the La Salle College golf team, had wiggled to the front of the six-deep crowd spanning the fairway and now feasted his eyes on every move the great man made, squinting through the filtered afternoon light to see what club Hogan had chosen. Finegan calculated that the Hawk had walked no less than nine miles since breakfast that morning.

Upstairs in the locker room above the pro shop, Skee Reigel and several other players came to the window overlooking the final green. Reigel remembers the scene being "unbelievably quiet—like 10,000 people sitting in a church." A few feet from Finegan, *Life* magazine photographer, Hy Peskin, a talented and aggressive New Yorker, suddenly plopped his camera on a fellow spectator's shoulder and insisted, "Don't move, pal."

Finegan watched Hogan take his stance, heard him inhale and exhale, then glance once at the distant flag for several seconds. His swing was a violent slash that "seemed like a blur" to the impressionable college boy. At that instant, Peskin's shutter lens opened and closed, freezing Hogan in his immaculate follow-through, a shot that became the greatest shot of Peskin's career and probably the most famous golf picture ever taken.

The elegant black-and-white photograph provides rich visual detail of what many consider to be the most marvelous clutch shot ever played in the throes of Open competition. The perfect balance of the slim, imperially tanned figure beneath the upraised hands and tilting white linen cap, the shadowed creases of Hogan's immaculately pressed tan gabardine trousers that suggest the faintest traces of the elastic supports within, the right foot en pointe, almost like that of a pirouetting ballet dancer—the signature thirteenth spike visible beneath the ball of his foot—and the way perhaps half of the solemnly watching multitudes (some wearing linen caps just like their hero) are turned away from the man striking the shot and already following the tiny white dot as it lifts toward the center portion of the green, while the greenside crowds stare intently back at Hogan, thousands of eyes attempting to pick out the tiny ball speeding at them from the sinking Pennsylvania sun. Four and a half seconds after the picture was snapped, Hogan's golf ball landed on the front portion of the putting surface and danced slightly left as it scooted a few yards up the slope to the left-hand corner of the green. His ball stopped rolling forty feet from the cup.

A surf of sustained applause and cheers rose along the fairway as Hogan slowly made his way toward the 72nd hole of the fiftieth United States Open Championship. As he did so, excited fans behind him broke and ran for a spot, any spot, close to the putting surface, oblivious to players still at work on the course, including Frank Stranahan, the former Augusta bad boy, who had his tee ball rudely knocked off its peg by overly enthusiastic Hogan fans as he prepared to hit his tee shot over on the 14th tee.

"Hogan," says Bob Sommers, "was a pathetic figure as he limped up the rise before the green. He had been on the course for six hours in this one round, and the last nine holes had been agony. He had thrown away a three-stroke lead over the last six holes, and right now he was as close to not caring as this tough, hard, determined man could ever be."

As deep quiet once again settled over historic Merion, Hogan took the measure of his forty-footer and rapped the ball firmly, believing it would fall off slightly to the right as it crossed the putting surface. Instead, the ball broke left and stopped four feet past the hole, sending anxious murmurs through the giant gallery. Moments later, whether out of disappointment with his collapse or a simple desire to get the ordeal over with one way or another, Hogan took half the time he normally required to size up a putt, assumed his crabbed stance, and rolled the ball into the left side of the cup to a burst of jubilant cheers.

There would be a play-off for the National Open between Mangrum, Fazio, and Hogan at 1:00 P.M. on Sunday, the sixth three-way tie in tournament history.

Hogan totaled and signed his scorecard, shook hands with and thanked Middlecoff, paid his caddie by the pro shop and asked the boy to leave his clubs there on the rack, then wearily mounted seventeen steps to Merion's players' locker room to collect his street shoes. He accepted congratulations from several players, Skee Reigel remembers, "but he looked completely beaten, as bad as I'd ever seen a man look after a tournament. I wouldn't have bet you a buck he was capable of playing any more golf that week."

At one point, Mangrum drifted by him and said, "See you tomorrow, Ben."

Hogan looked up, stone-faced.

"Yep," he replied, "see you tomorrow."

"I had given up on his being able to play in the play-off," Valerie told journalist Dave Anderson nearly five decades later. "But I couldn't tell him that."

While Hogan was putting on his street shoes and combing his hair, someone who clearly had a sense of history but no scruples pinched his one-iron from his golf bag. For years, the story went—proving how Hogan tales have a way of growing and changing shape with each telling—the thief supposedly also swiped his golf shoes from the same bag, even though he would clearly have worn them upstairs to the players' locker room.

To make matters even more confusing, there were some who later contended that the missing club was actually a two-iron Hogan fired so exquisitely to the final hole. Hogan himself said as much in *Five Lessons,* the famous instruction book he later wrote with Herbert Warren Wind, although Hogan eventually insisted that the club had been a one-iron and the copy in the book was a typographical error. George Fazio, for one, who stood nearby in the gallery and watched Hogan execute the shot, always maintained it was a two-iron he used, and so did veteran New York sportswriter Al Laney, who was also standing near the scene. Many years later, a member of Shady Oaks Country Club also swore Hogan personally told him it had been a two-iron. Future USGA president Bill Campbell, on the other hand, who was in the gallery directly behind golf's most mythical shot, says there's no doubt that it was a one-iron.

In hopes of clearing up the confusion, Merion members eventually wrote to the man himself, asking for clarification on the club he used that unforgettable afternoon, as well as for better particulars on how the club and shoes went wandering off into the mists of legend. Hogan wrote promptly back to the Merion membership: "It was a one-iron I played to the 72nd green. After hitting my shot, my one-iron was stolen. I haven't seen it since. Also, that night my shoes were stolen out of my locker and I haven't seen them either."

"This area," says Merion historian John Capers, fifty-two summers after the fact, "has created a real challenge to Merion's superintendents."

Kneeling by a modest granite marker set in the lush turf of Merion's 18th fairway (where, through a complex set of measurements it was eventually determined that Hogan hit the shot that got him into the play-off), Capers points to half a dozen recently repaired divots and explains that memorializing Hogan's feat with a modest stone plaque turned out to have a downside.

"Almost everyone who comes by here feels compelled to drop a ball and try and replicate the shot—measure themselves against Hogan that afternoon," he explains. The simple stone marker reads:

JUNE 11, 1950
U.S. OPEN
FOURTH ROUND
BEN HOGAN
ONE IRON

"I suppose you can't blame them," Capers allows with the fractional proprietary smile of a true flame-keeper, noting that even he has a cherished connection to that unforgettable Sunday on the cusp of the decade's first summer. His mother, Mary, a Merion ladies' club champion, was selected to serve as one of three scorers who accompanied Hogan, Mangrum, and Fazio on their historic play-off round.

But as Valerie Hogan pointed out, it was a play-off many doubted Hogan would be able to show up for.

After finishing his work that warm Saturday afternoon, Hogan returned to the Barclay Hotel and soaked his aching frame in bathwater for an hour, downed several martinis to cut the pain, ate an early dinner, and went to bed. "To make matters worse," Valerie said, "I woke up in the middle of the night to the noise of jackhammers slamming into the street below, but he slept so soundly he never heard them."

As luck would have it, Pennsylvania blue laws—in effect since the days of William Penn, they prohibited businesses and sporting events from operating until the last scheduled church service was concluded on Sunday morning—provided Hogan with extra hours to sleep in and rest his weary legs, enjoy a good breakfast, browse the *Inquirer,* and perform his ritual morning soak.

When he woke that morning, according to Valerie, "he was fresh as a daisy." Glancing out their hotel window at Rittenhouse Square, where a sunny day only slightly cooler than Open Saturday was developing, he showed few lingering effects of his brutal Saturday march and even casually remarked, "Isn't it a lovely day, Val?"

A pack of reporters and sportswriters waiting in the lobby of the Barclay was just as surprised as anyone when Hogan suddenly appeared among them a little before ten that morning, looking both refreshed and rejuvenated. Once again, they'd apparently underestimated the willpower of golf's most dominant figure since Bobby Jones, and many of the scribes offered him their hands and best wishes as he left the Barclay. A few even applauded his recovery.

Both Hogan and Mangrum finished the first nine holes in 36, while Fazio, who struck the ball better than either of his competitors but had less to show for it, completed his opening nine with a frustrating 37. With five holes left to play, Hogan, showing the first traces of fatigue (having to pause and rest with his hands on his knees) but no visible performance letdown, began to pull away from his competitors. As his adrenaline surged, Fazio began to overshoot greens and make bogeys, while Mangrum made a pair of poor approach shots that resulted in costly bogeys at 12 and 14.

"I've never seen a threesome with only one person in it," Mary Capers later commented to her young son John. "Hogan was in a separate world."

By the 16th tee, though, Mangrum was still hanging tough. A birdie at 15 put him only one stroke behind Hogan with the three tough finishing holes to go. Hogan hadn't cracked but looked just about ready to, Mangrum decided, figuring that if the little man made a mistake, he could pick up that stroke and maybe snatch the Open straight out from under Hogan at 18. Nothing would have given Lloyd Mangrum more pleasure than that.

Following a sloppy approach shot and a weak chip that left him nine feet to negotiate for his par on the 16th green, Mangrum marked his ball and waited for Hogan and Fazio to putt out. As he stood over his ball, Lloyd noticed a bug crawling on it and, without thinking, used the toe of his putter to mark the ball's position while he picked up his ball and blew off the critter. He replaced the ball and holed the putt, then proceeded on to the 17th tee, believing he was still only one stroke behind Hogan with two holes to play. Still within reach.

As he teed up his ball, though, USGA president and match referee Ike Grainger pushed through the crowd and called out, "Just a moment, Mr. Mangrum. Mr. Hogan has the honors."

Mangrum paused, perplexed, glaring at Grainger. Like many regular Tour journeymen, Lloyd generally considered the gentlemen who ran the United States Golf Association a bunch of overbred aristocrats who probably argued passionately over how many Greek olives made the perfect martini. Lloyd was a straight whiskey drinker who didn't care much for tournament officials and match referees.

Grainger, a suave New York banker by occupation and the sponsoring organization's in-house champion of what he called "the rule of equity"—the belief that a sense of fair play should always govern any decision—patiently explained to a visibly seething Mangrum that by illegally marking his ball a *second* time, he had incurred a two-stroke penalty.

(Curiously, like the other moments that were misreported or embellished in the aftermath of the most thrilling Open finish since Ouimet beat Vardon and Ray, news reports widely portrayed the "bug" incident as the source of the two-stroke infraction. As Ike Grainger was careful to explain to Mangrum, though, the USGA did not believe in "double jeopardy," so only the *first* infraction of the rules would be observed and penalized. In effect, under existing conditions, though he did improperly "clean his ball," as widely reported, it was marking his ball a second time that got Mangrum in trouble.)

For a long moment, Lloyd gave the USGA's gentle, fair-minded Solomon of the rules a cold and penetrating stare. Then he stepped back and shook his head. "I guess we'll all eat tomorrow," he muttered with a bitter little smile beneath his riverboat moustache, glancing off at the gallery.

Hogan, now three ahead, teed up his ball and wasted little time. He stroked his ball onto the 17th green and, minutes later, eased the pain of Grainger's ruling by sinking a mammoth uphill fifty-footer to ice the golden anniversary cake.

Not far away, Valerie Hogan, who was having her umpteenth glass of iced tea on the Merion porch, began softly crying. After hearing the gallery's roar on 17, someone had told her, "Ben won," and now another emissary explained to her that it was official. He had indeed won his second National Open. The "miraculous" comeback was complete.

An elderly couple seated at an adjoining table leaned over and politely inquired if they could do anything for her. She seemed so distressed.

"I'm all right," she replied, dabbing her eyes, before getting up to go join Ben for the awards ceremony. "I'm just happy for my husband. I'm crying with joy."

SENSING HISTORY about to be made, many of the tournament's biggest names came back to Merion that Sunday afternoon to watch how the drama played out. Skee Reigel remembers sitting in the locker room moments after the play-off's completion, having a celebratory cocktail with Demaret and Middlecoff ("We all wanted Ben to do it," he says) and several others, when they suddenly heard Hogan's name being paged on the club's public address system. Ben was being summoned for the formal presentation of the trophy and the first-place check of $4,000.

"Hell," Jimmy barked, rattling his ice cubes, "he's already up at Oakland Hills practicing for *next* year's Open!" The overwarm locker room erupted in laughter.

Minutes later, a large contingent of players joined one of the largest galleries ever to attend the awarding of the National Open gold medal and trophy. Hogan was more gracious than ever, his voice breaking slightly as he talked about what his Merion comeback meant. "I know a lot of people wondered if this could ever happen again," he said to Ike Grainger at one point. "I'm just so relieved to have it done."

Under the circumstances, even Lloyd Mangrum was reasonably gracious, making only a few choice comments about needing to learn the rules for marking his ball before he played in another National Open.

. . .

THE FOLLOWING WEEK out in Hollywood, as it happened, shooting began in earnest on the soundstages and back lots at Twentieth Century Fox on the Hogan film project, newly titled *Follow the Sun*.

Diffident, mumbling, politely inoffensive Glenn Ford and veteran film actress Anne Baxter had been picked by Lanfield and producer Sam Engle to play Ben and Valerie Hogan. Edward Hazlitt Brennan was putting the finishing touches on a script he had developed from his own swooning profile of Hogan in *Reader's Digest*, with helpful field notes from the scriptwriters at Riviera and Valerie Hogan's own substantial scrapbooks. Among the more unconventional terms of the movie deal, Hogan refused to sign a contract until the movie was completed entirely to his satisfaction.

After a train trip down to Palm Beach to play in the round robin with chum George Coleman, Hogan went north to suburban Detroit for the Motor City Open and then headed off to the golden West to make sure his life was properly conveyed to film.

According to the film's archivists, he became such a nuisance and perfectionist on Lanfield's set—once spoiling an entire day of filming by insisting that the clubs Ford was rather ineffectually swinging weren't the same models he used that particular year—that Sidney Lanfield began making rueful jokes about murdering the film's hero with his own pitching wedge.

By autumn, when Ben wasn't busy pestering Lanfield about some acutely minor detail of the bedroom set where the ailing Hogan character was struggling to get back on his feet and chase the Tour, he was coaching the distinctly unathletic Ford on Hogan swing principles out at Riviera, where most of the outdoor golf shots were filmed, or beating balls into a cage specially built on a back lot at Twentieth Century Fox.

Hogan thought Glenn Ford was a hell of a nice guy but a walking embarrassment when it came to filming his golf swing. So he personally worked with Ford for several days before permitting the swing sequences to be filmed.

At one point during a break in filming, Hogan and Ford, mentor and pupil, sat having a drink together in a studio bar when an excited publicity man rushed in to show them one of the studio's advertising fliers for the new film, which producers hoped to release early in 1951. Among other absurdities, the ad described Ben and Valerie as "two rollicking kids from Texas," at which point, Ford later recalled, Hogan became so angry he threatened to "wash his hands" of the entire movie debacle. "If somebody called us 'rollicking kids,'" Ford quoted the Hawk as fuming, "we'd have been laughed off half the courses in the country."

The ad copy was quickly changed. Moreover, unable to coach Ford to an acceptable level of competence, Hogan did all of the long shots himself on the film, as well as many of the close-ups. A special rubber mask was created that made the lower portion of Hogan's face resemble Ford's—a rather peculiar case of life imitating art imitating life. Or better yet, Ben Hogan simply playing himself.

ELEVEN

What *Is*
Ben Thinking?

SAM SNEAD LOVED to relate how Ben Hogan was on his way to play in the Greenbrier Festival of Golf in the spring of 1951—a non-official pro-am Tour soon to be renamed the Sam Snead Festival—when he passed the only movie house in town and glanced up to see that a new Hollywood block-buster had come to town. "Follow the Wind," announced the big black letters up on the marquee. "Starring Sam Snead."

The anecdote says something about the peaking rivalry between Snead and Hogan, though it's perhaps a little taller than the facts support. To begin with, as Hogan's own travel diaries indicate, he chose not to return to White Sulphur Springs to defend his Greenbrier title in 1951, and even if he had done so, he certainly wouldn't have been motoring over narrow unknown roads through the Blue Ridge Mountains.

Now slightly phobic about driving anywhere except around Fort Worth and neighboring Dallas, Ben and Valerie traveled to tournament sites almost exclusively by sleeper train, and on the four or five occasions a year when it

Overleaf: Movie poster, 1951 *(Courtesy of Alastair Johnson)*

was necessary to fly, he was able to suppress his anxiety about commercial air travel by traveling exclusively on the commercial airline he believed had the safest record—hometown American Airlines—and only on days when the weather appeared to be optimal for safety. Each spring before the Masters, he also flew to and from Palm Beach with George Coleman, a highly certified pilot whose skills he both trusted and admired. At train depots and airports, thanks to a man the Hogans hired to make arrangements ahead of their scheduled arrivals, a private car and experienced professional driver were always waiting to take them wherever they needed to go. Hogan kept the names of trusted drivers in one of his travel diaries and always tried to get the same driver in a particular location if at all possible.

As for Sam, coming off his finest season in pro golf in 1950, which included eight official Tour.wins and a host of lucrative unofficial pro-am titles, his second consecutive Vardon Trophy, and another Tour money title, an otherwise banner year was spoiled by the fact that his colleagues deprived him of a second-straight PGA Player of the Year honor, presenting the coveted accolade instead to his archrival on the basis of a *single* victory—Hogan's National Open comeback win at Merion Golf Club.

"If ever I should have won Player of the Year," Snead lamented to a reporter four decades after the fact, "it was 1950. I couldn't play any better than I did that year. Did I feel a little cheated? You bet I did. The award was called player of the *year*. The whole year. Not just one week."

Considering his own colorful rags-to-riches tale, Snead could perhaps be forgiven if he resented Hollywood's fascination with his archrival. Sam's own improbable rise to stardom through a rich man's game from the creased hills of the Old Dominion was in its own way as absorbing as Ben's and probably would have made an entertaining movie in its own right—a Capra-esque screwball comedy, say, about a witty hayseed who picks up a maple limb in a back holler and uses it to teach himself a golf swing (which he did, according to Sam), then beats the pants off the snobby golf establishment, achieving money and fame in the process, a sort of lower-case *Mr. Deeds Goes to Augusta*—were it not for the gravitas of Hogan's own saga, the kind of tear-jerker Hollywood simply couldn't resist.

Hogan's American life, by contrast, had everything a postwar movie scriptwriter could possibly want: a lonely runt rising above rural western poverty, a pretty girl helping him chase his impossible dreams, repeated years of failure and sacrifice, finally a breakthrough to the big time and all the rewards that come with it—fame, money, respect, a beautiful two-story house in the suburbs—then a life abruptly shattered by tragedy, a personal epiphany, a brave recovery, capped off by a comeback for the ages.

Ironically, perhaps the only thing left *out* of Hollywood's "inspiring true story of America's greatest athlete," as the film was being promoted during its early production stages, was the true source of Hogan's greatness, the shadowy events he permitted no one to see, the lost boyhood he never said boo about to anyone.

Valerie Hogan got the first glimpse of Sidney Lanfield's epic at a private screening held on Saturday, March 11, at the Seventh Street Theater in downtown Fort Worth, twelve days ahead of the picture's official release date. She went to see the movie dressed as if she were going to University Christian Church to hear one of Granville Walker's splendid sermons, and afterward, dabbing her eyes, she told a *Fort Worth Press* reporter that she found Lanfield's movie "terribly, deeply moving," admitting she wept through the scenes of the crash and Ben's struggling recovery. "For goodness' sake," she playfully chided the reporter, "Glenn Ford said he wept *too* when he saw the first cut of the film!" She added that she was "very pleased" with pretty Anne Baxter's portrayal of her, and speaking on behalf of her husband, who was out of town playing a lucrative exhibition match in Miami (with George Coleman), she emphasized that the producers got "all the facts exactly right" in making their movie and that she was even "startled but pleased" to see their actual mangled Cadillac used in the movie.

Marvin Leonard, who attended the screening with Valerie and a select group of Cowtown's ruling elite, had only one word for the film: "Terrific." Amon Carter, on the other hand, never one to miss an opportunity to hog the limelight, held forth on why Glenn Ford ought to receive an Oscar for his performance. "It's a marvelous movie," Carter drawled beneath the expensive felt cowboy hat he sported almost everywhere to remind folks of his connection to the spirit of the Old West. "Thoroughly enjoyable. Wasn't Ford particularly fine? He should win an Oscar. The picture should too."

The film had its gala opening on March 23, officially proclaimed Ben Hogan Day in Fort Worth by the mayor and a similar resolution by the Texas State Senate, filling three downtown theaters with overflow crowds estimated at upward of 6,000 patrons. Two other Hollywood films about the city were also about to premier in the Queen City of the Prairie, Warner Brothers' *Fort Worth*, a western starring Randolph Scott, and RKO's *High Frontier*, a movie about the production of the B-36 airplane, but they were dwarfed by the public fever over Ben's movie, which was announced via splashy full-page ads in both the *Press* and the *Star-Telegram*—"A Woman's Story of a Man's Great Comeback," buzzed the ad copy, ". . . And a Love Big Enough to Make the American Dream Come True—*Twice!*"

Gaines Cadillac (where Hogan purchased the Caddy he credited with saving their lives) and John L. Ashe and Son (the downtown clothier where Ben ordered his custom clothing, including the imported Egyptian cotton Alan Solley polo shirts he favored on the golf course, imported directly from England) both paid for congratulatory half-page ads, as did Hogan's equipment sponsor MacGregor Sporting Goods, Koslow's Furriers, and Marvin Leonard's legendary department store.

For its part, Twentieth Century Fox dispatched the movie's leading actors by plane and train to Texas with only director Lanfield and actress Anne Baxter, a recent Academy Award winner for *All About Eve*, sending their regrets. Marvin Leonard announced that he would be holding a private reception following the movie's debut at the Fort Worth Club and picking up the tab for a party of 200 invited guests at Colonial Country Club the following evening.

"This premier is the biggest thing to hit this town," trilled one of the city's society columnists, "since Amon Carter put on a cowboy hat and climbed up on a horse."

As searchlights by the venerable Worth Theater raked the evening sky on March 23 and thousands hovered behind velvet ropes to glimpse the arriving movie stars and dignitaries, the Carswell Air Force band serenaded a stream of tuxedo-wearing VIPs and their gowned wives as they arrived, including Mr. and Mrs. Ben Hogan, Jimmy Demaret turned out in a canary yellow dinner jacket, shyly smiling Glenn Ford, and beaming character actor Dennis O'Keefe. Other less recognizable luminaries included Dr. Alton Ochsner, Mary and Marvin Leonard, George and Elizabeth Coleman, General Hutchinson, Henry Cowen of MacGregor, Royal and Margaret Hogan, the Gordon Harrimans and daughter Valerie, Jesse and Claude Fox, and a smiling Mama Hogan herself, wearing a sensible moss green dress and flower corsage for the occasion.

In that afternoon's edition of the *Star-Telegram*, the sixty-one-year-old widow (who lived alone in a new efficiency apartment at the Lucerne Apartments near downtown) reminisced fondly about Ben's early job as a newspaper boy at the Texas & Pacific and his early obsession with golf, specifically how he beat golf balls through every yard in the neighborhood whenever she sent him to Parrott's Grocery for a stick of butter. She talked about the $40 golf clubs she sprang for when he was fifteen and the grave responsibility he felt to help support his family through those lean and difficult years of the Depression. She studiously avoided any mention of the reason *why* Ben was forced to go to work at such an early age. When the reporter briefly asked about Ben's father, she smiled tightly and replied, "It's a private matter. Hard work and sorrow won't kill you. I never live in the past." Before the reporter left her, though, she revealed that the debut of *Follow the Sun* was the "greatest moment of my life."

Perhaps it was. From Mama Hogan's perspective, Hollywood's secular canonization was nothing less than an affirmation of her pioneer belief that if you worked harder than the next guy and never complained or gave an inch, there wasn't any misery you couldn't outlive or at least put safely out of sight.

To make the story more palatable to mainstream American movie tastes, Lanfield's biopic chose to include no hint of the central childhood event—Chester's suicide—that shaped Ben's life and golf psyche. The film's narrative sweetly glossed over his family's resulting financial trauma, Hogan's years of humbling and dubious job hustling, and his multiple failures to make it as a regular Tour player—the very factors, in short, that made Hogan such an inscrutable champion to fans and foes alike.

Lanfield instead opted to convey his simplified tale purely from Valerie's worshipful, never-say-die perspective. The portrayal was that of a plucky small-town gal (played with steel magnolia pertness by Baxter) who props up the shy, doubt-riddled boy (played by mopey Glenn Ford, the Canadian actor "who radiates integrity and virtue," according to his own studio-written biography) she's adored since their Sunday school days together and to whom she gives the strength to chase his dream of being a big-time golf pro.

Lanfield drenched his sporting epic in the swooning violins and sentimental lyricism common to recent box-office smashes like *How Green Was My Valley* and, in search of an edgier subplot and a little comic relief, introduced an entirely fictional golf pro named Chuck Williams, a devil-may-care champion who parties as hard as he plays—Jimmy Demaret meets Clark Gable.

When success finally arrives for Ford's Hogan, he is unable to enjoy it or grasp why the game's fans don't cotton to him the way they do, say, to the backslapping, hard-drinking Williams (played by Dennis O'Keefe). In terms of acting jobs, O'Keefe steals Lanfield's show, capering over ottomans and quaffing bubbly from his own championship trophy cups. When the unlikely roadmates finally meet head to head à la Ben and Byron in "the Big One," a thinly disguised send-up of the U.S. Open, Williams is already in a tailspin of self-destruction. He drinks to mask a wild fear that he'll never win again, and even his recently acquired gold-digger bride is preparing to give him the heave-ho.

It's only when the "Texas Iceberg" is nearly killed by a marauding bus that baffled Ben's own private fog lifts and he conquers his doubts and finally discovers his humanity through the outpouring of an admiring nation—"You know, Val, I should have died to rate all of this," mumbles Ford wonderingly. "I had to get hit by a ten-ton bus to wake up."

As with many Hollywood epiphanies, Ben's collision has the curious effect of reforming his erring best friend too, who suddenly sees the light, goes on the wagon, saves his foundering marriage, and rededicates himself to Old Man Par. The movie reaches its dramatic climax with the gallant little Texan limping bravely toward the finish in the Los Angeles rain as he heroically attempts to mount his own "impossible comeback" before a gallery of true believers that includes Val, Chuck, and his newly returned wife, proving no champion ever walks alone.

"Somebody should *stop* him!" bleats the reformed gold-digger bride beneath their umbrella. "Chuck, why don't *you*!"

"Nobody can stop him," replies Chuck, eyes shining with grim admiration.

"Nobody *should*," murmurs Ben's wise gal Val, who happens to be out on the golf course where the real Valerie Hogan rarely set foot.

The film ends with Granny Rice, real-life dean of America's sportswriters, playing himself and introducing the tournament runner-up, a man whose "legs simply weren't strong enough to carry his heart around," to a raucous standing ovation by the very sportswriters who failed to understand and appreciate what a swell egg Hogan truly was until near-tragedy made him into something resembling a human being.

Proving art imitates life and sometimes even improves on it, *Follow the Sun* ends, aptly enough, with Hogan's famous smiling mug on the cover of *Time* magazine, to which the producers had added the helpful caption: "Wins 1950 U.S. Open."

MOST OF HOGAN'S FRIENDS and family liked the movie well enough, though Mama Hogan reportedly felt snubbed because Valerie Hogan got all the credit for Ben's eventual success. Hogan himself said little about the film (though decades later, when he saw it again on video, the story goes, tears ran down his cheeks as he watched it) as he graciously accepted congratulations and best wishes and mingled with movie stars and 400 guests at the Fort Worth Club afterward.

Cary Middlecoff and Jimmy Demaret, who made brief cameos in the movie, needled Hogan for weeks about not giving them big enough parts in the film, and Glenn Ford told anyone who would listen that coaching from Hogan had sliced ten strokes off his golf game. Sam Snead, who declined the invitation to the debut, claimed he never saw the movie until it reached West Virginia. "They got things pretty right," he said with a wink after finally seeing it. "But I wasn't in it as much as the sign outside said I would be."

The critics were more tempered in their judgments of the film. Most Texas dailies loved *Follow the Sun,* naturally enough, citing the movie's heartwarming message about faith and hard work overcoming any personal adversity, while many of the big-city reviewers found the film somewhat treacly and irritating. New York's *Herald-Tribune,* for example, complimented Ford's acting job but found Brennan's script "uneven . . . with lines that jump from cliché to cliché about a woman's place at a man's side." One influential Manhattan reviewer found Hollywood's Hogan and his running feud with a fictional sportswriter "contrived and somewhat irrelevant," a viewpoint dailies in Los Angeles and Chicago generally echoed.

Variety, Hollywood's newspaper of record, however, labeled the film "a basic human drama of love and courage with appeal to adult filmgoers" and predicted Hogan's tale would do a reasonably decent box-office business.

It did.

WHAT THE WORLD thought of his movie was basically irrelevant to the real Ben Hogan, who promptly started packing the day after Marvin's big premier party and boarded an eastbound train for unfinished business in Augusta, Georgia.

As it happened, the film hoopla cut directly into Hogan's cherished Seminole practice time, and he arrived in Georgia anxious to get straight out to the course and prepare his mind and game for mortal combat. As many have pointed out, in twelve previous appearances Hogan's ability to hit long and straight golf shots did him no great service over the bending fairways of Augusta National, and privately he grumbled to other players about the course "not suiting" his game, implying that his Masters "jinx" might extend indefinitely, a nearly unthinkable prospect to everyone. He'd grown to love the gracious Old South atmosphere and rubbing elbows with the elite gathering of golf legends, captains of commerce, and a future president named Ike.

Eisenhower had been coming to Augusta for regular golf vacations since Masters week of 1948, the year he was between paying jobs as supreme commander of Allied Forces in Europe and president of Columbia University. At that time, the old soldier and his bride billeted for eleven days in Bobby Jones's personal cottage on the 10th hole and fell deeply under the spell of Magnolia Lane. Like the azaleas that made the acreage resplendent with dazzling blooms, the Eisenhowers returned faithfully every spring for nearly a decade and a half, including twenty-nine visits during the eight years Eisenhower served the nation as First Golfer and Commander-in-Chief.

Hogan genuinely liked Ike, and "the General" greatly admired Hogan for his dedication to excellence and personal courage, his unwillingness to compromise or give up simply because he'd been run over by a bus. Like most Hogan admirers around Augusta, Ike took it on Cliff Roberts's infallible word that it was merely a matter of time before Ben beat his Masters drought. Hogan's Merion triumph showed beyond a shadow of a doubt that he still had the right stuff to win major championships, and there were no doubts about his ability to hit shots that mattered most in critical circumstances. On the contrary, close observers of the man had come to believe, as Jimmy Demaret had at L.A., that his near-death experience had made Hogan even more of an efficient scoring machine.

Ben's tournament preparation at Augusta that spring certainly displayed a thoroughness that was, if possible, more comprehensive than ever. During the ten days preceding the opening of '51 Masters play, in addition to his methodical, cocoonlike practice sessions with his caddie Willie Lee Stokes, Hogan hit hundreds of practice shots on the course and almost every bunker. He studied the swirling wind patterns on the golf course at various times of the day, developing a number of specific strategies, as well as various kinds of punch and knockdown shots to accommodate any conditions and maximize his approaches to the National's difficult, grainy Bermuda greens. "I remember playing a practice round or two with him about then," says Skee Reigel, "and thinking, if he was great before the accident, he was even better now. Ben's control of the ball was now basically unearthly."

Because the water hazard on the treacherous downhill 11th hole had recently been widened under the supervision of architect Robert Trent Jones, Hogan made up his mind, Reigel learned, to intentionally miss the green to the right in order to avoid any risk of a wet ball and a penalty stroke. "If you ever see me on that green in two," Hogan said when reporters saw him doing this earlier in the week, "I missed the shot."

For the fifteenth edition of golf's most cherished spring ritual, and Hogan's first tournament appearance of the year since withdrawing from the Phoenix Open owing to a bout of flu, spectators could simply amble up to the gates, shell out their 50¢ daily admission, and mosey straight up Magnolia Lane to grab a pimento cheese sandwich and watch the latest installment of Ben versus the world.

Hogan opened with solid rounds of 70-72 that left him a stroke back of Skee Reigel at the tournament's halfway post. As he sat taking off his shoes in the locker room after round two, one of the Roberts-approved scribes who was never far from Ben's elbow at Augusta National innocently wondered if, given the accident and his history of near-misses, winning this fifteenth Masters wouldn't mean as much as the National Open to Ben Hogan.

The Hawk studied his questioner for a moment. Before the accident, he would have ignored the reporter or reduced him to a quivering lump of flesh for such an idiotic and obvious question. "I try to win them all," he replied evenly, then softened a bit. "But you're probably right. This one may mean something special."

After three rounds, Ben remained one stroke shy of Reigel and Sam Snead, who shared the lead at 211, five under par. In the clubhouse, Hogan designated Sam as the man to beat to the reporters clustered around his locker. "The leaders usually fade," he cautioned, "but I can't depend on that. I've got to let go."

He was as good as his word. Playing with both confidence and caution, Ben issued a strong challenge to Snead early that final Sunday afternoon by birdieing consecutive holes at 3 and 4 on his outward nine. Reaching the 8th tee, he was informed that Skee Reigel had finished his day with 71, in a strong crosswind no less, for an impressive 282 total that would have won half the previous Masters championships.

Playing half an hour ahead, Snead heard the field reports too and decided he needed to give his partisans something to cheer about. At the dangerous 11th, the Slammer chose valor over wisdom and plunked a pair of foolish approach shots into the pond, scored a bloody quadruple eight on his card, and staggered home through Augusta's gently soughing pines to a miserable 80.

In the clubhouse, as Hogan made his turn in a tie for the lead, several players began to congratulate Skee Reigel. "I hope you boys are right," he said to them, looking wary. "But I'd feel a whole lot better if it was anybody but that little man out there."

Historically, Augusta's second nine has been a graveyard to many of the game's finest players, but Hogan ushered his ball strategically around the back nine that afternoon like a master chess player, reaching seven of the holes in regulation and two-putting safely for his par. On 11, true to the strategy he'd worked out and followed as closely as a Sid Lanfield movie script, he dropped his approach shot safely on the right side of the green and chipped with his six-iron to four feet, sinking the putt for par. On the bending 480 yard 13th, he lashed a drive far enough around the corner to momentarily tempt him to have a go at the green with a low iron, but then he changed his mind and lofted a six-iron short of Rae's Creek, pitched across with a wedge to seven feet, and drained the putt for a birdie 4 and a two-stroke lead over the nervously waiting Reigel.

"I never for a minute thought I was going to win that tournament," reflects Skee Reigel. "That was *Hogan* out there. He didn't make mistakes the same way some other guys did. He didn't back up. For years people asked me what my life might have been like if I'd won that '51 Masters. Gee, they say, you might have gone on and won a lot of big tournaments after that. Maybe that's true. But, golly, I have no regrets. That was Ben's time. I was just glad to be there and part of it."

Poignantly, as Hogan approached his ball in the final fairway, followed by the largest gallery in tournament history—8,000 fans were on the grounds that day, according to Cliff Roberts, who probably personally counted all of them—a playful Skee Reigel seized the microphone from Masters announcer Bill Sterns and announced Hogan's triumphant arrival at the 72nd green. "I just thought it would be a fitting touch, purely out of respect for Ben," he says.

Before he could make the announcement, however, the Hawk had to get safely through the final green in no worse than bogey. As Ben stood out in the fairway contemplating his final approach shot, memories of his costly three-putt in '46 and a similarly untidy three-putt finish in the Saturday round of the year before must have flickered like a bad movie trailer through his head. Looking grim and determined, he finally selected a six-iron and unexpectedly laid up thirty yards shy of the green.

"That stunned a lot of folks, including me," Reigel remembers. "Why would Ben play *short* on such a relatively easy shot? But then I realized he was taking no chance of being above that hole. It was the perfect illustration of

Hogan at his peak of control. He was probably the best wedge player alive and knew *exactly* what he wanted to do, and he did it."

With his vaunted "equalizer," Ben nipped his ball to a spot four feet below the hole, and he was preparing to putt when Demaret slipped up beside Valerie on the hillside and whispered impishly in her ear, "Did you hear, Val? Ben had a 12 on 18 and lost by six strokes."

As Ben's putt dropped, a sustained cheer rolled through the pines, and a hobbling Bobby Jones was one of the first people to reach the edge of the putting surface, extending his hand to welcome the newest member of Augusta's elite winner's circle. A short time later, standing with the assistance of a leg brace and a cane, Jones slipped the size 40-short kelly green Masters champion sports jacket on Hogan's 145-pound frame. The two men vigorously shook hands again and beamed at each other. Asked some years later which great player he would select if he needed one shot to win a major tournament, Jones unhesitatingly replied, "That's not hard for me to answer—Hogan." He thought a moment and added, "He had the intangible assets—the spiritual."

Minutes after overseeing the presentation of the green jacket, Cliff Roberts was more specific in his analysis of Hogan's brilliant final round at Augusta that afternoon, hailing it as "a classic in strategy and execution. Not a single one of those strokes would be called a missed shot or a mistake in judgment. And Ben made millions of golfers, and many others, very very happy."

A few days later, after playing a round with Augusta National's man in the White House, Hogan finally provided some thoughtful reflection on what winning the Masters meant to him. He sounded a little like Glenn Ford trying his best to sound like Ben Hogan.

"I got a big bang out of it. It wasn't so much winning the Masters. It was having all those people out there rooting for you—and then being able to come through for them. They're wonderful. I have had so much luck. If I never win again, I'll be satisfied."

But he wasn't. Not by a long shot.

THOUGH HIS SCHEDULE was reduced to just four tournaments for 1951 in order to preserve the strength of his legs, Hogan's game had never appeared more commanding. The wreck, he admitted to Marvin Leonard and Claude Harmon and precious few others, had shortened his ability to turn his hips out of the way on the downswing and thus reduced the length of his average drive by as much as a dozen yards. But the compensation for a shorter swing was that it gave him even more control over his clubs, particularly his irons.

Luck really had little to do with Hogan's success because he worked longer and harder than anyone to achieve this degree of technical proficiency, and he didn't intend to waste whatever time he had left playing for anything less than major championship titles.

Thus, after Augusta, he went back to Seminole for a little rest and a lot of practice in the stiff right-to-left Atlantic breeze on a course he enjoyed more than any other. The routine seldom varied. In the morning, he arrived about 9:00 A.M. and ventured out onto the empty golf course with his young shag boy in tow; after lunch he played a $10 Nassau with his buddies George Coleman, New York investment broker Paul Shields, and former Masters winner Claude Harmon. "Some of his matches with Claude were extraordinary," remembers Jerry Pittman. "I don't know if they even kept the cards because nobody would have believed the scores they shot."

As it's been from the beginning in 1894, the United States Open Golf Championship—popularly called the National Open in those days—is basically tournament golf's version of an Olympic marathon, a sustained ordeal of the fittest intended to separate worthy champions from would-be contenders, to weed out the very good from the truly great.

For its fifty-first edition, the greatest test in golf was returning to the old suburban Detroit battleground where Ralph Guldahl had set the record at 281 and Sam Snead let the first of many Opens slip maddeningly through his fingers. Back in 1937, on the cusp of the game's switch from hickory to steel shafts, Oakland Hills Country Club in the leafy Detroit suburb of Birmingham had played a whisker over 7,000 yards but failed to turn out to be the severe test many of the blazered aristocrats of the USGA had hoped it would be.

For 1951, embarrassed members set out to rectify this disappointment by hiring Robert Trent Jones to strengthen their fine Donald Ross golf course and bring it up to more modern Open standards. Curiously, English-born Jones, the self-promoting genius who innovated such concepts as platform tees, signature holes, and the strategy of a "risk-reward" approach to a hole ("Hard par, easy bogey," as he put it), responded by shortening the course to 6,927 yards, tightening fairways, and narrowing nearly every approach to the putting surfaces. Among other things, Jones installed large, flashed-up fairway bunkers that reduced the driving zones to frightening aisles of green, shifted and shrunk greens to sharpen the optimal approach angles, and ditched two reasonably bland par-5s in favor of making them brutally long and demanding 4-pars. The renovation work took well over a year to complete and scared the hell out of the first Tour players who ventured out to take a look at the results. "While no one denied that Oakland Hills was difficult," summarized Open historian Bob Sommers, "they questioned if it was good."

Hogan, for one, didn't think so. Length and control, Ben argued, were key elements every skilled golfer strived for, and by severely pinching the fairways and bunkering the greens so heavily, Jones and the well-meaning members of Oakland Hills, Hogan believed, had reduced the layout to a purely "defensive golf course where a player has to aim only for the heart of fairways and greens" rather than strategically attack pins the way a National Open "ought to be won." It didn't escape the notice of some that Hogan, a man who'd made a high Renaissance art form of making the fewest mistakes and playing his ball to the safest places, now complained that he felt cheated for having to do *exactly* that.

In a nutshell, many of the game's longest hitters, including Hogan, had difficulty carrying Oakland Hills' new arsenal of bunkering—they would simply have to pound the ball for all they were worth to reach the doglegs of several holes, hoping to thread the needle between Papa Jones's newly installed sand pits and avoid the USGA's punishing six-inch rough. As for those short hitters who couldn't manage this feat, they would simply be forced to play short of the traps and doglegs and face considerably longer and more daunting approaches to the greens.

Grumbling over these new challenges quickly reached a crescendo among the Open's 144 qualifiers. After following Snead and Demaret around the golf course and watching them flub shots during a final practice round, no less than wily old master Walter Hagen himself was moved to palm his hair, smile, and remark, "This course is playing the players instead of the players playing the course. It really *is* a monster."

For all his complaints, the record showed that Hogan, not too surprisingly, normally thrived on the toughest championship-caliber courses—a fact that statistically reduced most of the field's chances of winning and increased his own by an almost equal margin. It therefore surprised some seasoned Hogan watchers that after his own tour of the premises he rather tersely dismissed Oakland Hills as "completely ridiculous" and "probably much too hard" for most of the players in the field. The only player whose driving prowess and skill around the greens gave him a reasonable edge, he put forth soberly, was one Sam Snead.

"Don't believe a word of it," Sam countered with his lazy catfish smile, no small slouch at gamesmanship. "That's just Ben tryin' to get in everybody's heads like a swarm of wasps. Next thing, watch out, he'll be sayin' the course is really too easy and ought to be toughened up."

Sam knew his rival well. Following Ben's final practice round, and based on his superb record of accurately predicting winning scores in National Opens, Hogan appeared to reverse course and suddenly soften his opinion of Oakland Hills. He predicted that Ralph Guldahl's tournament record of 281 would in fact fall that week—a startling assertion that sent tremors of self-doubt through the club's tournament committee and prompted them to order the rough to remain uncut for the week. Tournament officials also agreed to set pins in their most impossible locations and further cinch fairways that were already tighter than a Victorian corset. As Snead pointed out to Charlie Bartlett and others on the eve of the start of play, as Oakland Hills was *now* set up it really favored one man and one man only—long-hitting, straight-driving Ben Hogan.

But the mental tennis match continued. As Ben left the locker room for the final time before the start of play, he shook his head and casually remarked, "If I had to play this damn course every week, I'd get into a new business."

His opening round certainly seemed to bear out this contention. Ben missed fairways, three-putted several greens, and finished the front nine with a miserable 39, four over par. After making an infuriating double bogey 6 on the concluding hole for 76, he took himself straight to the locker room and sat dejectedly on his locker bench.

"The stupidest round of golf I've ever played" was his unsparing verdict when he finally broke silence to reporters. True to his prediction, though, Sam Snead was leading after day one. The Slammer had fired 71.

National Opens are won by players who refuse to give ground, and unlike Snead, Hogan was the best in the business—maybe the best there had ever been—at not giving ground once it was taken. "I got the distinct feeling watching him that week," says West Virginia amateur ace Bill Campbell, "that his battle with Oakland Hills was something very personal, almost a blood feud for Ben."

Merion, Campbell says, was about proving he still had what it took to win major golf tournaments. "Many people were saying Oakland Hills, with all the Draconian changes, was simply beyond even Hogan's abilities. It became a contest within a contest for Ben—something he had to accomplish because no one thought he could possibly do it."

In round two, playing in steamy morning heat, Hogan improved to 73 for a halfway total of 149—five shots off the pace being set by the engaging South African Bobby Locke, he of the pleasant "muffin"-contoured face, traditional plus fours, formal necktie, and infallible wristy putter stroke. For his part, early leader Snead hiccuped his way around the golf course in round two, having to slash his way out of ankle-deep rough once or twice in transit to an untidy 78 and a 149 total that grouped him with Mangrum and Hogan. Fourteen other golfers lay between the three of them and the tournament lead. "I'd have to be Houdini now," Ben soberly assessed his midpoint chances. "It would take 140 to get the lead, and how can anyone shoot 140 on *that* course?"

The writers he said this to nodded their heads in solemn agreement, reluctantly already passing the torch from Ben to one of the names clustered near the top of the leaderboard—Locke or Demaret or perhaps the apparently ageless Paul Runyan, Julius Boros, maybe even beefy Clayton Heafner.

Not one player had beaten par during the opening two rounds (for the tournament the average round was 77), and only two men had managed to make 70. Despite a hook that sometimes forced him to aim at adjoining fairways, Bobby Locke's considerable chipping and putting skills suddenly made him the man to beat, in many opinions. Julius Boros was also displaying the kind of cool efficiency that winning National Opens required.

As for Ben, the finest final-round player of his era, he suddenly faced an even larger challenge than Merion: five strokes to make up in the Darwinist ordeal known as Open Saturday, the ultimate test of his course management on maybe the toughest golf course ever presented in defense of a National Open title.

On the strength of this beguiling proposition alone, a record 18,000 spectators turned out that Saturday morning in suburban Detroit, most if not all there principally to see if the Hawk could somehow pull off a miracle finish in the punishing heat.

Ben gave them something to cheer about right from the start, collecting birdies at the difficult 1st, 2nd, and 5th holes. Then he drove into a creek and lost a stroke at 7 but promptly made it back by rattling a bold forty-footer into the back of the cup on 8; he parred 9 and completed his first outward walk with a brilliant 32, sending seismic charges through the flocking multitudes. As word spread that Hogan was catching fire, thousands of fans peeled off the leaders and jogged back to see if slowly hobbling Ben could keep the magic going.

He ripped off a string of pars through the 13th hole but chipped poorly at 14 and made bogey. Hoping to miss the big bunker Trent Jones had placed outrageously in the heart of the fairway at 15—a hazard copied from the Principal's Nose at St. Andrews—Hogan attacked with his driver and ran his ball into the heavy rough on the right; a few minutes later, he compounded his miscalculation by firing his ball across the fairway into the opposing rough, staring expressionlessly after it, grunting, giving his head the faintest disbelieving shake. He lit a fresh cigarette off the butt of a dying one and trudged on. On his third attempt, the ball plugged in a bunker by the green. He blasted out and two-putted for double bogey 6.

On the 16th tee, he paused for several seconds, hands thrust on hips, the classic Hogan tournament pose, eyes alternately narrowed to slits and widening like a bird of prey sizing up a juicy rodent, cigarette smoke wreathing his hardened features. The tournament's sentimental favorite knew it was now or never on the dangerous so-called lake hole, a long and difficult dogleg right that finished with a small green tucked snugly against a pond, providing for one of the most intimidating pin positions in golf. A towering, well-placed drive was mandatory.

Hogan slashed his drive far down the right side of the 16th fairway, depositing his ball only inches from the first cut of rough. Abandoning his archconservative style of play for one of the few times ever in a major championship where he was contending, he attacked a flag that was positioned on a lip of green that protruded dangerously over the lake, aiming for a spot generally considered unreachable.

The ball bit hard into the green's firm flesh and spun, stopping five feet from the cup, sending up a gigantic hurrah from his camp followers. But he missed the putt. Then, to make matters worse, he bogeyed 17. He completed the morning round with 71, the second-best round of the entire tournament—but still three back of the leaders—and stalked off under his own private rain cloud.

Hogan left the 54th hole of the fifty-first National Open with his head down, pausing only to total and sign his card before slipping indoors for an aspirin, an iced glass of ginger ale, and some cool quiet privacy in which to reassemble his thoughts. His legs ached powerfully, but they *always* ached. The problem, for the moment at least, wasn't his legs. It was the Monster. He'd had the son-of-a-bitch of a golf course by the throat and somehow lost his grip on it.

When Hogan reappeared an hour or so later, he seemed far more composed and less annoyed with himself. "I'm going to burn it up, Ike," he told referee Ike Grainger on the 1st tee, following a modest lunch of cold roast beef and a little bouillon soup and a calming sit with his wife.

But he didn't do that—not at first anyway. An overcooked two-iron on the daunting 200-yard 3rd resulted in bogey 4, a one-shot deficit he was unable to erase until a birdie at 7. He concluded his final front nine of Open Saturday with a dead level 35, an acute disappointment until he heard that everyone ahead of him except Clayton Heafner was having similar difficulty and most were rapidly losing ground.

The Monster's 10th hole was widely regarded as the toughest par-4 on the course, one of the most unforgiving golf holes in the world, a 448-yard nightmare with a fairway that resembled a hotel corridor and rough that waved ankle-deep in spots. Ben put his tee shot 265 out into the short grass, then used his two-iron to rifle a low fade to within four feet of the flag. The crowds went crazy. "It was my best shot of the tournament," he explained later. "It went exactly as I played it, every inch of the way."

He putted in for his birdie 3, then parred holes 11 and 12. Another birdie came on 13—a fifteen-footer that curled gently into the heart of the hole, bringing on another ground-trembling cheer. When his bold three-iron approach flew over the green on 14, though, he visibly seethed with anger, burning his cigarette down to its filter in one long drag. He chipped and just missed the putt. Another damned bogey.

Hogan never forgot the way a hole treated him and illustrated the point beautifully at 15. This was the hole where he tried to miss the large bunker in the fairway with his driver and wound up in the deep rough that morning, resulting in a costly double bogey 6. He wasn't going to give the Monster any more chances like that. This time, selecting his three-wood, he swung hard, avoided the bunker, and nearly holed his six-iron approach to the green, draining the remaining three-footer for birdie.

He continued the artillery assault on 16, the potentially murderous lake hole, unleashing a 300-yard drive to the very edge of the lake itself before lofting a brilliant nine-iron shot to four feet of the cup. The putt singed the hole but stayed out. Hogan stared at it for a long moment "with eyes like volcano craters," said one eyewitness close to the action. He had to settle for par. Behind him, Bobby Locke recorded three consecutive bogeys to ruin his chances, and only Clayton Heafner, a man whose temper obscured his talent, was making a run at the title, playing steady and consistent golf that would net him a handsome 69 before the day was over.

After a surgical two-iron and two putts got him par at 17, Hogan calculated a par-4 might be good enough to win, but a birdie would definitely improve his chances. With a slight breeze at his back, taking a little more time than usual, he uncorked another 280-yard drive over the bunkered ridge of the dog-legging fairway—an extraordinarily gutsy play under the circumstances—and landed his shot in the fairway beyond the dogleg. A roar went up from the fairway and the fans ringing the final green. By this time, they were twenty and thirty deep, most of the paying customers through the gate that day.

With only a six-iron left to the green, he abandoned caution again and fired his approach shot straight at the flag instead of a spot safely below it. His ball settled softly fifteen feet above the cup.

For several minutes he studied the gentle downhill putt before taking his crouched position over the ball. All sound abruptly fell away. He lightly tapped the ball and watched it trickle down the baked slope toward the cup, gaining speed as it rolled, until it clattered into the cup. "It could do no less," says Open historian Sommers. The crowd lost its mind with joy.

"The way he played those closing three holes," says Bill Campbell, who was standing somewhere in the crush, craning to see the final putt, "illustrates something wonderful about Hogan—namely, that he could almost always hit exactly the shot that was needed at that moment. Great champions can all do that, of course, but I never saw anyone better at that than Ben."

Behind him out on the Monster, Bobby Locke and others heard the thunderous cheers coming from the direction of the clubhouse. They knew immediately what was up. Hogan was making his charge.

The birdie gave him 67.

"That took the starch out of the rest of us," Locke commented later, reflecting on the 73 he finished with, only good enough for third place. Clayton Heafner's brilliant 69 left him alone in second place.

Hogan's four rounds of 76-73-71-67 had gotten progressively better with each trip over Oakland Hills, and even though his 287 total came nowhere near to shattering Ralph Guldahl's old mark, his final round was already being hailed as a masterpiece of discipline and execution. "There have been other great finishes since then," says Sommers, "—Arnold Palmer's slashing 65 at Cherry Hills in 1960, the 65 by Jack Nicklaus at Baltusrol in 1967, Johnny

Miller's 63 at Oakmont in 1973, and the two 68s Cary Middlecoff put together at Inverness in 1957—but none compared to this one."

Hogan's 67 was the lowest score of the week and the second-lowest finishing round ever recorded by an Open champion, one stroke shy of matching Gene Sarazen's amazing final 66 at Fresh Meadow in 1932. Given the unprecedented difficulty of the golf course and the atmosphere of impossible expectations, Hogan's back-nine 32 made his finish one for the ages—and the most satisfying of his career.

Ironically, one of the first people to reach him and offer hearty congratulations as he came wearily off the 18th green was Ione Jones, the polished and highly educated wife of the man who transformed Oakland Hills into the Grendel of major tournament venues. Like 18,000 others sensing history that afternoon, she'd faithfully followed Hogan nearly every step of the way, rooting for him to win his third Open championship.

"Ben," she said to him, extending her elegantly tapered hand, "I'm so proud of you. You must be very pleased with the way you played."

Hogan paused and stared at her, then accepted her congratulations.

"Mrs. Jones," he replied calmly, "if your husband had to play the courses he designs for a living, I'm afraid you'd be in a breadline."

A few minutes later in the locker room, where he went to sweat out Heafner's and Locke's finishes, Ben sipped a cold beer and finally smiled with relief and admitted, "Under the circumstances, it was the greatest round I have played. To be honest, I didn't think I could do it. My friends said last night that I might win with a pair of 69s. It seemed too much on this course. It is the hardest course I've ever played. I haven't played all the courses in the world, mind you, but I don't want to, especially if there are any that are tougher than this one."

By the time he appeared to accept his third silver Open trophy and gold medal almost one hour later, showered and dressed in a fresh shirt and handsome tiny-check blazer, his inky black hair showing the first wisps of gray at the temples above his broad movie-star smile, Ben looked like a million bucks—or roughly what some wags calculated his third National Open title would mean to him once the commercial possibilities were totaled.

A giant horseshoe of humanity ringed the final green where the USGA's Joe Dey presented the trophy and medal and asked Hogan for his observations on the unforgettable finish. Hesitating slightly before he addressed the multitude, Hogan seemed almost prepared to speak from the heart, to reveal the depths of the powerful emotions churning inside him. He'd won three National

Opens in a row, tying Willie Anderson and leaving him one win shy of the overall Open record held jointly by Bobby Jones and Anderson. Suffice it to say, even most die-hard Hogan fans had largely accepted that mighty Oakland Hills was probably beyond their hero's grasp.

"I'm glad I brought this course," he said instead, resorting to the familiar protective comfort of a chilly postmortem, "this *monster*, to its knees."

AFTER NEARLY two full months off to recover his strength, a hiatus during which he made several television appearances and showed up to be feted at Toots Shors's restaurant in Manhattan, Hogan startled the golf world by suddenly entering George S. May's World Championship of Golf at Tam O'Shanter.

So unexpected was Hogan's call from Fort Worth that the Barnum of Golf personally took Ben's eleventh-hour entry over the phone and thanked him in advance for coming. Hogan's very name in a field meant a minimum of 10,000 more paying spectators, maybe 20,000 or 30,000 on the strength of events at Oakland Hills.

It was Hogan's first return to Tam O'Shanter since 1947, the year he carted home a silver-plated monstrosity called the International Cup for his trouble and privately criticized May for making a "side show" of the golf tournament by forcing caddies to wear numbers on their backs so spectators could identify the players. (At one point, in fact, May even outrageously proposed the players themselves wear numbers identifying them the way baseball players were identified—prompting a groundswell of protest from the players; the suggestion was ditched.) May's "side show" included handing out free admission tickets to nongolf types in Chicago's Loop simply to swell his galleries, and hiring magicians and minstrels to stroll through the crowds entertaining fans. At that time, Hogan vowed he would never return to a tournament where such ridiculous antics went on.

So why now?

As reporters puzzled over his possible motivations for entering a tournament put on by a man he reportedly disliked, on a golf course he didn't particularly care for (and where his other longtime nemesis Lloyd Mangrum served as touring pro no less), Ben quietly arrived in town and blitzed the field with a breathtaking sequence of rounds, 68-69-70-66, nimbly pocketing May's $12,500 first-prize money, his single biggest payoff ever. "Was the great Hogan even here?" mused one of the Windy City's more unimpressed sportswriters.

"He showed up, teed up, spoke to virtually no one, broke a scoring record or two then vanished. What," he wondered, "is Ben thinking?"

Clearly, something was on the Hawk's mind. Perhaps it was his much-talked-about "secret."

Weeks later, he helped Royal Hogan prepare for his first-round match in the U.S. Amateur Championship to be conducted at Bethlehem, Pennsylvania, and "Bubber" Hogan boasted to the *Fort Worth Press* that for the first time ever little brother Ben had revealed his "secret" swing wisdom directly to another mortal. "I'm the only one he ever showed it to," grinning and weather-beaten forty-one-year-old Royal boasted, though he declined to explain exactly *what* the "secret" consisted of. Whatever it was, Royal either quickly forgot it or couldn't make it work for him the way it did for his little brother. Days later, Bubber Hogan lost his opening match and was booted from the field of the National Amateur.

Ben spent November and most of December poking around at home, exercising his legs, and practicing and playing enough to keep the rust off his game at Colonial and Rivercrest. He and Val ventured out to only a few club holiday parties and early evening dinners with Marvin and Mary Leonard or Sarah and Gordon Harriman, who had moved into their new home on nearby Westover Road. Sometimes the W. A. Moncriefs and Earl Baldridges joined them, an expanding social circle that seemed to suggest Ben's growing desire for less travel and a more settled life. The social life of Westover Hills had its own "secrets" too, including the old Top of the Hill Terrace, a popular roadhouse out on the Arlington Road where Cowtown's elite often went to dance to an orchestra and gamble. Periodically, to keep up appearances in a town renowned for its frontier vices, local law enforcement officers would "raid" the well-known establishment, though not before the owners had been granted sufficient time to shove the blackjack table into the wall and give its better-known patrons ample warning to clear out. "Everyone went there, including my parents and Uncle Ben and Aunt Valerie," remembers Valerie Harriman. "It was all pretty innocent but really the thing to do for a while. I remember that once, though, rather amusingly to hear my mother tell it, they were all out there when the sheriff's men made one of their periodic raids. The charges, such as they were, of course, were quickly dropped and things went on pretty much as before. It added a little spice to their lives."

At club dinners, the women of Ben and Valerie's social set talked of debutante cotillions and hospital fund-raisers, the men about Korea and oil. Oil wasn't entirely on Ben's mind, though many of Ben's Rivercrest and Colonial cronies speculated that would be his next logical area of concentration and conquest.

No one but perhaps Valerie and Sarah understood that Ben's surprising World Championship entry and win had been purely, and rather calculatingly, about two things—robbing Snead and making money. Coming on the heels of his most impressive Open win to date, the win in Chicago gave Hogan victories in three of the four tournaments he'd entered in 1951, the only disappointment coming from a fourth-place finish at his hometown Colonial, an impressive total that gave him a reasonable shot of depriving rival Snead of another Player of the Year honor. Sam won just twice in 1951, the Miami Open and the PGA Championship.

If that was good enough to cinch a third Player of the Year Award, as he fully expected it to, not only would Hogan's commercial stock value soar and his exhibition fee rise to $2,000 a day, but he'd be in financial shape to pursue something he'd been thinking about doing for years—starting up his own golf equipment company.

Sure enough, days before Hogan arrived in Pinehurst in early November for the 1951 Ryder Cup, he was named PGA Player of the Year for the third time in four years. He sat down on the eve of the matches with a young sportswriter from the *Greensboro Daily News* to air some of his thinking about the future.

Among other things, he revealed that he was enjoying the pleasures of "family life" for the first time in memory and considering "significant other opportunities" beyond the grind of tournament golf—though, to no one's surprise, he refused to elaborate on what those "opportunities" might be.

Once again, he certainly didn't play like a man about to hang up his shooting irons and go dig oil wells.

Captained by rapidly balding Sam Snead, the American side dominated play and rolled to a 9½-to-2½ rout of Great Britain and Ireland. In the cup's opening foursomes, Ben and Jimmy Demaret teamed to demolish Fred Daly and Ken Bousfield, 5 and 4, and Hogan went on to whip Charles Ward, 3 and 2, in singles. The only true surprise of the lopsided victory was Jimmy Demaret's surprise announcement that *he* was retiring from Ryder Cup competition, leaving with the best unbeaten record in Ryder Cup history, a perfect 6-0-0.

As Henry Longhurst, swirling his whiskey, remarked to one of his American colleagues, the only real question in the aftermath of the Pinehurst debacle was whether Britain would ever be able to make Sam Ryder's matches an honest contest on American soil.

"Not as long as we've got Hogan," his American drinking companion replied.

ALL OF THIS—the brilliant bursts of tournament golf combined with hints of "significant other interests," Demaret's sudden Ryder retirement, and the persistent rumors of his own impending withdrawal—made Hogan's poor title defense of the Masters the following spring appear even more telltale—and pure anguish for his devoted followers to witness.

After opening with a pair of 70s that placed him in the hunt for a second green jacket, Ben posted distinctly *un*-Hogan-esque rounds of 74-79 and finished in a tie for seventh. The most obvious culprit was his putter.

Once the game's deadliest ball roller inside ten or twelve feet, Hogan's putting routine, particularly on shorter putts, suddenly became a source of visible frustration for the Hawk. At several points during this edition of the Masters, the reigning champion stood for unnatural lengths of time over his ball, staring coldly at the line, finally making a hesitant takeaway of his putter head and a short jabbing forward stroke. He missed putts left and right. Many years later, when the condition significantly worsened and effectively drove him from the game, Hogan's Shady Oaks friends found a nickname for this ailment: Ben's blind stares.

Sam Snead, the Masters winner that year, spotted the trouble early on. "Ben's ball-striking had never been better at that time, but a lot of folks don't realize that his putter really started acting up about '52 and '53. His problem wasn't a yip like mine. He simply couldn't pull back the putter and let it go. He told me later that he tried damn near everything to fix the problem—nerve pills [tranquilizers], relaxation exercises, even tried to get himself hypnotized a time or two I guess. Anyway, it got worse. Everything catches up to you in this game. That's where it started for Ben, though."

The Masters of 1952 would be the first of only three public appearances Ben made that year in regulation seventy-two-hole Tour events, and the 74-79 collapse of the most dangerous fourth-round player in history once again prompted a blizzard of reports and speculations that the Hawk was through. "Bantam's Round Causes Whispers," heralded a *Fort Worth Press* headline back home in Texas. "The gossip was thick late Sunday in the Augusta National clubhouse," reported former TCU link star turned *Press* sports reporter Dan Jenkins, noting that it was Hogan's worst finish in a major championship. "There was justification for the talk. Writers, golfers, and Masters committeemen all kept the room buzzing with talk of 'Hogan's blowup.' " The sobering consensus, according to Jenkins, expressed by a sportswriter for the local *Augusta Herald*, was "that Ben is through."

"No one knows what golf's greatest player is really thinking—though thoughts of hanging it up can't come easy for Hogan," chipped in a syndicated columnist from Chicago.

For the stubbornly quiet man at the middle of the storm, who would turn forty in a matter of months—an age when more than one great champion had suddenly seen his putting skills sharply decline—the lone highlight of the sixteenth Masters came on Tuesday night before the start of play when he hosted a special dinner at the clubhouse honoring all of the tournament's previous winners. Counting reigning champion Hogan, nine former Masters winners—Horton Smith, Henry Picard, Ralph Guldahl, Byron Nelson, Herm Keiser, Craig Wood, Snead, and Demaret—showed up on the eve of a similar dinner Bob Jones had hosted for years to honor distinguished amateur invitees.

Under the terms of the new "Champions Dinner" proposed by Hogan, the tournament's reigning winner got to select the evening's menu, and Hogan (who happened to be the reigning champion that spring) graciously offered to pick up the dinner's tab. Paying for the meal from his own pocket lasted two years until Hogan, as he later explained it, "realized the tab came to more than the winner's share of the purse," at which point he proposed that every preceding year's champion select the menu *and* pick up the check. The reason he finished runner-up at the Masters four times following the start of the Champions Dinner tradition, he joked some years later, was to avoid having to pay for so many expensive meals.

Looking back on Hogan's greatly diminished play in 1952, many would swear they saw other unmistakable signs of a passing of the guard that began in the pines of eastern Georgia that spring.

The great Jones was visibly fading fast—he would soon require the services of a motorized golf cart to transport him around the golf course—and stalwarts like Mangrum, Demaret, and even Claude Harmon were making noises about saying good-bye to the Tour.

The ageless Paul Runyan basically left the regular touring game that year. So did Henry Picard, Leo Diegel, and Craig Wood. George Fazio and Herman Keiser weren't far behind them. Ditto the Arkansas Traveler, Dutch Harrison. Though Sam Snead won his third green jacket that spring and some of his best scoring years were just ahead (in 1955, for instance, he won the Vardon Trophy for the lowest scoring average), the year 1952 would be the last time the Slammer captured more than four tournaments in a single season. Sam was cracking forty too, and already experiencing his own difficulties with the flatstick.

Seven weeks after the Masters, though, Snead's archrival Hogan won Marvin Leonard's Colonial Invitational for the third time and promised his fans he would play in the event as long as his legs would permit him to.

"If Ben wins the tournament again," his friend and mentor Marvin Leonard said, presenting Hogan with his third Colonial trophy, "I'll just *give* him the trophy."

Ben flashed his enamels, laughing easily.

"Is that a promise?"

"You bet it is."

A touching moment came in the opening round of this particular NIT when amateur sensation Bill Campbell, fresh from a failed bid for Congress from West Virginia, was unnerved to discover himself paired with Hogan and Demaret.

"I was so nervous," Campbell remembers, "I hit my opening drive off the heel of my club and struck a spectator in the hand. I felt awful about that and stood there asking myself *what* on earth I was even doing out there on the same golf course with the great Ben Hogan and Jimmy Demaret."

By the par-3 4th hole, the talented amateur's gloom had only deepened. He couldn't seem to find a fairway or a green and desperately wished a hole would open up so he could jump in and hide.

"But Ben suddenly did something extraordinary, almost as if he could read my thoughts. He knew I was losing it and walked over slowly and put his arm around my shoulders. He smiled and said very calmly to me, almost like an uncle, 'Now, Bill. You have just as much right to be out here as we do. So settle down. Take your time. And remember we're with you.' "

Campbell calmed down and shot 77, then went on to make Colonial's thirty-six-hole cut. On Sunday he finished with 72 to earn the tournament's low amateur honors and take home a Colonial bold Scottish plaid jacket of his own.

"I really owe that entirely to Ben," says the eight-time Walker Cup legend. "If he hadn't come over and spoken so kindly to me, I don't know what would have happened to me out there that week."

SIX DAYS AFTER stowing away another Colonial trophy, Hogan drove himself over to Northwood Club in Dallas for the first ever National Golf Day, an elaborate fund-raiser dreamed up by the PGA and *Life* magazine to raise money for the USO and the National Golf Fund and its related charity organizations.

Popularly called "Beat Ben Hogan Day," sponsors hoped that 100,000 golfers nationwide would be willing to shell out a buck for the chance to match their eighteen-hole scores at their home golf courses (using full handicap with five extra strokes for female participants) against Hogan's round on May 31 at Northwood Country Club, site of the approaching United States Open Championship, where defending champ Hogan would soon chase a record-tying fourth National Open.

Anyone who managed to "beat" Hogan's score at Northwood that day would receive a special bronze medallion stamped with the champ's likeness and the legend, "I beat Ben Hogan. May 31, 1952."

Northwood was a highly controversial choice for an Open venue. A five-year-old layout built on former ranchland just north of the Dallas city line, designed by a little-known Midwest course architect named William Diddel, it was owned by a membership that was largely made up of affluent newcomers to prosperous North Dallas, folks who didn't want to wait seven or eight years just to get into crowded Dallas Country Club or elite Brook Hollow Golf Club, where Sarah and Gordon Harriman belonged.

Like many traditionalists who believed the National Championship ought to be conducted only on golf courses with histories of proven toughness and rich tradition, Hogan felt that Northwood was simply too immature and unrefined for hosting the U.S. Open. That Northwood's boosters had unapologetically borrowed a page directly from Marvin Leonard's 1941 playbook (promising the USGA a guaranteed windfall of $25,000) didn't help its cause with many of its Fort Worth neighbors either. Rivalry between Dallas and Fort Worth preceded statehood and often fell—as it still does—along the fault lines of society and money. "Fort Worth is cows, trains, oil, and old Texas values," sums up one modern-day social maven with a foot in both cities. "It prides itself on being behind the times and paying cash. Dallas is foreign banks, new money, and big business. They buy on credit over there and think nothing of it."

A small army of print and broadcast journalists and 1,500 Hogan partisans, at any rate, turned out at Northwood to watch their man play the rest of "America." So did former Greensboro newsman John Derr, now a broadcast star for CBS Radio. It was Derr's job to stroll along with the champ and broadcast descriptions of his play. "Ben was perfectly cordial," Derr recalls, "but you could tell this wasn't his sort of thing, a made-up event that basically had no meaning on a golf course he clearly wasn't fond of. On the other hand, Northwood was where he had to defend his Open title in a couple weeks. He was clearly looking the place over with his usual thoroughness."

For his participation, Ben received $1,500 from the sponsors, and a controversy quickly developed when the Dallas papers reported that Hogan "refused" to donate his share of the proceeds back to the charities involved. In fact, he donated his check to University Christian Church but took his own sweet time in revealing this fact to the press, an indication of his need to protect his spiritual privacy.

As he warmed up on the practice range before his scheduled 11:00 A.M. tee time, Ben joked with the Northwood crowd about his aching legs and the effects of the "long drive to Dallas from home." He presented free golf balls to a group of kids who ringed the practice putting green, where he rapped putts for a solid half-hour before teeing off.

"The smile vanished as he walked to the 1st tee," John Derr remembers. "It was time for business. His face became absolute stone."

At the stroke of 11:00 A.M. CST, noon back east (where a cold heavy rain was pelting courses between Maryland and Maine), Ben and 14,000 wannabe Hogan beaters teed off on 1,200 golf courses from Pinehurst to Pebble Beach. Hogan used a butter knife to find the heart of the opening par-4 hole, and by the time he curled a twenty-five-footer into the cup at the 4th hole, he was two under par, cruising along on automatic pilot, the picture of machinelike poise and deliberation, hitting every fairway and missing not a single green in regulation. He went out in 34 strokes against a par of 36.

His first slip came on the 220-yard par-3 16th, where he pulled his one-iron shot into the trees, chipped out, and scored bogey. "That should cost *Life* another 10,000 medals," he remarked ruefully, marching on to the next tee. A second bogey there and a par finish left him two over for the nine—an even par 71 for the round.

Only 1,400 golfers— one-tenth of those who teed off against him—man-

aged to beat Ben Hogan that day. In Albuquerque, New Mexico, a local surgeon beat Hogan in the morning, then paid another buck and went out and
beat him in the afternoon to earn *two* medals, while auto magnate Henry Ford
II took Ben on at his home course at the posh Country Club of Detroit, shot
74, and just missed earning a medal. Playing through a downpour back east at
the Army-Navy Country Club, General Omar Bradley shot 85 for a net score
of 74—close but no cigar—while in the high country of Colorado, several
cowboy golfers were forced to push heavy spring snow off the greens and use
special putting strips in order to compete. Despite the conditions, a few of
them won "I Beat Ben Hogan" medals.

Out in sunny Hollywood, meanwhile, actor Bill Boyd—better known to
millions as "Hopalong Cassidy"—skipped out of filming his popular TV show
to try to beat Ben at the Los Angeles Country Club. After playing terribly for
several holes, the popular actor picked up his ball and went back to work.

The oldest player who won a medal that day was eighty-four-year-old
Mamie Cartwright, also of Hollywood, California, whose registered 45 handicap produced a winning net score of 71—thus a tie with her sporting hero
(ties counted too). "I didn't think I could beat Ben," she told *Life* magazine
with a husky laugh afterward. "My body and game are *both* a little out of
condition."

The youngest winner was plucky Diane Wilson, age eight, daughter of two
Kansas City golf professionals, who fired a nimble 117 against a handicap of
48 to wind up with a Hogan bronze keepsake. The best score was recorded by
Texas policeman Andy Sword, who went around his home course with a non-
handicap seven-under 64. Hogan personally presented the grinning patrolman
Sword with his medal.

At least four sitting governors and one elite member of the U.S. Senate—
Ohio's Robert Taft, a pretty fair stick—also gave it their best efforts, as did
the entire touring cast of *South Pacific* at a local country club in suburban
Cleveland. None earned a National Golf Day medallion, but Taft at least admitted later that participating in such a vast democratic enterprise probably
helped his national visibility. At that moment in time, he was the odds-on favorite to be named the Republican National Convention's nominee for president in 1952.

The first National Golf Day was simply fun and games compared to the
fifty-second United States Open Championship, which began on the same spot
exactly ten days later.

On paper at least, two factors made Northwood and Hogan a promising combination. The flattish course, as it was set up, wouldn't tax his legs too much and was said to be playing only slightly less difficult than Oakland Hills had—thus offering the intangible "severity" factor that always gave Hogan an edge over most any field. Also, during the ten days running up to the start of play, Ben logged no less than nine practice rounds on the golf course, identifying every possible strategic position where a National Open might be won or lost with a single swing of the club.

The final factor in his favor was his clear motivation to tie Bobby Jones's record of four U.S. Opens, a feat many believed might never be repeated, owing to radical equipment improvements and a rush of fine young players into the professional game. Still, despite their balking putters, Ben and Sam were the men to beat. "Northwood," predicted Charles Einstein of the International News Service a week before play began, relying on recent history as his Delphic oracle, "is the Open Hogan can't lose and Snead can't win."

Most observers agreed it would be nothing less than a coronation week down in Texas, especially with husband and wife radio personalities Phil Harris and Alice Faye, Ronald and Nancy Reagan, and other Hollywood sorts coming to "Big D" on the eve of play expressly to honor Ben Hogan at his induction into the Texas Sports Hall of Fame dinner at the Baker Hotel's Crystal Ballroom.

As it happened, Hogan was only the second man to be inducted into the two-year-old institution, the previous year's honor having gone to Texas baseball star Tris Speaker, and among the sellout audience of 400 paying dinner guests that evening was a grateful Bill Campbell, wearing his new Colonial sports jacket.

"For a man who was supposed to be so uncomfortable with words," Campbell remembers, "Ben gave an absolutely spellbinding acceptance speech about what the honor meant to him. He had that crowd eating out of his hand—and some folks wiping their eyes."

After being presented with his plaque by Tris Speaker, Hogan described his induction into the Texas Sports Hall of Fame as "the greatest achievement or honor I've ever received," then related an amusing anecdote about the only useful advice anyone had ever given him in golf.

It came from his wife, Valerie Hogan. "She is responsible for 75 to 80 percent of my success," he explained, nodding to the diminutive smiling woman seated on his right.

"I was complaining about missing putts," he pushed on, "and she told me, 'Ben, you're just going to have to get your second shot closer to the hole.'"

The audience laughed robustly at the obvious wisdom of her advice, and Hogan waited for them all to quiet back down.

"She is my inspiration and my helper," he summed up with a slightly wavering voice, adding, "I've tried to do that ever since."

As he sat down, the audience stood up, a thunderous ovation that lasted several minutes.

DIRECTOR SID LANFIELD was Ben's VIP guest at the tournament's various social festivities that week in Dallas, most of which the Hogans themselves chose to skip. Ben was looking forward to sleeping in his own bed and driving himself to and from the tournament site in his new Cadillac, a model that had one of the first passenger air cooling systems available in a luxury car.

The same night Ben was inducted into the Texas Sports Hall of Fame, *Follow the Sun* opened a lengthy run at Dallas's popular Lone Star Drive-in Theater.

BEFORE THE START of play, the pleasant balmy weather of recent weeks vanished and a large Bermuda high locked itself over the region and quickly stagnated the air, pushing both the temperature and the humidity level toward the century mark.

Many felt this environmental change would benefit Hogan, because he detested cold weather and thrived in heat that eased his body aches.

Initially at least, the Texas Iceberg scarcely appeared to notice the sweltering temperatures. He went out and fired back-to-back 69s that tied an Open thirty-six-hole record, a feat that led many in the huge corps of sportswriters laboring under fiercely hot canvas Army tents erected on Northwood's clay tennis courts to conclude that Hogan was on pace to set or break a scoring record and tie Jones and Anderson.

With only Saturday's double round to go, Hogan stood two strokes ahead of George Fazio, three ahead of a visibly struggling Johnny Bulla, and four ahead of the quiet, husky, former Bridgeport accountant now residing in Southern Pines, North Carolina, Julius Boros. After Ben and Val slipped off to have a lunch of cold soup and salad in private with Lanfield, Ben sat on a locker-room bench dusting his pant legs with sulfur powder to prevent chiggers from attaching themselves to his socks and joked about recently putting on some extra weight thanks to Valerie's constant attention. "Maybe I'll be the first 155-pound man ever to win the National Open," he said, smiling broadly.

An astute handicapper searching for a dark horse capable of halting the Hogan Express might well have settled on the thirty-two-year-old Boros, he of the liquid swing tempo and unhesitating putting stroke, a young buck who had briefly been a factor at both Merion and Oakland Hills. Weighing against Julius was the fact that he had officially been a touring pro for only two years, and no one expected the easygoing northerner to give a seasoned leader a fight in such a Texas steam bath. "The world was ready," as Robert Sommers sets the scene, "for another Hogan runaway."

On the Saturday morning after *Follow the Sun* opened at the Lone Star Drive-in, *Fort Worth Press* Dan Jenkins gamely predicted that Hogan, "the pharaoh of the fairways," would shoot no worse than 137 to break his own Open record of 276.

Boros was out early that morning, smoothly chipping and putting himself to a sensational morning round of 68. Paired with Pork Chops Oliver, Hogan was in the final group that headed to the 1st tee, and tellingly, his opening drive missed the 1st fairway by a couple of yards, diving into the thick grass on the right side of the fairway.

As late morning's temperatures edged steadily upward, Hogan's short game faltered; he missed several short putts early, grew visibly impatient with himself, and limped home from his morning circuit with an infuriating 74. He quickly retreated to the locker room for a shower and change of clothes. Darkhorse Boros now stood at 210, two ahead of Ben and the rest of the field.

"Even with that," remembers John Derr, "most people assumed the afternoon would belong to Hogan. I mean, for goodness' sake, they'd all gotten so *accustomed* to Hogan winning the National Open. Besides, the course was not only in his backyard but also one that rewarded straight drivers. Nobody was better at that, of course, than Ben."

For the first time since the fourth round at Merion, though, Hogan's legs and stamina betrayed him, and his famous iron will seemed to bend under the blast furnace conditions that greeted players over the final eighteen holes. Several times during his round Hogan paused and leaned on a club to rest and drink water in the punishing afternoon heat and humidity, his shirt and trousers showing huge spreading stains of salt and body sweat where his body was pouring off moisture. The air around him was perfectly still, hovering well above 100 degrees. Spectators fanned themselves with programs beneath straw hats or crowded into the paltry shade provided by Northwood's young cottonwoods. Baking inside the tournament press tent, reporters abandoned their typewriters and stood before pedestal fans brought in to try to cool down the air.

Save for knocking his ball out of bounds when he attempted to hook his approach shot around a tree to the 4th green, Hogan played reasonably well from tee to green that afternoon, but his putting was once again the agent of his undoing. With a cluster of costly three-putts, he completed his unsuccessful defense of the fifty-second Open with another 74, just good enough for third place behind Porky Oliver and Julius Boros.

It was the first time in four United States Open Championships that Hogan had not won, and many on the scene saw the same intimations of mortality that Dan Jenkins and others had seen at Augusta National months before. Within days, the national press corps was producing tribute pieces to Hogan as if they expected his official retirement announcement to come at any minute.

BY THEN, Ben Hogan was safely home again on Valley Ridge Road, settling in to plot his future both in and out of tournament golf and soberly taking stock of life on the eve of turning forty.

By almost any measure, Hogan was arguably the most materially successful athlete in America—possibly of all time. He owned several productive oil wells out in west Texas and a one-sixth interest in a new ranch-style luxury hotel being built in west Fort Worth. Thanks to Greyhound Bus and a constant flood of commercial opportunities, he was rumored to have more than a million dollars in the bank.

Among a host of lucrative possibilities, he was considering a six-figure offer to put his name on a chain of Ben Hogan teaching academies, discussing another instruction book deal with at least two prospective publishers, and personally managing a stream of income from several commercial endorsement deals that paid him five grand apiece each year just to use his name and likeness—Bromo Seltzer, Ben Gay, Chesterfield, and Pabst Blue Ribbon beer.

Furthermore, after more than a decade representing Hershey Country Club on tour, he had a sweet new deal that paid him ten grand to serve as director of golf at Tamarisk Country Club in sunny Palm Springs, a swank new desert club that had opened the previous February in Rancho Mirage. Under the terms of his new contract, all he had to do was show up for a few weeks every winter and play as little or as much golf as he chose to play.

Someone searching for a clue to what other "significant opportunities" Ben Hogan was pondering would not have had to look any further than the August 22 edition of the *New Bedford* (Massachusetts) *Standard-Times*, which ran a front-page account of the famous golfer's unexpected visit to a manufacturing firm in the tidy seaside city.

Eight days after his fortieth birthday, instead of playing in George May's World Championship of Golf (Hogan reportedly demanded a flat $5,000 appearance fee up front knowing full well May would balk. Ben braved a northeast squall and flew to New Bedford to pay a visit to the Acushnet Process Sales Company.

He was not in town to play golf, sign books, or even give one of the thoughtful "friendly" interviews he'd become rather known for since the accident. Asked by a local reporter when he might compete on tour again, Hogan smiled and simply replied, "Probably not until next year's Masters," and left things at that.

The truth was, Hogan was in New Bedford to see how Titleist golf balls were made. As soon as he could raise a couple hundred thousand dollars of investment capital and find the right financial partner who knew enough to stay the hell out of his way, Ben Hogan intended to start making the finest golf clubs anybody had ever played with—and eventually maybe even the balls to go with them.

TWELVE

Change

WRITER HERBERT WARREN WIND never forgot that winter morning in the California desert.

"I was on my way out west to cover the start of the new tournament season for 1953," remembers the former *Sports Illustrated* writer and future Hogan collaborator on *Five Lessons*, "and stopped off to see how Ben was enjoying his new club affiliation at Tamarisk Country Club. It was unannounced on my part. I was curious how he was faring, because no one had seen him for months. Based on his rather poor showings of late, there was widespread belief he was preparing to leave the Tour.

"In the pro shop, they informed me he was out practicing on the range, off by himself as usual, and I recall proceeding that way with, shall we say, great discretion—Mr. Hogan, as everyone knew, didn't like to be disturbed when he was practicing. I was prepared not to be received with much warmth. Ben and I were friendly, but I wouldn't have said we were friends. I couldn't have been more surprised by his greeting."

Overleaf: Ben Hogan and Sam Snead, 1954 Masters *(Corbis)*

The minute Hogan saw him, Wind says, a smile spread across his face, and the Hawk came walking briskly toward him with his hand thrust out.

"Great to see you, Herb," Hogan greeted him. "Say, do you have any plans for lunch?"

Pleasantly surprised, Wind stayed to watch Hogan hit balls for another hour or so, then joined him on the club's terrace for a conversation over lunch, touching on a broad range of topics, from the recent presidential elections to Ben's growing fascination with oil exploration, from National Open strategy to world affairs.

"I was deeply struck not only by how informed he was about many more things other than golf, but how relaxed and genuinely happy he seemed," Wind remembers. "This was a side of Hogan I'd heard about but had never seen. Few had. Here was a man who'd spent his whole life refining himself in the classic American way, learning to hit golf shots and win big tournaments, to speak and dress better, copying gracious, successful older men and finally becoming one himself. I remember thinking how ironic it was that as the world was pretty much writing him off, *this* Hogan was finally revealing himself. It was a welcome change from the past.

"As I watched him, though, I sensed an urgency about his practice, and I got the distinct impression he still had something important to prove—to himself if not others. The golf shots I watched him hit that morning were as fine as I'd ever seen him make. I recall thinking—I even remarked as much to him during our lunch—that this had to be unwelcome news to the rest of the Tour. He just smiled at that. Here he was out in the desert, with no one watching, getting himself into the finest playing condition of his career."

IF HOGAN was suddenly changing, so was the America around him.

During the autumnal election that sent Hogan's Augusta National friend Dwight Eisenhower to Washington (instead of Wind's preferred candidate, Adlai Stevenson for whom Wind, a graduate of Yale and Cambridge, had even done a spot of speechwriting), an unprecedented number of Americans had exercised their right to vote—over 61.5 million people, or a record 63 percent of the country's eligible voters, a historic turnout that probably had more to do with the nation's affection for Ike than his party's isolationist views. Throughout a campaign that was neither hard-fought nor particularly dramatic, as author David Halberstam points out in his marvelous book *The Fifties*, Eisenhower promised to end the Korean War but avoid "turning back the clock" on popular social reforms that had fed and housed millions of Americans through decades of depression and war, stressing that peace and prosperity would bring "wonderful new opportunities to daily American life."

As a result of Ike's genial style of governance and unapologetic admiration for the sporting life, some historians regard his tenure as a rather drowsy hiatus in national affairs, one long eight-year golf vacation between the social cataclysms of the '30s and '40s and the cultural and political upheavals of the 1960s. And yet, for better or worse, even as a protracted cold war replaced an intensely hot one, the entrepreneurial energy quietly unleashed by Ike's belief in consumerism and the politics of broader social mobility had profound effects on the way every American would live in the future.

In San Bernadino, that same winter Herb Wind called on Ben Hogan at Rancho Mirage, a pair of ambitious former carhops called the McDonald brothers opened a restaurant using a streamlined menu and a mechanized cooking process, offering cheap 20¢ hamburgers and milk shakes to a nation suddenly on the run. One national food critic quickly dismissed the California phenomenon as "assembly-line cooking" and predicted the novelty of "fast food" would lose its appeal before too long.

That following summer, former jukebox salesman Kemmons Wilson from Arkansas took his family on a car vacation to Washington, D.C., and was struck by the inferior conditions of most roadside motels. Upon returning home to Arkansas, Wilson drew up a business plan for a high-quality roadside accommodation that would offer travelers a clean spacious room, a free black-and-white TV set, and no unpleasant surprises—all for six bucks a night, double occupancy, with the kids staying free. Within just three months, borrowing a name from the popular Bing Crosby movie, Wilson opened his first new-fangled "Holiday Inn" on a busy federal highway between Memphis and Nashville.

Around business schools (which experienced a twofold increase from post-war levels in student applications, owing to the GI Bill), a new phrase suddenly came into vogue in 1953, identifying a class of Americans very much interested in the kinds of things Herb Wind was writing about and the good life Ben Hogan was living. "The new American middle class" had both the time and disposable income to purchase a new car (Ford's convertibles were the hottest thing going that spring), take a family vacation to Yellowstone, or subscribe to a record number of glossy magazines that appeared on newsstands that year catering to every taste from gardening to golf. For more serious reading, women flipped discreetly through Albert Kinsey's provocative treatise on female sexuality while their husbands followed dispatches of Sir Edmund Hillary's conquest of Everest, the planet's highest peak.

These couples were also buying homes in record numbers. In 1953, inspired by the sprawling planned community that former Seabee Bill Levitt erected on empty potato fields twenty miles east of Manhattan, American homeownership reached a summit too. If Levittown became an easy target for social critics who argued that brutally replicated neighborhoods would invariably undermine America's cultural diversity with "functional monotony," the overwhelming popularity of Levitt's innovation spawned a thousand copycats and sent millions of urban dwellers rushing headlong to the new American "suburbs" to try to grab their own little box of upward mobility. Golf course construction wasn't far behind. With a golfer in the White House, "country club" construction nearly doubled in a five-year span, and the first motorized golf carts appeared, alarming traditionalists who suddenly feared the old Scottish game would be overrun by rich fat men on wheels.

Bellwethers were everywhere in 1953. Aging, depressed Ernest Hemingway won the Pulitzer Prize for his depiction of the old man and the sea. Joseph Stalin died, and *Playboy* magazine was born. Chuck Yeager set a new airspeed record of 1,600 mph, and the first commercial jet airliner crashed. Jonas Salk produced a miracle vaccine for finally beating poliomyelitis, and the use of "vending" machines exploded. The pope gave his blessing to "psychoanalysis" as an effective tool for mental therapy. "Cinemascope" appeared, handsome young Jack Kennedy married *Society* photographer-ingenue Jacqueline Bouvier at her family's Newport estate, the Rosenbergs went to the chair, and shy Elizabeth was crowned queen of England.

On the plus side of this crowded news ledger, the Yankees won an unprecedented fifth World Series in a row. On the downside, the Russkies got the H-bomb too.

The biggest impact on emerging American values, however, came with the swipe of Ike's ink pen just weeks after Ben and Herb had their friendly chat on the patio at Tamarisk. Among his first actions as president, Ike signed a bill lifting Truman's freeze on the expansion of television stations, producing a blizzard of applications from prospective new station owners.

Within days, the Federal Communications Commission approved the sale of the first color TV sets to consumers, and ownership of television sets in general zoomed from 10 to 20 million in less than nine months, marking a sea change in the way the nation saw the world—and itself. Weeks after Ike installed the first putting green at the White House, Lew Worsham holed out his final-hole wedge shot for an eagle at George May's World Championship of Golf, the first golf tournament ever telecast coast to coast, to reveal a brave new world of commercial possibilities.

As Worsham was preparing to make his approach to the final green of May's extravaganza, trailing former PGA champion Chandler Harper by a stroke, Harper was already accepting congratulations from tournament officials and newly hired TV commentator Jimmy Demaret.

Worsham's shot was fat but thumped the front portion of the green and rolled directly into the cup for an eagle 2 and a one-shot victory. The crowd went nuts. "The son of a bitch *holed* it!" Demaret bellowed, without thinking, to the largest audience in history to witness a single golf shot.

Electrifying as that moment was, Worsham's shot was dwarfed by the enormity of the other great story in golf that season. In a year memorable for its stunning headlines, Ben Hogan made 1953 the most unforgettable year anyone ever had in golf, and perhaps in any sport.

IT BEGAN rather quietly.

Three weeks before the Masters of 1953, Ben tied for second at the Seminole pro-am and followed that up by finishing in eighth place at the Palmetto pro-am in Aiken, South Carolina. Whatever Herb Wind had seen at Tamarisk scarcely revealed itself in a pair of mediocre finishes at largely meaningless unofficial events.

Politely written off by the press and even many of his fans, the Hawk's usual low-key arrival in Augusta occasioned no great anticipation of another green jacket—though it did lead to a confrontation that had been building for months, if not years, one Hogan himself precipitated by switching to the Titleist golf ball.

During one of the tournament's early warm-up sessions, MacGregor Tour representative Toney Penna (who signed Hogan to his first MacGregor playing contract for $250 in 1937) approached Hogan on the practice tee—committing the ultimate faux pas—and wasted little time getting to the point.

"Ben," Penna said, "old man Cowen has sent out a directive saying all MacGregor players must use the Tourney ball. He wants to know if you plan to use it here."

"Hell, no," Hogan told him. "It's the worst ball ever made."

A few yards away, young Mike Souchak had to smile. The former Duke football star was one of several younger players, including Tommy Bolt, Cajun

Jay Hebert, and Jackie Burke Jr., Ben had taken a shine to. Souchak was also a MacGregor client who shared Ben's low opinion of MacGregor's new golf ball.

"MacGregor's custom club fitting shop was the best in the business," Souchak elaborates, "but probably half the new balls they were sending out to tournaments then were awful, really bad, an embarrassment. I know this for a fact because like lots of guys, including Ben, I carried an O-ring to check them with. The ones that weren't defective didn't stay that way long. One or two holes and they were worthless."

Hogan's feud with Cowen and MacGregor went much deeper than golf balls, though. To begin with, the Commercial model irons MacGregor sold under Ben's name weren't the company's top-of-the-line model. That distinction belonged to MacGregor's Tommy Armour Silver Scot model—the clubs Hogan himself used—and Ben flatly dismissed his own model as "department store junk," refusing to promote them in any way.

"In that case," Penna told him, "Henry says you're fired."

Hogan, according to witnesses, didn't bother looking up.

"Good."

As MacGregor sources tell it, however, the divorce officially took another six or seven weeks to happen.

Whatever the truth of the timing, Hogan's mind was clearly made up to break away from MacGregor and start his own equipment company by the time of his appearance at Augusta in the spring of 1953, where he was unapologetically using the new Acushnet Titleist red ball.

Whether it was the sudden liberation from MacGregor or the winter of steady practice on the beautiful turf out west at Tamarisk that lifted his spirits, or simply the fun and games beforehand at Seminole with George Coleman and Claude Harmon, many of Augusta's attending scribes quickly detected a new spring in Hogan's step—and a familiar determined glint in his eye.

The evening before play commenced, Ben and Valerie drove across the Savannah River to have an early dinner with Augusta member Bobby Goodyear and wife, Patty, at their elegant home in Aiken. Like Wind, Goodyear was struck by the relaxed and upbeat quality of Ben's mood. It was nothing like the remote little warrior he'd been once again reading about in the papers whose charm and game both had seemed to evaporate in 1952.

"Ben was wonderfully expansive that evening, talking up a storm. Couldn't have been more pleasant," Goodyear recalls with a chuckle. "But I learned firsthand how finicky he could still be about things. When I asked him if he wanted a martini, he replied, 'Yes. That would be nice.' But then he added, 'Say, would you mind if I made it myself?' So *he* made the martinis. Then came time to grill the steaks. I asked Ben how he preferred his fillet grilled. 'Medium rare,' he replied. Then damned if he didn't add, 'Look, would you mind terribly if I cooked the steaks?' So he did. Did a hell of a job too. That was Ben. Perfect gentleman but in control all the way, as usual."

Hogan began his tournament with a first-round 70, missing two short putts for par over the final two holes. That left him two strokes behind leader Chick Harbert and one behind Porky Oliver and Al Besselink, and one ahead of reigning champ Snead, who sank a monstrous putt for birdie 3 on the final hole for a round of 70 but erroneously signed his card for par and was forced to keep that score.

Hogan's usual Masters pattern was to assert himself in round two, which he did that Friday morning, tacking a brilliant 69 on the board for a halfway lead of 139, requiring just thirty-two putts to get around the golf course. Afterward, buoyed by his putter's unexpected revival, Hogan even agreed to pose beneath one of Augusta's gracefully arching hardwoods pointing to the number 139 spelled out in range balls.

Heavy rains soaked the course on the mornings of the third and fourth rounds, softening up the fairways and giving Augusta's greens just the kind of tackiness Hogan found ideal for precision shotmaking. But by the time he stepped to the 1st tee both afternoons, the Georgia sun was shining in glorious profusion and the air of the old horticultural nursery was perfectly still, presenting ideal scoring conditions. If it's true that great players make their own luck, even nature seemed to be rooting for Ben Hogan.

The Hawk's personal gallery swelled to over 10,000 people, and during round three both Hogan and playing partner Porky Oliver treated them to an exhibition of shotmaking. "Putts dropped everywhere," remembers an Augusta member who followed the pair around the course that afternoon. "When Ben wasn't making one, Porky was. It was like watching golf's version of a heavyweight boxing title. Little man versus big man."

On 13, Ben hammered his finest drive of the tournament—the best drive of his *life*, he told the Associated Press afterward—a curving rope that flew 270 yards and drew magnificently around the dogleg of the famous par-5 hole. At that point, Hogan abandoned the conservative play for which he was famous and uncharacteristically went for the green with a four-iron, successfully carrying Rae's Creek.

Pork Chops also got home in two, then rolled a twenty-footer into the cup for an eagle 3. The best Ben could manage was a three-putt for par, but he answered on the very next hole, curling a ten-footer into the cup for birdie. Then, at 15, he nearly replicated Sarazen's double-eagle four-wood shot of 1935, just missing the hole on the fly and two-putting for another birdie.

By the end of their two-man exhibition match, Oliver had assembled nines of 34-33 for 67, but Ben did him one better, going 32-34–66, his lowest round ever at the Masters. As someone noted, their best ball tally was a blistering 12 under par for the par-72 course, and at one point during their remarkable circuit several players heard what Hogan and Oliver were up to out in Amen Corner and hustled out to watch for themselves. "We can at least breathe the same air they are breathing," one of them supposedly observed, a bit of Masters lore that may or may not be true.

Ben's 205 total, at any rate, demolished Byron's old fifty-four-hole tournament record by two strokes and set the stage for a Masters finale a majority of the tournament's patrons had hoped would belong to the suddenly resurgent Hogan. His ball-striking had never appeared more commanding and, for the moment at least, was more than enough to compensate for a putter that caused its share of problems. If Ben hadn't three-putted twice and missed a trio of short birdie putts coming home that warm and sunny Saturday afternoon, someone calculated, he could easily have scored an unearthly 61.

As it was, going into the final round having levered open a four-stroke advantage over Oliver, the only real drama hinged on how many strokes Hogan could shave off Ralph Guldahl's seventy-two-hole Masters record of 279 set in 1937 and matched by Hogan friend Claude Harmon in 1948.

As Masters tradition dictated, the final-round leader was paired with a semiretired gentleman rancher from Roanoke, Texas, former Masters champion Byron Nelson, who later told reporters that he knew as he and Ben left the 1st green of their final round that the 1953 Masters belonged to his old friend and adversary from Glen Garden.

Moments before, Byron had watched Hogan pitch close to the pin, study the four-and-a-half-foot putt for a lengthy moment, assume his putting stance, and then back off, take his stance a second time, and then back away again. "You know how that goes," Lord Byron recounted the moment to reporters with a lazy smile. "Finally, in a kind of desperation, he just lunged at the ball. And it cut right in—perfectly." As he said this, Nelson used his hand to show how Ben's golf ball banged into the cup.

Anyone who'd listened to Hogan fret about his ailing putter stroke earlier in the tournament knew exactly what Nelson was getting at: even Ben's *worst* putts were somehow finding the hole that week in Augusta. Nobody was more aware of this good fortune (and rapidly advancing problem) than Hogan himself, of course. As he and Byron left that 1st green together, Hogan paused and observed with dry embarrassment, "Look at that, Byron. Now how can I *miss?*"

A bogey at hole 6 and a three-putt at 8 sent Hogan to the back nine with level par-36 on the card. Just ahead of him, Porky Oliver was having a decent Sunday as well, eagling the par-5 13th and fashioning a back-nine 35 that would give him two under 70 for the day and a brilliant, record-tying seventy-two-hole total of 279.

On his heels, though, Ben rolled birdie putts home on 13 and 15, then brought the huge gallery wedged around the 18th green leaping to its feet by rolling his final putt of the tournament into the cup for a birdie 3, a round of 69, and a new tournament record of 14 under par that blew away the old mark by five strokes.

In the crowded locker room, Hogan sipped a cold beer and admitted he'd never struck the ball better over seventy-two holes of competition. "How'd the legs hold up, Ben?" someone asked. "No worse than usual," he deadpanned, but then smiled graciously. "They never hurt as much when you're playing that well." Yards away, Gene Sarazen shook his graying aristocratic head and told an Associated Press reporter that Hogan's Masters assault amounted to the four greatest scoring rounds *anyone* had ever put together in golf.

Outside under the oaks, Cliff Roberts trumped Sarazen's remarks by calling Hogan's record 274 "the best seventy-two-hole stretch of golf ever played by anyone anywhere" and dismissed the winner's modest assertion that his record would "probably be broken next year," owing to recent improvements in club technology and "some of the better balls coming out now."

"It will be years, if not decades, before that happens," Roberts assured Herb Wind and others. "Ben's got the record for a while, I believe."

"There was very much a feeling that Ben was back," says Wind, recalling the popular fever unleashed by Hogan's historic, and largely unanticipated, Masters triumph. "And naturally everyone wanted to know where he was going to appear next."

A new seventy-two-hole Tour event was planned for Las Vegas, the Tournament of Champions, in two weeks. Would he go there?

"No," Hogan answered firmly when asked about his immediate plans. "I'm committed to go down to Mexico, fellas, and play the Pan American."

Former National Open champ Olin Dutra's swank new Club de Mexico in Mexico City was the host site for the second Pan American Open. Both Jimmy Demaret and Lloyd Mangrum, the tournament's defending champion, had positively raved about the conditions of Dutra's club, Mangrum calling it the "best golf course I've ever played."

A greatly hoped-for stretch battle between Lloyd, Jimmy, Sam, and Ben had failed to materialize at the Masters, so now the scribes would have to go south of the border if they wanted to witness a duel in the sun between the game's leading postwar money winners.

"How about the British Open?" someone asked. "Will you go over the pond?"

Hogan smiled and thought for only a moment.

"I have no plans to go to England," he replied, either forgetting that the tournament was to be played in Scotland that July or choosing to appear indifferent to it. He also neglected to mention that both Sarazen and Bobby Jones had recently urged him to seriously consider going after the Claret Jug, golf's oldest prize. No champion's résumé was complete, nor his greatness fully confirmed, both Bobby and Gene argued, until the game's oldest open golf tournament had been claimed.

Several factors weighed heavily against going abroad in Ben's mind, though. To begin with, there was no way he was going to repeat the miserable transatlantic boat trip that had made him so ghastly ill in 1949, and the prospect of flying so far over the open water made him positively queasy to think about.

Then there was the tournament's mandatory qualifying rounds to consider. Nobody was exempt, including three-time U.S. Open winners. Furthermore, British Open courses, he was repeatedly told by Snead and other veterans who'd made the difficult pilgrimage, didn't fit the American style of play Hogan had come to define in many minds—precision shotmaking that minimized the element of chance. Links land ground was uneven and hard, the bounces it produced far too quirky and unpredictable for the kind of game Hogan preferred to play.

Not to put too fine a point on the issue, but British Open courses were famous for blind holes, punishing bunkers, and haylike rough in midsummer, a wholly different animal than golf in the States. The wind blew hard and constantly off the sea, and the cool wet weather of the British Isles could drain a man of both strength and purpose in no time flat.

Hogan knew this much from his own journey to Ganton four years before.

He also knew that the food "over there" was lousy, the hotels drafty, and the prize money being offered by the sponsoring Royal & Ancient Golf Club of St. Andrews mere peanuts compared to what he could make doing a single exhibition match or public appearance back in warm and sunny Texas.

Before leaving his Augusta press conference, Ben made it perfectly clear to several of the prominent Tour writers like Wind and Fraley and Bob Brumby before they set off down the tournament trail that they should not expect to see him showing up in Britain come July.

"Don't you think you owe it to the game to at least try?" he was asked.

"No," Hogan answered firmly.

But during the train ride home to Fort Worth, obviously taking Jones's and Sarazen's advice to heart, he revealed to Valerie that if he won the National Open at Oakmont in June, he might have no option but to venture over to Carnoustie, thinking this revelation would probably come as both an unhappy surprise and unpleasant news to his wife. But she surprised him by coming back at her husband, "Ben, I should think you'd *want* to play in the British Open if you didn't win the U.S. Open." She'd obviously been talking to Squire Sarazen too.

Not since Willie Park in 1860 had a golfer won the British Open on his first attempt. But Valerie understood at least as well as Ben did that it was getting late in the game for making the kind of enduring mark Ben wanted to make before officially saying good-bye. From the beginning, she had been his only cheerleader and advice counselor; now, thanks to the accident and other factors, she was increasingly cast into the role of Hogan flame-keeper, a one-woman Royal & Ancient when it came to helping preserve her husband's costly odyssey through the game.

Over the next week and a half, with something at least as pressing as Carnoustie hanging fire in his brain, Ben scouted around Cowtown for a small manufacturing warehouse on the city's industrial south side that would be suitable for a clubmaking operation and, over lunch at Rivercrest, politely turned down local oil magnate W. A. "Monty" Moncrief's generous offer to help finance the golf equipment company most of Ben's closest friends now understood he was hell-bent on starting up as soon as he could find a building and hire and train the right workers. Ben thanked Moncrief for his offer and revealed that he'd already made the decision to go with Dallas real estate mogul Pollard Simons as a main partner in the Hogan equipment enterprise.

Over the course of several winter breaks in Palm Springs, Ben and Pollard had grown unusually close; Simons possessed the genteel manners and avuncular charm of a George Coleman or Marvin Leonard and had a positively gilded touch when it came to putting together business deals. As one of Pollard's friends remembered, "He always had the best of everything—the prettiest wife, the finest house, and the best kinds of friends. He was also a thoroughly decent and careful sort of man who loved golf and absolutely worshiped Ben."

During the interval before he left Fort Worth and flew south to the Pan American Open, Ben's telephone began ringing. Having heard through the grapevine that Ben was at least contemplating a trip to Carnoustie, the callers, including Hogan's own hero Walter Hagen, Bobby Cruickshank, and Tommy Armour, all expressed their belief that, win or lose at Oakmont, the Hawk should venture abroad. The Haig told Hogan flatly that he owed it to both his fans and "the good of the game" to try for the British title, while Cruickshank, a pleasant Scottish terrier of a man who won twenty Tour events and narrowly lost the U.S. Open in a play-off to Harvard-bound Bobby Jones at Inwood in 1923, informed Ben that the weather in that part of Scotland (where he happened to hail from) could be surprisingly warm and even rain-free in July.

As if this Greek chorus of famous petitioners weren't enough, Gene Sarazen followed up with a phone call of his own, urging Ben to get his hands on the smaller British ball and experiment with it before he made a decision one way or the other. When Hogan admitted that he was now inclined to think favorably about a trip to Carnoustie, Sarazen congratulated him and advised him to get to Scotland early enough to find a local caddie who knew what the hell he was doing and get accustomed to the firmer turf and the kind of "roll-up" shots a Yank would need to successfully compete on a links-style golf course.

Ironically, only Ben's friend and former Tour mentor Henry Picard phoned to talk about the other sizable obstacle facing Hogan even before he reached a final decision on Carnoustie—mighty Oakmont. "The only way to handle those greens," Henry advised, "is to play for the collars in front. Otherwise, you'll have no chance."

"I never felt such intense pressure from people everywhere to go over there and compete," Ben later admitted to reporter Bob Brumby, suggesting that even the public at large played a role in ultimately firming up his resolve to go to Carnoustie, a decision he didn't "officially" make until hours before the start of the U.S. Open in Pittsburgh.

Before shoving off for Mexico, Hogan scrounged up smaller British balls (which at 1.68 ounces weighed the same as American balls but were slightly smaller) and knocked them around Colonial, just to see how they reacted in the frisky Lone Star wind. He liked what he saw and resolved that if he could take enough comforts from home, including long underwear for any cold wet weather that might descend, the trip might not be so arduous after all.

"Valerie probably played the key role in finally making up his mind," remembers a family friend. "Every time Ben came home from practice or someplace, she'd been out shopping and brought something else she thought he would need over there, in hopes of persuading him to go to Scotland after all—canned foods you couldn't get in Britain, long-sleeved shirts and cotton sweaters, that sort of thing, even hand warmers from some hunting store in town. She was determined to make him go. I guess the stuff was piling up, and he told her to stop buying things or they would need a boat to carry it all over to Scotland."

"Does that mean you're going?" she supposedly said.

"That means I'm *thinking* about it," he replied.

BEN'S STRATEGIC PLANNING for making golf equipment and attacking Oakmont had scarcely begun to coalesce when another kind of storm erupted, with Hogan unexpectedly at its center. Twelve days before he was scheduled to depart for Olin Dutra's shindig in Mexico City, a news report, quoting unnamed sources inside the PGA, claimed Hogan had snubbed the new Tournament of Champions in Las Vegas in favor of going to Mexico simply because the Vegas tournament refused his "request" for an eye-opening $5,000 appearance guarantee. According to one major wire service report, quoting unnamed sources inside the PGA's upper hierarchy, Hogan had made the same request of the Mexicans and received the requested compensation. Compounding Hogan's apparent decision was news that the Las Vegas tournament was planning to set aside an unspecified percentage of its projected gate receipts for the Damon Runyon Cancer Fund, a charity donation that would clearly be hurt by the absence of golf's largest draw.

To many neutral observers, Hogan suddenly came off looking like a man more interested in making money in a foreign country than supporting cancer victims or even his own Tour back home.

Hogan's stubborn silence on the matter didn't help his cause one bit. As he often did whenever reports critical of his actions appeared in print, rather than confront the issue and *explain* his thinking, Hogan withdrew into a cocoon of silence and simply chose to ignore his gathering critics.

To make matters worse, within days the same wire services reported that Cary Middlecoff, Jimmy Demaret, Jack Burke Jr., and even defending champ Lloyd Mangrum had suddenly officially withdrawn from the Mexican tournament to protest Ben's demand for extra compensation.

In a rapidly widening brouhaha that played out over several days at the top of the nation's sports pages, the PGA stridently denied that any of its officials had criticized Hogan for choosing Mexico (a tournament outside the purview of the PGA) over Las Vegas, and Pan American officials countered with the argument that Hogan hadn't been paid anything like the five grand mentioned—only $750 plus expenses, according to the *New York Times*. A Mexican official fired back that Middlecoff and Burke had been "caught up in internal politics against one of the world's greatest players," in effect forced by the Tour to abandon the nonsanctioned Pan American tournament. Defending champion Mangrum, however, piqued because he hadn't been offered a fee that matched Hogan's, used the moment to address old wounds and make new ones. "Hogan never does anything for anyone else," he remarked bitterly. "Why should we go down there to help *his* exhibition?"

A day later, Lloyd attempted to soften his broadside by claiming his main gripe was with the Pan American sponsors, not Hogan personally. "Nothing has caused Ben and I to be any unfriendlier than we ever were," he explained a bit disingenuously, hoping to dampen reports of a developing blood feud between himself and Ben—which, in fact, there had been at least since Merion and probably a decade or more preceding that. "I've always been friendly with Ben until the past two years or so, but we haven't had much to do with each other. But then, Hogan doesn't have much to do with anyone."

That same day, in the *Houston Press*, Jimmy Demaret weighed in to defend his stubbornly silent four-ball mate. "Ben has only one thing to sell, and only one time in his life to sell it—when he's on top," Demaret told reporter Bob Rule, seeming to imply that Hogan had in fact been given five grand for appearing in Mexico and was bloody well entitled to every peso. Demaret also made it clear he was not part of any organized "boycott" and took pains to explain that Burke and Middlecoff weren't playing in Mexico primarily because of Burke's conflicting schedule and Cary's flaring allergies. The whole thing, he said with one of his happy-go-lucky laughs, was being "blown way the hell out of proportion." It was hurting Hogan, he added, and it was hurting the credibility of professional *golf.*

Almost ten days after the imbroglio erupted, Hogan finally sat down with the *Star-Telegram*'s Gene Gregston and told his side of the story. Denying he'd ever strong-armed the Las Vegas sponsors for appearance money, he added somewhat testily, "The whole thing was so idiotic, it wasn't even funny. I hated to have it come up because it hurt the feelings of the Mexican people, and Mangrum, and it wasn't good for golf in general. If they had asked me earlier [at Las Vegas], I'd have been delighted to play there, especially as it was in aid of the Damon Runyon Cancer Fund. Apart from that, I'm a free man living in a free country. I don't like being told where I have to play or can't play. If I have to take orders as to where I can or can't play, I suppose I might as well go to Russia."

Instead, the irritated Hawk went to Mexico City, fired 286 to win the tournament, and collected 30,000 pesos for his trouble, beating defending champion Mangrum and the rest of a fairly respectable field by a margin of three strokes. Revenge is a dish best served cold, he might have said (quoting Churchill)—were the Hawk willing to say anything more on the subject.

COLUMNIST RED SMITH summarized the Pan American debate as "querulous yapping from other pros resentful of their well-earned inferiority to Hogan." But fallout from the "Mexican affair" only fueled long-simmering resentments of Ben's chilly dominance of the game and even followed him to Sam Snead's Greenbrier Open.

When a reporter asked host Snead for his take on Ben's Pan American Open problems, the Slammer dryly observed, "I don't reckon it'll be much of a problem for him as long as he keeps on winning. With luck, however, it won't be here."

In fact, Sam and Ben were the only players to score four consecutive rounds in the 60s at that genial Greenbrier gathering, despite the fact that both men were beginning to have their acute difficulties with the flagstick.

At the final hole of the tournament, for example, Hogan rolled an eighteen-foot birdie putt (that would have tied the lead) two feet past the hole, then— visibly agonizing over the putt, battling his inability to draw back the putter—lurched and lipped out the short putt. Hogan finished with rounds of 67-68-68-69 to wind up third behind Jack Burke Jr. and Snead.

That same week, hoping to smooth ruffled feathers and put the damaging Mexican affair to rest once and for all, the PGA released an editorial from its forthcoming monthly magazine defending Hogan's honor and recent controversial decision to play south of the border, expansively noting that Hogan had also been widely (and unfairly, as it turned out) criticized for accepting his National Golf Day appearance fee when, in fact, every penny of that money went directly to his new church, a fact he apparently felt no need to explain to anybody.

Healthy competition was fine, but with the Colonial NIT next up, the last thing the field bosses of the PGA wanted was visible hostility between its leading stars or anybody else involved with the ridiculous Pan American dustup. Besides, golf was supposed to be a gentleman's game, and Hogan's unexpected resurgence to the top of the standings was pumping up galleries like never before.

Hogan had won three of the previous six Colonial tournaments, and to everyone's relief, the only mention of events south of the border that week came from a promising "young" professional—no one cared to name him— who admitted he'd become so smitten with "Hoganitis" down in Mexico that he'd actually gone around the golf course during practice rounds aiming his shots for Hogan's old divots and asking spectators to show him exactly where Hogan had stood so he could try to replicate his shots.

The day after Native Dancer won the Preakness, Ben battled a sharp west Texas wind and ninety-plus temperatures to fire a final round 67 and collect his fourth Colonial trophy. "Do I get to keep it this time?" he shot at tournament chairman Marvin Leonard, placing his hand on the ornate silver trophy, a replica of which would soon be made and presented permanently to Ben.

"No," Leonard replied with a paternal smile. "But you already *own* it."

Cary Middlecoff, who tied for runner-up honors with Doug Ford, accepted his $2,500 second-place check and wryly observed, "I feel honored to play in the Hogan Benefit here once again." He jerked a thumb at Hogan and added, "Maybe, one of these days, Ben will be too old to play in this tournament and the rest of us will have a chance."

The victory, his third in four starts, placed Ben atop the money race for 1953. More important to Hogan, it was his fourth Colonial title and the first time in fifty-four separate tournament championships that he'd won the same event four times. For a man who'd started the year widely rumored to be already out to pasture, Hogan was suddenly playing the best golf of his career.

In a matter of days—three weeks to be exact, though he didn't dare jinx his hopes by coming out and publicly saying so—Ben hoped to accomplish a similar feat at the United States Open Championship up in Pittsburgh, tying an elite record shared only by Bobby Jones and Willie Anderson.

Once again, though, he was dogged about Carnoustie. Someone showed Ben a recent copy of Britain's important *Golf Monthly*. The May issue contained an eloquent plea for his participation abroad. A simple headline neatly summarized a growing popular sentiment on both sides of the pond: "Hogan, the Master—Come Over."

Carnoustie, did he come and triumph, would impress the seal on Hogan's fame. In phantasy we see Hogan, the enigma, silent, austere, resolute, battling out the windswept links of the Angus seaboard, one of the massive tests of the game in the whole world of golf. Do not leave it too late, Ben, to take your place amongst the immortals of golf and the supreme honour of the game. Scottish golfers, and especially Carnoustie, whose sons did so much for golf in your homeland, will take you to their hearts.

"Do you suppose it's as tough as they say it is?" Ben asked an English golf writer who'd come across to cover his Colonial quest and keep an ear to the ground for any hints of the Hawk going to the fields of Angus.

"Probably none harder. All wind and few trees as far as you can see."

Ben smiled a little and nodded. The austerity of this description oddly appealed to him. Ironically for a man who managed tree-girdled Colonial so masterfully, Hogan disliked any kinds of trees on golf courses. He felt they were an unfair obstacle.

"You boys can go," he said with a mirthless laugh, "and tell me all about it later."

ON THE TUESDAY afternoon following his Colonial win, Ben and Valerie left home for Pittsburgh, Pennsylvania, making a brief detour through Cincinnati so Ben could officially part ways with Henry Cowen and MacGregor Sporting Goods. Though only a handful of Hogan intimates knew it, Ben and Pollard Simons had already signed the lease on a 15,000-square-foot building on West Pafford Street in south Fort Worth, and Ben had already begun talking with several experienced clubmakers from area golf clubs and scouting around for clubmaking machinery for his new operation.

That same day out in Hollywood, Twentieth Century Fox released *Follow the Sun* as a rerun feature, only now it was retitled *The Ben Hogan Story*. Glenn Ford confidently told *Variety* he believed the movie would do even bigger box office in its second run of theaters. It did.

For his part, Cowen was still quietly fuming about Ben's open defiance of his Augusta papal edict but had evidently backed off Toney Penna's tempestuous "firing" of Hogan on the practice tee, requesting that he simply be permitted the courtesy of making the case for the new MacGregor Tourney ball in person before "any rash decisions" were reached.

For three days, the story goes, Hogan was shown a battery of tests that had been done on the new MacGregor golf ball, all showing it to be superior in quality and performance, based on the use of a state-of-the-art mechanical driving robot. When Cowen finally asked what Hogan thought of all the evidence he'd been shown, Ben supposedly observed, "If it's so good, I recommend you enter that fucking machine in the U.S. Open," and walked out.

Who knows exactly what transpired. There is no formal record of the conversation, and people often recall the same event very differently. Hogan clearly had his mind made up before sitting down with Cowen, though, and the harshness of the parting certainly sounds like Hogan at his hard-edged best.

Ben pushed on to an exhibition match in Erie with young friend Jay Hebert and U.S. Amateur champion Sam Urzetta. Valerie took a train to New York, where she checked into the St. Regis, checked out Manhattan's smartest shops for a few days, then reunited with her husband and his broker Paul Shields at the "21" Club for dinner. Shields was one of Ben's Seminole inner circle and a frequent playing partner.

"Ben," Shields put it to him, according to Valerie, "have you given any thought to playing in the British Open at Carnoustie?" The question wasn't going to go away until Ben officially settled the matter one way or the other. Rumors were rampant that he was going but stubbornly refused to say so because he didn't want to be shadowed abroad by an army of reporters—or as he grumbled to someone, "Coxey's army following me everywhere I go these days, watching everything I do."

"I haven't given it much thought," Hogan replied, adding, "I really don't want to make the trip to Scotland. I think you just want to see me go over there and get beat. But if I win at Oakmont, maybe I'll think about it."

"Paul," Valerie interrupted, "I would think that even if Ben didn't win the U.S. Open, you would want Ben to go to the British Open."

According to Valerie, Shields patted her affectionately on the shoulder. "Spoken like a true wife," he said, at which point Valerie turned her serious brown eyes on Ben and said, "I would think you would have the curiosity to *want* to go."

He stared back at her. "Well, I'll do it," he said finally. "I'll send in my entry."

The next morning before leaving town, Hogan dropped into the USGA headquarters at Golf House and cabled his entry to the Royal & Ancient Golf Club of St. Andrews, mere hours before the entry deadline expired.

By the time Ben and Valerie went to Kiamesha Lake, New York, for an exhibition match with Jimmy Demaret at his new Concord International Club, then pushed on to Pittsburgh, the news of his Open entry leaked and a small army of reporters was waiting for the couple upon arrival at their hotel in downtown Pittsburgh. "From what I've heard, I think I'll probably need to get some comfortable long underwear for over there," Hogan said to a cluster of reporters, trying to downplay the excitement that his Carnoustie announcement had unleashed. "Does anyone make such a thing?"

Back on Wall Street, Paul Shields got a phone call from an official in John Foster Dulles's Defense Department who wondered if Ben had any interest in flying on to France after the British Open and playing an exhibition match at a U.S. Air Force base outside of Paris. The suggestion was made that Ike himself would be greatly pleased by this courtesy and the Defense Department would be willing to pay Hogan his usual exhibition fee and pick up all other travel and hotel expenses as well. Out of simple patriotic duty, not to mention his wife's fervent desire to see France, Hogan said yes.

Within days, Hogan's reluctant Scottish sojourn had taken on an exotic new appeal, at least in Valerie Hogan's mind.

"We've decided to take our first trip to Paris, our first real vacation together in years," she trilled to a wire service reporter who wondered how she felt about making her first trip to Europe. "We're both terribly excited about that prospect."

CONSTRUCTED BACK in 1905 by a steel magnate named Henry Fownes, who remarkably didn't take up golf until age forty, Oakmont Country Club included an assortment of terrors: greens that were created on just six inches of topsoil over a firm foundation of Allegheny River clay, rendering them unfathomably hard and fast; towering hardwood groves that made missing the twisting narrow fairways extremely penal; and bunkering that nearly every great player had cursed and condemned as being patently unfair.

At one point early in its life, Oakmont was home to more than 350 sand "pits" or roughly twenty bunkers per hole. Over the next half-century, as the howl of members' protests persisted, Fownes agreed to fill in more than half of them, but he steadfastly refused to give up the course's most distinguishing feature—its infamous furrowed bunkers. During Fownes's lifetime, in place of bunkers that were conventionally raked flat and smooth, Oakmont's sands were deep-ribbed affairs created by a special broad-toothed rake popularly called the "Devil's Backscratcher," a grooming instrument that produced deep and distinct furrows about the width of a golf ball in the sand, running perpendicular to the line of play. The furrows were easy to get into and brutal to get out of and gave Oakmont's bunkering the look of a plowed potato field— or a waiting burying ground.

One of the most feared bunker complexes on the course was aptly called the "Church Pews," a series of grassy ridges rising in a vast sandy wasteland next to the 3rd and 4th fairways, a forbidding landmark that players sometimes took five or six shots to extricate themselves from.

A player who survived Oakmont's infamous furrowed bunkers scarcely got any relief on the putting surfaces, which were so firm and fast that Sam Snead once joked that his marking dime slid off them. To compound matters, several greens tilted frighteningly away from the desired approach lines, making them all but impossible to hit in regulation under certain tournament conditions. During the 1935 National Open, Hogan's friend Grantland Rice watched a number of the world's finest players require *five* putts to finish their business on several closing holes, demolishing their hopes in the process.

That particular Open was unforgettably won by an appealing 200-to-1 long shot who'd never come close to winning anything of consequence but had a lot of local knowledge to rely upon. Pittsburgh golfer and future Oakmont member Sam Parks Jr. was the only man in the field who got around the saw-toothed golf course in less than 300 strokes that week (he shot 299 or 11 over par for seventy-two holes), largely by carefully steering his ball away from Oakmont's fierce and unforgiving bunkers and handling the greens with a deft and knowing putting stroke. Parks became a kind of local hero because he never won any other tournament and eventually abandoned professional golf for a steadier paying job as a salesman for U.S. Steel, finishing his days as a prominent member of the very golf club where he became a marvelous one-time wonder at the National Open.

In sum, Oakmont's reasonably short but treacherous 6,916-yard layout had never been humbled in competitive medal play of any kind. The tournament record was a rather intimidating 294, six over par, set by Willie MacFarlane at the Pennsylvania Open in 1934.

In short, it was Ben Hogan's kind of golf course. That much hadn't changed in American life.

BEN AND VALERIE arrived on June 2 from Kiamesha Lake, where, according to Jimmy Demaret, *he* was the one who finally persuaded Ben to submit his entry to the British Open. "I'm about the only guy in golf Ben will listen to," Jimmy told readers several weeks later in a broadly syndicated snippet from his forthcoming memoir of his early years on tour with Ben. "I talked Hogan into going to Scotland for the British Open when he was here for an exhibition."

Regardless of who prevailed on Ben to make the big decision, the only thing on Hogan's mind by the time he reached Pittsburgh was how to attack an Oakmont golf course that most people felt was utterly impregnable. Furthermore, he had less than a week to formulate a strategic plan before having to submit to the added ordeal of a thirty-six-hole qualifier, a new policy being tested that year by the sponsoring USGA, modeled after the British Open's required thirty-six-hole qualifying procedure, a move some felt made the Open fairer to all comers but less susceptible to being dominated by a one-shot wonder like Sam Park Jr.

While the USGA and club elders closeted themselves to intensely debate whether Oakmont's bunkers would be furrowed, as they were in '35, Lloyd Mangrum held court outside the locker room to air his complaints about Oakmont's punishing bunkers. "The traps are a disgrace," he gruffly complained to Oscar Fraley of UPI. "There is no premium here on real skill. Winning will be a question of sheer luck."

Minutes later, Hogan arrived by taxicab from his downtown hotel and paused and chatted pleasantly with spectators as he walked to the club pro shop with his golf shoes in hand to say a friendly hello to Oakmont's head pro, Lew Worsham, he of the wondrous "golf shot seen all over America" at Tam O'Shanter that same summer.

In stark contrast to Mangrum, Hogan appeared to be the soul of cordiality as he stood for several minutes giving his thoughts to local reporters and even collared a couple of the better-known scribes he'd tangled with over the years and invited them to lunch on the clubhouse porch, à la Herb Wind at Tamarisk. Most were genuinely disarmed by Hogan's sudden "niceness" and accessibility, though a few who'd felt the sting of Hogan's wrath suspected his sudden friendliness had more to do with his desire to secure his place in history than with forging better relations.

In recent years it had become a kind of parlor game among golf writers and even some top players to debate Ben's proper rank vis-à-vis Jones and Hagen. Up till now, few had ranked him ahead of Saint Bobby and Devil-May-Care Walter, but almost everyone agreed that the next two tournaments Ben was committed to play—believed to be the two toughest sites employed by Britain and America in defense of their national golf honors—would go a long way in determining Hogan's rightful place in the golf firmament.

"Who do I think has the best chance?" Ben replied when, as usual, someone asked him to make one of his predictions about the Oakmont ordeal ahead. "Well, maybe Sam Parks again. Who knows? I'm not kidding. It'll be somebody who can play these tricky greens. It could be Parks or any outsider."

Good old Sam Parks was now a genially spreading steel executive and far greater than a 200-to-1 long shot to repeat his Oakmont heroics, but he too was one of 300 qualifiers set to make a run for the title. The experimental thirty-six-hole qualifier was set for Oakmont and nearby Pittsburgh Field Club's slightly less daunting golf course. (Players were required to play a round on both courses.) Prior to his first practice round, Ben had never played the Field Club, and Oakmont only once, an exhibition in 1937, and he professed to have "no clear memory of the golf course" but only Oakmont's fearsome reputation and the advice of other players to go on.

In addition to a host of rising Tour stars like Burke, Bolt, Middlecoff, and Boros, this particular National Open field included an intriguing mix of grizzled elders out to try to recapture a bit of their former glory and a number of bright new faces hoping to make a splash. Gene Sarazen, Denny Shute, Paul Runyan, and Vic Ghezzi were among those hoping to qualify, as were Hogan's usual rivals: Snead, Mangrum, and Demaret. An assortment of lavishly talented newcomers included future stars like Bob Rosburg, Dave Marr, Art Wall, and Mike Souchak, along with amateur sensation E. Harvie Ward.

Lesser known among the familiar names, and set to begin his own quixotic quest at 10:24 in the morning on the first day of qualifying at Oakmont's 1st tee, was one Royal Hogan of Fort Worth. An hour behind him on the same tee, an unknown Hogan disciple named Jack Fleck would queue up to join the Open chase too. Also unnoticed in the field, fresh from big wins at the Ohio and Cleveland Amateur Championships and attempting to qualify for his first National Open, was a handsome twenty-three-year-old coast guardsman on special leave, a cocky Pennsylvanian named Arnold Daniel Palmer. Arnie, as his Latrobe High schoolmates liked to call him, would survive the Oakmont qualifier but miss the cut in the fifty-third United States Open Championship.

ACCOMPANIED ONLY by Arthur Daly of the *New York Times* and an Oakmont caddie for his initial practice round, Ben teed up on the downhill 495-yard par-5 1st hole and sliced one drive right, hooked another left, then hammered a third ball straight into the heart of the fairway. He made second shots from each of these strategic locations, chipped all three balls to separate parts of the green, then putted each ball from a different approach to gain a better understanding of the green's contours.

As Daly watched with a mixture of awe and fascination, the Hawk methodically studied the putting surface for every dent and undulation and even dropped and putted a couple of extra balls from even more formidable spots on the green, locations where he guessed the USGA might choose to insert pins come the weekend. Departing from his usual monkish silence, however, Ben liberally revealed his thinking about every hole to Daly, who dutifully scribbled throughout their walk together, providing a rare glimpse into the mind of sporting genius.

"It was an education to listen to Ben analyze every hole," Daly recounted later. "This one sloped away from the left so he'd deliberately hook into it. That one sloped away from the right so he'd fade a slice into it. On another he'd take the risk of landing in a trap because it was still the best way of getting at a hole." For several holes requiring low-iron or fairway wood approaches, recalling Henry Picard's useful advice that the only way to neutralize Oakmont's advantage was to land approach shots on front collars, Ben struck an array of high-flying four-wood shots that dazzled the reporter with their accuracy. "He put shots exactly where he said he would simply to see how they bounced or stopped," Daly reported. "I'd never seen anything quite like it."

At Oakmont's particularly dangerous 17th, for example, a short 4-par of just 292 yards where Ben calculated the Open might be won or lost with one swing, he first strolled the entire length of the fairway to examine the grassy approaches around the green, then walked slowly back to the tee and deliberately drilled the first of three shots into the rough just shy and left of the putting surface. When a fascinated Daly asked why he'd done this, Hogan explained to the reporter that the only sensible approach to a flag that was certain to be placed directly behind the largest and deepest bunker on the right was from the left-front rough. "The rough doesn't terrify me," Hogan told Daly as they proceeded, adding, "Oakmont requires as much thinking as any course I've ever seen."

Daly, who had not counted himself as a Hogan admirer up till then, thanked Hogan for permitting him to tag along and later admitted to colleagues, and his readers, that he was amazed by Hogan's display of mental cataloging, his astute calculations of the smallest details most players would scarcely notice. As other writers had also noticed, Hogan's damaged legs appeared to hold up remarkably well under the intensity of his field research. The charm offensive was apparently working pretty nicely too.

For the next five days, Ben's routine scarcely varied. He arrived at the course about nine o'clock each morning, climbing out of a taxi from downtown Pittsburgh, signed a few autographs on his way to the locker room, put on his spikes, and went straight to Misery Hill, where he smoked a pack of Chesterfields and hit a sack of balls for every club in his bag to a shag boy for at least two hours.

After a brief rest and light lunch (Ben was now trying to shed the fourteen pounds he'd put on since the wreck), he played practice rounds with Jack Burke, Mike Souchak, George Fazio, and Tommy Bolt.

On the sidelines, meanwhile, controversy flared again. This time Ben wasn't part of it. Or maybe he was.

Several players threatened to withdraw unless the USGA and Oakmont rescinded their decision to furrow the bunkers. The malcontents were led by none other than Lloyd Mangrum, who in addition felt that Oakmont's greens were too fast and that the Pittsburgh Field Club course across the Allegheny River had been artificially "tricked up" to match Oakmont's fierceness—all of this, Lloyd inveighed, for one reason only.

"Ben Hogan is the world's greatest golfer, and the rest of us have to qualify to play *him*. It's complete nonsense."

Responding to Mangrum's tantrum, club greens chairman Frank Magee issued a joint statement with the USGA stating that the practice of furrowing bunkers would continue "in a somewhat modified form," and course superintendent Bobby Loeffler, son of the legendary greenskeeper who helped Fownes design Oakmont's wicked layout, officially noted that, owing to an outbreak of heavy thatch and fungus, the club's greens were actually not as speedy as members normally played them. To preserve the greens, Loeffler added, they would not be rolled once competition began.

Mangrum was scarcely mollified by these explanations but failed to withdraw as threatened. When someone invited Hogan to comment on another controversy with Mangrum stirring the pot, he simply gave a wintry smile, leaked cigarette smoke from his nostrils, and replied, "Don't ask me that now."

About the only person who had anything nice to say about Oakmont in the early stages before qualifying began was ever-upbeat Jimmy Demaret. "I like it," he beamed after his first-round 71. "All this arguing has lifted the pressure from the dang thing already. I never enjoyed the start of an Open so much."

In the qualifying rounds (the USGA soon dumped this experiment, to overwhelming acclaim), Hogan carded 77 at Oakmont and a 73 at the weaker Field Club, an efficient 150 total that placed him safely in the middle of the pack of 157 players who qualified. When someone at dinner downtown paused by his table and wondered how his body was holding up to Oakmont's difficult terrain, Ben admitted that he felt a twinge of soreness in his lower back just above his left kidney. Perhaps he'd pulled a muscle slightly.

"I'll get some rest and be all right tomorrow," he said.

For the official start of play on Thursday morning, a pleasant sunny day on the cliffs above the Allegheny, only one man appeared wearing a sweater. Ben chose a long-sleeved white shirt and heavy gray cashmere sweater buttoned to the top. He also debuted an elegant black cigarette holder some found utterly incongruous for a chain-smoker. His playing partners were Sam Urzetta, the former U.S. Amateur champion from Rochester, and Peter Thomson, a promising young Australian with Hogan-like accuracy in his irons.

With a record first-day gallery of 8,000 spectators turned out in full force, Hogan cautiously attacked the penal golf course from the start, nabbing birdies at the 1st, 3rd, 6th, and 7th holes. The rest were fairly routine pars. He reached the turn at 33, having not missed a fairway and only one green, the 5th, in regulation. Just ahead of him, a brash amateur from Alice, Texas, named John Garrison went out in 34, made a casual remark about Oakmont being relatively easy, and blew to 39 on the back nine. Others suffered a similar fate. Jimmy Clark, the qualifying medalist, skied to 77 while Dr. Middlecoff, who was hot as a stovetop in practice and the qualifying rounds, three-putted five greens en route to 76. Defending champ Julius Boros, the man some were already calling the "forgotten champ," was one under for thirteen holes but three-putted the final four greens for 75. Host pro Lew Worsham staggered home with 78. Runyan and Sarazen fired 79 and 82, respectively, while young coast guardsman Arnie Palmer slashed his way into and out of Oakmont's killer rough to an awful 84.

Sam Snead, the only man most seasoned observers realistically expected to challenge the resurgent Hogan for the title, despite playing with a broken bone in his right hand, also three-putted three greens but sank a couple of clutch birdies to come home all square with par. The other headlines of day one belonged to a thirty-eight-year-old Pittsburgh amateur named Frank Souchak, who got around his hometown course with a score of 70, two under par, as did veteran Walter Burkemo and the balding George Fazio from Pine Valley. Triple Masters champ Demaret putted brilliantly to 71, and so did a curiosity named Bill Ogden, a former San Jose State collegian who needed Coke-bottle-thick spectacles to even see his ball sitting on the tee.

Hogan missed only one fairway on his opening back nine, a slightly hooked drive into the deep rough on 10, but missed no greens in regulation coming home. While Urzetta and Thomson were scrambling to make 77 and 80, respectively, Hogan, playing along in a world of his own, dropped a fifth birdie putt following a stunning tee shot to thirty inches on the daunting 234-yard par-3 16th. His brilliant 67 was one stroke shy of the course record. It gave him a commanding three-stroke lead over the field.

As the tournament leader sat changing into his street shoes in the locker room, one of the reporters horseshoed around him dared to ask him how his sore back had held up. Ben smiled a little and replied that it had been somewhat stiff for the first few holes but gradually got better. It was no big deal.

Someone else wondered how he got the sore back in the first place.

"I didn't," he replied sharply, displaying his first impatience with a question that week. "I'm forty years old. I'll have a new ache tomorrow, and I'll still have this one. I'm filled with ointment, and I kept my back warm with a sweater. I think I've got a cold in it."

An instant later, though, perhaps remembering the higher purpose of both his Oakmont and Carnoustie quests, he softened, smiled again, and reminded his questioners that he'd put out an all-points bulletin earlier that week for cashmere long underwear. If they arrived in time, he joked, maybe they would help keep his back loose and warm.

A few minutes later, pro Skip Alexander sauntered in. He'd been playing in the threesome directly behind Ben, watching Hogan surgically take apart one of the most difficult golf courses in America.

"I know how to shoot 67 on this course," Alexander announced to a group of young players loitering by their lockers, eyeing the reporters around Hogan at the end of the room.

"Yeah? How's *that*?" Bolt shot back at him.

"Hit every goddamned fairway and every green about ten feet from the hole," Alexander replied, jerking his head at the small gray figure heading for the locker-room door.

"Just like Hogan."

As he said this, one of the reporters taking notes jotted in his notebook: "This is the first Open in history decided on the first nine holes."

BEFORE ROUND TWO could be played, more controversy flared.

Because of Oakmont's severity, a number of groups had taken more than five hours to complete their opening rounds, and the USGA warned that penalties would be levied for continued slow play on Friday. After completing his morning round, however, Clayton Heafner and a few others, including former PGA champion Denny Shute, angrily denounced officials for openly favoring the tournament leader. "It took Hogan four and a half hours yesterday," Heafner fumed by his locker. "I told one USGA official I was going out and clock Hogan this afternoon and see how fast *he* played. I want to see them push Hogan along the way they did us."

That afternoon, mercifully, the assorted side dramas began to give way to some wonderful shotmaking. Snead required only eleven putts on the back nine and a chip-in with a seven-iron on the 18th hole to chalk 69. "I just snuck up on the holes," Sam drawled afterward. "You've got to sneak up on these things—put blinders on the ball. If you start going for holes on this course, you'll wind up in the next county."

Another huge gallery of 10,000 had turned out that Friday to see if Sam could catch Ben, and Hogan played with even more deliberation through the long sunny afternoon, swaddled in his heavy cashmere sweater and leaving a trail of cigarette butts in his wake, pausing to watch the treetops sway or note which way his cigarette smoke drifted in the light westerly breeze. Over most of his putts, he took as much time as he ever had in a tournament, immobile and staring at the line, giving some credence to Shute's and Heafner's contention that Ben was being indulged by tournament officials.

No one but Valerie, sitting patiently alone with a book and cup of tea inside Oakmont's elegantly timbered clubhouse, knew the source of Ben's struggle to pull the trigger on putts. The optic nerve of his left eye, damaged when his face struck the Cadillac dashboard, sometimes lost focus and depth perception on objects. As Demaret once noted, chief among Hogan's playing assets was his infinite patience, his willingness to suspend time until he felt completely ready to make the shot required. Until he could properly see the line, in other words, he simply refused to play. Thus, he waited for the muscles in his damaged eye to adjust, the hole to come into clearer focus, with hands unable to draw back the putter until his brain gave the go command.

Also contributing to Hogan's slow progress around Oakmont was the indisputable fact that most of the vast crowd was following Ben and only Ben, which slowed his pace to a crawl. Up ahead, both Snead and Mangrum finished fine second rounds, and suddenly Oakmont was producing exactly the kind of high drama everyone had hoped for—a battle for the National Championship among the best players in the game. Hogan still led, but Snead and Mangrum were half a length back, three-time Masters champ Demaret reasonably close on their heels.

As the USGA's Joe Dey posed it to Pittsburgh writer Bob Drum, did golf get any better than this?

"It's about time they quit grumbling and started playing," Drum growled back.

The grumbling continued, however, on Saturday morning, when Middlecoff and others complained that the leaders had been given preferential tee times starting at nine in the morning. "It's unfair," the normally amiable dentist protested, explaining how the course was being chopped to bits by the record foot-dragging galleries. "I don't think it's accidental either." Cary's remarks set the stage for a bizarre and ironic incident later that morning at Oakmont's 10th hole. Miffed by his late start and irked by the slow pace of play (pretty funny considering that Doc was so notoriously slow that players were known to carry stools to rest on while he fidgeted over his ball—Demaret once joked he could be measured for a suit between shots), Middlecoff jerked his approach shot into the adjoining Pennsylvania Turnpike, then picked up his tee and stalked back to the clubhouse to withdraw from the tournament.

By that point, Hogan was safely lunching on fruit and salad, looking surprisingly confident and comfortable with only a slim one-stroke lead over the ever-present Snead, clearly thinking about what he had to do to beat Sam in the afternoon closer.

Snead, by contrast, was pale and edgy, admitting as he ambled off to find something to eat during the short lunch break between rounds that his putter was acting up so badly he was thinking of trading for a new one that afternoon.

Going out several holes ahead of Snead, Hogan birdied the 1st hole of his final eighteen to go two up but remained only a stroke up over Sam through the 11th, owing to Sam's matching birdies behind him. During his lunch break, Hogan had repeated his assertion to a Chicago reporter that the tournament would "hinge on the final two or three holes." After putting his tee shot into one of Oakmont's infamously furrowed fairway bunkers at 15, blasting out into a greenside bunker, and having to hole a bending twenty-footer to salvage bogey, Hogan suddenly looked weary to some onlookers, his limp more pronounced, a man running out of steam—with those three critical closing holes yet to come.

Maybe the greatest lesson he'd learned in golf since withdrawing from his first professional golf tournament in 1930 and thumbing his way home to Fort Worth in shame and self-loathing was to reach down and focus harder when the chips were stacked against him. No one in any sport did this better than Hogan, and Hogan perhaps never did it better than over the final three holes at Oakmont in 1953.

Summoning whatever reserves remained in him, Hogan lashed a fairway spoon shot onto the tiny 234-yard 16th green and safely two-putted for par. At 17, where he'd explained his reasoning for strategically aiming at the left rough earlier in the week to Arthur Daly, he hammered his #2 Titleist onto the edge of the green and two-putted for a birdie 3. He followed up this display of strategic power by rifling a tee shot calculated to be 300 yards to the heart of the 18th fairway, then carved a slightly fading five-iron approach shot to within two feet of the cup. The giant gallery ringing the green released the lustiest cheer heard all week above the Allegheny and was still applauding and whistling when the grim-faced little man limped slowly onto the green and bent to mark his ball. A few minutes later, the vast multitude fell perfectly still and watched Hogan take his position over the short putt. According to one reporter, "He stayed there for a small eternity."

When the Hawk finally putted his ball, it rolled gently into the cup for a stunning birdie-birdie finish and a round of 71. In the locker room a short while later, golf writer Charlie Price approached Ben and wondered why he'd taken so long over such a relatively easy putt. Hogan stared at him blankly for a moment, then replied, "I never saw it go in, Charlie."

At the time, Price had no clue what Ben was getting at, no idea that Hogan's left eye at times was prone to lose focus.

Poor Sam. The massive roar he heard echoing through Oakmont's arching hardwoods as he was holing out on 14 told him, he admitted later, that everything was over but the shouting. The heart went straight out of him. He finished round four with three more bogeys, a too-familiar theme that left him bitterly mumbling to himself for decades, his fourth second-place finish at a National Open. "Enough," as he later put it in proper Sneadean context, "to make any thoroughbred feel like a farm mule."

Hogan's brilliant closing 71, capped off by the boldest finish in Open history, gave him 283 and shattered the old Oakmont tournament record by eleven strokes. It also gave him his coveted fourth National Open title, tying him with Willie Anderson and the great Bobby Jones in that elite category. Up on rainy Long Island, meanwhile, at almost the exact moment Ben was being presented the Open winner's medal and trophy (which he playfully pushed toward Sam, causing Snead to smile, roll his eyes, and pretend to swoon), Alfred Vanderbilt's grand three-year-old colt Native Dancer was hammering down the stretch to win the eighty-fifth Belmont Stakes, carving one-sixteenth of a second off the old track record set by the legendary Citation. It was a day of spectacularly historic sporting events, reserved for proven champions and thoroughbreds only.

But once again, it hadn't come without taking a toll. Just prior to the trophy presentation, Ben sat smoking a cigarette on a bench in the Oakmont locker room waiting for Snead to finish, the enormity of the moment finally settling on him. For the first time all week, someone said, he appeared physically and emotionally drained. He didn't smile much or even ask for a cold beer. He took off his spikes and put on his highly polished street shoes, washed up and combed his hair, and got dressed in a sports jacket and necktie in absolute silence.

When news came that Snead had faltered and the Open was his, applause broke out in the locker room. Before Hogan headed out to accept the tournament awards, a New Jersey sportswriter asked if he planned to return to Baltusrol and defend his title in '54. Ben looked at him and smiled as if the thought had never entered his mind until now. "I may not," he admitted gently. "I don't want to say I'm retiring. I love golf. I want to play it as long as I can. But I'm getting awfully tired. Someday there has to be a stopping point."

Not far away, standing outside the locker-room door in the lengthening shadows of the clubhouse in his old-fashioned plus fours, golf's elder states-man Gene Sarazen felt compelled to address the gathering debate over Ben's place among the greats of the game.

"This settles it in my mind," he told UPI's Oscar Fraley. "Ben's the best there ever was."

Fraley wasn't prepared to go quite that far, but hours later, as the newspa-perman sat at his post in the empty Open pressroom and rapped out his ac-count of Ben's remarkable Oakmont triumph to his five million readers, he conceded: "Ben Hogan stood one victory away today from universal recogni-tion as the greatest golfer of all time. If he wins the British Open late this month, the stubborn old guard finally will have to move the phenomenal lit-tle man up ahead of such storied heroes as Bobby Jones, Harry Vardon, and Walter Hagen."

By the next morning, Hogan was gone—off to another lucrative exhibition match before he and Valerie headed to New York to catch a transatlantic flight to Scotland.

It was exactly twenty-two days to the start of the British Open.

That same morning, legendary clothier Abercrombie and Fitch cabled Hogan's friend Paul Shields that it in fact had the very cashmere long handles Hogan had mentioned in a recent interview. They were ninety bucks a pair. Hogan asked Shields to pick him up a couple of pairs.

Meanwhile, down in Fort Worth, the A. J. Anderson Clothing Company made a media event out of dispatching several pairs of its fine wool and cotton long johns to New York via three pretty air hostesses on American Airlines, and not to be outdone, underwear manufacturer BVD also got into the act, promising to outfit the new National champ with three sets of its finest silk long underwear for his long journey to the game's birthplace.

THIRTEEN

The Longest Journey

Ben and Valerie arrived at Scotland's Prestwick Airport early in the afternoon of June 23. The couple consented to an impromptu news conference during which Valerie, as usual, declined to say anything and Ben—smiling, shaking hands, clearly relieved to be out of the air and back on dry land—initially had difficulty understanding the thick Scottish brogue of his questioners.

When a local man finally stepped in to serve as a translator, Ben fielded a number of questions about his health, his game, even the significance of his neckwear. Baffled by this question, he glanced down at his tie.

"It's red, white, and blue, sir," the translator elaborated a bit sheepishly. "Is there significance in that?"

"It's one of my favorite ties. That's all," Hogan told him.

The Hogans arrived at the Bruce Hotel overlooking the Carnoustie links, on the coast of Angus, near sunset. It was nine o'clock in the evening, the end

Overleaf: Ben Hogan Day, New York City, July 1953 (*AP/WideWorld*)

of a perfect Scottish summer day, and Ben was fascinated to see numerous players still out playing the golf course.

As for the course itself, as he later told Paul Shields and others, what he initially saw failed to impress him much: a vast landscape of green and brown mounds thrown into shadowed relief by the low angle of the sun, a few sand dunes scattered here and there, dense eruptions of head-high gorse and heather, only a few limp yellow flags to inform his eye that he was gazing upon an actual golf course, much less one of such distinguished reputation.

The hotel manager personally led the golf star and his wife upstairs to a comfortable double room overlooking the golf course, the Firth of Tay, and an unusually docile North Sea.

"Where's the bathroom?" Valerie asked him, looking around. "I don't see a bathroom."

"It's right this way," the manager replied, heading for the door. "It's down the hall, madam."

"No, no," Ben said. "If the bathroom is down the hall, we can't stay here. I'm sorry."

"Don't you have a room with a bath?" Valerie asked the manager.

The room next door had a bath, as it happened. But the room was much too small to accommodate both Hogans.

"Wait a minute, Ben," Valerie said. "Did you bring that card with the phone number of the other place that your friend gave you?"

A friend of Paul Shields's was a senior executive with National Cash Register, which owned a manufacturing plant in nearby Dundee. The company maintained a large private estate house on the outskirts of that town called Tay Park, a manor house used for entertaining company officials and traveling business executives. Knowing of Hogan's passion for comfort and privacy, the company had graciously offered the Hogans full use of the house, and when Ben dialed the telephone number on the card, he was pleased to get a Scottish lady calling herself Miss Pettie on the line informing him she was, in fact, expecting them at Tay Park.

"When we went over to Miss Pettie's that day," Valerie recalled, "it was just like Shangri-La, a big beautiful house with big beautiful grounds and a big beautiful upstairs room with a big beautiful bathroom."

"I can't believe this," Ben told her when he saw their room, a large double suite with full in-house bath and windows opening on lush private gardens.

An hour before, Valerie later said, her disgruntled husband was prepared to forget the British Open and fly directly home. "I've often thought it was fate that he kept the card with Miss Pettie's number on it," she added.

Later that evening, as they were getting settled, Miss Pettie even arranged for a rented Humber car and a company driver named John Campbell to drive the Hogans over the narrow lanes to and from Carnoustie, eleven miles away. "Their warmth warmed him," Valerie told Dave Anderson of the *Times* many years later, recalling how the staff and other Scottish guests of Tay Park never once asked Ben about his Carnoustie quest or his golfing exploits but gave him the privacy he craved and a comfort level that proved critical to his campaign.

He and Valerie dined alone at Tay Park their first evening, enjoyed a good red wine and fine roasted lamb, then joined in a conversation with other guests after dinner, Valerie later told her sister Sarah, staying up "a good bit later than expected" to hear amusing stories about local life and customs. Ben, she said, was charmed and visibly delighted to be at Tay Park, and during the course of the evening, among other things, he asked the indispensable Miss Pettie if she knew how he would locate a Carnoustie man named Cecil Timms, a young man Dick Chapman and Harvie Ward both recommended he consider as a caddie.

The book on "Timmy," as he was locally called, was that he was a bit talkative and slightly fidgety but also a fine amateur player who knew the championship course like the back of his hand. Miss Pettie promised to phone the links secretary and have Timmy found first thing in the morning.

Hogan repaid his gratitude for these and other courtesies by offering to put on a shot clinic for the NCR workers outside the company's Dundee factory before his practice rounds began.

When he got to Carnoustie's 1st tee to begin ten days of close scrutiny and practice on the championship course about midmorning on June 24, CBS broadcaster John Derr and fifty locals were already waiting there to accompany him around the golf course.

"The first thing he said to me was, 'John, why don't you get a rental set of clubs and play with me,'" remembers Derr, who declined the invitation but followed Ben for every round of golf he played before and during the tournament, unwilling to miss a moment of an effort he sensed had historic significance.

When the moment was right, he also wanted to ask Ben about his growing difficulties with the putter, a problem most seasoned Hogan watchers believed was the real reason their man was edging out of competition. Back at the Masters, Derr had used a stopwatch to time the painful intervals during which

Hogan hovered over his ball before striking the putt. "The shortest time was sixty-three seconds," he says. "And many times it was much longer than that. A small eternity for putting. I was dying to know *why*."

The two were old acquaintances. They shared a working friendship dating from Ben's breakthrough win at Pinehurst thirteen summers before, and Hogan felt comfortable enough with Derr during the inspections they made together of the championship course and adjoining Burnside course (where qualifying was scheduled to take place) to graciously offer Derr, a pretty fair stick in his own right, advice on his game.

"Several evenings after he was through practicing we stayed out on the course and Ben showed me what some were calling his 'secret.' The irony was, it wasn't just one thing. It had to do with five factors he said were critical to every golfer. And yet it was never the same five things with everybody. One day at lunch, after he'd shown me these moves," Derr recalls with a laugh, "he asked me not to ever tell all five things he'd told me until he was gone. That's exactly the way he put it too. *Until I'm gone*." The courtly broadcaster wasn't certain if Hogan meant until after he was "dead and gone" or simply until after he was gone from competitive golf. "At first I didn't have the nerve to ask him to clarify, but what he told me did get my handicap down to four. He meant, of course, that he didn't want those five general things known until he left active competition."

Derr did have the nerve to ask about Ben's increasingly lengthy spells over the putter. "Ben," he asked Hogan as they stood together once on a green, "you look to me like you're freezing over putts, almost as if you can't pull back the putter. If you don't mind me asking, what exactly are you thinking about? Are you trying to determine the direction or the speed?"

"Neither," Hogan admitted. "I don't putt until I'm ready, John. Any unnecessary movement in a golf swing is disastrous. But in a putting stroke it is a calamity. That's really all I'm doing, waiting and thinking about reducing any unnecessary movement."

So that was it: Hogan the perfectionist was unable to perform until he calculated the precise coordinates of movement required, like a violin virtuoso playing a sonata. Derr had to smile at this simple revelation. The truth was, everybody had a theory to explain Ben's blind stares. Some said it was the reverse of Sam Snead's tendency to "yip," a nervous jerky movement on the backswing that pushed or pulled his putter out of line. Others speculated that nerve damage from the wreck had ruined the smoothness of his stroke, a theory that came closer to the truth of a dominant left eye that simply refused to quickly focus on the target. In a sense, the "freezing" posture so many noted was simply Ben's effort to become completely still—reduce any unnecessary movement—and permit the eye to focus. It was, in many ways, a genuine blind stare.

Earlier that year at Colonial, Marvin Leonard had been dropping Derr off at his hotel when the broadcaster (who'd spent a great deal of time discussing the art of putting with Bobby Locke, an acknowledged whiz at that game within a game) mentioned to Leonard that he'd seen a flaw in Ben's stroke and wondered if Leonard thought it would be proper for Derr to approach Hogan with what he'd seen. It appeared to Derr that Ben was permitting the putter head to slide outside the line on the backstroke and having to pull it back in on the forward stroke.

"Everyone wants to help Ben with his putting," Leonard explained to Derr with a kindly smile. "He's getting 700 letters a week from people wanting to give him advice on nothing but his putting stroke. But I think it's all in Ben's head."

Derr was also present when Ben gave gangly, good-looking, affable thirty-four-year-old Cecil Timms the terms of his employment.

"I want you only to carry my bag, son, and keep very quiet."

"Aye, Mr. Hogan," said Timmy. "So you doona wish me to club ye, sir?"

The idea seemed utterly unthinkable to Timmy, a veteran looper who'd ushered many prominent golfing Yanks around Carnoustie's unforgiving links with bonny results.

"No. I want you to carry my bag, son. Keep the clubs clean and your mouth shut. Is that completely understood?"

"Aye." A pause. "Shall I read the greens for ye, then?"

"*No.*"

THE LITTLE GROUP that followed Ben around Carnoustie on his first practice round included Valerie Hogan, who followed along in a rare full outing onto a golf course, she later explained, both out of curiosity about the golf course and because she was worried about how her husband would handle the uncertain terrain and weather conditions.

She carried an extra sweater and a trench coat, but she needn't have worried. The Angus weather was balmy, breezes light off the Firth of Tay that morning. As Ben teed off, in the near distance, soft percussive thumps could be heard.

"What the hell is *that*?" Hogan asked Derr.

"Active artillery range just beyond the golf course there," Derr told him, pointing. Valerie smiled. "They're practicing too."

The locals were fascinated to watch Hogan play three balls on almost every hole, periodically pause and study the menacing sod-wall fairway bunkers, unlike anything seen stateside, and even bend over at one point and pick up a clump of the wiry sea grass that fringed the fairway, tilting in the endless breeze.

"He seemed to be taking a mental photograph of each hole," a sportswriter from Edinburgh who followed Ben that first day informed his readers, "and yet he was quite comfortable and at ease with his small group of spectators." Hogan also chatted pleasantly with fans and signed a few autographs. "Every time he prepared to hit a shot, though," the correspondent noted, "he was the Ben Hogan we've heard so much about, the wee Ice Man of golf, in a world all his own."

While the "Wee Ice Mon" was thus engaged, his nemesis Lloyd Mangrum checked into the Bruce Hotel and sped around the adjoining Burnside course with a score of 66 that snatched the first-day headlines of the Yanks' arrival in Carnoustie. Also arriving in town, via chauffeur-driven limo (with his dumbbells in tow), was two-time British Amateur champion and former Augusta bad boy Frankie Stranahan.

At the last minute, however, other famous American contenders sent their regrets. George Fazio, Johnny Bulla, Porky Oliver, and Gene Sarazen all cabled the Royal & Ancient Golf Club requesting that their names be scratched from the championship's roster of 180 entrants. Ditto Atlanta stockbroker and amateur sensation Harvie Ward (who was moving to San Francisco to take a job selling cars for Eddie Lowery) and even Ben's close friend George Coleman, a fine amateur who'd played in numerous British events over the years.

As Pork Chops Oliver reasoned on behalf of the other prominent American names conspicuously absent from the British Open in favor of the PGA Championship, which got under way in Birmingham, Michigan, the day before British Open qualifying commenced over in County Angus, not only was a trip overseas an expensive undertaking with no guarantee of a fellow breaking even, but Carnoustie was said to be the toughest test of seaside golf in all of Scotland. Who needed to travel that far just to lose a pile of dough and catch a cold?

Snead, Middlecoff, and Claude Harmon were also in Michigan, and there were some scribes who theorized that they declined to go abroad at least in part to provide their aging friend Hogan with easier pickings at Carnoustie. It was a sweet theory but, considering the competitive egos involved, highly unlikely. Still others back home blasted Hogan for once again choosing to play a "foreign tournament" over his own PGA Championship, a charge that proved there was no way the graying Texas legend could please even half the people half the time.

"As usual," said his sympathetic friend Jimmy Demaret, "old Ben is damned if he does and damned if he doesn't."

(Curiously enough, as events unfolded back home in Michigan, none of the Tour's established stars advanced to the tournament finals, leaving only journeyman Walter Burkemo to beat virtually unknown Felice Torza 2 and 1 for the Wanamaker Trophy.)

As he practiced, it became clear to Hogan that the minimalist nature of Scottish seaside golf wasn't his cup of tea, a fact he was initially careful to avoid revealing to his proud hosts. For the most part, the impressions he gave out were bland, carefully worded observations likely to offend nobody.

"The wind reminds me a little of the wind we have in Texas," he remarked pleasantly following his initial practice round. "The grass is very different, of course, and that will take some adjustment. But that's part of the fascination."

"The thing which strikes you most forcefully about this man," wrote a reporter from Glasgow after hearing these comments, "is his genuine modesty and sincerity. He seems utterly surprised by the excitement he creates wherever he goes. There is nothing cold or impersonal about this man, as we have been lead to believe. On the contrary, in his relations with fans he is cordial and even complimentary. On the course he is an admirable perfectionist, a stern man for a stern game. A personal trait any Scot is fully bound to admire."

And so it went.

On the streets of humble Carnoustie village, once the hemp-making capital of the British Empire, as Ben's daily practice time became the source of common knowledge and village pump conversation, shops closed early and his practice galleries swelled from 50 to 500 spectators. Schoolchildren took to halting any sun-tanned golfer they spotted on the street and decided must be American, in fervent hopes he might be the Wee Ice Mon himself.

"Hoganitis Strikes Carnoustie," announced a Dundee headline.

"Britain Smitten with Ben!" echoed London's *Daily Telegraph*.

Across the firth in County Fife, reading these dispatches, a twenty-year-old private learning Russian in the British Army's Special Intelligence Corps and stationed at Crail knew he had to somehow get over to Carnoustie and see the great Ben Hogan for himself.

"I'd been reading about this marvelous little man for years, and the belief was this was very likely to be his only trip over," remembers future CBS TV broadcaster Ben Wright. "I made up my mind that I should do whatever it took to see this great warrior who'd cheated death and come back to win the U.S. Open and Masters, even if it meant having to go AWOL to do it!"

Wright convinced five of his British Army mates to chip in five quid apiece to purchase an elderly, wheezing Austin automobile, persuaded his superiors to grant him a brief sick leave, then rambled straight to Carnoustie without benefit of a hotel reservation and only a few pounds sterling in his pockets. He got to the championship course just as Hogan was setting off on one of his final warm-up rounds.

"I shall never forget my first glimpse of the man. There was an absolute *aura* surrounding him, I tell you—the way he walked and held himself, the solemn manner in which he decided upon a shot and then made it. And his clothes! Remember, we in Britain were still coming out of the war and things were pretty rough. Hogan, on the other hand, was immaculate—the perfect crease of his trousers, the handsome multiple sweaters he wore, that famous checkered cap. He looked like a Greek *god* walking the earth! Just being near him gave one the deepest sort of thrill and chills."

Behind his cool mask of composure, Ben was having difficulty adjusting to the harder turf and the shorter flagsticks of British links golf. He admitted to Derr and Valerie that he might have misjudged his ability to compete and perhaps made a grave mistake by coming. "You never have a level lie," he later grumbled to writer Gene Gregston back in Fort Worth. "One time I'd be hitting with a baseball swing and the next time way down beneath my feet. Every fairway is rolling and full of mounds. I'd guess they mow the greens once a week maybe, and the fairways once a month. Usually they let goats in on the fairways and they never touch the rough.

According to Gregston, Hogan came off his early Carnoustie practice rounds disheartened and convinced he simply could not win. "The fairways were hard and pockmarked with divot holes. The greens were hard but heavy and slow where they appeared to him to be faster. This upset his putting rhythm and also forced him to play more hit-and-run approaches instead of flying the ball to the green."

According to Harry Andrew, the writer assigned by the *Scottish Sunday*

Express to shadow the golfer and produce a daily journal under Hogan's by-line, the Hawk had difficulty making his normal golf swing on the firmer seaside turf, especially with his short irons, which produced long divots and too much spin on balls. He was forced to teach himself to "nip" the ball off the turf, particularly from sandy lies, and to adjust upward as much as two clubs on any given shot, owing to the British ball's greater length. "In effect," says John Derr, who observed most of these last-minute adjustments, "Ben basically taught himself an entirely different sort of game. In my mind it was his most amazing feat ever."

As Derr later pointed out to his CBS Radio listeners, Hogan never bothered practicing shots from the heather and gorse. "A man who puts his ball there," Hogan told him, "won't be contending anyway."

As qualifying day loomed, Hogan asked Harry Andrew if there was someplace he could escape the growing crowds of onlookers and practice shots before his scheduled practice rounds each day. Andrew suggested the nearby Panmure links in the village of Barry, a fine private seaside club a few miles down the coast from Carnoustie. Andrew made inquiries and was told by the club secretary that Hogan would be most welcome to practice there, his privacy assured.

Hogan liked everything about Panmure. The turf was identical to Carnoustie's, the heather and gorse nearly as plentiful and intimidating, and finally something resembling a normal pretournament routine began to take shape. After breakfast at Tay Park, John Campbell drove Hogan to Panmure, where he practiced on an idle fairway with every club in his bag until about lunchtime, after which he showed up at Carnoustie's championship course for a practice round.

Hogan kept no official cards of his practice rounds—"They don't count," he explained when asked why—but the Scottish papers somehow deduced that he put together practice sequences of 70-69-69-70, and the London bookies initially listed Hogan at 9-to-4 odds.

On the Saturday before the start of the tournament, Hogan disappointed his multitudes by taking only his second day of rest since arriving in Scotland. "Hogan Rests to Dismay of Fans," reported the *London Times*. He and Valerie slept in, enjoyed a leisurely breakfast of eggs and bacon, pottered around the grounds at Tay Park through the afternoon, then took in an early movie in Dundee.

On Sunday, though, the day preceding the first qualifying round, Hogan spent the entire day at Panmure, hitting practice shots and studying what appeared to be a rising wind from the northeast, a sharper wind off the water. Timmy, casting an eye to the darkening east, informed him that rain and wind might be coming in off the cold North Sea.

Hogan lit another Chesterfield and nodded grimly, noting the way the smoke blew away, then got back to the business at hand. God might rest on Sunday in Scotland, but the Wee Ice Mon didn't have time to.

FROM REUTERS, JULY 4:

A stampeding gallery toppled several Scots into the drink Monday when Ben Hogan of Texas breezed through the first qualifying round of the British Open with a one-under par 70.

Fully 3,000 admirers overpowered golf stewards and scrambled to vantage points along the Barry Burn [brook] of Carnoustie's Burnside course. The crowd—most of them teenage Scottish bobbysoxers— shoved and pushed until several tumbled off the bank into the burn for a good soaking.

Hogan, hottest favorite to compete in the British classic, played leisurely with hardly a bead of perspiration to show for his day's work.

Dressed in a blue wool sweater and gray slacks, flanked by Derr and several stout uniformed Scottish policemen, Hogan officially began his British Open qualifying by scoring 70 at Burnside, a round that was impeded at several points by large and enthusiastic crowds.

The next afternoon, with heavy winds raking off the sea over the 7,200-yard championship course, Ben made five bogeys going out and left half a dozen putts short for a disappointing 41. It wasn't until the 18th hole, when he rolled a dramatic thirty-foot eagle putt into the hole for a distinctly *un*-Hogan-esque 75, that the first thing resembling a smile cracked his frozen gray features.

As he came off the final green, the Hawk briefly allowed himself to be taken captive by a group of local kids seeking his autograph. As he remarked over their heads to several Americans who'd followed his progress that afternoon, including old chum Sidney Lanfield and a few friends from back home in Texas, "These Britishers sure have given me a great welcome. I just wish I was giving them a better show. I don't know what's wrong with me. I've kind of lost my edge since Oakmont."

Even so, he qualified easily. As he prepared to leave the tournament grounds that afternoon, however, he was asked to give his impressions of conditions now that "more typical" Carnoustie weather had arrived.

"Those greens are like putting on putty," he replied without fully calculating the effect of his words. "I think I'll get them a lawn mower sent from Texas so they can cut them real close."

Many who heard the comments insist they were Hogan's attempt to be witty, to let off a little steam built up during an intensely frustrating round. But several newspapers took whatever the Hawk said as gospel, and some took offense at Hogan being his same old frigid self. When an offended local reporter pointed out that Carnoustie's greens had been cut *twice* each day, Hogan smiled grimly and replied, "It would have helped if they had put the blades in the mowers."

"Ben Thinks Texas Lawn Mower Would Do Trick," said Scotland's leading daily.

"Hogan Insists Greens Need Mowing," echoed Reuters.

THE NEXT MORNING, wrapped in two sweaters, Ben officially began his quest for the Claret Jug by splitting the opening fairway with his three-wood against a strong easterly wind, escorted by half a dozen Scottish policemen struggling to keep a gallery estimated at 3,000 from blocking his progress.

Part of the charm of the British Open was the intimacy that fans still enjoyed with players. Unlike in America, there were no gallery ropes, and spectators were permitted the luxury of walking directly along fairways with tournament competitors. Many in the gallery wore neckties and carried umbrellas as if they were headed to church, a sign of the high respect most Scots accorded their national golf championship.

Carnoustie's greens were hard, but once again, several Hogan birdie putts came up maddeningly short, while others slid past the holes. At several points during the round, Cecil Timms actually dipped his head and covered his eyes so he wouldn't have to watch his employer anguish over these efforts. He waved his lanky arms too and more than once sighed loudly with exasperation as putts stopped short or missed the target.

"If it's so damned hard to watch," Hogan finally snapped at him, "just stand there, Timmy, and look away. Don't make such a show out of it. For God's sake, calm down."

"Aye, Mr. Hogan."

"And *quit* eating my candy. I'll bring you your own tomorrow."

For a boost of energy between cigarettes, Ben had brought along a sack of lemon drops. Timmy was nervously helping himself to them.

"Aye, sir."

Considering the difficult conditions, Ben's opening 73 was a highly respectable score in an international field of qualifiers that was far better than most Americans watching from afar appreciated. It included defending champion Bobby Locke (future multiple British Open winner), Australian Peter Thomson, Argentinean stars Antonio Cerda and Roberto De Vicenzo, Americans Mangrum and Stranahan, former British Open champ Max Faulkner, Welshman Dai Rees, Scotsman John Panton, and the talented Irishmen Christy O'Connor and Fred Daly.

Hogan's 73 placed him three strokes back of Stranahan and one back of De Vicenzo, Locke, Thomson, and Rees. Mangrum and Faulkner followed Hogan. The only other American in the field, D. W. Fairfield of Jacksonville, Florida, shot 82, followed up with 79 on Thursday, and went home.

Following Thursday morning downpours that drenched the early starters, Ben and his playing partner, Italian Ugo Grappasonni, initially enjoyed nearly perfect conditions for scoring as they ventured out to the first nine—plenty of sunshine and surging, appreciative crowds estimated at 7,000 strong.

Hogan's irons were sharp, but half a dozen birdie putts just grazed the hole. A key moment occurred on the 4th hole when he intentionally hammered his tee shot across the 15th fairway to a chorus of gasps, then nimbly carved a middle-iron shot to within six feet of the hole, dropping his first birdie of the round. "The dunes around him reverberated with hearty cheers," reported the *Scotsman*.

Two more birdies followed, and Hogan's solid 71 finish could easily have been 67, according to Derr and others on the scene. That left the crowd favorite just two strokes shy of Scotland's own Eric Brown and Welshman Dai Rees at 142.

Twice during the second round the skies had briefly opened up on Hogan and his playing partner, soaking Ben's standard gray sweaters. By the end of the round, he was repeatedly pausing to blow his nose, turning grayer as the minutes passed, feeling the onset of a nasty head cold that would develop into something much worse by nightfall.

On the eve of Friday's thirty-six-hole finale, with the field neatly halved to fifty players, Ben was tied for second place with fellow American Frank

Stranahan, who slipped to 74 in round three and savagely kicked open a club-house gate in self-disgust as he departed the grounds, trailed by several deeply sympathetic bobby-soxers.

Back at Tay Park, Ben bathed and slept fitfully, waking several times during the night. "Every night when Hogan got back to his hotel," Harry Andrew later told his son Bryan, "he could hardly move. He had to be lifted into a warm bath just to get the circulation going." Nevertheless, by Friday dawn the Hawk was up and bathed and bandaged, dressed in a roll-neck shirt and a pair of light wool sweaters, dizzy with fever but dismissing his wife's firm opinion that he was in no condition to play.

A local physician was summoned by Miss Pettie, and Hogan agreed to take an injection of penicillin to try to stall the advance of the infection. By an hour before his 10:27 tee time, Ben's body temperature had soared to 103. "He'd lost a lot of weight over there," remembers John Derr, who learned about Ben's flu but chose not to mention it to his live American radio audience because Hogan asked him not to. "As for Valerie," Derr remembers, "she was a nervous wreck with worry. None of us could frankly believe Ben was going to go out there and try to walk thirty-six holes in that kind of weather."

Once again, over the early holes, Hogan's putter did him no favors. He missed relatively short-level birdie opportunities on 2 and 4, parred 5, then came to the daunting 6th hole, a 570-yard torture chamber that forced players to hit their tee shots well right of a pair of deep fairway bunkers, lay up shy of a narrow-shouldered burn that crossed the fairway, then punch a low-running chip shot safely onto the green.

There was a shorter approach few dared to attempt, a line directly to the left of the fairway bunkers, a strip of brown fairway grass measuring just twenty feet wide and bordered dangerously to the left by the fenced practice ground and out-of-bounds stakes.

One of the more engaging stories to arise from Hogan's Carnoustie quest was the way he chose to play the difficult par-5 sixth hole. Every golfing schoolboy knows how Hogan threw caution to the wind and fired his teeball in all four rounds to a narrow strip of turf between a fierce fairway bunker and the left out-of-bounds, a shorter but far more dangerous approach to the green that might, under certain conditions, have permitted Hogan to get home in two.

According to Hogan's own caddie, however, it didn't happen that way at all. As Cecil Tims eventually related to Royal and Ancient historian Donald Steel,

Hogan struck his tee shot cautiously to the center and right side of the fairway during the first three rounds, and only during the final round—primarily because the wind was sharply off the water—aimed for and reached the narrow strip of turf on the left.

The success of such a gutsy play, with golf's oldest championship hanging in the balance, apparently grew over the decades with the telling—another indication of how everything Hogan did added another layer of the mythic.

In any event, whichever "eyewitness" account is true, reflecting afterward on his spectacularly accurate driving in the rounds of the championship—he missed just *one* fairway in qualifying and none during the championship itself, shades of his breakthrough win at Pinehurst in 1940—Ben told Harry Andrew that he "never hit a drive more than ten feet from where I wanted it," a bravura performance that underscored his growing legend as the finest shotmaker of his time, and perhaps all time.

Once again his second shot at 6 carried the burn but came up just shy of the green, whereupon he smartly chipped to within a few feet of the cup and rolled the putt home for a birdie that ignited his gallery. Despite a costly three-putt at 17, Ben limped to the clubhouse with a one under 70 that placed him in a tie for the lead with the gentlemanly Argentinean Roberto De Vicenzo, a gentle bull of a man who resembled a prizefighter and was capable of extraordinary bursts of low scoring.

A stroke behind them were Thomson, Tony Cerda, and Dai Rees.

Valerie, who brought a bottle of the prescription medicine aureomycin along with Ben's lunch of ham sandwiches and orange wedges, asked Timmy to take these items to Ben in the gents locker room across the Links Parade Road, where he quickly retreated to get warm, wash up, and rest for a spell.

When Timmy came back, he reported to Mrs. Hogan that her husband declined to take the medicine because he was feeling "slightly better." Timmy sat down on a bench to watch his employer's wife eat her lunch. "I felt so sorry for him," Valerie explained later, "so I offered him half of my sandwich, which he gladly accepted." That evening the Hogans compared notes and discovered that Timmy had mooched half a sandwich off Ben Hogan as well. "So he ate a full lunch while Valerie and I ate half a lunch each," as Ben later recounted the tale—one of his favorites—to friends back home in Fort Worth.

"I kept thinking of the job at hand," he later explained about the break between rounds. "I felt that my original plan had to be changed somewhat. As the tournament progressed, the pressure kept building up, and although I didn't feel well physically, having taken the flu the night before, the excitement of being tied for the lead with one round to go was offsetting my physical discomfort, and I actually felt stronger moving into the afternoon round."

THE ONLY TIME Hogan ever altered an original game strategy, as he explained to Gene Gregston several months later, was in the last round of a tournament where he knew he needed to make up ground. "If you're in front, you can make the other fellow make the mistakes. But if you're behind and running out of holes," he said, "you've got to go." As the Northwood Open had proved, however, an attacking strategy didn't always work for Hogan. Still, at Carnoustie he knew he had to *go* the way he had at Oakmont just weeks before.

Through four holes at level par that afternoon, beneath skies that spit cold pellets of rain one moment and leaked weak rays of watery sunshine the next, Ben heard that Tony Cerda had dropped a birdie behind him on the 3rd hole to go one up. Ben's winning prediction of 283 was in sight, but he calculated that he needed at least one under 70 to stave off Cerda and the others. With the hardest parts of the course yet to come, where would he get *two* birdies?

The first came on the very next hole, the slight doglegging 4-par of just 390 yards. He began by slamming a 300-yard drive that easily cleared the fairway bunker, then hit his approach to about fifteen feet shy of the flag on the rising double-terraced green. As he watched, though, his ball began to trickle backward down the slope, picking up speed as it rolled off the green, stopping on the edge of a bunker in a patch of sandy rough maybe thirty-five feet from the cup. His shoulders fractionally dipped.

Hogan swore softly and lit a new cigarette, trudging over to examine his unlucky lie. Not only had the greens been ridiculously slow all week, holding almost everything thrown at them, but now he had to manufacture a shot he rarely if ever had practiced. Blasting out in a conventional manner was far too risky, he decided, since the ball could easily fly the green and leave him an impossible downhill follow-up for par. So after a moment of thinking it over, he asked Timmy for a nine-iron. That was "something I would ordinarily never do. I've never been able to chip out of sand successfully," he later explained. "Usually I either leave the ball there or hit it too far."

This time he hit it just right, however, a small brisk stroke that nipped his Titleist off the sandy patch and sent it briefly spinning through the air. The ball bounced twice on the green, pitched against the bank, skidded a little ways uphill, banged the back of the cup, leapt up three inches in the air (the *Scotsman on Sunday* claimed it was a "foot"), and fell back into the cup. The gallery let out a tumultuous roar, and Hogan cracked the faintest smile. It was his first birdie of the final round, and moments later, when Cerda made bogey, Hogan held the solitary lead for the first time in the tournament. As he later admitted to Derr, the effects of his head cold suddenly vanished, and he actually felt an unexpected surge of confidence and strength as all of his inner reserves suddenly came to bear. The other fine Argentinean challenger, De Vicenzo, was now three strokes back.

Following a second brief burst of rain and hail, Hogan threaded a perfect drive between the fairway bunkers and the dangerous out-of-bounds line of the 6th, according to the most popular account, nearly placing his tee shot in an earlier divot—"The only ones there were *his*, for goodness' sake," says Derr—then drilled another fairway wood to the edge of the green, chipped to within three feet, and sank his second birdie.

As he marched off to 7, Hogan had no firm idea where those around him stood, but he finished the outward nine calculating he might need at least one more birdie in order to win.

It was at about this point that someone told him Frank Stranahan and Dai Rees had finished with matching scores of 286 and that Peter Thomson could probably do no better than them. If Ben didn't do anything stupid and managed to par his way to the house, he would have 284 and probably golf's oldest championship sewn up. But as Hogan heard from a marshal, Tony Cerda was hanging tough, making clutch putts that kept him still within striking range.

A scary moment came at 10. As Ben took his stance and prepared to drive his ball, a black-and-white sheepdog sauntered across the tee directly in his line of fire. Hogan glanced up, stepped back, and even smiled slightly as the huge gallery chuckled and murmured. Silence settled, and Hogan took his stance a second time. As he drew back his driver, the dog loped out of the crowd again, crossing back maybe twenty yards directly in front of him. Ben's ball whistled two inches over the dog's head and landed 260 yards out in the fairway. The crowd collectively gasped, sighed with relief, then quickly applauded for both survivors of the incident.

Hogan showed no emotion whatsoever, prompting one reporter to wonder if he'd even noticed the beast. He had. "If it had hit him," Hogan said later, "it probably would have killed the dog, could have messed up my score pretty badly, and there might have been a different ending to this story."

As it was, following sensational approach shots at both 10 and 11, Ben narrowly missed recording birdies. At 12 he missed the green with a rare wayward iron approach shot but recovered beautifully with a seventy-five-foot pitch that let him putt a three-footer to save par.

On 13, the 167-yard par-3, he carved a slightly fading shot to twelve feet and sank the putt for a deuce birdie. It was the moment, he later confided to John Derr, when he knew he was going to win the British Open Championship.

On 15, Ben rolled another fine birdie attempt half an inch past the cup and settled for a tap-in par. Walking off the green, lighting a fresh cigarette ("I hardly smoke now on the golf course," he told the *Sunday Post*, "but this week I guess I've gone through a dozen packs, a hundred a round between us," meaning himself and Timmy the caddie), he glanced over at Derr.

"Where are they, John?"

He meant Cerda and any other late chargers. Frank Stranahan had made a heroic final-round charge, one-putting each of his last six greens, including a forty-foot eagle putt on 18. His best was not good enough, though, leaving him at 286.

"De Vicenzo's finished with 73. Cerda is three under," Derr reported.

"What hole is he on?"

"13."

"Tee or green?"

"He's through 13. Playing 14."

There were no scoreboards at Carnoustie, only scoring tents along the way manned by volunteers and military personnel conveying scores to the clubhouse via walkie-talkie. The workers called it "bush telegraph."

Across Britain, in cars and shops and homes, a million BBC Radio listeners already knew that Cerda had struck a spectator on 12 and Hogan was leading him now by three strokes. Like young Ben Wright in the surging gallery, which often broke into a dead run to gain a good view of Hogan's next shot, they sensed there was no denying the Wee Ice Mon his Claret Jug. "The excitement running through that crowd was greater than anything I'd ever seen or witnessed," remembers Wright. "It was comparable to having the new queen on the throne and Hillary reaching the top of Everest. That moment was positively *electrifying* . . . all those adoring fans going home each step of the way with Hogan. It confirmed something very fine indeed about this game of golf, the obstacles one must overcome to achieve such a championship. In that regard, there had never been anything like Hogan at Carnoustie. And I daresay there never shall be again."

At 16, the long par-3, Ben drilled a magnificent four-wood shot to twenty-five feet of the cup. "John," he remarked almost casually to Derr as they walked side by side toward the green, "you can go get ready for that interview now. This tournament is over."

"It gave me goose bumps when he said that," Derr recalls. "The certainty in his voice was absolute, almost chilling."

No champion ever played better with a lead than Hogan. That's what Henry Picard said about him when Ben won his first tournament at Pinehurst in 1940, and that's what the entire world understood best about the Hawk now on the threshold of capturing the British Open on his first attempt. After safely parring the next two holes, Ben arrived at Carnoustie's 18th tee and was greeted by an extraordinary sight: 20,000 spectators packed both sides of the 503-yard par-5 hole, ten deep in places, all standing with quiet respect as the greatest player of the age prepared to strike his final drive.

Ben unleashed a corker, a searing 280-yard drive into the wind that missed the top of the fairway bunker by a mere two yards, another gutsy approach that left him the best possible angle for going at the green. Moments later, he used his beloved four-wood to drill his ball spectacularly onto the putting surface in two, leaving his ball just thirty-five feet shy of the cup. He paced around the green and finally hunched over his ball, rapping his eagle attempt firmly across the green. The ball rolled to a stop eighteen inches from the cup—a final effort that came up frustratingly short again. With no visible hesitation or difficulty, however, he rolled the remaining putt of the tournament into the cup for birdie 4 and a final-round 68, giving him a seventy-two-hole total of 282. His 68 was a new single-round record for Carnoustie, a 282 total that beat the course's previous tournament record by a whopping eight strokes. His seventy-two-hole score was also the best ever in a British Open Championship.

As the roar from the largest gallery in Open history rose through the damp and breezy afternoon air, Hogan removed his checkered wool cap and acknowledged the crowd with a wave and a smile. "I'd never seen a grayer and more exhausted-looking figure," Ben Wright remembers. "People said he smiled as he came up the final fairway, but I never saw any kind of smile until he removed his cap. He looked utterly and completely drained, a man on the verge of collapse. Still, the way the crowd quietly and respectfully parted as he approached—well, it reminded me of passing royalty. We in Britain had just lost our golf-mad king George, remember. Young Elizabeth was fresh upon the throne. But now we had true golfing royalty in Ben Hogan."

As the changeable skies loosed rain upon the scene, the new British Open champion retreated to the small broadcast shed, where Derr was waiting to go on the air live to a national audience of CBS listeners back in America. "It was rather strange," Derr picks up the tale. "I noticed as we started talking that Valerie was standing just outside in the rain, which was picking up its pace. So I asked Ben to tell the listeners about his final magnificent round of 68 and then left my seat to go and invite her in out of the rain. Ben kept talking as if I were still seated beside him. 'Valerie,' I said to her, 'please come on inside out of the rain. I'd love to have you say a few words too.' She looked at me rather aghast at this suggestion. 'Oh, no, John. I really *couldn't*,' she said, and then made it very clear she wasn't budging from her spot in the rain. So she just stood out there waiting, and Ben and I finished the interview."

After the broadcast, the new champion ruffled a few feathers by refusing to return straightaway to the trophy presentation, leaving thousands of his fans and the press waiting in a light Angus rain. What some decided was vintage Hogan rudeness was really Hogan's old-fashioned sense of propriety exerting itself—his refusal to accept the Claret Jug until he was wearing a proper sports jacket.

The problem was that the clubhouse at Carnoustie was little more than a municipal starter shed with no changing rooms and Ben's jacket was hanging in a locker room at a clubhouse across Links Parade Road. Several players, including De Vicenzo, quickly left to catch a departing train.

The problem was finally solved when Hogan turned to his Boswell for that week, Harry Andrew of the *Sunday Express*, and said, "Harry, can you lend me your jacket?" Moments later, the Hawk went out to accept his trophy, dressed in another man's coat.

"I didn't come here to take home a trophy," he said after accepting the Claret Jug. "Whether I won or lost was incidental. I came over here because a lot of people back home wanted me to and some people over here did too."

When a London reporter wondered if he planned to go on to the Ryder Cup matches at Wentworth and if he would return to defend his title in 1954, Hogan replied that he was simply too tired to play the Ryder Cup. "I'm definitely not retiring yet," he said, then added almost wistfully, "But I've been traveling nineteen years now, boys. I'm forty, and there isn't much mileage left in this old frame. It's time I took it easy."

He concluded his remarks by describing Scottish fans as "the greatest galleries I've ever seen," thanked the people of Carnoustie and Scotland in general for the "warm hospitality they have extended to both Valerie and me," then admitted he probably wouldn't return to Britain to defend his crown.

Before leaving home, Hogan had been asked by the USGA's Joe Dey to bring home one of his golf balls for the organization's Golf House museum, regardless of the outcome. Before Ben went off to accept his trophy, Derr reminded Ben of this promise, and Hogan instructed the newsman, "Go ask Timmy about it, and ask him about the other ball too."

The elegant broadcaster had no idea what this meant but went out and found Hogan's caddie, who was giving his client's clubs a final polishing rub before he packed them into the boot of the Humber for the drive back to Tay Park. From Scotland, Ben and Valerie were scheduled to fly directly to Paris for their much-publicized French vacation.

"Timmy," said Derr, "Ben asked me to get that ball for the USGA."

"Aye, sir." Timmy reached into his pocket and pulled out the #4 Titleist that Hogan had finished his record-breaking round with. He gave it to Derr.

"He said to ask you about the other ball as well . . ."

Timmy smiled and nodded. "Aye."

He fished another ball out of his pocket, this one a #2 Titleist, and handed it over to the broadcaster, who examined it and wondered where Ben had used it on the golf course. Ben, Derr knew, had used a three-hole rotation system, placing a new ball in play every third hole.

"That's the one he made his only deuce with," explained the caddie. "He wanted *you* to have it, sir."

For a moment, Derr was speechless. It was the ball Ben was using when he made the critical birdie on 13 and knew he'd won the British Open.

"It was the kind of thoughtful thing Ben Hogan did for people without the world ever hearing anything about it," Derr says. "That was Ben's nature. I think it was simply his way of saying thank-you to me for being there for all those years."

Derr took the ball home and gave it to his young daughter, Cricket.

SHORTLY AFTER the trophy presentation, Ben Wright was thumbing his way out of Carnoustie town, headed back to Panmure to try to coax his dying Austin back to life, when he saw Hogan's Humber approaching on the coast road as it set out for Dundee.

"I'd met and become friendly with his driver John earlier that day, and he'd said to me he would see if Mr. Hogan would mind giving me a lift back to my car, especially a young man in uniform."

The Humber slowed but then sped on.

"Apparently the driver asked to stop and pick me up but a weary Hogan instructed him to drive on," says Wright. "When I met Hogan again many years later in Texas, I told him this story and we had a nice laugh about it. I recall him saying that, in retrospect, he wished he'd stopped and picked me up, and I explained that the walk back to my car wasn't too terribly far, a mile or two at most. It gave me ample time to think about the marvelous things I'd witnessed—and what I was going to tell my superiors about my whereabouts being unknown for several days on end."

Upon their arrival at Tay Park, Ben and Valerie were pleased to discover that Miss Pettie had put up an American flag beside the British one, and a dozen members of her staff, including chefs, chambermaids, and groundskeepers, had assembled beside the driveway. The women kissed Ben on the cheek, and the men shook his hand good-bye. Then one of the men began unzipping the pockets of his golf bag.

"No," Ben protested gently, "I'd love for you to see it, but everything is still in there." He thought the man was trying to see the Claret Jug.

"Aye, sir. But there's something we'd like to show you."

One by one, a number of personal trinkets and good-luck charms were extracted from one of the bag's lower pockets—amulet stones, personal notes, an ancient British coin, a treasured family locket.

"They placed them there for good luck," Miss Pettie explained, beaming.

"Ben was so touched he couldn't even speak," Valerie confided to her sister, Sarah, later. "I've never seen him so deeply moved by anything. He couldn't believe they would do something like that, and he had tears in his eyes saying good-bye to them all."

No one had ever seen the great Ben Hogan shed a tear in public. But the Wee Ice Mon melted as he said good-bye to the staff at Tay Park.

THE LONGEST JOURNEY any man can make, someone once said, is the distance from head to heart.

Ben's Merion triumph would always be his most prized tournament because it proved he could still play and win major championships, Oakland Hills his most satisfying because of the way he finished to bring the monster to its knees. "But the British Open gave me my greatest pleasure," he explained to Jim Tinkle of the *Star-Telegram* several years later. "Certainly the others were pleasurable, but none of them gave me the feeling, the desire to perform, that gripped me in Scotland."

That same afternoon at the train station in Edinburgh, a homeward-bound John Derr encountered Bernard Darwin, the aging dean of British golf writers and Charles Darwin's nephew, standing in the rain, waiting for his own train home to London. Darwin had just covered his final British Open for the *London Times*.

"You know, John," the famous journalist mused, "I don't think we'll ever see the likes of Hogan again. I distinctly got the feeling he could have done whatever was required of him in order to win. He could have shot 65 if he had needed it."

"That's what makes him Ben Hogan," Derr agreed.

The world press, meanwhile, was already unleashing every superlative imaginable on Hogan's Carnoustie conquest and searching for the proper context for a year unlike any in memory. With rounds of 73-71-70-68 that got progressively better over the toughest links in Scotland, missing only one fairway in 108 holes of golf, Ben's Carnoustie triumph matched any championship in Open history for drama and courage, and editorialists on both sides of the Atlantic were already hailing his record for 1953—seven tournaments, five wins, three majors titles—as the finest since Jones's "impossible quadrilateral" conquest of the U.S. and British Amateur and both nations' Opens in 1930.

"And who shall say he is *not* the best of all time?" former Walker Cupper Leonard Crawley of the *Daily Telegraph* essayed, prompting Gene Sarazen from his grape farm in upstate New York to repeat his assertion to the wire services that Hogan had proved, once and for all, "that he is the greatest player of all time. No ifs, ands, or buts about it, boys. Got that? Good. Print it."

When a vacationing Sir Walter Hagen down in Florida was asked about Hogan's Carnoustie triumph, he only smiled like he'd known something all along. "Did you think he *wouldn't* win?" he playfully volleyed back at the Miami reporter.

Even Bobby Jones, wracked by pain but clearheaded as ever, was moved to concede: "What Ben has done is extraordinary. His career has been like no other I've seen or heard of."

THE DAY BEFORE the Hogans left Leuchars Royal Air Force base for a brief stop in London (where he met the new queen, Elizabeth, and was presented a letter entitling him to play in the British Isles anytime he wished), Harry Andrew wondered if Ben might not wish to slip twelve miles over the lanes to take a peek at the Old Course at Saint Andrews, the celebrated home of the Royal & Ancient Golf Club and the popularly acknowledged birthplace of the game.

"What for?" Hogan replied. "It's just another golf course."

Andrew looked hurt. Hogan smiled at him.

"Tell you what, Harry. When that plane takes off tomorrow, it'll fly right over the course. I promise you, if the weather's clear, I'll take a real good look at it."

The next morning, though, Hogan's Humber just missed making the ancient paddle-wheeled ferry connection across the Firth of Tay, and John Campbell was forced to detour through Perth, delaying their scheduled departure by half an hour from Leuchars. "I guess I'll have to build a bridge," Ben joked to the military staff waiting to see them off to London and Paris.

Harry Andrew was there to say good-bye too. While their bags were being loaded, Andrew commented to Valerie on Ben's unusually relaxed frame of mind that week, and she told him: "I do all of the worrying for him, Harry. He can play so much easier when he knows I am with him in his mind. I have always done this. When you are lucky to be alive, a missed shot does not really seem so important. That thought is always with us."

"Life for Valerie Hogan has been one long spell of tension," the man from the *Sunday Express* wrote after the Hogans were gone, never to return. "It shows in her eyes; her hands are never still. There are lines on her forehead, there is gray in her hair. Ben saved her in the car crash which crippled him four years ago. And she repays the debt every day."

A little while later, the bomber on loan from General Norstad, American air commander in Europe, banked low over the Old Course, and Ben peered out over one of the oldest golf courses on earth, the game's most hallowed teeing ground, a place where virtually every immortal before him had walked and triumphed.

"Very interesting," he remarked, in perfect Hoganese, and said no more about the subject.

THIRTY MILES outside Paris the following Wednesday afternoon, at Fontainbleau Golf Club, a fine old Tom Simpson layout, the new British Open champ gave "lessons" to several enthusiastic American airmen stationed at a nearby base and teamed with the base commander to lose a "best ball" match 3 and 2 to the club's pro, one "Fifi" Cavalo, and Henri de Lamaze, France's top amateur golfer. Hogan shot 69 and displayed only traces of his recent bout of flu. For three days he and Valerie had billeted at the plush Paris Ritz, "resting, walking around Paris a bit, sightseeing and eating lots of good French cooking, the usual things one does on vacation," as he summed it up to the man from the *Herald Tribune* before teeing off.

Before returning to Paris that afternoon, word came from military brass that the city of New York was preparing a hero's welcome and a ticker-tape parade for the Hogans upon their arrival home.

Ben and Valerie were scheduled to depart for home the next morning on the boat train for Le Havre. Rather than fly directly from Paris to New York, as originally planned, at the last minute the Hogans chose to book passage on the ocean liner *United States*, a crossing that would take five days.

"Really?" he said, breaking out his photogenic California smile. "Sure, that's fine with me. I'm flattered they would do that."

The next afternoon, as he boarded the passenger liner, a reporter for Reuters wondered, in parting, if Hogan "perfected" the game. The question seemed to catch Hogan off-guard and even embarrass him a little.

"It's real kind of folks to say so," he replied. "It's nice to know they have so much confidence and faith in you. But I hope I never become perfect. Because then, where do you go from there? Down, that's where."

When these comments filtered back to America, only the Tour's current leading money winner, one Lloyd Mangrum, felt compelled to take issue with the accolades pouring Hogan's way. "It's hogwash," he declared some weeks later in Chicago at George May's season-closing Tam O'Shanter event. "Sure Hogan's a good player, but he's a long way from being the best golfer that *ever* picked up a club. Just let him play on the Tour like the rest of us do week in and week out, and he'd place eighth or ninth occasionally, and it wouldn't surprise me if he finished out of the money once in a while."

As Derr and others noted, this was a different-sounding Lloyd Mangrum than the one who sat in the plush George V Hotel in Paris just days before the start of play at Carnoustie and intimated to *New York Daily News* golf writer Bob Brumby that he probably couldn't beat "the little man" in head-to-head competition. The only reason he was going to Carnoustie, Lloyd allowed, was because his employer, George May, had guaranteed him an extra five grand in his pay packet if he could somehow capture the Claret Jug and haul it home to Chicago. As it happened, Lloyd finished nineteen strokes behind Hogan and caught the first plane out of Scotland. The latest broadside from Mangrum was probably aimed at trying to prevent Hogan from winning a fourth Player of the Year honor. It didn't work.

Half a dozen weeks later, Ben collected a record-breaking 803 ballots from PGA members and the nation's sportswriters to win his fourth PGA Player of the Year Award.

Remarkably, Lloyd Mangrum, who won the Vardon Trophy but just lost the Tour money title to Lew Worsham, had no comment on the landslide.

FIVE DAYS on a tranquil sea with only his wife and his thoughts and the remnants of a nasty head cold was perhaps exactly what Ben Hogan needed to come to terms with his Carnoustie triumph and the unshakable feeling that his long journey through golf was rapidly drawing to a close.

At 5:30 sharp on the morning of July 21, a steward discreetly knuckled the Hogans' stateroom door and notified Valerie, who appeared in her formal French dressing gown, that a press party had assembled and was waiting to greet Mr. Hogan in the ship's main salon. Fifty reporters and photographers had been ferried out from New York Harbor to meet the liner by a U.S. Coast Guard cutter.

Fifteen minutes later, the Hogans entered the salon to the sustained applause of the reporters and a handful of their curious fellow early-rising ship travelers who'd come to watch the press conference. Valerie appeared a little strained, but Ben merely blinked with sleepy surprise and appeared (to the reporters) even skinnier than he had on departing America several weeks before. "Gee, I can't imagine you fellas getting up so early to do this just for me," he said, shaking his head.

Someone brought him a cup of coffee. He lit the day's first cigarette, picked a fleck of tobacco off his tongue, and patiently submitted to the usual stream of questions about his latest triumph, health, and tournament plans.

"Now that you've got all the major championships," a man from the *Newark Star-Ledger* put it to him, "do you plan to give up golf?"

"Golf is my whole life—golf and competition. I've been playing since I was twelve, and I hope to be playing it my whole life. I have no plans to retire yet," he replied, pausing to consider. He added, "And I am certain I will play again in the National Open. Whether I play in a British tournament is a question. That is a long way off. Right now I am very tired of traveling and very tired of playing golf."

Someone asked when he might play again.

"Probably the Masters next spring."

"Anything else?"

"I've committed to play a few exhibitions. That's all, fellas."

When asked if he would reconsider his decision to skip the forthcoming Ryder Cup at Wentworth outside London, he quickly said no—then wondered if there had been any "good rain down in Texas" to ease the punishing two-month drought the Lone Star State was suffering through. No one knew for sure.

"Hey, Ben. You thinking of buying a ranch like Byron?" someone asked him playfully, producing chuckles around the salon.

"No. But I am going to start making golf clubs," he explained simply.

The reporters were delighted to have a "scoop." Heretofore, Hogan had remained maddeningly silent about whatever "significant opportunities" he was pursuing outside of tournament golf. A few persistent rumors held that he wanted to start making golf equipment and take on the likes of Spalding, MacGregor, and Wilson. But the man himself had never confirmed such daring thinking until this very moment. The scribes couldn't write fast enough.

"I think I have a revolutionary way of making clubs," he explained to them that morning at sea. "We have made several experimental models and hope to be in production soon. I expect the factory to be set up in Texas, probably around Fort Worth."

In fact, as he said this, his company was already up and running at the production facility he and Pollard Simons were setting up on West Pafford Street. Recently, he hired a woman he'd gone to grade school with way back in Dublin to be his secretary. But true to form, Hogan didn't mention any of this because he didn't want any reporters nosing around his unopened factory, bugging people and potentially causing costly delays.

"Won't this interfere with your playing golf?" one of the writers wondered.

Hogan smiled fractionally, leaking smoke from his nostrils.

"I don't expect to be a desk man."

A reporter standing next to Valerie wondered how she felt about Ben starting up his equipment company and probably being around home more often.

"I would like to see him not try for any more big championships if he has to work as hard as he did for these," she admitted. "I'd rather he just started playing for fun."

Ninety minutes later, as the lens of a newsreel camera focused on them, Ben and Valerie Hogan stood together like a couple of newlyweds at the rail admiring the Statue of Liberty as their ship eased into New York Harbor. An armada of tugs and private boats blew their horns, and several city fireboats shot streams of water into the air as a salute to the arriving hero and his bride.

A while later, the "Hogan team," as Ben had taken to calling them, was met at pier 86 by a police escort detail, an official representative of the mayor, and a sea of popping flashbulbs. They were promptly driven by limo to the Park Lane Hotel, where they were permitted to "rest" for a few hours before being placed in a pair of separate, open Chrysler limos and driven to lower Manhattan for the official start of a Lindbergh-style ticker-tape parade to city hall with an escort of fifty motorcycle policemen and both the city's Fire Department and Sanitation Department marching bands.

For the day, July 21, Broadway's Great White Way was officially renamed "Hogan's Alley," and just after noon on the hot, steamy summer day a crowd estimated at 150,000 office workers, surprised tourists, and Hogan fans lined the sidewalks as a cascade of shredded phone books and brokerage ticker tape filtered down on Ben and Valerie's motorcade.

The Hawk sat on top of the lead limousine, dressed in an expensive gray businessman's suit, looking like a million bucks. Valerie rode in the car directly behind him with PGA president Horton Smith, Linc Werden of the *New York Times*, and USGA vice president Ike Grainger. As the crowd cheered and called out his name, Ben turned and waved with one hand, then repeated an identical movement in the opposite direction with his other hand. He later confessed to Valerie that he was disappointed that he didn't see a single soul he knew.

The parade ended on the steps of city hall, where mayor Vincent Impellitteri presented an official citation to Ben and slightly mangled legendary mayor James Walker's famous words of greeting to Bobby Jones when he received his ticker-tape fete in July 1930: "Here you are, the world's greatest golfer, and I am probably the worst." (Walker's actual quote: "Here you are, the greatest golfer in the world, being introduced by the worst one.")

The official proclamation, in any case, lauded Hogan for being a great champion whose achievements were an inspiration "to the youth of the nation." But the real showstopper came when Impellitteri opened and read a telegram from Hogan's sometime Augusta golf partner, the new president of the United States.

Millions of Americans would like to participate with the New Yorkers today who are extending their traditional welcome upon your return from your magnificent victory. We are proud of you not only as a great competitor and a master of your craft, but also as an envoy extraordinary in the business of building friendship for America. With best wishes to you and Mrs. Hogan, [signed] Dwight D. Eisenhower

The sweating crowd of 5,000 erupted in applause and cheers as Hogan accepted the telegram and stood blinking at it in the bright filtered sunlight falling through canyons of concrete and steel. For a lengthy moment, even after the crowd quieted back down, he was unable to find his voice. Finally, he motioned Valerie to his side and draped an arm around her shoulders. "It would take me forever to tell you what was . . . in my heart right now," he began, then cleared his throat. "Only in America and in New York City could such a thing happen to a little guy like me."

He paused again and glanced at Valerie. She beamed encouragingly up at him.

"I have a tough skin," he resumed, his voice audibly cracking with emotion, "but I have a soft spot in my heart and . . . and . . . this tops anything that *ever* happened to me. Right now I feel like crying. This is the greatest moment of my life."

"Then Ben Hogan choked up," wrote Associated Press sportswriter Will Grimsley. "Nobody had ever seen Ben Hogan choke up before. But he did. This was the grim, hard-bitten master of the fairways—rawhide and cold steel, the man without nerves, the mechanical man, they called him. It was too much for the Fort Worth, Texas, blacksmith's son."

From city hall it was on to lunch at Toots Shors's, Hogan's favorite Manhattan haunt, where he lunched with Grantland Rice, former heavyweight boxing champ Gene Tunney, and baseball great Stan Musial and learned he had just been named the thirteenth member of the PGA Hall of Fame, the first of his era to receive such an honor.

After promising Ed Sullivan he would soon make a second guest appearance on the top-rated TV show, it was then on to a press conference at Golf House, where Ben presented executive secretary Joe Dey with the winning golf ball that Timmy had saved at Carnoustie.

About that same moment, down in Washington, inside the steamy un-air-conditioned Senate chamber of the U.S. Capitol, the Honorable Lyndon Baines Johnson got to his feet and read a lengthy editorial from the tiny *Lufkin* (Texas) *Daily News* hailing Ben Hogan as the world's greatest golfer ever, then asked that his remarks and the newspaper editorial itself be entered into the

Congressional Record for July 21, 1953. It was immediately ordered to be so entered by the Senate's presiding president, Vice President Richard M. Nixon.

Ben's big day in the Big Apple ended with a prime rib dinner (Texas beef, of course) at the Park Lane Hotel thrown by the USGA and attended by a host of stars from golf's galaxy, including Sarazen and Jones, Denny Shute and Claude Harmon, Francis Ouimet and Johnny Farrell (Open champs from 1913 and 1928, respectively), amateur sensation Harvie Ward and Oakmont pro Lew Worsham. "It was the kind of night that should have forever laid to rest any of this business about Ben Hogan being a cold and unsociable fellow," Ike Grainger remembered decades later. "I think old Ben laughed and talked with every person in the house, and some of them two or three times, sharing stories. He couldn't get enough of it."

A profound hush fell over the room when the great Bobby Jones rose to make his dinner remarks, perhaps to shed his own light on Hogan's rightful place in the game's pantheon. According to Harvie Ward, "everything got so doggone quiet, it felt like the president was about to address Congress."

In gracious remarks that were full of praise for Ben's incomparable Carnoustie triumph, Jones artfully declined to say one way or another whether he thought Hogan was the greatest player ever. But the ailing god nearly went that far.

"Without a doubt people are running faster, jumping higher, and jumping farther than ever before. I can't see any reason why they can't play golf better today. Ben, you're the best because you're willing to work the hardest of all."

The party went late into the evening, the laughter and storytelling, the toasting and celebration of Ben's final journey from head to heart.

When Ben and Valerie finally got back to their hotel room and shut the door, Valerie confided a few days later to her sister, Sarah, Hogan loosened his necktie, sighed, and smiled wearily.

"This has been the hardest day of my life," he said.

FORTY-EIGHT HOURS later, at 5:15 in the afternoon on Friday after two nights of heavy rains began to refill depleted local reservoirs, the fete was continued down in Texas. Mama Hogan was the first to lurch forward and give her youngest son a brisk kiss for a job well done after he and Valerie stepped off an American Airlines flight and onto a bright red carpet at Amon Carter Field, where seventeen uniformed American Airlines stewardesses held placards spelling out WELCOME HOME HOGANS and Ben's old Glen Garden boss

James "Captain" Kidd, a son of old Carnoustie himself, pranced merrily about wearing a vivid Scottish tam and waving a little Scottish flag.

The Carswell Air Force band blared out "The Eyes of Texas" and Cowtown's Mayor Deen officially welcomed "Fort Worth's most famous man" home and ushered the arriving hero into the newly built and air-conditioned terminal building for a scheduled ten-minute news conference.

Valerie stood arm in arm with her sister, whispering about the recent whirlwind of days.

Then it was home by police escort to the swank Western Hills Hotel, where the Hogans, part-owners of the establishment, had been residing in a spacious apartment since putting their Valley Ridge house on the market the previous spring. Privately, friends of the couple talked about how Valerie had never warmed to the house on Valley Ridge, and while she waited in the background for Ben's press conference to wind up, she revealed to a *Star-Telegram* society writer that she and Ben "expect to build a new house somewhere in town" within two years, one she thought Ben might even take a hand in designing.

The following Monday, the Queen City of the Prairie presented Ben and Val with their own version of a Texas ticker-tape parade and a big luncheon at the Hotel Texas, where one local dignitary after another got up to talk about the glory Hogan had brought to his hometown. Colonial Country Club's president presented Ben with an honorary membership to the club.

"This means you don't have to pay dues anymore, Ben," he said, breaking up the ballroom. "I know that will please you a great deal."

The most powerful speaker was Ben's friend Granville Walker, who talked about Hogan's trek toward immortality and his undaunted courage in overcoming adversity, sprinkling quotes from Kipling and Ecclesiastes as he wrapped the room in his oratorical magic.

"If there is anything more remarkable than Ben Hogan the golfer," Walker concluded, "it is Ben Hogan the *man*."

When it was finally Hogan's turn to speak, once again he couldn't find the words to do it. He hesitated, gripping the lectern, and allowed his once-cold Hawk eyes to float over the expectant faces of the room as surfacing emotions threatened to reveal him in a way no golf course ever had.

His voice "wavered and almost broke as the champion found it difficult to express all that was stored up within him," wrote *Fort Worth Press* writer Bud Shrake.

"My heart is completely filled with gratitude, humility, and pride," Ben finally told the crowd. "After this week I don't think anything better could happen."

Carnoustie had been, he admitted, the high point of the finest year of his life, the culmination of everything he had ever dreamed about and worked for. But now he was looking forward to going home and "doing nothing but loafing a bit."

The crowd had a good laugh at this parting remark. They knew Ben Hogan had never loafed a day in his life.

Early the next morning, sure enough, a member on his way to breakfast at Colonial glanced over and spotted Fort Worth's most famous citizen putting on the practice green, trying to work the bugs out of his ailing stroke. In six days' time, Ben and Valerie were flying up to visit Ike in the Oval Office, then play an exhibition match outside Washington, D.C.

After lunch with Marvin, however, Ben didn't venture out to the golf course as he customarily did following lunch. He got in his Cadillac and drove over to see how work was coming on the somewhat dilapidated, single-story, brick-fronted warehouse he and Pollard Simons had recently begun renovating on West Pafford Street near the campus of Southwestern Baptist Seminary.

That was where the rest of his life was waiting.

FOURTEEN

Fleck

V ALERIE HOGAN abruptly stopped clipping newspaper articles in 1954. Her amazingly ordered scrapbooks, her meticulous cataloging of Ben's extraordinary journey through golf, suddenly ceased, almost as if she understood—or had been told—there would be little her husband accomplished on the golf course worthy of remembering from that time forward.

In fact, Hogan would win just twice more in his career, teaming with rival Sam Snead to take both the team and individual honors of the 1956 Canada Cup, followed by a fifth and final Colonial NIT title in the spring of 1959.

True to his word after Carnoustie, he didn't play again in tour competition until the Masters of 1954, the tournament best remembered as the major contest in which amateur Billy Joe Patton nearly swiped a green jacket from under the noses of the game's top players.

William Joseph Patton, aka "Billy Joe," of Morganton, North Carolina, a brawny twenty-eight-year-old lumber salesman with a humble nature and a

Overleaf: Jack Fleck and Hogan following play-off, Olympic Golf Club, United States Open Championship, 1955 *(Corbis)*

rapid homemade swing, qualified by the slimmest of margins for golf's most elite invitational—as an alternate from the preceding year's Walker Cup team. But he made his presence known even before the tournament began by entering the Wednesday "clinic" and winning the annual Masters driving contest with a bash of 338 yards that reached the back of the club practice range. In the process, he made himself an instant gallery favorite by whistling between shots and entertaining fans with a stream of witty down-home comments.

Patton made an even bigger impression the next afternoon by shooting 70 and tying for the Masters lead with veteran Dutch Harrison. By Augusta standards, the weather that opening day was awful, cold and blustery, snapping concession tents apart and keeping all players except two from breaking par—Lloyd Mangrum and Jack Burke Jr., both of whom had 71s. Hogan finished a stroke back of them. Friday's weather was even more disagreeable, with stinging darts of rain causing Harrison to slide to a woeful 79 and Hogan to finish with one over 73. Billy Joe had 74 but gained sole possession of the lead heading into Saturday's round, whistling all the way.

Glancing at the leaderboard and Patton's impressive 144, normally cordial Cary Middlecoff, five strokes back, grumbled, "If this guy wins the Masters, it'll set golf back fifty years."

The good dentist wasn't the only guy not having any fun. Earlier in the week, when Bill Campbell was grouped with Hogan and Skip Alexander in a practice round, Campbell had clearly heard Ben mutter, "I'm ready to leave."

Campbell and Alexander exchanged glances. Skip heard it too.

"Are you talking to us, Ben?" Campbell probed gently.

"No," Ben replied, head down, "I'm just thinking out loud."

Campbell had noticed something significantly different about the Hawk's golf swing that day. "That remarkable little fade of his that used to hover and then drop beneath the hole was more like a slider now. It still finished below the hole most of the time, but its flight wasn't nearly as penetrating or effective as before. Ben was following his normal plan, but I got the impression he was simply going through the motions. You could tell his head was somewhere else."

Ironically, that same week *Life* magazine published a survey of seven prominent golf professionals who speculated on the key to Ben's fabled accuracy, his so-called "secret." Coming up with seven entirely different theories, they sounded, as Hogan biographer Curt Sampson puts it, "like a freshman philosophy class" trying to explain and reduce Hogan's success to a technical formula. Walter Burkemo claimed Ben dropped his hands at the top of the swing, while pro Fred Gronauer insisted the key to his extraordinary accuracy was all "in his pivot." Mike Turnesa believed the secret was Hogan's grip, the way it permitted him to open the face on his backswing and thus prevent the dreaded hook. Ben's Seminole golf pal Claude Harmon was certain the secret was in his left hip turn—"If you clear the left hip early," Hogan once assured him, "you can hit it as hard as you like with the right hand"—while George Fazio believed it had to do with shoulders that maintained a level attitude.

For his part, Sam Snead scoffed at the very notion Ben even had a secret. "Hell, it's easy to have a 'secret' when you won't tell anybody about it," he said, while Gene Sarazen only smiled and pointed to his head, identifying the primary locus of Ben's major advantage. "He *thinks* better than anyone who has ever played this game," Sarazen declared, getting closest to the truth.

True to form, Hogan himself remained silent as a sphinx on the debate, golf's version of angels dancing on the head of a pin, and not for the first time a feeling persisted among his colleagues that Ben was not only withholding vital information on the subject but rather enjoying the confusion of so many people trying to figure him out.

Partly because he'd been repeatedly snubbed and even ridiculed by some members of the press early in his career struggles and partly because everything in his nature had been shaped around a singular unspeakable event he was bound and determined to keep hidden from view at all costs, Hogan was emotionally hardwired not to really give a damn what people thought of his silence on any subject, including and maybe especially his acquired ability to hit a golf ball better than anyone.

If a chilly public demeanor had successfully kept the inquiring world at arm's length for decades, withholding vital information was his final bulwark against the kind of intimacy he had been denied at every phase of life save one, his early childhood. He also wasn't above intentionally obfuscating answers and explanations either, like the time many years after his withdrawal from the Tour when he reportedly told a young and worshipful Ben Crenshaw that the key to hitting a low running shot was to hit it "on the second groove." More than once, to throw pursuers off his track, he gave interviewers an erroneous birth year and didn't bother correcting the impression that Fort Worth was his actual hometown. "As long as I knew him," says Mike Souchak, "Ben never felt comfortable talking about himself, what he'd accomplished, or where he'd come from. Whether it was modesty or embarrassment, I don't know. But it was like the past, in many ways, simply didn't exist. He was not going to explain himself to anybody—or if so, maybe only Valerie. Maybe she knew his real secrets."

For all the absurdity of *Life* trying to reduce Hogan's incomparable swing to a master formula, on the other hand, Ben had a new dream to finance and pragmatically didn't reject the magazine's offer of ten grand to eventually "reveal" all about his secret at some future date. Most of Ben's contemporaries found the media fandango surrounding his alleged secret laughable, ribbing Ben to his face (and grumbling behind his back) about taking the editors of *Life* for an expensive joy ride. As biographer Sampson and others have pointed out, however, something serious and lasting did evolve from the episode—in the form of the most influential swing instruction book in history.

When a new Time-Life publication called *Sports Illustrated* borrowed drawings from the original *Life* article without Hogan's written permission, Ben personally phoned *Life* and threatened to sue the magazine for a breach of contract. According to one insider, the only thing that mollified Ben was another compensation fee of ten grand and a written apology for the oversight. Somewhere in the course of their negotiations, perhaps coming from Time-Life founder Henry Luce himself, the initial suggestion to "update" Hogan's best-selling instruction book, *Power Golf*, grew into the idea to pay Ben an additional $30,000 for an entirely new kind of instruction book based directly on a new series of instruction pieces yet to be written.

To complete the transaction, Luce, a wealthy publisher of periodicals, purchased Hogan's former book publisher, A. S. Barnes and Company, and reportedly encouraged editors for both *Life* and *Sports Illustrated* to subsequently compete for the rights to serialize the new project in future issues. When *Sports Illustrated* won out, Hogan's new Tamarisk lunch companion Herbert Warren Wind was selected to provide the words for the new serialized instruction series. "Ben and I had always been on fairly friendly terms," Wind says. "Especially after our afternoon together in the desert in early 1953. But I must admit feeling a little, well, nervous about the project we were undertaking. I knew he was a perfectionist and could be extremely difficult if he had a mind to be. But having said that, he turned out to be simply delightful to work with—keen, friendly, and full of helpful insights."

In June 1956, Wind and medical illustrator Anthony Ravielli flew to Fort Worth and met with Hogan in his newly refurbished equipment company's office on West Pafford. "There was a very fine chemistry between the three of us, particularly between Ben and Tony," Wind remembers, "and a mutual respect that made our jobs so much easier." For several days, Wind and Ravielli interviewed and photographed Hogan at Colonial and talked about the physics of the golf swing. They returned the following autumn to show him Ravielli's detailed steel ink pen drawings, employing an "eyelash" technique found in the better illustrated medical texts, and Wind's proposed outline for the book, as well as some rudimentary writing on Ben's swing principles—more or less the same five swing ideas he'd mentioned to John Derr at Carnoustie. As Wind recalls, Hogan made only a few basic revisions and expressed pleasure at Ravielli's drawings of his hands and body at work. Between the three of them, a title was finally settled upon: *Five Lessons: The Modern Fundamentals of Golf.*

As Ben told Marvin Leonard and others, he trusted Wind to translate the fundamentals of a golf swing that had grown to nearly mythic proportions to the printed page primarily because of Wind's reputation as a thorough journalist who wrote with care and a clear understanding of the game rather than a sensational edge.

"We worked exceedingly fast on the project, a series of months really," Wind amplifies, "and I was struck not only once again by the mental thoroughness of Ben, his grasp of a wide variety of subjects from science to current events, but his great enthusiasm for getting it down as accurately as possible. I remember quite vividly him saying he believed this book, if we produced it properly, would help people not only understand the proper mechanics of the golf swing but maybe also better understand how he had accomplished so much. Though he refused to come out and say it, I believe he was very proud of what he had been able to accomplish in golf." Wind adds, "More than once he commented to me that this book and his golf equipment company were simply his way of sharing that success with people."

When the first serialization of the project appeared in the pages of *Sports Illustrated* in March 1957, Wind reportedly reached Hogan at Seminole for his reaction. "I haven't really seen it yet, Herb," Ben told him. "I admit I wasn't prepared to see the members of the club here on the practice tee, holding up the magazine."

Whatever else was true, the disciples of Ben Hogan now had a bible upon which to build their golf swings, a master plan to emulate and refine and somehow make their own through tireless application, and critics who found the book to be either too detailed for the average Joe to comprehend or deathly dull thanks to its somewhat plodding straightforward style clearly didn't understand the unique psychic connection Hogan enjoyed with his ardent fans.

True believers understood what Hogan meant when he said, "All that is really required to play good golf is to execute properly a relatively small number of true fundamental movements."

The clear message was:

"I dug it out of the dirt, friend. So can you."

FOR THE THIRD round of the '54 Masters, Hogan wasn't pleased to discover himself paired with the tournament's unlikely new star, the delightfully homespun lumber salesman Billy Joe Patton, and even less happy when the friendly upstart outdrove him over the opening three holes.

The Hawk turned even more glacial when some of Billy Joe's possum-hunting buddies from the Carolina high country playfully called out as Hogan and Patton strode past them: "Hey, Billy Joe, who's that *little* guy in the funny white cap?"

The comments probably weren't malicious, aimed more at keeping their unlikely Lochinvar loose and free-swinging than at insulting the game's only Greek god. But they clearly reminded Ben of the summit he'd reached and the physical decline that was already setting in. The sum effect was to briefly summon forth the Hawk of old. On the back nine, Ben hit the heart of every fairway and green while Billy Joe's driving was long and wild off the tee, often in and out of the pine trees. The engaging amateur made several miraculous up-and-downs, however, and after yet another amazing escape, several fans heard Hogan mutter through his clenched teeth, as he started for the next tee, "I can't *stand* this."

Nevertheless, he shot 69 to Billy Joe's 75 to take a five-stroke lead over the colorful amateur, and Sam Snead suddenly breathed new life into his own hopes by marking a 70 on the card to also lead Patton by two. "Most assumed that was it for Billy Joe," says the tournament's other prominent amateur, Bill Campbell. "The feeling was that he'd been fun to watch and root for, but now it was time for proven champions to settle the matter."

As Ben walked down the 3rd fairway of his final round, however, a thunderous roar echoed from the tranquil pines ahead at 6. Hogan spotted a wire service reporter who held up one finger and explained, "Patton. An ace at 6."

Hogan grimaced. Then, as he waited to tee off at 6, another mighty roar erupted from the grove of trees obscuring the 8th green. Another glance and inquiry. Patton had made birdie 4.

After a fine drive on 7, a third roar filtered down from up the hill at 9. Billy Joe had birdied that hole too. The unknown country boy was back in harness and apparently plowing up Augusta National. He and Hogan were now dead even and leading the tournament.

As Ben drove off 10, Billy Joe hammered his tee ball at 13—a poor slice that wound up under a pine tree well back of where most players would normally consider having a go at the short but lethal par-5 green sitting above the rocky waters of Rae's Creek.

"But Billy Joe was an amateur," points out Augusta historian Charlie Price, "and he knew such circumstances arise maybe once in an amateur's lifetime, not every spring." Amid rebel yells and glandular whoops of "Go for it, Billy Joe!" Patton reasoned, not incorrectly, that he hadn't gotten that far in Bobby Jones's sacred invitational by playing it safe. So he drew out a three-wood and hesitated only a moment before drilling his second shot into the creek, pin-high to the hole. To his gallery's horrified fascination, he removed his spikes and waded barefoot into the water to hit his ball out, then suffered second thoughts and picked up his ball and waded out, dropping his ball behind the hazard. Before putting his shoes back on, barefoot as a September lad, he pitched his recovery shot into the shoulder of the green and watched his ball bounce backward into the brook.

The smile vanished from his handsome features for the first time that week. Patton finished the hole with a devastating double bogey 7. (A fascinating footnote: Thirty years later, Ben Crenshaw, leading the 1984 tournament, came to the same spot on the 13th, and faced an identical tantalizing choice—to go for the green or cautiously lay up. Crenshaw initially pulled out his three-wood and made up his mind to go for the green. But being a student of history, he was well aware of what had happened to Billy Joe Patton from the same spot. As he hesitated, glancing around the gallery for his father, Ben later said, he thought he saw a shaft of Georgia sunlight fall on a familiar face in the crowd, one Billy Joe Patton. He put back his fairway wood, laid up, and won the Masters that year.)

Meanwhile, behind Billy Joe's debacle, at 11, the hole where Ben always intentionally aimed right of the green to avoid putting a ball in the water, the same man who once said he didn't mind mis-hitting a shot but absolutely detested missing one *before* he hit it, made one of the most costly mental errors of his career. Unaware of Billy Joe's misadventure ahead at 13, and believing he needed to make up ground, Ben violated his own cardinal rule at 11 and fired a three-iron approach directly at a flag tucked dangerously down front and left on the slick bank above the still black waters, pulling the shot ever so slightly. His ball dropped twenty feet shy of the pin into the drink. The gallery groaned and remained deathly silent as Ben took the penalty drop and made six.

Up ahead, still reeling from his mistake at 13, Billy Joe took a costly bogey

6 on 15 just as the gallery up the hill at 18 was giving Sam Snead a rousing ovation. The Slammer had finished with 289 and now had sole possession of the lead in the clubhouse. An hour later, Hogan limped home with 75 to tie him, having blown a three-shot lead over Snead in the space of ninety minutes, shades of Masters past, a collapse that would chew at him like an ulcer for years.

As for Augusta's unlikely leading headline-grabber that week ("A new kind of hero was born," Charlie Price says, "a give-'em-hell amateur"), Billy Joe Patton finished a stroke behind the two titans of golf and smiled as if he still heard the angels singing. On the way out of Magnolia Lane, he paused for photographs and signed little kids' autograph books like there was no tomorrow.

The tournament itself was the real winner that week. Because of Patton's brilliant play and the excitement it generated, the Masters (which was two years shy of its first live television coverage) received more press coverage than at any time since Jones had competed, and the outcome simply reinforced the growing belief among golf's cognoscenti that the Masters always brought out the best in pro and amateur alike. "As a result, the Masters tournament," says Price, "now had tradition, despite its lack of age."

The next day's play-off was a golf junkie's dream come true, the world's top two players going head to head with the intimacy of a match-play club final. As it played out, both Sam and Ben played steady if somewhat uninspiring golf through twelve holes, but then Sam birdied 13 and Ben, showing the strain of yet another overtime, three-putted for bogey from inside twenty feet on 16.

It was essentially over at that point, despite Sam's untidy bogey at 18, which left him only a stroke better than Hogan—but that was all it took to earn a third green jacket. Hogan's putting stroke was once again the culprit, and the tale lay in the numbers. During their match, Ben reached every green in regulation while Sam hit only fourteen greens. But Hogan needed thirty-six putts to Snead's thirty-three, and there was the difference between winning and losing a tenth major.

"It's nice of you to let me have another one," Sam quipped pleasantly to Ben at the presentation ceremony, then narrowed an eye playfully and remarked, "Say, Ben, I thought someone said you were going to retire. Did you forget?"

"Only how to putt, Sam," Hogan, by at least one account, deadpanned.

"When you beat that guy," Snead remarked to a wire reporter as Hogan strode away, "brother, you've *done* something."

Behind the scenes of the most memorable Masters in years, the Golf Writers Association of America presented a new award called the Ben Hogan Award, honoring an individual who continued to be active in the game despite a physical handicap or serious illness. The first winner was Hogan's close friend Babe Didrikson Zaharias, who had recently battled ovarian cancer and was fighting her way back to form. Later that same summer, in fact, she would capture the Women's U.S. Open at Salem Country Club by the runaway margin of twelve strokes, one of the most dominant performances in the history of the game. That turned out to be Babe's last hurrah, though. A year later, doctors in Texas diagnosed another inoperable tumor and gave her six months to live. While spending time with friends in Fort Worth that final Christmas, growing weaker by the day, Babe rallied her strength and dined at Colonial with Ben and Valerie and several others. The next day, her devoted husband George Zaharias brought her back to the club, dressed in pajamas and a robe, and carried her in his arms to the nearest putting green, where she got down and laid both palms flat on the grass, smiling peacefully. Six months later, her doctors severed her spinal cord to relieve her pain, and in September 1956, the first Ben Hogan Award honoree, golf's great Babe, passed away.

THE FIRST SETS of Ben Hogan irons came off the production line at the West Pafford Street plant about the time Ben was defending his title at the 1954 Colonial. He opened with rounds of 69 and 71 and suddenly withdrew, explaining that he'd pulled a muscle in his left knee. That may well have been true, but the larger aggravation was unexpected developments at the Ben Hogan Company, where the first sets of clubs coming off the line didn't please the boss. The traditional soft, forged blade heads—designed and shaped personally by Hogan and his clubmaker George De Julio—were essentially fine, beautiful examples of traditional clubmaking at its finest. But the borings, the holes drilled to insert the club shafts, were terribly inconsistent. "Some of them looked absolutely awful," remembers Ronnie McGraw, a local club pro who managed to get his hands on one of the few first sets that escaped the building; McGraw later went to work for Hogan as a clubmaker. "Some of the holes looked as if they'd been drilled by people who had no idea what they were doing."

Ben promptly ordered production halted until he could hire and train better assembly workers, no small problem since the buzz was strong and his new Hogan sales staff was already accepting orders for the premium-priced irons and a few dozen sets were already trundling out the door to the more respected club pros around the country. While Hogan wrestled with his production dilemma, chief investor Pollard Simons calculated a potential loss of $150,000 in revenue and suddenly got cold feet. He asked for a meeting with Ben; the pair went behind closed doors at West Pafford Street and, a little while later, agreed to part ways. Both men described the split as "amicable," and Simons told friends it was one of the saddest days of his life.

Hogan went straight downtown to the Fort Worth National Bank and borrowed a reported $450,000, using his name and personal fortune to guarantee the note. A short while later, Marvin Leonard put together a small group of investors that included George Coleman, Bing Crosby, San Francisco auto dealer Eddie Lowery, New York Yankees owner Dan Topping, and Wall Street broker Paul Shields and cleared Ben's name off the loan, putting the company financially back on track.

What happened to the scuttled irons? One bit of fanciful Hogan folklore holds that the Boss ordered them buried in an unmarked grave in a field directly behind the plant, another that he had the forged heads melted down and sold for scrap to Cadillac Motor Company. When a young municipal pro from rural Iowa named Jack Fleck showed up at the plant before the start of play in the Colonial NIT in the late spring of 1955, shortly after the new and improved Hogan irons were coming off the line, hoping to get his hands on one of the first production sets available, he claims to have seen dozens of sets of the rejects sitting in old oil drums, being regripped and prepared for shipment to Japan for use at driving ranges. It's possible some of the better defects were indeed sent abroad, though most of the improperly drilled clubs, according to several longtime company employees, were dispatched to a local foundry where they were chopped up and melted down. A few sets sat gathering dust in a storage bin over the company men's rest room near the grinding shop in the factory, others say, for decades.

THE NATIONAL OPEN that summer was on the Lower Course at Baltusrol, the fabulous old Tillinghast layout in suburban New Jersey, a landmark occasion due to several related developments in the rapid growth of the game. For the first time ever, the National Open would be broadcast live to a nationwide television audience by NBC-TV, producing un-heard-of revenues for the golf establishment and its civic sponsors alike, a projected windfall that occasioned a steep escalation of tournament prize monies in general and a gold rush of promising college-boy talent into a game where graying journeymen like Sarazen, Snead, and Hogan had always ruled. Furthermore, ambitious TV execs promised it would only be a matter of years before golf would be broadcast and seen in "living color," a moment that would instantly make the black-and-white photos and grainy newsreels of the recent past—not to mention stars like Hogan and Snead themselves—seem like postcards from another era. In 1958, just four years down the pike, perfectly timed to coincide with Arnold Palmer's first major win and the social frenzy that particular edition of the Masters unleashed, the first commercial tournament sponsors— auto manufacturers, insurance firms, toothpaste makers, and so on—would also appear, replacing civic organizations and heralding a sea change in the way tournaments would be promoted and conducted in the future. Many of these newcomers borrowed more from the management style of George S. May than Clifford Roberts, who warned in the early 1960s that the only thing that could damage his beloved Masters—and professional golf in general— was the influence of "too much money" flowing through the game, a view Ben Hogan passionately shared with Augusta's majordomo.

With these and other changes anticipated, for the first time ever at Baltusrol spectators were no longer free to roam at will over the golf course. In an agreement worked out among Tour officials, the USGA, and television moguls who didn't want some big-headed palooka standing between Ben Hogan's winning putt and ten million television viewers, it was decided that fairways and greens would be roped off even more than usual, keeping galleries safely on predetermined corridors through the rough. Even though several notable players complained about this policy change, insisting that golf was a game meant to be viewed from the player's own perspective, it quickly became clear that TV money talked louder than tradition.

As if to underscore these sea changes, that same summer at the Country Club of Detroit in Grosse Point Farms, Wake Forest dropout and former coastguardsman Arnie Palmer whipped jet-set Seminole member Bob Sweeny—one of the few men Hogan genuinely feared playing for dough—to capture the United States Amateur Championship. Within a year, warm and magnetic Palmer, a go-for-broke style of player whose approach to the game couldn't have been more unlike Hogan's, would win the Canadian Open and begin to generate unprecedented popular interest in the game.

With his mind on other things, not too surprisingly, Hogan was never really a factor at Baltusrol. Though he lay only a stroke behind leader Ed Furgol after thirty-six holes, Ben putted miserably and shot 76 in the morning round of

Open Saturday and wilted under a blanket of thick moist Atlantic heat, failing to mount any kind of rally in the afternoon. His 289 summary was merely good enough for a tie for sixth place, five strokes behind Furgol, a man whose personal story rivaled Ben's for tenacity of spirit and will to overcome adversity.

As a child, Furgol had suffered a broken arm that was improperly set, a mistake that left him with a permanently bent and rigid arm that was useless to golf. Rather than abandon his favorite sport, though, he developed an oversized left-hand grip for his golf clubs, a short but powerful golf swing that sent the ball flying a mile, and a fabulous short-game touch. Following a distinguished amateur playing career, Furgol had his finest year as a pro in 1954, when he won the Open at Baltusrol and was named PGA Player of the Year.

The next year he proved these achievements were no fluke by taking both the team and individual honors at the Canada Cup while teamed with Chick Harbert. Not long after he won the National Open, however, and not unlike the legendary little man he replaced as Player of the Year in 1954, Furgol grew weary of the transient glamour of the pro Tour life and retired to the more settled life of a club pro.

AFTER BALTUSROL, Ben admitted to Valerie and Sarah and Gordon Harriman that he wasn't certain he had many—maybe any—National Opens left in him.

In a matter of weeks, he would be forty-two. His legs ached more than ever, especially around the knees, and the blurriness in his left eye was only deepening his gloom with the putter. If nothing else, National Opens required stout legs and an unhesitating putter stroke, and Ben could count on neither anymore when the game was on.

Aside from significant physical challenges, Hogan's putting woes—his game's only visible flaw to most astute observers—revealed a growing inability to "relax" over the ball and make the kind of smooth and confident transfer of the putting stroke that had won him sixty-seven Tour events and nine major championships. It was about this time that the Hawk, an avid reader of scientific data, began experimenting with mild tranquilizers and even consulted with an expert on hypnosis, hoping to beat back the advance of the Blind Stares.

He would certainly need to find a way to relax and once again perform at his peak if he intended to capture an unprecedented fifth National Open in 1955. Given his steadily shrinking tournament schedule and rapidly growing involvement in making what he liked to call "the Stradivarius of golf clubs," most of Ben's friends correctly deduced that, aside from the ritual practice and process of constant refinement he found so soothing and necessary for emotional well-being, the prospect of leaving the game with an elusive fifth National Open in his grasp, something no mortal had ever been able to achieve in golf, was his sole reason for submitting to another Open ordeal.

An unprecedented fifth would leave no room in anyone's mind for discussion about who rightfully stood atop golf's Mount Olympus.

Complicating matters in 1955, though, was the USGA's selection of an entirely unknown venue for the national championship, the Lakeside Course at San Francisco's Olympic Club, a place named for the faraway home of the gods themselves. If Baltusrol's ten national championships made it one of the game's most venerated layouts, the Olympic Club, near but not in sight of the Pacific Ocean, winding pleasantly through heavily wooded stands of pine, cedar, and eucalyptus trees that stood as much as one hundred feet high and narrowed fairway corridors to sixty yards in places, was a largely unknown factor and a place with no revealing and helpful golf history to rely upon.

When Olympic was opened in 1921, the 6,400-yard gem was believed to be an adequate test of golf for just about anyone, but after witnessing the Brinks job Hogan did on Riviera in the summer of 1948, a committee of worried Olympic members contracted with Robert Trent Jones to make major alterations over the year leading to the '55 Open. Among other things, Jones nudged the course back several hundred yards, tightened almost every driving line and approach, added new strategic bunkering and dangerous mounding to the layout's easier holes, and permitted rough to creep into unheard-of places. Based on early reviews of his revisions, the common opinion was that Olympic was now only slightly less difficult than Oakland Hills four years before and a walking nightmare for the player who couldn't hit fairways. In other words, it was Ben Hogan's kind of place.

Though the nearby ocean was unseen, blocked by the estimated 45,000 eucalyptus, pine, and cypress trees planted on the formerly barren dunes that lay between Lake Merced and the Pacific, prevailing breezes produced strange and eerie sound effects on the Lakeside Course—some described it as a ghostly moaning—and the layout was often cloaked in layers of mist and fog, which constantly "watered" the fairways and made the rough, a unique variety of rye grass (with single blades measuring three-eighths of an inch in width) imported from Italy thirty-three years before, impenetrably dense in spots. It was a bunchy, grabby kind of rough, heretofore unseen in Open competitions.

Ben as usual arrived two weeks early and in the course of his strategic preparations on the course decided to alter his game to better fit Olympic's quirks, especially the unknown rough. Among other adjustments, though only a handful of people realized what he was doing at the time, he flattened his swing angle and shortened his backswing significantly, sacrificing distance for greater accuracy, and simultaneously adopted an even more defensive putting posture, swing changes his collaborator Herb Wind immediately noticed in his early practice rounds and speculated upon to his readers. "The old sense of attack was missing in his putting. He seldom opened up with his full cut, and when he did he had trouble getting through on the shot. He was swinging faster too, sort of punching into the short shots with his forearms forcing the blow."

Many decided these changes, particularly the absence of his signature sweeping, upright follow-through, were telltale signs of Hogan's suddenly declining shotmaking skills, aging legs, and uncooperative muscles. "In our ignorance," admitted the fine sportswriter Al Laney afterward, "we thought Ben had adjusted his game to his own physical limitations and that he was at last playing with impaired weapons. We ought to have known better, to understand that he was adjusting to the new conditions just as he had at Carnoustie."

Two days before the start of play in the fifty-fifth National Open, with his plan of attack set and the dangerous course's topography and landmarks fully committed to memory, Hogan chose not to play any more practice rounds at the Lakeside Course. Instead, he and Seminole partner Claude Harmon chose to slip over to the tamer Ocean Course to practice a variety of specialty shots they believed they would need come tournament time.

By Open standards, the field was a superb one and included the usual betting favorites Snead, Hogan, and Middlecoff, the heroic reigning Open champ Furgol, a smattering of wily and still-dangerous veterans like Lawson Little and Lew Worsham, a rare appearance by Byron Nelson, a host of established young stars like Burke, Bolt, and Boros—the "killer bees," one columnist labeled them—plus rising Australian star Peter Thomson (now playing the American tour full-time) and a number of promising newcomers like local San Francisco star Bobby Rosburg and his Palo Alto houseguest for the week (former National Amateur champ and new papa) Gene Littler, former collegiate standouts Dow Finsterwald and Mike Souchak, the renowned amateurs Stranahan and Ward, and even a couple of hungry gunslingers from Ben's own backyard, Fort Worth's Ernie Vossler and Dallas pro Shelley Mayfield. Lloyd Mangrum was a last-minute scratch due to a separated rib, but he assured everyone he would stick around Olympic to watch the proceedings. He was particularly interested in seeing how Snead and Hogan handled such an unknown and unforgiving track.

With all of this accumulated firepower, despite Trent Jones's ingeniously wicked alterations, most reporters were surprised when only one man managed to break par 70 in the tournament's opening round—Ben's delightfully volcanic pal Tommy ("I don't throw my clubs much farther than the average guy") Bolt, who shot a sizzling three under 67 and triggered the annual outcry from the field that the USGA was once again aiming to embarrass the world's best players. Among the tournament's more memorable opening disasters, after missing a trio of short putts and barking at photographers for ruining his concentration, perpetual Open victim Sam Snead, alternately whistling and baring his teeth, jerked out the heavy lumber and quit trying to finesse Olympic's frightfully narrow corridors. He sprayed monstrous tee shots all along the course's back nine and tromped from one calf-deep patch of rough to another, muttering to himself about never playing in "another goddamned Open," and finished opening day with a dismal 79, one behind his amiable young playing partner Bobby Rosburg. Before any of the reporters could reach Sam for what was certain to be a colorful assessment of the course, the seething Virginian set off across the concrete parking lot still wearing his playing spikes, clattering for the safe haven of the nearest hotel watering hole.

If misery indeed loves company, it was scant consolation to the Slammer that out of 162 hopefuls who began the day in Olympic's sea mist, only 62 players managed to make their way around the course in eighty blows or less. Former Open champs Middlecoff, Furgol, and Boros all placed 76s on their cards, Byron and Lew Worsham embarrassing 77s. Lawson Little's 81 prompted him to say Olympic would be his last Open. Massaging his temple in the press tent following his awful opening 76, defending champ Furgol politely retracted his earlier "foolish" comments about Olympic "seeming much easier" than Baltusrol and pointedly noted that any player who got off to the kind of miserable start he did—hooking his spoon into an unplayable lie on the first drive, spending much of his early round hacking out of the eight-inch rough—was going to have a difficult three days at the fifty-fifth National Open.

Playing with an unhurried deliberation that for anyone else would have threatened to bring on a sanction for slow play—most players now accepted the fact that the USGA cut Ben slack simply to have golf's largest gate attraction in the field—Hogan required thirty-three putts to get home with a respectable 72, leaving him one behind his friend Burke and one ahead of his friend Souchak. Even with his altered swing, Ben's ball-striking had been superior, but he left several short putts hanging on the lips of half a dozen cups. "I haven't figured out whether these greens are slow or fast," he admitted after his first round, showing only a little fatigue. "Maybe I'll know more after tomorrow."

By then, the tournament's halfway mark, a surprising score of 155 was sufficient to qualify for the Open's rugged Saturday finish, one of the highest midpoint totals in decades. "This place isn't a golf course," said Snead, attempting to make light of his own near-disaster after fashioning a brilliant comeback 69 in round two. "It's really just a pretty graveyard by the sea."

As the fog rolled in off the Pacific that Saturday morning, Hogan's 72–73 start had positioned him just one stroke behind Bolt and Harvie Ward (who lived across the street from the club and captured the United States Amateur championship later that summer). Tied with Ben was perennial Open threat Julius Boros and a pair of unknown tourists, twenty-five-year-old Augusta (Georgia) native Walker Inman and his traveling partner, an angular, almost Lincoln-esque muni pro from Davenport, Iowa, called Jack Fleck, the very same young man who had showed up a year before at the nascent Ben Hogan Company looking for a set of Hogan clubs he could call his own.

Fleck's journey to the National Open was probably the most improbable in the field. The quiet, dignified, thirty-three-year-old former caddie had been playing the Tour full-time only since January of that year, having promised his wife, Lynn, that if he didn't make a successful go on the pro circuit in 1955, he would abandon his dream of big-time tournament golf and return to Iowa and settle down to run the local municipal golf course. One of the club affiliations Fleck listed on his résumé upon registering for the tournament was a driving range. And unlike almost every professional in the field, Fleck, whose best finish that season was an invisible tenth place at Baton Rouge, had no official equipment sponsor or commercial endorsement deal of any sort.

Only the clubs he was using were special, a gift of the man who made them—one William Ben Hogan. The only other set in play that week at Olympic belonged to Hogan himself.

The opening script of Olympic's otherworldly drama, in fact, may really have begun back in the late winter of the Tour season. Fleck had written to his hero Hogan, wondering if he could somehow obtain a set of the new Ben Hogan clubs he'd recently heard pro Skip Alexander raving about down in Florida. Ben Hogan Company general manager Charley Barnett wrote Fleck back, inviting him to send along his equipment specs and drop by the Fort Worth factory if and when he earned an invitation to the Colonial NIT in May.

Every year, Colonial's tournament committee extended a special invitation to a pair of promising professionals deemed by former Colonial champions to have a reasonable shot at finally breaking through on tour. It was a tournament policy Ben had a direct hand in shaping, no doubt recalling his own years of struggle when an invitation to a quality event like Colonial would have meant the world to his confidence.

Though Fleck had never met his hero face to face, Jack was convinced beyond a shadow of a doubt that the "surprising" Colonial invitation that found its way to Davenport was a direct result of his hero's influence. The other special invitation that year went to tour newcomer Dow Finsterwald.

On the Monday morning of Colonial week, Fleck turned up at the Ben Hogan Company on West Pafford Street to pay his respects, say thank you, and check on the progress of his new clubs with Charley Barnett. Barnett hadn't reported to work yet that morning, but the Boss, as usual, had.

"Mr. Hogan came out and greeted me very warmly," Fleck remembers. "He seemed to take a great deal of interest in my progress, and I think he appreciated the fact that, like him, I'd had a long tough road to the Tour but I hadn't yet given up. Hogan respected that. We didn't talk long, but he let me know that he was very happy for me to be playing his new clubs—which, incidentally, he refused to accept a penny for. I would gladly have paid for them, but he wouldn't take anything. I left there with a full set of irons and woods, and on top of the world. He promised to get a wedge and sand club to me as soon as possible." Fleck made no particular impression with his shotmaking or scoring at the Colonial, finishing far back of the leaders, but says he knew even then that those clubs, and the modest confidence Ben expressed in him, would transform both his game and his life.

Unlike his hero, who billeted downtown at the plush Saint Francis Hotel for the two weeks he was in the Bay Area for the U.S. Open, Fleck stayed at the modest El Camino Real Motel in blue-collar Daly City with his portable record player and his beloved Mario Lanza records. Fleck was something of a health enthusiast in the style of Frank Stranahan, but he also had his own Hogan-esque rituals of tournament preparation. To begin with, he always rose early to stretch and exercise and often listened to Mario Lanza sing while he was shaving. He also tried to pray every morning of his life.

The product of a fairly strict Presbyterian upbringing, two things happened early on during Open week that told Jack, he says, that it wasn't going to be any ordinary week. "To begin with, I was at my Olympic locker several days before the start of things when Hogan suddenly comes in all by himself. 'F' and 'H' were fairly close to each other, see, and Ben had something special with him—my new wedges. He couldn't have been friendlier or more encouraging to my hopes, wishing me the best of luck with them. It was almost like he knew something unusual was going to happen. What a boost of confidence *that* was.

"Then, on Tuesday before start of play, an older man I knew who'd been following me around some during the practice rounds pulled me aside and asked me a strange question. 'Jack,' he said, 'do you ever pray to win a golf tournament?' 'Of course not,' I told him. 'That just wouldn't be the right thing to do. God doesn't care who wins or loses a golf tournament.' Well, he thought about it a little and came back to me later and said, 'Jack, here's what I think you ought to do. I want you simply to pray for the power and strength to compete, to play the best you can possibly play. That way, win or lose, you'll have done your best.' I thought about it and told him I thought I could do that."

So Fleck got on his knees and prayed. But he also practiced like a man about to meet his maker on the 1st tee.

In advance of the tournament, he knocked out forty-four practice holes a day, two full eighteen-hole loops plus eight more holes that left him standing beside Olympic's magestic white clubhouse. From Hogan he'd picked up the habit of memorizing every feature of a hole's landscape, but he took his own preparations one step further by meticulously pacing off distances and compiling yardage books for later reference. "I used to tell people later that my memory just wasn't as good as Ben's," Fleck jokes. Many of his contemporaries point out that the lanky Iowan was among the first in tournament play to use a homemade yardage book, which Jack Nicklaus often gets credit for introducing to competitive play and which eventually became standard practice on Tour. A few days before Olympic's National Open got under way, in any event, Fleck felt so confident in how he was playing with his new Hogan clubs that he wrote a letter to the editor of his hometown newspaper boldly predicting the Open's top ten finishers. Hogan was naturally listed as one of Jack's favorites to win. He also listed his own name as a "sleeper" choice to surprise the field and capture the National Open of 1955.

A sympathetic Davenport editor might not have doubled over at such an outrageous suggestion, but most of the seasoned reporters assembled at Olympic would have. The field, after all, was top-heavy with several former Open champions and a host of fearless flatbellies, maybe the best ever from top to bottom. Against this vast array of talent, many newsmen even wondered how a guy who had no amateur career to speak of and had never come close to winning a professional golf tournament of any significance—a player who reportedly couldn't even break 80 during any of his practice rounds—even managed to sneak into the field. "Fleck," commented one national columnist when he was asked to handicap the players individually, "sounds a lot like 'fluke' to me."

Such hard handicapping makes for entertaining copy, but the bit about Fleck's practice rounds was in fact erroneous. Like Hogan, Fleck never bothered keeping score during his Olympic preparations, usually hit multiple balls on every hole, and seldom had any firm idea what he might have scored. "A few of the Open reporters demanded to know what kind of scores I'd been shooting in practice," he explains, "and I casually replied something like, 'Oh, I don't know. For all I know it could be 80 or 85.' That's why some of them wrote that I never broke 80. It wasn't true. I knew my ball-striking had suddenly reached a new level, and so did anybody who watched me practice that week."

According to the statistics that course doctor Robert Trent Jones began compiling beneath his famous bucket hat at the start of play, the average driving distance off the tee during the opening round was just 216 yards, which meant players were having to strike long and accurate low irons to the greens, which looked no bigger than billiard tables, something Ben Hogan still did better than almost anybody in the business.

AS THE IMPRESSIVE field faltered around him, plodding Ben's Saturday morning round was a model of conservative play and productive consistency. He fashioned another 72 and started the final loop one stroke ahead of the field. Only Sam Snead, Bobby Rosburg, and the equally unheard-of Bud Holscher got through Olympic's punishing rough with a better score on Open Saturday morning. The invisible man Fleck, who looked as if his clothes came from Ben's closet, missed several key putts with his cherished Bull's-Eye putter and slipped back several notches to 75.

By the lunch break, Fleck remembers, the buzz among reporters and even other players was that Hogan was on the threshold of making history again. No one played better with a lead, after all, or more commandingly when it counted most, than Hogan. His chances appeared undeniable.

But Fleck says he wasn't worried because that morning an angel spoke to him in the bathroom mirror.

"I was shaving, and suddenly a voice came out of the glass, clear as a bell. It said, 'Jack, you are going to win the Open.' At first I thought I'd imagined it, or maybe somebody was in the room with me. I looked around, then went back to shaving. By golly, if it didn't come a second time—straight out of the mirror. Clear as day. 'Jack, you are going to win the Open!' I had goose bumps on me, as if electricity was going through my body."

As it happened, this was the second "visitation" of sorts for Fleck at Olympic. During his second round of play in the biggest tournament of his life, Fleck, a spotty putter at best, had suddenly felt "a very good feeling" in his hands, which helped him drain several key putts for his day's low round of 69—a sparkling score largely ignored by the press or simply dismissed out of hand as a fluke that sounded like Fleck.

Had an angel visited Jack in the bathroom of the El Camino Real Motel to let him know something truly extraordinary was going to happen that Saturday at Olympic? Fleck thought so—and still does.

"I didn't talk about this for a long time after it all happened," he explains. "It sounds so crazy, people hearing voices from a mirror and so forth. But I know what I heard, and given how I'd been praying that week, I knew it was the Lord speaking to me, telling me to have faith in myself and everything would work out fine. I didn't mention it to a soul, however, and actually tried to put the voice out of my head once I got to the golf course."

That Saturday morning Fleck was paired with Gene Littler, the wry little Californian whose cultured buttermilk swing matched Snead's and who would soon start mopping up championships on the Tour; Jack and Gene were in the next-to-last group out at midmorning, almost two hours behind Hogan and his partner Charlie Harris, teeing off with only a handful of their friends from back home following. One of the helpful presences following Jack was his childhood friend from Davenport, a fine amateur player and dentist named Paul Barton. As a youngster, Fleck had caddied for Dr. Barton. "He was like a father to me, a very calming presence," Fleck says.

Jack's untidy third-round 75, though, gave him a fifty-four-hole total of 220 that left him three behind Hogan, two behind the resurgent Snead and Boros, and one behind Rosburg and Bolt. At this late juncture in the game, as with Billy Joe Patton at Augusta, most seasoned heads never gave the pleasant muni pro from Iowa another passing thought.

"Normally after a round where I slipped the way I did Saturday morning, I would have been upset with myself and blown any hope I had of coming back. This time, however, as Littler and I went off to have a little lunch, I felt entirely different. Not a bit jittery or mad. Quite calm. This was new. Hard to explain."

As Jack went off to find a tuna sandwich and glass of iced tea, Hogan was making the turn of his final round followed by his usual multitudes, a gallery that included a Stanford philosophy student named Mike Murphy, recently returned from studying in India, the handsome son of a Salinas lawyer whose father had been pals with writer John Steinbeck. Murphy had first followed Hogan at the Crosby in '46 and later been positively mesmerized by the sight of Hogan hitting practice balls in the winter dusk by the sea at Pebble Beach. He once watched Hogan for nearly six hours at Pasatiempo too.

"Watching Hogan was like watching the great teachers of the East," says Murphy. "In India, in Sanskrit, they have a word that applied perfectly to Hogan—*diksha*. Literally translated, it means 'initiation' or even 'transmission.' Anyone who ever watched Ben practice or play felt this diksha, a field of extraordinary psychic energy, a powerful presence that explains why top players and ordinary fans alike found watching him so irresistible—would just stand for *hours* without saying a word, almost as if they were in church. If you ask anyone who did this, who experienced Hogan's diksha, they'll tell you the silence surrounding him at these times was profound, holy. We in America don't produce mystics. But Hogan was close."

After tapping in his final putt at Olympic's 18th hole for a masterful final round of 70 that gave him 287 and, most on hand believed, an insurmountable lead and historic fifth Open championship, America's little guru of golf did something quite revealing. Visibly exhausted, he raised both his arms into the damp late afternoon air to try to silence the roaring gallery so his playing partner, Bob Harris, could finish.

After Hogan and Harris shook hands, Gene Sarazen, who was doing color commentary for NBC-TV, strutted forward to congratulate Hogan on winning a record fifth Open. "Ben," said the beaming Squire, "would you do everybody a favor and put up five fingers?" The symbolism momentarily escaped a weary Hogan.

He presented his ball to the USGA's Joe Dey, another totem for the association's Golf House museum, shook hands, and unthinkingly began to put up his hand when it suddenly came to him what Sarazen was getting at. Instead, he shook his head and commented, "It's not over yet, Gene."

"You got the feeling that the only person there who didn't think Ben was going to win was Ben himself," remembered Herb Wind. "That's how much excitement his four rounds generated, especially the final one."

Mike Murphy, meanwhile, bolted for the clubhouse, slipping past the badged security guard and finding his way upstairs to a quiet corner of the club lounge, where Valerie Hogan was seated alone on a couch. He sat down on the same couch, hoping to observe a reunion when the apparent champion came upstairs. She scarcely noticed him; she was in a trance of her own.

As 15,000 spectators milled around in the long shadows outside Olympic's bunting-draped clubhouse, wondering if the Open was effectively over, word spread that there was still one man left out on the golf course who had an outside chance of catching Hogan—the unknown muni pro from Iowa. The longest shot in the field. Mr. Unknown himself.

Fleck.

One pressroom sage hurriedly calculated Jack's chances of catching Hogan at 8,000-to-1. "Most of us, I regret to say, decided it was really over," says Herb Wind. "Who would have believed Fleck could do what he did?"

It was nearly 8:00 P.M. back in the East, and several wire reporters disappeared to their posts in the press tent to begin cobbling early edition leads describing Hogan's incomparable feat, his historic fifth National Open.

Back on the 14th tee, Fleck, a survivor of the Normandy invasion who once told his wife, Lynn, that tournament golf held absolutely no terror for him, felt unnaturally calm and in control of his fate. At 11, a marshal had informed him that he stood only one stroke off Hogan's 287 lead, adding, "All you have to do, Jack, is play safe and get one more birdie."

A few feet away, Gene Littler drolly commented, "He'll need a few pars too."

Fleck told himself he had worked too hard that week to "play safe" on the home stretch, and with adrenaline surging through his veins, the Iowan overclubbed and scored a costly bogey on 14, dropping him two back of the man waiting in the clubhouse locker room. Now he needed two birdies in four holes to catch Hogan.

At the turn he'd had maybe fifty people following him; by the 15th, there were 3,000. "That bogey didn't bother me. Again, I can't exactly say why, but that good feeling, that tingling from the second round, was back in my hands." He made a beautiful six-iron shot to the 15th green and smoothly sank an eight-foot putt for a deuce birdie.

In the locker room, the leader heard the muted roar from out on the course.

"Ben Hogan sat heavily on a bench," recounts Wind, and took a scotch and water from somebody's hand. It seemed certain that his 287 had clinched his fifth championship. He sipped his drink, shook his head and said slowly: "Boys, if I win it, I'll never work at this again. It's just too tough getting ready for a tournament. This one doggone near killed me. Besides, I don't think it's fair to drag Valerie around and put her through this every time." Someone asked if his leg had bothered him. "Only my knee," said Ben. "The more I walked, the more it hurt."

At that moment, an attendant burst into the silent locker room and excitedly called out, "Jack Fleck is on 16, and he needs one birdie on the last three to tie!"

Hogan calmly sipped his drink, staring at nothing. He lit a fresh cigarette and inhaled deeply, as usual slowly leaking smoke from both nostrils.

"Good for him," he breathed.

A reporter asked Hogan which hole he thought he'd won the tournament on. Hogan's head turned. He gave his questioner a cool stare.

"There's no one hole. You don't win tournaments on just *one* hole. There's seventy-two holes." He took another long drag and released the smoke slowly. "Nobody's won anything yet."

The emissary reported Fleck's par at 16.

Olympic's long uphill 17th hole, a short par-5 converted to a long par-4, had yielded only two birdie 3s that day, both of them on holed-out wedge shots. No one had reached the green in two regulation shots, but Fleck now scorched his three-wood approach to within twenty feet of the cup, prompting Lawson Little to whistle and tell a national radio audience that he'd just witnessed one of the finest clutch shots ever. At his post, NBC-TV announcer Lindsay Nelson was signing off the air, describing Ben Hogan as the probable new national champion once again.

"Fleck's parred 17! Just missed his birdie. Needs a birdie on 18 to tie!"

Hogan stood up and unzipped his trousers and hung them neatly on the locker hook.

"I've got to take a shower, boys," he declared and walked stiffly and unhurriedly toward the shower room. "There was small talk," Wind recalled, "then the group was silent until Ben returned."

Upstairs, Valerie Hogan sat perfectly still, closing her eyes for lengthy periods of time. A few moments before, the club's public address system had called out, "Telephone call for Mr. or Mrs. Hogan. Telephone call, please. . . ." But she had completely ignored whoever was calling the club to congratulate Ben on his record-breaking win.

When a steward approached her, she glanced at him and simply shook her head, refusing to accept the call. Earlier that year at Oakmont she had decided she'd had enough of major golf tournaments. The toll was simply now too high on both of them—his frail legs and her frail nerves.

"You could see the worry in her face," remembers Mike Murphy, recalling Harry Andrew's observation after Carnoustie. "She obviously wasn't overjoyed to be there."

Out on the beautifully elevated 18th tee, in the coolness of early evening, Jack the giant killer was staring at the thousands standing four deep along the final Olympic fairway. It was a stirring sight that led his gaze to the multitudes waiting on the hill below the magnificent white clubhouse, to see if the tournament's most unheralded player could pull off the most dazzling upset since Ouiment beat Vardon and Ray.

"The clouds let a few streaks of sunlight shine through," Fleck later wrote in his memoirs. "And I said to myself, 'If this isn't heaven, I don't know what is.' "

With that, Fleck calmly laced a three-wood shot into the first cut of rough, the two-inch fringe about six inches off the fairway, 150 yards from the green, on a gentle upslope of the hourglass fairway. Fleck called the fringe "long fairway," a nearly perfect spot from which to attack the flag positioned back right over the green's facing pot bunker.

Another courier dashed into the locker room, where Hogan was now unhurriedly buttoning up his John L. Ashe and Son trousers and slipping on his English-made Cordovan shoes.

"Fleck's in the rough on 18!"

Ben began patiently knotting his Italian silk necktie.

A wire service writer found the tension nearly unbearable. He casually asked Hogan if he'd used his own clubs in the tournament. "I mean, of course," he quickly added, "the ones you're now manufacturing."

"Yes," Hogan replied, without looking at his questioner.

Jackie Burke Jr. suddenly appeared a dozen yards away, banging open his locker.

"What did you do, boy?" Hogan said gruffly to him. If Ben liked you, everyone understood, he called you "boy." If he didn't, or was still making up his mind about you, you were either "fella" or simply ignored.

Burke grimaced. He'd blown to 77 that afternoon.

"No good, Ben. Drove in the rough all day."

At that moment out on the gentle upslope of Olympic's 18th fairway, the regal and slender Fleck, who even resembled his hero from certain angles, was now standing by his ball, which was sitting up nicely on the barbered fringe. It was a beautiful lie. He pulled his new Ben Hogan seven-iron from the bag.

Just then, Tommy Bolt blew into the locker room, telling someone over his shoulder, "I can't stand to watch." He spotted his buddy Hogan putting on his sports jacket and hurried over to stick a needle in him the way nobody but Thunderbolt could do.

"Hey, Benny," Bolt snarled, "you got me all fouled up down there at Fort Worth. You got me to fix that hook. Now, goddamn it, I'm slicin' the ball everywhere! I bet you did that on purpose, you son of a bitch."

Hogan only smiled. He began taking extra clubs out of his locker.

Cary Middlecoff was on his way out, hurrying away from the gathering tension. He paused long enough to extend a gracious hand to the apparent winner. "Wonderful tournament, Ben," he said softly. "Really wonderful. A damn good score."

Hogan thanked him without smiling.

Fleck struck his shot. Thirteen thousand sets of eyes squinted to follow the high spinning ball as it flew through the heavy evening air, carrying the pot bunker and landing on the front portion of the green, whereupon it bounced twice and rolled to a stop eight feet from the flag, producing a thunderous cheer from the gallery. Most of them were absolute Hogan die-hards hoping and praying Ben got his fifth. But they were also ardent golf fans who appreciated a brilliant clutch shot when they witnessed one.

Hogan suddenly dropped several clubs on the locker-room floor, picked up a head cover that came loose, and glanced around at those seated around him. "Anybody want a club cover?" he joked ruefully.

The emissary was back.

"Fleck's got eight feet to tie!"

Someone asked Hogan how many sets of golf clubs his Fort Worth factory could produce in a single day.

"It comes to 450 sets per month, Bill," Ben told him quietly, gathering up his sticks.

"Is it true that you threw away a hundred thousand clubs because they weren't perfect?"

Hogan nodded. "I've got at least $150,000 worth of clubs I won't ship," he explained quietly. He sighed and sat down on the bench again. The group around him grew perfectly still and silent, staring at the warm close air. In a moment or two, the noise from outside would tell them all they needed to know.

Jack Fleck wasted no time sizing up his putt. He took his position and stroked the ball smoothly on a bending arc directly into the hole, unleashing a wild ovation on the steep grassy slopes around him. He stood for a moment looking a little dazed, then cracked a lopsided smile.

As the gallery outside the locker room roared, one of the reporters waiting with Ben whispered with disbelief, "Damn. The kid sunk it."

Hogan's eyes fractionally dropped, according to Herb Wind, his shoulders sinking the way Valerie said they always did when the cause was lost. A play-off was the last thing on earth Hogan wanted to endure at that moment in his life. Upstairs, someone broke the news to Valerie, and she continued sitting perfectly still, looking out the window at the light Pacific fog in the treetops, like a woman in the early stages of grief.

"Son of a bitch," Ben quietly swore.

Then he lifted his head and glanced around at the somber faces around him. They looked like men attending a funeral—not unlike the stunned partisan visages that would greet Arnold Palmer at precisely the same spot eleven years later after he blew a commanding seven-stroke lead over Olympic's final nine holes and numbly wondered if he had the strength to face a play-off with Bill Casper. He did, and lost—forever identifying Olympic as a place where very peculiar things happened to front-runners and legends in the sea mist.

"I was wishing he'd either make a 2 or a 4," Ben admitted a few moments later. "I was wishing it was over—all over."

With that, he stood up, forced a smile, and motioned the locker-room attendant over. "Might as well get those things back in the locker, son. Gotta play tomorrow, looks like."

Mike Murphy was still seated beside Valerie Hogan when her husband came up to collect her. "She hadn't moved when we heard the roar that told us Fleck had made the birdie. She just sat very still. He, on the other hand, was smiling. I later heard how bitterly disappointed he was in the locker room, but I saw none of that when he came upstairs. He was beautifully dressed, the soul of graciousness, that commanding presence very much evident. If anything, he seemed a little relieved, as if he welcomed an extraordinary ending like this."

AFTER DARKNESS settled a little while later, Fleck phoned his wife, Lynn, to tell her about his unforgettable day, then went out for a private celebratory dinner with Dr. Barton and his wife. At the restaurant, cartoonist Cal Bailey presented the Iowan with an amusing character sketch that, in retrospect, was an eerie foreshadowing of things to come. The picture shows a smiling Jack Fleck clutching a sickle and a baffled-looking, flat-capped "Hogan" standing in the deep rough at Olympic's 18th hole. "Fore!! Mr. Hogan," the cartoon Fleck is saying. Was it a picture of things to come?

Back at the El Camino Real, Fleck listened to Mario Lanza sing "I'll Walk with God" one last time before turning in, got on his knees and said his prayers, then slept like a baby for nine and a half hours. In the morning, before going to the golf course, he drove to a public beach and walked along the tide line, praying for the strength to play his best against a man he admired more than anyone in golf.

"As I was walking from the parking lot to the locker room a couple hours before the play-off," Fleck recounts, "Ben suddenly appeared, carrying his shoes. We walked together to the locker room having a very pleasant conversation." A little while later, Jack went over to Hogan's locker and explained to Ben, who was seated lacing up his shoes, that he'd been driving from El Paso that winter day back in '49 when two motorcycle policemen and the ambulance bearing Hogan had passed him, racing for the hospital in El Paso.

"I did not know it was you, Ben, until I read the next morning's paper. But I wanted you to know I prayed for you along with thousands of well-wishers."

Hogan thanked him. Fleck put out his hand.

"So good luck and whatever happens out there today, Ben, you'll know what I mean."

The two shook hands. It was an odd remark, Fleck's awkward way of trying to say he sensed they were both caught up in something beyond normal events, a moment that in many ways was larger than them both. But Fleck claims he saw the same aura of spirituality surrounding Ben that Murphy and others glimpsed for an instant that week in the Pacific sea mist. He thought Hogan might even acknowledge this shared awareness.

"Thanks, Jack." A long pause, their eyes searching each other's. "Good luck to you too."

A short time later, as the two players were waiting to be announced on the 1st tee, Fleck was summoned into the pro shop for a last-minute phone call. It was Porky Oliver on the other end, an old Hogan victim. "Jack," Porky growled, "you beat the little man or I will kick your ass up to your shoulders! Good luck and good-bye!" Fleck had to smile as he walked back to the 1st tee.

Hogan later told friends he'd never seen anyone as nervous as Jack was on the first tee, a fact the Iowan proved by skulling his first two shots. He was fortunate to get his third shot on the putting surface and two-putt for a par-5.

On the par-3 3rd hole, Ben hit his tee shot to about twelve feet from the hole. Fleck buried his tee shot in the greenside bunker. His bunker shot was too strong and went over the green to its far edge. As Jack walked by the waiting Ben, he apologized for his "poor play."

"Jack, take your time," Hogan told the suddenly nervous Iowan. "Don't worry about a thing."

Fleck holed his next shot with his putter to save par. Then Ben missed his twelve-footer and got his par. According to Shelley Mayfield, Hogan later conceded that the calming remark to Fleck had been a strategic mistake because, from that point on, Fleck became even calmer and didn't miss a shot that mattered for the rest of the round.

The playoff for the fifty-fifth National Open began to get interesting at the 5th hole. Hogan put his drive in the trees and made bogey 5. Fleck put his drive in the fairway and made par to go one up.

On the 6th hole, following a poor bunker shot, hands tingling, Fleck rolled a spectacular twenty-five-footer into the cup to save par. After matching pars at 7, Hogan drained a monstrous, bending, downhill fifty-foot putt for birdie 2 on the 8th hole. Fleck coolly responded by rolling his own eight-footer into the cup for a tying deuce. Then at 9, Fleck made a fifteen-footer for birdie, and Hogan, hovering for a long moment over the putt, grazed the hole with his tying effort to go two strokes down at the turn.

Fleck ignited the trailing gallery of 5,000 by draining a similar birdie putt on 10; he was suddenly three up, putting daylight between himself and his hero.

But Ben gamely battled back on 11, blasting a bunker recovery shot to six feet and making the par while Fleck bogeyed. They reversed roles on 12, when Ben hooked his drive into the eucalyptus trees and Fleck struck one of his long "slider" shots down the right side of the fairway. Ben missed a short putt for par; Fleck made his. The margin was back to three strokes with six to go.

For the play-off, the USGA relaxed its rope policy and the gallery was permitted to traipse along well behind the players. Both men seemed entirely in their own worlds, silent and poker-faced as they walked. According to reporter Al Laney, who was trailing the players by a few yards, the unknown Iowan appeared to "be in a dream state" and playing the golf of his life, completely unfazed by his famous competition and the obvious fact that virtually no one on the premises, whether they would admit to it or not, wanted to see Hogan denied his fifth Open championship.

After matching pars at 13, Hogan finally mounted the charge most of his fans had been expecting all day. He birdied the 410-yard 14th to shave one stroke off Fleck's lead. Both men narrowly missed birdies on the par-3 15th and again matched scores on 16, the infamous double dogleg hole, with par-5s. At the long 17th hole, Olympic's most treacherous hole, Hogan reached the fringe in two swats and nearly canned his twenty-five-footer for birdie. Fleck finally made a mistake—he missed his first short putt of the day and departed the green with a bogey that left him just one stroke in the lead.

The gallery bolted ahead of them to line the final fairway and green, one of the finest short finishing holes in all of golf with its magnificent elevated tee and beautiful bull's-eye green just 350 yards away. As he launched his tee shot, Ben's foot slipped on the slightly sandy top-dressed surface of the tee, and he yanked his drive sharply to the left off the neck of his driver. His ball dived into the wet and dense rye grass about 250 yards out, disappearing from view. Gasps rippled along the fairway. This was something most had never heard of Ben Hogan doing—choking on the final tee shot of a major championship.

For those who contend there truly was something otherworldly about Fleck's upset win at the fifty-fifth Open, spookily foreshadowing Arnie's unimaginable freefall there in 1966, Ben's impossible lie in the left rough certainly underscored the metaphysical dimensions of the place, a case of life imitating Cal Bailey's sketch from the evening before.

After grimly assessing his situation, Ben motioned Fleck and the tournament officials to move back twenty yards so he could use his sand iron to advance his ball safely sideways back to the fairway and take his chances on either holing out or Fleck blowing his approach shot. As the golf world held its collective breath, the finest wedge player in history took a harsh cut and advanced his ball only a few inches before it vanished again in the cabbage.

Hogan appeared almost impassive, a grim spectator at his own funeral. He paused only a moment before making a second harder swipe, the severed grass clinging to the sharpened leading edge of his lashing wedge like hay off the end of a farmer's sickle. The ball moved a few yards closer to the fairway. His fourth effort got him back to the short grass, and his fifth swing to the rear of the steeply tilted putting surface, where, several minutes later, he sized up the forty-footer for double bogey and almost nonchalantly sent his ball running down the slope and into the heart of the cup for a meaningless six.

Fleck, meanwhile, easily made his par and stood for a moment as if he simply couldn't believe what had transpired. The voice in the mirror had been right. Sustained applause broke out, and his famous adversary limped forward to offer his firm handshake and congratulations, smiling with the same tinctured air of relief Mike Murphy had seen in the clubhouse lounge. Moments later, as news cameras snapped furiously around them, Hogan peeled off his famous flat cap and used it to playfully fan Fleck's red-hot Bull's-Eye putter.

WAS THERE, in fact, something metaphysical about Fleck's extraordinary upset of Hogan at Olympic, a place named for the home of the ancient battling gods? Or was it simply one of the statistical inevitabilities, Father Time announcing his eternal presence and a necessary changing of the guard—the way color television, say, would herald the sudden coming of Palmer and Nicklaus?

Whichever answer comes closer to the truth, many historians and game junkies list Fleck's Open play-off win as one of the biggest upsets in all of sports history. Fleck, for one, remains fully convinced that under the circumstances the level his game attained that week was nothing shy of miraculous. "I honestly feel like something deeply spiritual happened at Olympic for Ben and me both," he reflects, nearly half a century later. "I almost feel as if God intended me to be the instrument that brought Ben's extraordinary career to a close. He couldn't have had a more sympathetic winner, that's for sure."

The classical purity of such an upset—the greatest player of the age knocked off by his most humble disciple, the only other man in the field using Hogan clubs—didn't elude one Mike Murphy either.

After Olympic, Murphy went on to help found the Esalen Institute in Big Sur and ultimately wrote one of the most enduringly popular golf books of all time, *Golf in the Kingdom,* which includes a vivid account of Fleck's mythical heroics.

"There's no question in my mind that we witnessed a rare and amazing transmission of psychic energy," Murphy says, explaining that all "masters" eventually reach a point where they select a "pupil" to whom they can pass their psychic energy and accumulated wisdom, theorizing that Hogan's "secret" (which he calls "true gravity" in *Golf in the Kingdom*) was simply his incomparable mental energy and self-discipline, a presence the Hawk was destined to convey and see manifested in a selected pupil.

At the awards presentation, Hogan seemed to be thinking somewhat along the same lines.

"I'm through with competitive golf," he announced with a cracking voice, leaving the multitudes briefly speechless on the hillside, smiling a little to try to cover the deepest disappointment of his life.

"I came here with the idea of trying to win. I worked harder, I think, than ever before in my life." He added that he just couldn't put himself and Valerie through the grind of preparation any longer, though he might someday try his luck at another Open.

"From now on," he elaborated to reporters, "I'm a weekend golfer. I want to play just for the pleasure of it because I want to be around the fellows and around golf."

With that, like a man already changing form from mortal to myth, he politely lifted a hand, said good-bye, and vanished.

HOGAN'S NEXT APPEARANCE had an element of the supernatural surrounding it too. Ten days into the new year, according to the most common account of events, just days before the start of the '56 Crosby pro-am, while attending a Monday night cocktail party at George Coleman's house near the Lodge at Pebble Beach, his host sidled over and said, "Hey, Ben, the two kids want to play you and Byron."

The "kids" Coleman meant were young Kenny Venturi, son of San Francisco's Harding Park Golf Course starter and one of the top amateur players of the day, and Harvie Ward, the lavishly talented reigning National Amateur champion and 1952 British Amateur titleholder.

In George Coleman's own account of the proposed match, told to several friends over subsequent years, it didn't happen during the Crosby but at another time of the year. While Eddie Lowery and Byron Nelson and their wives were having drinks at Coleman's house, Lowery told George that he had two amateurs (Venturi and Ward) who could beat any two pros George could get together. Ben and Valerie were staying at the Pebble Beach Lodge but were not at the cocktail party. Neither were Venturi and Ward. George called Ben, as Coleman relayed events, and passed along Lowery's challenge, which Hogan promptly took up. It was agreed from the start that the match would be played at nearby Cypress Point Golf Club.

Venturi was Byron's protégé, but he'd met Ben at the '54 Masters before he went off to Korea to fulfill his military service. Three holes into their Augusta practice round together, Ben invited the awestruck twenty-three-year-old to quit calling him "Mr. Hogan" and simply call him "Ben." At the 4th hole, when young Venturi drilled a three-iron shot to twelve feet and Hogan put his own three-iron shot in the bunker, Hogan glanced over at the amateur's bag and grunted. "You've got a bag of one-irons. Serves me right for looking into an amateur's bag, I guess."

"Should I call you Mr. Hogan now?" a startled Venturi asked him.

"No. But when you get in," Hogan deadpanned, "give me your address and I'll send you a decent set of clubs."

He did too. Their friendship had grown from there.

"I'll play," Ben supposedly told Coleman in the most popular version of how the match came to pass, "but I don't know if Byron will."

Across the room (in the first version of the story), Eddie Lowery was making an identical sales pitch to Nelson and getting the same response. "Sure," said the affable Nelson, "but I don't know if Ben will want to do that."

When all finally agreed to play, Hogan instructed Lowery to make a tee time at Pebble Beach for eleven sharp in the morning.

"But, Ben," Lowery reminded him, "we're planning to play at Cypress at ten o'clock."

"I know," Hogan replied. "But I don't want people seeing us playing with two damn amateurs."

"With that," Kenny Venturi remembers, "Ben glanced over at me and winked. If Ben really liked you, he would glance at you and wink."

George Coleman's account differs in that Cypress Point was the agreed meeting spot from the beginning, that Pebble Beach was never used as a decoy—yet another example of how Hogan stories tend to change and grow with each telling.

What is clearer is that six players went out the following morning at Cypress, the legendary pros against the hungry young amateurs, with Lowery and Coleman along for a side match. Only a handful of spectators were on hand. No reporters were notified.

Ward and Venturi birdied nine of the first ten holes but found themselves one down in the match because Hogan and Nelson matched their scoring stroke for stroke until Ben holed an eighty-five-yard pitch on the 10th, an up-hill 5-par of 500 yards.

At eleven, Nelson nailed a two-iron to twelve feet and made the putt; his protégé Venturi promptly halved him. "I don't remember anyone saying much more than the occasional 'Good shot' or 'You're away,'" says Ward. "It was a match played in near-total silence. Truthfully, I don't even really remember the details very clearly—just one birdie after another happening in a kind of fog."

"There may have been a card. But I don't know who kept it," recollects Byron. "But then, nobody needed to."

On it went, the amateur challengers hitting one brilliant shot after another in the misty Monterey sea air, the wily old pros matching them every step of the way to retain their one-up lead.

At the postcard 16th hole, the famous long par-3 over the churning cove of water, both Nelson and Ward hit drivers and halved the hole with birdies. In Coleman's version, Byron alone birdied the sixteenth to go dormy 2, then the players tied 17 for a 2 + 1 Hogan-Nelson win. In Ken Venturi's memory of events (which became the popular account) the group came to the short but steeply canted 18th fairway, often described as the only weak hole at Cypress, with Hogan and Nelson clinging to a one-up lead. Venturi coolly pitched his approach shot to twelve feet, Ben to ten. Newly returned infantry sergeant Venturi calmly rolled his ball into the cup. Hogan squatted and then paced for several moments, then settled over his ball. One bit of Hogan lore holds that he gritted his teeth and mumbled, "I'm not about to be tied by two goddamn amateurs," and promptly holed the putt, though none of the other players recall Hogan saying a thing, just rolling home the winning ball. Curiously, in his recollections some years later at a USGA function honoring Byron, George Coleman maintained that the match ended when Hogan-Nelson went two up at 17. None of the other competitors recalled it that way, though. The truth remains lost in the Monterey mist.

Both Ward and Nelson shot 67s, Venturi a 65. The vanishing Hogan had 63.

The amateur team's better-ball score was 59, thirteen strokes under par, one more than Ben's and Byron's 58.

As a group, they scored twenty-seven birdies and one eagle—Hogan's spectacular pitch-in at 10.

"Ben and I talked about it, off and on, for several years," Venturi says. "Coming when it did, at the start of my playing career and near the end of his, it was deeply meaningful to us both. Whatever else can be said, I don't think the world will see anything quite like that again."

FIFTEEN

Shady Oaks

TAKE IT FROM ME, fellas. There's nothing like this place anywhere else in the world," boasted a relaxed and smiling Ben Hogan as he greeted local reporters on a hot summer morning in 1958, just days after his friend Tommy Bolt won the United States Open Championship at Southern Hills in Tulsa. Hogan and Marvin Leonard were standing together in the spacious "air-conditioned" pro shop of Fort Worth's newest architectural masterpiece, the Shady Oaks Country Club.

Spread over 200 acres of real estate that Marvin Leonard had purchased from Amon Carter on Roaring Springs Road in the northwestern reaches of Westover Hills, Shady Oaks featured a beautiful, modern-style clubhouse with Italian marble shower stalls in its men's locker room, a Grecian-style swimming pool for families, a dining room filled with the work of southwestern artists, and a pro shop believed to be the best stocked in all Texas. The jewel in the crown, however, was its Robert Trent Jones 6,320-yard par-71 golf course, a sporty layout designed for the average country club player who could

Overleaf: Ben and Valerie, Shady Oaks Country Club, 1990 *(Courtesy Hogan Estate)*

hit the ball 190 yards reasonably straight but didn't want his lip bloodied by a championship test like Colonial's. Almost as important to Ben Hogan, who actually had the major hand in shaping both designs, was the new club's nifty par-28 "little" practice course, where he could retreat and practice unseen and undisturbed for hours on end. Those members who didn't care to have to walk in the hot Texas sun could also use one of the club's new fleet of "motorized golf scooters," one of the first clubs in Texas to have them.

According to the *Star-Telegram*, Citizen Leonard had spared no expense in creating his golf retreat beneath the oaks, shelling out more than $4 million of his own money to produce what he believed to be the finest private "members" country club anywhere in America, a place where Cowtown's social elites and most successful businessmen and their invited guests could gather to eat lunch, hatch deals, and hit golf balls in the privacy of their own kind. Unlike at Colonial, which now boasted more than 700 members and had become something of a secular shrine to the illustrious playing career of Ben Hogan, there were no irksome tee times and very few rules of any kind at Shady Oaks. It was a true "members" club with a fabulously attentive staff and a golf course that suited Hogan to a tee. Regal Colonial Country Club would forever be the place most associated with Hogan's shining public life. But for the rest of his days, beautiful Shady Oaks would be his true home.

The club was merely the first phase of a more ambitious plan Leonard had in mind to develop 1,200 additional surrounding acres into a community of luxurious private homes, the city's finest new neighborhood. To no one's particular surprise, one of the first-choice double lots Leonard sold on a densely shaded ridge with a lovely glimpse of the surrounding forested hills, on a newly cut residential street called Canterbury, less than a five-minute Cadillac ride from the front gates of Shady Oaks itself, was to Ben and Valerie Hogan.

In less than a year's time, the couple would hire a local architect to design a tasteful ten-room house with a swimming pool and barbecue and adjoining servant's bungalow in an elegant rustic style Valerie Hogan described as "country French." The house wouldn't be ready for almost two years—early 1961—in part because Ben meticulously oversaw every aspect of its construction both inside and out, à la the making of *Follow the Sun*, beginning with the structure's 80,000 bricks made by hand on the premises and used to construct the walls and three separate fireplaces, two of which Ben had pulled down and rebuilt from scratch at least three times until they satisfied his exacting eye. He also hand-selected the pecan floor panels and personally monitored their installation. When the home was finished, George Coleman supposedly couldn't resist asking Ben if he and the house's architect (a man Hogan had known since World War II) had been friends before building the house together.

"Yep," Hogan replied.

"How about when you finished?"

"Nope."

By Fort Worth's somewhat showy residential standards, the house at 1917 Canterbury Drive would turn out to be a reasonably conservative affair, its white bricks and timbered front porch posts conveying the look of a fine California desert ranch house rather than that of a country retreat found, say, in rural Provence or Picardy. The home's interior walls and carpets would be done in designer off-white, and its furnishings were mostly formal French Provincial pieces Valerie chose through consultations with the area's leading interior decorators.

In the coming decades, much would be inferred from the fact that the beautiful residence featured only one master bedroom, a design peculiarity that led many to assume that Ben Hogan wanted no overnight houseguests. In fact, the house had at least two additional rooms that could be, and were, converted for use as guest rooms on several occasions. But the absence of official bedrooms—and overnight guests themselves, for that matter—was less an indication of Hogan's wariness of people, as widely perceived, than of his reluctance to reveal a strained home life he felt was nobody else's business.

The only visible evidence that the world's greatest golfer resided there for a number of the home's early years was a large ceremonial military drum Hogan had a New England designer find and make into a glass-topped table for his den. It was an idea he got while visiting with the Duke and Duchess of Windsor at their chateau outside Paris days after his Carnoustie triumph. In the chateau's stables, which had been converted into the Duke's office, Ben was deeply impressed by a pair of coffee tables his royal Seminole friend had made from a pair of his old regimental drums, used to display his letters abdicating the throne for the woman he loved.

For many years Hogan's own drum table displayed several of his most cherished possessions too, including all his U.S. Open medals and similar mementos from his cherished North and South, Masters, and Western Open campaigns, until Hogan (increasingly worried about burglary) was persuaded by Leonard to move them, along with other trophies and memorabilia—including his prized Hickok Belt for being named America's top athlete for 1953—to a special new Hogan display Leonard had built at Colonial Country Club. After that, Ben displayed his favorite club heads under glass at Canterbury Drive, including every model he'd designed and marketed since the company's inception.

IN THE THREE years since being upset at Olympic, the quality of Ben's tournament performances had seriously declined. In 1956 he delighted fans and confounded critics again by charging out of the ether at Oak Hill in Rochester to nearly seize that historic fifth Open. Needing just two pars on the tournament's concluding holes to tie a nervous and waiting Cary Middlecoff in the clubhouse, Ben's putter once again agonizingly betrayed him. Freezing and withdrawing over a critical three-foot par putt on the 71st hole, he finally made a stab at the ball and missed the cup, then managed only par on the 18th for a 282 total that left him in second for the second time in two years. "As he limped from the green," says Open author Robert Sommers, "the 13,000 fans watching him finish applauded and cheered. So many of them had wanted so badly for him to win a fifth Open, and they knew his time was running out."

By the end of 1957, it looked as if Hogan's extraordinary lease atop the game had finally expired. He entered only five events, two of which officially counted, both painful affairs for Hogan die-hards to behold. At the Masters, he missed his first cut ever, followed by a woeful eleventh-place finish at Colonial, and he chose to skip the U.S. Open at Inverness altogether.

His next campaign was only marginally better. Entering a handful of events in 1958, only three of which he deeply cared about, he placed a distant fourteenth at Augusta and tenth at the U.S. Open at Southern Hills. The best he could muster at Colonial was a faltering tie for fifth. For the year, he took home just $4,484 in official Tour dollars, scarcely enough to cover his traveling expenses for the year.

"It surprised a lot of us to see Ben suddenly playing so poorly," says Bob Rosburg, the young Californian who began to break through about that time. "He told us he was retiring, but I don't think we believed he would ever really do it. He'd been on top so long. Maybe we just couldn't stand the thought of not seeing him there, of knowing he was finally going."

Going but not gone. This was Hogan, remember.

After struggling to thirtieth place at Augusta in April 1959, Ben went to his friend Jimmy Demaret's tournament in Houston and finished in a tie for twenty-sixth place. "It was painful for us to watch Ben's game struggle the way it did," says Billy Casper, who styled much of his own game after Hogan's technique and succeeded Bolt as National Open champion later that summer.

"But every time they would write him off, he would suddenly do something extraordinary—something only Hogan could do."

Less than a week later, forty-six-year-old Hogan hammered out a course record 63 during a Colonial practice round, then opened the tournament with blistering rounds of 69-67. The blind stares nearly derailed him in round three—he skied to a miserable 77, a round that included five three-putts from inside twenty feet—but finished with a strong 72 to take his fifth Colonial title in another place that had come to be known as Hogan's Alley.

Billy Casper won the National Open at Winged Foot that summer with his extraordinary putter. The solemn twenty-seven-year-old Californian, widely regarded as the best putter in the game, missed half a dozen shots in regulation but one-putted eight greens to open with 71. Ahead of him stood Gene Littler, Dick Knight, and Gary Player, the cheerful, intensely fit, young South African who would capture his first British Open in just a few weeks' time.

After blazing out with a 32 over Winged Foot's treacherous opening nine, Ben Hogan completed the back side with 37 and wound up in a tie for the first-day lead with 69. He pieced together two more solid rounds of 71 before blowing up on Open Saturday afternoon to 76 and finishing the tournament with 287, a tie for eighth place. It wasn't a performance for the ages, but it would never be forgotten.

Two days before play began at Winged Foot, a highly successful commercial photographer named Jules Alexander decided he would slip out to Mamaroneck from his Manhattan studio to see if he could find an interesting subject to shoot. He knew nothing about golf or golfers; Alexander's usual subjects were glamorous magazine cover girls, movie stars, and famous personalities in the news. He arrived at Winged Foot on a Tuesday afternoon, the next-to-last practice day before the Open's start, with three cameras over his shoulder and no press credentials. Unlike abrasive Hy Peskin, who took the famous Hogan one-iron shot at Merion and sometimes nudged people out of the way to get his picture, Alexander was a reserved and polished man who relied on a quick study and unobtrusive manner to get his photograph.

"I hadn't been there long when I saw this man putting on his rain pants before climbing into a sand trap," Alexander remembers. "A lot of people were watching him, so I watched too. I'd heard about Ben Hogan, naturally, but I'd never seen him. I used my 300-millimeter lens to shoot him and basically followed him the rest of the round. I used a lot of film that day."

Alexander was back the next day too, when the afternoon sun was shining in Mamaroneck. Hogan was playing his final warm-up round with his good friend Claude Harmon, Winged Foot's head professional. "By then I was totally absorbed by the man, the way he moved and played, even the way he smoked a cigarette. There was something so quietly powerful about him. He was utterly oblivious to what was going on around him, and yet he knew I was there every step of the way photographing him. He never once looked at me or spoke. And I made no move toward him. We just both did our jobs. But I felt a strong intimacy with my subject. I now understood what people *meant* about seeing Hogan."

At the 15th green, after Hogan returned from slipping into Freddie Corcoran's house for a moment—Alexander thinks he went there to use the toilet— Ben lit a cigarette and leaned on his putter, casually crossing his left foot over his right in a posture of brief parade rest, serenely waiting to putt, the faintest smile playing on his face as he stared off into the near distance of a fine summer day. The lens of Alexander's silent Leica camera opened and shut, and the photograph that graces the cover of this book was taken. It was one of many marvelous black-and-white photographs the studio photographer took of his subject that week—arguably the finest and most revealing pictures ever taken of Hogan in his element—but it would be another thirty-five years before the two men officially met and spoke to each other. (An amusing footnote. According to Alexander, the small gray flap visible below Hogan's right hand in the photograph may have been the result of improperly buttoned fly trousers. "I have a hunch Claude Harmon said something to him about it," says Jules with a laugh, "because by the next tee, when I shot him again, the little flap wasn't visible.")

AFTER WINGED FOOT, it was months before anyone saw the Hawk again in public. Most of his days were spent working on new head designs at the Ben Hogan Company in the morning and going to Shady Oaks for lunch and practice in the afternoons, a developing pattern that would characterize the balance of his days. His equipment company was producing 200 sets of premium-quality irons and woods a week and basically selling every set as quickly as they could package and ship them. The manufacturing triumvirate of Wilson, Spalding, and MacGregor, for the record at least, weren't willing to admit being worried about Hogan cutting into their sales, but club pros around the country reported that Hogan irons were flying off the shelves into the hands of better players.

At Shady Oaks, Ben normally lunched with Marvin Leonard and W. A.

Moncrief, and sometimes with Regan Carraway and oilmen Earl Baldridge and Gary Laughlin.

Laughlin in particular was Hogan's kind of guy. Twenty years younger than Ben, a former Marine pilot who'd served in Korea but now worked in the oil rig leasing business with his older brother Phil, Laughlin and Hogan first met at the Rivercrest member-guest in 1953. "We primarily got together because he knew I was in the oil drilling business and that was a subject that increasingly fascinated him," recalls Laughlin. "I was struck by the diligence of his research on the subject. For instance, he would go back and get old drilling logs—they're public record—and study them with a fine-tooth comb for evidence of remaining hydrocarbons in the soil, a good way to locate oil deposits others might have missed, if you've got the patience to do that sort of thing. Ben obviously did. And he found some oil. A great deal in some cases."

Their first modest oil deals were done in the mid-1950s, but a strong personal friendship quickly evolved from the business relationship. Laughlin's reserved manner, high intelligence, and respectable single-digit handicap clearly attracted the older Hogan, and Laughlin found Hogan's earthy wit and unexpected warmth both disarming and irresistible. As one decade ended and another began, their friendship deepened and Hogan began to invite Laughlin to play with him in money matches around Dallas and Fort Worth, often against two of the region's leading club professionals, Eldridge Miles and Shelley Mayfield.

Says Laughlin, who served for a time with Hogan on the new country club's board of directors: "Ben was never much for playing rounds for fun at Shady Oaks or really anyplace else. He loved that place more than anywhere on earth, mind you, but playing was always serious business for him. Especially then. If he played a casual round with some of the fellas, it was usually only nine holes, rarely more than that. He loved to slip out and practice shots against the wind on certain holes and stay all afternoon out at the little nine testing new clubs. When he felt like a bit of serious competition, he would phone me up at the office and say, 'Gary, I want you to call Miles and Shelley. Tell 'em we'll be there at one o'clock sharp.'"

Mayfield, head pro at Dallas's prestigious Brook Hollow, was a former Tour player (four wins in three years out on the circuit) and future Texas Golf Hall of Famer. Eldridge was the beloved head man at Dallas Country Club and an enthusiastic early seller of Hogan clubs. "The games we played were $5 Nassaus, never much money on the matches," says Mayfield. "But you'd have thought the National Open was riding on the outcome the way Ben went after them. I think he used them to keep his competitive edge." Most of these matches took place at Mayfield's Brook Hollow, a fine course designed by A. W. Tillinghast in 1920.

"I recall many afternoons riding back to Fort Worth with Ben when he simply didn't speak because we'd lost by a stroke or two," remembers Laughlin with a laugh. "He loved Shelley and Miles. But it just ate Ben up to lose to them. It was only a few bucks, mind you. But money was never the issue."

The big money game, Laughlin says, was waiting for Ben at Shady Oaks.

In the early sixties, something called "the Swing" started, a game that resembled one Sam Snead used to play against five or six pigeons simultaneously. In the Shady Oaks version, however, whoever chose to "take the Swing" against the field had to match scores with upward of fifteen or twenty players using full handicaps that were computed daily. A man who was on top of his game and had the nerve to take the Swing could make a handsome pile of dough in an afternoon. Or lose a small fortune.

"Ben hated handicaps, detested the very word 'net,' " says Laughlin. "That was because early on in the Swing some of the regulars at Shady Oaks really began to get into Ben's pockets. He just hated having to give a good player strokes. For instance, he always gave me one a side on the holes *he* thought were toughest, not what was printed on the card. He was always correct in this regard. For what it's worth, some of the guys also took him apart in gin rummy. Ben's normal partner in the Swing was Earl Baldridge, who Ben called Ziggy, a wonderful old guy with a profane mouth, an ugly swing, and a wonderful sense of humor. Ben adored him. Earl was CEO of Champlin Oil. His father had made a fortune and then lost every penny in the Great Depression. Earl went to work as a kid in the oil fields and paid off every one of his father's debts. He was about the homeliest man you ever saw, but with a heart of gold and as honest as the day. He gave Ben hell, and Hogan loved every minute of it. When Earl was in the hospital dying many years later, Ben was there to see him every day. That's how close they were—what kind of friend Ben was if he liked you.

"Anyway, whenever Ben would send his eggs back to the kitchen at Shady Oaks, which was fairly often, Earl would growl at him, 'Hogan, a couple years ago you couldn't rub two nickels together, and now they can't get the béarnaise sauce right for you!' "

Ziggy's eleven handicap didn't stop him and his partner Hogan from taking some terrible beatings in the Swing, according to Laughlin and others, and finally one day Ben had suffered enough. He announced that he planned to take the Swing, and several hotshots who heard about this made plans to come over from Dallas.

"When everybody got out to the course," Laughlin continues the tale, "they discovered that the flags had basically been placed in impossible spots on the greens—in places only one guy was capable of getting close. You know who. What they didn't know until later was that Ben came out early and personally had the course superintendent put the pins exactly where he wanted them.

"He ate them all alive that day," Laughlin concludes with a chuckle. "They always called it the day of the Big *Fugh*."

HOGAN'S FINAL professional appearance of the 1950s came in Dallas in September 1959. Before the start of a tournament that would soon be renamed by the Salesmanship Club in honor of his old Glen Garden rival Byron Nelson, Hogan played three practice rounds at Oak Cliff Country Club with a nervous young caddie named Rayburn Tucker on his bag.

Tucker knew Oak Cliff like the back of his hand. He also knew that Ben Hogan seldom asked a caddie's opinion on any subject. At the 6th hole, however, the young man screwed up his courage and brazenly asked Hogan if he wanted assistance reading the course's tricky greens or yardage to the green.

Hogan smiled a little.

"No, son. Just keep the balls clean with a damp towel, be at the ball when I arrive, and keep the bag far enough from the ball so that the bag or clubs will not touch the ball if the bag inadvertently drops. That's all. Got that?"

Tucker nodded. Hogan studied the distance to the flagstick, then glanced at his eager young caddie.

"So what club should I hit?"

Tucker didn't hesitate.

"It's a three-iron, sir."

Hogan chose that and hit his ball inside the leather.

When Tucker asked him what time he should be ready to go the next morning, Hogan asked him what time their tee time was.

"Ten-thirty, sir."

"Then be here at nine-thirty. You'll recognize me—I'll be wearing a white cap."

With that, Hogan flashed his young caddie another smile, climbed in an Oldsmobile 98 with paper mats on the floor, a loaner he was using while his Caddy was being serviced. During the tournament, he asked the young caddie to confirm distances and club selection on almost every shot except for driver and fairway woods and whenever he was obviously in range with a nine-iron or wedge. "He asked me to help him read only one putt, at the 71st hole, whether it was uphill or downhill," Tucker recalls, noting that some years later George Coleman speculated that the only reason Hogan collaborated with him was due to failing eyesight and Ben's reluctance to wear eyeglasses on the golf course. Even so, Hogan hit sixty-eight greens in regulation, drank one cold Schlitz beer in the locker room after every round, and finished six strokes behind the eventual winner, Julius Boros.

"It was the most amazing week of my life," says Tucker, who memorized every detail about his hero that week, from the Faberge foot powder he put in his $1,500 Maxwell Brothers golf shoes to the way he kept a beautiful sports jacket and fresh dress shirt and silk tie waiting in his locker on the outside chance he won and needed to dress for a trophy presentation.

The two men weren't destined to cross paths again until Gary Laughlin reintroduced them in 1981. But like Jules Alexander up at Winged Foot, the Oak Cliff caddie's brief time with Hogan would eventually turn into a gift to Hogan fans everywhere.

VALERIE HARRIMAN graduated from Arlington Heights High School in 1958 and enrolled at Texas Christian to study psychology. She had her mama's good looks and her grandmother Jesse's spirited and open personality, not to mention a deep passion for horses and a talent for barrel riding on her beloved pony Twinkles. "Much to the dismay of my mother and Aunt Valerie," she explains, "I was really a cow girl at heart, just like my grandmother Jesse. I was more interested in roping goats than dating the nice boys from the country club where my parents and Uncle Ben and Aunt Val all went. But they expected me to do the whole debutante thing, so I became known as the deb with the blue jeans beneath her party dress."

About this same time, Jesse and Claude Fox legally separated and Valerie's grandmother Jesse spent a great deal of her time with her granddaughter at the house Sarah and Gordon Harriman rented near Rivercrest Country Club while their new home was being built within sight of Valerie's and Ben's custom home on Canterbury Drive. "We could literally look out the back window of my parents' new house on Indian Creek and see Aunt Valerie standing at her kitchen window looking down at our house," remembers Valerie Harriman with a laugh. "Unlike my mother, Aunt Valerie only had a few close friends in Fort Worth. Uncle Ben and my mother were increasingly her primary outlet to the outside world."

Sarah Harriman, on the other hand, busied herself in a host of social and charitable activities, volunteering at Harris Hospital, serving as a garden club officer, and playing golf at Shady Oaks or Brook Hollow in Dallas whenever possible. Not long before the family moved into their new house, Gordon Harriman legally adopted Valerie as his daughter.

"Having my grandmother come visit so often was an absolute joy, a real hoot," says Valerie Harriman. "We became great pals and confidantes, and when my parents went over to the Swiss House on Camp Bowie for dinner or out to club dances with Uncle Ben and Valerie, she would make us a drink from their liquor cabinet and tell me these wonderful Wild West stories about the family that nobody else would dare talk about—including the crazy stuff that went on down in Mineral Wells that so embarrassed Aunt Valerie and my mother. I came to understand that both ladies were quietly terrified by the strain of mental illness that manifested itself somewhere back in the family history, that unknown cousin who ran through the family money and caused such a scandal."

It was Jesse Fox, Valerie Hogan's own mother, who pointed out that her oldest daughter's narrowing world was putting strain on the Hogan marriage. "Everyone knew Aunt Valerie was tough on domestic servants and shop clerks, demanding and not terribly tolerant. That was probably Fort Worth's poorest-best-kept secret. She would fire cooks or maids, and Uncle Ben would sometimes go and hire them back. But I was shocked to learn Uncle Ben had apparently moved out of their house for a while as they were preparing to move into their new house on Canterbury. He moved over to the Western Hills Hotel and later a place called the Green Oaks Inn, where my grandfather stayed for a time before he found someplace else to live. I guess he was cooling off from a fight, but it really worried my grandmother. She used to say she thought Aunt Valerie was going to blow it if she wasn't careful."

Initially, at least, only a handful of Hogan's closest social friends knew about the brief separations, and none of them dared speculate on their deeper meaning, though in retrospect some feel it fully explains Ben's desire for one master bedroom in their Canterbury dream house. As Ben Hogan withdrew from public life, his daily routine between work and Shady Oaks became his primary focus and source of happiness.

So much of Valerie Hogan's life, by contrast, had been defined by being her famous husband's fiercest cheerleader and career adviser, his counselor at large and arbiter on all subjects. Now, increasingly, there was little more for her to do in their lives beyond selecting the designer wallpaper and tasteful furnishings that would best complement the new pecan wood flooring. Friends who came to the house for dinner parties admired Valerie's decorating eye and never found her anything but a gracious hostess.

"Unlike my mother, who had a million friends and a hand in dozens of things socially, entertaining people wasn't a natural or easy thing for Aunt Valerie. She worked hard at creating a formal air of graciousness," says Valerie Harriman. "In some ways, it was like Uncle Ben out on Tour. What guests saw was what she wanted guests to see, a woman very much in control of the situation, the essence of Texas sophistication. But her natural wariness of people exceeded Uncle Ben's, and with each passing year, as his company and Shady Oaks became more important to him, that really began to quietly assert itself."

"To most folks in town, Valerie was the picture of gracious charm, though I doubt anyone but her sister and Ben were really close enough to understand what sort of things she was wrestling with—a need to manage things the way she always had," says Dr. Jim Murphy, who became Ben and Valerie's personal family physician about this time.

"Things got worse for Valerie once Ben left the Tour and stayed home. I think her sense of duty changed. She went from someone who'd given just about everything to support his career to someone now bent on protecting what he—or they—had built together over the decades. As she got older, if you crossed her in the slightest way, she was as unforgiving as anyone I ever knew. She became jealous of anyone who got close to Ben at this time. She treated me fine, but as the years went along anyone who got close to Ben, or tried to, became a threat. I think that's what led to whatever domestic problems they had. I always thought this was sad, totally unnecessary paranoia. People loved Ben, and they knew he loved her, no matter what."

"Everybody knew Ben and Valerie were very private people," echoes Gary Laughlin. "There was talk of strain at home, but when they showed up at club dances and functions as a couple, you could see that Ben enjoyed being out on the town, among people he knew well and liked. He'd really let his hair down and dance with every woman in the place. In my opinion, shared by others, he became even *more* friendly and accessible during this time period. People were drawn to him, and of course, his company was going great guns."

"You got the feeling that whatever was going on between Ben and Valerie behind closed doors," adds Tex Moncrief, whose wife Deborah was one of Valerie's few close friends, "it was something between a man and a woman and they were somehow working it out privately. Ben didn't quit on golf or his marriage."

Near the end of one of the elaborate deb parties her mother and aunt insisted she attend about this time, just as a new decade broke, Valerie Harriman saw a sight that cracked her up and warmed her heart. "There was Uncle Ben, the famous Ice Man, dancing with some other debs on *top* of a ballroom table. They were doing the "Twist," laughing, and having the time of their lives."

A RECORD 40,000 spectators moved through the pines on Masters Sunday in 1960, hoping to watch the two most exciting players of the era duel it out for another green jacket.

Chain-smoking L&M cigarettes and swigging Cokes, hitching up his pants and winking at kids behind the gallery ropes, lean and charismatic Arnie Palmer entered the final round of the springtime classic with a razor-slim lead over four hungry young lions and one rapidly aging one: Finsterwald, Venturi, Boros, Player, and the slowly limping Ben Hogan.

The Bon-Air bookies had Palmer at 4-to-1 odds to win for good reason. In the three weeks leading up to the Masters, the good-looking son of a Latrobe golf pro had been on a scoring juggernaut, winning tournaments at Texas, Baton Rouge, and Pensacola. Before that, he'd won the first-ever Desert Classic in California too.

With the coming election of the youngest president in history and talk of space exploration pressing the popular consciousness toward new frontiers, Americans seemed eager to find new paths and new heroes to admire. Ironically, before the start of the 1958 Masters, Ben Hogan helped give them one in the cocky, confident form of young Palmer. Following one of the tournament's warm-up sessions, Hogan turned to Jack Burke Jr. in the locker room and casually remarked, "Tell me something, Jackie. How the hell did *Palmer* get an invitation to the Masters?" A few yards away, Arnold heard the question and felt his ears glowing with rage. Like many other young guns on tour, he'd always been in awe of Hogan's accomplishments and skills, but the stinging remark—which he believes Hogan wanted him to hear—absolutely set the son of Latrobe on fire. When play began, Palmer fired rounds of 70-73-68-73 for a 284 and hoisted a green jacket straight off Kenny Venturi's back, the first of Palmer's major titles.

As Palmer's star rose and Hogan's set, the resentment between the two had grown more apparent over time. During the third round of the 1959 Masters, the second year the tournament was televised—when Ben finished in a dismal thirtieth place—hard-charging Arnie glanced up at a scoreboard above Rae's Creek and saw a soldier from nearby Camp Gordon clutching a handmade sign that proclaimed, ARNIE'S ARMY. "That gave me an electric thrill, I can tell you," he wrote in his memoirs. "To think that in just five years' time my fans had grown from a few hometown folks following me around the Country Club of Detroit to a whole *army* politely rooting for me at Augusta."

There was no stopping him, and the differences between golf's two most galvanizing personalities, its storied past and thrilling future, were apparent to anyone with working eyes in the spring of 1960. The younger star was brash, muscular, and perpetually smiling and waving, a good-looking hombre who took every sort of risk to please galleries with his swashbuckling style of play. On top of that, he preferred bright cheerful colors and looked damned good on TV.

The older star was torturously slow and deliberate, stone-faced throughout his exertions, chaste in his utterances, a graying legend who clearly didn't give a damn what the galleries thought of his actuarial style of play. He looked, by contrast, almost out of place on TV.

The final round of the 1960 Masters held the thrilling promise of seeing Palmer and Hogan duel it out for another green jacket. Boros and Player fell back early that final spring Sunday of the new decade, but Dow Finsterwald and Kenny Venturi put on a show of match-play excellence that ended with Venturi's par on 18 that got him into the columned clubhouse with a leading score of 283.

Hogan, who had the biggest galleries of the day, put on quite a show too. He hit nearly every fairway and green in regulation that afternoon and played beautifully save for four short putts that wreaked havoc on his scorecard. He finished with a disappointing 76 and admitted in the locker room, somewhat ghoulishly, "Every time I stand over the ball I feel like the hole is filled with my corpuscles"—as if his blood and cells were draining out of him and filling up the hole. His faltering 289 left the Hawk in a tie for sixth place.

As Arnold was heading toward the 17th tee, he glanced over at a scoreboard where another young soldier was holding up a sign: Go ARNIE! ARNIE'S ARMY. The television cameras saw it too. He needed one birdie to catch Venturi or two to beat him. Twice he took his stance on the 17th green, sizing up a thirty-foot birdie putt, and twice he stepped back for a second look. Finally, he assumed his peculiar knee-knocking stance over the ball and slapped it hard across the green, sending it racing up the incline to the very edge of the cup, where it wavered for an instant before dropping in for birdie, unleashing battle cries from his new field recruits. Hearing the roar from inside the locker room, Hogan puffed a cigarette and dryly commented, "I hope that's not Palmer."

After one of the best drives of his life, Arnie drilled a low-flying six-iron shot that checked up five feet from the cup. Minutes later, he settled over his putt and lazily curled his ball into the hole for his second Masters title in three years. He hesitated a moment, glanced around for his wife, Winifred, grinned, and leapt into the air with joy.

Ben Hogan, by golly, had never done anything like *that*. The cheering, someone estimated, lasted nearly three and a half minutes.

A few days after Palmer's triumphant second win at the Masters and his first round of golf with presidential lame duck Ike, *Sports Illustrated* called Palmer an "authentic and unforgettable hero," and another national magazine declared he was the most "thrilling thing to happen to American sports in years, maybe decades."

The Age of Hogan was officially over.

ANY LINGERING doubts about this were erased forever by events at the National Open of 1960 at Cherry Hills, outside Denver, eight weeks later.

Reemerging from his Fort Worth seclusion two weeks prior to the first round of the Open, Ben entered the Memphis Invitational as a warm-up and chiseled three sensational rounds in the 60s, a third-round 73 providing his only blemish for the week. On the concluding hole of regulation play, putting like the Hogan of old, he smoothly holed a clutch birdie that vaulted him to a tie with Tommy Bolt and Gene Littler. In the next day's play-off, Hogan sank an eighteen-foot eagle putt to shave Bolt's lead to one, then squared what was essentially a two-man match with a short birdie putt at 16, sending the Memphis fans into a frenzy.

After Ben put his tee shot on the long par-3 17th twenty feet from the cup, Bolt, a supreme shotmaker whose marvelous skills were unfairly colored by his choleric tantrums and club-throwing antics, choked down on a two-iron and nearly aced the hole.

Ben just missed his birdie try; Tommy dropped his seven-footer. When Hogan's ten-foot birdie attempt on 18 also grazed the hole, the forty-two-year-old Bolt had the Memphis title in his hands, his fourteenth Tour win. "That

Hogan is tough coming down the stretch," he brayed, grinning with relief. "I don't like to play him at all." Bolt paused a moment, then added warily, "The National Open is coming up, and the little man is playing very well. I better get my money down on him."

Because of the 5,280-foot elevation and thin Rocky Mountain air at Cherry Hills, many prognosticators believed Hogan's twelve-year-old tournament record of 276 was in jeopardy because the golf ball flew, on average, five to fifteen yards farther through the air.

That was the upside of the equation. The downside was that after several practice rounds, competitors, including Hogan, began to complain of headaches and shortness of breath. To combat this gathering public relations quandary, tournament officials hurriedly scrounged up and offered small portable oxygen canisters to the players at special stations set up around the course.

Arnold Palmer was in trouble from his very first swing of the tournament, but not because of the thin mountain air.

Cherry Hills' opening hole was a slightly downhill 4-par of just 320 yards, with a small creek running parallel to the fairway. During his practice rounds, Arnold had driven the green several times and made up his mind to go for broke on the tournament's opening shot. Unfortunately, he pushed his tee shot into Little Dry Creek, took a drop, ricocheted his next shot off a tree, and finished the 1st hole of the sixtieth United States Open with a double bogey 6. "You could have fried an egg on my forehead at that moment," he said later.

Young Jack Nicklaus, the reigning U.S. Amateur champion who had turned twenty the previous January, immediately set spectator tongues wagging by needing only a wood off the tee and either a nine-iron or wedge to reach most of Cherry Hills' long par-4 holes. Jack's unearthly length was the early buzz of the tournament, especially after he entertained practice-round spectators by hammering several driver shots *over* the range fence, silencing jokes about his chubby frat boy physique.

In fairness, the broody-looking, squeaky-voiced junior at Ohio State had reportedly spent a fair amount of his collegiate leisure time at a certain Columbus rathskeller draining Blatz beer cans and earning the nickname "Blob-o" from his Phi Gamma Delta brothers. But his spectacular playing record of 1959, during which he won twenty-nine of thirty matches, beat the accomplished amateur Charlie Coe in the National Amateur final (a man Ben Hogan considered one of the toughest opponents ever), and won the North and South Amateur and basically everything else he pursued, indicated to most seasoned heads that "Fat" Jack's eventual career stop would be the PGA Tour.

In March 1960, days ahead of Arnie's trump of Hogan at Augusta, though no one who didn't follow college golf paid much notice, Nicklaus and his Walker Cup teammate Deane Beman teamed to win the International Men's Four-Ball Tournament in Hollywood, Florida, and just weeks later Nicklaus matched the nova-like Billy Joe Patton for low-amateur honors at the Masters itself, prompting the ailing Bob Jones to observe, "He has the finest potential of any player I've seen in years."

HOGAN MISSED his first scheduled practice tee time at Cherry Hills on Thursday, June 9. Still dragging from the Monday play-off with Bolt in Memphis, the Hawk delayed his arrival in Denver by one day, leaving himself only six days to prepare for the start of the Open.

His first practice round came on Friday with Jay Hebert, a one-under score of 70 that Hogan himself quickly dismissed as "meaningless." In the process of studying the course and memorizing its various landmarks, hitting his usual complement of balls to greens and so forth, practice scores remained irrelevant to Hogan.

His main gripe, which showed up in the *Rocky Mountain News* only days before the start of play and indicated that he was up to his old Open habits, was that Cherry Hills was playing "too easy" for a National Open. In his spare appraisal of the place, the Hawk complimented the course's conditioning but noted that the fairways were ridiculously wide, the rough was too thin, and several out-of-bounds lines had either been shifted or removed completely, sharply reducing the penalty for a wayward drive. He predicted players would embarrass the USGA, but not everyone took the bait. "Hogan's using that old psychology again," warned Cary Middlecoff with a low smile. "I've seen that headline before at other Opens." One of the few players who agreed with Ben and expressed a similar opinion was Jack Fleck.

Hogan opened the sixtieth United States Open with a mediocre 75, the culprit once again being his shaky putting stroke.

Palmer survived his opening disaster and came home with 72, trailing his old college rival, former Duke footballer Mike Souchak, by four strokes. In the warm press tent after his round, Souchak, who carried a famous Jesuit prayer for good luck in his money clip, credited his lead to a putting lesson

Jack Burke had recently given him in Oklahoma City. Mike had needed just twenty-eight putts to finish with a sterling round of 68. The rest of the first-day leaders were names that few outside the press tent in the record first-day crowd of 14,067 were overly familiar with—Henry Ransom (69), amateur Don Cherry (69), promising Australian Bruce Crampton (70), unknown Huston Leclair Jr. (70), and so forth.

Jack Fleck, though, got around Cherry Hills in 70, as did the relentlessly upbeat Gary Player. ("Wonderful," he enthused to a reporter as he bounced off the 18th green on the balls of his feet, showing few if any effects from the thin oxygen. "Don't you just *love* this clean mountain air?") Bill Casper and Dow Finsterwald were both at 71, as were former Open champ Furgol, relatively new pro Kenny Venturi, and the most promising Phi Gamma Delta golfer in history, Jack Nicklaus.

When the day's final grouping completed play, speculation about where the cut might fall come Friday centered on the number 147. That score would set a record for the lowest cutoff mark in Open history. So maybe Hogan hadn't just been trying to get inside USGA's wooly heads after all.

Round two was no thing of beauty for the newly crowned King of Golf. Palmer shot even-par 71, while Souchak rode his blazing putter around the course for 67 and a new record halfway total of 135.

Hogan's group went off at 9:04 and included Dow Finsterwald and the young '56 Australian Open winner Bruce Crampton, who holed a blind bunker shot on 12 en route to 71 and a halfway total of 141. The early drama of the trio centered on Dow Finsterwald, the elegant lawyer's son from Athens, Ohio, who chipped in twice to finish the front nine with 33, but then had a disagreement with a volatile caddie, who unceremoniously dumped his bag and stalked off at the 15th hole. A Hogan fan enthusiastically stepped forward from the gallery so Dow didn't have to lug his own bag home like a weekend duffer. With order restored, Finsty went on to birdie holes 16 and 17 and finish with 69, briefly giving him the thirty-six-hole lead in the clubhouse.

As for Ben, not too surprisingly, his concentration was so intense that some say he actually failed to notice the dustup between Dow and his caddie. Before the start of the round, worried about falling behind the leaders, the Hawk simply remarked to Marvin Leonard's daughter Marty and her new husband John Griffith (who came up via train with a group of other Hogan loyalists from Fort Worth), "I've got to *go* today."

Thus resolved, he went out and blistered the course like the Hogan of old, scored birdies on four of the first seven holes, and was out in 32 and home again in 67. When the press found and encircled him in the locker room afterward, Hogan complimented Dow on his play—"He's a magician on the greens"— and admitted he was having trouble judging distances. Even so, as someone was quick to point out, he'd had *seven* one-putts and required just twenty-eight putts to get around the course, one of his best putting performances in years. "That's perhaps true," he conceded darkly, a bit incomprehensibly against all visible evidence, "but I haven't gotten a feel for the course yet."

A chip shot away in the official press tent at that very moment, however, Dow Finsterwald was busy describing Hogan's performance as "the finest exhibition with irons I've ever seen."

As he mopped his brow with a towel and bantered lightly with the reporters in a manner that would once have been unthinkable, joking about his age and frayed nerves, someone naturally wondered if Hogan was physically up to the challenge of Open Saturday's thirty-six-hole finisher in such thin overheated air. In the distant past, Ben might have frozen his questioner with a look. *This* Hogan, however, seemed perfectly at ease, replying that he didn't think thirty-six holes tomorrow would be too much for his forty-eight-year-old body, which he allowed was in "pretty good shape under the circumstances.

"What I need," he added a touch ruefully, "is someone to put a rubber band on my putter. And I don't know why. Short putts or long putts—I can't bring the putter back." With that, he told the tale of his early traveling companion "Wild Bill" Mehlhorn, the colorful Tour pioneer who once dragged his misbehaving putter on the pavement behind his car after a tournament, a tale attributed to a number of other early tourists, including Hogan's own early traveling pal Ky Laffoon. One of the finest players ever from tee to green, according to Hogan, Mehlhorn once yipped a two-foot putt into a bunker several yards away. The Cherry Hills reporters all laughed at Ben's little cautionary tale of another champion's woe with the flatstick, half a lifetime ago.

"None of the writers whom Hogan had eating from his hands," writes Cherry Hills historian Julian Graubert, "made much of the anecdote; none drew the obvious comparison between the Mehlhorn of the story and the Hogan of 1960. All they—or anyone else—cared about was that Ben Hogan was off life support."

ARNOLD PALMER, the darling of the golf media, the tournament's prohibitive favorite, wasn't having a very good time at the National Open.

In the first round, he calculated, poky play by Fleck and Middlecoff had cost him at least four strokes, and it didn't help his mood one bit that for the first time since his "breakthrough" his wife, Winnie, was back home in Pennsylvania. Arnold's frustrating 71 in round two only intensified his longing for Winnie and a feeling that he was "falling a country mile behind Souchak and others."

If that weren't enough, Palmer's newspaper nemesis and occasional drinking friend Bob Drum from the *Pittsburgh Press* had begun goading him about his aggressive style of play. "You dumb bastard, you're blowing yourself straight out of the tournament," Drum growled affectionately at Palmer. "Why the hell you're going for that green on one, I sure don't know."

Young Nicklaus had his problems with Cherry Hills' opening hole in round two, drilling his tee shot into the creek on the fairway's right flank. Unlike Arnie, though, he made a beautiful recovery shot that salvaged his par and concluded with a highly respectable 71 that had Drum and others duly taking notice, especially after his playing partner Casper, the defending champ, gushed: "Jack is so long and straight off the tee, and he has a good stance like a real veteran. He has to become one of the greatest if he continues to improve."

As for Casper himself, Billy's day was a smorgasbord of sprayed tee shots, lovely recoveries, missed short putts, and breathtaking long putts that tumbled into the cup. He also had 71, six strokes back of Souchak heading into Open Saturday.

THE ROCKY MOUNTAIN sun was sparkling and warm on Saturday morning, June 13. The most intriguing pairing of the day, Hogan and Nicklaus, appeared on the tee at 9:00 A.M. sharp.

To judge by appearances alone, the thick-necked college boy wasn't the slightest bit intimidated to be chasing the National Open in the company of the game's most revered figure, with the hottest players on the Tour on their heels no less. Both men lay at 142.

As Jack later told it, he'd been led to believe from other Tour players that playing with Hogan was a draining and difficult experience. "He was cold, they said, and he concentrated so explicitly on his own game that he was hardly aware that anyone else was on the course. This, I discovered early in the day, was absolutely wrong. Ben couldn't have been pleasanter to play with. He didn't talk a great deal, but whenever I produced a better than average stroke, he'd say, 'Good shot,' and in a way that you knew he meant it. In a word, he treated me like a fellow competitor, and I liked that."

One subtle irony of the pairing, though naturally neither man reflected on this at the time, was their mutual connection to Jack Grout, the former Glen Garden assistant pro who traveled west with Ben when he began his career and may have had some influence in shaping Ben's early golf swing. Many years later, Grout wound up at Scioto in Columbus, where he shaped the golf swing of a promising youngster named Jackie Nicklaus. And there was more.

"Hogan had a lot of influence on my left-to-right ball flight," Nicklaus said later, explaining that Grout had talked a great deal about Hogan's battles with the hook off the tee and worked hard to convince Nicklaus, as he matured, of the value of playing a more precise left-to-right shot pattern. "Grout and I worked very hard against the hook," he said, "and Hogan had a lot to do with that."

The Hawk put on a shotmaking seminar in the thin sunny air of 1960's Open Saturday, incredibly hitting his first eighteen greens in regulation, something almost unheard of in the championship. He made no costly three-putts and dropped two birdies for a 69 that could have been much lower if several other putts hadn't just grazed the cup. "If ever Nicklaus were going to crumble," says Graubert, "this would have been the time. There he was, the chubby, pink-faced man-child playing on the game's greatest stage, accompanying arguably the greatest player in history." But the college boy with the overpowering game refused to buckle. Before wandering off to find lunch, Nicklaus tacked his own impressive 69 to the card.

That same morning, Palmer woke up telling himself he was still within striking range at 143. Once again he went for broke on the dangerous 1st hole, and once again he nearly drove the green but walked off the putting surface with a disappointing bogey. The rest of his round was equally maddening. He turned in five birdies but wound up with a 72, signed his card, and stomped off to get a Coke and a cheeseburger and try to compose himself for the afternoon action.

"At that moment, with eighteen holes to play," he said, "I was exactly where I had been at the start of the third round. I was still eight back of Souchak, and on top of that, four players in the two pairings that finished just ahead of me— Boros, Player, Hogan, and the kid Nicklaus—had all gained ground on Mike."

As Arnold stood talking with Bob Drum, Ken Venturi, and Fort Worth

writer Dan Jenkins, Souchak hooked his drive on 18 out of bounds and finished the morning with an expensive double bogey. He stood at 208, with thirteen players clustered on his heels. Palmer, the fourteenth player back at 215,
grabbed a cheeseburger and munched it, wondering aloud what would happen if he shot 65 on the afternoon round. "Two-eighty," he theorized, "always
wins the Open."

Drum snorted.

"Two-eighty won't do you a damn bit of good," he growled and laughed.

Arnold abruptly stopped chewing. Then swallowed hard.

"Oh yeah?" he declared. "Watch and see."

Palmer stalked to his bag, yanked out his driver, and proceeded to the driving range, where he hammered two or three monster drives to the back of the
range before he heard his name being paged for the start of the afternoon
round. A few minutes later, funneling his rage into an explosive swing, he
nailed his drive to the front edge of the first green.

Finally.

HOGAN, JUST THREE back of Souchak at the break, had a little soup, an
iced tea, and a single aspirin for lunch. He went into the men's locker room
and washed his face and hands, then reapplied the supportive elastics on his
legs. He changed his socks and combed his hair.

By the time he was back on the tee for his 1:30 tee time, the buzz of a fifth
Open was building everywhere on the grounds at Cherry Hills. "There was
genuinely a feeling that he simply could not be denied," said Herb Wind. "He
had defied all the odds and here he was once more, contending for that elusive
fifth Open. Some of us felt fate would be kind to him this time."

Overhead, there was something new to golf: a "news" helicopter hovering
above the grounds to tape footage of the first Open in history where maybe
twenty different men stood a reasonable chance of winning with just eighteen
holes to play.

Oblivious to it all, Hogan lit a fresh cigarette, laced his three-wood tee shot
to the heart of the 1st fairway, and picked up where he'd left off that morning,
playing the game the same way he'd started playing back in 1940—one shot at
a time, one fairway after another, making no unforced errors, picture-perfect
golf.

Above him, the helicopter pilot must have been thinking this too, because
he hovered closer to look at the featured Nicklaus-Hogan pairing until Ben,

finally distracted, stepped back from a shot, glanced balefully up, and asked an official to chase away the pilot. Apparently unfazed by this noisy intrusion, the Hawk didn't miss a green in regulation on the outward nine, but neither did he make a birdie, staying right where he'd been at two-under par for the championship.

Walking along beside him, showing not the least sign of wilting under the pressure, young Nicklaus eagled the 538-yard 5th and lopped three strokes off par by the turn to leap into a tie with the faltering Souchak. For the first time in what would eventually become one of the most celebrated careers in golf, Jack Nicklaus held a share of the lead in a U.S. Open.

The real heroics, though, belonged to Palmer. Seven strokes back at the start of his final eighteen, he hitched up his pants and fired one extraordinary shot after another, his gallery growing by the hundreds with each slash of his club. After lipping out his eagle putt at the 1st, he clipped off four consecutive birdies that almost caused the ground to tremble from the stampede of fresh recruits racing to join his army.

Arnie went out in a breath-catching 30 that placed him smack in the heart of the race, four under for sixty-three holes, just one behind the surprising new leader Nicklaus, and tied with a logjam of players that included Hogan, Souchak, Boros, Fleck, Finsterwald, Jerry Barber, and Don Cherry.

The scuttlebutt on Cherry Hills was that the 7,004-yard course bared its teeth from the 8th hole on. "I always said that if this course had been built at sea level," says Dow Finsterwald, "it would have compared favorably against the toughest Open courses anywhere." Dow personally found out how tough on hole 9 of his final round when he hit his tee shot under a spruce, scored double bogey, and freefell out of contention.

As Julian Graubert notes, in eighteen previous Open appearances Hogan had never played so magnificently from tee to green. By the twelfth hole of his final round, he'd hit 30 greens in regulation numbers, an extraordinary feat under the circumstances. With precision iron play that rivaled anything he had ever done, golf's living legend had given himself more than a dozen relatively easy birdie opportunities, but holed only a handful.

With six holes left to play, momentarily holding a two-stroke lead over Hogan and the rest of the field, Nicklaus had a thought that probably would have terrified any other twenty-year-old college boy: he thought he was going to win the National Open.

At hole 13, though, standing over a critical eighteen-inch putt above the cup, Jack's inexperience cost him dearly. With the Hawk watching in stony silence, he was tempted to pause and ask an official if a ball mark directly in his putting line could legally be repaired. It could indeed, but Nicklaus was too embarrassed to ask. Instead, when he delicately stroked his ball, the tiny indentation turned his ball just enough from the hole to miss.

Hogan had his own bad luck at the hole, striking the flagstick on his approach, which left his ball ten feet from the cup. If he hadn't hit the flag, he calculated, the ball would have stopped three inches from the hole. After a protracted time over the putt, the Hawk missed another excellent opportunity for birdie. One pairing behind them, when Arnie heard that Jack had bogeyed 13 and *he* was suddenly tied with three others (Nicklaus, Boros, and Fleck) for the Open lead, the newly designated King of Golf simply smiled and murmured, "How sweet it is."

Shaken by his mistake at 13, Nicklaus three-putted from forty feet on the 14th green, resulting in another costly bogey. Hogan made par, and now he and Jack were tied at three under for the tournament, one behind Palmer and Boros, and Fleck.

Amazingly, with only a handful of holes left to decide the issue, at least eight men statistically remained in contention.

FINALLY, at 15, Ben rolled a 15-foot putt into the cup for his second birdie of the round, creating a three-way tie for the lead between Palmer, Fleck, and Hogan. In the press tent, a buzz began about a reprise of Olympic in 1955. But it was not to be.

At the tournament's 67th hole, after laying down an onslaught of birdies nearly matching Arnold's assault, Jack Fleck left himself a seven-foot putt to take sole possession of the lead. He missed, then incomprehensibly stubbed the tiny come-backer for a bitter bogey. That lapse dropped him one behind Hogan and Palmer.

Ahead at 16, Ben's approach stopped twelve feet from the pin, Jack's less than six feet. Both men misjudged the break and missed their birdie putts. Only Ben appeared to labor over the tap-in, freezing for nearly a minute before he thumped the ball into the cup. As he walked off the green, he was shaking his head.

Two holes remained, and Hogan, the greatest closer of his era, had a share of the lead with Palmer, at four under. Nicklaus, Fleck, and Boros were just one back of them, grinding for everything they were worth.

It was just before five in the afternoon, and the warm Rocky Mountain air had grown very still. Hogan and Nicklaus moved to the 17th tee almost eight hours after Open Saturday had begun for them. Ben's greens-in-regulation count, incredibly, was now up to thirty-four straight, and he knew he was tied for the lead but, oddly enough, didn't know with whom.

Lighting a fresh cigarette, he asked a spectator and was informed that his coleader was now Arnold Palmer. For a moment he looked surprised, maybe a little shaken too. "*He's* not a contender, is he?" Hogan responded narrowly. The gallery nodded.

Composing himself, Ben lashed a drive down the long tree-lined 17th fairway and followed that up with a beautiful three-iron shot that left him fifty yards shy of the watery moat that circled the island green on the long par-5 up-hill hole. Nicklaus laid up too. Each man then stood for a moment, surrounded by silence and shadows, trying to calculate his next shot.

The hole on the 17th green was cut only twelve feet from the front edge, just above a firm bank of grass that rose abruptly above a twenty-foot-wide channel of still water. It was a typical flag placement for the Open's penultimate hole, daring a desperate contender to go for broke or play it safe and shoot for the middle of the green.

Out in the fairway, Ben was a familiar figure. The hands on hips, smoke swirling, dark gray eyes studying every feature of the green as he tried to make up his mind what to do. It was only fifty yards to the pin, half a wedge swing at most. His ball was sitting up nicely, but to get it anywhere close to the hole the finest wedge player of his day would have to pinch the ball sharply on the downswing and put a fierce backspin on it to keep it from running well beyond the flagstick.

It was a wildly risky strategy that flew in the face of everything Hogan believed about seizing and holding a championship's lead.

Nicklaus opted for safety, pitching his ball safely beyond the slope and permitting it to roll twenty feet past the cup. He would count on his putter to get a long birdie, uncommon wisdom in talent so fresh. Jack then turned and stood still to see what Hogan would do.

A slight breeze blew into Ben's impassive face—a help, he decided, slowly pulling his "equalizer" from the bag.

Taking his position over the ball, he struck a crisp arching half wedge shot that looked absolutely perfect coming off the club face and rising toward the green. Gallery applause, in fact, began and increased like an ocean surf even before the ball bit the flesh of the green's forward slope.

When it struck the top of the slope, though, the terrific backspin pulled the ball back several feet to the edge of the bank, where it wavered for an instant before beginning a torturous slow descent down the slope into the water. The huge gallery gasped. Hogan stood rigidly, as if he simply couldn't believe it either.

Twenty yards to his right, standing behind the gallery rope, Marty Leonard turned her head away and began to cry. Others in the crowd did too. It took several moments, in fact, for the hubbub created by Ben's staggering miscalculation to die away.

Hogan looked ashen, more resigned than angry. He took a drag of his cigarette and thumbed it away in disgust.

Two decades later, when a friend at his Shady Oaks lunch table casually wondered if the shot had perhaps been a mistake, Hogan replied quickly, "No. I hit that shot perfectly. It went exactly where I planned it to go."

So what, then, went wrong? Most witnesses believed that another three or four inches of carry would have put him within a foot or two of the cup, all but guaranteeing a record fifth Open title. Even for Hogan it would have been a reasonably easy putt for birdie. Had the forty-seven-year-old Hawk not *seen* the distance properly or simply put a little more mustard on the backspin than needed?

Neither, according to the Hawk.

The collective agony of the moment, in any case, matched anything he'd ever experienced on a golf course, he later told someone.

Now, 15,000 disbelieving witnesses knew exactly the same thing Ben was thinking: he would never have this chance again.

Hogan limped slowly over the little causeway to the green and examined his lie at the water's edge. It wasn't as bad as initially thought. His golf ball lay halfway into the water, showing well above the water line. In the poised silence, Nicklaus waited and watched from up the slope on the green, while behind him in the fairway Boros and Gary Player paused and waited to play their third shots, watching too. Three hundred yards behind them on the tee, Arnold Palmer could tell something had gone awry up ahead. Moments later, someone told him Hogan was in the water.

"No kidding," he murmured, inhaling half an L&M.

Hogan sat down on the bank and removed his right shoe and sock. Applause began to ripple along the gallery ropes when people realized what the Hawk intended to try to do. When his gingerly placed bare foot slipped on the soft lake bottom, however, Ben sat down again and replaced his shoe minus the sock, then took all the time he needed to make a proper stance, finally lashing violently at the ball. Following the explosion of water and mud, his ball flew up and landed several feet past the hole, running another dozen feet toward the rear edge.

The gallery was still applauding as he walked onto the green to mark his ball and collectively groaned again minutes later when his gallant par-save slid past the cup. He tapped in to bogey 6, suddenly in a tie with the young, frowning Nicklaus.

"I think the fight went out of Ben right there," speculates Palmer, who heard his father's admonition to concentrate only on *his* next shot, not somebody else's. "Though he technically still had a chance and never gave up, I think he knew in his heart it was over."

And yet, a closing birdie on 18 by either Hogan or Nicklaus would have forced Palmer to make pars on two of Cherry Hills' toughest holes. But as Nicklaus acknowledged some years later, even his concentration was shattered by the unexpected development at 17. Mistakenly assuming he was out of the contest, Jack choked down on his driver and punched his fading tee shot over the lake into the deep right-hand rough.

Hogan took an entirely different approach to self-destruction, a far more uncharacteristic one, aiming to cut off as much of the long uphill fairway as possible by picking a spot directly across the widest part of the lake. He threw himself into the shot, the ball exploding off his club face and rocketing toward the far shore, drawing slightly as it flew. Mere feet from the far side, his ball plunked into the water.

Hogan limped slowly up 18, the tournament's 72nd hole, with his head down ever so slightly, lost in the swirl of his own thoughts, unseeing eyes fixed only on the turf just ahead of him—the attitude of resignation Valerie had so poignantly described to a reporter on the porch of the Carolina Inn all those years ago.

To some, it was an eerie reprise of his devastating Open play-off loss to Fleck, only worse. This time there was no defiant downhill forty-footer to finish like a champion. His fourth shot just missed the green and he three-putted for seven, nearly topping the ball on his second putt. A triple bogey was a sad end for a man who only minutes before had stood on the threshold of making golf history. Now that opportunity belonged to a younger man named Palmer.

After tapping in for seven, Hogan leaned down to retrieve his ball and straightened up to shake hands with the promising blond youngster from Ohio. He thanked Jack for the round and limped off, oblivious to the sustained and respectful applause that lasted until he disappeared from sight.

Twenty minutes later, following a clutch chip on the same green with its long afternoon shadows, Arnold Palmer took his time making his final two-foot putt for a remarkable score of 65 that would seal his 280 and, assuming it held up, amount to the most dazzling final-round comeback in Open history. When his ball tumbled into the hole, he took two quick steps forward, snatched up his ball, glanced around with a huge smile, and flung his visor into the air. "Palmer has won!" cried the excited NBC commentator, forgetting there were at least three other contenders still out on the course. "Palmer has won!"

It wasn't until Mike Souchak failed to pull off a miracle eagle at 18, Don Cherry topped his approach shot into the moat on 17, and poor fate-wounded Jack Fleck couldn't summon another Open miracle when he needed it most that the verdict was in and Bob Drum and others were scrambling to check the record books.

On his way to what many were already hailing as the greatest finish in National Open history, Arnold had passed fourteen of the finest players on earth—including the finest—and achieved the third-lowest seventy-two-hole total in Open history (the second-lowest total was Jimmy Demaret's 278 at Riviera, while the record belonged to Hogan, whose breakthrough 276 was shot at the same tournament).

"Hi ya, lover!" the beaming new King of Golf barked happily to pretty Winnie way back in Shawnee-on-the-Delaware when he finally got her on the telephone at her family's summer cottage.

"Guess what? We *won*!"

BY THEN, Hogan was showered and dressed, calmly seated by his locker, fielding polite questions, and trying to explain his reasoning for the failed shot at 17. Hadn't the Hogan principle, someone wondered, always been to make the safe and intelligent play and let others force the costly errors? "Maybe I should not have done it, but I wasn't more than this far from finishing with 279," he explained to Larry Robinson of the *New York World Telegram and Sun*, holding his hands only a foot apart. He sighed a little. "I'm just a dumb guy, I guess. I figured I needed to finish five under for 279 to win the tournament and gambled for a birdie 4 on the 17th." He thought a moment more and added, "Maybe I should have played it safe."

"For what my opinion is worth," his playing partner Nicklaus weighed in some time later, "I feel that under the circumstances Ben made the right move. . . . A birdie there might possibly win for him—even Palmer wouldn't be able to reach the 17th in two. I am, of course," he admitted, "just guessing at Ben's thoughts."

"It was a good shot, a *good* damn shot," Hogan told Larry Robinson before he left the Cherry Hills clubhouse that afternoon. "I missed my spot by about two feet from fifty yards out. I would do it exactly the same way again."

Twenty-three years later, however, in a rare television interview under the eaves at Shady Oaks with his friend Kenny Venturi, the graying legend admitted he was still haunted by that moment out in Cherry Hills' 17th fairway.

"I wake up at night thinking about that shot right today," he admitted quietly, eyes shining with emotion. "It's been twenty-three years, and there isn't a month that goes by that it doesn't cut my guts out."

In the early 1970s, when Hogan's portrait was unveiled at Golf House, a rules official who was on duty at the 71st hole that afternoon confessed to Ben that, given the circumstances and the player involved, he might not have had the nerve to call a penalty on Ben if he'd mistakenly touched the water on his backswing.

"You wouldn't have had to," Hogan reassured the man with a consoling smile. "I'd have called it on myself."

DURING THE LENGTHY train ride home to Fort Worth, Hogan didn't say more than a few words to anyone, including Valerie. He appeared to be a man with a great deal weighing on his mind. Construction of his new home was under way, and his playing career was effectively over. A further indignity greeted Hogan at the train station in Cowtown when he discovered that a clumsy porter had somehow mishandled his clubs and bent his favorite driver.

As devastating as Cherry Hills had been, business was also pressing on his mind.

Earlier in the year, Hogan had been approached by the American Machine and Foundry Corporation about buying his rapidly growing equipment company, and in a matter of weeks the sale of the Ben Hogan Company to AMF was consummated for an undisclosed amount of money—one source says it exceeded $3 million—that made Hogan one of Fort Worth's wealthiest citizens.

By all accounts, the deal was a sweet one for both parties. Hogan gained a powerful corporate parent and unparalleled distribution network, and AMF got the hottest equipment company in golf to add to its growing portfolio of sport-related companies. Ben agreed—actually demanded—to stay on as chairman of the board, retaining the right to develop products and run the company as he saw fit. As part of his deal with AMF, Hogan agreed to occasionally play tournaments that kept his name in public view, though after Cherry Hills his primary focus sharply shifted from playing golf to innovating bold design refinements that dramatically changed the ways in which clubs were both manufactured and sold.

In 1961, for example, the company developed and introduced a faster reactive carbon steel shaft called the Hogan Flash Reaction, the first significant improvement in shaft technology in almost half a generation. One of the industry's early proprietary golf shafts, it paved the way for other manufacturers to follow suit. Working with an AMF engineer named Dr. Fred Dunkerly, Hogan also created and introduced the first alloy-added lightweight steel shaft in 1969. The Apex shaft, as it was called, was expanded to five different flexes and became the second-largest private-label shaft in golf. "The game," as Hogan liked to say, "is all about feel."

About this same time, the company's innovative "speed-slot" toe groove on its wooden-headed clubs and an innovative "curved-sole" design that greatly increased the sole radius of its woods made Hogan, for a time, the most sought-after fairway woods among better golfers.

Designer Gene Sheeley left Kenneth Smith Golf and joined Hogan as his top designer and clubmaker in 1964. "Gene and Mr. Hogan were basically the company's entire R&D [research and development] team," says Ronnie McGraw, who worked under Sheeley for many years. "They were quite a team. The old man would sketch out something on paper, come up with a design he wanted to try out, and give it to Gene. Gene would have the head made and shaft it up, then give it back to Mr. Hogan, who would take the club over to Shady Oaks and try it out. If the club came back in a day, it was no good. If it was gone a whole week, Sheeley knew he'd be making up a whole set. Everything was done slowly, by hand, and once the club head was tweaked to the old man's satisfaction and was exactly the way he wanted it, Gene would put the master design in a leather briefcase, lock it, and personally carry that club head to the Cornell Foundry up in Chicago. Mr. Hogan told him, 'Don't let those club heads out of your sight,' and Gene personally stayed there to watch while it was copied. The sample was then brought back to West Pafford Street, and if it passed close inspection by the old man, it went into production. All the final grinding, chroming, polishing, stamping, and assembly went on in Fort Worth, where Mr. Hogan could personally supervise the production.

As he used to say, those clubs had *his* name on them. There was no way he would let them out of here anything less than perfect."

By the time colorful Bostonian Terry Freschette came on board as Northeast sales rep for the company in 1966, the company employed nearly 400 workers in its various plants and Hogan was something of a beloved despot. "The people in the plants absolutely loved the guy," Freschette remembers. "He walked the floor every day of his life, checking in on people and just saying hello. He wasn't overly chummy, but he obviously cared and had an amazing knack for seeing talent and understanding small things about the people who worked for him. If a guy's wife was in the hospital, say, and he was in a tight situation financially, Mr. Hogan would slip him a C-note and say, 'Do something nice for your wife or family,' or if he heard about somebody's kid in trouble . . . ditto. They called him 'the Boss.' And he liked to tell them they weren't making golf clubs, they were making 'jewelry.' I'd never seen company loyalty like the Hogan workers had, even when the union tried to get in. And I've never seen anything like it since."

Freschette, who became national sales manager and eventually vice president of sales for the company, says the Boss was particularly fond of his field reps. "They were the backbone of the company, and he made them feel very special. Knew all their names, families, likes and dislikes, the whole nine yards. Everything was done with a handshake, very few contracts of any kind. That was how Hogan believed business should be run. Your word was your bond. Loyalty and trust were paramount. When I got there in the mid-sixties, the company's primary marketing strategy was to sell exclusively through the club pros around the country, so every year the sales guys—we're talking twenty-five or thirty guys, mind you—brought a home pro to Fort Worth for three days of golf and meetings. They toured the plant, learned in detail about the development of our products, and always wound up playing golf at Colonial or out at Shady Oaks." For most of the guys, he adds, the concluding dinner with Mr. Hogan was the highlight.

For a man who supposedly had little to say, says Freschette and other Hogan sales veterans, the Hawk dazzled his reps with unscripted talks that "had them laughing their asses off one minute and then wiping their eyes the next. When he talked about his principles as both a golfer and a man, I tell you, there wasn't a dry eye in the place. They'd have laid down in front of a delivery truck for that little guy."

At the company's peak in the early '70s, the company had 600 or 700 accounts with nearly every top club professional in the country, and Hogan took particular pride in hosting his annual company sales meeting—another multi-day extravaganza for which he put up his salesmen in style, unveiled the company's latest technical innovations and marketing campaign for the coming year, and even let his hair down a little.

Remembers another former salesman: "If you were a Hogan guy, you wore a dress shirt and tie to everything, no matter how hot it was in Texas—the sales meeting, the marketing strategy, the technical talks, everything but golf at Shady Oaks. That was just Mr. Hogan. He liked to say, 'I'm not Mr. Wilson. My name is Ben Hogan, and you are representing the finest company in golf, so you'd better look like it.' This naturally extended to hair. The Boss hated long hair of any kind. It drove him absolutely crazy."

On one memorable occasion, to drive the point home, Hogan arranged to have his entire sales staff bused to a downtown Fort Worth hotel for individual haircuts—"real buzz jobs," as Terry Freschette remembers it. That evening at their dinner, a shabbily dressed long-haired guy suddenly appeared at the head table, seizing the microphone and talking nonsense.

"The guys were stunned, wondering how the hell *he* got in. Then the wig came off, and it was the old man himself," Freschette says. "He just busted up the place with that stunt."

Hogan and Freschette enjoyed a particularly close relationship during these go-go years of the Ben Hogan Company.

"I don't know why he took a shine to me the way he did. I mean, he was so serious and quiet, and I'm this loud Boston guy. He had a way, though, of recognizing people who were loyal and worked as hard as he did."

One morning while Freschette was shaving, the phone rang and it was the Boss on the other end, voice wavering, wondering if Terry would come over immediately to Canterbury Drive. "He sounded so frightened I wiped off my face, jumped into some chinos and loafers, and sped over to his house and found he'd somehow driven his Cadillac through his garage door."

Directly across the street from the Hogan house was a man hitting golf balls in an empty lot. "He was a club pro from somewhere, I guess—a real Hogan nut. There were a lot of them around by then. When Ben had come out to go to work, the crazy sucker pounced on him, claiming he could show Ben how to cure his putting problem forever. Ben was so frightened he put his car in drive and plowed through the garage door as it came down. That was the kind of thing that started to happen about then. People would show up at the company door or even out at Shady Oaks, trying to meet Mr. Hogan. Scared the hell out of Valerie. She always thought he might be kidnapped."

Others called him in the middle of the night.

One night toward the end of the sixties, Hogan's home phone rang, rousing him from a dead sleep. It was Gary Player on the opposite end, calling from Rio de Janeiro.

When Player asked if Hogan would help him sort out his equipment problems if he traveled to Fort Worth, Hogan groggily wondered, "What equipment are you playing now, Gary?"

"Dunlop," Player replied.

"Then I suggest you call Mr. Dunlop," Ben said and hung up on him.

Darkly amusing as the popular story is, what seldom gets mentioned are the circumstances surrounding the incident. The source of the information is George Coleman, Ben's closest friend. According to Coleman, Gary Player had made a gentleman's agreement early, sealed by a handshake, to join the Hogan staff and use Ben Hogan Company equipment. Hogan had irons made to Player's specifications and sent them to the South African, at no charge. Meanwhile, Player received a better offer from a competing company, possibly upstart First Flight (which also wooed Arnold Palmer), and reportedly agreed to a deal without informing Hogan. According to Coleman and Gary Laughlin, Hogan was furious to learn that Player had his new equipment company copy his Hogan irons and never forgave Player for reneging on their gentleman's agreement.

"The next day I was sitting in my office when the phone rang," Gary Laughlin picks up the story. "It was Ben on the other end, all hotter than hell."

"Gary, do you know how Gary Player got my home phone number?"

"Why, I gave it to him, Ben," Laughlin admitted.

"Well, damn it, don't do that ever again!"

With that, Hogan slammed the phone down on Laughlin too.

As THE "swinging sixties" moved along, one night in the spring of 1965 Ben and Valerie invited a dozen of their closest friends to Canterbury Drive to help celebrate their thirtieth wedding anniversary. On that night, there was no trace of whatever was troubling the Hogan marriage. As Sinatra crooned on the hi-fi, a congenial Ben mixed the martinis and grilled the steaks and somewhere near the end of the evening got to his feet and proposed a toast, looking at his wife.

"This is to my only friend and partner all these many years," said the Sinatra of golf, then kissed her on the cheek. Days before, Mr. and Mrs. George

Coleman had given Ben and Valerie a small miniature poodle they named Duffer. Ben took an immediate shine to the little dog.

Though he still periodically slipped over to the Green Oaks Inn after spats, friends and family who knew of these brief interruptions came to accept them simply as part of the couple's lifestyle, one more apparent contradiction in a life poignantly full of them.

"There was never any question about Ben's devotion to Valerie. He made that clear," says insurance man Gene Smyers, a Shady Oaks regular who insured the Ben Hogan Company and sometimes visited Ben at the Green Oaks and joined him for dinner at the Swiss House and other places around Cowtown. "These were nothing more than little calming-down periods. Every marriage of any significant length goes through tough spells. If you survive them and work it out, the marriage is normally stronger. Could Valerie be difficult? Absolutely. But so could Ben. These were two complex individuals with a lot of history between them. It speaks well of them both that they managed their problems and kept their relationship alive."

That same spring, *Golf World* named Hogan "Golfer of the Century," and the Hogans made their annual winter pilgrimage to Seminole, where someone remembered that he made a point, rather sentimentally, of seeking out young caddies who hadn't managed to get a bag that day and tipped them $20. Weeks later, Ben put in his twenty-third appearance at the Masters, shot 291, and finished in a tie for twenty-first place.

This particular edition of the Masters, which was won for the second time by Jack Nicklaus, was notable for two portents of change. During the practice sessions prior to the start of play, a short, neatly bearded engineer from Phoenix, Karsten Solheim, wandered around the practice tee and pressroom showing off a newfangled style of cavity-back putter, a radical concept design that would soon begin to alter the direction of the game and have a direct impact on the way golf clubs were manufactured and marketed.

At this same Augusta gathering of eagles, *Sports Illustrated* writer Alfred Wright was amazed by the open reverence players young and established now accorded Ben Hogan, conferring on him the status of an almost holy figure. "The touring pros are fascinated by Hogan," Wright wrote. "They talk about him a lot, as if he were some combination of natural and supernatural phenomenon—a strange cross between Mount Rushmore and the Headless Horseman. His accomplishments and attitudes made him a legend of the game, but his peers helped perpetuate the legend." Wright even gave this proper phenomenon a name. He called it the "Hogan Mystique."

• • •

"THERE WAS NO question," says Ken Venturi, "that this was really Ben's long good-bye to the game. It broke your heart to watch at times." During the next year's edition of the National Open, which returned to Olympic for the first time since Fleck's great upset, Venturi and Hogan were playing one of the early rounds together when Ben struck a magnificent shot to the 2nd green, leaving himself a twelve-footer for birdie. "I watched him stand over the ball for the longest time," Venturi remembers. "It was pure anguish for him—and anyone who saw it. Finally he comes over to me and says, 'Ken, I just can't take it back.' He meant his putter, of course. I looked at him and said, 'Ben, forget it. Who gives a damn? You've beaten us all long enough.' He just gave me that long penetrating look of his, and afterward, in the locker room, he came over and thanked me for saying what I'd said to him." This became Kenny Venturi's most cherished memory of Hogan.

"My sense of it," adds Venturi, "was that he was at that place where his desire to keep playing in U.S. Opens was matched by his embarrassment of having people see him putt like that. It was really over."

It was a week of other final encounters too.

At one point before the start of play, while Ben was walking into the Olympic's clubhouse alone, with his expensive golf shoes in hand, deep in thought, he ran smack into none other than Jack the Giant Killer.

Fleck's career path hadn't been an easy one since his stunning upset of Ben at the Open. He had won only twice and never lived up to anything near the promise of that glorious June week just over a decade before, primarily because of his own tyrannical putter. Once again their lockers were just yards apart. "We said hello and exchanged pleasantries and went into the locker room together. Just before he went out to play, though, he came over and offered me his hand. He held it, I guess, for thirty or forty seconds, almost clung to it, maybe even a minute, staring at me as if there was something he badly wanted to say. But then he just released my hand and said, 'Well, Jack. Good luck. Good-bye.' "

Fleck says he spent many years trying to guess what Hogan might have wanted to say to him that final time together at Olympic. "I think he was about to ask me about the comment I made to him before we went out for the play-off—where I said to him, 'Good luck, Ben. And you'll know what I mean.' What I meant by that, was, of course, that God's hand was directing events of that Open. I could really feel that, and I believe Ben did as well. He was far more spiritual than most people knew."

For all his putting snares, Hogan finished in a highly respectable tie for twelfth place at Olympic in 1966, the Open best remembered as Billy Casper's almost equally supernatural upset of Palmer. Fleck, for the record, wound up twenty-seventh.

Both legend and mystique grew immeasurably ten months later when Ben, approaching fifty-five years of age, returned to Augusta and nailed 66 to the leaderboard during the third round, briefly ball-striking and putting like the steely champ of old, positively electrifying Masters patrons. As the sweet ironies of fate would have it, this turned out to be the first telecast of the Masters in full color, and Hogan's final appearance at the Champions Dinner he started.

"The ovation Ben received as he limped up that final fairway on Sunday matched just about anything I ever heard at Augusta," remembers Frank Chirkinian, the longtime boss of CBS's broadcast team. "I don't think there was a dry eye on the grounds." By late Sunday afternoon, Hogan's jerky, ugly putting stroke had reasserted itself, and he limped home with 77, still good enough for tenth place.

"Even those players who didn't care for him personally were awed by his presence," says Arnold Palmer, that summer's National Open runner-up on the lower course at Baltusrol. "Whenever he appeared, usually suddenly and without warning, a definite charge went through the place. You could feel it in the air, especially among the younger players."

Palmer felt that charge, and the sting of Hogan's still-potent wrath, that October at the Ryder Cup matches down at Jackie Burke's club in Houston. For the third time, Hogan had been unanimously selected as (nonplaying) captain of the American squad, and for the second time the diametrically opposite personalities of Hogan and Palmer collided like a cold front and tropical air on a humid Texas afternoon. It began when Arnold showed up a couple of days late for practice rounds at Champions Golf Club, then took Tony Jacklin and several other British team members for a spin in his new Jet Commander plane, at one point zooming them up 8,000 feet in the air and dramatically rolling the aircraft, then circling dangerously low over the course itself on his final approach. "When Arnold came over us," remembers Billy Casper, who was on the 17th green at the time, "his wheels were down. I could have hit a wedge over that plane." "The only time I've ever seen a plane fly *under* the eaves of a clubhouse," quipped host Jimmy Demaret.

Neither the Federal Aviation Agency nor Captain Hogan was particularly amused by the stunt. The FAA launched an inquiry that resulted in a letter of severe reprimand, and Hogan made it clear he wanted no hotdogs on any team of his.

"Hey, Cap. What ball are we playing?" Arnold supposedly asked Hogan just prior to his announcement of the event's opening foursomes, a reference to the option players had to use either the British- or American-sized ball.

Hogan gave him an arctic stare. "Well, Mr. Palmer, I don't know what ball *you're* planning to use. You haven't made the team yet."

On a team bristling with talent that included Casper, Boros, Johnny Pott, Gay Brewer, Al Geiberger, Doug Sanders, Bobby Nichols, Gene Littler, and Hogan disciple Gardner Dickinson, Arnold the King, after winning two matches on opening day, was noticeably absent from the important second-morning four-balls. In his final-day singles matches, a visibly seething Palmer polished off Jacklin 3 and 2 in the morning and demolished Brian Huggett 5 and 3 in the afternoon. The resulting 23 1/2-to-8 1/2 victory was one of the largest routs in Ryder Cup history. One more bit of lore before the Hawk vanished again from sight.

A year later, Hogan reluctantly underwent the first of a series of surgeries to remove scar tissue from the calcium deposits that had accumulated over time in the joints of his left shoulder. Dr. Robert Dunn, the physician who performed the operation, had hoped to work on Hogan's increasingly fragile left knee as well. But as work proceeded, it was decided that the risk of operating on Hogan's gimpy knee and possibly further crippling the champ was simply too great. Following a slow recovery, Hogan continued wearing a rubber knee brace beneath his trousers, but he played only ten full rounds of golf in 1968, none of them in tournament competition.

In place of the competition he craved, his life increasingly revolved around the comforting routine of driving to West Pafford Street every morning, five days a week, parking the Cadillac in the same reserved slot, and walking through the assembly plant to greet workers and check up on production, discussing design ideas with Gene Sheeley before retreating into his office to sign photographs or business letters his secretary Clarabelle Kelly (an old school chum from Dublin) always had positioned in a neat stack on the corner of his desk.

The volume of requests—for autographs, for public appearances—picked up steadily with each passing year. "Look at that," Hogan once fretted to Terry Freschette, pointing to a large stack of items awaiting his attention on his desk.

"I either have to say no to them all or sign every damn thing they send. And if I do sign them, they just keep coming."

Decades further along, though, Hogan's personal secretaries Pat Martin and Doxie Williams never had any trouble convincing him to sign items. "I think he enjoyed doing it because it gave him a connection to people at a time when he so rarely went out in public," says Williams. She remembers that he particularly liked sending letters of encouragement to athletes and young people who'd been through some kind of personal trauma. Another time, upon learning that the local chapter of the ASPCA was out of funds and about to close its doors, Hogan signed "dozens" of photographs and offered them to the organization for its fund-raising efforts.

"It always surprised him," Martin echoes, "that people even remembered who he was and what he did. For some strange reason, I think he honestly felt he would eventually be forgotten."

OVER AT Shady Oaks, at the large round table that was set aside for Hogan and his friends in the men's grill room, that same brand of quiet generosity frequently asserted itself.

"I remember Ben passing the hat around the lunch table on numerous occasions," says Gene Smyers, "taking up donations for somebody he'd heard about or simply just read about in the newspaper—people, you know, who had been in some kind of accident or suffered misfortune and didn't have much, even if he'd never met 'em."

Smyers particularly recalls a Shady Oaks waitress named Rosalinda who was gravely wounded by would-be robbers after cashing her paycheck and pushing her grocery cart home. "That was on a Saturday. On Tuesday, Ben went around the table asking every man there to put in four or five hundred apiece. He raised $10,000 for her hospital expenses in about five minutes. That was Ben. Those kind of things really hit him hard."

The Hawk's routine seldom varied. By noon each day, Hogan was out the door of his company and on his way to lunch at Shady Oaks, where he would often order scrambled eggs and toast for lunch and then slip off to a favored spot on the golf course to hit balls and test clubs undisturbed for hours. When a reporter asked him about this routine in 1968, he explained, "I often find it's better for me to be off by myself. That way, I don't intrude on their games and they don't intrude on me."

"Though he preferred to be alone a lot of the time, you always got the sense around here that little happened without Ben knowing it," says Gary Laughlin, who served on the club's board with Hogan about this time and recalls a funny and revealing incident.

"Ben got it in his head that the club should quit giving out free golf tees in the pro shop. The reason was, people were leaving their tees all over the ground. Littering. He hated that and thought that if they had to *buy* their tees they wouldn't be so wasteful. He actually proposed that tees be sold, but when the board voted down his proposal, he resigned. When I asked him why, he told me, 'They aren't listening to me. I've got better things to do.' "

The caretaker in him didn't stop there, however. When Hogan heard that many of Shady Oaks' older members were having difficulty hitting shots out of the club's deeper bunkers—most of which he had personally designed, by the way—he had special sand wedges with extra bounce made up and presented to every member.

When Hogan gave Gary Laughlin a copy of Harvey Penick's *Little Red Book* some years later, he signed it, "To Gary, Best Wishes, Henny Bogan."

"That's who he really was by then, I think," muses Gene Smyers. "Henny Bogan was the man we knew. He could be a pain when he sent his scrambled eggs back to the kitchen three times in a row because they weren't perfect. But nobody ever had a bigger heart than Henny Bogan."

IN 1969 Hogan put in a surprise appearance at the sixty-ninth United States Open, which was held that summer at Champions Golf Club. For the first time ever, though, Ben Hogan came to the competition purely as a spectator. He had hoped to compete, but his shoulder and knee simply weren't up to the rigors of the competition.

He also came to see if young Lee Buck Trevino could capture a National Open in his own backyard. The pair had played several "casual" rounds in Dallas and Fort Worth, and like Hogan, Trevino was a born outsider with a homemade golf swing and a class chip on his shoulder, a gifted underdog and hustler who'd come up the hard way pounding pesos out of the dirt.

Though the "Merry Mex" quipped and joked his way around the golf course, Trevino's ball-striking was almost peerless, and his verbose charm was largely a defense mechanism employed to keep his nerves loose and the gallery at arm's length—his own version of Hogan's protective cowl of concentration. The moment he vacated the golf course, Trevino switched off his chatty wit and became a serious man who zealously guarded his privacy. "That boy," Hogan told Demaret and Burke and others, "has the best damn game in golf."

While having cocktails in the locker room during the Open, Jimmy Demaret casually mentioned to Ben that several of the older Tour veterans were thinking of pulling their sticks out of mothballs and playing a few exhibition tournaments for the heck of it. There was even talk circulating of starting up some kind of pro tour for seniors, though it would take nearly a decade more for such a tour to formally materialize. Hogan, someone recalled, "looked at Jimmy as if he must have had one too many see-throughs."

"There's no way on earth I'm going to let people see my game," he grumbled, explaining that he was through playing in public, underscoring why Shady Oaks meant so much to him.

"Nobody but me should have to suffer through *that*."

SIXTEEN

Letting Go

B∪T HE DID come back.

Two weeks prior to the start of the 1970 Champions tournament in Houston, in late April, following a return to Seminole, Hogan suddenly showed up for some intensive practice sessions with a caddie and moved into a private cottage across the street from the club. By the time the Tour rolled into town in the first week of May, Hogan's game from tee to green was its normal thing of beauty, and even his putter paralysis was momentarily subdued. By the time Valerie arrived for tournament weekend, waiters in the clubhouse knew how to make Hogan's favorite vodka martini, and the Hogan table was set for dinner every evening at seven sharp. Tournament hosts Demaret and Burke made sure Ben and Valerie were treated like visiting royalty.

The players were astonished to see him there. "Word of Hogan's entry," reported *Sports Illustrated*'s Walter Bingham, "caused the normally blasé golfers to react like sightseers on Hollywood and Vine. None of them were immune. Hogan was there waiting for them, and everywhere he went clusters of play-

Overleaf: A young Ben and Valerie, 1939 *(Courtesy Hogan Estate)* ers stopped talking and gawked." Adds host Jack Burke: "Just having him there elevated everyone's mood. There were guys, after all, who'd never seen Hogan play, only heard the stories. For them, for all of us really, it was something special."

Tom Weiskopf was one of the lucky ones selected to play practice rounds with the master. He later confessed that he was so terrified at the start of their first round he had difficulty teeing up his ball. "I knew from following Hogan back in college back in Ohio how totally intimidating he could be, just his demeanor and the way he played. But he told me to call him Ben straight off the bat, and we had a wonderful time playing together. I've never seen anyone, in fact, who was more of a perfect gentleman. Privately, I think this worshipful stuff the guys were doing embarrassed him, really got under his skin." After their practice round, Weiskopf told his friends Frank Beard and Bert Yancey that he'd never seen anyone hit a golf ball the way Hogan did. "He never missed a fairway or green. He hit one ball left, one ball right, and one straight down the middle of the fairway. If he could have putted, he probably would have shot 61 or 62."

When the distraction of being idolized finally became too much for the Hawk to bear, he and his caddie simply commandeered a cart and rambled off to practice alone on the club's second course—shades of Panmure and Carnoustie—prompting the perpetually edgy Dave Hill to complain, "He's not a friendly man, that's all there is to it. But if that's what makes him happy, he's entitled to it."

Hogan opened the Champions tournament with a solid 71, a round during which he hit every green in regulation but missed eight relatively short birdie putts. By day's end, pro Bob Goalby had counted 31 of his fellow Tour pros who doubled back to follow Hogan after they'd completed their own rounds. Ben's putter grew colder in round two, however, resulting in 75, but a decent third round of 71 placed him within striking range of the Sunday lead.

Tournament officials paired him with Lee Trevino. "Two Texans, two Open champions," quoth Bingham, "two guys with killer instincts." In the first seven holes, Hogan nailed four birdies and made no worse than par, generating "Palmer-like" whoops from the Houston galleries. "Suddenly Hogan was not only giving Trevino a lesson on how to win *four* U.S. Opens," Bingham duly noted, "he was in a position to win this tournament." When Hogan's tee shot on the par-3 8th hole just missed striking the pin and rolled back to the far edge of the green, however, his game's only major weakness was once more painfully revealed. Despite rapidly declining eyesight, Hogan stubbornly refused to wear eyeglasses on any golf course but Shady Oaks and every now and then was forced to quietly ask his caddie about the precise pin location because his depth perception was very poor—a condition that made his Houston performances all the more remarkable.

Hovering indecisively over his Hogan golf ball (Ben's ball was now the leading ball on tour, being used by more than a third of the players assembled in Houston), he made a desperate lunge that sent his ball sliding several feet past the hole, producing his first three-putt of the day. "The magic was gone," Bingham concluded. "But what a performance it had been."

When a reporter asked Trevino for his impressions of Hogan's performance, the Merry Mex explained that with nine holes left to play he was certain the tournament belonged to Ben. "He gave us all a lesson out here this week, didn't he?" Trevino mused, shaking his head wonderingly. As things played out, Hogan wound up five strokes back of first place, in a tie for ninth.

Though no one knew it, Ben's left knee was also a casualty of his quest for one more win, a strained ligament that made his limp even more pronounced. Even so, four days later, he teed off at Colonial in pursuit of his sixth Leonard trophy, prompting Red Smith to hail his surprising resurrection effort as the "top sports story of the year in America."

"Tee to green," says Gary Laughlin emphatically, "Ben was probably as good as anyone out there, including Trevino. That's remarkable when you realize he was approaching sixty years old. Somewhere in his mind I think he realized the putting wasn't ever going to come back, but tournament competition was his life, and I think he genuinely felt that if he practiced as diligently as he always had, he could somehow beat the problem. He just couldn't let go."

The gods were not kind at Colonial. After opening with a smart 69 that could easily have been three or four strokes better and briefly challenging for the lead, the blind stares returned with a vengeance and exacted a heavy toll that breezy spring Friday—a 77 from which he never recovered. Limping even more slowly than usual, he produced respectable rounds of 73 and 72 to finish out in a tie for fifty-sixth place.

But still he couldn't let go.

In August he showed up at Westchester Country Club for a tournament he'd always fancied owing to its proximity to Manhattan, where he and Valerie could dine with Paul Shields and Valerie could shop. Ben politely requested a late morning starting time for the first round in order to complete his morning preparations, the elaborate bandaging and stretching rituals that had been part of his life now for nearly two decades.

His request, not unreasonable under the circumstances, either got misplaced or was simply ignored owing to the heightened sensitivity of tournament officials to charges by a handful of malcontents that Hogan always received preferential treatment, a charge that wasn't without some merit. But Hogan was *Hogan*, a larger majority argued, and the fact that the Hawk had even come to play at all should have warranted tournament managers cutting him some slack. In any case, the fifty-seven-year-old limped off through the heavy dew at one of the tournament's earliest tee times, carded a miserable 78, and withdrew from the tournament.

ON AUGUST 26, a serious blow of another kind came when Marvin Leonard passed away in his sleep. Leonard had been ill for months, suffering the effects of bleeding ulcers and cirrhosis of the liver. The last time Ben saw his surrogate father alive was weeks before at one of their regular grill room lunches at Shady Oaks prior to the Colonial tournament. The two men sat alone together at their customary table by the window, chatting quietly and looking out at the golf course like a pair of lions in winter.

Two days after Marvin's death, Ben served as one of his honorary pallbearers at First Methodist Church in Fort Worth, a duty fulfilled on what Valerie described to her sister Sarah as "one of the most difficult days of Ben's life."

Both the *Press* and *Star-Telegram* were full of tributes to Citizen Leonard. Even after selling Leonard's Department Store to Tandy Corporation in 1967, the "Merchant Prince of Fort Worth," as he was often called, fought hard to keep his flagship store open downtown to serve the working people who'd always been his best customers, remaining true to the small-town values that had made him Fort Worth's most beloved public figure.

Just a year or so prior to his death, unwilling or unable to slow down, Leonard presided over the start of several new commercial developments that would, he believed, greatly benefit the residents of Cowtown: the creation of a large regional shopping center for a blighted section of town where there had been little in the way of commercial development; a luxury hotel aimed at boosting local convention trade; and various middle-income apartment buildings to ease a city housing crunch. He also transferred many of his personal assets to local charities, and in one final act of personal generosity, he sold Shady Oaks to its members for a fire-sale price of $2.7 million, or roughly what the club's unimproved land value was worth. At a time when property taxes were rising steeply and several new country clubs had opened in the Metroplex area,

Leonard's final move guaranteed the financial health of Shady Oaks for decades to come. Not long after his death, however, Tandy sold Leonard's Department Store to the Dillard's department store chain for $5 million, and the big friendly "country store" that had touched so many lives, including and maybe especially Ben Hogan's, was no more.

The congenial atmosphere of Shady Oaks, however, made Citizen Leonard a happy man almost up to the day of his death. For days following his interment at the family mausoleum at Greenwood Cemetery, out White Settlement Road west of downtown, Ben and several round table regulars sat in the men's grill room drinking "see-throughs" and telling stories about "Mr. Marvin's" extraordinary business acumen and common touch with people. When it came Ben's turn to reminisce, the others remembered, he talked fondly and unhurriedly about the day a young and distinctly unathletic Marvin came out to Glen Garden to see if he couldn't ease his stress pains with a little golf and paid a left-handed runt with an absurdly strong grip to tote his golf bag, the two of them setting off together in the early morning dew before other members arrived. "If he hadn't come along then," Ben told Smyers, Laughlin, and the others, "who knows how I might have ended up."

MARVIN LEONARD's death hit Ben extremely hard. In many ways, I don't think he was ever quite the same again," says Eddie Vossler, then a junior on the TCU golf team. Almost every day of his college years from 1969 to 1973, upward of 1,200 times during the years of his formal higher education, Eddie shagged Ben's golf balls at Shady Oaks, an opportunity created when Ernie Vossler, Eddie's papa, the former Colonial caddie and Tour player who was now in the real estate development business in California, had phoned Hogan to mention that his son had decided to go to TCU, whereupon Ben had suggested Eddie spend his free afternoons out at Shady Oaks "where I can keep an eye on him for you," a kindness the senior Vossler never forgot.

"My entire class schedule was set around caddieing for Mr. Hogan. In four years I never took a class after ten in the morning so I could be at the club by noon when Mr. Hogan arrived to have lunch with Mr. Leonard and the other regulars. By one-fifteen every day they were headed back to work and Mr. Hogan was headed out to hit balls with me."

During a thousand afternoons together, Eddie saw another change creep into Hogan's daily routine. When Eddie began his service as Hogan's shag boy in 1969, a moment when Ben still entertained thoughts of competing on tour, Hogan rarely drank more than a single glass of white wine or a vodka martini during lunch with the boys. But beginning about the time of his mentor's death, the level of alcohol Ben consumed, particularly later in the day, increased. "It wasn't a big increase at first. He'd never been much of a drinker. But the others would come back to the club around four o'clock for evening cocktails and a little gin rummy, and by then Mr. Hogan had usually finished his practice and taken a long hot shower. Sometimes he got into the gin game, but you could tell his mind and heart weren't really in it. I always felt, based on things he said to me during our practice sessions, that his drinking increased because of his physical pain. I also think Mr. Marvin's death, and others that started happening about then, took a major toll on him."

"Ben didn't like pills of any kind, especially pain pills," confirms Dr. Jim Murphy, who became Hogan's personal physician after Dr. Howard Ditto, the husband of Ben's sister, suffered a massive heart attack and died the summer of 1970. It was another emotionally devastating blow to Hogan, who adored his older sister and admired her accomplished surgeon husband, both of whom were heavy drinkers and smokers. "There's no question Ben started drinking more alcohol to ease the pain in his legs and shoulders, and maybe some of the mental frustration that went with it. Pain medications just weren't his thing. This contributed to the strain at home."

Valerie, Murphy and others say, was convinced that her husband's fame and familiar routine might lead to unfortunate consequences, perhaps a kidnapping or something worse. Patty Hearst's ordeal was in the news, and both Hogans were regular television watchers—Valerie and her afternoon soap operas, Ben and his evening news.

More pragmatically, however, Valerie was increasingly worried about the combination of Ben's drinking and driving his own Cadillac around town. "She was obsessed with the fact that if he had an accident, given who he was, somebody could take everything they had," recalls Valerie Harriman. "It was a valid concern, but as with most things where Aunt Valerie was concerned, it was greatly overblown—that old fear of going broke and having to start over that people from the Depression had, and her own almost pathological need to keep control of everything in their lives. Uncle Ben's drinking and driving became her holy obsession, a reflection of how little else she had in her life except worrying about Ben and trying to prevent him from doing something she believed would injure their reputation."

Echoes Murphy: "Ben was a very strong man, and a strong-willed one. So was she, in her own way. In fairness to Valerie, I think she was only doing what she'd always done—simply trying to protect Ben the only way she knew how. Obviously she overdid it at times. But as his golf career ended and his body gave out and alcohol affected him more easily than ever, this became a problem for them both, a real struggle of wills."

Golf Digest writer Nick Seitz caught a glimpse of this domestic strain when he showed up for an exclusive interview on Canterbury Drive before the Colonial in 1971. "It surprised me to discover that he was staying over at the Green Oaks Inn at the time. There were rumors of problems at home. But when I finally got to Canterbury Drive, they were particularly gracious, especially Valerie, formal but polite and welcoming. Aside from the formality, you wouldn't have guessed anything was going on."

Reporter and subject, Seitz explains, got off to an unpromising start. "The interview came out of a story *Golf Digest* planned to run after Hogan suddenly appeared at Houston in 1970. A collection of Hogan Tour stories was put together in article form and sent to him for comment. He replied that half of them weren't true but said if we sent someone down to interview him in Fort Worth he'd tell us the real story. So there I was. The first couple days didn't go well at all, I'm afraid. I asked him questions, and he gave very guarded replies. I was terribly frustrated. When I finally pointed out to him that we weren't getting anywhere and said that if he didn't want to open up, I certainly didn't wish to waste his time, he looked at me with those eyes that seemed to bore right through you. But then he smiled and said, 'Very well. Let's start again.' "

As the two men got to know each other better, their conversations shifting from a sterile office environment to Shady Oaks and finally Canterbury Drive, Seitz was pleased to discover a much friendlier Hogan than he'd been led to expect, a man of droll, earthy wit who relished his privacy and practice sessions and daily roundtable fellowship at Shady Oaks, enjoyed a needling joke at his own expense, and exhibited a surprising taste for collecting antiques and original art. "Ben loves art," Valerie explained to Seitz during a brief tour of their house, which was done in off-white with shades of blue and yellow. "When we're in New York he goes gallerying." Besides the famous regimental drum table containing Hogan club heads, the only evidence that the world's greatest golfer resided on Canterbury Drive, the future *Digest* editor-in-chief noted, as others before him had, was a cluster of golf prints hanging above the bar.

Had Seitz had the opportunity to investigate a little more closely, he would have seen a number of golf titles sitting on the shelves of a bookcase beside the den fireplace. They included first editions of *Five Lessons*, *Power Golf*, and several of Herb Wind's books. The other titles were mostly history and biography, but there was one curious little tome, a slim, dog-eared volume called *How to Relax: Scientific Body Control* (1945) by William "Little Bill" Miller. Following Hogan's wreck and rehabilitation in 1949, someone had given the Hawk this book. It was written by one of the nation's foremost "relaxation" experts, who claimed to have studied several super athletes—notably Jim Thorpe, Honus Wagner, Joe DiMaggio and Babe Ruth—and discovered a vital link between their peak performances and their ability to relax under stressful playing conditions. The theories of the "Miller Method" simply confirmed what Hogan had dug out of the dirt and learned entirely on his own. Namely, that his ability to block out the world's distractions and place himself in a mental state that replicated the peace and comfort he felt on the practice tee was the final key to unlocking his greatest performances. The little book was one that Hogan dipped into from time to time for the rest of his life.

Sitting with the reporter in his private study, the Garbo of Golf lowered his guard and opened up even more. He explained that he was looking around to buy a cattle ranch, contemplating the writing of a new instruction book, and working as a consultant on an updated version of *Follow the Sun*. He was uninterested in a proposal to name a professional golf tour after him, and he spoke of a major swing change he'd recently made to accommodate his aching left knee but admitted that Augusta's hilly terrain no longer made the Masters a realistic goal. Sam Snead and Byron Nelson and even Gene Sarazen still showed up each spring to thrill the crowds at Augusta, but without Hogan. Moving on to other topics, the aging Hawk revealed his plan to design a championship golf course in the very near future and gently inveighed against a host of other small things, including rising property taxes, pros with too much hair on their heads, and his own need to wear eyeglasses in order to see flag positions. When Seitz asked this apparently "mellowed" Hogan if he had any interest in playing senior golf, the legend stiffened and looked at him, as if debating whether to dignify the question with an answer. "Not until I'm a senior," he finally replied to Seitz.

When the editor asked the Hawk about his sudden and unexpected return to tournament life, Hogan reflected, "Time's runnin' pretty short if I don't play now. I enjoy practicing and playing in tournaments." He paused and thought for a moment. "Besides," he added, "I haven't really done what I wanted to do yet."

"What is that?" the editor wondered.

Hogan stared at him.

"I haven't won enough tournaments."

THE COMMONLY HELD view is that Ben Hogan made his final public tournament appearance in the spring of 1971 when he magically appeared at Houston for a second time. After scoring four consecutive pars on the course's unremittingly long opening holes during the first round, the hobbling Hawk attempted to fade a low flying three-iron shot into the front portion of the 190-yard par-3 4th hole and dumped his ball in a deep creek ravine that guarded the green. To the surprise and then astonishment of his playing partners Dick Lotz and Charles Coody and a gallery of Hogan loyalists who seemed to materialize every time he appeared in a public setting, Ben dropped two more balls on the spot and drilled them into Cypress Creek as well. To compound matters, while climbing down the slope to hunt for his wayward shots, his weak left knee buckled and he nearly toppled into the creek.

With a limp that was noticeably more pronounced with every step, Hogan climbed out of the ravine and finished the hole with a woeful nine, completing his opening nine with 44. Following a double bogey at 10 and a bogey at 11, his knee gave way again on the tee shot at 12, and he nearly spilled to the ground a second time. His ball lay in the fairway, though, and a few minutes later he sent it sailing over a small pond to the heart of the green, one fine farewell shot to a lifetime of competition.

"As if he had at least convinced himself he could still hit a couple decent golf shots," wrote his early biographer Gene Gregston, "Hogan called it a day and a career." He stood for a moment in the classic Hogan pose: hands on hips, white cap shading his eyes as his caddie walked around the pond to pick up his ball. He turned to his playing partners and said, "I'm sorry, fellas. I'm through." A few minutes later, Hogan climbed on a motorized cart and rode silently back to the locker room with his head tilted down, the pose of defeat from so long ago, a sad, ignominious ending to the most accomplished career in professional golf.

But the curious thing is, it didn't end there.

The following week at Colonial, despite the throbbing knee, Hogan was hell-bent on somehow chasing a sixth Colonial title. After practicing on the club's 15th fairway most of Tuesday afternoon, he spotted his old friend Mike

Souchak in the tournament locker room and invited him to play a practice round the next morning. Souchak, who left the Tour after 1966 to take the head pro job at Oakland Hills, was in Fort Worth by special invitation—in other words, at Hogan's request—and jumped at the opportunity to play with Ben.

"It ran through my mind that it might be the last time I'd get to see him play," Mike says. "So we get to the 1st tee around noon the next day, Wednesday, and there are, like, ten or twelve top pros with their caddies hanging around—every one of them just dying for Hogan to ask them to join us. You could just see it on their faces. But Ben doesn't say a peep to them, hardly acknowledges their presences."

On his approach shot to the 7th hole, Hogan swung hard and felt his left knee buckle the way it had a week before at Champions. "He damn near fell down on his face, and I asked him if he wanted to quit. He shook his head and said, 'No. Let's keep going.' He was visibly in a great deal of pain."

On the par-3 8th hole, Hogan nearly shanked his tee shot into the creek. "That's enough," Hogan declared quietly, sending the caddie ahead once again to pick up his ball. "I played on through nine, he watched, and we walked in together without saying much of anything," Souchak remembers. "I hated to think this was the end, and that same thing must have been running through Ben's head too."

After Mike putted out on 9, Hogan limped toward him with his hand extended.

"Look, Mike, I enjoyed it," Hogan said quietly, "but I'm not going on."

When Souchak finished his practice round, he went to find his old friend but discovered Hogan had cleaned out his tournament locker and was gone. He did not register to play in the Colonial that year.

He never again played in public.

BOB JONES PASSED away early the following winter.

The air was justly full of tributes to Saint Bobby, golf's most revered figure. The Hogans considered attending the memorial service in Atlanta, but upon learning that Jones was to be buried in his family's Oakland Cemetery plot in a private service, they sent flowers and a note of condolence instead. Though they still made the annual spring pilgrimage to Seminole to see George Coleman and his second wife, Dawn, neither Hogan had any interest in traveling anymore, and Ben for the most part wanted nothing to do with the flood of honorary dinners and requests to pay him homage that constantly streamed his way.

It was the beginning of a difficult time. Hogan was on the shoals of sixty but physically felt much older than his chronological years. Not long after Jones's death, Princess Hogan Ditto succumbed to years of cigarettes and alcohol. "She and Doc had been even more inseparable than Ben and Valerie," says Jackie Towery of her aunt. "Real lovebirds. I think she mostly died of a broken heart, missing Doc."

Hogan took his sister's death harder than Marvin Leonard's, burrowing protectively into the only routines that gave his life shape and meaning now: three hours of office work every morning followed by lunch at Shady Oaks, two hours of hitting balls if the weather was warm enough, long hot showers and a few cocktails and a little gin rummy in the afternoon with the boys.

As the seventies progressed, he rarely played a full nine holes of golf, choosing only to slip out to the course now and then in his riding cart to join select groups of friends for a few holes. If he spotted Gary Laughlin on the tee, he would grab a seven-iron and walk nine holes with the younger oilman for exercise and conversation. Several times a week the Hogans showed up for early dinner at the club, dressed as if headed to University Christian Church. As age came on, Hogan's church attendance tapered off, especially following the retirement of Granville Walker. They normally dined alone at Shady Oaks, talking quietly at their customary table against the wall. They were unfailingly kind to the club's waiters and waitresses, particularly Charles Hudson, the dining room's genial headman, who always had Mr. Hogan's chilled vodka martini waiting when Hogan arrived at his table.

One afternoon in late 1973, Hogan invited Laughlin out to the site in Grapevine where he was consulting with architect Joe Lee (earlier an associate of Dick Wilson, Hogan's favorite architect of the '50s and '60s) on the construction of the Trophy Club, a private development that was supposed to feature two championship golf courses, residential house lots, luxury apartments, shopping centers, parks, and even its own schools, a sprawling, ambitious project that one Hogan round table member jokingly nicknamed "Hoganville."

"I couldn't believe what I saw when I got out there," Laughlin recalls with a laugh. "That whole area was woods, but Ben had had the trees cut back hundreds of yards from the fairways. There were trees down as far as you could see. When I asked him about it, he said trees were an unfair hazard to have on any golf course. He hated trees—so there weren't going to be any trees in the way at the Trophy Club."

By the next year, the Trophy Club was in trouble. House lots weren't moving, and the financial backers were balking at any more construction until a number of problems got sorted out. "It was a bitter disappointment to Ben," says Laughlin. "The course eventually got built, but it never satisfied Ben. I think the perfectionist in him drove the owners crazy, and I know the problems out there made him very unhappy. Fortunately, he didn't have any of his own money in the project. But still, it never came out the way he'd envisioned it. He wasn't one bit happy with it."

But life had not equipped Ben Hogan to be happy; it had equipped him to survive and succeed beyond his own boyhood dreams or anyone's expectations of him, to grab hold and never let go, to forever outrun an unspeakable moment in the winter dusk on the eve of Valentine's Day in 1922. Now, as it became clear he would never accomplish what he told Nick Seitz he hoped to—"I haven't won enough golf tournaments"—the very idea of venturing away from these narrow and protective routines of life became an almost paralyzing thought to the Hawk. Early in 1974, Jack Fleck phoned Ben wondering if he might agree to simply appear at a charity golf tournament named for the late Vince Lombardi. The cause was a good one and directly benefited children. "I don't play in front of people anymore, Jack," Hogan told him flatly, and sent a few autographed photographs instead.

That same year, however, he steeled himself and flew to Pinehurst to be one of the thirteen honorees at the opening of the World Golf Hall of Fame. Before heading home to Fort Worth, he was asked by a young reporter how it felt to be a "living legend" and if he planned to write his memoirs. He bristled at the question, but quickly softened. "No, I don't. I'm not sure why anyone would want to read that," he joked darkly. On the way home, he confided to Valerie that he detested being thought of as a "living legend," an elder statesman of the game, a golden has-been. "In another five or six years," he told one of his Shady Oaks cronies, "no one will even remember or give a damn who I was."

Even so, about this same time, principally at the urging of his circle of friends and a few influential reporters like Herb Wind and John Derr, Hogan at least considered the possibility of writing his memoirs, setting down an account of his remarkable odyssey on paper. The themes were clear: the rise from humble beginnings in former Indian territory, the runt of the caddie yard who became one of the most celebrated figures of his day, the little man who struck it big by never giving up. He hoped either Wind or Fort Worth writer Dan Jenkins might eventually collaborate on the project with him, or possibly Los Angeles columnist Jim Murray (who for a time was rumored to be working on a revised script for *Follow the Sun*, a project that never got off the boards). "For a while," confirms Jenkins, whose colorful sports novels struck pay dirt about that time, "Ben and I got together to talk about doing his autobiography. But either I was busy with one of my projects or he just wasn't ready to begin . . . something always got in the way. In any case, I don't know if he felt ready or willing to expose and examine his own life the way you would want him to." Adds Jackie Towery, who was especially close to her uncle during this period of time: "It would have meant he had to open doors and look in rooms where he hadn't looked for a very long time, consider things he'd hoped to forget. Looking back, I think it might have brought him a measure of peace to finally be able to reflect on those terrible circumstances. But I think he was too honest to try and write about something he couldn't even bring himself to talk about. And of course, Valerie would never have encouraged that. She lived in terror that somebody besides a handful of friends would find out Ben wasn't always happy with his home life. There's no way she would have encouraged him to write about Chester Hogan."

So the seventies swept on, a volatile, bright-hued decade characterized by angry gas lines and the first commercial airline hijackings, Watergate's protracted melodrama, Saigon's fall, wide neckties, Elvis's overdose, and orange golf balls, a golf era highlighted by Johnny Miller's brilliant 63 at Oakmont and otherwise thoroughly dominated by Jack Nicklaus Throughout it, Ben Hogan stayed home, wrapped in his protective routine, rarely if ever seen beyond a few miles of Shady Oaks.

Shady Oaks was officially closed on Mondays, but Sandy and Gary Laughlin frequently met Ben there for lunch and conversation anyway. The Laughlins usually brought lunch from one of Cowtown's celebrated barbecue joints, and the three of them sat at the Hogan table in the empty grill room, talking about news of the day and oil wells. "Ben was exceedingly fond of Sandy," Laughlin explains. "She made him laugh at a most difficult time of his life. Those quiet Mondays at Shady Oaks meant a great deal to Ben, I think, because he simply couldn't abide the thought that there might be no place where he could go."

On Saturday and Sunday afternoons, Laughlin says, Hogan particularly loved watching college football games and PGA events on TV at the club. The

Hawk was an enthusiastic fan of several rising stars, particularly Tom Kite, Ben Crenshaw, John Mahaffey, and Lanny Wadkins.

"I remember we were once sitting there watching Tom Kite in some major tournament," recounts Gene Smyers, "and Tom's got the lead with only a few holes to play. So what does he do? He attempts to pull off the kind of low percentage shot Ben Hogan *never* would have attempted unless he was trying to make up ground. I remember Ben shaking his head and grumbling, 'That dumb son of a bitch. He'll never win a major until he learns not to do stupid things like that.'

"Mind you, Ben loved Tom Kite," Smyers adds with a laugh. "And of course, he turned out to be right."

IN THE SPRING of 1977, not long before his friend Bing Crosby collapsed and died on a golf course in Spain, Hogan did something quite extraordinary during one of his final visits to Seminole. "Sometimes in the late afternoon or early evening," Dawn Coleman explains, "George and Ben used to hit balls from our back lawn directly into the ocean. We had just gotten this new movie camera, and George thought it would be nice to have his own copy of Ben's swing on film."

Hogan agreed to be filmed on one condition—that the film never be seen by anyone but the Colemans and their closest friends.

The Coleman house, a mansion built by Henry Ford II, was on Ocean Boulevard, facing the Atlantic. The two men went out to the wide yard overlooking the water while the Colemans' longtime butler, Franco Rosiello, held the movie camera. "Ben still had a beautiful swing, but he didn't want anyone but us or a few people at Shady Oaks or Seminole to see him hit balls anymore. I don't know why that was. As George later said to me, his swing hadn't changed much at all. But George loved Ben dearly, and he abided by Ben's wishes." Unfortunately, she adds, many years later a pirated copy of the home movie got out and Hogan pounding balls into the sea eventually wound up on the Internet. "I'm so glad both George and Ben were gone by then," says Dawn Coleman. "Ben would have been heartbroken to know strangers were looking at that."

During this same sojourn to Florida, Ben supposedly played at least one final eighteen-hole round at Seminole with Coleman. If they wrote down their scores, they didn't bother keeping the card. Someone remembered that Ben tipped several caddies lavishly before saying good-bye to his favorite golf course in the world. There is no memory of him playing there again.

Before a Legends of Golf four-ball tournament the following year, however, in 1978, Jimmy Demaret phoned Hogan to ask if he would consider teaming up for a senior professional four-ball event. "C'mon," Demaret ribbed him playfully. "It'll be just like the old days. Me horsing around and you not saying a damn thing to anybody."

But Hogan declined. "There's nothing left of my game, Jimmy," he explained. "I'm through with golf."

But golf wasn't through with the Hawk. His mystique was growing with each passing year.

During the previous summer's edition of the National Open at Southern Hills in Tulsa, reporter Dave Anderson asked former winner Tommy Bolt how Jack Nicklaus's domination of the game compared with the career of Ben Hogan.

"Well," Bolt drawled, needing only a moment to think, "I've seen Nicklaus watch Hogan practice. I've *never* seen Hogan watch Nicklaus practice."

For Christmas that year, Dawn and George sent Valerie and Ben a special gift: a female poodle puppy. Several months before, Duffer had died and Ben was still deeply in grief over the little dog's death. The Hogans kept the new poodle puppy for several days and then had it shipped back to Florida. "Thank you," Ben wrote George and Dawn, "but we're just too old to handle a puppy now."

The Colemans decided to keep the dog and named her Bunker. "She lived many years and was much beloved in our household," Dawn Coleman says.

IN THE SPRING of 1983 came some unexpectedly welcome news. A classic-club dealer named Bobby Farino had purchased a vintage set of MacGregor irons at the Tournament Player Championship, and noticed two intriguing things about the set's one-iron. That particular club was stamped "Hogan Personal Model," and the one-iron had a precise well-worn sweet spot in the inside face. "Obviously," says Farino, "it had belonged to a fine shotmaker and it didn't take me long to realize it might have been Hogan's famous missing one-iron from Merion." Farino sent the club to the Colonial via Tour player Lanny Wadkins. "Mr. Hogan took it straight to the range and hit only a few balls with it before he declared, "This is it." End of story. The prodigal one-iron had finally come home. Hogan, says his former secretary Pat Martin, "couldn't have been more pleased to have it back."

Mama Hogan fell and broke her hip in 1983. Up till then, the health of the hardworking pioneer woman who insisted on living alone and never retiring had been extraordinary. She entered the hospital and declined rapidly, though, passing away on July fourth. Over the last few days of her life, Ben Hogan was constantly at his mother's bedside.

Ben and Royal exchanged words over details of her funeral and suffered a brief falling-out. "I don't know what the disagreement was about exactly, but being the older brother," speculates Jackie Towery, "I think my father wanted to control everything. In the end, Uncle Ben just let him have his way."

Passing years hadn't been overly kind to Royal Hogan. Like his mother, he lived alone in a house on Alton Road just behind the stadium where the TCU Horned Frogs played football. Soon after his wife, Margaret, passed away in 1976, owing to complications from alcohol, his only son, Royal Dean Jr., died in an unfortunate accident, slipping and falling down his own apartment house steps. "My mother and brother were such gentle souls," says Towery, "and my father was such a tough and overbearing man who insisted on everything being done his way. My mother was thoroughly intimidated by him and drank behind doors to drown her sorrows. I don't recall my father ever hugging anyone in the family or telling them what a good job they'd done. That was the Hogan way. When his mother said he missed his calling being a prison warden, she knew exactly what she was talking about. In many ways, I blamed him for both their deaths."

Royal Hogan's wrath, she says, was particularly hard on his son, a sweet-natured boy called Royal Dean, Jackie's junior by fifteen years, an artistic and free-spirited young man who loved art and fiddled with old cars.

"But my father believed any son of his—a Hogan—had to be perfect. There was no room for him to be anything other than a successful businessman. Art was nothing in my father's opinion, and Royal Dean wasn't allowed to be who he wanted to be." When the teenage Royal Dean's grades slipped, his father packed him off to military school. And when that failed to get the desired re-sults, their estrangement grew. The younger Hogan dropped out of high school, grew his hair, and moved to Aspen, Colorado, with hopes to start an art studio, living primarily off the proceeds of oil leases Royal had placed in his son's name. There, his sister says, her younger brother fell in with the wrong crowd and drifted into drugs and alcohol. "When I told my father that Royal

Dean needed professional help," Towery relates, "he simply refused to listen. No Hogan could possibly have a drinking or drug problem because they were *Hogans*. That's exactly how he thought."

After the troubled youth phoned his sister asking for her help one evening in the early 1980s, Jackie Towery took charge and got Royal Dean into a drug and alcohol rehab hospital in Wichita Falls. After he successfully completed the program, she helped move him into a new apartment near the Ridglea Theater that Claude Fox had managed for many years after his divorce from Jesse Fox. "For a while he was just doing beautifully," Jackie Towery says. "He got his GED and was talking enthusiastically about opening his own design studio, even though my father always dismissed it as 'just a bunch of junk.' Still, many of us had great hope for Royal Dean." But her father's continued distance from his own son, she says, caused Royal Dean to revert to old habits and eventually resume drinking.

One morning after he'd been partying all night, Royal Dean drove his car into a fence at the apartment complex where he lived, then panicked and fled. The police were summoned and found the young man at his apartment. An officer asked him to move his car, but as he was walking down the steps, he slipped, fell, and severely fractured his skull. He never regained consciousness and died a short time later. Royal Dean Hogan was thirty-six years old.

"It was just another tragedy in a family where tragedy was at the heart of things never discussed," says Towery. "And we even had words over my brother's funeral. My father wanted him buried in a coat and tie, and I had to laugh because Royal Dean was such a free spirit he didn't even *own* a coat and tie. Didn't matter. My father had it his way."

By the late '80s, Royal Hogan's own health was rapidly deteriorating too, and many nights, despite their differences, Jackie Towery picked up her ailing father and drove him out to dinner.

In downtown Fort Worth, Hogan Office Supply was also dying a slow but inexorable death. The problem was not unlike the changing times that contributed to the death of his own father, Chester Hogan, more than six decades before: an inability to adapt to changing times. As chain warehouse superstore office supply firms began their incursions into the city's rapidly growing suburbs, Royal Hogan simply couldn't match their prices or hope to compete. "In a nutshell," says David Corley, who left Hogan Office Supply about this time to start his own interior design firm, "Royal simply refused to change with the times and alter how he did business. He believed there was only one way to go, and that way eventually took its toll."

Reflective of this stubbornness, after Jackie and David Corley had divorced and she decided to marry a prominent attorney named Robert Towery, her father reacted by angrily denouncing her decision and even blaming his equally strong-willed daughter for David Corley's decision to strike out on his own in business. As a way of striking back at her, he demanded that she return a car he'd once given her. When the pair argued over her desire to take a vacation, Royal, who didn't believe in taking vacations, fired his daughter from her part-time job at Hogan Office Supply.

"Imagine that," Jackie says, with a little laugh. "He fired his own daughter. That's a Hogan for you."

Father and daughter did not speak again for almost three years.

TIMES WERE RAPIDLY changing in the golf equipment business too. Fifteen years after Karsten Solheim showed up at Augusta National to show off his newfangled putter, Ping golf clubs were revolutionizing the way the game was played. They were also knocking holes through the traditional iron market Ben Hogan had once dominated. Though Hogan was still chairman of the board and actively involved in the day-to-day operations of his company, owing to technical innovations in material construction—principally the introduction of Surlyn and more durable two-piece balls—as well as constant management changes in Fort Worth, the Hogan golf ball had lost its supremacy on tour and would soon vanish altogether.

In golf club technology, investment cast irons (made of molten steel poured into club-head molds) were far cheaper to manufacture than conventional hand-forged club heads (made through a traditional process that involved a single piece of high-grade steel shaped and finished by hand). Even though Tour players and low-handicappers typically preferred the greater "feel" of traditional forged irons, that market was rapidly dwindling as popular demand for more forgiving "cavity-back" designs (which feature larger "sweet spots") was growing by leaps and bounds with each passing year.

Introduction of the aptly named Hogan "Edge" irons was meant to halt advancing red ink on West Pafford Street. Unveiled in the fall of 1988, the result of four intensive years of hard research and collaboration between the Hogan design brain trust and Cornell Forge Company, the Edge was billed as the world's first true forged cavity-back iron.

But it didn't come without a struggle inside the palace gates.

The hybrid iron was the baby of new Hogan president Jerry Austry, a dynamic, straight-talking, former Wilson exec who took the reins of the company shortly after Minnesota investor Irwin Jacobs bought Hogan from AMF in 1984 and folded it into his parent Minstar Corporation. "The company was losing about two and a half million dollars a year at that point," Austry says, "and was actually hurt by its principal image as a manufacturer of high-quality golf clubs for better players, essentially the low-handicapper at the country club. But as I pointed out to Ben, how big is *that* market?"

Hogan, Austry says, thought Ping was "absolute junk"—Hoganspeak for investment cast irons with little or no feel in them. "But I walked into his office one day, shut the door, and showed him the hard data, then told him he might not like it, but Karsten Solheim was basically kicking our asses with his cavity-back irons. I said the only way we were going to get out of the black hole we were in was for him to get more actively involved again and produce an iron the rest of the golf world could get excited about. He didn't like what I told him, but he finally looked at me and said, 'Okay. Let's do it.' He was a very smart guy, and he knew the choice was either to make the change to perimeter-weighted technology or die. Otherwise, as I told him, Hogan was going to be out of business within three or four years."

As work on the new product began in earnest, Austry realized he had the perfect marketing tool for introducing the new forgiving iron sitting right before him—Ben Hogan himself. In the spring of 1987, Austry convinced Hogan to board his first airplane in seven years and fly out to Los Angeles to appear in a television commercial for the new Edge irons. Over three days, the spot was shot on the 4th hole at Riviera ("The best par-3 on earth," Hogan once called it) with the seventy-four-year-old Hawk striking balls and preaching his gospel of the importance of "feel" in a golf club. Longtime Riviera professional Art Rios pretended to be his caddie, and despite the heavy layer of secrecy imposed over the proceedings, several hundred fans and curious Riviera members slipped out to watch the filming. At one point when Hogan was taking a break between shoots in one of the two production trailers hauled to the site, he asked Austry why so many people were interested in the making of a television commercial. Didn't that happen every day of the week in L.A.?

"They're here to see *you*, Ben," Austry told him with a laugh.

Hogan sipped his vodka and shook his head.

"I don't know why," he muttered, sounding genuinely baffled.

During another break in the filming, Riviera member Bob William ferried a vodka martini to Hogan in his set trailer. The two were old friends from the filming of *Follow the Sun* (William had served as publicist for the film), and William, an avid golfer, couldn't resist the temptation to ask Hogan about a problem he was having with his own golf swing. Before he could finish his question, Hogan ordered him to put down his drink and go to the top of his backswing and stop. "From there," William recounted to Riviera members later, "I received the best lesson I ever had, but he warned me, 'If you tell anybody, I will kill you!'" Hogan, he concluded, seemed far more relaxed and contented than he'd ever been before.

At the Beverly Wilshire Hotel each evening, Hogan plied Austry with tales of his early life on the rough-and-tumble golf tour—his failed attempts to make it on tour, the car tires swiped out from under him and Val in Oakland, the breakthrough win at Pinehurst, his wreck and glorious comeback. "He talked, I listened, and it was simply one of the marvelous experiences of my life. Meanwhile, I was a nervous wreck trying to make sure everything went off okay with the commercial," Austry remembers. "Ben, however, seemed to get a kick out of it all—the attention, the fans, and being back in California." Whenever fans asked him to pose for photographs or sign his autograph, Austry remembers, Hogan happily obliged them.

The Hawk's three-day trip to California, his first trip out of Fort Worth since his final sojourn to Seminole, resulted in an unforgettable TV spot that pushed Ben Hogan Company sales the next year from 50 million to 70 million after it started airing in early 1988. More than 100,000 sets of the Edge irons were produced and sold, and the Hogan Company got back into the black— just in time to be sold again.

The buyer that year, Far Eastern businessman Moruri Isutani, reportedly paid $58 million for the Hogan Company. A short time later, his American buying spree also included the purchase of the Pebble Beach golf resort for a whopping $835 million. When Isutani came to pay a call on the living god whose prestigious name he'd purchased, Hogan reportedly shook the man's hand before sitting down to lunch at Shady Oaks, leaned toward his guest, and told him with no ambiguity, "You've just bought the family jewels, Mr. Isutani. Please don't screw it up."

That same summer, Jack Nicklaus tried to convince Hogan to fly up to Columbus and be honored at his Memorial Golf Tournament. Former honorees had included Bob Jones, Walter Hagen, and Byron Nelson.

Hogan politely declined.

"Why would I want to go up there are be *eulogized*?" he pointed out to Laughlin, Smyers, and others around the big round table at Shady Oaks. "Hell, I'm not even dead yet."

KRIS TSCHETTER'S parents gave both her and older brother Mike memberships at Shady Oaks in 1983. Kris was a promising young golfer and incoming freshman at TCU that autumn, and soon her afternoons were devoted to practicing out at Shady Oaks and trying her best to ignore the club's most celebrated member.

"When I got there," she recalls, "the first thing people said to me was, 'Don't bother Mr. Hogan or speak to him unless he speaks to you,' and for a while I tried that. Unfortunately, that's just not my personality, and one day I simply walked over to him and introduced myself, and the next thing I know he starts to show up to watch me hit balls on the little nine. Sometimes he would carry his six- or seven-iron and three balls while I played. He wasn't the least bit cold or unfriendly. He was just *shy*."

A strong friendship developed between the pair. "He was by nature a tinkerer and loved to try this and that in a golf swing, and I think one reason he liked me so much was, I wasn't particularly in awe of him. Also, we needled each other a little bit, which both of us enjoyed."

Once, for example, Tschetter had a friend who was terribly anxious to meet her friend Ben Hogan. When she mentioned it to him, he frowned and replied, "No, thank you. I've met all the people I want to meet in life, Kris."

"But, Mr. Hogan," she fired sweetly back at him, "you said the same thing five years ago—before you met *me*."

Hogan glared at her for a moment, she recalls, and then his eyes twinkled with mischief.

"Worst day of my life," he snapped, cracking both of them up.

Another time he posed for a photograph with her in the club's men's grill room, playfully holding his nose as he pointed to Tschetter.

When Kris made it to the LPGA Tour in 1988, Hogan was among the first to congratulate her. "He was so proud of me and didn't hesitate to say so. But unlike almost everybody else, when my game slumped a little bit, he didn't ask me what was wrong. He used to say, 'I know how hard it is out there. You just keep practicing and playing. Don't give up. Work harder.'" When she phoned him to say hello from the Women's U.S. Open in Atlanta one summer, while going through a particularly rocky patch, he gave her an aggressive little pep talk about getting back to basics and not fooling around. A few days later, he phoned her back.

"He wanted to know if he'd hurt my feelings," she recalls. "He said Mrs. Hogan wasn't speaking to him because she had overheard our conversation and thought he was being tough on me. I told him, on the contrary, I didn't take offense at all. That was just our way of needling each other, a real sign of affection."

Sometime later, when Tschetter and Hogan were hitting balls out on the club's little nine, she admitted to him that she was blue from breaking up with her boyfriend.

"He was very sympathetic, listening and then talking about how you have to work hard at a relationship in order for it to survive. Kind of like a golf swing. You just keep at it and don't give up. I was very grateful to him. I remember he said he and Mrs. Hogan had been through a lot together, including some particularly tough times, but they'd stayed together and worked things out, and he said he was lucky to have her."

MIKE WRIGHT arrived at Shady Oaks in 1984. He was from San Antonio, twenty-one and recently married, a bright, polite young first assistant who had the unenviable task of giving lessons to members and their children while the finest shotmaker in history watched from his grill room table.

"He took a great interest in what I was doing, and over the next couple of years, whenever it was cold outside or there was a slow moment at the club, he would come over and start to talk to me about all kinds of things about being a club pro—how to run the shop and monitor the 1st tee, sales per square foot, ratios over inventory, the importance of pleasing the members, that sort of thing. It was fascinating, like having a private tutor on being a club pro."

Art Hall, Shady Oaks' longtime head professional, was in declining health and about to take an early retirement, and it eventually dawned on Wright that a grooming process was quietly under way by his friend, Ben Hogan. "We would sit and talk for hours. I would ask questions and he would answer them. It was just so . . . comfortable." When the club's board announced that interviewing would begin to find Hall's replacement, most—including Mike Wright—assumed he was too young to occupy the post. Wright was just twenty-three.

"The club president asked me to come downtown for a formal interview with the board. That was going to be on Friday. On Thursday, Mr. Hogan came to me and asked to see my résumé and letter of application. After I wrote those up, we sat in the office and he proofread them both, fixing a few things, finally suggesting that I add a clause that said that if after one year the membership wasn't happy with me as head pro, I would step aside and give somebody else the opportunity.

"It was an unusual thing to put in a letter of application," Wright says, "but he knew I was young and they would be taking a chance on me. He knew exactly what would ease their concerns and give me the opportunity to show them what I could do."

On Friday, just hours before the big interview downtown at Tex Moncrief's office, Hogan came to Mike to ask what he planned to wear.

"I'll just wear a nice white shirt," Wright told him. "I didn't bring a jacket because they don't see me in a jacket and tie all of the time. I don't want to be presumptuous."

Hogan shook his head. "Mike, I want you to go over to Neiman's and buy a sports jacket and new tie and have them put it on my account. You need to look your best, son."

Wright thanked his mentor but said he simply couldn't do that.

"So he stares at me and says, 'All right then. Take mine.' He takes off his own sports coat and hands it to me." The jacket was too small, but Wright took it with him anyway; then, on the way to the interview, the young pro stopped off at Sears and bought himself a new coat and tie. When he returned to Shady Oaks later that afternoon, Hogan was waiting for him, demanding to know how the interview went.

"I told them what I lacked in experience I would make up with hard work," the young assistant explained.

"Good," Hogan replied, smiling. "That was good."

The next day, a Saturday, Tex Moncrief pulled Wright almost casually aside and informed him the board had unanimously decided to appoint him Shady Oaks' new head professional.

"I couldn't wait for Mr. Hogan to come in that afternoon. I was bursting to tell him. When I did, he just smiled as if he knew it all along, shook my hand, and said, 'Do a good job, Mike. That's all they can ask.'"

ONE OF Mike Wright's first steps at the club had been over a napping mixed breed mutt named Buster, his second over a black-and-white border collie called Max.

Buster and Max were the club's dogs and Ben Hogan's pampered friends. After Duffer's death, Hogan told Gary Laughlin he just couldn't take the pain of owning—and losing—another dog. But when Max started coming around the club in the late '70s, Hogan took an immediate shine to him. Max's official home was oilman Phil Laughlin's house off the club's 8th fairway. But once Max hopped on Hogan's riding cart and accompanied the Hawk to the little nine, where the dog would patiently sit and watch Hogan hit balls, the pair became inseparable. Ben rewarded his companion with burgers from the club kitchen and eventually suggested that a separate feeding account be established for the dog, which he and other members paid for. When the Ben Hogan Company introduced the Edge iron, Hogan agreed to be photographed for the marketing campaign with Max by his side.

A short time later, perhaps as a direct result of Max's budding celebrity, the Laughlins had to hire a lawyer and go to court to get Max back from a local resident who secured the dog on his property and claimed the friendly border collie actually belonged to him. A trial of ownership wound up before a local magistrate. "It was like a scene from some old movie," remembers Gary Laughlin. "The judge had the dog brought into the courtroom and released and Max came straight over to Phil, wagging his tail. That was the end of that. Ben was like a child on Christmas when he heard the decision."

Not too long after Max charmed his way into Hogan's heart, Buster the schnauzer showed up at the club. Someone had found him wandering one of the burgeoning city's new freeways, and member Tex Moncrief paid for a doggie door to be installed in the club bag room so Buster could have a decent place to sleep at night. A maintenance account was set up for him too. Buster roamed through the club at night, pretty much going wherever he saw fit. "There were ten or so members he favored, but Mr. Hogan was definitely his favorite," says Mike Wright. "Every day after lunch we had Mr. Hogan's clubs in the cart, angled just the way he liked them, and the dogs would wait for him to go out to the course. Max jumped up in the seat beside him, and Buster preferred to trot along beside the cart. They were quite a trio for a number of years."

Hogan was devastated when Max was struck and killed by a UPS truck. "You could see how deeply it affected him emotionally," says Mike Wright. "After that, Buster became even more important to him."

NOT LONG AFTER his sentimental journey to Riviera, Hogan attended a wedding reception for Gary Laughlin's daughter Cary at Shady Oaks and wound up sitting in a quiet corner of the ballroom with Rayburn Tucker, his grown-up caddie from the 1959 Dallas Open, now a successful real estate man and ardent student of the game. "We had a lengthy conversation," Tucker recalls, "that opened with my telling him that Herb Wind and I had become friends and pen pals. Ben said he was thinking of having his memoirs written, and I asked if he would consider Wind as the author. Ben said he thought Herb was an excellent writer but he hadn't really decided who would do the book."

The thrust of the memoirs, Hogan told Tucker, would be an account of his life with Valerie, conveying the principles of married life they had refined during half a century of being together. "He very much wanted it to be a 'legacy' to young people, particularly young married couples, setting out things he and Valerie had learned about faith, dedication, and loyalty to each other. I encouraged him to do it. So did others, like Dawn and George Coleman."

The book was never written, though the episode seems to suggest the peace Ben had made with his marriage, the admiration and devotion he clearly felt toward the woman who devoted her life to his search for acceptance. Tucker soon played another role, however, in the perpetuation of the Hogan legacy.

About this time, several irreplaceable Hogan items disappeared from the Hogan Trophy Room at Colonial and were later recovered by authorities. (This was the second theft of Hogan memorabilia; his famous Hickok belt was stolen and recovered in 1980.) During a visit to Fort Worth by USGA Museum curator Karen Bednarski, after viewing Hogan's safely returned artifacts, an idea came to Tucker, a member of the USGA museum committee: to explore the possibility of mounting an exhibit of some of Hogan's trophies, medals, and other memorabilia at Golf House, as part of an effort to raise public interest in the organization's fine museum. With the help of Doxie Williams, Tucker, Bednarski, and USGA Executive Committee member Bob Russell were able to convince Hogan that the exhibit was a good idea. Herb Wind and USGA president Grant Spaeth also added their voices of support.

On the day the items were to be removed, Tucker recalls with amusement, "Ben asked me to meet him at Colonial that morning. We met in the trophy room, and when the packers began to remove the five U.S. Open medals from the trophy case, Ben turned to them and said, 'You fellows be careful with those, they're hard to come by!' "

The exhibit, "Golf: The Lifework of Ben Hogan," helped set a new annual attendance record for Golf House.

• • •

NOT LONG AFTER his final trip west in 1987, Hogan felt a sharp pain in his lower abdomen and for several days simply ignored it. "Ben's threshold for pain was considerably higher than most people's," says his physician, Jim Murphy. "He walked around for a week or so just ignoring that pain while his appendix grew bigger by the day. When it did burst, by golly, it nearly killed him."

Hogan was rushed to Harris Hospital in Fort Worth, treated aggressively with painkillers and antibiotics, and kept there for nearly seven weeks. During that time he lost thirty pounds, complained incessantly about being denied cigarettes, and demanded to go home.

The moment he got home, friends remember, Hogan couldn't wait to hop in his Cadillac and resume familiar routines—mornings at the office and afternoons at Shady Oaks. But Valerie was more worried than ever about something happening to him if he operated his own car. He'd begun to suffer lapses in memory, failing to recall where he'd been or who he'd spoken to just an hour ago, unmistakable early symptoms of what Jim Murphy soon believed was dementia or possibly even Alzheimer's disease.

"They weren't big things at first, but anything out of the ordinary routine totally worked up Valerie. She was convinced that the painkillers and anesthesia the doctors gave Ben during his appendix operation had caused his memory loss. She absolutely refused to accept the fact that the condition was growing worse as the years came on, and she flatly rejected any idea that he had Alzheimer's."

THERE WAS CERTAINLY nothing wrong with Hogan's long-term memory when he made a surprise public appearance at the Waldorf Astoria in New York the day after Curtis Strange defeated Nick Faldo in their play-off for the 1988 U.S. Open at Brookline. The event was a black-tie birthday fete celebrating the one-hundredth anniversary of golf in America, a star-studded gala highlighted by *Golf* magazine's selection of the "One Hundred Heroes of Golf." Forty-eight of the hundred designees turned out to see who would be named "Player of the Century," including Snead and Nelson, Palmer and Nicklaus. Earlier in the day, Hogan appeared at a reception at the St. Andrew's Golf Club at Hastings-on-Hudson and spent hours chatting, signing autographs, and posing for photographs. "It was amazing to watch," says George Peper, *Golf*'s editor-in-chief, the architect of the affair. "People couldn't believe he was really there, and he couldn't have been more gracious. For a man who supposedly didn't want to be honored and made a fuss over, he certainly appeared to get a charge out of the whole thing."

That evening at the dinner, Peper convinced Sam Snead to get to his flat country feet and tell a few "colorful" stories just to get things rolling. Then one by one, the other honorees on the three-tier dais felt obliged to come to the microphone and express a few extemporaneous thoughts about their careers. When it was Hogan's turn, the room fell silent. Staring down at a golfer's silhouette printed on the evening's program, with no prepared remarks, Hogan mistook the form of Charles Blair MacDonald (one of the founders of the USGA and a moving spirit of the Chicago Golf Club) for Harry Vardon. Over the next twenty-five minutes or so, Hogan gave an impromptu lecture on the beauty and importance of a good Vardon golf grip. "It was the closest thing a thousand people ever got to a personal golf lesson from Ben Hogan," Peper says. "The crowd was absolutely mesmerized. When he was finished, people went crazy. Nobody who was there will ever forget it."

In the aftermath of the gala, news circulated that Hogan felt snubbed when Jack Nicklaus was named "Golfer of the Century." But friends of Hogan's say this wasn't the case, and several Hogan fans who waited in the long line to exchange a few words with golf's most elusive superstar found him surprisingly talkative and in excellent spirits.

One of them was Jim Finegan, the college boy who'd crouched just yards from Hogan at Merion, now one of the premier wordsmiths in the game. "The public adoration of Hogan really began during the cocktail hour before the dinner," Finegan remembers. "I watched as, one by one, a procession of the game's great names made their way to have a few moments with the great man. Arnold and Jack. Raymond Floyd. Johnny Miller. Tom Watson and the others. On they came, awestruck, each waiting their turn and smiling shyly, almost like schoolboys, gently inching forward and then backing away when their moment was through, like homage being paid to the aging king."

Waiting his turn in a similar queue after the dinner, Olympia Fields head professional Brian Morrison from Chicago finally got to shake hands with his childhood hero. "When I explained to Mr. Hogan that I'd started my club career at a club near where he'd worked back in the nineteen thirties, he seemed so pleased to learn this. He asked me wonderful questions about the business, and we talked for several minutes about how operations had changed. I couldn't believe how much he had to say on the subject—how much he *knew* about a club pro's life. He signed my dinner program and seemed in no rush to go anywhere, savoring every minute of the attention."

OTHER FANS, famous and unknown, made their own pilgrimage to Shady Oaks in hopes of catching a magical glimpse of golf's most mythic figure.

For years during the annual telecast of the Colonial on CBS, Ken Venturi drove out to Shady Oaks for lunch at Ben's table, a tradition that started in the late 1980s. One year he invited director Frank Chirkinian and commentators Ben Wright and Gary McCord along. After introductions were made and the trio was seated, Hogan glanced neutrally at McCord and asked him what he did for a living. The colorful course commentator was a little taken aback. "I work for CBS and I'm a pro and I'm on the Tour, Mr. Hogan," McCord politely replied.

Hogan nodded and fell silent for a few minutes. A few minutes later, he glanced at McCord again. "How long have you been on Tour?"

"Sixteen years."

"What have you won?"

"I haven't won anything, sir."

Hogan snorted gently and abruptly turned his attention to Venturi and Chirkinian. Several minutes passed and he glanced at McCord again. "What the hell are you *doing* on Tour?"

In 1992 former Shady Oaks caddie and Hogan shag boy Jody Vasquez arranged for British Open champion Nick Faldo to come for lunch at the round table. Faldo and his agent, John Simpson, flew to town and were driven by Vasquez to Hogan's West Pafford Street office. "I suggested to Nick beforehand that he write out the questions he wanted to ask Mr. Hogan, explaining to him that you didn't sit and chat with Hogan the way you do with most people. I told him Mr. Hogan preferred straight questions and gave direct answers, and if there was a lull in things or he got bored or his mind started to drift, well, that could be it."

The three men took a seat in Hogan's office, and Faldo glanced at Vasquez, who nodded to indicate Faldo should begin. A multiple winner of the British Open and the Masters who had come close on several occasions to bagging Hogan's beloved National Open as well, Nick leaned affectionately toward his host's desk and smiled. "Well, Mr. Hogan, how do you win a U.S. Open?"

"Shoot the lowest score," Hogan replied as if that much should be perfectly obvious.

The three visitors laughed. Hogan didn't. Finally Hogan cracked the faintest smile.

"I'm not kidding," he said, adding, "I promise you, son, if you shoot the lowest score by Sunday night, they'll give you the medal. I know because I've got five of them." (As the incident in the Colonial trophy room indicated, Hogan counted the unofficial '42 Hale America in his total of National Opens, even if the USGA refused to.)

After lunching with Hogan at Shady Oaks, Faldo wondered if his host would mind watching him hit balls on the range. Hogan declined. When Faldo went out to hit balls anyway, a Hogan Company official reminded Hogan that Faldo had come all the way from England just to pay his respects, hinting it might not be such a bad thing to go watch the Pride of Britain swing a golf club.

"What clubs does he play?" Hogan wondered.

"Mizuno."

Hogan thought for a moment. He'd been down this road once before with a talented foreign player who wanted his insights but not his golf clubs.

"No," he said. "I don't think so."

Word of the exchange reached the tee where Faldo was hitting balls.

"Go get me a set of Hogan clubs and tell him I'm considering changing," Faldo reportedly told Simpson.

But Hogan never came out.

THE BEN HOGAN COMPANY was in trouble.

Shortly after purchasing Hogan in the late '80s, the new owner, Moruri Isutani, offered to put up $3 million in support of a new developmental tour and proving ground for the pro stars of tomorrow (thirty events at $100,000 apiece), the new Ben Hogan Tour. When Hogan president Jerry Austry balked at such a large financial commitment with little or no apparent direct marketing value to product sales, he was fired by Cosmo World, Isutani's company, and replaced by former National Golf Foundation executive David Heuber, who was promoted to oversee the changes. In late 1990, Cosmo World formed the Ben Hogan Property Company and also purchased Pebble Beach for a reported $835 million. Soon afterward, Cosmo announced plans to sell private memberships to the Monterey landmark, setting off a backlash of protest among local residents and golf purists everywhere. Facing a public relations nightmare of monumental proportions, the membership plan was eventually scrapped, sending Cosmo World into a financial tailspin. The domino effect was felt in Fort Worth, insiders say, because Cosmo World failed to deliver promised funds for new research and development, stalling innovation and damaging sales. As a result of the moves, the Ben Hogan Company had difficulty meeting its financial obligations to the new Hogan Tour, which soon found a new sponsor and changed its name. By the following February, cash-strapped Cosmo World was forced to unload Pebble Beach to Lone Cypress Company for a fire-sale price of $500 million (an estimated $335 million loss), and several months after that Isutani also unloaded the Ben Hogan Company to the AMF Companies of Richmond, Virginia, which promptly announced that the Fort Worth factory would be shut down and all of the company assets relocated to Virginia.

Thus, within four years, the once-proud Ben Hogan Company had its fourth owner, a firm that specialized in making bowling balls. "What the hell is going on?" Hogan wrote in a personal memo to David Heuber, who soon departed the company to pursue other opportunities. Friends say Ben, who was by this time little more than a figurehead, was heartbroken, angry, and dejected by his inability to save the company and keep it in Fort Worth.

NOT LONG AFTER Nick Faldo came to Shady Oaks and the Ben Hogan Company prepared to close its doors and move to Virginia, Hogan purchased head waiter Charles Hudson a new suit of clothes. One noontime while Hogan was lunching with his round table cronies, Valerie Hogan phoned the club to ask Hudson if he would mind driving Mr. Hogan down to John L. Ashe and Son to be fitted for a new suit. She revealed to Hudson that she didn't want her husband driving his Cadillac anywhere but from home to the club, a distance of just under three miles. "As you may have already seen, Charles," she explained, "Mr. Hogan is a little forgetful these days. I don't want him to get lost."

Her fears were growing stronger every day. For this reason she hired Elizabeth Hudson (who was no relation to Charles) as a full-time companion and caregiver to her husband. The sister of the Hogans' longtime cook, Willie Mae Green, Elizabeth was an experienced, no-nonsense caregiver with an impressive résumé that included several prominent Fort Worth families. She came to Canterbury Drive with impeccable credentials, but nearly didn't take the job.

"The first thing Mrs. Hogan did when I stepped into the house was order me to remove my tennis shoes. She had this white wool carpet in her hallway and didn't want me getting any dirt on it. Then she started right away on her list of dos and don'ts. I had to get new shoes and a white uniform, and so forth. On and on she went. Well, naturally, I'd heard how difficult she could be from my sister. But I asked myself if I could tolerate being ordered around like that." Part of her duties was to drive Hogan wherever he needed to be driven and to keep him off cigarettes.

"She was terrified of that man getting behind the wheel, and didn't want him touching cigarettes—both things he really loved to do. To be honest, I was prepared to turn down the job until I met Mr. Hogan. He was so sweet and considerate to me straight off, and we immediately had something special between us, some kind of private chemistry. There was this little twinkle in his eye, kind of like a child's. I remember she left us alone to talk. He asked me if I knew what he'd done in his life. I knew he was some kind of famous golfer but admitted I didn't know much about that, and he laughed and said that was all right because he would tell me all about it if I wanted to hear. I said I did, and we agreed I would go to work for them as soon as possible—as soon as I could get some new shoes Mrs. Hogan approved of.

"He told me my old tennis shoes would be fine, not to pay any attention to his wife. But I told him I would get those new shoes and that uniform because I wanted to work for him. I loved that man right off."

HOGAN COMPANY secretaries Sharon Rea and Pat Martin remember the week the West Pafford Street factory closed in June 1993, putting 300 employees on the street.

"It was like a death in the family, especially for Mr. Hogan," says Rea. "He'd always taken such pride in the work we'd done and the people who worked for him. It was such a personal place to work. That final week he just walked around in a kind of daze, saying good-bye to people in the factory and thanking them, looking as downcast as I'd ever seen him." Adds Martin: "By that point he made none of the decisions about the golf equipment, and you could see how this deeply distressed him. He couldn't understand, at times, how such a thing could have happened."

Rea and Martin moved Hogan's office furnishings—his executive desk and beloved blue leather chair—to a small two-room office in the Western Build-

ing, not far from Canterbury Drive. "It was so sad to see him sitting in that little office with nothing really to do except reply to letters and autograph pictures and look at clubs he no longer had anything to do with making. He'd
turn and stare out the window with this faraway look in his eye, and you knew
he was thinking something," says Rea.

"Don't ever grow old, Sharon," Hogan repeatedly told his secretary.

"About the only thing left for him to do in terms of business," says Martin,
"was keep up with his other business interests, his oil wells and the rest."

Shortly before Elizabeth Hudson was hired by Valerie Hogan to be her husband's driver and constant companion, Ben failed to return home from the
club at his appointed hour. When Valerie phoned Shady Oaks, she was startled to learn from Charles Hudson that her husband had left the club not long
after lunch and hadn't been seen since. Her next frantic phone call was a panicked one to the Westover Hills and Fort Worth police, who immediately
commenced searching for Hogan's familiar black Cadillac.

A while later, "about cocktail hour," according to one of the grill room regulars, Ben suddenly reappeared at Shady Oaks, asking Charles Hudson for a
martini and wondering what all the fuss was about. "Mrs. Hogan was about
out of her mind," remembers Sharon Rea, "but he'd been driving around out
west of town searching for land to buy. When I asked him why, he told me he
planned to build a new factory and rehire all of his laid-off workers."

It took several days, Martin and Rea say, and some serious conversations
with company lawyers, before Hogan accepted that the terms of his contract
with the new owners legally prevented him from starting a new golf equipment company under his own name.

"I think that was the final straw," says Sharon Rea. "That just finally broke
his heart and spirit."

ONE AFTERNOON not long after the Ben Hogan Company decamped for
Virginia, Charissa Christopher drove over to see her grandfather Royal
Hogan at his house on Alton Road, near the TCU campus. Like his mother
before him, Royal, who was well into his eighties and suffering from advanced
stages of lung cancer, stubbornly insisted on living alone. Since "firing" his
daughter Jackie, the two of them had mended their fences, but it was really
Jackie's middle child, Charissa, a spunky, plainspoken young woman who
managed a catering firm called Festivities, who looked after her grandfather's

needs on a daily basis. Charissa also regularly checked in with her great Aunt Valerie and brought prepared gourmet food to the house on Canterbury Drive, as well.

"My grandfather was such a mess," she says, "but his dying gave us both something special—an opportunity to grow close and understand each other, and maybe Uncle Ben and Aunt Valerie too. My grandfather would fire his caregivers, and I would have to get up and go over in the middle of the night to calm him down and check his medication, and we would just sit and talk. Even more than my great Uncle Ben, Royal had this hidden sweetness he couldn't or wouldn't let others see. He told me family stories I'd never heard, a genuine unburdening that touched my heart, as if he felt he needed to make peace with things. He talked about the struggles he and Ben had growing up, about why life made their mother so difficult and hard. He showed me old photographs, and we talked about how lonely and difficult it had been for them all after his father Chester's death, especially for Ben. But he never once mentioned the suicide itself."

One afternoon while the pair was seated in the living room on Alton Road, the doorbell rang. "I went to answer it, looked out, and holy cow, it was Uncle Ben. He was just standing there holding his hat and smiling. I turned to my grandfather and said, 'Pops, Uncle Ben is here! Do you think something is wrong?' He just smiled as if he knew something and said, 'No. He comes by every now and then. Let him in.' "

Listening to the famously coldhearted Hogan brothers pleasantly reminisce about this or that, Charissa Christopher had a revelation. "I realized most people had it completely wrong about them. Supposedly they'd never been close. But that wasn't the least bit true. That was just the impression they gave out— one more thing hidden from view. There was such respect and love buried beneath all that stubbornness. My grandfather had done so much for Ben, and Ben clearly felt a deep gratitude to him.

"I remember thinking how they just expressed their love in a very different way than most people did. Perhaps we'd simply misunderstood them."

ATTORNEY DEE KELLY saw how rapidly Ben's memory was ebbing when he paid a call on Ben and Valerie to revise their final wills. "Ben could impressively remember in detail everything he'd ever done on a golf course or an oil well deal he'd made forty years ago, but he couldn't remember what he said to me five minutes before," says the prominent Fort Worth attorney the Hogans selected to update their legal documents.

"When we talked about his estate and wishes for it, it was very clear that Ben wanted Valerie to have total control of everything because she knew his wishes better than anyone. I'll never forget when he walked me out to my car after our meeting, and he asked me for the third or fourth time that afternoon if I fully understood that after his death everything was to go directly to Valerie—that she knew what his wishes were and would follow through with them. I assured him I understood this. They'd been married almost sixty years and through everything together. 'Good,' he replied. 'She knows exactly what I want.' "

Following his disappearing act in the Cadillac, Valerie took to hiding Ben's car keys so he couldn't get up and go for a drive in the middle of the night. She also made certain Elizabeth Hudson drove him anywhere he wanted to go, but she also began to curtail his daily sorties to Shady Oaks, fearing he might somehow embarrass or injure himself there. "Her intentions were honorable," says Dr. Jim Murphy, "but it had the effect of confusing and saddening Ben. In trying to protect him so aggressively, she took him away from the very people and places he loved most, the things that always gave him comfort. She refused to believe it was Alzheimer's or something that couldn't even be treated. I tried to convince her to let more people see Ben. In my opinion, that wouldn't have injured his reputation one bit. People understand these things happen in every family and are naturally sympathetic. It would have done him a world of good to be with more people, but Valerie didn't see it this way."

When Valerie Harriman came home to Texas from rural Colorado to be with her ailing mother Sarah about this time, she was startled by her Uncle Ben's mental decline. There was no doubt in her mind that he was suffering from Alzheimer's disease. "There were new treatments that could have helped him. I know because I'd researched them and already spoken to specialists in the matter. I'd also talked to psychologists about Aunt Valerie's handling of Uncle Ben. As I told my mother, there were new treatments that would have eased her anxiety and made life better for both of them."

Sarah Harriman was dying of lung cancer, and her grandchildren, Lisa and Sean, accompanied their mother to their grandmother's bedside. So did Valerie Harriman's boyfriend John Anderson.

Old tensions came to a head in the hallway outside Sarah Harriman's bedroom when Valerie Hogan chastised her niece for bringing a boyfriend home while her mother was dying. "I guess it was that old sense of appearance exerting itself again, her proper view of right and wrong. She was furious with me and really chewed me out in front of my own children, and I remember saying something to her like, 'Well, Aunt Valerie, if my mother and kids like John, I really don't give a toot what you think.' It was so unnecessary, under the circumstances. I wasn't going to allow her to try and control *my* life too."

Sarah Harriman passed away in her sleep the next morning. With her passing, says Valerie Harriman, went any hope of getting Valerie and Ben Hogan the kind of help she believed would have made their remaining years easier. A further tension arose when Valerie Harriman discovered her aunt had already gone and collected Sarah's golf clubs at Shady Oaks. "On her deathbed, my mother asked me to give her clubs to one of her special buddies at Shady Oaks. But Aunt Valerie refused to let them go. It was just one more thing she couldn't let go of. I decided not to push the issue."

After Sarah's funeral, Valerie Harriman watched her Uncle Ben limp up to her mother's casket in the empty chapel, placing his hand on the polished wood. "He had the biggest, sweetest tears in his eyes. And then he did something that broke my heart. He rapped gently on my mother's coffin and said softly, 'Sarah, can you hear me? C'mon out. I want you to come back.'"

NOT LONG AFTERWARD, Buster the dog died too.

One winter evening when Valerie brought Ben to Shady Oaks for one of his increasingly rare dinners out, Mike Wright had something special to show to Hogan, a small stone marking Buster's grave just outside the pro shop.

"He stood there looking at it, and then he did something extraordinary," Wright says. "He removed his hat and gently knelt, kissed his hand, and placed it on the stone."

It was about this time that Wright glanced up one warm slow summer afternoon and discovered Ben Hogan walking out to the 10th tee with his driver and three golf balls in hand, to hit the final golf shots of his life—three balls, each one better than the last, an echo of his incomparable shotmaking at Carnoustie or perhaps simply the customary practice routine he'd innovated and transformed from ritual into legend.

Gene Smyers remembers having lunch alone with Hogan about this time at Shady Oaks when the National Open came up. "Gene, I won five Opens," Ben told him, pausing. "I just can't remember where."

Another time, Marty Leonard arranged for Jules Alexander to finally stop by Shady Oaks and meet the man his beautiful black-and-white photographs helped illuminate. "He was sitting alone at the round table in the grill room when I came in," recalls Alexander. "He motioned me over, shook my hand, and knew exactly who I was. We chatted for several minutes and I was touched when he told me he and Mrs. Hogan believed my photographs of him were their favorites."

After Ben endured colon surgery and a bout of bronchitis in May 1995—a trauma that among other things caused a special Hogan Day tribute being mounted by Dee Kelly to be canceled—Valerie curtailed his daily trips to Shady Oaks. He just "wasn't up to seeing people," as she described her decision to permit him only occasional outings to his favorite place. When Jim Murphy sent over medicine for Hogan's blocked sinuses, Hudson says, her employer put them in the garbage, believing medicine would only boost Hogan's short-term memory loss. The only painkiller he continued to take was a single Tylenol or aspirin.

"He simply didn't understand what was happening to him," says Hudson. "He would ask me, 'Elizabeth, where *is* everybody?' and that would tear at my heart. I told him they were still there, just waiting to see him. People would call the house or come by, and Mrs. Hogan would say he wasn't up to having visitors. It was always the same. Every day they came, seems like, every day she said no. And he got a little bit sadder each time."

Not long after his colon surgery, she remembers, Arnold Palmer phoned to offer his best wishes; so did Jack Nicklaus, Mike Souchak, Ken Venturi, and others. Only a few were permitted a few moments on the phone with Hogan. At one point, according to Hudson and Dee Kelly (who says Valerie told him she listened to their conversation), Tiger Woods phoned and asked to speak with Hogan. The two spoke for only a few moments, and Valerie supposedly heard her husband at one point remark, "I feel the same way about you too, Tiger."

"She was so worried about him getting out and doing something to injure himself, she just never let that poor man out of the house," says Hudson. "He was dying to just go over to Shady Oaks and see his friends and eat some scrambled eggs and bacon, have a cigarette, and ride in that Cadillac he loved so much. But all she would let the cook and me feed him for breakfast was Special K and fresh-squeezed orange juice and a little black coffee. 'Elizabeth,' she would say to me ten times a day, 'we can't let people see Mr. Hogan like this.' "

Before Hogan's colon surgery, according to Pat Martin and Sharon Rea, Valerie Hogan rarely came by the company office. But after the factory closed and Ben's office was moved to the Western Building, followed soon after by cancer surgery that perhaps diminished his mental and physical capacities, Valerie Hogan assumed a direct role in her husband's business affairs.

"She really committed herself to understanding their financial situation," says Martin. "Every month we would go over the oil reports, and she would make the decision to close this oil well or that one, based on how it was doing. She didn't want anyone taking advantage of him—and they did, I'm afraid. They would hold hands in the office, and it was clear to Sharon and me both that by that point he relied on Elizabeth Hudson and Mrs. Hogan for everything."

Valerie put out word that she no longer wished Hogan's Shady Oaks friends to call or even come by the house to say hello. "I don't think she intended to hurt him, but she did," reflects Elizabeth Hudson. "Little by little she took away things that man loved—Shady Oaks, his friends, even his cigarettes and that Fleetwood Cadillac he loved so much."

Whenever Valerie Hogan left the house in the morning, Hudson began sneaking Hogan out to sit in his beloved automobile. "The two of us would sit in that car, never leaving the driveway, just him and me, talking up a storm. I let him smoke all the cigarettes he wanted to. She never knew about that, but it made him extremely happy. We talked about everything, his life, his golf, his friends at Shady Oaks. He told me about growing up in Morningside, in a little house on the south side of Fort Worth, and about his mama and his daddy, about going to church there and selling newspapers at the train station before he got so famous, how his older brother would come and get him every night to walk him home. He asked me if I would drive him over there to show me the house. Naturally I said I would be delighted to, but Mrs. Hogan didn't want us going anywhere.

"He told me about his big golf tournaments too. I didn't know anything about golf, you understand, but he just talked and talked about how this shot won that big tournament and so forth. It made him so happy. There was always such a smile on his face whenever he talked about playing golf. Whenever a golf tournament came on TV, him and me would watch it together. I don't think Mrs. Hogan particularly liked that—I reckon she thought it would make him want to go over to Shady Oaks, which it did. She also asked me not to pray with him but when she left, we did that too. He told me he loved going to church. One more thing he missed."

At one point, Hogan asked his caretaker to read to him from *Five Lessons*, his classic book on the shotmaker's art. "He closed his eyes and just listened, like a baby hearin' a lullabye. Then he opened them and looked at me and smiled and said, 'I practiced a lot, Elizabeth. And when I practiced, I practiced to get it *right*!' "

One day, out of the blue, Hogan began talking about his father, Chester.

"I was startled when he told me about how his daddy had shot himself. It just suddenly came out when we were sitting together and talking about the past. He was a child when it happened, and never got over it. He said he spent his whole life wondering why his daddy did that because he loved his father very much. He loved his mama too, but it wasn't quite the same. You could tell that he'd spent his whole life tryin' to figure that out, why his father did that. It bothered him terribly, not knowing."

After this conversation, Elizabeth Hudson says, Ben Hogan seemed a little more at peace with his father's death.

"It was almost like he'd always needed to sit and talk with somebody who understood what a terrible thing that must have been. He just needed to finally let all of that go," she says. "He smiled at me and thanked me for listening."

VALERIE HOGAN gave Elizabeth Hudson firm instructions that, in the event she passed away before her husband, Hudson was to continue caretaking her husband exactly as she had done for almost five years.

Hudson agreed but made up her own secret contingency plan.

"I promised God that if Mrs. Hogan passed first, the first thing I was going to do was get that man a big comfortable double bed to sleep in and then paint the walls of that house a nice cheerful color. After that, I would go over to that club of his and get as many of his golf trophies and photographs as I could and put 'em up all *over* the walls of that house just so he'd have 'em to look at when he was watching golf on TV. I planned to drive him *everywhere* in his Cadillac too—carry him to church, and let him smoke all the cigarettes he wanted to smoke. If she passed first, why, I planned to let him see all of his old friends, have 'em come to the house or meet him over at Shady Oaks. Anything he wanted, just to make his final days easier."

But God, she says, had other plans in mind.

NEAR CHRISTMAS of 1996, Royal Hogan died.

"I can't believe Bubber's gone," Ben said simply, when Valerie broke the news to him. Elizabeth Hudson recalls that news of his brother's death made Hogan withdraw even more. "It was like the last person he knew besides Mrs. Hogan was gone."

Early one morning that July, Valerie Hogan phoned Hudson at her house on the city's south side, a bungalow mere blocks from where Ben had lived as a boy.

"Elizabeth, Mr. Hogan has fallen," she said. "You need to come right away."

Hogan was taken to All Saints Hospital and placed in a private suite. "He was very calm and alert," Hudson says. "But I think both of us knew he wouldn't be coming home again. I patted his hand and assured him he would be fine, Jesus was taking care of him now. And I'd be here waiting for him, saying my prayers. He just looked back at me and smiled a little."

Jackie Towery got to see her uncle before he passed away too. "The moment he saw me," she remembers, "he raised up a little out of the bed, and I put my hands in his. He squeezed and whispered, 'Jacqueline, where have you been?' and my eyes just filled up with tears."

The following morning, Friday, July 25, 1997, Ben Hogan asked his wife. "When am I going to get something to eat in here?"

"Well, honey, they're about to feed you now," Valerie told her husband, then left the room to go check on his breakfast. When she returned moments later, Ben had slipped away. He was eighty-four year old. It was the eve of Valerie Hogan's eighty-fifth birthday.

Just days ahead of him, his friend George Coleman died too. Days later, one of Hogan's favorite sportswriters, seventy-eight-year-old *Los Angeles Times* columnist Jim Murray, passed away as well.

VALERIE HOGAN asked Sam Snead and Ken Venturi to be among the honorary pallbearers for the funeral at University Christian Church. Several of Hogan's friends from Shady Oaks were asked to serve, including Gene Smyers and Mike Wright, and so were Tommy Bolt, Dee Kelly, Shelley Mayfield, and PGA Tour commissioner Tim Finchem. It bothered some of Hogan's longtime friends that Jackie Burke and Mike Souchak weren't asked, and one omission seemed to dwarf the rest: Byron Nelson.

"I know exactly why Mrs. Hogan didn't want Mr. Nelson," says Elizabeth Hudson. "I asked her, and she told me Mr. Nelson had once said some unkind things about Mr. Hogan in a newspaper—least *she* thought so. She didn't forgive much if she thought you did wrong."

Nelson and his wife, Peggy, came anyway, sitting in the overflow crowd of luminaries and friends who attended the Hawk's funeral service on a hotly flaring summer afternoon. Other familiar faces included Ben Crenshaw, Los Angeles pro Eddie Merrins, and John Mahaffey.

"It was dignified and simple, no parade of stars," says Rayburn Tucker, who also served as an honorary pall bearer. "That's what most struck me about the service. Only the minister spoke, and he talked far more about Ben the man than Hogan the champion."

The Scripture minister Charles Sanders chose to read came from Romans 5: "We glory in tribulation," the verse goes in part, "knowing that tribulation worketh patience; and patience, experience; and experience, hope."

It was the perfect coda for a little man who never gave up hope of his own personal salvation through hard work.

VALERIE HOGAN was very clear on what should be done with her late husband's estate, which was estimated to be worth about $30 million at the time of his death, not counting oil leases and stock holdings.

A million dollars was earmarked for donation to Cook's Children's Hospital in Fort Worth, another million to University Christian Church. The bulk of the estate went directly to designated Hogan heirs, Valerie's great-niece Lisa Scott and her brother Sean Anderson. For a while, Dee Kelly and estate executor Tex Moncrief explored options with Hogan's widow about setting up a trust or charitable foundation that would have perpetuated Hogan's name and significantly lessened the inheritance tax penalty incurred for skipping a generation. "Valerie's mind was very clear and firm on the issue," says Kelly. "She would not change her mind on the subject."

Elizabeth Hudson stayed on to look after her employer.

"She grew kinder to me, giving me china dishes and other things she no longer had need of. She paid me well too. I took to worrying about her the way I'd worried about Mr. Hogan. She was the tiniest little thing who ate hardly anything."

"She would call me sometimes at night," remembers Sharon Rea, "and talk for *hours* about Mr. Hogan—how they traveled here or there, the people they met, the wonderful life they had together. She missed him so much. Whatever else is true, she gave her life to that man, and he returned her love for all that loyalty."

A year after her husband's death, Valerie received a telephone call from book publisher Martin Davis. In late 1995, Davis had published *The Hogan Mystique*, a coffee table book celebrating Hogan's playing career through the black-and-white photographs of Jules Alexander, with related essays and commentary by Dave Anderson, Ben Crenshaw, Ken Venturi, and Dan Jenkins. The book sold over 60,000 copies and, though unauthorized by the Hogans, prompted the Hogans to send thank-you notes to the editor and his contributing writers.

The success of *The Hogan Mystique* convinced Davis and Anderson that a more detailed look at Hogan's storied playing career, specifically through the eyes of his surviving widow, was in order. Valerie Hogan agreed to work with Dave Anderson, and the two began an ongoing conversation about the past.

There were three things she needed to do before she died, Valerie told Elizabeth Hudson, Dee Kelly, and even Dan Jenkins, who signed up for another of his colorful essays on Hogan for the latest Davis project, *The Man Behind the Mystique*.

The first thing was to attend Jack Nicklaus's Memorial Golf Tournament in Ohio and finally accept the honor her husband had been so reluctant to accept in the late '80s. The second thing was to oversee the completion of the spectacular new Hogan Room at Golf House in Far Hills, New Jersey. Following the second burglary and recovery of Hogan artifacts in the early 1990s, inspired by the huge crowds drawn by the first Hogan exhibition at Golf House, Tucker, Bednarski, Bob Russell, Andy Mutch and USGA executive director David Fay helped convince Valerie to move most of her late husband's trophies, medals, and other memorabilia to a special Hogan Room at Golf House. The new Hogan Room was scheduled to open its door to the public in early June 1999.

Overcoming her own reluctance to travel, in May 1999, she went to Jack Nicklaus's memorial ceremony in Ohio, then on with Sharon Rea and Rayburn Tucker to the opening of the Hogan Room at Golf House in early June. "She was so tired and extremely frail," remembers Rea, "but she somehow just kept going. It was amazing. She ate almost nothing. I would buy her Blue Belle ice cream and Ensure and make them into a milk shake for her, and she would talk to me for hours about the things she and Mr. Hogan had done together in their long life together. That was the only thing on her mind— opening that museum room and getting that last book done on Mr. Hogan."

Back home in Fort Worth, there was talk of renaming Roaring Springs Road (the route Ben took from his house to Shady Oaks) Ben Hogan Boulevard. And additional good news arrived when Spalding announced its purchase of the Ben Hogan Company from Virginia businessman Bill Goodwin, with plans to eventually move the firm back to its rightful home and even rehire many of the old Hogan workers.

"That really picked up Mrs. Hogan's spirits," recalls Rea. "She said over and over how pleased Mr. Hogan would have been by this news."

Three weeks after the opening of the Hogan Room at Golf House, on the eve of accompanying Sharon Rae out to Los Angeles to attend a memorial scholarship golf tournament for Jim Murray, Valerie Hogan and Dave Anderson spoke a final time by telephone, going over a few more reminiscences that expanded her memories of the Hawk's career from 3,000 to 13,000 words.

"She was clearly exhausted by this point," says Anderson, "but you could hear the relief in her voice. She wanted to get it all down before finally letting go."

The next morning, Elizabeth Hudson was cleaning up the breakfast dishes in the kitchen on Canterbury Drive when she heard a soft thump and went to investigate. At the end of the hallway, she discovered Valerie Hogan's tiny body slumped against a wall where she had collapsed. Moments before, Valerie had finished writing a thank-you letter to the USGA official who oversaw the creation of the Hogan Room.

"I knew before I even touched her that she was gone," says Hudson softly. "I believe she had done all the Lord had sent her here to do."

Valerie Hogan had finally let go.

ON THANKSGIVING morning of 2002, a small fire broke out in the mechanical room at Shady Oaks Country Club. The damage was minor, but the fire loosened asbestos that got into the structure's circulation system and blew throughout the clubhouse. After months of cleanup and a fairly vigorous debate among the membership, a decision was reached to tear down the existing clubhouse and build a new one. Several longtime members expressed sadness and outrage at this decision, wondering what the club's most distinguished member would have felt.

The famous round table from the men's grill room—which was officially renamed the Hogan Room several years back—was put in storage, and most of Hogan's personal effects, including his fedora hat and his beautifully polished golf shoes with the thirteenth spike, were sent for safekeeping to the

Golf World Hall of Fame in St. Augustine, Florida, until further notice. One of Hogan's double lockers, containing his clubs and other personal grooming items, was also sent to the Hall of Fame. Another club locker was sent to the USGA's Golf House in Far Hills, to be replicated and eventually displayed in the museum's marvelous Hogan Room.

When it was revealed in late 2003 that the Ben Hogan Company's new parent company was Callaway Golf and the Fort Worth plant was to be closed and moved a second time to Callaway's factory in southern California, it was decided that Hogan's office furniture and other personal effects would be sent to Colonial Country Club, for a permanent display in the famous club's pro shop.

The symbolism of all this wasn't lost on Mike Wright, the young club professional Hogan helped coach to his first big job in golf—now in his twentieth year as Shady Oaks' head professional. If everything goes according to plan, sometime in late 2004 a new, smaller Shady Oaks clubhouse will reopen to its membership.

"I feel a great responsibility to keep Mr. Hogan's legacy—what he taught me and the values he stood for—alive around here," says the young man who fittingly witnessed the final golf swings of the game's most wondrous ball-striker.

The famous round table, Wright adds, will soon be returned to its sacred spot in the club's new Hogan Room, only now it will be located on the second floor of the rebuilt clubhouse, ten or twelve feet higher than before.

"That will allow whoever sits there to have a much finer view of the golf course," says Wright. "Somehow I just know that would please Mr. Hogan."

BOOKS

Allen, Frederick Lewis. *Only Yesterday*. New York: Harper & Row, 1931.

————. *Since Yesterday*. New York: Harper & Row, 1939.

Alter, Judy, and James Ward Lee, eds. *Literary Fort Worth*. Fort Worth, Tex.: TCU Press, 2001.

Barkow, Al. *Golf's Golden Grind: The History of the Tour*. New York: Harcourt Brace Jovanovich, 1974.

————. *Gettin' to the Dance Floor: An Oral History of American Golf*. Springfield, N.J.: Burford Books, 1986.

Barr, Art, Jr. *Ben Hogan and Buster*. Privately published, 2002.

Bolt, Tommy, with Jimmy Mann. *The Hole Truth: Inside Big-Time, Big-Money Golf*. Philadelphia: Lippincott, 1971.

Buenger, Victoria, and Walter L. Buenger. *Texas Merchant: Marvin Leonard and Fort Worth*. College Station: Texas A&M University Press, 1998.

Corcoran, Fred, and Bud Harvey. *Unplayable Lies*. New York: Duell, Sloan and Pierce, 1965.

Davis, Martin, ed. *The Hogan Mystique: Classic Photographs of the Great Ben Hogan*.

Photographs by Jules Alexander; essays by Dave Anderson, Ben Crenshaw, and Dan Jenkins; commentary by Ken Venturi. Greenwich, Conn.: American Golfer, 1994.

———. *Ben Hogan: The Man Behind the Mystique*. Greenwich, Conn.: American Golfer, 2002.

Demaret, Jimmy. *My Partner, Ben Hogan*. London: Peter Davies, 1954.

Derr, John. *Uphill Is Easier*. Pinehurst, N.C.: Cricket Productions, 1995.

———. *Don't Forget to Wind the Clock*. Pinehurst, N.C.: Cricket Productions, 1996.

Dickinson, Gardner. *Let 'er Rip: Gardner Dickinson on Golf*. Atlanta: Longstreet Press, 1994.

Evans, Harold. *The American Century*. New York: Alfred A. Knopf, 1998.

Fehrenbach, T. R. *Lone Star: A History of Texas and the Texans*. New York: De Capo Press, 2000.

Fleck, Jack. *The Jack Fleck Story*. JC Publishing, 2002.

Graffis, Herb. *The PGA*. New York: Thomas Crowell Co., 1975.

Graubert, Julian I. *Golf's Greatest Championship*. New York: Donald Fine Books, 1997.

Gregston, Gene. *Hogan: The Man Who Played for Glory*. Englewood Cliffs, N.J.: Prentice-Hall, 1978.

Hagen, Walter. *The Walter Hagen Story*. New York: Simon and Schuster, 1952.

Halberstam, David. *The Fifties*. New York: Ballantine Books, 1994.

Hogan, Ben. *Five Lessons*. New York: A. S. Barnes and Co., 1957.

———. *Power Golf*. New York: A. S. Barnes and Co., 1948.

Keeler, O. B. *The Bobby Jones Story*. Chicago: Triumph Books, 2003.

Knight, Oliver. *Outpost on the Trinity*. Fort Worth, Tex.: TCU Press, 1990.

Laney, Al. *Following the Leaders*. New York: Ailsa, Inc., in agreement with the Michael Laney Trust, 1991.

Lawrenson, Derek. *The Complete Encyclopedia of Golf*. London: Carlton Books, 1999.

McCormack, Mark. *The World of Professional Golf*. Annual 1970–71. London: Hodder and Stoughton, 1970.

Macdonald, Charles Blair. *Scotland's Gift—Golf*. New York: Charles Scribner's Sons, 1928.

Miller, William. *How to Relax*. New York: Smith and Durrell, 1945.

Morrison, Alex, ed. *The Impossible Art of Golf: An Anthology of Golf Writing*. New York: Oxford University Press, 1994.

Murphy, Michael. *Golf in the Kingdom*. New York: Arkana, 1992.

Nelson, Byron, and Peggy Nelson. *How I Played the Game*. Dallas: Taylor Publishing, 1993.

Ouiment, Francis. *A Game of Golf*. Boston: Houghton Mifflin, 1932.

Owen, David. *The Making of the Masters*. New York: Simon & Schuster, 1999.

Pace, Lee. *Pinehurst Stories*. Pinehurst, N.C.: Pinehurst, Inc., 1999.

Palmer, Arnold, with James Dodson. *A Golfer's Life*. New York: Ballantine Books, 1999.

Peper, George. *Golf in America: The First 100 Years*. New York: Harry N. Abrams, 1988.

Price, Charles. *A Golf Story: Bobby Jones, Augusta National, and the Masters Tournament*. New York: Atheneum, 1986.

Sampson, Curt. *The Eternal Summer: Palmer, Nicklaus, and Hogan in 1960, Golf's Golden Year*. Dallas: Taylor Publishing, 1992.

———. *Hogan*. Nashville: Rutledge Hill Press, 1996.

———. *The Masters: Golf, Money, and Power in Augusta, Georgia*. New York: Villard, 1998.

Shackelford, Geoff. *The Riviera Country Club: A Definitive History*. Los Angeles: Riviera Country Club, 1995.

Shorter, Edward. *A History of Psychiatry: From the Era of the Asylum to the Age of Prozac*. New York: John Wiley & Sons, 1997.

Snead, Sam, with George Mendoza. *Slammin' Sam*. New York: Donald Fine, 1986.

Snead, Sam, with Al Stump. *The Education of a Golfer*. New York: Simon & Schuster, 1962.

Sommers, Robert. *The U.S. Open: Golf's Ultimate Challenge*. New York: Atheneum, 1987.

———. *Golf Anecdotes*. New York: Oxford University Press, 1995.

Strickland, Art. *A History of Northwood Club*. Virginia Beach, Va.: Donning Co., 2002.

Towle, Mike. *I Remember Ben Hogan*. Nashville: Cumberland House, 2000.

Ward-Thomas, Pat. *The Lay of the Land*. New York; Ailsa, Inc., 1990.

Wilson, Mark. *The Golf Club Identification and Price Guide IV*. Newark, Ohio: Ralph Maltby Enterprises, 1999.

Wind, Herbert Warren. *The Story of American Golf*. New York: Simon & Schuster, 1956.

———. *Following Through*. New York: Ticknor & Fields, 1985.

Wright, Ben, with Michael Patrick Shiels. *Good Bounces and Bad Lies*. Chelsea, Mich.: Sleeping Bear Press, 1999.

ADDITIONAL SOURCES

Owing to the precision of Valerie Hogan's clipping books, many of the periodical sources used in the research of this biography were missing their title source. What follows is a list of known periodicals the tale was drawn from:

Arizona Republic, Asheville Citizen, Associated Press, *Atlanta Constitution, Augusta Chronicle, Baltimore Evening Sun, Boston Evening Transcript, Boston Globe, Chicago Daily News, Chicago Tribune, Christian Science Monitor, Cleveland Plain Dealer, Columbus Dispatch, Dallas Morning News, Dallas Times-Herald, Denver Post, Detroit Free Press, Detroit News, Dublin Progress, El Paso Herald-Post, El Paso Times, Forth Worth Press, Fort Worth Star-Telegram, Glasgow Herald, Golf Digest, Golf Illustrated, Golfing, Golf Journal, Golf Magazine, Golf Monthly (United Kingdom), Golf World, Greensboro Daily News, Greensboro Record, The Guardian*, International News Service, *Life, London Daily Express, London Daily Herald, London Daily Mail, London Daily Telegraph, London Mirror, London Times, Los Angeles Evening Herald, Los Angeles Times, Louisville*

528   SELECTED BIBLIOGRAPHY AND SOURCES

Courier Journal Magazine, Miami Herald, Newark Ledger, New York Daily News, New York Herald-Tribune, New York Journal American, New York Times, New York World Telegram and Sun, Oakland Tribune, PGA Magazine, Pittsburgh Press, Reader's Digest, Reuters, Rocky Mountain News, San Antonio Light, San Antonio News, San Diego Union, San Francisco Chronicle, The Scotsman on Sunday, Sports Illustrated, St. Louis Star-Times, St. Paul Pioneer Press, St. Petersburg Independent, Time, United Press International, *Washington Star*, and *Weekly Scotsman*.